MODEL   **MIDI Implementation Chart**

Function . . .		Transmitted	Recognized	Remarks
Basic Channel	Default Channel			
Mode	Default Messages Altered			
Note Number	True Voice			
Velocity	Note ON Note OFF			
Aftertouch	Key's Ch's			
Pitch Bender				
Control Change				
Prog Change	True #			
System Exclusive				
System Common	Song Pos Song Sel Tune			
System Real Time	Clock Commands			
Aux Messages	Local ON/OFF All Notes OFF Active Sense Reset			
Notes				

Mode 1: OMNI ON, POLY   Mode 2: OMNI ON, MONO   O: Yes
Mode 3: OMNI OFF, POLY   Mode 4: OMNI OFF, MONO   X: No

FIGURE 1: *The first column in Figure 2 indicates the function or message category for each row. The "Transmitted" and "Recognized" columns correspond to the transmission and reception functions. An X at the intersection of one of these columns and a function row indicates that the corresponding MIDI category is implemented. Conversely, an O indicates that the category is not handled by the instrument.*

For every kind of computer user, there is a SYBEX book.

All computer users learn in their own way. Some need straightforward and methodical explanations. Others are just too busy for this approach. But no matter what camp you fall into, SYBEX has a book that can help you get the most out of your computer and computer software while learning at your own pace.

Beginners generally want to start at the beginning. The **ABC's** series, with its step-by-step lessons in plain language, helps you build basic skills quickly. Or you might try our **Quick & Easy** series, the friendly, full-color guide.

The **Mastering** and **Understanding** series will tell you everything you need to know about a subject. They're perfect for intermediate and advanced computer users, yet they don't make the mistake of leaving beginners behind.

If you're a busy person and are already comfortable with computers, you can choose from two SYBEX series—**Up & Running** and **Running Start**. The **Up & Running** series gets you started in just 20 lessons. Or you can get two books in one, a step-by-step tutorial and an alphabetical reference, with our **Running Start** series.

Everyone who uses computer software can also use a computer software reference. SYBEX offers the gamut—from portable **Instant References** to comprehensive **Encyclopedias**, **Desktop References**, and **Bibles**.

SYBEX even offers special titles on subjects that don't neatly fit a category—like **Tips & Tricks**, the **Shareware Treasure Chests**, and a wide range of books for Macintosh computers and software.

SYBEX books are written by authors who are expert in their subjects. In fact, many make their living as professionals, consultants or teachers in the field of computer software. And their manuscripts are thoroughly reviewed by our technical and editorial staff for accuracy and ease-of-use.

So when you want answers about computers or any popular software package, just help yourself to SYBEX.

For a complete catalog of our publications, please write:

SYBEX Inc.
2021 Challenger Drive
Alameda, CA 94501
Tel: (510) 523-8233/(800) 227-2346 Telex: 336311
Fax: (510) 523-2373

The Musician's Guide to MIDI

The Musician's Guide

to

MIDI

Christian Braut

Paris

San Francisco

Düsseldorf

Soest

ACQUISITIONS EDITOR: David Clark
DEVELOPMENTAL EDITORS: Ken Brown and Steve Lipson
TRANSLATOR: H.B.J. (Heather Barbara) Clifford, Tristan Translations
EDITOR: H.B.J. Clifford
TECHNICAL ASSOCIATE: Stephen T. Satchell
PROJECT EDITOR: Kathleen Lattinville
BOOK DESIGNER AND CHAPTER ARTIST: Claudia Smelser
TECHNICAL ARTISTS: Cuong Le and John Corrigan
TYPESETTER: Dina F Quan
PROOFREADERS/PRODUCTION ASSISTANTS: Lisa Haden and Kristin Amlie
INDEXER: Matthew Spence
COVER DESIGNER: Ingalls + Associates
COVER ILLUSTRATOR: Max Seabaugh

Authorized translation from the French language edition.
Translated from the French by H.B.J. (Heather Barbara) Clifford.
Original copyright © SYBEX S.A.R.L. 1992.
This edition was revised and updated by Adolfo Garcia and Christian Braut.
Translation copyright ©1994.

Library of Congress Card Number: 93-83899
ISBN: 0-7821-1285-4

Manufactured in the United States of America

10 9 8 7 6 5 4 3 2 1

This book is dedicated to Adeline, Fanny, Lise, Gabriel… and Satanas.

Acknowledgments

MY THANKS TO Adolfo Garcia, Michel Geiss, David Korn, Alain Mangenot, Patrick Moulou, Bruno Valenti, and Christian van Houcke; to *Keyboards* magazine, and to the Bank of France.

Contents at a Glance

Table of Contents

CHAPTER 3

The MIDI Language

59

CHAPTER 5   Synthesis and Sampling Methods   213

CHAPTER 8   MIDI Recording: Advanced Techniques   315

CHAPTER 9

Recording and Synchronization   377

CHAPTER 10

Working with MIDI Devices: Memory, Dump Messages, and Data Formats   437

CHAPTER **11**

Working with MIDI Devices: Managing SysEx Messages 485

CHAPTER 12   Using GenEdit   541

CHAPTER 13   An Editor/Librarian for the Yamaha TX81Z   609

CHAPTER 14   Recent Extensions: General MIDI and MIDI Show Control   679

CHAPTER **15** MIDI Machine Control: Data Formats,
Messages, and Commands   **767**

CHAPTER **16**

MIDI Machine Control: Responses and Applications

APPENDIX C **GenEdit Commands at a Glance**   **1011**

Foreword

by JEFF RONA

MIDI has forever changed the way music is made. This simple technology has become the universal glue which holds together the worlds of music, the personal computer, and a new creative process. It is a wonderfully enabling technology that has become the de facto standard for electronic instrument and audio equipment networking around the world in an amazingly short period of time.

MIDI offers musicians the ability to work with any number of sophisticated instruments with relative ease. It allows any personal computer to be used as a central controller for an entire arsenal of devices. It allows musicians to interact with each other and exchange music in an entirely new way.

MIDI has grown far beyond its original musical uses, tying together the worlds of audio and video devices, theatrical stage and lighting automation, film and video postproduction, and a host of other unusual applications.

The main ingredient that has made all this possible is software. MIDI-based application programs have been created for a vast number of musical and other uses: From MIDI sequencers that record, edit, and replay musical ideas, to recording studio automation.

When MIDI first appeared in 1983, there was only a handful of keyboard instruments employing the new technology. MIDI was used simply as a link to layer a few musical instruments together. However, within just a couple of years, an entirely new cottage industry was born: music software. The creative options now available to the musician or audio engineer are truly vast. There are not only applications fulfilling a wide range of needs, but also the tools to allow advanced users of MIDI devices to create their own custom systems with any MIDI-compatible PC.

I doubt that many of MIDI's founding fathers had any idea that what they were designing would become a creative wildfire that would span the globe. MIDI can be found on everything from the least expensive hobbyist keyboards available to the most expensive electronic music systems made; from CD players to digital multitrack recorders; from guitar amps to personal computers. MIDI is a tool of our time.

This book will give you an in-depth tour of every aspect of the MIDI protocol, from its use as a basic musical instrument networking technology to its many uses for timbre editing and custom studio applications. The author has gone far to show you the diversity of MIDI's capabilities, so that you can do it yourself, from the perspective of either a musician or a software designer.

Finally, I believe it helps to keep the right perspective when learning about MIDI and related technologies. The topics covered in this book are merely tools for creative exploration. They should be treated with the same reverence you might give to a good hammer or screwdriver. You need good tools to build a structure of your design, but the structure is not made out of hammers or screwdrivers. The goal is to be able to create something that did not previously exist. Something that is yours. And to have some fun along the way. Enjoy.

 Jeff Rona is a Los Angeles-based composer and musician and is the founder and past president of the MIDI Manufacturers Association.

Introduction

"MIDI" STANDS FOR "Musical Instrument Digital Interface." Along with analog synthesizers (which started appearing on the market toward the end of the 1960s) and digital audio, the MIDI standard is one of the richest and most far-reaching innovations in the history of musical electronics. Officially introduced in 1983, the standard was designed to regulate communications between different types of devices: synthesizers, samplers, drum machines, computers, tape recorders, and others. It's a truly universal language.

Developed through data-processing and digital technologies, these MIDI-compatible devices are having a direct effect on the evolution of music. Available at first only to an elite, these devices have since become democratized. This democratization has given birth to a household production tool: the so-called "home studio."

However, the beginning wasn't easy. Before committing to MIDI, many manufacturers hesitated for a long time. The first MIDI synthesizers (the Sequential Circuits Prophet 600 and the Yamaha DX7) even aroused a certain amount of skepticism among users. But in a very short time this was transformed into an unprecedented infatuation. Today it's inconceivable for a manufacturer to bring even the most modest keyboard to market without building a MIDI interface into it. For 1989 alone, MIDI sales were estimated at more than $300 million. Its universal nature, together with its low cost of implementation, is one of the main reasons for its huge commercial success.

MIDI and its applications have continued to evolve over the years. The specifications book is a lot thicker now, and we've come a long way from the simple instrument-to-instrument connections for which the interface was originally designed. If today's musicians want to extract the maximum advantage from this potential, they need to acquire more and more in-depth knowledge. Far from being a drag on creativity, mastery of the MIDI standard will help musicians focus on the artistic aspects of their work, by giving them ways to optimize their use of these new tools.

The early chapters of this book are dedicated to a theoretical review of the acoustic phenomena related to the production of sound and to general information about the evolution of musical instruments over the last twenty years, along with an introduction to the principles of the interface.

The middle chapters of the book are an in-depth study of the MIDI standard, in terms of software as well as hardware, based on the official documentation provided by the International MIDI Association (in Version 4.1 and Version 4.2 of the MIDI 1.0 Detailed Specifications).

Subsequent chapters deal with MIDI hardware and its many related applications, in terms of instruments, sequencers, recording, synchronization, editors, librarians, and so on. Because of the very small amount of documentation that exists on the subject, the emphasis here is on the programming of System Exclusive messages and on the applications that use them.

The book closes with a look at recent additions to the standard, namely General MIDI, MIDI Show Control, and the MMC (MIDI Machine Control) commands.

CHAPTER

1

Sound:

The Stuff That Music's Made Of

VERY MUSICAL instrument—in other words, every sound-production system—has to obey the laws of acoustics. Whatever the instrument is, its sound is made up of the same elements, and is represented by the same parameters. A few basic concepts in acoustics—the science of sound—are the key to approaching and mastering all the MIDI instruments.

Strictly speaking, sound is an auditory sensation generated by an acoustic vibration. This acoustic vibration is a back-and-forth movement that happens in a molecular medium, such as air. The term "oscillatory phenomenon" refers to back-and-forth motion around an equilibrium position, known as the "rest" or "resting" position. The air molecules that are in direct contact with the excitatory system (i.e., the system that causes the vibratory phenomenon) start to oscillate with the same motion, transmitting the motion to their neighboring molecules, and so on. Thanks to this chain reaction, or *propagation*, the sound progressively and eventually reaches an ear (the receiving system). The amount of time the sound needs to travel from the excitatory system to the receiving system is a function of this propagation speed (which is also known as the *velocity of the sound*). In air, sound waves travel at about 1085 feet per second.

As shown in Figure 1.1, the best way to illustrate the phenomenon of vibratory propagation is to throw a pebble into water and watch the concentric circles which move away from the point of impact. We see that the water is not displaced linearly (as it is with a flowing stream). Instead, the troughs (rarefactions) and peaks (compressions) gradually propagate outward. To verify this fact, all you have to do is observe the position of a floating object (such as a cork bottle-stopper), which will oscillate up and down without moving so much as a millimeter along a horizontal

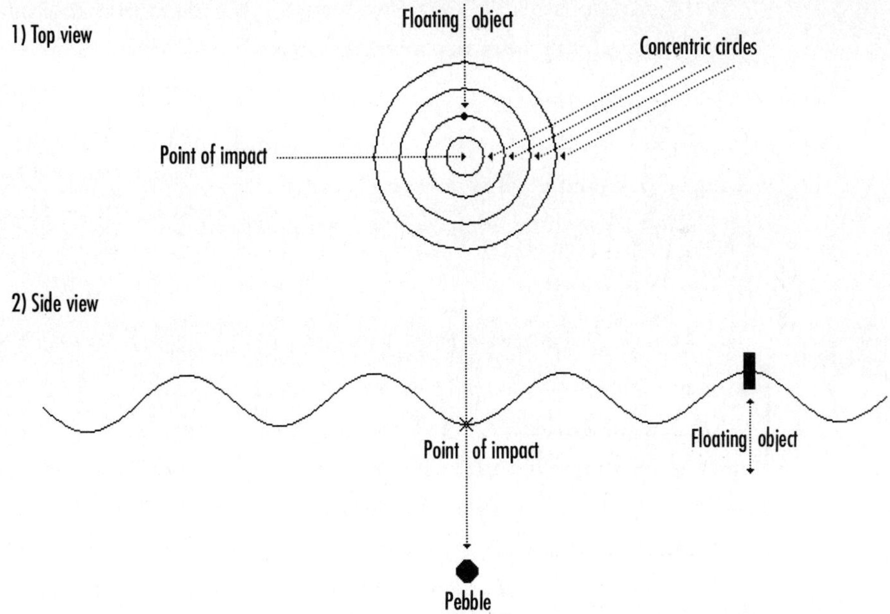

FIGURE 1.1: *The act of throwing a pebble into water causes compression and rarefaction of incompressible molecules, which propagate away from the point of impact in the form of concentric circles. As the alternating peaks and troughs indicate, the water doesn't move in a linear way; instead, it moves up and down, so that an object floating on it is displaced vertically rather than horizontally.*

axis. The principle works exactly the same way in air: an oscillatory motion causes greater or lesser changes in pressure (i.e., a variation in the density of the air molecules), while the air as a whole doesn't move. The linear motion of a flowing stream is comparable to the motion of a current of air, which, of course, produces no sound.

Showing Sound in Two Dimensions

Hearing sound is one thing. But how do you show sound on paper? Easily, it turns out. As shown in Figure 1.2, by drawing a graph with the time along the abscissa and the changes in pressure along the ordinate, you can show the sound in its two-dimensional form: i.e., its waveform. If the durations of the successive trough/peak pairs in the waveform are identical, the vibratory motion is *periodic*.

The simplest periodic waveform is the sinusoidal waveform. This waveform represents the most elementary possible vibratory physical phenomenon. For example, as shown in Figure 1.3, you can get this waveform (leaving aside the damping effect) with an excitatory system consisting of

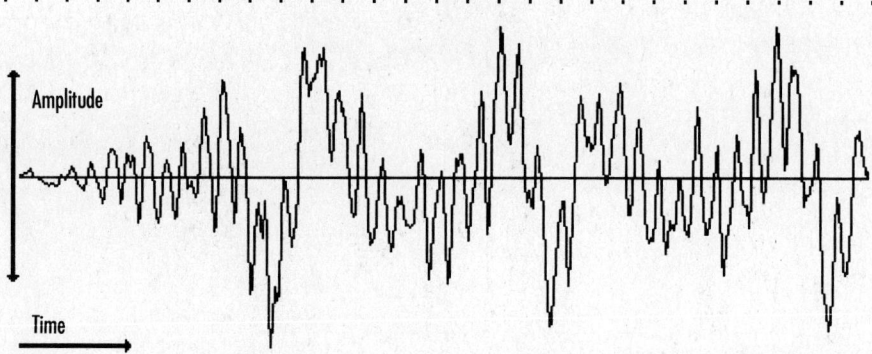

FIGURE 1.2: *A two-dimensional graph of a waveform. The horizontal line corresponds to the rest position of the molecules, and the amplitude of the compressions and rarefactions is shown above and below the line.*

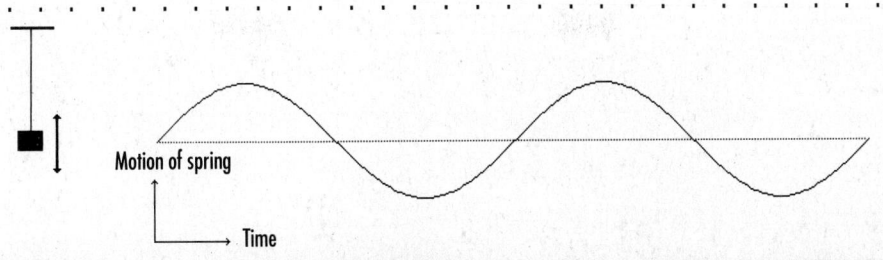

FIGURE 1.3: *The sinusoidal graph traces the temporal displacement of the weight attached to the spring. This graph represents the most elementary possible periodic motion.*

a vertical spring attached at its upper end to the ceiling and at its bottom end to a weight. By pulling the weight downward and then suddenly releasing it, and then taking the graph shown in Figure 1.2 and replacing the changes in pressure with the vertical movement of the spring, you get a perfect sinusoidal waveform.

Musical Building Blocks

Whatever a sound is, from the roar of a rocket launch to the pluck of a single guitar string, three parameters are all it takes to define its characteristics. Although different sound generators may call them by slightly different names, you'll find them referred to most often as *pitch*, *amplitude*, and *timbre*.

Pitch

The concept of pitch is based on the fact that any given tone is heard as being more or less "high" or "low" (see Figure 1.4). The faster the oscillations, the higher the tone. Conversely, the slower the oscillations, the lower the tone.

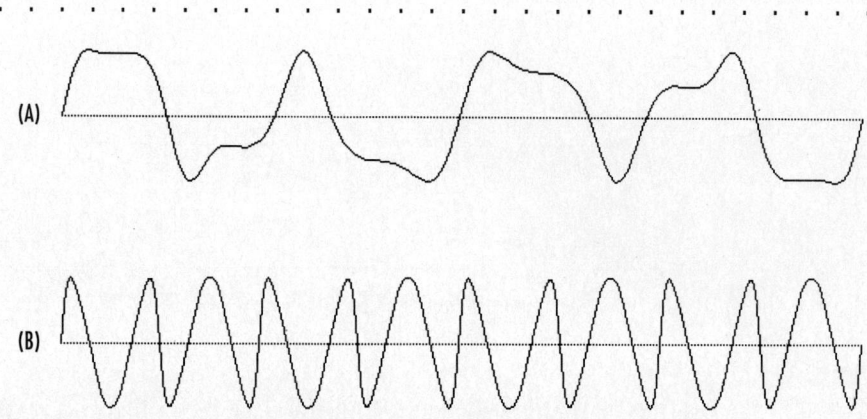

FIGURE 1.4: *The pitch of waveform (A) is lower than the pitch of waveform (B).*

A tone whose oscillations are periodic is perceived by the human ear as having a fixed pitch (a C, an A, etc.), as shown in Figure 1.5. The part of the waveform (i.e., the peak/trough pair) that's reproduced identically is known as its *cycle*. The pitch of a tone is a function of the number of

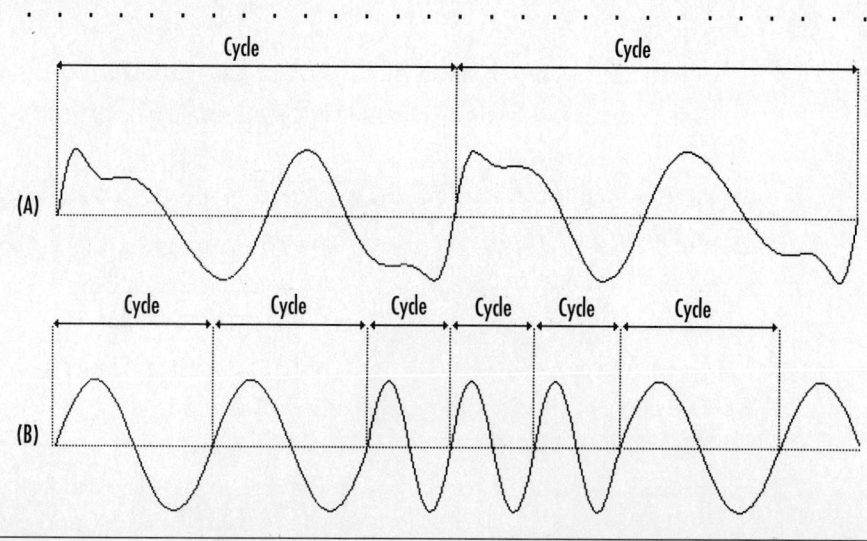

FIGURE 1.5: *The pitch of waveform (A) is fixed, unlike the pitch of waveform (B), whose cycles have different durations.*

cycles per second, or *frequency*. Frequencies are expressed in hertz (a unit derived from the name of the German physicist Heinrich Hertz). The abbreviation "Hz" is customary.

Even in the best of cases, the frequencies the human ear can hear are limited to the range between 20 and 20,000Hz (i.e., from 20 to 20,000 cycles per second). Most of the data sheets for microphones, amplifiers, speakers, and other audio equipment call this frequency range the "pass-band" or "pass-range." Frequencies below 20Hz are known as infrasonic frequencies, and the ones above 20,000Hz are known as ultrasonic frequencies. It's worth noting in passing that the frequency of the tuning or concert pitch has arbitrarily been set to the frequency of an A at approximately 440Hz (i.e., 440 cycles per second).

Frequencies and Intervals: Tuning the Octave

A one-octave interval is defined by a ratio of 2 between the frequency of the highest note and the frequency of the lowest note. For instance, the frequency of the A immediately above the tuning or concert A is 880Hz, and the frequency of the next higher A is 1760Hz. The frequency of the next A below the tuning A is 220Hz, and so on.

The scale most commonly used today—the so-called well-tempered scale—divides every octave into twelve equal semitones. Because human pitch perception is logarithmic, and because the one-octave difference is represented by a multiplication factor of 2, you have to multiply or divide a given frequency X by the 12th root of 2 (i.e., 1.059463094) to get the frequency of the next higher or next lower semitone. For instance, $440 \times 1.059463094 = 466.163$, which corresponds to an A-sharp.

The following list gives the numbers by which you have to multiply a given frequency in order to get the next twelve higher halftones:

$1.059 \ (1.059^1)$	Minor second
$1.121 \ (1.059^2)$	Major second
$1.188 \ (1.059^3)$	Minor third
$1.258 \ (1.059^4)$	Major third
$1.332 \ (1.059^5)$	Fourth
$1.411 \ (1.059^6)$	Diminished fifth
$1.494 \ (1.059^7)$	Fifth
$1.582 \ (1.059^8)$	Minor sixth
$1.675 \ (1.059^9)$	Sixth
$1.774 \ (1.059^{10})$	Minor seventh
$1.879 \ (1.059^{11})$	Major seventh
$2 \ (1.059^{12})$	Octave

Most of the noises you hear in the natural environment are *aperiodic*. This means that the compressions and rarefactions of the air molecules are irregular; in other words, that the frequency varies over time. This doesn't keep you from interpreting the noises as being relatively high or low, because you can intuitively estimate their average or mean frequency. The noises of a closing door, a jet aircraft, and a breaking glass are examples of aperiodic sounds. On the other hand, likewise because of their variable pitch, these sounds can't be "sung" by human voices.

Amplitude and Dynamics

Amplitude involves the concept of the volume, or loudness, of a tone. For instance, the graph in Figure 1.6 indicates that the amplitude of a

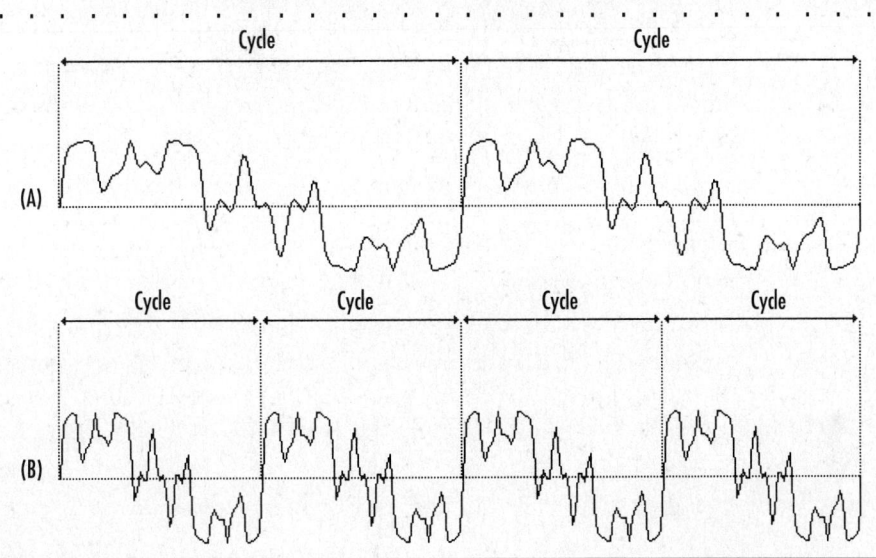

FIGURE 1.6: *Waveform (B) is one octave higher than waveform (A), in which each cycle lasts half as long.*

sinusoidal waveform is characterized by the maximum difference in the variation in pressure with regard to the ordinate axis. The farther the troughs and peaks are from the resting position (i.e., from the horizontal axis), the louder the tone is perceived to be. Considering again the example of the pebble thrown into the water, the more the cork rises and falls, the greater the amplitude of the motion. In this case, amplitude is a direct result of the force with which the pebble was thrown.

The human ear perceives amplitude logarithmically. In fact, generally speaking, for most of the human senses "the intensity of a sensation varies directly as the logarithm of the numerical value of the stimulus." This rule is known as Fechner's Law. For instance, if you had an instrument with a value of, say, 10 and you wanted a volume that was twice as loud, you'd need a value of 100 (that is, 10 to the second power, or 10^2).

In the same way that the pass-band measures the performance of a piece of audio equipment over the range of frequencies that the equipment can handle, the dynamics measure the response of the equipment in terms of amplitude. Dynamics, which are expressed in decibels (dB), indicate the difference between the minimum volume and the maximum volume. As indicated in Figure 1.7, the higher the dynamics, the more faithfully the nuances between a soft tone and a loud tone are reproduced.

Dynamics are a relative characteristic. For example, in a hi-fi amplifier with limited dynamics, the difference in volume between the soft and loud tones in a piece of music will be diminished. The decrease in volume of a fixed waveform has a characteristic progression, as shown in Figure 1.8.

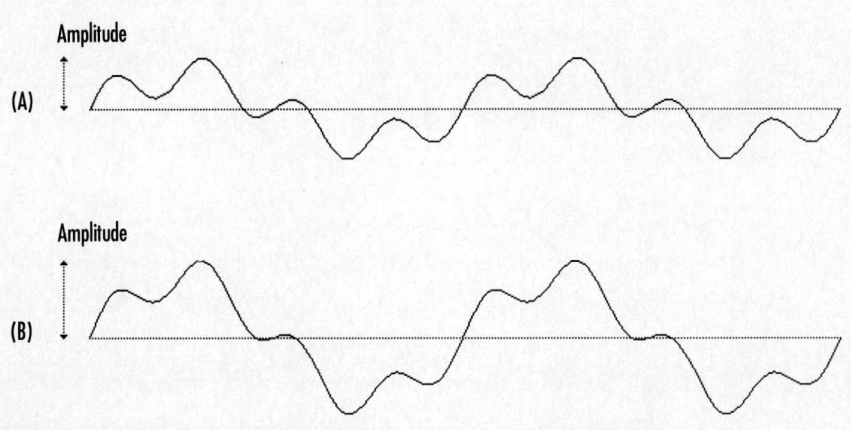

FIGURE 1.7: *Waveform (B) is identical to waveform (A), but the volume of the sound which it represents is greater.*

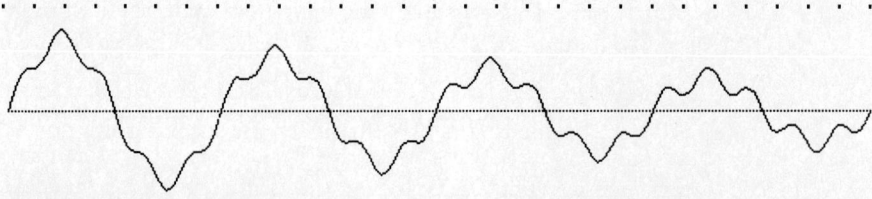

FIGURE 1.8: *The volume of the waveform for a fixed pitch gradually decreases.*

Timbre

Of the three parameters of a sound, timbre is without a doubt the most subtle and the most subjective. It's what gives a tone its "color." In fact, as shown in Figure 1.9, the same note (pitch) played at the same volume (amplitude) by different instruments will not produce the same auditory sensation, and the corresponding waveforms will not have the same shape.

That's about as far as anyone can go toward understanding timbre without a little more knowledge of the science of sound. Fourier's law is good place to start.

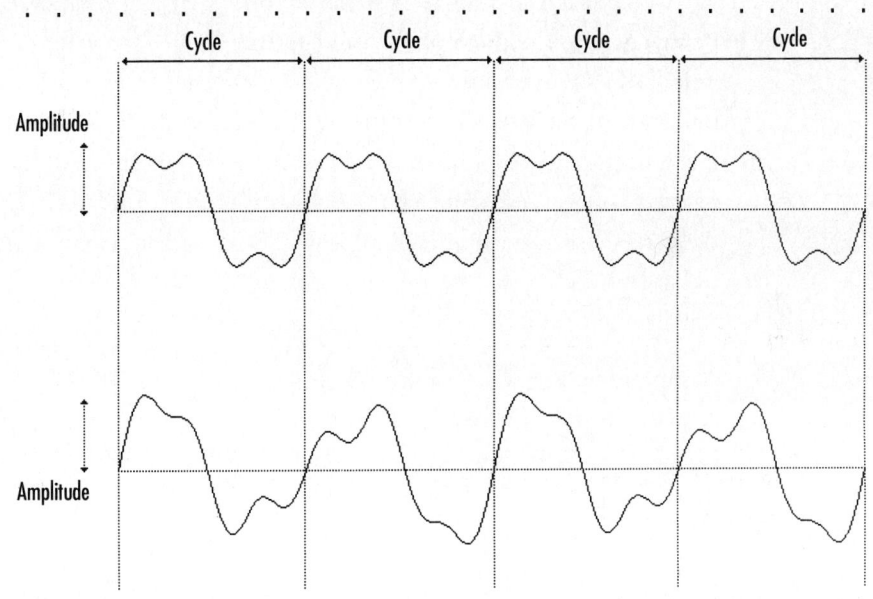

FIGURE 1.9: *Waveforms (A) and (B) are equivalent in terms of pitch and amplitude but do not have the same shape; therefore, their timbre is different.*

Fourier's Law and Harmonic Series

It was in 1822 that the noted physicist Joseph Fourier discovered a law that would revolutionize signal processing. The law is general and applies to all periodic signals, whether the signals are sound waves or some other kind of wave. Here's the definition:

> Fourier's Law: All complex periodic movements can be broken down into a series of simple periodic (sinusoidal) movements, known as harmonics, whose frequencies are integral multiples of the lowest or fundamental frequency.

That's the secret of timbre. A periodic tone (that is, a tone with a fixed pitch, equal to the pitch of the fundamental) actually consists of a given number of sinusoidal waveforms whose frequencies are whole-number multiples of the frequency of the fundamental tone. The richest timbre includes the entire harmonic series, while the thinnest timbre has the appearance of a simple sinusoidal waveform (i.e., the fundamental tone). Between these two extremes, any and all intermediate combinations are possible. In other words, the harmonic components of a complex periodic signal, as shown in Figure 1.10, determine the timbre of the signal.

An aperiodic signal (i.e., a variable-pitch signal) also consists of a multitude of sinusoidal waveforms. However, the frequencies of an aperiodic signal aren't necessarily whole-number multiples of the frequency of the fundamental tone. In order to distinguish them from the harmonic frequencies, these frequencies are known as "*partials*."

In short, two tones that have the same pitch and the same amplitude can be distinguished by their harmonic content. To see how this theory works, consider the example of a sinusoidal waveform whose pitch is 1000Hz. A periodic tone based on this fundamental will contain some or all of the harmonics that are multiples of this frequency and that are audible up to the 20th harmonic (because $20 \times 1000\text{Hz} = 20,000\text{Hz}$),

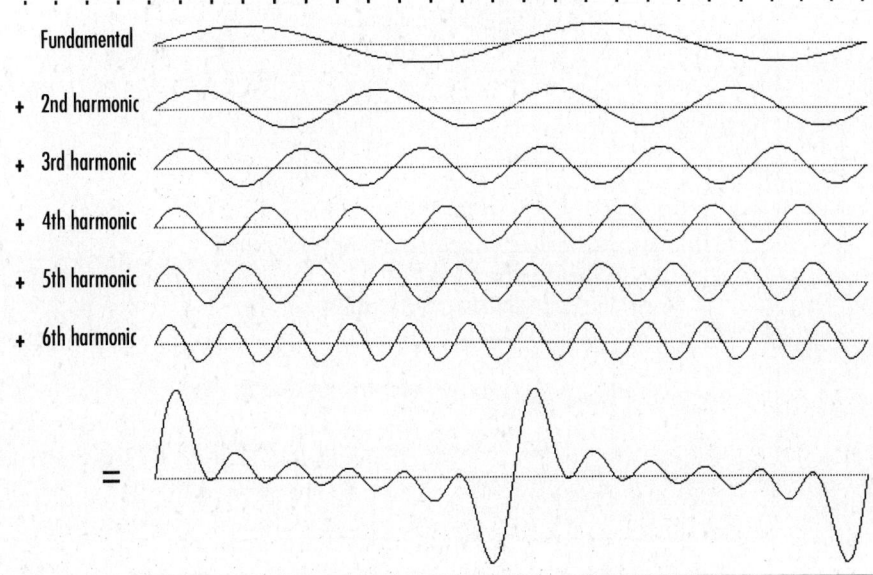

FIGURE 1.10: *A periodic signal consisting of its fundamental and its first five harmonics is built by adding together the six sinusoidal waveforms. In this example, all of the harmonics have the same amplitude.*

which is the theoretical limit beyond which human ears can't hear sounds. It's customary to use the term "Xth harmonic" to refer to the harmonic that's formed when the fundamental frequency is multiplied by X. Likewise, the term "harmonic series" is used to describe the set of sinusoidal waveforms that make up a periodic tone. So in this example, a tone consisting of the 2nd, 3rd, 6th, and 9th harmonics will contain, in addition to the 1000-Hz fundamental, the simple periodic movements at 2000, 3000, 6000, and 9000Hz.

This analysis leads to another two-dimensional representation of sounds, namely, the "spectral content." As indicated in Figure 1.11, the frequencies are shown along the abscissa, and their amplitudes along the ordinate. The frequency scale can be either linear or logarithmic, whichever you prefer.

B

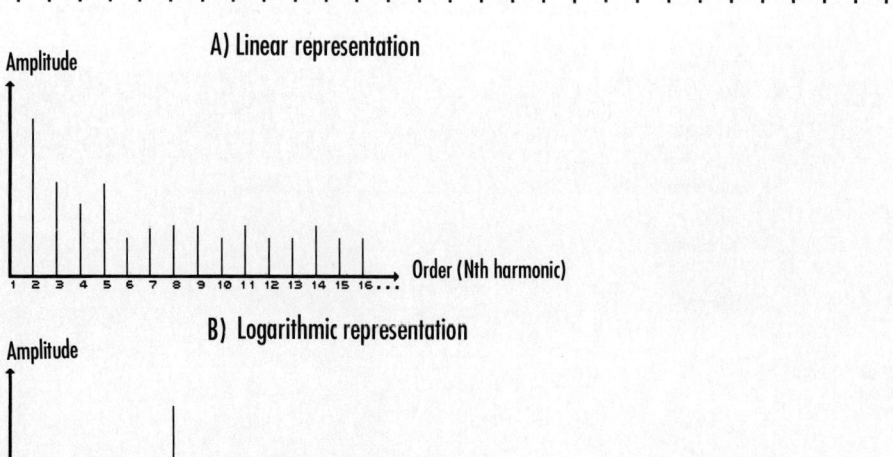

FIGURE 1.11: *A two-dimensional representation of the frequency content of a tone describes the various harmonics and their respective amplitudes. Two methods can be used: linear representation (in which any two successive harmonics are separated by the same distance) and logarithmic representation (in which two consecutive octaves are separated by the same distance). In this example, the tone contains the first through the 16th harmonics.*

Now take a look at the musical intervals that separate each harmonic from its fundamental. As you saw earlier, a frequency has to be doubled in order to be repeated in the next higher octave. In the example just given, the 2nd, 4th, 8th, and 16th harmonics (i.e., the frequencies at 2000, 4000, 8000, and 16,000Hz) represent intervals of one, two, three, and four octaves with regard to the fundamental. For a series of 32 harmonics and for pitches that are expressed not in terms of hertz but in the form of ratios with regard to the intervals within an octave, almost all of the harmonics correspond approximately to standard intervals. The exact ratios for these intervals are multiples of 1.059463094, and appear in the next-to-last column of Table 1.1.

TABLE 1.1: *Harmonic Ratios*

HARMONIC	ABSOLUTE RATIO	OCTAVE RATIO (LESS THAN 1:1)	DECIMAL RATIO	NEAREST MULTIPLE OF 1.059	CORRESPONDING DEGREE OF THE SCALE
OCTAVE 1					
1	1/1	1/1	1	1	fundamental
OCTAVE 2					
2	2/1	1/1	1	1	fundamental
3	3/1	3/2	1.5	1.494	fifth
OCTAVE 3					
4	4/1	1/1	1	1	fundamental
5	5/1	5/4	1.25	1.258	major third
6	6/1	3/2	1.5	1.494	fifth
7	7/1	7/4	1.75	1.774	minor seventh
OCTAVE 4					
8	8/1	1/1	1	1	octave
9	9/1	9/8	1.125	1.121	major second
10	10/1	5/4	1.25	1.258	major third
11	11/1	11/8	1.375	1.411	diminished fifth
12	12/1	3/2	1.5	1.494	fifth
13	13/1	13/8	1.625	1.582	minor sixth
14	14/1	7/4	1.75	1.774	minor seventh
15	15/1	15/8	1.875	1.879	major seventh

TABLE 1.1: *Harmonic Ratios (continued)*

HARMONIC	ABSOLUTE RATIO	OCTAVE RATIO (LESS THAN 1:1)	DECIMAL RATIO	NEAREST MULTIPLE OF 1.059	CORRESPONDING DEGREE OF THE SCALE
			OCTAVE 5		
16	16/1	1/1	1	1	octave
17	17/1	17/16	1.062	1.059	minor second
18	18/1	9/8	1.125	1.121	major second
19	19/1	19/16	1.187	1.188	minor third
20	20/1	5/4	1.25	1.258	major third
21	21/1	21/16	1.312	1.332	fourth
22	22/1	11/8	1.375	1.411	diminished fifth
23	23/1	23/16	1.437	1.411	augmented fourth
24	24/1	3/2	1.5	1.494	fifth
25	25/1	25/16	1.562	1.582	
26	26/1	13/8	1.625		minor sixth
27	27/1	27/16	1.687	1.675	major sixth
28	28/1	7/4	1.75	1.774	minor seventh
29	29/1	29/16	1.812		
30	30/1	15/8	1.875	1.879	major seventh
31	31/1	31/16	1.937		
			OCTAVE 6		
32	32/1	1/1	1	1	octave

· ·

Without going into a study of the various tempering methods, most of which are beyond the scope of this book, it's worth mentioning that the Zarlin scale (which is also known as the "physicists' scale" or "pure scale") is built from intervals that are determined by this harmonic series. This scale has the major disadvantage of applying only to a single tonality (i.e., the tonality, or musical key, of the fundamental of the harmonic series on which it is based), because the twelve halftones are unequal. This is why the well-tempered scale is used today. It's not as pure as the Zarlin scale, but it doesn't have the single-tonality problem. In practical terms, that means you can modulate, or change from one key to another, without disrupting the acoustic or musical structure of a piece.

Starting arbitrarily with a fundamental that's equal to C1, the harmonics in the series correspond to the following notes: C1, C2, G2, C3, E3, G3, Bb3, C4, D4, E4, Gb4, G4, Ab4, Bb4, B4, C5, etc.

With acoustic (natural or nonelectronic) sounds, the amplitude of the harmonics has a tendency to decrease gradually over time, in proportion to the order of the harmonics. This is why, when several one-octave intervals (i.e., harmonics 1, 2, 4, 8, 16, 32, and so on) are present, the ear hears an overall pitch instead of a cacophony resulting from the superimposition of many different pitches.

The process of breaking down a tone into a set of sinusoidal waveforms is actually much more complicated than it might seem. The amplitude of each of the harmonics in the tone evolves over time, and this evolution is what determines the richness of a tone. So by listening closely to a note played on an acoustic instrument, such as a piano, you can hear the timbre and the amplitude diminishing as the tone decreases.

What this means is that Fourier's Law is accurate only for a "snapshot" of a tone. Analytical engineering procedures such as Discrete Fourier Transform or the more recent Fast Fourier Transform (FFT), discovered in 1965 by J.W. Cooley and J.W. Tukey, make it possible to break down a sound mathematically into set of sinusoidal waveforms throughout the course of its duration. Speedier than its predecessor, as its name implies, the FFT algorithm has invaded the domain of musical data processing. It leads directly to the three-dimensional representation of sound (i.e., the evolution over time of the frequency and amplitude of each harmonic), as shown in Figure 1.12.

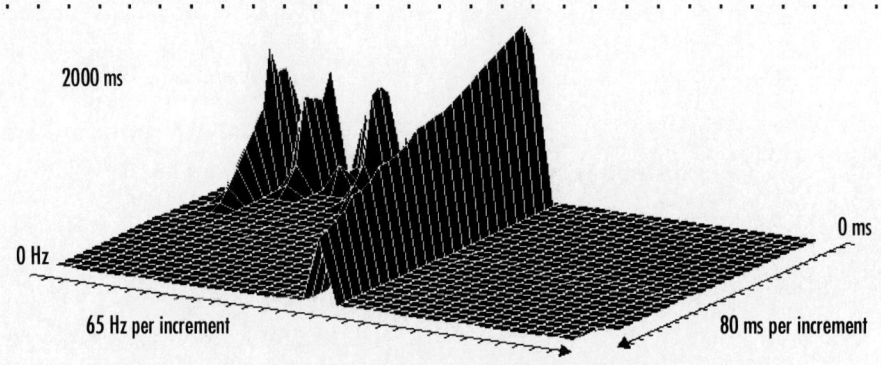

FIGURE 1.12: *A three-dimensional illustration of the evolution of a tone over time.*

In theory it's easy. But sound synthesis runs up against plenty of other difficulties. In addition to the evolution of the pitch and particularly of the amplitude of each sinusoidal waveform in a complex periodic signal, there are always also a few partials (i.e., sinusoidal waveforms whose frequencies are not whole-number multiples of the fundamental). At the beginning of any tone produced by an acoustic instrument, a short transition period precedes the stabilization of the harmonic content of the tone. During this period, for instance, the brass player blows into his instrument, and the column of air takes a certain amount of time to stabilize (which also causes a slight change in pitch); the piano keys strike the hammers, producing a characteristic noise just before the strings begin to vibrate regularly, etc. The harmonic content is unstable, and, in spite of a predominance of harmonics, many partials are generated. These are the so-called "attack transients." At the auditory level, these short periods are the ones which, more than any other, characterize an instrument (and on which, more than any other, the fidelity of a synthesized sound depends). Not surprisingly, these transients are also the hardest phenomena to imitate.

Chapters 5 and 6 of this book address the way the major families of sound generators and the way they handle pitch, amplitude, and timbre. Meanwhile, this brief overview of the principal characteristics of a tone should let you make good use of the specialized MIDI messages about the acoustic management of synthesizers.

Making Music, Then and Now

In conventional acoustic (i.e., non-electronic) instruments, the production of a tone is related to two fundamental concepts. The first involves the physical object that produces the auditory phenomenon, and the second involves the type and amount of energy the musician has to impart to the physical object in order to make it vibrate. These two concepts correspond respectively to the concept of an instrument and the concept of the person who plays it. The first concept is governed by the laws of acoustics, while the second is generally symbolized by a system of musical notation.

Conventional instruments, in the broad sense of the term (whether woodwinds, strings, or percussion instruments) have in common a physical structure which is in direct contact with the musician. This physical structure lets the musician activate the sound-production mechanism. In musical data processing, this portion of the process is known as the *controller*. For example, it consists of the keyboard and pedals of a piano, the neck and strings of a guitar, the sticks and skins of a drum—or, more generally, everything that lets the musician influence the production of the tone. The materials used in the construction of an acoustic musical instrument are directly responsible for the way the instrument produces the sound, whether these materials are part of the controller (as in a guitar or percussion instrument) or whether they're interconnected mechanically (such as the hammers, springs, and dampers of a piano, or the bellows of an organ). The controller portion of the instrument and the sound-generation portion are inseparably linked.

A New Breed of Instruments

Instruments have evolved dramatically since the middle of this century. Up till then, the controller portion had a physical effect on the quality of the sound that the instrument produced. The subsequent development of electrical techniques, followed by electronic and then digital techniques, made it possible to simulate or reproduce given acoustical conditions independently of any physical controller. These new instruments, which were designed to create waveforms of all kinds, are known as *sound generators*. They include synthesizers, samplers, and other instruments.

The output of these generators is a signal which represents the sound wave in electrical form. The signal is sent to an amplifier circuit, which forwards it to speakers. Inside the generator, various procedures are activated in order to determine the pitch, the amplitude, and the timbre of the sound signal to be created. Unlike acoustic instruments, in which physical energy must be transmitted by the controllers, these procedures need no physical energy in order to be implemented. A synthesizer may have a keyboard; but in this case the keyboard doesn't control a hammer mechanism that causes strings to vibrate. Instead, the keyboard simply sends the sound generator a command to produce a given tone. This command is sent by means of an electrical signal, which can be either analog or digital. These commands are the notorious "MIDI messages." As you'll see, this type of controller doesn't have to look like a keyboard (although, for obvious reasons of convenience, a keyboard is what it usually looks like).

Musical data-processing assumes that musical performance involves three necessary sequential stages, as opposed to the two stages that a conventional acoustic instrument requires. In these three stages,

1 ▪ The musician physically transmits energy to the controller (by pressing keys, etc.)

2 ▪ The controller converts this energy into a control signal intended for the sound generator. This conversion consists simply of encoding the mechanical action transmitted to the controller by the musician.

3 ▪ When the sound generator receives the control signal, it reproduces the sound (by using electronic and/or digital components to simulate given acoustical conditions).

Without getting too far ahead of the discussion, it's easy to imagine the range of possibilities that an electronic musical instrument can offer as a result of the fact that stages 1, 2, and 3 are independent of one another. For instance,

▪ Substituting, in Stage 1 or Stage 2, a different but equivalent control signal, to automate the implementation procedure for the sound generator

▪ Driving several sound generators from the same controller

▪ Driving a sound generator from any given controller, etc.

Toward an Interface

This separation between the controller and the sound generator implies the use of a protocol (i.e., an *interface*) that lets these two modules communicate with one another. The concepts outlined in this section provide a brief introduction to the principles that govern the interfaces for electronic musical instruments, retracing the history of the systems which characterized the pre-MIDI period. In broad terms, there are three major categories of information that are necessary and sufficient for any musical interface, and particularly for the MIDI interface. They are:

- The data used to encode what the musician plays
- The synchronization data
- The data representing the parameters of a tone

Encoding What the Musician Plays

Dividing a musical instrument such as a synthesizer into two clearly separate modules (i.e., the controller and the sound generator) implies the existence of an interface system that lets the two modules talk to each other. The interface converts into encoded signals the motions that the musician applies to the controller (i.e., the instrumental execution), in order to drive the sound generator (i.e., the production of tones).

The first synthesizers were analog devices. The interface system was nothing more or less than an electrical signal whose voltage varied as a function of the note played on the controller (i.e., the keyboard). This voltage provided power to the sound generator, thereby determining the frequency (i.e., the pitch) at which the oscillator should produce the waveform.

Physically, this system was easy to implement. An electrical signal having a given voltage was sent from one end of the keyboard to the other, passing through a resistor for each note it encountered. The farther this signal traveled, the more resistors the voltage passed through, and therefore the more the voltage decreased. Every time a key was pressed, the corresponding voltage was transmitted to the sound generator, thereby indicating the frequency to be produced. The frequency was actually physically produced by the oscillator or waveform generator.

Although this principle is simple, right from the beginning it ran up against the problem of the lack of standardization. As shown in Figure 1.13, some keyboards used a linear voltage-variation method (i.e, the hertz/volt system), and others used a logarithmic method (i.e., the volt/octave system).

The hertz/volt system

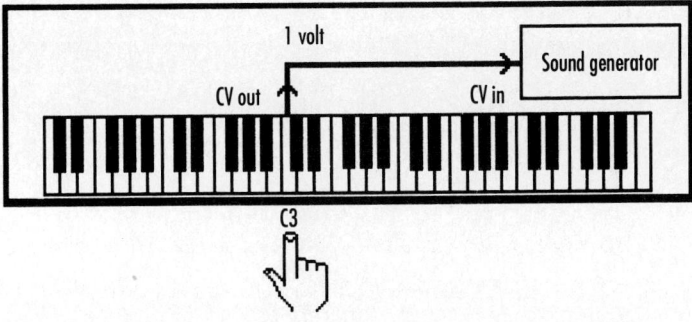

The volt/octave system

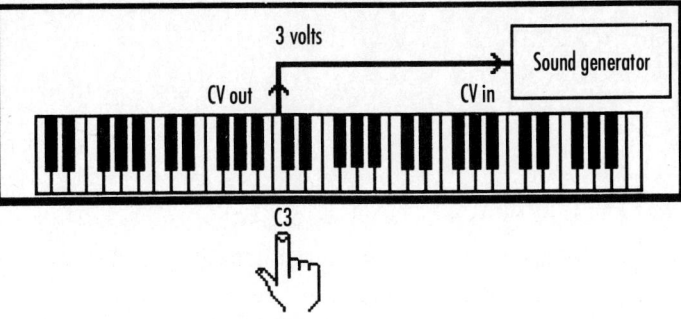

FIGURE 1.13: *When the C3 key is pressed, the keyboard sends the sound generator a voltage of either 1 volt (in the hertz/volt system) or 3 volts (in the volt/octave system).*

In the linear method, the voltage doubled with every octave. Because an octave is divided into 12 semitones, all you had to do to obtain the voltage of the next semitone was to multiply a given voltage by the twelfth root of two (i.e., by 1.059463094). In the volt/octave system, each successive octave corresponded to a one-volt increase in the voltage, or an increase of 0.0833 volts per semitone. Table 1.2 shows the correspondence between these two systems over a range of five octaves.

TABLE 1.2: *Correspondence between the Hertz/Volt System and the Volt/Octave System*

NOTE	FREQUENCY	HERTZ/VOLT SYSTEM	VOLT/OCTAVE SYSTEM
C	1	65.406 0.250	1.000
C#	1	69.296 0.265	1.083
D	1	73.416 0.281	1.166
D#	1	77.782 0.297	1.250
E	1	82.407 0.315	1.333
F	1	87.307 0.333	1.416
F#	1	92.499 0.353	1.500
G	1	97.999 0.374	1.583
G#	1	103.826 0.396	1.666
A	1	110.000 0.420	1.750
A#	1	116.541 0.445	1.833
B	1	123.471 0.471	1.916
C	2	130.813 0.500	2.000
C#	2	138.591 0.530	2.083
D	2	146.832 0.561	2.166
D#	2	155.563 0.595	2.250
E	2	164.814 0.630	2.333

TABLE 1.2: *Correspondence between the Hertz/Volt System and the Volt/Octave System (continued)*

NOTE	FREQUENCY	HERTZ/VOLT SYSTEM	VOLT/OCTAVE SYSTEM
F	2	174.614 0.667	2.416
F#	2	184.997 0.707	2.500
G	2	195.998 0.749	2.583
G#	2	207.652 0.794	2.666
A	2	220.000 0.841	2.750
A#	2	233.082 0.891	2.833
B	2	246.942 0.944	2.916
C	3	261.626 1.000	3.000
C#	3	277.183 1.059	3.083
D	3	293.665 1.122	3.166
D#	3	311.127 1.189	3.250
E	3	329.628 1.260	3.333
F	3	349.228 1.335	3.416
F#	3	369.994 1.414	3.500
G	3	391.995 1.498	3.583
G#	3	415.305 1.587	3.666
A	3	440.000 1.681	3.750
A#	3	466.164 1.781	3.833
B	3	493.883 1.887	3.916
C	4	523.251 2.000	4.000
C#	4	554.365 2.119	4.083
D	4	587.330 2.245	4.166
D#	4	622.254 2.378	4.250

TABLE 1.2: *Correspondence between the Hertz/Volt System and the Volt/Octave System (continued)*

NOTE	FREQUENCY	HERTZ/VOLT SYSTEM	VOLT/OCTAVE SYSTEM
E	4	659.255 2.519	4.333
F	4	698.456 2.668	4.416
F#	4	739.989 2.827	4.500
G	4	783.991 2.996	4.583
G#	4	830.609 3.174	4.666
A	4	880.000 3.363	4.750
A#	4	932.328 3.561	4.833
B	4	987.767 3.774	4.916
C	5	1046.502 4.000	5.000
C#	5	1108.731 4.238	5.083
D	5	1174.659 4.490	5.166
D#	5	1244.508 4.757	5.250
E	5	1318.510 5.040	5.333
F	5	1396.913 5.339	5.416
F#	5	1479.978 5.657	5.500
G	5	1567.982 5.993	5.583
G#	5	1661.219 6.349	5.666
A	5	1760.000 6.727	5.750
A#	5	1864.655 7.127	5.833
B	5	1975.533 7.551	5.916
C	6	2093.005 8.000	6.000

Regardless of the system that's used, the voltage command sent to an oscillator is known as the "*CV*" (control voltage). Although this signal indicates the pitch of the note that was played, it tells you nothing about how long the note lasts. The idea of duration is addressed by a signal known as the "gate signal," which is triggered when pressure is placed on a key and released when the pressure is removed from the key. This way the gate signal indicates to the sound generator's envelope generator (i.e., the section that controls the development of volume over time) the length of time during which the note (i.e., the waveform produced by the oscillator) should be played. Physically, the gate signal is an all-or-nothing electrical signal. As shown in Figure 1.14, a positive voltage (usually +5 volts)

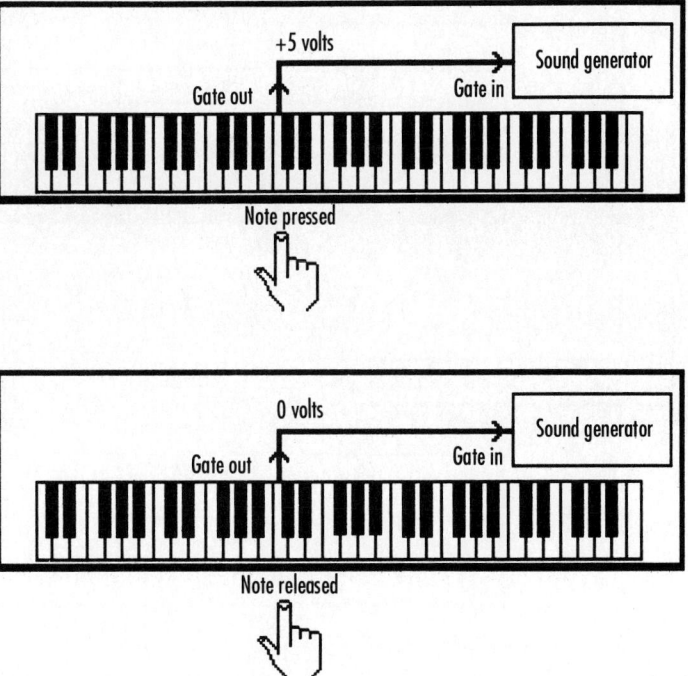

FIGURE 1.14: *When pressure is applied to a key, the gate voltage changes from 0 to +5 volts. The voltage drops back to zero as soon as the key is released.*

corresponds to a key that's being pressed, and the absence of voltage corresponds to the resting state. Together, CV and gate signals form the most elementary kind of interface between a keyboard and a sound generator.

This interface inspired the idea of driving several sound generators from a single keyboard. All that was needed was to install ports in each synthesizer for the CV-out and gate-out signals (i.e., the signals sent from the keyboard) and for the CV-in and gate-in signals (i.e., the signals intended for the sound generator). This way, as shown in Figure 1.15, if the CV-out and gate-out ports of a first synthesizer were connected to the CV-in

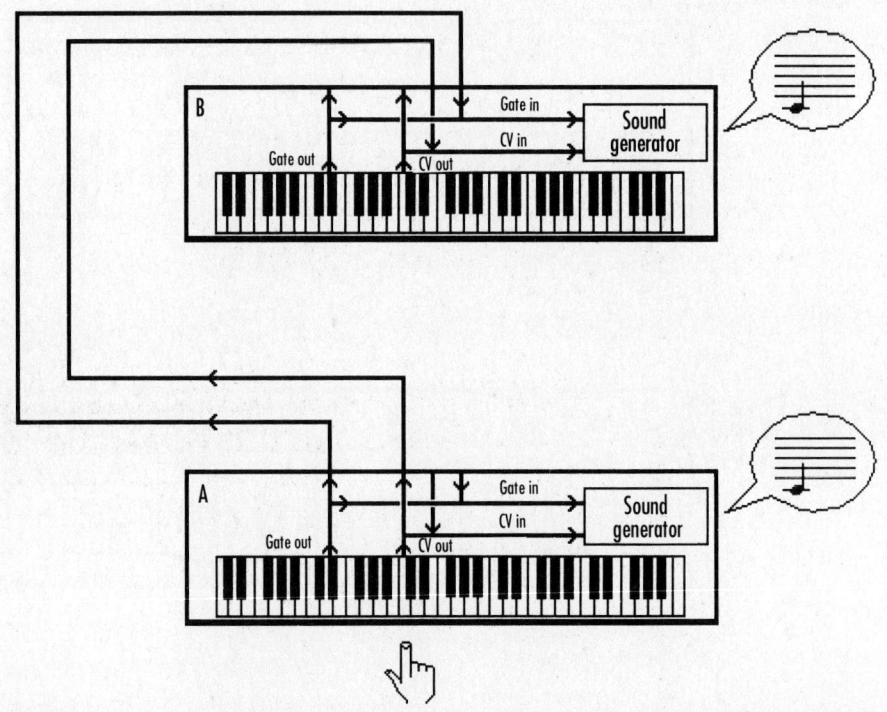

FIGURE 1.15: *The keyboard of instrument A sends CV and gate information to the sound generator of instrument B.*

and gate-in ports of a second synthesizer, the keyboard of the first synthesizer could drive both sound generators (provided of course the CV standards were the same, or an interface was used to convert hertz/volt signals to volt/octave signals or vice versa).

This principle of controlling a sound generator by means of voltage was extended by the addition of other interfaces, such as the Pitch to Voltage Converter, which made it possible to convert the pitch of a signal obtained at the output of a microphone into a CV signal in real time.

The Dawn of the Digital Era

It became obvious early on that the unstable nature of electrical voltages made them less than ideal for controlling pitches. Experimental electronic musicians also found it was virtually impossible to obtain accurate and consistent agreement between voltage-controlled oscillators (VCOs). The appearance of microprocessors, which at the time were not a part of analog synthesizers, provided a solution to the problem, and new interfaces saw the light of day.

Instead of sending a variable voltage as a function of the notes played on a keyboard, the keyboards started sending numbers, at a rate of one number per note (hence the term "digital interface"). This procedure solved the problems caused by the instability of the pitch command. But here again, in spite of every attempt at standardization, certain manufacturers developed their own proprietary communications protocols, sometimes in conjunction with an interface between the digital system being used and the CV/gate-signal system. These protocols included the Borland DCB (Digital Communication Bus) interface. The term "DCO" (Digitally Controlled Oscillator) replaced the term "VCO." Some time later the MIDI standard appeared and put an end to these incompatibilities.

Sequencers and Synchronization

The first sequencers were devices which could replace a keyboard in order to drive a sound generator automatically. To do that, it was necessary first of all to program a set of CV and gate (i.e., sequence) voltages and store them in the sequencer's memory. When these voltages were forwarded from the CV-out and gate-out ports of the sequencer to the CV-in and gate-in ports of a sound generator, the sound generator automatically played the programmed musical "score." This method became known as "step-by-step programming."

In order to program each CV and gate voltage in accordance with a musical meter (i.e., a musical tempo), the sequencer included a clock which divided a quarter-note into a given number of memory spaces, with each space either sending or not sending the CV and gate signals. This was the principle that governed the operation of the first rhythm boxes, which contained in a single housing a sequencer and a sound generator that specialized in imitating percussion instruments.

Techniques evolved, and real-time sequencers rapidly replaced their step-by-step counterparts. Instead of programming each voltage one after another in the sequencer's memory, it was much easier to connect the signals produced by the keyboard to the sequencer's memory. This way, what a musician played could be recorded directly and in real time by storing the CV and gate voltages corresponding to the keys that were being pressed and released. In short, real-time sequencers were a lot like specialized tape recorders—ones that simply recorded and reproduced a certain number of control signals intended to automate the playing of one or more sound generators. Real-time sequencers stored the CV and gate messages issued by the keyboard in order to forward them later to the sound generators. Thanks to MIDI, this type of sequencer has managed, little by little, to achieve a certain degree of popularity. (For a detailed look at sequencer operations, see Chapter 7, "MIDI Recording: The Basics.")

Long before MIDI, however, machines existed that were designed to drive sound generators in real time and at a given tempo (not only rhythm boxes, but also arpeggio generators and other devices). In order to make several of these devices operate together, it was necessary to synchronize them extremely accurately. Hence the appearance of a second family of signals, i.e., the synchronization signals.

Like gate signals, synchronization signals (also known as *triggers* or clock signals) are represented as alternating series of null and positive voltages. As shown in Figure 1.16, this alternation of voltages occurs at a rate of a given number of *pulses per quarter note* (PPQN).

FIGURE 1.16: *A square-wave synchronization signal at 24 PPQN (pulses per quarter-note).*

When the trigger input of a slave machine is synchronized with the trigger output of a master machine, the two units will keep the same tempo throughout a piece. As always, thanks to the lack of coordination, the procedures in use were multitudinous: 24, 48, 96, and 384 PPQN, to name a few. But here again the MIDI standard put paid to the lack of standardization.

Programming the Shapes of Sounds

In the earliest analog synthesizers, the parameters of sound (i.e., variations in pitch, timbre, and amplitude) were programmed in real time with the aid of many, many *switches* and potentiometers (*pots* or *faders*), all of which acted directly on the electronic components of the synthesizer. At first, it was virtually impossible to store all of these settings, and only one tone could be worked with at a time. The only way to verify the fruits of one's labors was to note on a piece of paper the position of all the switches and pots.

Once again, microprocessors made it possible to store and recall instantaneously a given number of sounds (i.e., the entire collection of synthesizer settings). In the same way that voltage commands (i.e., VC signals) were replaced by digital commands, the positions of switches and pots began to be digitized. Unfortunately, even in the best of cases the amount of memory available for all these positions was limited to several tens of sounds. Hence the appearance of a third type of interface, namely, the sound-memory storage interface. When normal memory filled up, its contents could be saved on external media for reloading later. At the time, in the absence of floppy disks or hard disk drives, the mass storage function was fulfilled by a simple cassette reader/recorder (like those used by many microcomputers of that era). But because each synthesizer used a proprietary synthesis procedure, the parameters for a given sound on any two given instruments were utterly incompatible. In fact, the settings for a given synthesizer X had nothing in common with the settings for a given synthesizer Y, thereby making it impossible to standardize anything at all. Meanwhile, the reliability of data storage on cassettes left something to be desired, and this method was soon replaced by data storage on floppy disks. Naturally, the MIDI standard didn't drag its feet when it came to increasing synthesizers' memory-management potential.

The point of this short summary of the earliest synthesizers and their interfaces is that musical interfaces center around three axes:

1 • encoding what the musician plays (including the step of recording the resulting codes)

2 ▪ synchronizing the recorders with each other, and

3 ▪ managing the tone-creation parameters.

So much for the past, burdened as it was with a multitude of incompatibilities. It's time now to look at the welcome changes that the MIDI standard brought, and see how those changes relate to hardware as well as to software.

IV V VI VII VIII IX X XI XII

CHAPTER 2

XIII XIV XV XVI A B C D E F G H I

The MIDI

Hardware
Interface

N INTERFACE, in the data-processing sense of the term, can be defined as "a hardware and software device by means of which information is exchanged between two systems." Microcomputers are a good illustration of this concept. Thanks to specialized interfaces, the computer's CPU (central processing unit) can exchange information with keyboards, screens, mass storage devices (floppy disks, hard disk drives, etc.), printers, etc.

For example, when you tap the "1" key on a calculator and the digit is displayed onscreen, you're dealing with three systems and two interfaces. The three systems are the numeric keyboard of the calculator, the calculator's CPU (microprocessor), and the display screen. The first interface converts the pressure on the key into a code which the microprocessor can understand. Then the microprocessor uses a second interface to convert the code into a piece of data that can be displayed on the screen.

As a general rule, an interface is defined by both hardware characteristics (i.e., the "transport mechanism" for the data and the format in which the information is conveyed) and software characteristics (i.e., the language in which the information is expressed). The role of the MIDI interface is to carry musical information among several systems (keyboards, tone generators, etc.). We'll examine the hardware specifications first.

ᏜIDI: A Serial Asynchronous Link

The MIDI interface is a bidirectional (i.e., one wire for each direction) serial asynchronous link which transfers data at a rate of 31,250 bits per second (bps) with a tolerance of plus or minus 1 percent. Information is transmitted in binary form, i.e., coded as zeros and ones. As shown in Figure 2.1, the information is grouped in bytes (groups of eight bits, numbered from D0 to D7). Each byte is enclosed by a *start bit* (logical 0) and a *stop bit* (logical 1). The start and stop bits let the receiving unit identify the beginning and end of a byte as it comes in, bit by bit. In other words, these bits are the first and last elements of the byte. Therefore, in order to obtain 8 bits of useful information, you have to send a group of 10 bits. (This 10-bit group is also known as a byte even though this use of the term can be confusing, since "byte" generally refers to a group of 8 bits.) These 10-bit MIDI bytes are grouped into packets (which can contain any number of bytes, from 1 to infinity) according to a well-defined syntax that is the subject of later chapters. The result of this grouping is known as a "MIDI message."

The concept of a *serial* interface means that bits are transmitted one after another, through a single wire. At a data rate of 31,250 bps, it takes 320 microseconds to transmit one useful byte (10 bits). Thus, in one second

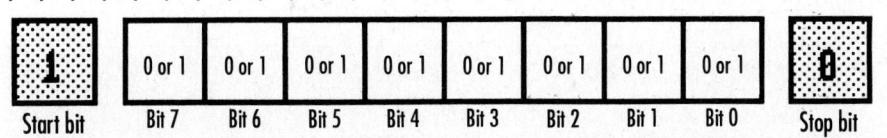

1	0 or 1	0 or 1	0 or 1	0 or 1	0 or 1	0 or 1	0 or 1	0 or 1	0
Start bit	Bit 7	Bit 6	Bit 5	Bit 4	Bit 3	Bit 2	Bit 1	Bit 0	Stop bit

FIGURE 2.1: *A MIDI byte consists of eight useful bits enclosed by a start bit and a stop bit, which make it possible to tell where the active information begins and ends.*

the MIDI interface can transmit more than 3000 bytes. There is another procedure, known as a *parallel* link, which requires at least as many wires as there are bits to be transmitted at once (see Figure 2.2). Because a parallel link sends each byte as a single block, the byte can be transferred eight times faster than in a serial link.

Serial `0 1 1 1 0 1 1 0` ⟶

Parallel
`0` ⟶
`1` ⟶
`1` ⟶
`1` ⟶
`0` ⟶
`1` ⟶
`1` ⟶
`0` ⟶

FIGURE 2.2: *A serial interface transfers the bits in a message one after another over the same line, while a parallel interface uses the same number of lines (generally, eight) as there are bits to be transmitted simultaneously.*

The start and stop bits are to a large extent related to the asynchronous nature of the MIDI link. These bits let the receiver detect the presence of data without requiring that the receiver take into consideration the time at which the information arrives. Conversely, with a synchronous interface, the clock of the sender and the clock of the receiver are synchronized. More specifically, the clock of one of the two devices is sent to the other device by means of a separate link, which requires an additional line. This way, the receiver knows the exact time at which it should expect data to arrive (see Figure 2.3). Synchronous links are much trickier and harder to implement than asynchronous interfaces. What's more, synchronous links are not well suited to MIDI, because with MIDI the time at which information is issued is a function of the musician, and therefore completely unpredictable.

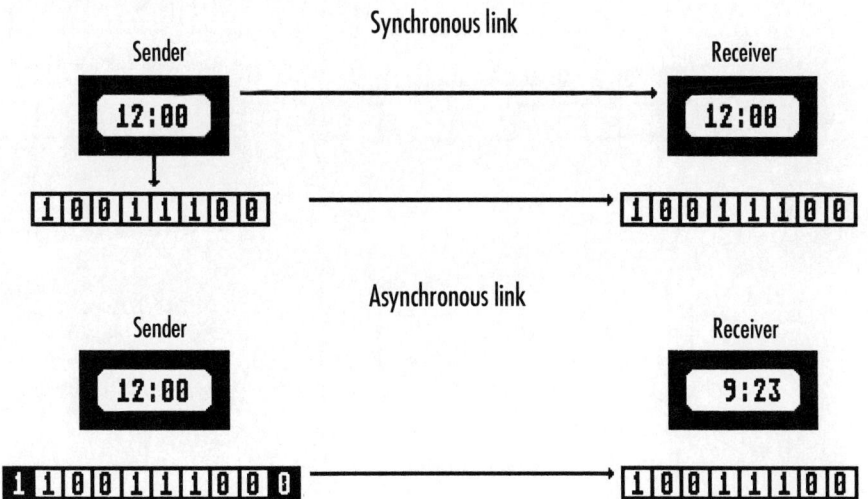

FIGURE 2.3: *In a synchronous link, the clock time of the sender is transmitted to the receiver. In this example, the receiver knows that at exactly 12:00 noon the sender will transmit a piece of data.*

Speed and Density

As noted above, MIDI messages travel at a constant rate of 31,250 bits per second. Thus, when a receiving unit receives a start bit, it waits until the first useful bit in the byte (i.e., bit D0) arrives 320 microseconds later, and so on until the stop bit arrives. However, nothing regulates the time interval between two MIDI bytes in the same message. In theory, in order to optimize transmissions, this interval should be as short as possible (i.e., 320 microseconds) (see Figure 2.4). In reality, however, if a message contains several tens of bytes—the way MIDI's System Exclusive messages do—some MIDI devices don't transmit the data at full speed.

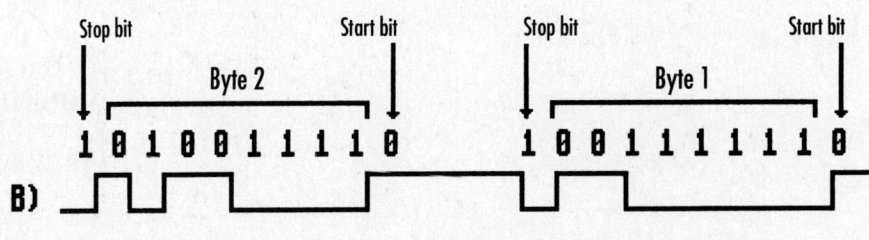

FIGURE 2.4: *Device A uses the maximum pass-band for a given transfer speed. Device B does not.*

Other MIDI devices overflow during reception, due to an insufficient amount of buffer space, if the maximum transmission density is used.

Connectors

Physically, the MIDI standard requires 5-pin, 180-degree DIN connectors, such as the Switchcraft 57 GB5F. (Octave Plateau instruments use Canon XLR sockets, and Lake People uses jacks.) The DIN standard isn't well known among musicians, and the distinctive MIDI connectors are easy to tell apart from audio connectors (see Figure 2.5).

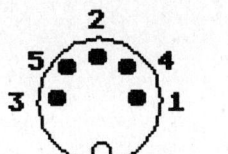

FIGURE 2.5: *The pin pattern of a DIN socket*

Functionally, the MIDI interface consists of three types of sockets, known as "ports": MIDI In, MIDI Out, and MIDI Thru. Their roles are explained in detail later in this chapter. Pins 1 and 3 are not used. Pin 2 in the MIDI Out and MIDI Thru ports is reserved for ground. (The MIDI In port has no ground.) Pins 4 and 5 carry a 5 milliampere current loop. A logic voltage of +5 volts represents a bit set to 0, and a logic voltage of 0 volts represents a bit set to 1 (see Figure 2.6).

Although specific MIDI cables exist, it is perfectly all right to use conventional hi-fi cables, provided however that two pins are not inverted or "strapped" (i.e., soldered in pairs) at the ends of the cable, as shown in Figure 2.7. In any event, a MIDI cable should be no more than about 45 feet long. Longer cables can adversely affect the data they carry.

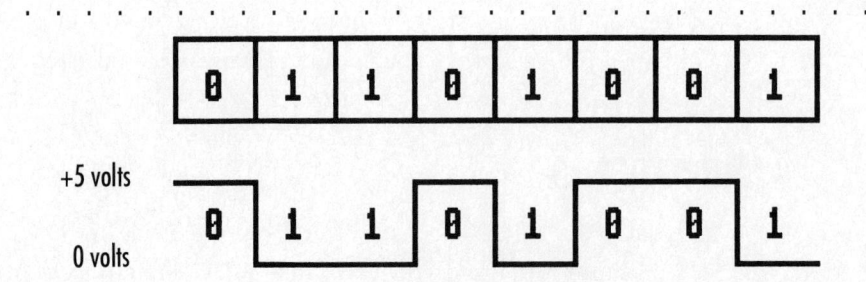

FIGURE 2.6: *A byte shown as a series of logic voltages*

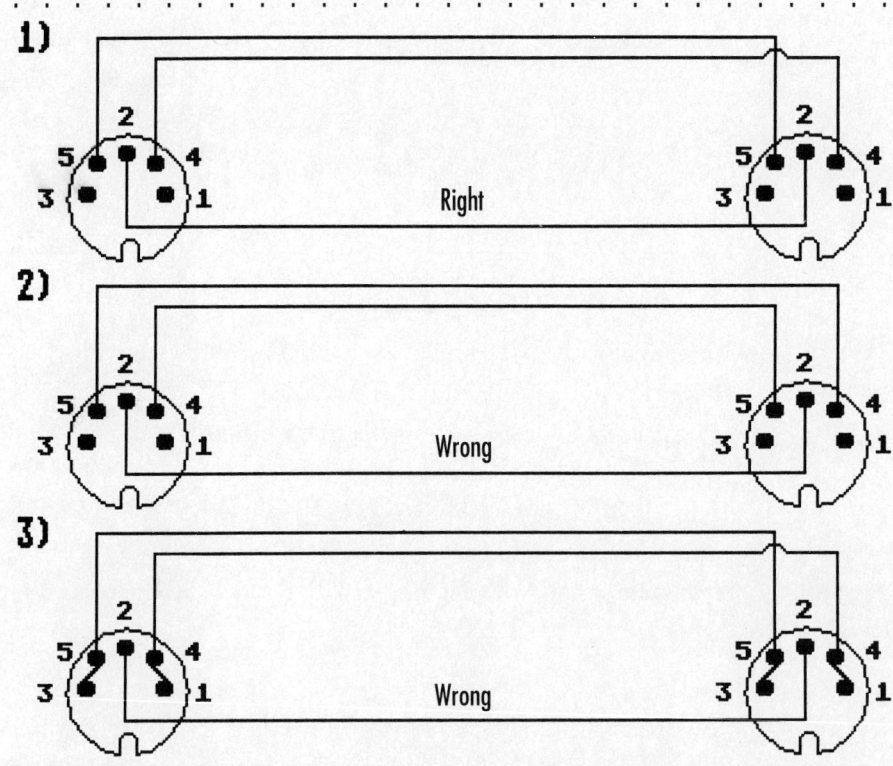

FIGURE 2.7: *Only the first of these three MIDI connections (with the ground on pin 2 and the conductive lines on pins 5 and 4) is correct. Pins 5 and 4 in the second connection are inverted, and the pins in the third connection are "strapped" (i.e., pins 5 and 3 are soldered together, as are pins 4 and 1).*

Optoelectrical Isolation

In order to avoid electrical interference, and particularly ground loops, each MIDI In port is equipped with a optoelectrical isolator. The principle consists of providing power to an LED (light-emitting diode) by means of the current loop. Depending on its voltage state, the LED either lights or doesn't light a photoelectric transistor, which in turn either does or doesn't allow current to pass. Thanks to this isolation, the risk of interference between the MIDI data and the instrument circuits is eliminated.

The capability of an optoisolator is a function of its transfer ratio, i.e., the ratio between the strength of the incoming current and the strength of the outgoing current. For example, a strength of 2.5 mA (milliamperes) measured at the output of the transistor corresponds to a ratio of 1:2. It is strongly recommended that optoisolators be used which have a ratio of at least 1:1 and a response time of less than 2 microseconds. The Sharp PC-900 and the Hewlett-Packard 6N138 (or equivalent) optoisolators are recognized by the MIDI standard (see Figure 2.8).

The purpose of the diode placed upstream of the optoisolator circuit is to protect the LED from polarity inversion and from self-induction phenomena caused by the high transmission speed. As shown in Figure 2.9, a set of 220-ohm resistors regulates the strength of the current loop and protects the components against potential short-circuits.

The Serial/Parallel Interface

In order for MIDI instruments to communicate with computers, you need an interface that converts data from the MIDI device (for use by the microprocessor) and converts data from the microprocessor (for use by the MIDI device).

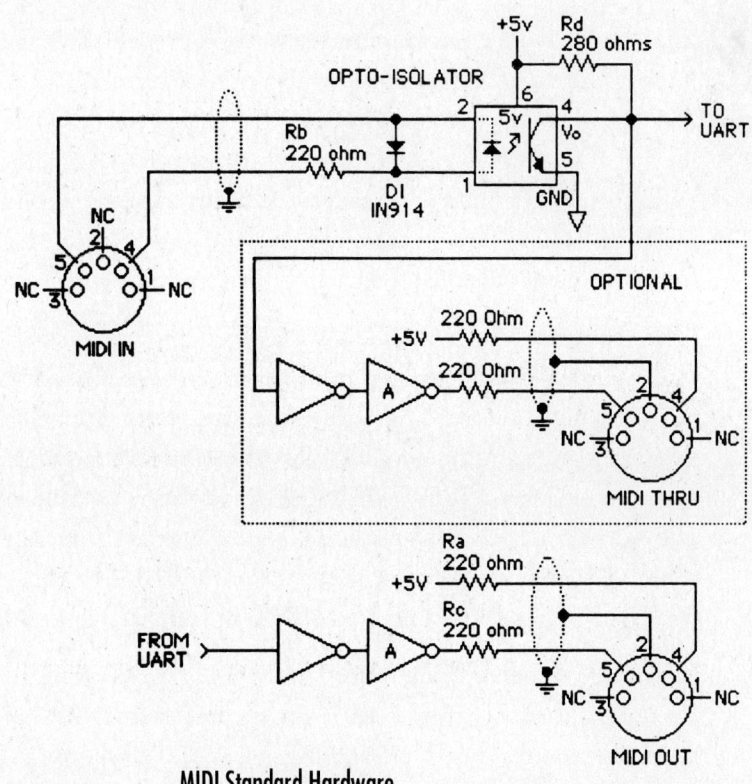

MIDI Standard Hardware

NOTES:

1. Optoisolator currently shown is Sharp PC-900
   (HP 6N138 or other optoisolator can be used with appropriate changes).

2. Gates "A" are IC or transistor.

3. Resistors are 5%.

FIGURE 2.8: *The physical description of the MIDI standard, taken from the official documentation. Copyright ©1988 MIDI Manufacturers Association—used with permission.*

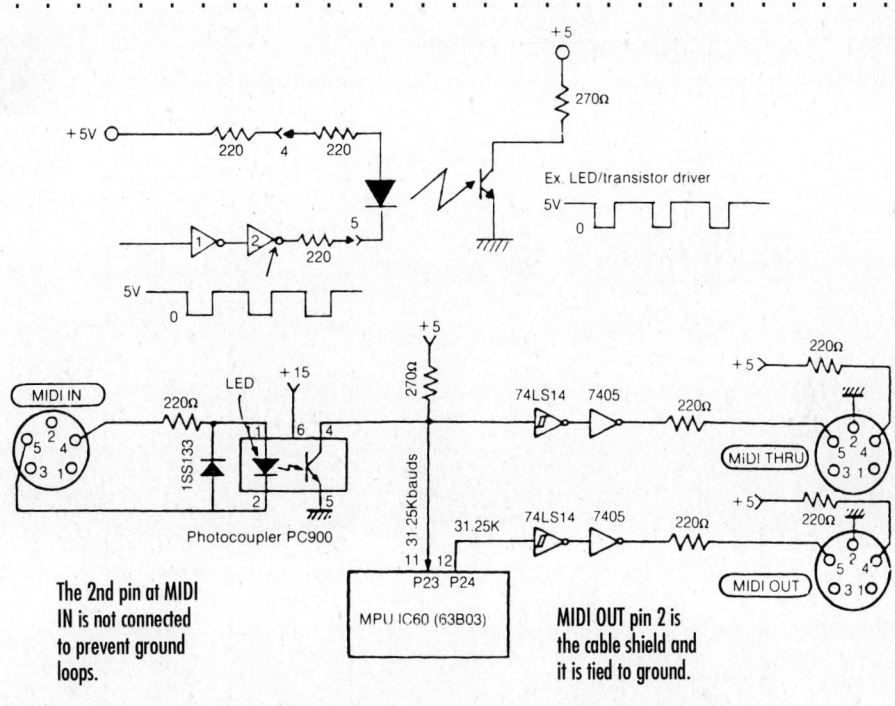

FIGURE 2.9: *The MIDI interface of the Yamaha DX7*

Conversions: Playing Both Ways

As shown in Figure 2.10, the conversion takes place with the help of a specialized circuit known as a UART (Universal Asynchronous Receiver/Transmitter) or ACIA (Asynchronous Communications Interface Adapter). When a start bit is received at the MIDI In port, the serial/parallel interface waits until it has received 8 bits, one after another, and then stores them one by one in its internal memory (i.e., in a memory register).

Serial-to-parallel interface

UART

Microprocessor

`0 1 1 1 0 1 1 0` → MIDI In

0
1
1
1
0
1
1
0

Parallel-to-serial interface

UART

Microprocessor

`0 1 1 1 0 1 1 0` ← MIDI Out

0
1
1
1
0
1
1
0

FIGURE 2.10: *The serial-to-parallel interface sends the 8 bits of a MIDI byte to the microprocessor over 8 separate wires. The parallel-to-serial interface sends the byte over a single wire.*

Once the stop bit tells the MIDI In port that the entire byte has been properly transmitted, the MIDI In port is then ready to send the 8 bits all at once to the microprocessor (over 8 separate lines, known collectively as the *data bus*). Once this transmission has been completed, the UART switches back to WAIT mode for the next start bit, and so on.

The Interrupt Buffer System

Imagine the UART and the microprocessor are two telephones. If your phone (i.e., the microprocessor) had no ringer, you would have to pick up the handset in order to tell whether someone was calling you (i.e., if information was being sent to the UART and forwarded by the UART to the microprocessor). The ringer lets you pick up the handset only when you have a good reason to, i.e., when you know someone is waiting to talk to you. This is an example of an interrupt system which lets you carry on any other activity at the same time, even if you are waiting for a call. The concept in data processing is exactly the same.

Such an interrupt system, as shown in Figure 2.11, keeps the microprocessor from spending most of its time waiting for the MIDI bytes output by the UART. As soon as the UART receives MIDI data, the system uses a direct line to warn the microprocessor that the UART is ready to

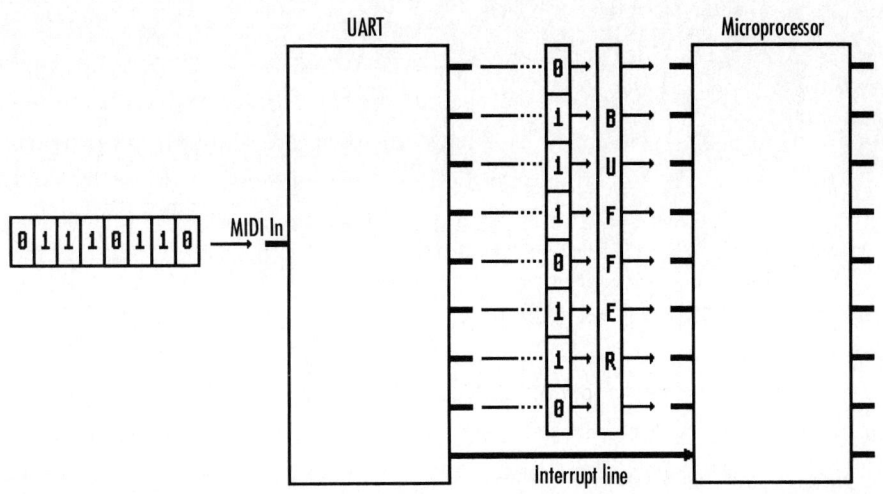

FIGURE 2.11: *The interrupt line warns the computer that a MIDI byte is about to arrive. If the computer is busy with another task (such as a screen display, calculations, etc.), the byte (and its arrival time) is stored in a buffer to await processing.*

send the data to it. Then the microprocessor interrupts whatever it was doing and gives priority to the reception operation, if necessary storing the MIDI byte in a buffer memory in order to handle it later.

The buffer memory is like a telephone answering machine that stores calls (i.e., data) while you're doing other things. This association of the interrupt principle with a buffer memory has three advantages. First, the microprocessor can tend to its business without having to monitor the MIDI In port; second, each byte is handled immediately upon arrival; and third, there is no risk of an unrecoverable data loss unless the buffer over-flows. In other words, in the same way that the incoming message cassette of a telephone answering machine can hold only a certain number of mes-sages, the buffer memory can overflow if it receives an excessive amount of data and isn't emptied fast enough. If that happens, the next bytes in the transmission are irretrievably lost. Warning messages such as "MIDI overflow," "buffer overflow," and "MIDI buffer full" let you know a problem is about to happen. Obviously, it's worthwhile for MIDI instru-ments to have good-sized buffers.

When the microprocessor sends data, the UART works the opposite way. As soon as it receives a byte from the microprocessor, the UART issues a start bit, "serializes" the byte (i.e., sends the bits one after another, starting with the low-order bit and ending with the high-order bit), and ends the operation with a stop bit. The UART then lets the mi-croprocessor know that it's ready to handle the next byte. In order to send the bits at the proper speed (i.e., 31,250 bps), the serial/parallel in-terface generally divides an internal 1MHz or 500kHz clock signal (the values currently used in microcomputer data processing) by 32 or by 16.

MIDI Connections: How the Music Moves

Before getting into the principles of MIDI connections, it's worth taking a moment to review the different types of links for an interface system.

In any interface between two units A and B, there are three possible types of data transfer: from A to B, from B to A, and in both directions at once (simultaneously or otherwise). In the first two cases, the links are one-way. In the third case, the link is bidirectional. In order to operate, the bidirectional link needs one line for each transfer direction. (Sometimes a single physical line contains both of these logical lines.) The computer/screen interface is an example of a one-way link (from the computer to the screen), and the computer/floppy-disk reader interface is an example of a bidirectional link (in this case, for data storage and data loading).

In a bidirectional link, data can travel independently in both directions, like cars on the two sides of a highway. With the help of a dialogue system, it can also be transferred by means of exchanges, as in a telephone conversation. The interface between a computer and a printer is a perfect example of a bidirectional link that uses a single dialogue-type connection. Schematically speaking, the computer sends the first string of characters to be printed via one of the lines of the connection, and waits until the printer reports back, by means of another line, that the printing task has been completed. Then the computer sends the next string, and so on. The data travels in both directions via a single connection, in accordance with a well-defined communications protocol.

Up till now we've been limited to an exchange of data between two units. However, there's no reason why more units couldn't be connected to form a true network. This is exactly the case with MIDI, which theoretically lets you connect an infinite number of instruments, depending on what you want to do.

MIDI In and MIDI Out–The Elementary Links

At a minimum, as shown in Figure 2.12, every MIDI device has two parts: an output port (MIDI Out) and an input port (MIDI In). The simplest link between two MIDI devices, MIDI A and MIDI B, takes the form of a one-way link: from A to B or from B to A. By connecting the MIDI Out port of synthesizer A to the MIDI In port of synthesizer B, synthesizer B will respond automatically to keys pressed on the keyboard of synthesizer A. In this case, you only need one wire.

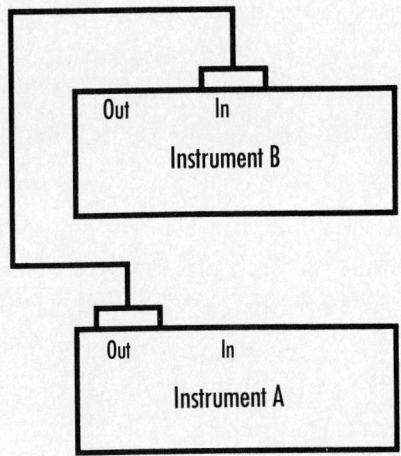

FIGURE 2.12: *In a one-way link, the MIDI Out port of instrument A transmits data to the MIDI In port of instrument B.*

By connecting the two devices from A to B and from B to A (i.e., the MIDI Out port of device A to the MIDI In port of device B, and vice versa) as shown in Figure 2.13, you get a bidirectional link that uses two wires. This type of connection is known as a *handshake link*. In addition to having the option of controlling synthesizer B from synthesizer A and synthesizer A from synthesizer B, you can also carry on dialogue-type exchanges (e.g., via MIDI System Exclusive messages).

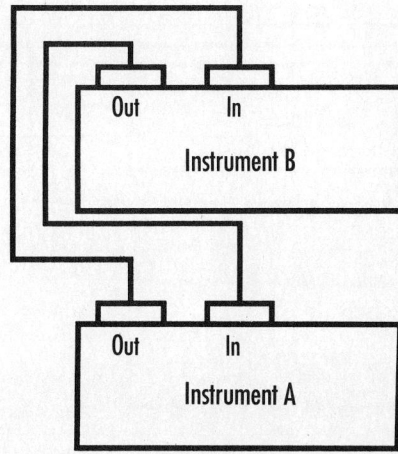

FIGURE 2.13: *The handshake link is represented by two one-way links between two instruments (with MIDI Out of instrument A connected to MIDI In of instrument B, and vice versa). This way, the MIDI bytes can travel in both directions, simultaneously or otherwise.*

But why stop there? Why not connect three MIDI devices (A, B, and C) by means of two one-way links? By connecting the MIDI Out port of device A to the MIDI In port of device B, and connecting the MIDI Out port of device C to the MIDI In port of device A, device A can drive device B, and device C can drive device A. With the addition of a cable connecting the MIDI Out port of device B to the MIDI In port of device C, as shown in Figure 2.14, device B can control device C.

The MIDI Thru Port

The system described above has the disadvantage of not letting a single device (i.e., one MIDI Out port) control two other devices (i.e., two MIDI In ports). This is why most MIDI devices have a third type of port, known as the MIDI Thru port. This port retransmits the MIDI codes that are received by the MIDI In port. In a manner of speaking,

The MIDI Hardware Interface

```
┌──────────────────────┐      ┌──────────────────────┐
│  Out      In          │      │         In           │
│                       │      │                      │
│   Instrument B        │      │    Instrument C      │
└──────────────────────┘      └──────────────────────┘

┌──────────────────────┐
│  Out                  │
│                       │
│   Instrument A        │
└──────────────────────┘
```

FIGURE 2.14: *In this configuration, device A drives device B and device B drives device C, but device A does not drive device C.*

the codes received by the MIDI In port are "photocopied" and sent immediately to the MIDI Thru port.

For example, by connecting the MIDI Out port of device A to the MIDI In port of device B and connecting the MIDI Thru port of device B to the MIDI In port of device C, devices B and C can be driven by device A. In this case the information received by device B is duplicated by the MIDI Thru port and sent to device C. This type of link, as shown in Figure 2.15, is known as a "daisy-chain" or cascade-type link.

The number of devices that can be connected this way is theoretically unlimited, because there's nothing to keep us from connecting the MIDI Thru port of device C to the MIDI In port of device D, and so on. A long cascade-type link induces virtually no delay (an average of 2 microseconds per instrument, depending on the response time of the optoisolators). On the other hand, the leading and trailing edges of the signal have a strong tendency to break down (see Figure 2.16) and become munged beyond recognition—a state that makes for faulty interpretations of

666

FIGURE 2.15: *In this daisy-chain link, the information sent from instrument A to instrument B is "photocopied" and sent immediately to instrument C, which in turn transmits it to instrument D, and so on.*

FIGURE 2.16: *Because the MIDI signal has to pass through the optocouplers, the leading and trailing edges of the signal tend to break down.*

MIDI messages. This is why it's advisable for a daisy-chain link not to contain more than three instruments.

Connection Boxes

A truly humongous variety of boxes are available that are intended to improve the performance of a MIDI network by mixing, separating, or "routing" signals. Later chapters examine how these boxes are implemented. Meanwhile, here's a short introductory overview of their capabilities.

The MIDI Thru Box

The MIDI Thru box is an alternative to the daisy-chain link. It consists of a MIDI In port and several MIDI Thru ports. Incoming signals are duplicated as many times as there are MIDI Thru ports in the box. This technique prevents the breakdown of the signals, simplifies connections, and frees the MIDI Thru ports on the linked instruments for the addition of more daisy-chained devices. This configuration, shown in Figure 2.17, is known as a *star network*. Figure 2.18 shows a combination of a star network and a cascade network.

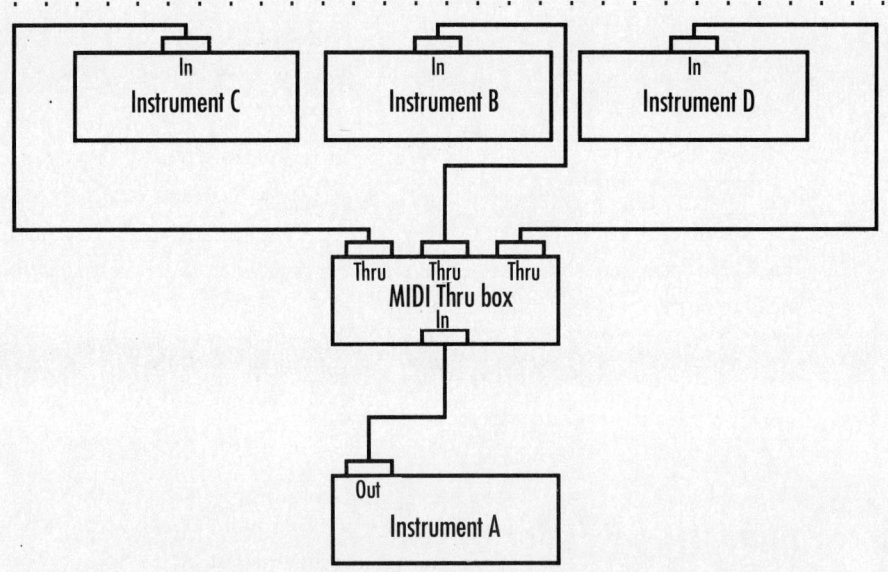

FIGURE 2.17: *The MIDI Thru box duplicates a signal received at its MIDI In port, creating one copy for each of its outputs (MIDI Thru ports). The box makes it possible to create a star network, as an alternative to a cascade-type (daisy-chain) link.*

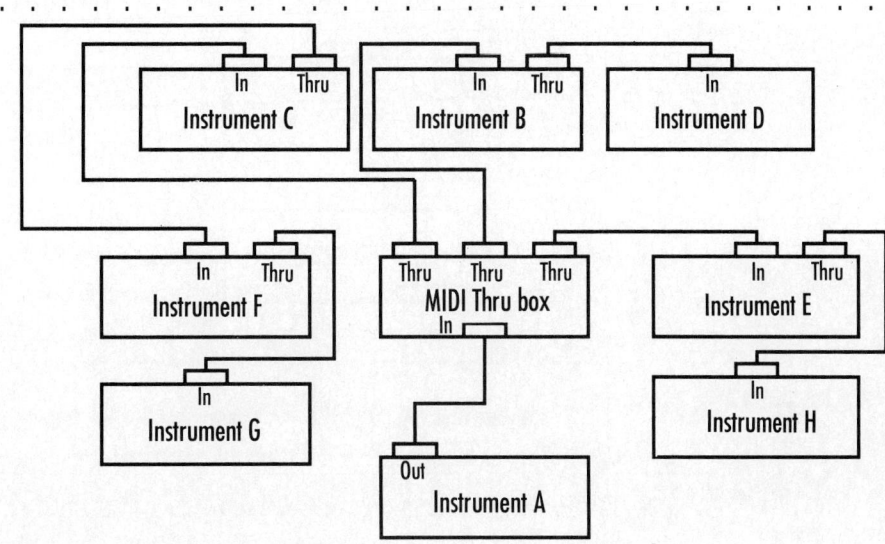

FIGURE 2.18: *A combination of star and cascade networks. Instruments B, C, and E are connected in a star network (via a MIDI Thru box) and are the sources of the cascade links with instrument D, instruments F and G, and instrument H, respectively.*

The MIDI Merger

Suppose you want to drive an instrument C simultaneously from two other instruments, A and B. To do so, you have to mix (merge) the signals from the MIDI Out ports of instruments A and B in order to send them to the MIDI In port of instrument C, as shown in Figure 2.19. (Caution—this mixing of MIDI messages has nothing to do with the mixing of audio signals, such as the signals output by mixing boards!)

Because of its characteristics, the MIDI interface transmits the messages one after another (i.e., in series). If two messages from instruments A and B arrive at the input of the merger at the same time, then the merger has to give priority to one message or the other, making the non-priority message wait while the first message is sent. Some mergers can mix more than two MIDI signals.

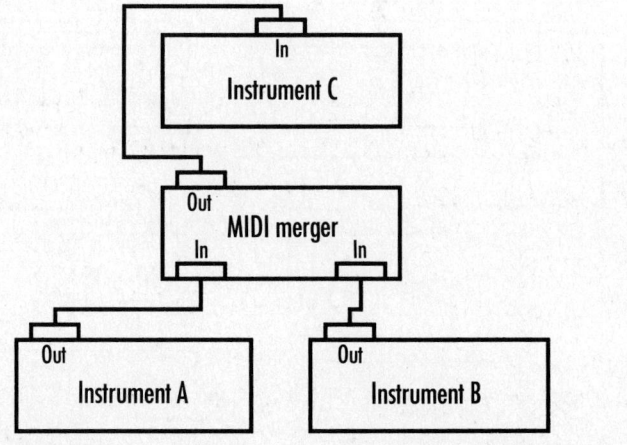

FIGURE 2.19: *With a MIDI merger, instruments A and B can drive instrument C.*

The MIDI Patch

The MIDI patch is a connection matrix consisting of a given number of MIDI In and MIDI Out ports: an 8×8 patch (8 inputs and 8 outputs), a 16×16 patch (16 inputs and 16 outputs), etc. Figure 2.20 shows an 8×8 patch.

After connecting the MIDI Out ports and the MIDI In ports of the instruments to the MIDI In and MIDI Out ports of the patch, all you have to do is program each MIDI In port of the patch, in such a way as to direct the signals to one or more of the MIDI Out ports. Each MIDI Out port accepts signals from only one MIDI In port, unless the patch includes a merger function. On the other hand, the signals from a MIDI In port can be sent to several MIDI Out ports (i.e., the MIDI Thru function). Most MIDI patches let you store several assignment schemes in memory. This way, you can modify the configuration of a MIDI network simply by calling up the corresponding stored program.

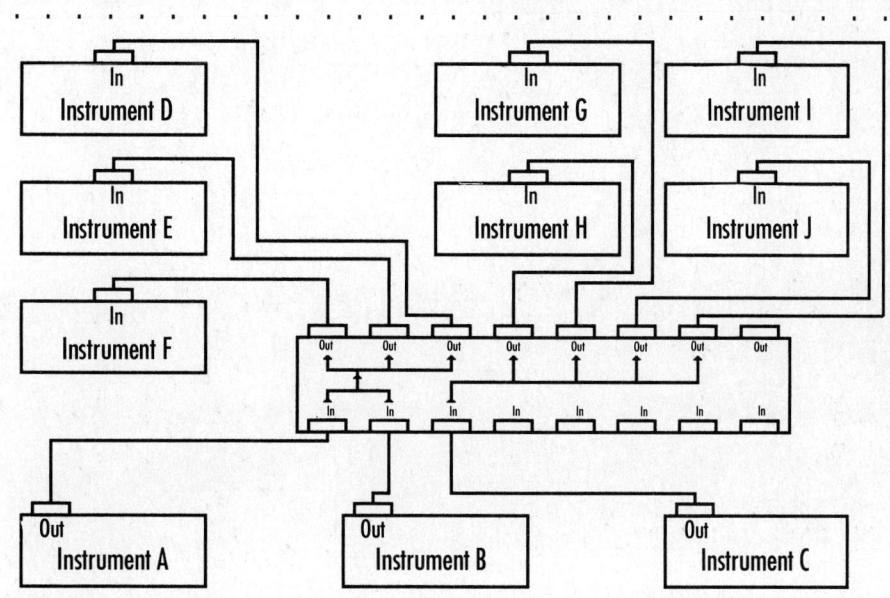

FIGURE 2.20: *The way this patch is programmed, instruments A and B drive instruments D, E, and F (the inputs of A and B are "merged"), while instrument C drives instruments G, H, I, and J.*

CHAPTER

3

XIII XIV XV XVI A B C D E F G H I

The MIDI
Language

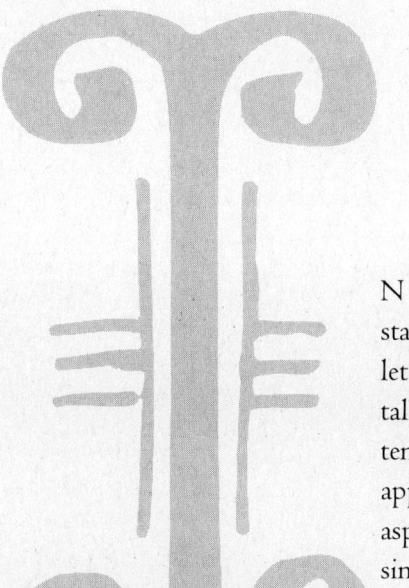I N THE BEGINNING, the MIDI standard was designed essentially to let keyboards and sound generators talk to each other. At most, it was intended for use in modest sequencer applications. Although the hardware aspect of the interface hasn't evolved since then (for the obvious reason of preserving compatibility), that's by no means the case with the software aspect of MIDI—namely, its language.

Within a very short time the notorious MIDI ports had made their way into many families of equipment. Today they're found in every peripheral device in the audio signal-processing field. Mixing boards, tape recorders, special-effects processors, microcomputers, and synchronization units are some of the products that have been infected by the MIDIfication virus. Meanwhile, the capabilities of sound generators have been expanding (with memory storage, polyphony, and multitimbral features), samplers have become democratized, and so on. In other words, if the MIDI language hadn't grown beyond its original incarnation, by now technological progress certainly would have made it obsolete.

Happily, though, in those early days the MIDI designers developed an extremely flexible language that was especially well suited to continuing evolution. Putting it another way and drawing a parallel between the MIDI language and the human vocabulary, you could say that the MIDI dictionary can always be enriched by new idioms. This capability has made it possible to add extensions to the standard as the need for them became apparent, while still preserving complete forward compatibility.

An Evolving Document

The NAMM conferences held yearly in the United States provide the context for privileged meetings attended by members of the two manufacturers' organizations—the MMA (MIDI Manufacturers' Association) and the JMSC (Japan MIDI Standards Committee)—that are responsible for administering the MIDI standard. At these meetings new versions of the language are generally approved, as were the addition of the sample dump standard in 1986, the MIDI time code in 1987, and MIDIfiles in 1988. In the wake of these improvements, in June 1988 the IMA decided to prepare a complete revision of the official document and issue it as Version 4.0 of the *MIDI 1.0 Detailed Specifications*. Version 4.2 which covers General MIDI, was released in January, 1993.

The Format of MIDI Bytes: Status and Data

The MIDI interface carries information that translates a musician's playing into digital events. To do that, the interface uses bytes, and therefore finite numbers, as opposed to analog electrical or magnetic signals, which can represent an infinite number of values. These bytes, which in a sense are the MIDI alphabet, provide some insight into how the MIDI language—that is, its words and sentences—is built.

First of all, the MIDI standard divides data into two categories: *status* information and *data*. Generally speaking, status information indicates the actions performed by the musician. The pressing or releasing of a note or sustain pedal, and the shifting of a pitch wheel or modulation wheel, are typical examples of status information. However, in most instances such an action or command requires more information—for instance, the number of the note being pressed or released, an indication of the beginning or end of a sustained tone, or the new position of the pitch wheel or modulation wheel. The responsibility for providing this information falls on the data bytes that accompany the status indicator.

With no exceptions, all MIDI information is transmitted in the form of a "status plus data" structure known generically as a *message*. The number of data bytes in a message (from 0 to n) varies, depending on the type of status byte. To draw another analogy with human language, just as every word in English has a well-defined role in a sentence (as an adjective, verb, etc.), each MIDI word (or byte) has a well-defined role in a message: as either a status word (i.e., the definition of a musical command) or a data word (i.e., the value of the command). In order for the syntax of a MIDI sentence (i.e., a MIDI message) to be correct, the MIDI message has to consist of one status word followed by 0 to n data words.

At the binary level, each byte represents one of 256 possible different values (from 0 to 255). In order to be able to tell the difference between a status byte and a data byte (which are nominally identical), MIDI uses bit 7 of the byte as an indicator. This bit is known as the high-order bit or *most significant bit* (MSB). Depending on whether bit 7 is set to 1 or to 0, the byte is either a status byte (1xxxxxxx) or a data byte (0xxxxxxx) (see Figure 3.1 below).

In fact, for a microprocessor, testing one of the bits in a byte is the fastest way to tell the difference between the two types of messages. As a result, in the MIDI language there are only 7 bits (that is, bits 0 through 6) that can be used to represent information. What this means is that instead of

Status	**1**	0 or 1	0 or 1	0 or 1	0 or 1	0 or 1	0 or 1	0 or 1
	Bit 7	Bit 6 2^6 (64)	Bit 5 2^5 (32)	Bit 4 2^4 (16)	Bit 3 2^3 (8)	Bit 2 2^2 (4)	Bit 1 2^1 (2)	Bit 0 2^0 (1)

Data	**0**	0 or 1	0 or 1	0 or 1	0 or 1	0 or 1	0 or 1	0 or 1
	Bit 7	Bit 6 2^6 (64)	Bit 5 2^5 (32)	Bit 4 2^4 (16)	Bit 3 2^3 (8)	Bit 2 2^2 (4)	Bit 1 2^1 (2)	Bit 0 2^0 (1)

FIGURE 3.1: *Status bytes and data bytes are differentiated by the value of bit 7.*

being able to represent any one of 256 different values, a MIDI byte is limited to representing any one of 128 different values (i.e., from 0 through 127). As far as data is concerned, this 128-value limit is easy to work around, because several data bytes can be associated with any given single status byte. On the other hand, the status bytes are by definition limited to a maximum of 128—but that number is more than ample for coding musical actions.

In short, then, each MIDI message consists of a status byte, which can have any of 128 possible different values and which represents a command or an action (1xxxxxxx), followed by 0 to n data bytes (0xxxxxxx) that indicate the nature of the action.

Because the MIDI language consists of status bytes and data bytes grouped together, before going any further it's worthwhile to describe the various types of status messages and examine the types of data associated with each of them.

The MIDI Channel and the Concept of Addressing

As you saw in the chapter that dealt with In, Out, and Thru connections, a MIDI network is not limited by the number of units that are connected in it. With Thru ports and/or connection boxes, it's theoretically possible to interconnect an infinite number of MIDI instruments. The only limitation is the density of the information circulating within the network: i.e., the maximum speed of the interface.

You've seen that several instruments in a network can be connected cascade-style (in a daisy-chain link, in which the MIDI Out port of the first instrument is connected to the MIDI In port of the second instrument, and the MIDI Thru port of the second instrument is connected to the MIDI In port of the third instrument, and so on), or in a star configuration (in which the MIDI Out port of the first instrument is connected to the MIDI In ports of the other instruments by means of a MIDI Thru box). In any case, every message sent via the MIDI Out port of the transmitting unit (such as a message from a keyboard indicating that a note has been pressed) passes through the entire network (for instance, a series of sound generators). Under normal circumstances, all of these sound generators should start to play this note in unison—which may not necessarily be the intended result.

To take a more concrete example, suppose a network consists of a keyboard connected to three sound generators and all three sound generators receive exactly the same information. What can you do, without changing the connections, to drive the sound generators sequentially instead of simultaneously? Simply apply the concept of *logical addressing*. For instance, if you want to drive just one of the generators (call it generator 1) from the keyboard, you would assign the keyboard a transmission address X and assign generator 1 a reception address X, and assign each of the other two generators a reception address that's anything other than X. This way, even though all three generators receive all of the messages transmitted by the keyboard (remember, all of these messages travel over a single cable in a daisy-chain network, or over as many cables as there are instruments to be driven in a star network), each generator ignores the messages that aren't addressed to it. This concept of addressing is an integral part of the status byte, and is known as the *MIDI channel.*

The Daisy-Chain Link

It's possible to draw a parallel between a MIDI network and a railroad line by representing the instruments as stations and the MIDI messages as trains of data (with the locomotive, the cars, the engine driver, and the passengers respectively indicating the status information, the data, the status byte, and the data bytes). A MIDI keyboard (the "departure station") is located upstream of the daisy-chain network. When a key is pressed, a train leaves the departure station via the MIDI Out port of the keyboard. The engine driver (i.e., the status byte) specifies that a note-press command has been addressed to a particular instrument (as a function of the transmission channel, which we set beforehand on the keyboard). Behind the engine driver, the passengers in the cars (i.e., the data bytes) carry the information relating to the note-press command. (This information includes the number of the note as well as the speed at which the note is to be pressed.)

The train is a local, and stops at the first station it reaches (i.e., the MIDI In port of the first sound generator). The sound generator then analyzes the address (i.e., the channel) contained in the engine driver's message (i.e., the status byte), in order to decide whether the passengers' messages

(i.e., the data bytes) are intended for it. In other words, the sound generator asks itself whether it has been assigned the task of playing the note in question (provided of course that the channel of the status information in question corresponds to the generator's reception channel).

Regardless of whether the generator decides to play the note, the train and its passengers depart via the MIDI Thru port and continue along the track to the next station (i.e., the MIDI In port of the next sound generator). The chain reaction continues until the train reaches the final station (i.e., the last sound generator in the daisy-chain), as shown in Figure 3.2 below.

In short, the status byte of the transmitting unit incorporates the concept of addressing, or, in other words, the capability of letting the sound generator evaluate the message. By examining the channel of the status byte, the generator can decide whether or not to perform the corresponding action.

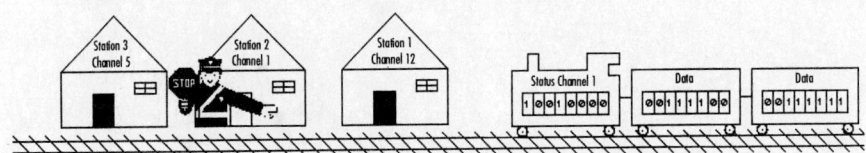

FIGURE 3.2: *In a daisy-chain link, represented symbolically by a railroad network, the message from the transmitting instrument passes through all of the other instruments, the same way the train passes through all the stations. If the channel of the message (indicated by the locomotive) corresponds to the channel for a station, the message is transmitted for execution. In any event, the message circulates until it reaches the last instrument in the daisy-chain link (indicated by the last station in the figure (Station 3)).*

In order for a dialogue to be established between two MIDI instruments, the transmitting instrument and the receiving instrument have to be set to the same channel.

The Star Network

To illustrate the concept of channels in a star network, another parallel can be drawn: this time, with television. When a viewer is watching the small screen, its antenna port and the antenna ports of neighboring TVs simultaneously receive signals from several channels. This pattern, illustrated in Figure 3.3 below, is analogous to the way every instrument in a

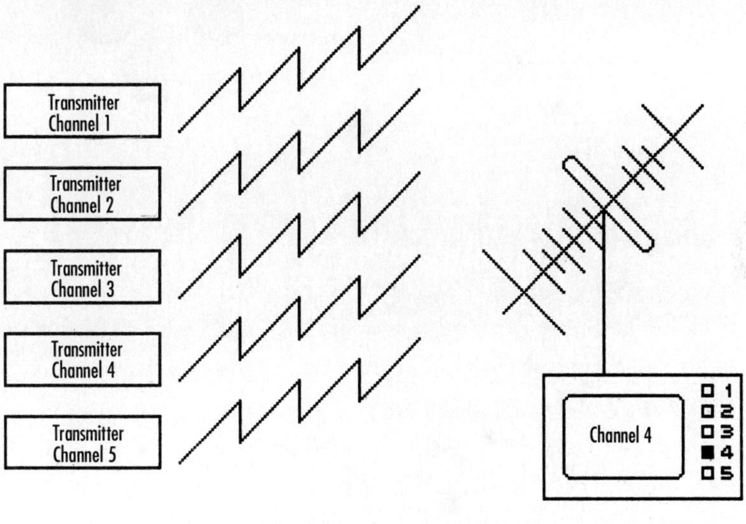

FIGURE 3.3: *Even though a TV set (i.e., a tuner) receives all of the channels being sent by the transmitter, the viewer sets the channel to the one he wants to watch. MIDI instruments work the same way, except that (as we'll see later on) a MIDI instrument can receive all of the channels simultaneously. The effect is somewhat like the mosaic pattern that the broadcast signals form on a TV screen.*

star network receives messages from the transmitter, regardless of the MIDI channels the receiving instruments may be set to. However, each TV is set to select one channel at a time, according to the viewer's preferences, filtering out everything but the information that interests it without keeping the other TVs from receiving that information. Among all the channels broadcasting to it, each TV pays attention to only one, adjusting its receiver accordingly.

This is the principle that MIDI messages use. The messages include channel-identification information (analogous to the number of a TV channel) that lets each receiver decide whether any particular message concerns it. If the information in a message doesn't involve a given receiver (for instance, if channel 3 is broadcasting but you want to watch channel 2 instead), neighboring units (analogous to the other instruments in the star network) can still use that information. The MIDI Thru box "sprays" information to all the instruments on the network, the same way the TV transmitter "sprays" signals to all the antennas in its broadcast area.

Channel Messages and System Messages

Information intended for the entire MIDI network is an exception to the rule that says MIDI messages must include channel identifiers. This information is distributed in the form of *System messages*, which don't implement the concept of channels.

Another type of message does include the concept. These are known as *Channel messages*. Each of these two categories is further divided into sub-categories.

The Seven Channel Messages

The number of MIDI channels is limited to 16. The representation of 16 values in binary notation (i.e., the values from 0 to 15) requires four bits. As shown in Figure 3.4 and Table 3.1 below, in the status byte of a MIDI message, bits 0 through 3 (i.e., the right-hand half-byte) carry the

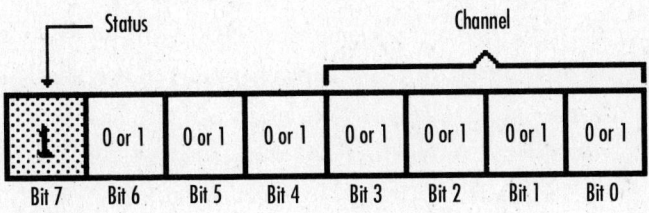

FIGURE 3.4: *Bits 0 through 3 in a status byte indicate the MIDI channel.*

TABLE 3.1: *The Four-Bit Representation of MIDI Channels*

BITS	CHANNEL NUMBER	BITS	CHANNEL NUMBER
0000	Channel 1	1000	Channel 9
0001	Channel 2	1001	Channel 10
0010	Channel 3	1010	Channel 11
0011	Channel 4	1011	Channel 12
0100	Channel 5	1100	Channel 13
0101	Channel 6	1101	Channel 14
0110	Channel 7	1110	Channel 15
0111	Channel 8	1111	Channel 16

code for the MIDI channel. Because bit 7 is already designated as the status indicator, only bits 4 to 6 (i.e., 8 possible values) are available to specify the content of the musical command.

In reality, however, the MIDI standard uses only 7 types of status bytes associated with the concept of a channel, with bits 4 to 6 taking on values from 000 to 110. In increasing numerical order, these commands are: note released (*Note Off*, 000), note pressed (*Note On*, 001), *Polyphonic Key Pressure* (010), *Control Change* (011), *Program Change* (100), *Channel Pressure (aftertouch)* (101), and *Pitch Bend* (110). Each type of status byte is duplicated 16 times, once for each channel, for a total of 112 messages for 7 types of status bytes. For instance, if a note was pressed (*Note On*), the status byte for this piece of information on channel 3 would be written "10010010". (Note: In binary notation, channels 1 to 16 are numbered from 0 to 15.)

The Two Types of Channel Messages: Voice and Mode

MIDI Channel Messages are divided into: *Voice messages* and *Mode messages*. Sound generators (synthesizers, samplers, etc.) can reproduce simultaneously a given number of notes, in what's known as *polyphony*. You could say that a 16-note polyphonic sound generator consists of 16 sound generators for any given note. The MIDI standard applies the so-called "*voice*" terminology to each of these generators. Voice messages have a direct effect on how the sound generators produce sounds. Mode messages (which are categorized as Control Change messages) define the instrument's response to Voice messages.

The Three Types of System Messages

Unlike channel messages, *System messages*, which are intended to be received by the entire MIDI network, don't use the channel concept. What this means is that the right-hand half-byte of the status byte of a system message is always equal to 1111 (FH). Bits 4 to 6 (which could have served as the identifier for an eighth status message, 111) leave 16 possible values for the right-hand half-byte (which otherwise could have contained channel information). These 16 values belong to this second category of status bytes: namely, the category that contains the system messages. These messages don't use the channel concept; therefore, they can be sent an entire MIDI network all at once. These messages are in turn subdivided into three sub-categories: six *System Common messages*, eight *System Real Time messages*, and two *System Exclusive messages*.

Receiving Status Information

Generally speaking, every receiving MIDI unit has to pay attention to the most recent status byte it has received, even if the preceding message is incomplete. MIDI instruments also have to ignore status bytes that haven't yet been defined (i.e., status bytes that are reserved for extensions that will be implemented in the future). The various types of MIDI bytes and MIDI messages are summarized in Figure 3.5 below, and listed in detail in Table 3.2 and Table 3.3.

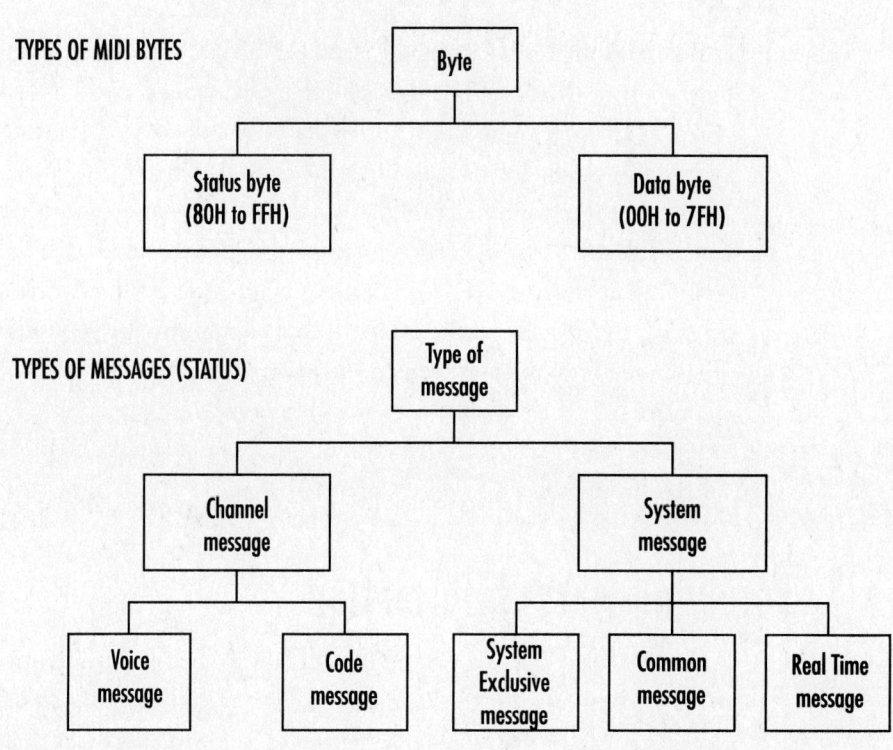

TYPES OF MIDI BYTES

Byte

Status byte (80H to FFH)

Data byte (00H to 7FH)

TYPES OF MESSAGES (STATUS)

Type of message

Channel message

System message

Voice message

Code message

System Exclusive message

Common message

Real Time message

FIGURE 3.5: *Data bytes and status bytes*

TABLE 3.2: *Status Information in MIDI Messages*

BINARY	HEX	DECIMAL	MEANING
10000000	80H	128	Note Off channel 1
10000001	81H	129	Channel 2
10000010	82H	130	Channel 3
10000011	83H	131	Channel 4
10000100	84H	132	Channel 5

TABLE 3.2: *Status Information in MIDI Messages (continued)*

BINARY	HEX	DECIMAL	MEANING
10000101	85H	133	Channel 6
10000110	86H	134	Channel 7
10000111	87H	135	Channel 8
10001000	88H	136	Channel 9
10001001	89H	137	Channel 10
10001010	8AH	138	Channel 11
10001011	8BH	139	Channel 12
10001100	8CH	140	Channel 13
10001101	8DH	141	Channel 14
10001110	8EH	142	Channel 15
10001111	8FH	143	Channel 16
10010000	90H	144	Note On channel 1
10010001	91H	145	Channel 2
10010010	92H	146	Channel 3
10010011	93H	147	Channel 4
10010100	94H	148	Channel 5
10010101	95H	149	Channel 6
10010110	96H	150	Channel 7
10010111	97H	151	Channel 8
10011000	98H	152	Channel 9
10011001	99H	153	Channel 10
10011010	9AH	154	Channel 11
10011011	9BH	155	Channel 12
10011100	9CH	156	Channel 13

TABLE 3.2: *Status Information in MIDI Messages (continued)*

BINARY	HEX	DECIMAL	MEANING
10011101	9DH	157	Channel 14
10011110	9EH	158	Channel 15
10011111	9FH	159	Channel 16
10100000	A0H	160	Polyphonic Key Pressure channel 1
10100001	A1H	161	Channel 2
10100010	A2H	162	Channel 3
10100011	A3H	163	Channel 4
10100100	A4H	164	Channel 5
10100101	A5H	165	Channel 6
10100110	A6H	166	Channel 7
10100111	A7H	167	Channel 8
10101000	A8H	168	Channel 9
10101001	A9H	169	Channel 10
10101010	AAH	170	Channel 11
10101011	ABH	171	Channel 12
10101100	ACH	172	Channel 13
10101101	ADH	173	Channel 14
10101110	AEH	174	Channel 15
10101111	AFH	175	Channel 16
10110000	B0H	176	Control Change channel 1
10110001	B1H	177	Channel 2
10110010	B2H	178	Channel 3
10110011	B3H	179	Channel 4
10110100	B4H	180	Channel 5

TABLE 3.2: *Status Information in MIDI Messages (continued)*

BINARY	HEX	DECIMAL	MEANING
10110101	B5H	181	Channel 6
10110110	B6H	182	Channel 7
10110111	B7H	183	Channel 8
10111000	B8H	184	Channel 9
10111001	B9H	185	Channel 10
10111010	BAH	186	Channel 11
10111011	BBH	187	Channel 12
10111100	BCH	188	Channel 13
10111101	BDH	189	Channel 14
10111110	BEH	190	Channel 15
10111111	BFH	191	Channel 16
11000000	C0H	192	Program Change channel 1
11000001	C1H	193	Channel 2
11000010	C2H	194	Channel 3
11000011	C3H	195	Channel 4
11000100	C4H	196	Channel 5
11000101	C5H	197	Channel 6
11000110	C6H	198	Channel 7
11000111	C7H	199	Channel 8
11001000	C8H	200	Channel 9
11001001	C9H	201	Channel 10
11001010	CAH	202	Channel 11
11001011	CBH	203	Channel 12
11001100	CCH	204	Channel 13

TABLE 3.2: *Status Information in MIDI Messages (continued)*

BINARY	HEX	DECIMAL	MEANING
11001101	CDH	205	Channel 14
11001110	CEH	206	Channel 15
11001111	CFH	207	Channel 16
11010000	D0H	208	Channel Aftertouch channel 1
11010001	D1H	209	Channel 2
11010010	D2H	210	Channel 3
11010011	D3H	211	Channel 4
11010100	D4H	212	Channel 5
11010101	D5H	213	Channel 6
11010110	D6H	214	Channel 7
11010111	D7H	215	Channel 8
11011000	D8H	216	Channel 9
11011001	D9H	217	Channel 10
11011010	DAH	218	Channel 11
11011011	DBH	219	Channel 12
11011100	DCH	220	Channel 13
11011101	DDH	221	Channel 14
11011110	DEH	222	Channel 15
11011111	DFH	223	Channel 16
11100000	E0H	224	Pitch Bend Change channel 1
11100001	E1H	225	Channel 2
11100010	E2H	226	Channel 3
11100011	E3H	227	Channel 4
11100100	E4H	228	Channel 5

· ·

TABLE 3.2: *Status Information in MIDI Messages (continued)*

BINARY	HEX	DECIMAL	MEANING
11100101	E5H	229	Channel 6
11100110	E6H	230	Channel 7
11100111	E7H	231	Channel 8
11101000	E8H	232	Channel 9
11101001	E9H	233	Channel 10
11101010	EAH	234	Channel 11
11101011	EBH	235	Channel 12
11101100	ECH	236	Channel 13
11101101	EDH	237	Channel 14
11101110	EEH	231	Channel 15
11101111	EFH	239	Channel 16
11110000	F0H	240	System Exclusive
11110001	F1H	241	MIDI Time Code quarter frame
11110010	F2H	242	Song Position Pointer
11110011	F3H	243	Song Select
11110100	F4H	244	– undefined –
11110101	F5H	245	– undefined –
11110110	F6H	246	Tune Request
11110111	F7H	247	End of Exclusive (EOX)
11111000	F8H	248	Timing Clock
11111001	F9H	249	– undefined –
11111010	FAH	250	Start
11111011	FBH	251	Continue

TABLE 3.2: *Status Information in MIDI Messages (continued)*

BINARY	HEX	DECIMAL	MEANING
11111100	FCH	252	Stop
11111101	FDH	253	– undefined –
11111110	FEH	254	Active Sensing
11111111	FFH	255	System Reset

. . . .

TABLE 3.3: *Status-Byte Families*

HEX STATUS	BINARY STATUS	NUMBER OF DATA BYTES	DESCRIPTION
		CHANNEL VOICE MESSAGES	
8cH	1000cccc	2	Note Off
9cH	1001cccc	2	Note On
AcH	1010cccc	2	Polyphonic Key Pressure
BcH	1011cccc	2*	Control Change
CcH	1100cccc	1	Program Change
DcH	1101cccc	1	Channel Aftertouch
EcH	1110cccc	2	Pitch Bend
		CHANNEL MODE MESSAGES	
BcH	1011cccc	2**	

. . . .

TABLE 3.3: *Status-Byte Families (continued)*

HEX STATUS	BINARY STATUS	NUMBER OF DATA BYTES	DESCRIPTION
		SYSTEM MESSAGES	
F0H	11110000	***	System Exclusive
	11110sss	0 to 2	System Common
	11111ttt	0	System Real Time

cccc = the MIDI channel, from 1 to 16, with a value for cccc of 0 (0000) to 15 (1111), inclusive

sss = value from 1 (001) to 7 (111), inclusive

ttt = value from 0 (000) to 7 (111), inclusive

* The first data byte is from 0 to 119, inclusive

** The first data byte is from 120 to 127, inclusive

*** <the number of variable data bytes> F7H

. . . .

Voice Messages

This section gives detailed descriptions of the MIDI voice messages, starting with the Note On and Note Off messages.

The Note On Message

Name:	Note On
Format:	1000cccc (9cH) 0nnnnnnn 0vvvvvvv
Type:	channel Voice message

cccc	channel number
nnnnnnn	Note Number
vvvvvvv	velocity

The Note On message, shown in Figure 3.6 below, is transmitted after a key on the keyboard has been pressed, and, more generally, whenever any physical action is applied to a MIDI controller (such as a saxophone, violin, accordion, etc.) in order to trigger the production of a sound. When it receives this message, the sound generator plays the note that has the corresponding number.

FIGURE 3.6: *The Note On message*

The Note-Off Message

Name:	Note Off
Format:	1000cccc (8cH) 0nnnnnnn 0vvvvvvv
Type:	channel Voice message
cccc	channel number
nnnnnnn	Note Number
vvvvvvv	Velocity

The Note Off message, shown in Figure 3.7 below, is transmitted when a key value, or fret is released. When it receives this message, the sound generator stops playing the corresponding note.

FIGURE 3.7: *The Note Off message*

The MIDI Tessitura

The Note On and Note Off messages consist of three bytes (one status byte and two data bytes), for a total transfer time of 960 microseconds (msec). The first data byte (0nnnnnnn) indicates the number of the note. The MIDI range consists of 128 notes (ten and a half octaves from C–2 to G8)—a generous amount of auditory real estate. In contrast, the range of a piano keyboard is a little more than seven octaves. In MIDI and in decimal notation, this range corresponds to notes 21 (A–1) to 120 (C8).

Velocity

The third byte indicates the speed with which the note was pressed (i.e., the Note On message) or the speed with which the note was released (i.e., the Note Off message). This speed is known as the *velocity* of the pressure or release, and its values range from 0 to 127. Velocity is often confused with the striking force, which, although physically related to it, isn't quite the same thing.

Each note has two contacts. The first contact detects the pressure applied to the note, and the second detects the end of the movement (i.e., the point at which the key reaches its pressed position). The time between the activation of the first contact and the second contact determines the pressure speed, while the time that elapses between the activation of the second contact and the first contact determines the release speed.

The MIDI standard specifies that a non-dynamic keyboard (that is, a keyboard that's not sensitive to velocity) should transmit a constant value of 64 (40H). However, there's no reason why the sound-generator part of a non-dynamic keyboard shouldn't respond to velocity messages transmitted by a dynamic keyboard.

The velocity of a Note On message is also known as *attack velocity*, and the velocity of a Note Off message is also known as *release velocity*.

Finally, a Note On message with a velocity 0 means the same thing as a Note Off message. As a result, you can feel free to substitute either of these messages for the other one. The technique is explained in greater detail in the section in this chapter that discusses Running Status.

The Velocity Response Curve

The way a dynamic keyboard indicates the speed of attack in terms of velocity isn't regulated or governed by the MIDI standard. Although the minimum speed is indicated by 1 and the maximum speed is indicated by 127, what happens between these two values is up to each manufacturer. In other words, for a linear response curve, velocity acts like a constant function of the speed of attack. However, an exponential response is generally preferable, because it's more like a human touch. In some MIDI instruments the velocity response curve is programmable, for transmission and also for reception. Programmability makes it possible to adapt this parameter to a musician's playing style.

The Three Interpretations of Note On and Note Off Messages

A non-dynamic keyboard uses the following messages to indicate the attack and release of a note:

```
note-on: 1001cccc 0nnnnnnn 01000000 (40H)
note-off: 1000cccc 0nnnnnnn 0vvvvvvv (a value of 40H is
recommended)
```

or even:

```
1001cccc 0nnnnnnn 00000000
```

A keyboard that's dynamic only with regard to attack uses the following messages:

```
note-on: 1001cccc 0nnnnnnn 01000000 (40H)
note-off: 1000cccc 0nnnnnnn 0vvvvvvv (a value of 40H is
recommended)
```

or even:

```
1001cccc 0nnnnnnn 00000000
```

A keyboard that's dynamic with regard to both attack and release uses the following messages:

```
note-on: 1001cccc 0nnnnnnn 0vvvvvvv
note-off: 1000cccc 0nnnnnnn 0vvvvvvv
```

Assigning Note Messages

Although at first it may seem obvious, it's essential that the transmitting instrument send a Note Off message for every Note On message. For instance, under certain circumstances (such as with a sequencer) a sound generator may receive two identical Note On messages (i.e., messages having the same number) one after the other on the same channel. When it receives the second of these messages, the generator can either cut off the first note in order to play the second, or use another one of its polyphonic voices to superimpose the two notes. This second option shows

how important it is for the transmitting instrument to send two Note Off messages. Otherwise, one of the notes would be sustained indefinitely.

When a sound generator receives two identical Note On messages, one from its keyboard and the other through its MIDI In port, the generator has to make sure that a Note Off message that arrives from the keyboard cuts off only the note that was triggered by the keyboard, and, conversely, that a Note Off message that arrives through the MIDI In port cuts off only the note that was triggered via the MIDI interface.

Table 3.4 shows the correspondence between MIDI note numbers (in binary, hexadecimal, and decimal), the various types of notation currently in use, and also the corresponding frequencies and pitch cycle times.

TABLE 3.4: *MIDI Note Numbers, Notation, Frequency, and Cycle Time*

BINARY	HEXADECIMAL	DECIMAL	NOTATION	FREQUENCY, IN HZ	CYCLE TIME, IN MILLISECONDS (MSEC)
00000000	00	0	C −2	8.176	122.3122
00000001	01	1	C# −2	8.662	115.4473
00000010	02	2	D −2	9.177	108.9678
00000011	03	3	D# −2	9.723	102.8519
00000100	04	4	E −2	10.301	97.0793
00000101	05	5	F −2	10.913	91.6306
00000110	06	6	F# −2	11.562	86.4878
00000111	07	7	G −2	12.250	81.6336
00001000	08	8	G# −2	12.978	77.0519
00001001	09	9	A −2	13.750	72.7273
00001010	0A	10	A# −2	14.568	68.6454
00001011	0B	11	B −2	15.434	64.7926

· ·

TABLE 3.4: *MIDI Note Numbers, Notation, Frequency, and Cycle Time (continued)*

BINARY	HEXADECIMAL	DECIMAL	NOTATION	FREQUENCY, IN HZ	CYCLE TIME, IN MILLISECONDS (MSEC)
00001100	0C	12	C −1	16.352	61.1561
00001101	0D	13	C# −1	17.324	57.7237
00001110	0E	14	D −1	18.354	54.4839
00001111	0F	15	D# −1	19.445	51.4259
00010000	10	16	E −1	20.602	48.5396
00010001	11	17	F −1	21.827	45.8153
00010010	12	18	F# −1	23.125	43.2439
00010011	13	19	G −1	24.500	40.8168
00010100	14	20	G# −1	25.957	38.5259
00010101	15	21	A −1	27.500	36.3636
00010110	16	22	A# −1	29.135	34.3227
00010111	17	23	B −1	30.868	32.3963
00011000	18	24	C 0	32.703	30.5781
00011001	19	25	C# 0	34.648	28.8618
00011010	1A	26	D 0	36.708	27.2419
00011011	1B	27	D# 0	38.891	25.7130
00011100	1C	28	E 0	41.203	24.2698
00011101	1D	29	F 0	43.654	22.9077
00011110	1E	30	F# 0	46.249	21.6219
00011111	1F	31	G 0	48.999	20.4084
00100000	20	32	G# 0	51.913	19.2630
00100001	21	33	A 0	55.000	18.1818

TABLE 3.4: *MIDI Note Numbers, Notation, Frequency, and Cycle Time* (continued)

BINARY	HEXADECIMAL	DECIMAL	NOTATION	FREQUENCY, IN HZ	CYCLE TIME, IN MILLISECONDS (MSEC)
00100010	22	34	A# 0	58.270	17.1614
00100011	23	35	B 0	61.735	16.1982
00100100	24	36	C 1	65.406	15.2890
00100101	25	37	C# 1	69.296	14.4309
00100110	26	38	D 1	73.416	13.6210
00100111	27	39	D# 1	77.782	12.8565
00101000	28	40	E 1	82.407	12.1349
00101001	29	41	F 1	87.307	11.4538
00101010	2A	42	F# 1	92.499	10.8110
00101011	2B	43	G 1	97.999	10.2042
00101100	2C	44	G# 1	103.826	9.6315
00101101	2D	45	A 1	110.000	9.0909
00101110	2E	46	A# 1	116.541	8.5807
00101111	2F	47	B 1	123.471	8.0991
00110000	30	48	C 2	130.813	7.6445
00110001	31	49	C# 2	138.591	7.2155
00110010	32	50	D 2	146.832	6.8105
00110011	33	51	D# 2	155.563	6.4282
00110100	34	52	E 2	164.814	6.0675
00110101	35	53	F 2	174.614	5.7269
00110110	36	54	F# 2	184.997	5.4055
00110111	37	55	G 2	195.998	5.1021

. . . .

TABLE 3.4: *MIDI Note Numbers, Notation, Frequency, and Cycle Time (continued)*

BINARY	HEXADECIMAL	DECIMAL	NOTATION	FREQUENCY, IN HZ	CYCLE TIME, IN MILLISECONDS (MSEC)
00111000	38	56	G# 2	207.652	4.8157
00111001	39	57	A 2	220.000	4.5455
00111010	3A	58	A# 2	233.082	4.2903
00111011	3B	59	B 2	246.942	4.0495
00111100	3C	60	C 3	261.626	3.8223
00111101	3D	61	C# 3	277.183	3.6077
00111110	3E	62	D 3	293.665	3.4052
00111111	3F	63	D# 3	311.127	3.2141
01000000	40	64	E 3	329.628	3.0337
01000001	41	65	F 3	349.228	2.8635
01000010	42	66	F# 3	369.994	2.7027
01000011	43	67	G 3	391.995	2.5511
01000100	44	68	G# 3	415.305	2.4079
01000101	45	69	A 3	440.000	2.2727
01000110	46	70	A# 3	466.164	2.1452
01000111	47	71	B 3	493.883	2.0248
01001000	48	72	C 4	523.251	1.9111
01001001	49	73	C# 4	554.365	1.8039
01001010	4A	74	D 4	587.330	1.7026
01001011	4B	75	D# 4	622.254	1.6071
01001100	4C	76	E 4	659.255	1.5169
01001101	4D	77	F 4	698.456	1.4317

TABLE 3.4: *MIDI Note Numbers, Notation, Frequency, and Cycle Time (continued)*

BINARY	HEXADECIMAL	DECIMAL	NOTATION	FREQUENCY, IN HZ	CYCLE TIME, IN MILLISECONDS (MSEC)
01001110	4E	78	F# 4	739.989	1.3514
01001111	4F	79	G 4	783.991	1.2755
01010000	50	80	G# 4	830.609	1.2039
01010001	51	81	A 4	880.000	1.1364
01010010	52	82	A# 4	932.328	1.0726
01010011	53	83	B 4	987.767	1.0124
01010100	54	84	C 5	1,046.502	0.9556
01010101	55	85	C# 5	1,108.731	0.9019
01010110	56	86	D 5	1,174.659	0.8513
01010111	57	87	D# 5	1,244.508	0.8035
01011000	58	88	E 5	1,318.510	0.7584
01011001	59	89	F 5	1,396.913	0.7159
01011010	5A	90	F# 5	1,479.978	0.6757
01011011	5B	91	G 5	1,567.982	0.6378
01011100	5C	92	G# 5	1,661.219	0.6020
01011101	5D	93	A 5	1,760.000	0.5682
01011110	5E	94	A# 5	1,864.655	0.5363
01011111	5F	95	B 5	1,975.533	0.5062
01100000	60	96	C 6	2,093.005	0.4778
01100001	61	97	C# 6	2,217.461	0.4510
01100010	62	98	D 6	2,349.318	0.4257
01100011	63	99	D# 6	2,489.016	0.4018

TABLE 3.4: *MIDI Note Numbers, Notation, Frequency, and Cycle Time (continued)*

BINARY	HEXADECIMAL	DECIMAL	NOTATION	FREQUENCY, IN HZ	CYCLE TIME, IN MILLISECONDS (MSEC)
01100100	64	100	E 6	2,637.020	0.3792
01100101	65	101	F 6	2,793.826	0.3579
01100110	66	102	F# 6	2,959.955	0.3378
01100111	67	103	G 6	3,135.963	0.3189
01101000	68	104	G# 6	3,322.438	0.3010
01101001	69	105	A 6	3,520.000	0.2841
01101010	6A	106	A# 6	3,729.310	0.2681
01101011	6B	107	B 6	3,951.066	0.2531
01101100	6C	108	C 7	4,186.009	0.2389
01101101	6D	109	C# 7	4,434.922	0.2255
01101110	6E	110	D 7	4,698.636	0.2128
01101111	6F	111	D# 7	4,978.032	0.2009
01110000	70	112	E 7	5,274.041	0.1896
01110001	71	113	F 7	5,587.652	0.1790
01110010	72	114	F# 7	5,919.911	0.1689
01110011	73	115	G 7	6,271.927	0.1594
01110100	74	116	G# 7	6,644.875	0.1505
01110101	75	117	A 7	7,040.000	0.1420
01110110	76	118	A# 7	7,458.620	0.1341
01110111	77	119	B 7	7,902.133	0.1265
01111000	78	120	C 8	8,372.018	0.1194
01111001	79	121	C# 8	8,869.844	0.1127

TABLE 3.4: *MIDI Note Numbers, Notation, Frequency, and Cycle Time (continued)*

BINARY	HEXADECIMAL	DECIMAL	NOTATION	FREQUENCY, IN HZ	CYCLE TIME, IN MILLISECONDS (MSEC)
01111010	7A	122	D 8	9,397.273	0.1064
01111011	7B	123	D# 8	9,956.063	0.1004
01111100	7C	124	E 8	10,548.082	0.0948
01111101	7D	125	F 8	11,175.303	0.0895
01111110	7E	126	F# 8	11,839.822	0.0845
01111111	7F	127	G 8	12,543.854	0.0797

Program Change Messages

This section discusses Program Change messages: their syntax, the way they're numbered, how they're stored, and how they're reassigned.

The Program Change Message

Name:	Program Change
Format:	1100cccc (CcH) 0ppppppp
Type:	channel Voice message
cccc	channel number
ppppppp	Program Number

In MIDI jargon, the Program Number (0xxxxxxx) indicates the location of a memory area (such as a patch, a program, a performance, a timbre, or a preset) that contains all the parameters for one of the functions of a

MIDI unit. What this means is that there's a total of 128 addressable locations (i.e., from 0 to 127). For example, when a Program Change message is received, a synthesizer will switch to the corresponding sound. Conversely, if the number of a sound is manually selected on the synthesizer, this same message will eventually be transmitted to the MIDI Out port. Most MIDI devices (such as special effects processors, patches, mixing boards, etc.) can receive and transmit Program Change messages. The format of Program Change messages is shown in Figure 3.8 below.

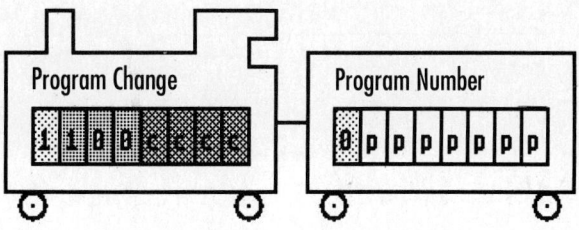

FIGURE 3.8: *The Program Change message*

When Program Change Messages Are Received

Not all sound generators react the same way when they receive a Program Change message. Some of them cut off all of the voices that correspond to notes that are being played on the channel in question, while some immediately assign the new sound to that channel (in which case undesirable noises sometimes occur during the transition). Others don't select the new sound until all of the notes have been released that were being played when the Program Change was received. Yet others assign the new sound to new notes, while the notes that were being played when the Program Change was received go on producing the earlier sounds.

The Different Numbering Systems Currently in Use

Some makers start program changes with 0, while others start with 1. Still others use the octal system (base 8). This is especially true of the Roland company, which arranges the memory areas in most of its products in groups of 8 per bank. Under this scheme, the first memory area (0 in MIDI) is number 11 (i.e., area 1 in bank 1), the eighth memory area is number 18 (i.e., area 8 in bank 1), the ninth memory area is number 21 (i.e., area 1 in bank 2), and so on. Table 3.5 shows examples of numbered program change messages.

TABLE 3.5: *Examples of Numbered Program Change Messages*

DECIMAL (0 TO 127)	DECIMAL (1 TO 128)	HEXADECIMAL	OCTAL (1, 2, AND 3)	BASE 12
0	1	00H	A11 I11 INT A1	INT A1
1	2	01H	A12 I12 INT A2	INT A2
2	3	02H	A13 I13 INT A3	INT A3
3	4	03H	A14 I14 INT A4	INT A4
4	5	04H	A15 I15 INT A5	INT A5
5	6	05H	A16 I16 INT A6	INT A6
6	7	06H	A17 I17 INT A7	INT A7
7	8	07H	A18 I18 INT A8	INT A8
8	9	08H	A21 I21 INT B1	INT A9
9	10	09H	A22 I22 INT B2	INT A10
10	11	0AH	A23 I23 INT B3	INT A11
11	12	0BH	A24 I24 INT B4	INT A12
12	13	0CH	A25 I25 INT B5	INT B1
13	14	0DH	A26 I26 INT B6	INT B2

· · · · · · · · · · · · · · · · · · ·

TABLE 3.5: *Examples of Numbered Program Change Messages (continued)*

DECIMAL (0 TO 127)	DECIMAL (1 TO 128)	HEXADECIMAL	OCTAL (1, 2, AND 3)	BASE 12
14	15	0EH	A27 I27 INT B7	INT B3
15	16	0FH	A28 I28 INT B8	INT B4
16	17	10H	A31 I31 INT C1	INT B5
17	18	11H	A32 I32 INT C2	INT B6
18	19	12H	A33 I33 INT C3	INT B7
19	20	13H	A34 I34 INT C4	INT B8
20	21	14H	A35 I35 INT C5	INT B9
21	22	15H	A36 I36 INT C6	INT B10
22	23	16H	A37 I37 INT C7	INT B11
23	24	17H	A38 I38 INT C8	INT B12
24	25	18H	A41 I41 INT D1	INT C1
25	26	19H	A42 I42 INT D2	INT C2
26	27	1AH	A43 I43 INT D3	INT C3
27	28	1BH	A44 I44 INT D4	INT C4
28	29	1CH	A45 I45 INT D5	INT C5
29	30	1DH	A46 I46 INT D6	INT C6
30	31	1EH	A47 I47 INT D7	INT C7
31	32	1FH	A48 I48 INT D8	INT C8
32	33	20H	A51 I51 INT E1	INT C9
33	34	21H	A52 I52 INT E2	INT C10
34	35	22H	A53 I53 INT E3	INT C11
35	36	23H	A54 I54 INT E4	INT C12
36	37	24H	A55 I55 INT E5	INT D1

TABLE 3.5: *Examples of Numbered Program Change Messages (continued)*

DECIMAL (0 TO 127)	DECIMAL (1 TO 128)	HEXADECIMAL	OCTAL (1, 2, AND 3)	BASE 12
37	38	25H	A56 I56 INT E6	INT D2
38	39	26H	A57 I57 INT E7	INT D3
39	40	27H	A58 I58 INT E8	INT D4
40	41	28H	A61 I61 INT F1	INT D5
41	42	29H	A62 I62 INT F2	INT D6
42	43	2AH	A63 I63 INT F3	INT D7
43	44	2BH	A64 I64 INT F4	INT D8
44	45	2CH	A65 I65 INT F5	INT D9
45	46	2DH	A66 I66 INT F6	INT D10
46	47	2EH	A67 I67 INT F7	INT D11
47	48	2FH	A68 I68 INT F8	INT D12
48	49	30H	A71 I71 INT G1	EXT A1
49	50	31H	A72 I72 INT G2	EXT A2
50	51	32H	A73 I73 INT G3	EXT A3
51	52	33H	A74 I74 INT G4	EXT A4
52	53	34H	A75 I75 INT G5	EXT A5
53	54	35H	A76 I76 INT G6	EXT A6
54	55	36H	A77 I77 INT G7	EXT A7
55	56	37H	A78 I78 INT G8	EXT A8
56	57	38H	A81 I81 INT H1	EXT A9
57	58	39H	A82 I82 INT H2	EXT A10
58	59	3AH	A83 I83 INT H3	EXT A11
59	60	3BH	A84 I84 INT H4	EXT A12

TABLE 3.5: *Examples of Numbered Program Change Messages (continued)*

DECIMAL (0 TO 127)	DECIMAL (1 TO 128)	HEXADECIMAL	OCTAL (1, 2, AND 3)	BASE 12
60	61	3CH	A85 I85 INT H5	EXT B1
61	62	3DH	A86 I86 INT H6	EXT B2
62	63	3EH	A87 I87 INT H7	EXT B3
63	64	3FH	A88 I88 INT H8	EXT B4
64	65	40H	B11 C11 CRT A1	EXT B5
65	66	41H	B12 C12 CRT A2	EXT B6
66	67	42H	B13 C13 CRT A3	EXT B7
67	68	43H	B14 C14 CRT A4	EXT B8
68	69	44H	B15 C15 CRT A5	EXT B9
69	70	45H	B16 C16 CRT A6	EXT B10
70	71	46H	B17 C17 CRT A7	EXT B11
71	72	47H	B18 C18 CRT A8	EXT B12
72	73	48H	B21 C21 CRT B1	EXT C1
73	74	49H	B22 C22 CRT B2	EXT C2
74	75	4AH	B23 C23 CRT B3	EXT C3
75	76	4BH	B24 C24 CRT B4	EXT C4
76	77	4CH	B25 C25 CRT B5	EXT C5
77	78	4DH	B26 C26 CRT B6	EXT C6
78	79	4EH	B27 C27 CRT B7	EXT C7
79	80	4FH	B28 C28 CRT B8	EXT C8
80	81	50H	B31 C31 CRT C1	EXT C9
81	82	51H	B32 C32 CRT C2	EXT C10
82	83	52H	B33 C33 CRT C3	EXT C11

· ·

TABLE 3.5: *Examples of Numbered Program Change Messages (continued)*

DECIMAL (0 TO 127)	DECIMAL (1 TO 128)	HEXADECIMAL	OCTAL (1, 2, AND 3)	BASE 12
83	84	53H	B34 C34 CRT C4	EXT C12
84	85	54H	B35 C35 CRT C5	EXT D1
85	86	55H	B36 C36 CRT C6	EXT D2
86	87	56H	B37 C37 CRT C7	EXT D3
87	88	57H	B38 C38 CRT C8	EXT D4
88	89	58H	B41 C41 CRT D1	EXT D5
89	90	59H	B42 C42 CRT D2	EXT D6
90	91	5AH	B43 C43 CRT D3	EXT D7
91	92	5BH	B44 C44 CRT D4	EXT D8
92	93	5CH	B45 C45 CRT D5	EXT D9
93	94	5DH	B46 C46 CRT D6	EXT D10
94	95	5EH	B47 C47 CRT D7	EXT D11
95	96	5FH	B48 C48 CRT D8	EXT D12
96	97	60H	B51 C51 CRT E1	
97	98	61H	B52 C52 CRT E2	
98	99	62H	B53 C53 CRT E3	
99	100	63H	B54 C54 CRT E4	
100	101	64H	B55 C55 CRT E5	
101	102	65H	B56 C56 CRT E6	
102	103	66H	B57 C57 CRT E7	
103	104	67H	B58 C58 CRT E8	
104	105	68H	B61 C61 CRT F1	
105	106	69H	B62 C62 CRT F2	

. . . .

TABLE 3.5: *Examples of Numbered Program Change Messages (continued)*

DECIMAL (0 TO 127)	DECIMAL (1 TO 128)	HEXADECIMAL	OCTAL (1, 2, AND 3)	BASE 12
106	107	6AH	B63 C63 CRT F3	
107	108	6BH	B64 C64 CRT F4	
108	109	6CH	B65 C65 CRT F5	
109	110	6DH	B66 C66 CRT F6	
110	111	6EH	B67 C67 CRT F7	
111	112	6FH	B68 C68 CRT F8	
112	113	70H	B71 C71 CRT G1	
113	114	71H	B72 C72 CRT G2	
114	115	72H	B73 C73 CRT G3	
115	116	73H	B74 C74 CRT G4	
116	117	74H	B75 C75 CRT G5	
117	118	75H	B76 C76 CRT G6	
118	119	76H	B77 C77 CRT G7	
119	120	77H	B78 C78 CRT G8	
120	121	78H	B81 C81 CRT H1	
121	122	79H	B82 C82 CRT H2	
122	123	7AH	B83 C83 CRT H3	
123	124	7BH	B84 C84 CRT H4	
124	125	7CH	B85 C85 CRT H5	
125	126	7DH	B86 C86 CRT H6	
126	127	7EH	B87 C87 CRT H7	
127	128	7FH	B88 C88 CRT H8	

The first method is used by, among others, Korg (in its M and T series equipment) and Oberheim (Matrix 6), which number their sounds from 00 to 99. The second method is in use in most MIDI devices; the third is almost never used; the fourth (and its variants) is favored primarily by Roland (in its D-10/D-20/D-110, D-50, and MKS-70 devices); and the fifth is popular with Kawai (in its K5 synthesizer).

Data Storage

When power is turned off, some MIDI devices store in memory the most recently selected patch number. Other devices initialize themselves at power-on with the number of the first memory area (0, 1, 11, etc.).

Instruments with More than 128 Programs

A problem comes up when an instrument has more than 128 memory locations. In fact, there's no way to call sound 129 using MIDI, because the corresponding Program Change message doesn't exist.

One solution uses an intermediate storage layer consisting of 128 locations that respond to Program Change messages. Each of the locations in this virtual layer is responsible for calling one of the sounds in the device (for example, sounds located above number 128). Roland uses this method, particularly in synthesizers such as the D-10 and D-20.

Another solution is based on a set of memory banks, each of which contains 128 sounds. The shift from one bank to another is done by assigning any MIDI message (Control Change, System Exclusive, etc.) to the indicated bank before sending the Program Change message. (See also the discussion of the Bank Select message, which was implemented in 1990, at the end of Chapter 4.)

Multitimbral Mode

Multitimbral MIDI instruments are a little more complicated. Depending on the circumstances, the same type of message can be used in two very different ways. In fact, the Program Change message has the effect of either changing the sound number of one of the generators (i.e., one of the multitimbral voices) on its own channel, or changing the entire configuration (i.e., the sound produced by each generator) on the global channel.

Program Change and Autoloading

It's worth noting that for some samplers, reception of a Program Change message automates the loading into RAM (random-access memory) of the contents (a sample, program, volume, etc.) of the corresponding memory location in mass storage This autoloading function is particularly well suited to live performances.

Aftertouch

Aftertouch or key pressure is an expressive parameter related to variations in the amount of pressure applied to keys on a MIDI keyboard after the keys have reached their pressed position. In practice, aftertouch generally controls one or more of the real-time parameters (for instance, amplitude, pitch, or timbre) of a sound. The MIDI standard distinguishes two types of aftertouch: *Polyphonic Aftertouch* and *Channel Aftertouch*.

Polyphonic Key Pressure

Name:	Polyphonic Key Pressure
Format:	1010cccc (AcH) 0nnnnnnn 0aaaaaaa
Type:	channel Voice message
cccc	channel number
nnnnnnn	Note Number
aaaaaaa	value of the aftertouch

Like the velocity value, an aftertouch message is related to the Note Number represented by the first data byte (0nnnnnnn). The second data byte (0aaaaaaa) indicates the variation in aftertouch. For example, for each note in a three-tone chord, three series of aftertouch messages can be transmitted independently of one another:

```
90H 3CH 69H: Note On channel 1/Do 3/velocity 105
90H 40H 5FH: Note On channel 1/Mi 3/velocity 95
90H 43H 77H: Note On channel 1/Sol 3/velocity 119
A0H 3CH 12H: polyphonic key pressure channel 1/C3/pressure 18
A0H 40H 1FH: Polyphonic Key Pressure channel 1/E3/pressure 31
A0H 43H 11H: Polyphonic Key Pressure channel 1/G3/pressure 17
A0H 3CH 13H: Polyphonic Key Pressure channel 1/C3/pressure 19
A0H 40H 20H: Polyphonic Key Pressure channel 1/E3/pressure 32
A0H 43H 12H: Polyphonic Key Pressure channel 1/G3/pressure 18
... ... ...
... ... ...
... ... ...
... ... ...
A0H 3CH 63H: Polyphonic Key Pressure channel 1/C3/pressure 99
A0H 40H 70H: Polyphonic Key Pressure channel 1/E3/pressure 112
A0H 43H 62H: Polyphonic Key Pressure channel 1/G3/pressure 98
... ... ...
90H 3CH 00H: Note On channel 1/C3/velocity 00 (= Note Off)
90H 40H 00H: Note On channel 1/E3/velocity 00 (= Note Off)
90H 43H 00H: Note On channel 1/G3/velocity 119 (= Note Off)
```

The format of the Polyphonic Key Pressure message is shown in Figure 3.9 below.

FIGURE 3.9: *The Polyphonic Key Pressure message*

Channel Aftertouch

Name:	Channel Pressure (Aftertouch)
Format:	1101cccc (DcH) 0aaaaaaa
Type:	channel Voice message
cccc	channel number
aaaaaaa	value of the aftertouch

In this case, a single pressure sensor is used for a single MIDI channel (that is, physically for the entire keyboard). As a result, the note number is no longer necessary and the information can be represented adequately by a single data byte (0aaaaaaa).

Channel Aftertouch messages have the same effect on every note in a chord. For example:

```
9FH 3CH 69H: Note On channel 15/C3/velocity 105
9FH 40H 5FH: Note On channel 15/E3/velocity 95
9FH 43H 77H: Note On channel 15/G3/velocity 119
DFH 12H: Channel Aftertouch channel 15/pressure 18
```

```
DFH 1DH: Channel Aftertouch channel 15/pressure 29
... ...
... ...
... ...
DFH 03H: Channel Aftertouch canal 15/pressure 3
... ...
9FH 3CH 00H: Note On channel 15/C3/velocity 00 (= Note Off)
9FH 40H 00H: Note On channel 15/E3/velocity 00 (= Note Off)
9FH 43H 00H: Note On channel 15/G3/velocity 00 (= Note Off)
```

It's easy to see that with Channel Aftertouch, the 9 messages (27 bytes) that were needed to indicate the polyphonic key pressure in the preceding example can be replaced by a total of 3 messages (6 bytes). The format of the Channel Aftertouch message is shown in Figure 3.10 below.

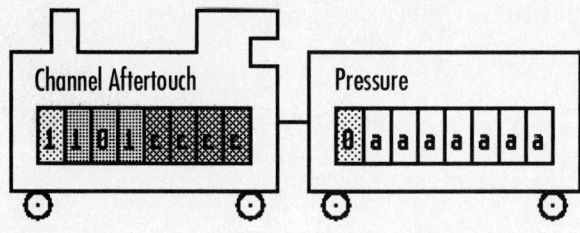

FIGURE 3.10: *The Channel Aftertouch message*

Pitch Bend

This section examines Pitch Bend messages: their syntax, their variations, and the different ways they're sent and received.

The Pitch Bend Message

Name: Pitch Bend

Format: 1110cccc (EcH) 0xxxxxxx 0yyyyyyy

Type:	channel Voice message
cccc	channel number
xxxxxxx	value of the Pitch Bend (least significant byte, LSB)
yyyyyyy	value of the Pitch Bend (most significant byte, MSB)

This message indicates the position of the Pitch Bend wheel (also called the *pitch wheel*) that's found on MIDI keyboards. The wheel's job is to produce a real-time upward or downward change in the pitch of a tone. (Some instruments, such as the Akai S3000, have a mode in which no pitch change is imposed on notes that are released before the wheel is shifted and that are still audible.) The Pitch Bend message occupies two bytes, and its 14 data bits can represent any one of 16,384 different values. The least significant byte (LSByte) is sent first, followed by the most significant byte (MSByte). In other words, the value of the Pitch Bend message is 00yyyyyy yxxxxxxx (because bit 7 of each data byte is set to 0 and therefore is not available for use in coding information), or even 128 × 0yyyyyy + 0xxxxxxx. The format of the Pitch Bend message is shown in Figure 3.11 below.

Because the purpose of this message is to produce an upward or downward change in pitch, the wheel will be shifted to one side or the other of

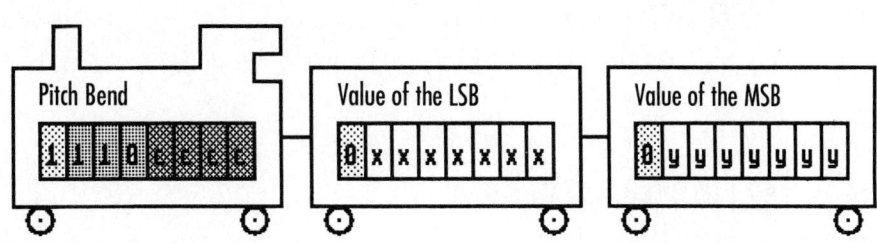

FIGURE 3.11: *The Pitch Bend message*

a central or rest position. The central, minimum, and maximum positions correspond respectively to bytes 00H 40H (00000000 01000000), 00H 00H (00000000 00000000) and 7FH 7FH (01111111 01111111). Coded in the form of 14 useful bits, and in proper order (i.e., the LSByte first, followed by the MSByte), their values are 2000H (00100000 00000000), 0000H, and 3FFH (00111111 11111111).

Resolution for Transmission and Reception

Even with 14-bit resolution, most pitch wheels only use 7 bits (128 values), 8 bits (256 values), or 9 bits (512 values). In such cases, the high-order bits are used (i.e., bits 8 to 14, 7 to 14, and 6 to 14, respectively). In equal shifting, the number of messages to be transmitted increases proportionally as a function of this resolution. The density of the messages transmitted is also a factor, and corresponds to the minimum time interval separating the transmission of two successive Pitch Bend messages.

In setting the resolution and density of Pitch Bend messages, a manufacturer reaches a compromise between the way the human ear hears the change in pitch and a reasonable degree of congestion in the MIDI network's pass-band. During reception, most sound generators ignore certain bits, such as the ones in the least significant data byte. Likewise, during transmission the low-order bits are the ones that get truncated. Unfortunately, users' manuals don't mention these characteristics very often. At power-on some MIDI keyboards automatically issue a Pitch Bend message at 00H 40H in order to initialize the sound generators to which they're connected.

The Pitch-Variation Range

Although the Pitch Bend message indicates the position of the pitch wheel, it does not in any way describe the correspondence between the value of the shift and the resulting dissonance. In effect, it's up to the user to program the pitch-variation range on the receiving machine (i.e., the sound generator), in terms of a number of semitones (generally from 1 to 12). For instance, if the range is set to 12, the minimum and maximum values (00H 00H and 7FH 7FH) of the pitch wheel will produce a dissonance of −12 and +12 semitones, respectively.

The pitch interval separating two consecutive Pitch Bend values depends on the precision of the pitch wheel, and therefore is a function of the value of the variation range. Some sound generators let you set different numbers of semitones for the positive and negative shifts (for example, +7 and −11 semitones respectively). Finally, as explained in the following section, the Pitch Bend Sensitivity message lets the sound generator know the extent of the pitch bend.

Transmitting Pitch Bend Messages

The following examples show how a MIDI instrument transmits Pitch Bend messages coded as 9, 7, and 14 bits.

Example 1

Pitch Bend coded as 9 bits (0yyyyyy 0xx00000), i.e., over 512 values:

a) Upward movement of the pitch wheel (256 messages, including the message indicating the central position); see Table 3.6:

TABLE 3.6: *Upward Movement of the Pitch Wheel*

PITCH BEND MESSAGE	MOST SIGNIFICANT BYTE (MSB)	LEAST SIGNIFICANT BYTE (LSB)	PITCH BEND CODED AS 14 BITS IN BINARY	HEXADECIMAL	DECIMAL
EcH 00H 40H	01000000	00000000	00100000 00000000	20H 00H	8,192
EcH 20H 40H	01000000	00100000	00100000 00100000	20H 20H	8,224
EcH 40H 40H	01000000	01000000	00100000 01000000	20H 40H	8,256
EcH 60H 40H	01000000	01100000	00100000 01100000	20H 60H	8,288
EcH 00H 41H	01000001	00000000	00100000 10000000	20H 80H	8,320
EcH 20H 41H	01000001	00100000	00100000 10100000	20H A0H	8,352
EcH 40H 41H	01000001	01000000	00100000 11000000	20H C0H	8,384
EcH 60H 41H	01000001	01100000	00100000 11100000	20H E0H	8,416
EcH 00H 42H	01000010	00000000	00100001 00000000	21H 00H	8,448
EcH 20H 42H	01000010	00100000	00100001 00100000	21H 20H	8,480

TABLE 3.6: *Upward Movement of the Pitch Wheel (continued)*

PITCH BEND MESSAGE	MOST SIGNIFICANT BYTE (MSB)	LEAST SIGNIFICANT BYTE (LSB)	PITCH BEND CODED AS 14 BITS IN BINARY	HEXADECIMAL	DECIMAL
EcH 40H 42H	01000010	01000000	00100001 01000000	21H 40H	8,512
EcH 60H 42H	01000010	01100000	00100001 01100000	21H 60H	8,544
...	...	...	...	...	...
EcH 00H 7EH	01111110	00000000	00111111 00000000	3FH 00H	16,128
EcH 20H 7EH	01111110	00100000	00111111 00100000	3FH 20H	16,160
EcH 40H 7EH	01111110	01000000	00111111 01000000	3FH 40H	16,192
EcH 60H 7EH	01111110	01100000	00111111 01100000	3FH 60H	16,224
EcH 00H 7FH	01111111	00000000	00111111 10000000	3FH 80H	16,256
EcH 20H 7FH	01111111	00100000	00111111 10100000	3FH A0H	16,288
EcH 40H 7FH	01111111	01000000	00111111 11000000	3FH C0H	16,320
EcH 60H 7FH	01111111	01100000	00111111 11100000	3FH E0H	16,352

b) Downward movement of the pitch wheel (257 messages, including the message indicating the central position); see Table 3.7:

TABLE 3.7: *Downward Movement of the Pitch Wheel*

PITCH BEND MESSAGE	MOST SIGNIFICANT BYTE (MSB)	LEAST SIGNIFICANT BYTE (LSB)	PITCH BEND CODED AS 14 BITS IN BINARY	HEXADECIMAL	DECIMAL
EcH 00H 40H	01000000	00000000	00100000 00000000	20H 00H	8,192
EcH 60H 3FH	00111111	01100000	00011111 11100000	1FH E0H	8,160
EcH 40H 3FH	00111111	01000000	00011111 11000000	1FH C0H	8,128
EcH 20H 3FH	00111111	00100000	00011111 10100000	1FH A0H	8,096
EcH 00H 3FH	00111111	00000000	00011111 10000000	1FH 80H	8,064
EcH 60H 3EH	00111110	01100000	00011111 01100000	1FH 60H	8,032
EcH 40H 3EH	00111110	01000000	00011111 01000000	1FH 40H	8,000
EcH 20H 3EH	00111110	00100000	00011111 00100000	1FH 20H	7,968
EcH 00H 3EH	00111110	00000000	00011111 00000000	1FH 00H	7,936
EcH 60H 3DH	00111101	01100000	00011110 11100000	1EH E0H	7,904
EcH 40H 3DH	00111101	01000000	00011110 11000000	1EH C0H	7,872
EcH 20H 3DH	00111101	00100000	00011110 10100000	1EH A0H	7,840

TABLE 3.7: *Downward Movement of the Pitch Wheel (continued)*

PITCH BEND MESSAGE	MOST SIGNIFICANT BYTE (MSB)	LEAST SIGNIFICANT BYTE (LSB)	PITCH BEND CODED AS 14 BITS IN BINARY	HEXADECIMAL	DECIMAL
EcH 00H 3DH	00111101	00000000	00011110 10000000	1EH 80H	7,808
...	...	...	...	...	...
EcH 60H 01H	00000001	01100000	00000000 11100000	00H E0H	224
EcH 40H 01H	00000001	01000000	00000000 11000000	00H C0H	192
EcH 20H 01H	00000001	00100000	00000000 10100000	00H A0H	160
EcH 00H 01H	00000001	00000000	00000000 10000000	00H 80H	128
EcH 60H 00H	00000000	01100000	00000000 01100000	00H 60H	96
EcH 40H 00H	00000000	01000000	00000000 01000000	00H 40H	64
EcH 20H 00H	00000000	00100000	00000000 00100000	00H 20H	32
EcH 00H 00H	00000000	00000000	00000000 00000000	00H 00H	0

Example 2

Pitch Bend coded as 7 bits (0yyyyyy 00000000), i.e., over 128 values:

a) Upward movement of the pitch wheel (64 messages, including the message indicating the central position); see Table 3.8:

TABLE 3.8: *Upward Movement of the Pitch Wheel*

PITCH BEND MESSAGE	MOST SIGNIFICANT BYTE (MSB)	LEAST SIGNIFICANT BYTE (LSB)	PITCH BEND CODED AS 14 BITS IN BINARY	HEXADECIMAL	DECIMAL
EcH 00H 40H	01000000	00000000	00100000 00000000	20H 00H	8,192
EcH 00H 41H	01000001	00000000	00100000 10000000	20H 80H	8,320
EcH 00H 42H	01000010	00000000	00100001 00000000	21H 00H	8,448
EcH 00H 43H	01000011	00000000	00100001 10000000	21H 80H	8,576
...	...	...	...	...	...
EcH 00H 7EH	01111110	00000000	00111111 00000000	3FH 00H	16,128
EcH 00H 7FH	01111111	00000000	00111111 10000000	3FH 80H	16,256

b) Downward movement of the pitch wheel (65 messages, including the message indicating the central position); see Table 3.9:

TABLE 3.9: *Downward Movement of the Pitch Wheel*

PITCH BEND MESSAGE	MOST SIGNIFICANT BYTE (MSB)	LEAST SIGNIFICANT BYTE (LSB)	PITCH BEND CODED AS 14 BITS IN BINARY	HEXADECIMAL	DECIMAL
EcH 00H 40H	01000000	00000000	00100000 00000000	20H 00H	8,192
EcH 00H 3FH	00111111	00000000	00011111 10000000	1FH 80H	8,064
EcH 00H 3EH	00111110	00000000	00011111 00000000	1FH 00H	7,936
EcH 00H 3DH	00111101	00000000	00011110 10000000	1EH 80H	7,808
...			...	...	...
EcH 00H 01H	00000001	00000000	00000000 10000000	00H 80H	128
EcH 00H 00H	00000000	00000000	00000000 00000000	00H 00H	0

Example 3

Pitch Bend coded as 14 bits (0yyyyyy 00000000), i.e., over 16,384 values:

a) Upward movement of the pitch wheel (8,192 messages, including the message indicating the central position); see Table 3.10:

TABLE 3.10: *Upward Movement of the Pitch Wheel*

PITCH BEND MESSAGE	MOST SIGNIFICANT BYTE (MSB)	LEAST SIGNIFICANT BYTE (LSB)	PITCH BEND CODED AS 14 BITS IN BINARY	HEXADECIMAL	DECIMAL
EcH 00H 40H	01000000	00000000	00100000 00000000	20H 00H	8,192
EcH 01H 40H	01000000	00000001	00100000 00000001	20H 01H	8,193
EcH 02H 40H	01000000	00000010	00100000 00000010	20H 02H	8,194
EcH 03H 40H	01000000	00000011	00100000 00000011	20H 03H	8,195
...			...	...	...
EcH 7EH 7FH	01111111	01111110	00111111 11111110	3FH FEH	16,382
EcH 7FH 7FH	01111111	01111111	00111111 11111111	3FH FFH	16,383

b) Downward movement of the pitch wheel (8,193 messages, including the message indicating the central position); see Table 3.11:

TABLE 3.11: *Downward Movement of the Pitch Wheel*

PITCH BEND MESSAGE	MOST SIGNIFICANT BYTE (MSB)	LEAST SIGNIFICANT BYTE (LSB)	PITCH BEND CODED AS 14 BITS IN BINARY	HEXADECIMAL	DECIMAL
EcH 00H 40H	01000000	00000000	00100000 00000000	20H 00H	8,192
EcH 7FH 3FH	00111111	01111111	00011111 11111111	1FH FFH	8,191
EcH 7EH 3FH	00111111	01111110	00011111 11111110	1FH FEH	8,190
EcH 7DH 3FH	00111111	01111101	00011111 11111101	1FH FDH	8,189
...	...	...	...	...	...
EcH 01H 00H	00000000	00000001	00000000 00000001	00H 01H	1
EcH 00H 00H	00000000	00000000	00000000 00000000	00H 00H	0

Example 4

Some MIDI instruments transmit Pitch Bend messages coded as 14 bits, without using the 16,384 values that are available. In the case shown in the following table, the messages are transmitted at intervals of 32 units, and 33 units every four messages.

a) Upward movement of the pitch wheel (256 messages, including the message indicating the central position); see Table 3.12:

TABLE 3.12: *Upward Movement of the Pitch Wheel*

PITCH BEND MESSAGE	MOST SIGNIFICANT BYTE (MSB)	LEAST SIGNIFICANT BYTE (LSB)	PITCH BEND CODED AS 14 BITS IN BINARY	HEXADECIMAL	DECIMAL
EcH 00H 40H	01000000	00000000	00100000 00000000	20H 00H	8,192
EcH 20H 40H	01000000	00100000	00100000 00100000	20H 20H	8,224
EcH 40H 40H	01000000	01000000	00100000 01000000	20H 40H	8,256
EcH 60H 40H	01000000	01100000	00100000 01100000	20H 60H	8,288
EcH 01H 41H	01000001	00000001	00100000 10000001	20H 81H	8,321
EcH 21H 41H	01000001	00100001	00100000 10100001	20H A1H	8,353
EcH 41H 41H	01000001	01000001	00100000 11000001	20H C1H	8,385
EcH 61H 41H	01000001	01100001	00100000 11100001	20H E1H	8,417
EcH 02H 42H	01000010	00000010	00100001 00000010	21H 02H	8,450

TABLE 3.12: *Upward Movement of the Pitch Wheel (continued)*

PITCH BEND MESSAGE	MOST SIGNIFICANT BYTE (MSB)	LEAST SIGNIFICANT BYTE (LSB)	PITCH BEND CODED AS 14 BITS IN BINARY	HEXADECIMAL	DECIMAL
EcH 22H 42H	01000010	00100010	00100001 00100010	21H 22H	8,482
EcH 42H 42H	01000010	01000010	00100001 01000010	21H 42H	8,514
EcH 62H 42H	01000010	01100010	00100001 01100010	21H 62H	8,546
...	...	...	...	...	...
EcH 1EH 7EH	01111110	00011110	00111111 00011110	3FH 1EH	16,158
EcH 3EH 7EH	01111110	00111110	00111111 00111110	3FH 3EH	16,190
EcH 5EH 7EH	01111110	01011110	00111111 01011110	3FH 5EH	16,222
EcH 7EH 7EH	01111110	01111110	00111111 01111110	3FH 7EH	16,254
EcH 1FH 7FH	01111111	00011111	00111111 10011111	3FH 9FH	16,287
EcH 3FH 7FH	01111111	00111111	00111111 10111111	3FH BFH	16,319
EcH 5FH 7FH	01111111	01011111	00111111 11011111	3FH DFH	16,351
EcH 7FH 7FH	01111111	01111111	00111111 11111111	3FH FFH	16,383

Receiving Pitch Bend Messages

The following examples show how a MIDI instrument that can receive Pitch Bend messages coded as 8 bits (from 0 to 256, and more precisely from −127 to +128 with respect to the central point, as indicated in the "Offset" column in the table) would interpret the preceding three examples.

Example 1 (pitch bend distributed over 9 bits)

a) Upward movement of the pitch wheel; see Table 3.13:

TABLE 3.13: *Upward Movement of the Pitch Wheel*

PITCH BEND CODED AS 14 BITS IN BINARY	HEXADECIMAL	DECIMAL	CODED AS 8 BITS	DECIMAL	OFFSET
00100000 00000000	20H 00H	8,192	10000000	128	0
00100000 00100000	20H 20H	8,224	10000000	128	0
00100000 01000000	20H 40H	8,256	10000001	129	+1
00100000 01100000	20H 60H	8,288	10000001	129	+1
00100000 10000000	20H 80H	8,320	10000010	130	+2
00100000 10100000	20H A0H	8,352	10000010	130	+2
00100000 11000000	20H C0H	8,384	10000011	131	+3

TABLE 3.3: *Upward Movement of the Pitch Wheel (continued)*

PITCH BEND CODED AS 14 BITS IN BINARY	HEXADECIMAL	DECIMAL	CODED AS 8 BITS	DECIMAL	OFFSET
00100000 11100000	20H E0H	8,416	10000011	131	+3
00100001 00000000	21H 00H	8,448	10000100	132	+4
00100001 00100000	21H 20H	8,480	10000100	132	+4
00100001 01000000	21H 40H	8,512	10000101	133	+5
00100001 01100000	21H 60H	8,544	10000101	133	+5
...	...	...	...	...	...
00111111 00000000	3FH 00H	16,128	11111100	252	+124
00111111 00100000	3FH 20H	16,160	11111100	252	+124
00111111 01000000	3FH 40H	16,192	11111101	253	+125
00111111 01100000	3FH 60H	16,224	11111101	253	+125
00111111 10000000	3FH 80H	16,256	11111110	254	+126
00111111 10100000	3FH A0H	16,288	11111110	254	+126
00111111 11000000	3FH C0H	16,320	11111111	255	+127
00111111 11100000	3FH E0H	16,352	11111111	255	+127

b) Downward movement of the pitch wheel; see Table 3.14:

TABLE 3.14: *Downward Movement of the Pitch Wheel*

PITCH BEND CODED AS 14 BITS IN BINARY	HEXADECIMAL	DECIMAL	CODED AS 8 BITS	DECIMAL	OFFSET
00100000 00000000	20H 00H	8,192	10000000	128	0
00011111 11100000	1FH E0H	8,160	01111111	127	−1
00011111 11000000	1FH C0H	8,128	01111111	127	−1
00011111 10100000	1FH A0H	8,096	01111110	126	−2
00011111 10000000	1FH 80H	8,064	01111110	126	−2
00011111 01100000	1FH 60H	8,032	01111101	125	−3
00011111 01000000	1FH 40H	8,000	01111101	125	−3
00011111 00100000	1FH 20H	7,968	01111100	124	−4
00011111 00000000	1FH 00H	7,936	01111100	124	−4
00011110 11100000	1EH E0H	7,904	01111011	123	−5
00011110 11000000	1EH C0H	7,872	01111011	123	−5
00011110 10100000	1EH A0H	7,840	01111010	122	−6

TABLE 3.14: *Downward Movement of the Pitch Wheel (continued)*

PITCH BEND CODED AS 14 BITS IN BINARY	HEXADECIMAL	DECIMAL	CODED AS 8 BITS	DECIMAL	OFFSET
00011110 10000000	1EH 80H	7,808	01111010	122	−6
...	...	...	...	...	...
00000000 11100000	00H E0H	224	00000011	3	−125
00000000 11000000	00H C0H	192	00000011	3	−125
00000000 10100000	00H A0H	160	00000010	2	−126
00000000 10000000	00H 80H	128	00000010	2	−126
00000000 01100000	00H 60H	96	00000001	1	−127
00000000 01000000	00H 40H	64	00000001	1	−127
00000000 00100000	00H 20H	32	00000000	0	−128
00000000 00000000	00H 00H	0	00000000	0	−128

Example 2 (pitch bend distributed over 7 bits)

a) Upward movement of the pitch wheel; see Table 3.15:

TABLE 3.15: *Upward Movement of the Pitch Wheel*

PITCH BEND CODED AS 14 BITS IN BINARY	HEXDECIMAL	DECIMAL	CODED AS 8 BITS	DECIMAL	OFFSET
00100000 00000000	20H 00H	8,192	10000000	128	0
00100000 10000000	20H 80H	8,320	10000010	130	+2
00100001 00000000	21H 00H	8,448	10000100	132	+4
00100001 10000000	21H 80H	8,576	10000110	134	+6
...		...		...	...
00111111 00000000	3FH 00H	16,128	11111100	252	+124
00111111 10000000	3FH 80H	16,256	11111110	254	+126

b) Downward movement of the pitch wheel; see Table 3.16:

TABLE 3.16: *Downward Movement of the Pitch Wheel*

PITCH BEND CODED AS 14 BITS IN BINARY	HEXADECIMAL	DECIMAL	CODED AS 8 BITS	DECIMAL	OFFSET
00100000 00000000	20H 00H	8,192	10000000	128	0
00011111 10000000	1FH 80H	8,064	01111110	126	-2
00011111 00000000	1FH 00H	7,936	01111100	124	-4
00011110 10000000	1EH 80H	7,808	01111010	122	-6
...	...	...	...	...	...
00000000 10000000	00H 80H	128	00000010	2	-126
00000000 00000000	00H 00H	0	00000000	0	-128

Example 3 (pitch bend distributed over 14 bits)

a) Upward movement of the pitch wheel; see Table 3.17:

TABLE 3.17: *Upward Movement of the Pitch Wheel*

PITCH BEND CODED AS 14 BITS IN BINARY	HEXADECIMAL	DECIMAL	CODED AS 8 BITS	DECIMAL	OFFSET
00100000 00000000	20H 00H	8,192	10000000	128	0
00100000 00000001	20H 01H	8,193	10000000	128	0
00100000 00000010	20H 02H	8,194	10000000	128	0
00100000 00000011	20H 03H	8,195	10000000	128	0
...	...	...	...	...	...
00111111 11111110	3FH FEH	16,382	11111111	255	+127
00111111 11111111	3FH FFH	16,383	11111111	255	+127

b) Downward movement of the pitch wheel; see Table 3.18:

TABLE 3.18: *Downward Movement of the Pitch Wheel*

PITCH BEND CODED AS 14 BITS IN BINARY	HEXADECIMAL	DECIMAL	CODED AS 8 BITS	DECIMAL	OFFSET
00100000 00000000	20H 00H	8,192	10000000	128	0
00011111 11111111	1FH FFH	8,191	01111111	127	−1
00011111 11111110	1FH FEH	8,190	01111111	127	−1
00011111 11111101	1FH FDH	8,189	01111111	127	−1
...	...	...	...	...	...
00000000 00000001	00H 01H	1	00000000	0	−128
00000000 00000000	00H 00H	0	00000000	0	−128
...					

Control Change Messages

This section is limited to a discussion of Voice messages, starting with the Control Change messages, since Mode messages are the subject of the next chapter.

The Control Change Message

Name:	Control Change
Format:	1011cccc (BcH) 0xxxxxxx 0yyyyyyy
Type:	channel Voice message for X from 0 to 120
	channel Mode message for X from 121 to 127
cccc	channel number
xxxxxxx	controller number
yyyyyyy	controller value

Control Change messages are intended to have a real-time effect on various parameters. Thanks to their very open structure, the development of these messages has unquestionably been the liveliest in the history of MIDI status information. These messages have been, and still are, extendable. Each update of the standard expands their capabilities. Overall, 121 controllers are available (from 0 to 120). These controllers are allocated in the following way:

- From 0 to 31: the most significant byte (MSByte) for the basic continuous controllers.
- From 32 to 63: the least significant byte (LSByte) for the basic continuous controllers.
- From 64 to 69: switches.
- From 70 to 95: additional continuous controllers coded as a byte.

- From 96 to 101: incrementing and decrementing, for Registered and Non-Registered parameters.

- From 102 to 120: undefined controllers.

The format of Control Change messages is shown in Figure 3.12 below.

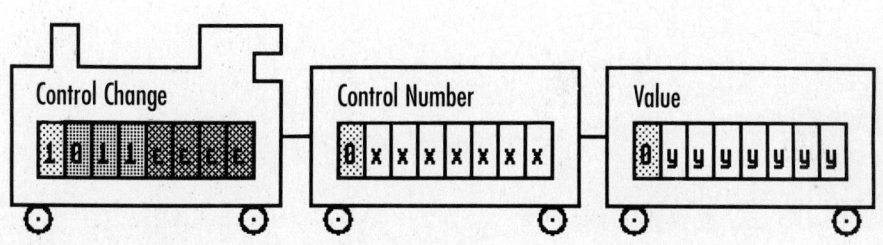

FIGURE 3.12: *The Control Change message*

Continuous MSB/LSB Controllers

The MIDI standard currently defines only 14 of the 32 continuous controllers (from 0 to 31 and 00H to 1FH). The information that these controllers carry theoretically indicates the movement of *pedals, wheels, levers,* and potentiometers or *faders.* The result is an uninterrupted stream of data (hence the term "continuous controller"). For example, by shifting the modulation wheel (controller 01) of a keyboard from its minimum position to its maximum position, you should in theory get the following messages:

```
BcH 01H 00H
BcH 01H 01H
BcH 01H 02H
BcH 01H 03H
... ... ...
... ... ...
BcH 01H 7EH
BcH 01H 7FH
```

In the same way as for the Pitch Bend message, the keyboard processor analyzes the position of the modulation wheel a given number of times every second. This number of analyses per second (usually from 50 to 100) corresponds to the update speed of that controller (i.e., the *data update rate*). If you shift the modulation wheel within half a second, the result should be something like this:

```
BcH 01H 00H
BcH 01H 05H
BcH 01H 0AH
BcH 01H 0FH
... ... ...
... ... ...
BcH 01H 7AH
BcH 01H 7FH
```

In these examples only the MSB of the continuous controller was operative, because 128 values were enough to quantify the pitch-wheel shift. In order to indicate the movements more accurately, you could call on the services of the corresponding LSB of the continuous controller (which, for modulation, would be 33). However, very few constructors make use of this option, and as a result you get a resolution of 16,384 possible values (i.e., from 0 to 16,383) for a transmission that consists of 14 useful bits (rather than 16, because bit 7 in each of the two bytes is by definition set to zero).

In hexadecimal notation coded as two bytes, the maximum value that can be quantified by 14 bits is equal to 3FFFH (i.e., 00111111 11111111). This report, consisting of two MIDI data bytes and 14 bits, is linked to the data-identification and status-identification constraints (i.e., the setting of bit 7 to 0 or 1). As you saw earlier, if these 14 useful bits are represented by the letters "a" through "n," then the conversion takes place in the following way:

```
Oabcdefg Ohijklmn = OOabcdef ghijklmn
```

For example:

```
01111111 01111111 (7FH 7FH) = 00111111 11111111 (3FFFH)
```

or even:

```
01010011 01110001 (53H 71H) = 00101001 11110001 (19F1H)
```

Here's an illustration of how modulation messages are transmitted in the form of two bytes, with conversion for 14 useful bits:

```
BcH 01H 00H MSB modulation
BcH 21H 00H LSB modulation (MSB + LSB = 0000H = 00 decimal)
BcH 01H 00H MSB modulation
BcH 21H 40H LSB modulation (MSB + LSB = 0040H = 64)
BcH 01H 01H MSB modulation
BcH 21H 00H LSB modulation (MSB + LSB = 0080H = 128)
BcH 01H 01H MSB modulation
BcH 21H 40H LSB modulation (MSB + LSB = 00C0H = 192)
... ... ...
... ... ...
BcH 01H 7FH MSB modulation
BcH 21H 00H LSB modulation (MSB + LSB = 3F80H = 16,256)
BcH 01H 7FH MSB modulation
BcH 21H 40H LSB modulation (MSB + LSB = 3FC0H = 16,320)
```

In this case, if a slight readjustment of the position means that only the least significant status byte needs to be retransmitted, then the most significant status bit doesn't need to be retransmitted ahead of it.

The transition from:

```
BcH 01H 02H MSB modulation
BcH 21H 4FH LSB modulation (MSB + LSB = 014FH = 335)
```

to:

```
BcH 01H 02H MSB modulation
BcH 21H 7AH LSB modulation (MSB + LSB = 017AH = 378)
```

is equivalent to:

```
BcH 01H 02H MSB modulation
BcH 21H 4FH LSB modulation (MSB + LSB = 014FH = 335)
BcH 21H 7AH LSB modulation (the stored MSB + the new LSB at 017AH = 378)
```

The Continuous Controllers, in Detail

What follows is a detailed explanation of the 14 currently available continuous MSB/LSB controllers. The 19 controllers that haven't yet been defined by the MIDI standard are reserved for future extensions.

Modulation (1/01H): Modulation on a MIDI keyboard is done by means of a wheel or a lever. Some manufacturers, such as Roland, provide a tetrapole joystick. As such, pitch bend and modulation can be controlled simultaneously and single-handedly by diagonal movements of the joystick. Manufacturers of MIDI instruments have the option of assigning modulation to parameters of their choice in order to create tremolo (i.e., a variation in amplitude), vibrato (i.e., a variation in pitch), or any other effect they may consider desirable.

Breath Controller (2/02H): The role of the breath controller (i.e., control by means of breathing) is similar to those of aftertouch and modulation. It takes the form of a plastic nozzle into which the user exhales, in such a way as to convert variations in pressure into MIDI messages. Because of its similarity to the embouchure of wind instruments, the breath controller is particularly well suited to imitating these instruments.

Foot Controller (4/04H): The purpose of this controller is identical to that of the breath controller. The only difference is that this controller works by means of a foot command.

Portamento Time (5/05H): Portamento makes it possible to make a gradual pitch transition between two notes, the same way a violinist slides a finger along a string of the instrument. The Portamento Time message regulates the duration of this transition.

Data Entry (6/06H): In analog synthesizers, each sound-editing parameter is implemented by physical access and control means (potentiometers, switches, etc.), whereas in most digital synthesizers, certain keys are reserved for selection of the parameter to be edited. The parameter can be displayed on a liquid-crystal display (LCD) screen, and its value can be changed by a single and unique command (entered by means of a potentiometer, alpha dial, or other control device).

Main Volume (7/07H): This controller relates to the output volume of a sound generator. The most widespread use of this controller is in automating MIDI volumes (for example, during mixing).

Balance (8/08H): Balance corresponds to the equilibrium in terms of volume (i.e., the mixing) between two tones. In order to build a sound, some synthesizers use a stack of two timbres, known as the *upper tone* and the *lower tone*. Balance values of 0, 64, and 127 are understood to refer to the lower tone alone, the lower tone and the upper tone in equal proportions, and the upper tone alone, respectively.

Pan (10/0AH): This controller should not be confused with the Balance controller. The Pan message affects the spatial localization of a sound in stereo (i.e., panoramic) space. The values, which range from 0 to 127, sweep the stereophonic range from left to right.

Expression (11/0BH): This controller involves a volume adjustment whose purpose is to refine the Main Volume controller.

General Purpose (16-19/10H-13H): This class of controllers is reserved for non-standardized applications. Four of these controllers (16 to 19) are characterized by resolution over 14 bits (with optional LSBs for 48 to 51), whereas four others (80 to 83) are limited to a single 7-bit data byte.

Switches

Controllers 64 to 69 are assigned to serve as *switches*. In other words, these controllers represent the *on* and *off* states. For the 128 values authorized by the data byte, values 0 to 63 (00H to 3FH) correspond to the OFF position, and values 64 to 127 (40H to 7FH) correspond to the ON position. However, it's advisable to use only the minimum (00H) and maximum (7FH) values.

Damper Pedal (64/40H): This controller is the sustain pedal, which is used in exactly the same way as the damper pedal of an acoustic piano. The MIDI sustain pedal prolongs the continuation period of the amplitude envelope of a sound generator. When Note Off messages are received after pressure has been applied to the sustain pedal, these messages wait for the pedal to be released before they go into effect.

Portamento (65/41H): This controller turns the portamento on and off.

Sostenuto (6/42H): Unlike the sustain function, the Sostenuto function prolongs only the notes that are played after pressure has been applied to the pedal.

Soft Pedal (67/43H): This pedal is identical to the muting pedal of an acoustic piano.

Legato Footswitch (68/44H): When a Legato Footswitch On message is received, the sound generator switches into monophonic mode. When a Note On message is sent to it before the

Note Off message for the "current" note, the pitch of this latter note changes as a result, without any "re-attack" of the sound. When a Legato Footswitch Off message is received, the sound generator switches back into the mode it was in before it received the Legato Footswitch On message.

Hold 2 (69/45H): This controller duplicates the function of the sustain pedal when two holding functions need to be implemented at the same time.

Additional Continuous Controllers Coded as a Byte

Apart from the "General Controllers 5 to 8" (that is, 80 to 83/50H to 53H) mentioned earlier, here's the meaning of the additional Continuous Controllers for a byte.

Sound Controllers 1 to 10 (70 to 79/46H to 4FH): You are free to assign the functions of your choice to these ten controllers. However, by default, the Timbre Variation, Timbre/Harmonic Intensity, Release Time, and Attack Time parameters are associated respectively with the first four of these controllers, described in more detail below.

Timbre Variation (70/46H): This controller selects one of two variations of a sound, such as a muted trumpet as opposed to an unmuted one, a pizzicato violin as opposed to a bowed violin, and so on. The selection doesn't affect notes that are being played. A sound for which only one variation is available will respond to the following two messages:

```
BcH 46H vvH (with vvH from 00H to 3FH): the original sound
BcH 46H vvH (with vvH from 40H to 7FH): the variation
```

while a sound for which three variations are available will respond
to the following four messages:

```
BcH 46H vvH (with vvH from 00H to 1FH): the original sound
BcH 46H vvH (with vvH from 20H to 3FH): the first variation
BcH 46H vvH (with vvH from 40H to 5FH): the second variation
BcH 46H vvH (with vvH from 60H to 7FH): the third variation
```

and so on.

Timbre/Harmonic Intensity (71/47H): This controller has a
real-time effect on the harmonic contents of a sound (e.g., the cut-
off frequency of a low-pass filter in subtractive synthesis, the amplitude of a modulator in FM synthesis, the equalizer in a
processor, etc.). This message, which acts on either side of a central value, never affects parameters that are stored in memory.

```
BcH 47H vvH (with vvH from 00H to 3FH): less and less brilliant
BcH 47H vvH (with vvH = 40H):           no change
BcH 47H vvH (with vvH from 41H to 7FH): more and more brilliant
```

Release Time (72/48H): This controller has a real-time effect
on the duration of the release segment for some or all of the envelopes of a sound. This message, which acts on either side of a central value, never affects parameters that are stored in memory.

```
BcH 48H vvH (with vvH from 00H to 3FH): shorter and shorter duration
BcH 48H vvH (with vvH = 40H):           no change
BcH 48H vvH (with vvH from 41H to 7FH): longer and longer duration
```

Attack Time (73/49H): This controller has a real-time effect on
the duration of the attack segment for some or all of the envelopes
of a sound. This message, which acts on either side of a central
value, never affects parameters that are stored in memory.

```
BcH 49H vvH (with vvH from 00H to 3FH): shorter and shorter duration
BcH 49H vvH (with vvH = 40H): no change
BcH 49H vvH (with vvH from 41H to 7FH): longer and longer duration
```

Portamento Controller (84/54H): When a subsequent Note On message is received, a portamento effect is produced between the note whose number is specified by the Portamento Controller and the note whose number is named in the Note On message, at a speed determined by the Portamento Time continuous controller. For example:

MESSAGE	DESCRIPTION	MEANING
9cH 40H 39H	Note On A2	A2 is pressed
BcH 05H 01H	Portamento time = 1	Slow speed
BcH 54H 3CH	Portamento Controller C3	The portamento will start at C3
9cH 40H 40H	Note On E3	E3 is pressed; execution of the portamento, from C3 to E3
9cH 40H 3DH	Note On D3	D3 is pressed
8cH 40H 40H	Note Off E3	E3 is released
8cH 40H 39H	Note Off A2	A2 is released
8cH 40H 3DH	Note Off D3	D3 is released

The Portamento Controller affects only the first Note On message that arrives. It never affects the pitch of subsequent notes, nor the pitch of notes that are being played. Furthermore, if the note number that it carries is the same as the number of a note that's being played, the portamento will start with this note when the next Note On message is received, without the involvement of any other polyphonic voice (in other words, without any "re-attack" of the note that's being played).

For example:

MESSAGE	DESCRIPTION	MEANING
9cH 40H 3CH	Note On C3	C3 is pressed
BcH 05H 20H	Portamento time = 32	Average speed
BcH 54H 3CH	Portamento Controller C3	The portamento will start at C3
9cH 40H 40H	Note On E3	E3 is pressed; execution of the portamento, from C3 to E3
9cH 40H 3DH	Note On D3	D3 is pressed
8cH 40H 40H	Note Off E3	E3 is released
8cH 40H 3DH	Note Off D3	D3 is released

There's no need to send a Note Release message to C3, because this note has been transformed into E3.

The preceding examples have assumed that the sound generator is polyphonic. Now suppose that it's monophonic and that it's just received a Legato Footswitch message. In this case, the reception of a Portamento Controller will have an immediate effect on the pitch of the note that's being played. For example:

MESSAGE	DESCRIPTION	MEANING
9cH 40H 39H	Note On A2	A2 is pressed
BcH 05H 60H	Portamento time = 96	High speed
BcH 54H 3CH	Portamento Controller C3	A2 is transformed into C3, and the portamento will start at C3

MESSAGE	DESCRIPTION	MEANING
9cH 40H 40H	Note On E3	E3 is pressed; execution of the portamento, from C3 to E3
8cH 40H 40H	Note Off E3	E3 is released

This message is especially important to MIDI guitarists because it lets them work in polyphonic mode, whereas up till now they'd been forced to use Mode 4 (monophonic mode, with one channel per string).

Effects 1 Depth through Effects 5 Depth (91 to 95/5BH to 5FH): Formerly known as External Effects Depth, Tremolo Depth, Chorus Depth, Celeste (Detune) Depth, and Phaser Depth, today these five controllers have a wider range of action, in the sense that they can control the effects of their choice. However, their former designations are still their default values.

Incrementing and Decrementing Data

The role of the *Data Increment* (96/60H) and *Data Decrement* (97/61H) controllers is identical to that of the Data Entry controller. Rather than causing continual changes in the value of a parameter to be edited, these controllers simply add a unit to the value or remove a unit from the value. Unlike the Data Entry controller, whose effect is absolute (in that it indicates the position of the cursor), these two controller work in relative mode.

Registered and Non-Registered Parameters

The purpose of *Registered* and *Non-Registered* parameters is to make it possible to select a specific parameter on a MIDI instrument. In order to edit the value of a parameter once the selection has been made, a Data Entry,

Data Increment, or Data Decrement message must be sent. Registered Parameter numbers (100/64H LSB and 101/65H MSB) and Non-Registered Parameter numbers (98/62H LSB and 99/63H MSB) are coded in the form of 14 bits (i.e., 16,384 values). When that's enough to select a new parameter, it is possible to transmit just one of the two messages (MSB or LSB). For instance, after a Non-Registered Parameter 0 has been selected (BcH 62H 00H, BcH 63H 00H), the following message can advantageously be used to select a parameter 5: BcH 62H 05H. The Registered and Non-Registered Parameter messages are among the later additions to the MIDI standard. They provide access to a total of 32,758 (that is, 2 × 16,384) new controllers.

Manufacturers are free to use Non-Registered Parameter numbers as they see fit, provided that the functions of any such numbers are listed in the operating documentation. On the other hand, the parameters assigned to registered numbers are defined by the MIDI standard. There are currently five such parameters:

> **Pitch-Bend Sensitivity (MSB 00/LSB 00):** This parameter is used to specify the range of action of the pitch bend (i.e., the pitch variation) in one direction or the other from its central position. The value of the Data Entry MSB corresponds to adjustment by semitones, and the value of the Data Entry LSB corresponds to adjustment by *cents* (i.e., hundredths of a semitone). The following example deals with a variation of plus or minus 5 semitones and 3 cents:

```
BcH (1011cccc) 65H 00H: MSByte for the registered parameter number
BcH            64H 00H: LSByte for the registered parameter number
BcH            06H 05H: data-entry MSB (5 semitones)
BcH            26H 03H: data-entry LSB (3 hundreds)
```

Fine Tuning (MSB 00/LSB 01): This parameter modifies the smaller-scale adjustment of a sound generator. At the resolution level, the data-entry divides 100 cents into 8,192 steps:

```
BcH 06H 00H: Data Entry MSB
BcH 26H 00H: Data Entry LSB → -8192
BcH 06H 40H: Data Entry MSB
BcH 26H 00H: Data Entry LSB → 0
BcH 06H 7FH: Data Entry MSB
BcH 26H 7FH: Data Entry LSB → +8192
```

Coarse Tuning (MSB 00/LSB 02): Identical to fine tuning, but for a larger-scale adjustment (at 100 cents per bit):

```
BcH 06H 00H: Data Entry MSB
BcH 26H 00H: Data Entry LSB → -64
BcH 06H 40H: Data Entry MSB
BcH 26H 00H: Data Entry LSB → 0
BcH 06H 7FH: Data Entry MSB
BcH 26H 7FH: Data Entry LSB → +63
```

The last two currently defined registered parameters are explained in the section in Chapter 4 that describes the MIDI Tuning Standard. Meanwhile, Table 3.19 lists all of the currently defined controllers.

TABLE 3.19: *Controllers*

DECIMAL	HEXADECIMAL	DESCRIPTION
00	00H	Bank Select
01	01H	Modulation
02	02H	Breath Controller
03	03H	– undefined –
04	04H	Foot Controller
05	05H	Portamento Time
06	06H	Data Entry MSB

TABLE 3.19: *Controllers (continued)*

DECIMAL	HEXADECIMAL	DESCRIPTION
07	07H	Main Volume
08	08H	Balance
09	09H	– undefined –
10	0AH	Pan
11	0BH	Expression Controller
12	0CH	Effect Control 1
13	0DH	Effect Control 2
14 to 15	0EH to 0FH	– undefined –
16 to 19	10H to 13H	General-purpose controllers (1 to 4)
20 to 31	14H to 1FH	– undefined –
32 to 63	20H to 3FH	LSB for controllers 0 to 31
64	40H	Damper pedal (sustain)
65	41H	Portamento
66	42H	Sostenuto
67	43H	Soft Pedal
68	44H	Legato Footswitch
69	45H	Hold 2
70	46H	Sound Controller 1 (default: Timbre Variation)
71	47H	Sound Controller 2 (default: Timbre/Harmonic Content)
73	48H	Sound Controller 3 (default: Release Time)
74	49H	Sound Controller 4 (default: Attack Time)
75 to 79	4BH to 4FH	Sound Controllers 6 to 10

TABLE 3.19: *Controllers (continued)*

DECIMAL	HEXADECIMAL	DESCRIPTION
80 to 83	50H to 53H	General-purpose controllers (5 to 8)
84	54H	Portamento Control
85 to 90	54H to 5AH	– undefined –
91	5BH	Effects 1 Depth (formerly External Effects Depth)
92	5CH	Effects 2 Depth (formerly Tremolo Depth)
93	5DH	Effects 3 Depth (formerly Chorus Depth)
94	5EH	Effects 4 Depth (formerly Celeste (Detune) Depth)
95	5FH	Effects 5 Depth (formerly Phaser Depth)
96	60H	Data Increment
97	61H	Data Decrement
98	62H	Non-Registered Parameter Number LSB
99	63H	Non-Registered Parameter Number MSB
100	64H	Registered Parameter Number LSB
101	65H	Registered Parameter Number MSB
102 to 120	66H to 78H	– undefined –
121 to 127	79H to 7FH	Mode messages

CHAPTER

4

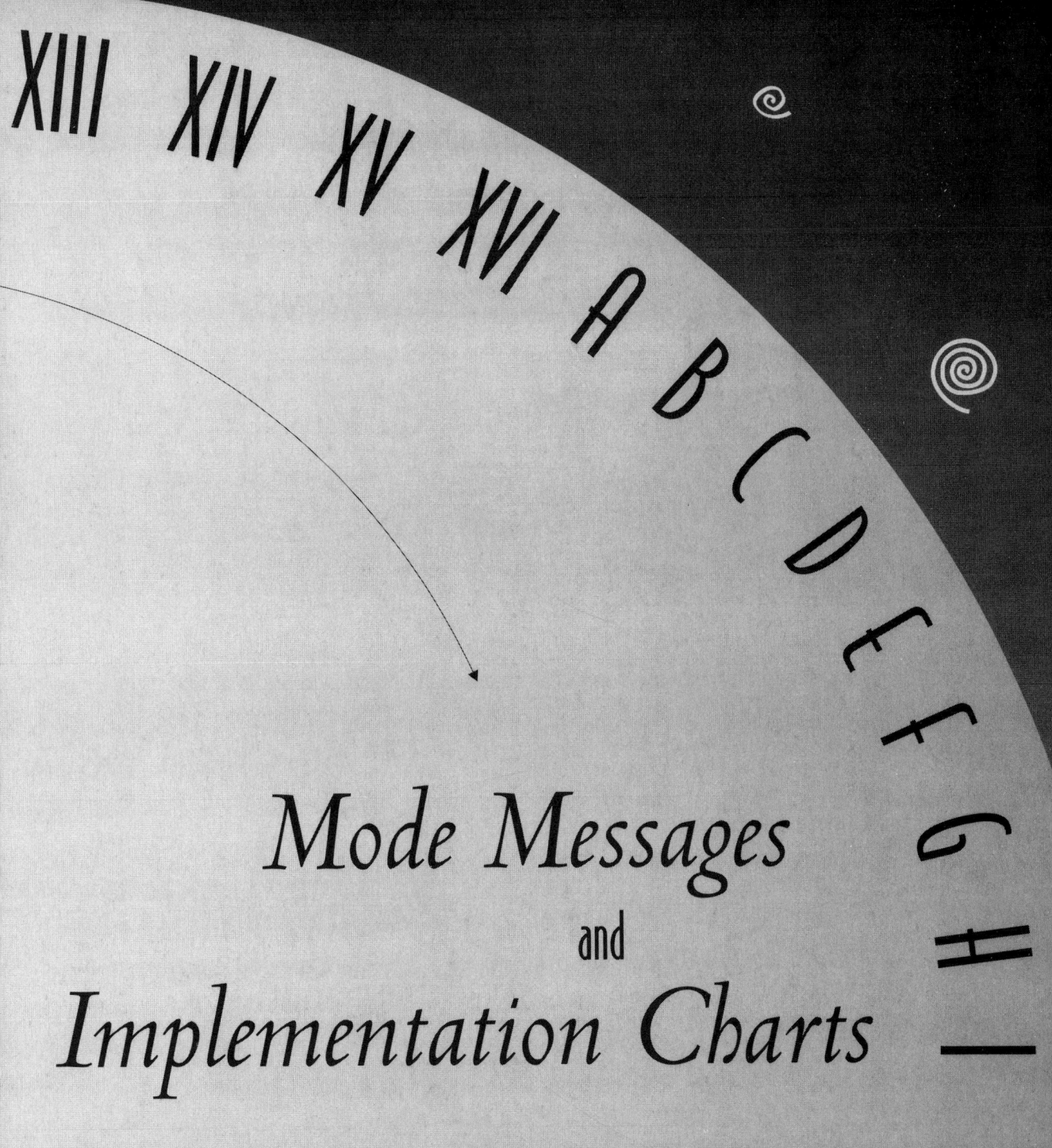

XIII XIV XV XVI A B C D E F G H I

Mode Messages
and
Implementation Charts

HANNEL MODE MESSAGES are the second of the two types of *Channel messages*. (The other type, as you saw in the last chapter, consists of the *Channel Voice messages*.) The seven Mode messages occupy the last numbers (121 to 127) that are assigned to Change Control messages.

The All Sound Off, Reset All Controllers, Local Control On/Off, and All Notes Off Messages

For clarity, Mode messages can be divided into two categories. The first group contains the *All Sound Off, Reset All Controllers, Local Control On/Off,* and *All Notes Off* messages, and the second group contains the *Omni On, Omni Off, Poly,* and *Mono* messages.

All Sound Off

Format:	1011cccc (BcH) 01111000 (120/78H) 00000000
Type:	Channel Mode message

The All Sound Off message forces the sound generator to cut off all voices on the indicated channel (which is equivalent to 128 simultaneous Note Off messages; see below). You should never use this message as a replacement for an All Notes Off message or messages; however, you can also use it to silence an effect processor (reverb, delay, etc.), to turn off a set of lights that are controlled by MIDI, and so on.

The Reset All Controllers Message

Format:	1011cccc (BcH) 01111001 (121/79H) 00000000
Type:	Channel Mode message

The Reset All Controllers message reinitializes all of the continuous controllers (i.e., controllers 1 to 120), along with Pitch Bend, Polyphonic Key Pressure, and Channel Aftertouch. The reinitialization values are generally the defaults set by the manufacturer. In most cases, the switches (Sustain, etc.) move to the OFF position, with the controllers (Pitch Bend, Balance, and Pan) functioning more or less around a central value and recreating this position. Except for certain controllers such as Main Volume, the controllers that start from zero (Modulation, the Breath Controller, etc.) return to that value. A receiving unit set to mode Omni On (modes 1 and 2) should obligatorily ignore a Reset All Controllers message.

When a piece of software (such as a sequencer) wants to reinitialize all of the controllers of different instruments, including the controllers of instruments that don't implement the Reset All Controllers message, the MIDI standard recommends the following procedure:

- First, send as many independent messages as there are controllers to be initialized (with Pitch Bend centered, Modulation and Aftertouch set to zero, etc).

- Then send a Reset All Controllers message.

The reinitialization values selected by the software for sending independent messages aren't necessarily identical to the values selected by the instruments that receive Reset All Controllers messages. That's why it's important to follow the chronological order indicated above, so as to give priority to the reinitialization values of the Reset All Controllers message with respect to the reinitialization values of the independent messages.

The Local Control On/Off Messages

Format:	1011cccc (BcH) 01111010 (122/7AH) 0xxxxxxx
Type:	Channel Mode message
0xxxxxxx	00000000: Local Control Off
0xxxxxxx	01111111: Local Control On

The Local Control message first involves MIDI devices that have a keyboard and a sound generator in the same physical unit. In normal operation, when the user presses a note on the keyboard, a Note On message is sent simultaneously to the MIDI Out port (and from there to any other connected devices), and to the sound generator (telling it to play the note immediately internally). In addition to responding directly to notes played on the keyboard, this sound generator reacts to data it receives through the MIDI In port. The purpose of the Local Off message is to disconnect the internal link between the keyboard and the sound generator, as shown in Figure 4.1 below. Conversely, the Local On message re-establishes this link. When an instrument is turned on, it should be in Local On mode.

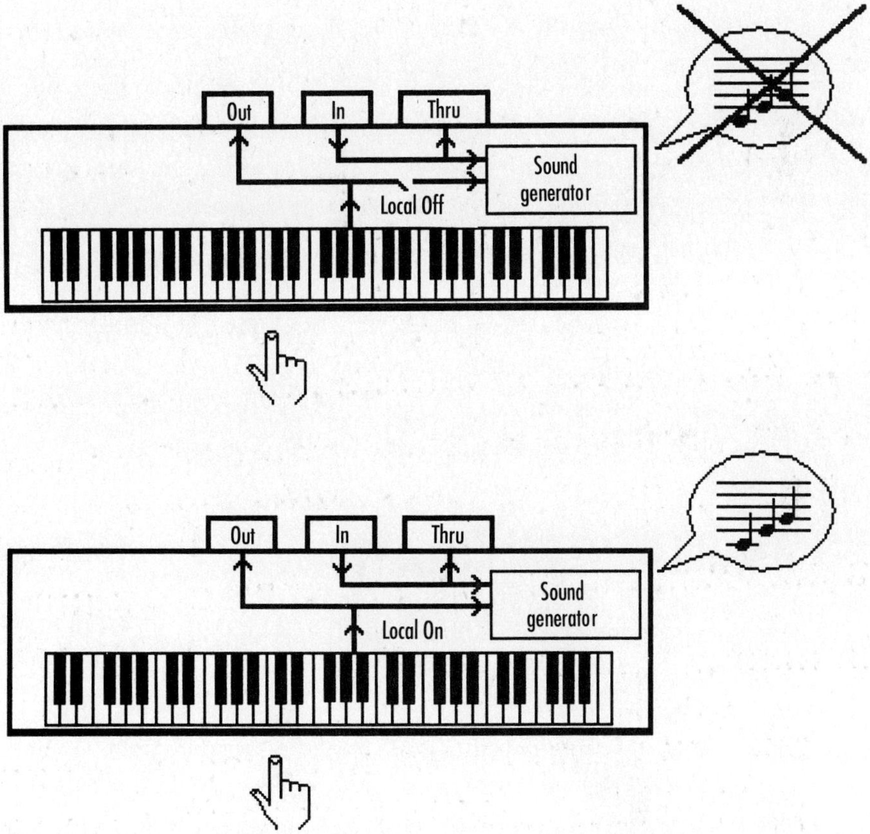

FIGURE 4.1: *This diagram shows a keyboard and a sound generator in the same unit. MIDI messages from the keyboard are sent to the sound generator via the local link and also via the MIDI Out port.*

When an instrument is in Local Off mode, you can think of it as two modules: a control keyboard and an expander. In such a case, the instrument remains mute, because its expander portion (i.e., the sound generator) is not connected to the keyboard. In order for the sound generator to function in this configuration, its MIDI In port has to be connected to the MIDI Out port of the master keyboard. Because these two MIDI ports are located in the same physical unit, this approach has no practical value. It's given here only to help illustrate the principle of local modes.

When this same link between the MIDI Out port of the keyboard and the MIDI In port of the expander is present when the instrument is in Local On mode, it has the effect of duplicating all the notes played by the sound generator, thereby reducing polyphony and inducing slight phase shifts (i.e., the so-called chorus effect), caused by the superimposition of identical notes separated by a time lapse of a few milliseconds. In point of fact, the generator receives Note On information through its internal link with the keyboard and also via its MIDI link, as shown in Figure 4.2 below. The usefulness of Local Mode is especially useful when you're working with sequencers, as you'll see in later chapters.

The All Notes Off Message

Format: 1011cccc (BcH) 01111011 (123/7BH) 00000000

Type: Channel Mode message

Used in exceptional situations (when one or more notes are hung, or when the Stop key of a sequencer is pressed, sometimes causing a simultaneous Reset All Controllers message to be sent), this message forces the sound generator to cut off all of its voices on the corresponding channel.

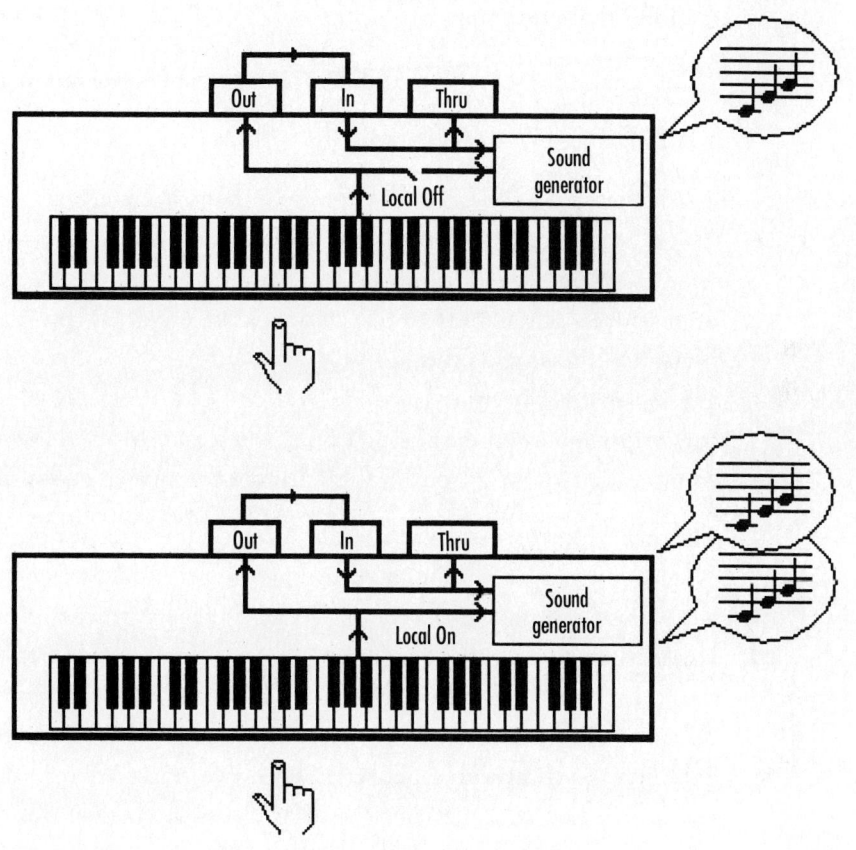

FIGURE 4.2: *In Local Off mode, MIDI messages are sent to the sound generator via the external MIDI Out/MIDI In link. In Local On mode, the same notes are played twice: once by the external link and once by the local link.*

Transmission of this message is equivalent to sending 127 note-release messages (one per note number).

When a piece of software (such as a sequencer) wants to cut off all of a sound generator's voices, without knowing whether the sound generator

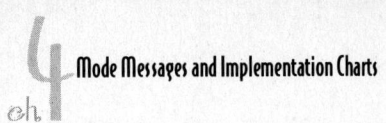

implements the All Notes Off message, the MIDI standard recommends the following procedure:

- First, send 127 Note Off messages (one per note number).

- Then send an All Notes Off message.

Remember that in addition to their own meanings, which are described in the next section, the Omni Mode Off, Poly, and Mono messages can also serve as an All Notes Off message. However, a receiving unit that has been set to Mode Omni On (i.e., Mode 1 and Mode 2) ignores All Notes Off messages. When an All Notes Off message is sent to a receiving unit that has been set to Mode 3 (Omni Off, Poly), the message only cuts off the notes on the basic channel, whereas in Mode 4 (Omni Off, Mono), it cuts off the notes on the channel over which it was transmitted.

Although the substitution of an All Notes Off message for one or more Note Off messages is strongly discouraged, some keyboards do send an All Notes Off message instead of a Note Off message when a note is released when no other note has been pressed—for instance, each time the musician's hands leave the keyboard. (This is the case with many Roland devices.) This nonstandard interpretation runs the risk of causing incompatibilities, such as with sequencers, when two tracks are recorded that are intended to drive the same sound on the same channel (for instance, when the left-hand and right-hand parts of a piano piece are recorded separately). After the two tracks have been recorded, an All Notes Off messages transmitted by one of the tracks will automatically cut off all the notes on the other track.

Using the All Notes Off message in conjunction with the sustain pedal can also cause problems. Some sound generators give All Notes Off messages priority over the sustaining action. By doing that, they suddenly cut off their voices while the pedal is still pressed. According to the standard, these generators theoretically should wait for a sustain-release message before implementing the All Notes Off message.

Under no circumstances should an All Notes Off message received at the MIDI In port of a keyboard instrument that includes a sound generator cut off the notes being played at the keyboard—only the notes being received via MIDI. It is recommended that any instrument that can't respond this way should ignore such an All Notes Off message.

The Omni, Omni Off, Poly, and Mono Messages

While the Voice messages (such as Note On and Note Off) directly affect the notes played by the sound generator, the Omni Mode On, Omni Mode Off, Poly, and Mono messages regulate the allocation of the Voice messages, as a function of polyphony and of the MIDI channels. The combination of Omni Mode On and Omni Mode On messages, and the combination of the Poly and Mono modes, determine how a MIDI instrument transmits or receives Voice messages.

With Mode messages, the concept of an "instrument" doesn't apply to a physical instrument but rather to a logical instrument. For example, a multitimbral sound generator consisting of eight virtual monotimbral generators represents eight clearly distinct instruments. As you'll see with regard to modes 1, 2, and 4, an instrument can receive Voice messages over different channels. However, to avoid any risk of confusion, the instrument has to receive or transmit these four Mode messages over a single channel. This channel is known as the *basic channel*, and is indicated by the letter N. (Mode messages transmitted to a receiving instrument over a MIDI channel other than the basic channel are ignored.) Furthermore, the user can't modify the basic channel except through System Exclusive messages, or else directly from the control panel of the device.

Before describing the combinations, here's a look at the meaning of these four messages.

Omni Mode Off (+ All Notes Off)

Format: 1011cccc (BcH) 01111100 (124/7CH) 00000000

Type: Channel Mode message

With Omni Mode Off, a MIDI unit set to receive voice messages over a given channel X ignores messages whose channel is different from the selected channel. For example, a generator that receives on Channel 1 with Omni Mode Off will not pay attention to any messages it receives over channels 2 to 16.

Omni Mode On (+ All Notes Off)

Format: 1011cccc (BcH) 01111101 (125/7DH) 00000000

Type: Channel Mode message

With Omni Mode On, the receiving unit responds to all the voice messages that arrive at its MIDI In port, regardless of their channel number.

Mono Mode On (+ All Notes Off)

Format: 1011cccc (BcH) 01111110 (126/7EH) 0vvvvvvv

Type: Channel Mode message

vvvvvvv   the MIDI channel number

With Mono Mode On, the receiving unit plays only one note at a time per channel. What this means is that a polyphonic sound generator converts itself into as many monophonic sound generators as its polyphony allows. This mode is used when several note messages should not be sent simultaneously over the same channel.

Poly Mode On (+ All Notes Off)

Format: 1011cccc (BcH) 01111111 (127/7FH) 00000000

Type: Channel Mode message

With Poly Mode On, each channel in the receiving unit plays as many notes at once as its polyphony allows. This mode is used when several note messages should be sent simultaneously over the same channel.

The combination of Omni Mode On, Omni Mode Off, Poly, and Mono messages defines what are known as the "MIDI modes." There are four of them:

- Mode 1: Omni On, Poly

- Mode 2: Omni On, Mono

- Mode 3: Omni Off, Poly

- Mode 4: Omni Off, Mono

These four modes determine how the receiver will react to Voice messages, and also how the transmitter will send the messages. (When a transmitter and a receiver are located in the same device, each has its own mode setting.) It is recommended that when a MIDI device is turned on, it should be initialized in Mode 1. In changing from one mode to another (which also triggers the cut-off of the voices linked to the Note On messages received at the MIDI In port), the two messages don't have to be sent back. In other words, the transitions from Mode 1 to Mode 2, from Mode 4 to Mode 3, from Mode 1 to Mode 3, and from Mode 4 to Mode 2 only require retransmission of the Mono, Poly, Omni Mode Off, and Omni Mode On messages. The receiver should store permanently the two messages that make up a Mode message.

Mode 1: Omni On/Poly

In this mode, the instrument accepts all Voice messages regardless of their channel (Omni On), up to its polyphony limit (Poly). This limit corresponds to the number of notes that the instrument can play simultaneously. For example, if the instrument receives a chord consisting of four notes, it will play these four notes—provided that its polyphonic capability is greater than three voices.

```
90H 20H 40H: Note On channel 1/G#0/Velocity 64
95H 77H 54H: Note On channel 6/B7/Velocity 84
9CH 24H 20H: Note On channel 13/C1/Velocity 32
92H 59H 6AH: Note On channel 3/F5/Velocity 106
```

Mode 3: Omni Off/Poly

In this mode, the instrument accepts only the Voice messages corresponding to the selected reception channel (Omni Off), up to its polyphony limit (Poly).

Mode 4: Omni Off/Mono

The usefulness of Mode 4 becomes clear when an alternate controller such as a MIDI guitar controller is used. MIDI guitars transmit not only note messages, but also different expression parameters. For instance, when the pitch of a note varies, Pitch Bend messages are transmitted. It's easy to see that, if the musician plays a six-note chord and, inside the chord, independently varies the pitch of one of the six strings, only the note that corresponds to that string should respond to the pitch bend. Otherwise the entire chord would be affected by the change in pitch. If the six note messages were transmitted over the same channel, the pitch bend would be applied, and applied awkwardly, to the entire chord.

This is why Mode 4 forces the sound generator to act as though it consisted of a set of monophonic sound generators, each of which is set to its own channel. When driven by a MIDI guitar, each of these monophonic generators responds on its own channel and with the same type of sound to the messages sent by the corresponding string. In other words, a MIDI expression message triggered by one of the strings will only affect the appropriate voice.

The third byte of a Mono message (0vvvvvvv) specifies the number of different MIDI channels the transmitter uses to send the Voice messages, and also specifies the number of different MIDI channels over which the receiver receives the Voice messages (in the above example, six). If you let M represent this number of channels and let N represent the basic channel (as indicated by the right-hand half-byte of the status byte), then your MIDI guitar will transmit over N to $(N + M - 1)$ channels (where M = 6). Of course, in any case the value of $(N + M - 1)$ can't be greater than 16. As a result, to obtain 16 different channels, N has to be set to 1. A MIDI instrument that receives a Mode 4 message therefore assigns its voices in a monophonic way, one per channel, from N to $(N + M - 1)$.

A Mono message with M = 0 is an exception. This message forces the receiver to assign its voices at a rate of one per channel, until it reaches its polyphony limit or channel 16, whichever comes first.

With a polyphonic sound generator, for a value of M equal to 1, Mode 4 can imitate monophonic instruments such as the brasses, which can't play more than one note at a time. However, Mode 2 is still the easiest to use.

Mode 2: Omni On/Mono

During reception, all the Voice messages, regardless of the channel they're on, are assigned to a single voice of the sound generator, which then converts itself into a monophonic generator (equivalent to the previous mode with M = 1). In Mode 2, the role of the third byte (0vvvvvvv) in the

Mono message loses all of its significance. This mode is used fairly infrequently and is not the subject of a great deal of interest.

A transmitter has no way of knowing whether the receiver to which it's sending a Mode message is or isn't implementing the message. If the receiver doesn't implement the message, it can ignore it or else switch to the nearest mode.

Summary of the MIDI Modes for Receiving Units

Mode 1
(Omni On, Poly)

Voice messages are received regardless of the channel they're on, and control as many voices as polyphony allows.

Mode 2
(Omni On, Mono)

Voice messages are received regardless of the channel they're on, but control only one voice at a time.

Mode 3
(Omni Off, Poly)

Only the Voice messages whose channel corresponds to the basic channel of the receiving instrument (i.e., channel N) are taken into consideration. These Voice messages control as many voices as polyphony allows.

Mode 4
(Omni Off, Mono)

Only the voice messages whose channels correspond to the N to $(N + M - 1)$ channels of the receiving instrument are taken into consideration. Each channel plays only one voice at a time.

Summary of the MIDI Modes for Transmitting Units

Mode 1 (Omni On, Poly)	All the Voice messages are transmitted over channel N.
Mode 2 (Omni On, Mono)	The Voice messages are transmitted monophonically over channel N.
Mode 3 (Omni Off, Poly)	All the Voice messages are transmitted over channel N.
Mode 4 (Omni Off, Mono)	Voice messages from 1 to M are transmitted over channels N to $(N + M - 1)$, monophonically on each channel.

All Mode messages have the same status byte (BcH, or 0100cccc), and the data bytes of Mode messages all have the format 0xxxxxxx 0yyyyyyy. The contents of the data bytes are described in Table 4.1 below.

TABLE 4.1: *Contents of the Data Bytes in Channel Mode Messages*

VALUE OF DATA BYTE oxxxxxxx	VALUE OF DATA BYTE oyyyyyyy	MEANING
xxxxxxx = 120/78H	yyyyyyy = 0	All Sound Off
xxxxxxx = 121/79H	yyyyyyy = 0	Reset All Controllers
xxxxxxx = 122/7AH	yyyyyyy = 0	Local Control Off
xxxxxxx = 122/7AH	yyyyyyy = 127	Local Control On
xxxxxxx = 123/7BH	yyyyyyy = 0	All Notes Off
xxxxxxx = 124/7CH	yyyyyyy = 0	Omni Mode Off (All Notes Off)

TABLE 4.1: *Contents of the Data Bytes in Channel Mode Messages (continued)*

VALUE OF DATA BYTE 0xxxxxxx	VALUE OF DATA BYTE 0yyyyyyy	MEANING
xxxxxxx = 125/7DH	yyyyyyy = 0	Omni Mode On (All Notes Off)
xxxxxxx = 126/7EH	yyyyyyy = M	Mono Mode On (Poly Mode Off) (All Notes Off), with the number of channels equal to M
xxxxxxx = 126/7EH	yyyyyyy = 0	Mono Mode On (Poly Mode Off) (All Notes Off), with the number of channels equal to the number of voices in the receiver
xxxxxxx = 127/7FH	yyyyyyy = 0	Poly Mode Off (Mono Mode Off) (All Notes Off)

cccc = the basic channel (1 to 16)

xxxxxxx = the controller number (121 to 127)

yyyyyyy = the value of the controller

Running Status

Running Status is a way to compress MIDI data in real time (to avoid the delay problems caused by high throughput produced by intensive use of continuous controllers, etc.). In any case, for sequencers it's desirable to be able to disconnect Running Status manually, so as to preserve compatibility with the (relatively small number of) machines that don't accept it. On the other hand, it's the receiver that's responsible for detecting whether incoming data has been compressed. Some devices only implement Running Status when the density of messages transmitted by the keyboard exceeds a given threshold.

Running Status only compresses Channel messages (i.e., Voice and Mode messages), compressing them in the following way: for purely consecutive messages, which have the same status byte and which use the same channel, the status byte is transmitted only for the first message, without being repeated for the following messages. This procedure is shown diagrammatically in Figure 4.3 below.

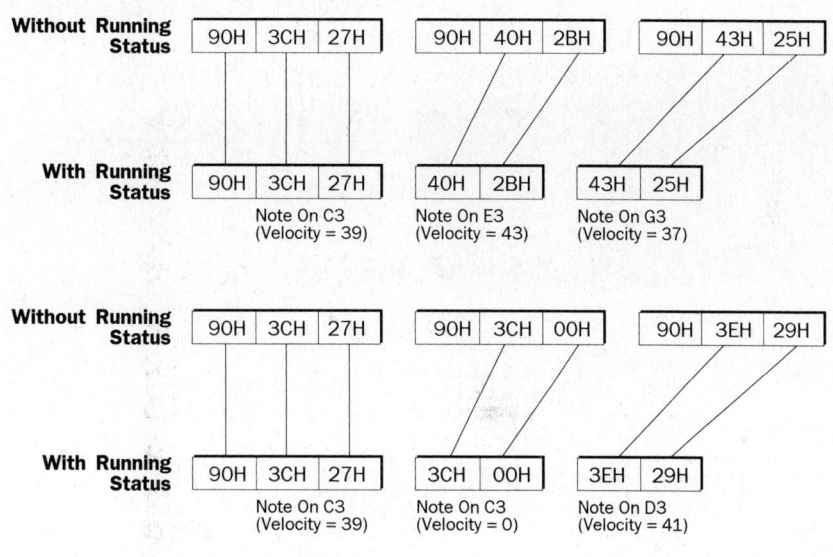

FIGURE 4.3: *Data compression*

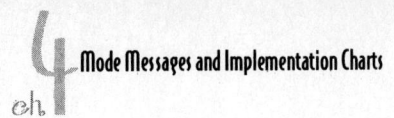

With compression, a series of three Note On messages followed by three Note Off messages only needs 14 bytes instead of 18.

Without Running Status:

```
90H 3CH 69H: Note On channel 1/C3/Velocity 105
90H 40H 5FH: Note On channel 1/E3/Velocity 95
90H 43H 77H: Note On channel 1/G3/Velocity 119
80H 3CH 40H: Note On channel 1/C3/Velocity 64
80H 40H 40H: Note On channel 1/E3/Velocity 64
80H 43H 40H: Note On channel 1/G3/Velocity 64
```

With Running Status:

```
90H 3CH 69H: Note On channel 1/C3/Velocity 105
    40H 5FH: Note On channel 1/E3/Velocity 95
    43H 77H: Note On channel 1/G3/Velocity 119
80H 3CH 40H: Note On channel 1/C3/Velocity 64
    40H 40H: Note On channel 1/E3/Velocity 64
    43H 40H: Note On channel 1/G3/Velocity 64
```

These examples show how useful it can be to send a Note On status byte followed by a Velocity of 0 instead of by a Note Off message. This way, the compression feature doesn't differentiate between a series of Note On status indications, some of which play the role of a Note Off message. In the example given above, Running Status stays in effect, also applying to the three released notes (in this case, using 13 bytes instead of 18):

Without Running Status:

```
90H 3CH 69H: Note On channel 1/C3/Velocity 105
90H 40H 5FH: Note On channel 1/E3/Velocity 95
90H 43H 77H: Note On channel 1/G3/Velocity 119
90H 3CH 00H: Note On channel 1/C3/Velocity 00 (= Note Off)
90H 40H 00H: Note On channel 1/E3/Velocity 00 (= Note Off)
90H 43H 00H: Note On channel 1/G3/Velocity 00 (= Note Off)
```

With Running Status:

```
90H 3CH 69H: Note On channel 1/C3/Velocity 105
    40H 5FH: Note On channel 1/E3/Velocity 95
    43H 77H: Note On channel 1/G3/Velocity 119
    3CH 00H: Note On channel 1/C3/Velocity 00 (= Note Off)
    40H 00H: Note On channel 1/E3/Velocity 00 (= Note Off)
    43H 00H: Note On channel 1/G3/Velocity 00 (= Note Off)
```

Naturally, Running Status is more effective with note messages, Pitch Bend messages, and continuous controllers than it is with a Sustain Pedal message or a Program Change message. Nevertheless, it requires a little more intelligence on the part of the receiver, which has to store in memory the last status byte analyzed (in a specific buffer, called the *Running Status buffer*), until a different status byte arrives, so that it can assign a meaning to the compressed data that follows. The receiver also has to know how many of these data bytes are expected (i.e., one or two), as a function of the type of status byte, without counting the Real Time status bytes (see the following section) which can interrupt a MIDI message in the middle (between a status byte and a data byte, or between two data bytes). Under no circumstances should these Real Time messages be stored in the Running Status buffer.

Assume for instance that an instrument in Mode 1 (Omni On, Poly) receives a Mode message, such as an Omni Off message (whose status byte indicates a Control Change), over a channel not intended for it (i.e., a channel other than the basic channel), followed by a second Control Change message (such as a modulation) which should be taken into consideration and compressed by the Running Status feature. If the receiver decides at the start not to store the Control Change status message in its buffer, under the pretext of ignoring the reception of an Omni Off message over a channel that doesn't concern it (because that channel is different from channel N), then the receiver will also lose the following modulation data bytes (because it no longer knows what status to assign to them):

- B0H 7CH 00H: because the basic channel is channel 3, the message is ignored and the status byte is not stored.
- 01H 7HH: this message (modulation over channel 1 with Running Status) is lost for good.

The MIDI standard recommends that the Running Status buffer be managed in the following way:

1. Erase the contents of the buffer (i.e., clear the buffer) when the device is turned on.
2. Store the status byte when a Channel message is received.
3. Clear the buffer when an Exclusive or Common message is received.
4. Do not touch the buffer when a Real Time message is received.
5. Ignore data bytes when the buffer has been set to zero (i.e., cleared, with its contents erased).

During a long compression, the transmitting instrument should regularly re-send the status code. In fact, a receiver that's turned on in the middle of a transmission of compressed data has to wait for the next status byte in order to determine the nature of the data (that is, to identify the status group to which the data belongs).

System Real Time Messages

| F8H | Timing Clock |
| F9H | – undefined – |

FAH	Start
FBH	Continue
FCH	Stop
FDH	– undefined –
FEH	Active Sensing
FFH	System Reset

There are six *System Real Time messages*. Their status bytes are from F8H to FF8. Unlike most MIDI messages, the Real Time messages do not contain data bytes. Furthermore, like Common messages, they are sent to the entire MIDI network; therefore they don't include a channel number. The first four status bytes in Real Time messages handle the synchronization of MIDI devices.

Synchronization Messages

At this writing, the standard provides two synchronization methods: one that uses Real Time messages, and one that uses the MIDI Time Code (MTC). The Real Time messages are based on relative (i.e., variable) temporal measurements (tempo), while the MIDI Time Code is based on absolute (i.e., fixed) temporal measurements (clocktime). This section considers only the four Real Time synchronization messages.

When two or more devices (rhythm boxes, sequencers, etc.) are synchronized, a master unit drives one or more slave units, transmitting metronome information to them (in the form of a certain number of pulses per quarter note, or PPQN), and also transmits commands (Start, Stop, etc.). Most synchronizable MIDI devices don't mind which role they play, and can act as either master or slave. To switch a device from one role to the other, in most cases all you have to do is set the clock of the device to internal (master) mode or to external (slave) mode.

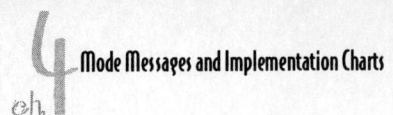

Because operating in internal mode doesn't automatically cause a device to send a synchronization code to other devices, sometimes the device has to be asked for the code explicitly. It's not unusual for an instrument operating in external mode (i.e., ready to receive Real Time messages at its MIDI In port) to ignore internal commands (Start, Stop, Continue, etc.), or for an instrument operating in internal mode to ignore Real Time messages that arrive at its MIDI In port.

Timing Clock Messages

Format: 11111000 (F8H)

Type: System Real Time message

The purpose of Timing Clock messages, as shown schematically in Figure 4.4 below, is to synchronize two or more MIDI units to the same basic tempo. The timing messages, in the form of clock ticks, are sent to the slave units by the master unit (in reading mode, after transmission of a Start or Continue message), at regular intervals and at a rate of 24 messages per quarter note. As a result, the transmission frequency varies depending on the tempo.

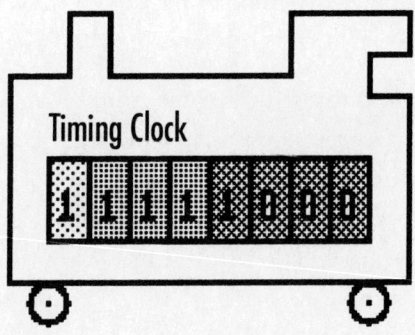

FIGURE 4.4: *The Timing Clock message*

Some units operating in master mode even send Timing Clock messages when they are stopped. This capability makes it possible for slave units to analyze the tempo (that is, to prepare themselves), while waiting for a Start command or a Continue command, in order to synchronize themselves more efficiently.

Finally, Table 4.2 below shows the correspondence between note values and the number of clock ticks in Timing Clock messages:

TABLE 4.2: *How Note Values Correspond to Clock Ticks*

NOTE VALUE	NUMBER OF CLOCK TICKS
Dotted whole note	144
Whole note	96
Whole note (triplet)	64
Dotted half note	72
Half note	48
Half note (triplet)	32
Dotted quarter note	36
Quarter note	24
Quarter note (triplet)	16
Dotted eighth note	18
Eighth note	12
Eighth note (triplet)	8
Dotted sixteenth note	9
Sixteenth note	6
Sixteenth note (triplet)	4

TABLE 4.2: *How Note Values Correspond to Clock Ticks (continued)*

NOTE VALUE	NUMBER OF CLOCK TICKS
Thirty-second note	3
Thirty-second note (triplet)	2
Sixty-fourth note (triplet)	1

The Start Message

Format:	11111010 (FAH)
Type:	System Real Time message

When a master unit switches into reading mode at the start of a piece, a Start message, as shown schematically in Figure 4.5 below, is sent to the slave units. To synchronize themselves, these units should wait to receive a MIDI clock message. Unfortunately, some MIDI device mistakenly interpret the Start message as a Timing Clock message. In such a case, these slave units "advance" by one more MIDI clock signal. In order to give these units time to react (that is, enough time to keep them from missing the first clock message), the Start message should be spaced at least one millisecond apart from the next Timing Clock signal. In spite of the fact that a slave unit set to internal mode theoretically shouldn't accept any real time messages, in practice it sometimes happens that some of these units start up when they receive a Start command—but with their own rhythm, and therefore without synchronizing themselves according to the Timing Clock messages they receive.

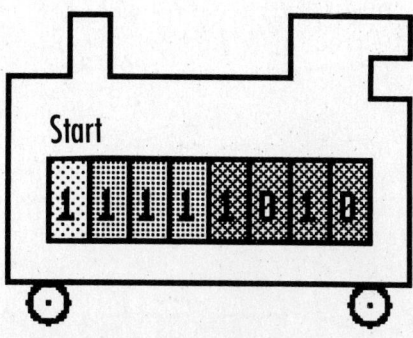

FIGURE 4.5: *The Start message*

The Stop Message

Format: 11111100 (FCH)

Type: System Real Time Message

When pressure is applied to the Stop key (or the Pause key, etc.) of a master unit, a *Stop* message, as shown diagrammatically in Figure 4.6 below, is sent to the slave units. The slave units should stop immediately, storing in memory their current position. (Slave units that react to Song Position Pointer messages, as explained in the next section, should store their current position in a register provided for that purpose.) Because the current position is stored in memory by both the master unit and the slave units, the master unit is in position to restart the slave units from the same position by sending a Continue message, instead of having to use SPP messages. On a completely different level, the master unit sends a Note Off message for each note that's active when a Stop message is sent

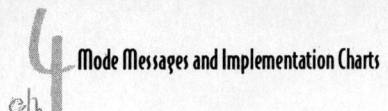

(taking care not to replace a Note Off message with an All Notes Off message, which some machines don't recognize). The MIDI controllers of the slave units are reinitialized the same way.

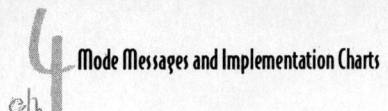

FIGURE 4.6: *The Stop message*

The Continue Message

Format:	11111011 (FBH)
Type:	System Real Time message

When the *Continue* key of the master unit is pressed, the Continue message, as shown diagrammatically in Figure 4.7 below, is sent to the slave units. Some sequencers group the Start and Continue functions in the form of a single separate Read key. In such a case, a Read command triggered at the start of a piece causes a Start message to be transmitted, while a Read command triggered at any other point causes a Continue message to be transmitted.

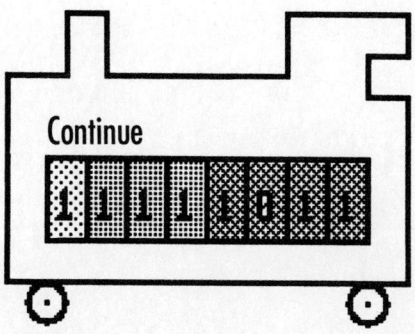

FIGURE 4.7: *The Continue message*

The slave units should wait to receive a MIDI clock message in order to synchronize themselves, starting with the position at which they were stopped. In order to give them enough time to react (that is, enough time to keep them from missing the first clock message), the Continue message should be spaced at least one millisecond apart from the next Timing Clock signal.

The receiving units ignore the redundancy of the Start, Stop, and Continue messages. To maintain perfect synchronization between two or more MIDI units, priority has to be given to the four preceding messages. This way, if necessary a transmitting instrument (such as a sequencer) can place these messages ahead of any other messages (Note On, Note Off, etc.), or even insert these messages between two MIDI bytes in any single given message, as shown diagrammatically in Figure 4.8.

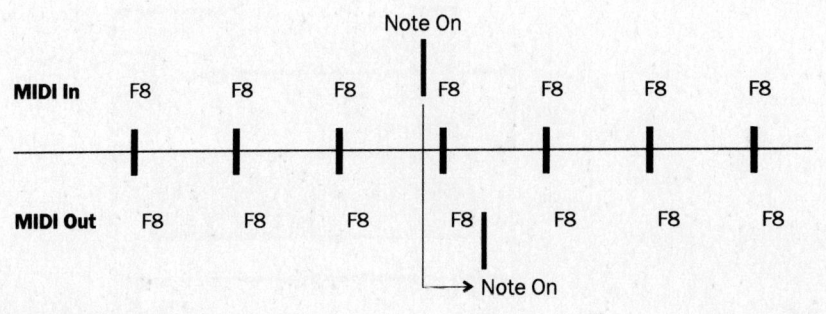

FIGURE 4.8: *Prioritizing Synchronization Messages*

Other Real Time Messages

The last two messages in this section are the Active Sensing message and the very powerful, potentially hazardous System Reset message.

The Active Sensing Message

Format: 11111110 (FEH)

Type: System Real Time message

The *Active Sensing* message, as shown diagrammatically in Figure 4.9 below, is an optional message whose purpose is to monitor, in real time, the proper operation of a MIDI link. This byte is sent from a transmitter to a receiver at a maximum interval of 300 milliseconds, provided that no other message is being transmitted. If the receiver recognizes Active Sensing messages, then as soon as it receives a first Active Sensing message it waits logically to receive the message at regular intervals (up to 300 milliseconds apart) when no other MIDI message is arriving. If this is not the case, then the receiver treats the link as defective, cuts off all of its voices (All Notes Off), and goes back to its initial operating mode. This message is especially effective in the event of an untimely disconnection of the MIDI cables.

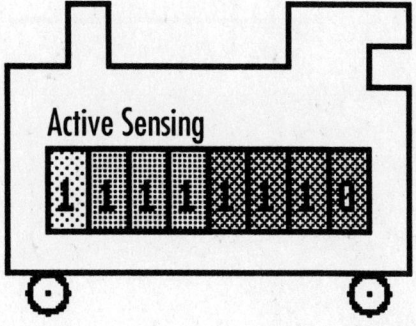

FIGURE 4.9: *The Active Sensing message*

The System Reset Message

Format: 11111111 (FFH)

Type: System Real Time message

This message, shown diagrammatically in Figure 4.10 below, is the last of the status codes. You don't see it implemented very often. In any event it should be handled with extreme care; ideally, it should be reserved for extreme situations. Under no circumstances should it ever be retransmitted via a MIDI Thru port.

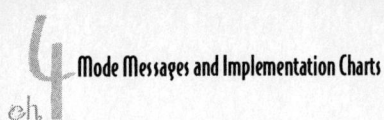

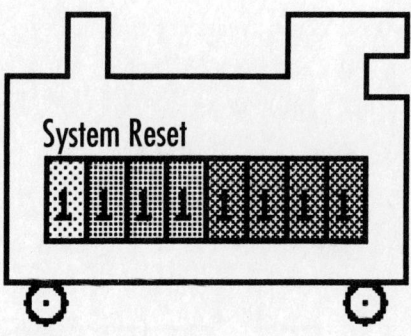

FIGURE 4.10: *The System Reset message*

Why so many cautions? Because the message is so powerful. In essence, it reinitializes a MIDI unit. To do that, it performs all of the following operations:

- Switching the unit to Mode 1 (Omni On, Poly)

- Switching the unit to Local On

- Cutting off all the voices

- Reinitializing all of the controllers

- Forcing the Song Position Pointer to zero

- Stopping the playing (sequencer, rhythm box, etc.)

- Clearing the Running Status buffer

- Forcing the parameters to the values that they had when the unit was turned on

As a general rule, none of the System Real Time messages should be stored by a sequencer. Imagine what would happen during a reading if synchronization codes recorded on one track were mixed with synchronization codes transmitted by a sequencer…!

System Common Messages

System Common messages are characterized by the fact that they don't contain a channel number, and therefore are sent to the entire system. The status bytes for *System Common messages* range from F1H to F7H. The MIDI Time Code Quarter-Frame (F1H) and End of Exclusive (F7H) messages, which have particular characteristics, are discussed in sections of their own.

F1H	MIDI Time Code Quarter Frame
F2H	Song Position Pointer
F3H	Song Select
F4H	– undefined –
F5H	– undefined –
F6H	Tune Request
F7H	End Of Exclusive (EOX)

The Song Position Pointer Message

Format:	11110010 (F2H) 0xxxxxxx 0yyyyyyy
Type:	System Common message
xxxxxxx	value of the song pointer (Least Significant Byte/LSB)

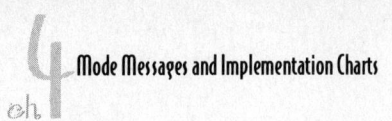

yyyyyyy value of the song pointer (Most Significant Byte/MSB)

The purpose of this message, shown diagrammatically in Figure 4.11 below is to position MIDI devices (such as rhythm boxes and sequencers) at a specific point in a piece. It's used in conjunction with synchronization messages based on Clock Signal, Start, Stop, and Continue messages.

The Song Position Pointer (SPP) is nothing more than a counter that's incremented by one unit at each MIDI beat, starting at the beginning of the piece. By design, a MIDI beat corresponds to six Timing Clock signals, and therefore is equivalent to a sixteenth note. With two data bytes you can represent 16,384 sixteenth notes, or almost 35 minutes of music at a tempo of 120 quarter notes to the minute. The first time a Start command is activated, the value of the SPP is set to zero. The value is incremented by one unit every six Timing Clock messages until a Stop command is received. At that point, the current value of the SPP is stored. This value is reincremented when a Continue command is received, or reinitialized (reset to zero) when a Start command is received.

Functionally, the Start message is like a Continue message sent at the same time as an SPP that's set to zero. As usual, the least significant byte (0xxxxxxx) is sent first.

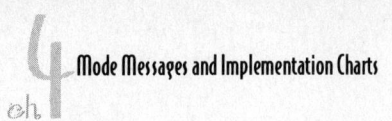

FIGURE 4.11: *The Song Position Pointer message*

If a device receives an SPP message followed by a Continue message and MIDI clock signals, it should store the number of clock signals so that it will know where to position itself in order to start in perfect synchronization. For example, assume the device receives an SPP message with a value of 8 (i.e., 48 MIDI clock signals), and that during the positioning operation it receives a Continue message followed by two clock signals. In this case, the receiving device should start at the position that corresponds to the fiftieth (50th) clock signal.

The Song Select Message

Format: 11110011 (F3H) 0xxxxxxx

Type: System Common message

xxxxxxx   song number

This message, shown diagrammatically in Figure 4.12 below, is a sort of Program Change message. Its function is to select one of the 128 *Song Numbers* on a sequencer or rhythm box. The time it takes a MIDI unit to

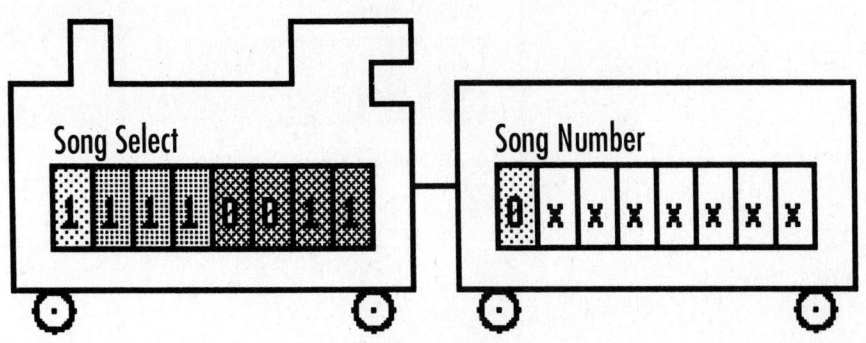

FIGURE 4.12: *The Song Select message*

react to an SPP message or a Song Select message depends on how fast the unit can locate the piece or the location in the piece where it's supposed to start playing. If the MIDI unit receives a Start message at the same time, then in order to start in exact synchronization the MIDI unit has to store the number of Timing Clock messages it receives during the positioning operation (i.e., to make up the delay by skipping X clock signals).

The Tune Request Message

Format: 11110110 (F6H)

Type: System Common message

This message, shown diagrammatically in Figure 4.13 below, is transmitted to analog sound generators in order to ask the generators to tune their oscillators.

FIGURE 4.13: *The Tune Request message*

System Exclusive Messages

The third and last category of system messages contains the *System Exclusive messages*. The purpose of these rather special messages is to transmit so-called "nonstandard" manufacturer-specific information. All of the MIDI messages you've met up till now (Channel Voice, Channel Mode, System Common, and System Real Time messages) have a universal meaning. In other words, for example, the format of a Note On message, indicating that a key had been pressed, is always the same, whether the message is sent from a Yamaha, Roland, Korg, or any other type of keyboard. This kind of information can be standardized because all the keyboards have the same function—namely, to trigger notes. In the same way, all the sound generators respond to these note messages.

On the other hand, two sound generators that are based on different synthesis principles (such as Yamaha frequency modulation, Roland linear arithmetic, or Korg advanced integration) are incapable of exchanging sound parameters (i.e., memory contents). In fact, strictly speaking, the so-called "frequency modulation" language has nothing in common with the so-called "linear arithmetic" and "advanced integration" languages. However, two Yamaha, Roland, or Korg synthesizers that are identical or similar (i.e., that are members of the same family) *can* send these parameters to one another, thanks to System Exclusive Messages. Generally speaking, the function of these messages is to transmit all the information that's specific to a given MIDI device. System Exclusive messages have the following format:

11110000 (F0H) 0xxxxxxx <data bytes> 11110111 (F7H)

which is illustrated diagrammatically in Figure 4.14 below.

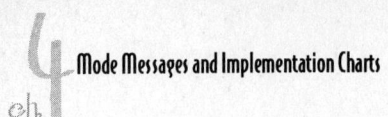

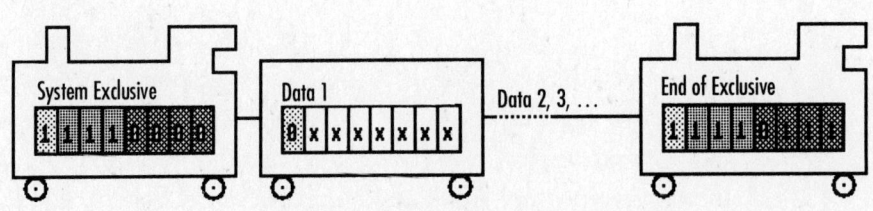

FIGURE 4.14: *The Format of System Exclusive messages*

Contrary to the rule that says that a MIDI message has to consist of a single status byte that may or may not be followed by one or more data bytes, a System Exclusive message is enclosed by two status bytes (F0H and F7H). The reason is simple: as soon as a MIDI message is standardized, for a given status byte X the receiving unit waits to receive a specific number of data bytes Y. This way, when a sound generator receives a Note On status byte, it knows for sure that two data bytes (namely, the Note Number and the Velocity) will follow. On the other hand, a System Exclusive message can transmit as many data bytes as it needs to. This is why the message has to include a final status byte (F7H)—in order to alert the receiving unit to the end of the message. This final status byte, which is known as an End of Exclusive (EOX), is a System Common message.

Because any examination of System Exclusive messages is inevitably linked to the way each manufacturer uses these messages, this section is limited to a few general observations.

Manufacturers' Messages

In the System Exclusive messages that are proprietary to each of the manufacturers, the first data byte (0xxxxxxx) identifies the company. This byte is the so-called "Manufacturer's ID," or maker's identification. This code is assigned by the MMA and the JMSC. It obligates the manufacturer to publish the format of the System Exclusive messages used by a device, within one year after the device's introduction on the market. The list of Manufacturer's IDs is published in the MIDI standard distributed by the IMA. As with all data bytes, the number of possible values is limited to 128. In view of the growing number of companies that would like to be assigned identification codes, the decision was made to increase this number of values to 16,384 by developing a variable-size system according to the following rules:

- For 00H < 0xxxxxxx < 7DH, 0xxxxxxx corresponds to the manufacturer's ID as coded in one byte, as shown below:

```
11110000 (F0H) 0xxxxxxx <data bytes> 11110111 (F7H)
```

- For 0xxxxxxx = 00H, the manufacturer's ID consists of three bytes, of which only the last two are significant. In other words, the 16,384 values are coded in 14 bits, as shown below:

```
11110000 (F0H) 00000000 0yyyyyyy 0zzzzzzz <data
bytes> 11110111 (F7H)
```

Because of their special meaning, the values 7DH, 7EH, and 7FH are examined separately in the next section. Meanwhile, the following chart shows how MIDI manufacturers' IDs are grouped by families.

FAMILY	SINGLE-BYTE ID	THREE-BYTE ID
The American group:	01H to 1FH	00H 00H 01H to 00H 20H 00H
The European group:	20H to 3FH	00H 20H 00H to 00H 3FH 7FH

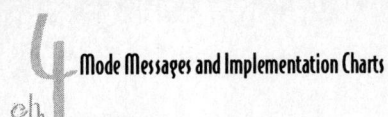

FAMILY	SINGLE-BYTE ID	THREE-BYTE ID
The Japanese group:	40H to 5FH	00H 40H 00H to 00H 5FH 7FH
Others:	60H to 7CH	00H 60H 00H to 00H 7FH 7FH

Appendix D contains a list of all the officially recognized manufacturers, as published in Version 4.2 of the MIDI standard.

Universal Exclusive Messages

Three of the identifiers for Exclusive Messages, known as Universal Exclusive Messages, have nothing to do with manufacturers.

- The 7DH identifier is reserved for noncommercial use (such as by universities and researchers).

- The 7EH ID is reserved for Universal Non-Real Time use. The format is:

```
1110000 (F0H) 01111110 (7EH) <device ID> <sub-ID#1>
<sub-ID#2> <data bytes> 11110111 (F7H)
```

Table 4.3 below lists all the currently defined Universal Non-Real Time SysEx IDs.

- The 7FH ID is reserved for Universal Real Time use. The format is:

```
1110000 (F0H) 01111110 (7FH) <device ID> <sub-ID#1>
<sub-ID#2> <data bytes> 11110111 (F7H)
```

TABLE 4.3: *Universal Non-Real Time (7EH) System Exclusive IDs*

‹sub-ID#1›	‹sub-ID#2›	DESCRIPTION
00H	—	– not used –
01H	– not used –	*Sample Dump Header*
02H	– not used –	*Sample Dump Packet*
03H	– not used –	*Sample Dump Request*
04H	nnH	*MIDI Time Code*
04H	00H	Special
04H	01H	Punch In Point
04H	02H	Punch Out Point
04H	03H	Delete Punch In Point
04H	04H	Delete Punch Out Point
04H	05H	Event Start Point
04H	06H	Event Stop Point
04H	07H	Event Start Point with additional info
04H	08H	Event Stop Point with additional info
04H	09H	Delete Event Start Point
04H	0AH	Delete Event Stop Point
04H	0BH	Cue Point
04H	0CH	Cue Point with additional info
04H	0DH	Delete Cue Point
04H	0EH	Event Name in additional info

TABLE 4.3: *Universal Non-Real Time (7EH) System Exclusive IDs (continued)*

‹sub-ID#1›	‹sub-ID#2›	DESCRIPTION
05H	nnH	*Sample Dump Standard extensions*
05H	01H	Multiple Loop Points
05H	02H	Loop Points Request
06H	nnH	*General Information*
06H	01H	Identity Request
06H	02H	Identity Reply
07H	nnH	*File Dump*
07H	01H	Header
07H	02H	Data Packet
07H	03H	Request
08H	nnH	*MIDI Tuning Standard*
08H	01H	Bulk Dump Request
08H	02H	Bulk Dump Reply
09H	nnH	*General MIDI*
09H	01H	General MIDI System On
09H	02H	General MIDI System Off
7BH	– not used –	*End of File*
7CH	– not used –	*Wait*

TABLE 4.3: *Universal Non-Real Time (7EH) System Exclusive IDs (continued)*

‹sub-ID#1›	‹sub-ID#2›	DESCRIPTION
7DH	– not used –	*Cancel*
7EH	– not used –	*NAK (negative acknowledge)*
7FH	– not used –	*ACK (acknowledge)*

Table 4.4 below lists all the currently defined Universal Real Time SysEx IDs.

TABLE 4.4: *Universal Real Time (7FH) System Exclusive IDs*

‹sub-ID#1›	‹sub-ID#2›	DESCRIPTION
00H	—	– not used –
01H	nnH	*MIDI Time Code*
01H	01H	Full Message
01H	02H	User Bits
02H	nnH	*MIDI Show Control*
02H	00H	MSC Extensions
02H	01H to 7FH	MSC Commands (see Chapter 14)
03H	nnH	*Notation Information*
03H	01H	Bar Number
03H	02H	Time Signature (immediate)

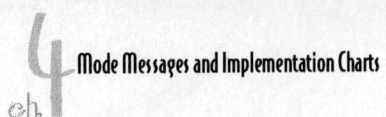

TABLE 4.4: *Universal Real Time (7FH) System Exclusive IDs (continued)*

‹sub-ID#1›	‹sub-ID#2›	DESCRIPTION
03H	42H	Time Signature (delayed)
04H	nnH	*Device Control*
04H	01H	Master Volume
04H	02H	Master Balance
05H	nnH	*Real Time MTC Cueing*
05H	00H	Special
05H	01H	Punch In Points
05H	02H	Punch Out Points
05H	03H	– reserved –
05H	04H	– reserved –
05H	05H	Event Start Points
05H	06H	Event Stop Points
05H	07H	Event Start Points with additional info
05H	08H	Event Stop Points with additional info
05H	09H	– reserved –
05H	0AH	– reserved –
05H	0BH	Cue Points
05H	0CH	Cue Points with additional info
05H	0DH	– reserved –
05H	0EH	Event Name with additional info

TABLE 4.4: *Universal Real Time (7FH) System Exclusive IDs (continued)*

‹sub-ID#1›	‹sub-ID#2›	DESCRIPTION
06H	00H to 7HF	*MIDI Machine Control Commands* (see Chapter 17)
07H	00H to 7HF	*MIDI Machine Control Responses* (see Chapter 18)
08H	nnH	*MIDI Tuning Standard*
08H	02H	Note Change

· ·

Back in the early days, the Device ID byte was known as the "channel byte." Now, however, the Device ID byte in Universal SysEx ID messages generally refers to a device in terms of a physical unit (the "hunk of metal and plastic," as it's often known) rather than to a channel or a virtual device inside a physical device.

This isn't a hard and fast rule, though—just the default. Some devices, such as multi-transport tape decks or computer with card slots, may have more than one Device ID. It's up to the manufacturer to indicate any exceptions to this general practice.

The protocols that require universal SysEx messages—such as the Sample Dump Standard, the MIDI Time Code, General MIDI, MIDI Show Control, and MIDI Machine Control—are described in later chapters. Meanwhile, here are the descriptions of the other messages in the Real Time and Non-Real Time SysEx categories.

The General Information Messages

There are two MIDI General Information messages: the Identity Request and the Identify Reply message. The Identity Request, which asks what kind of MIDI device the inquiring device is connected to, looks like this:

Format: F0H 7EH <device ID> 06H 01H F7H

Type: Universal Non-Real Time System Exclusive message

```
F0H          : System Exclusive ID
7EH          : category = Non-Real Time
<device ID> : the device ID number
<sub-ID#1>  : 06H = general information
<sub-ID#2>  : 01H = ID request
F7H          : EOX
```

In response to this request (which is a sort of ID check), the receiving unit sends the Identity Reply message, which looks like this:

Format: F0H 7EH <device ID> 06H 02H mmH ffH ffH
             ddH ddH ssH ssH ssH ssH F7H

Type: Universal Non-Real Time System Exclusive message

```
F0H          : System Exclusive ID
7EH          : category = Non-Real Time
<device ID> : the device ID number
<sub-ID#1>  : 06H = general information
<sub-ID#2>  : 02H = ID reply
mmH          : manufacturer's ID code, in either one
               or three bytes
ffH          : the family of the device within the
               manufacturer's group (i.e., the 14-bit
               Device Family Code), expressed over two
               bytes (an LSbyte and an MSByte)
```

```
ddH           : the type of device within the family
                (i.e., the 14-bit Device Family Member
                Code), expressed over two bytes (an
                LSbyte and an MSByte)
ssH           : the version number of the operating-
                system software
F7H           : EOX
```

For example, in response to such a request, an Ensoniq VFX-SD Version 1.32 synthesizer would transmit the following bytes:

F0H	Start of Exclusive
7EH	Non-Real Time
0cH	basic MIDI channel
06H	Sub-ID #1
02H	Sub-ID #2
0FH	Ensoniq identification
05H	Device Family Code (LSB)
00H	Device Family Code (MSB)
01H	Device Family Member Code (LSB)
00H	Device Family Member Code (LSB)
00H	software version information
00H	– not used –
xxH	version number (integer portion)
01H	version number (decimal portion)
20H	EOX

The Bar Marker

This message, transmitted by a sequencer, a rhythm box, or any other device, indicates that the next MIDI clock signal (F8H) or the next MTC frame (F1H xxH) marks the start of a new bar. If the receiving unit is stopped, then it can place itself at the corresponding position and immediately display the bar number in question. It is strongly recommended that the bar marker be sent immediately after the last MIDI clock signal or the last MTC frame—that is, so that no delay separates these two messages.

Format: F0H 7FH <device ID> 03H 01H aaH aaH F7H

Type: Universal Real Time System Exclusive message

```
F0H:          System Exclusive ID
7FH:          category = Real Time
<device ID>:  device ID number (default = 7FH = all)
<sub-ID#1>:   03H = "notation"-type message
<sub-ID#2>:   01H = Bar Marker message
aaH aaH:      bar number, in the form LSB/MSB
              00H 40H =   at the stop
              01H 40H --> 00H 00H = countdown
              01H 00H --> 7EH 3FH = bar number
              7FH 3FH =   while running, unknown bar
                          number
F7H:          end of exclusive (EOX)
```

The way bar numbers should be interpreted needs some explaining. In the order MSB/LSB, these numbers represent the following values:

```
4000H                   : when stopped
from 40001 to 0000H : deduction
from 0001H to 3F7EH : bar number
3F7FH                   : when running, unknown bar number
```

Or, in binary:

```
01000000 00000000                                   : when stopped
from 01000000 00000001 to 00000000 00000000 : deduction
```

```
from 00000000 00000001 to 00111111 01111110 : bar number
00111111 01111111                           : when running, unknown bar
                                              number
```

Expressed in the form of 14 useful bits (because by definition bit seven in a MIDI byte is set to zero), these values are indicated in the following way:

```
100000 00000000                            : when stopped
from 100000 00000001 to 000000 00000000 : deduction
from 000000 00000001 to 011111 11111110 : bar number
011111 11111111                          : when running, unknown bar number
```

Or, in hex:

```
2000H                   : when stopped
from 2001H to 0000H     : deduction
from 0001H to 1FFEH     : bar number
1FFFH                   : when running, unknown bar number
```

The negative data bytes, which are used to make the deduction, are represented in accordance with the so-called "twos complement" method. As you'll recall, this approach consists of starting with the equivalent positive value and inverting all of the bits, then adding 1 to the result. The number of bars deducted is also equal to the number expressed in this way plus 1. In other words, the number of bar 2001H (100000 00000001) corresponds to a deduction of 8,192 bars (−8,191), because after having inverted the bits for the value +8,191 (1FFFH in hex, or 011111 11111111 in binary) in order to add 1, you get:

```
  100000 00000000  (the bit inversion)
+               1
  ---------------
= 100000 00000001
= 2001H
```

In the same way, bar number 2002H (100000 00000010) corresponds to a deduction of 8,191 bars (−8,190), because after having inverted the bits of the value +8,190 (1FFEH in hex, or 011111 11111110 in binary), in order to add 1, you get:

```
100000 00000001 (the bit inversion)
+              1
---------------
= 100000 00000010
= 2002H
```

And so on, until you get a deduction of two bars, corresponding to bar number 3FFFH (111111 11111111), because after having inverted the bits of the value +1 (0001H in hex, or 000000 00000001 in binary), in order to add 1, you get:

```
111111 11111110 (the bit inversion)
+              1
---------------
= 111111 11111111
= 3FFFH
```

Finally, the value 0000H indicated a deduction of one bar, after which positive values take over in order to count the number of bars in the piece, from 0001H (+1) to 1FFEH (+8,190).

The Time Signature

This message, as transmitted by a sequencer, a rhythm box, or any other device, indicates the time signature of a piece (2/4, 4/4, 6/8, 5/4, whatever). The message exists in two forms: one in real time, in which the receiving unit immediately adopts the new time signature, and the other in non-real time. In this form, the receiving unit can display the new time signature right away, but doesn't adopt it until it receives the next Bar Marker message.

Format: F0H 7FH <device ID> 03H 02H lnH nnH ddH
            ccH bbH [nnH ddH ...] F7H

Type: Universal Real Time System Exclusive message

```
FOH          : System Exclusive ID
7FH          : category = Real Time
<device ID>  : ID number of the device (default = 7FH
               = all)
<sub-ID#1>   : 03H = "notation"-type message
<sub-ID#2>   : 02H = immediate change in the time
               signature
lnH          : number of bytes to follow
nnH          : numerator of the time signature
ddH          : denominator of the time signature
               (expressed as a negative power of 2)
ccH          : number of MIDI clock signals per
               metronome tick
bbH          : number of thirty-second notes per MIDI
               quarter-note
[nnH ddH ...] : groups of two additional bytes
               (numerator and denominator) that define
               a bar created within a given bar
F7H          : EOX
```

Format: F0H 7FH <device ID> 03H 42H lnH nnH ddH
              ccH bbH [nnH ddH ...] F7H

Type: Universal Real Time System Exclusive message

```
FOH          : System Exclusive ID
7FH          : category = Real Time
<device ID>  : ID number of the device (default = 7FH
               = all)
<sub-ID#1>   : 03H = "notation"-type message
<sub-ID#2>   : 42H = deferred change in the time
               signature
lnH          : number of bytes to follow
nnH          : numerator of the time signature
ddH          : denominator of the time signature
               (expressed as a negative power of 2)
ccH          : number of MIDI clock signals per
               metronome tick
```

```
bbH           : number of thirty-second notes per
                MIDI quarter-note
[nnH ddH ...] : groups of two additional bytes
                (numerator and denominator) that
                define a bar created within a given bar
F7H           : EOX
```

For more information about the nnH, ddH, ccH and bbH bytes, see Chapter 8.

Master Volume

This message, which is intended primarily for instruments that are compatible with the General MIDI standard, affects not just the volume of one channel or another (which is the job of Control Change 7), but on the overall volume of the device as a whole.

Format: F0H 7FH <device ID> 04H 01H vvH vvH F7H

Type: Universal Real Time System Exclusive message

```
F0H          : System Exclusive ID
7FH          : category = Real Time
<device ID>  : device ID number
<sub-ID#1>   : 04H = message of the "device control" type
<sub-ID#2>   : 01H = master volume
vvH vvH      : value of the volume over 14 bits (LSB/MSB)
F7H          : EOX
```

Master Balance

This message, which is intended primarily for instruments that are compatible with the General MIDI standard, affects not just the balance of one channel or another (which is the job of Control Change 10), but on the overall valance of the device as a whole.

Format: F0H 7FH \<device ID\> 04H 02H bbH bbH F7H

Type: Universal Real Time System Exclusive message

```
F0H            : System Exclusive ID
7FH            : category = Real Time
<device ID>    : device ID number
<sub-ID#1>     : 04H = message of the "device control" type
<sub-ID#2>     : 02H = master balance
bbH bbH        : value of the balance over 14 bits (LSB/MSB)
F7H            : EOX
```

File Dump

This protocol lets files be exchanged (dumped) between two computers by means of MIDI links—for example, to transfer a piece in MIDI Files format (see Chapter 8) between a hardware sequencer and a computer, or to transfer any file between different kinds of computers. To do this kind of transfer, it's recommended (but not required) that you establish a bidirectional link between the sending unit and the receiving unit by connecting the MIDI Out port of one to the MIDI In port of the other, and vice versa.

Here's the general syntax of the messages:

Format: F0H 7EH \<device ID\> 07H \<sub-ID#2\> ssH
                ... F7H

Type: Universal Non-Real Time System Exclusive message

```
F0H            : System Exclusive ID
7EH            : category = Non-Real Time
<device ID>    : ID number of the unit for which the message is intended
<sub-ID#1>     : 07H = file dump
<sub-ID#2>     : the type of message, i.e.,
                 01H = dump header
                 02H = data packet
```

```
                  03H = dump request
ssH :             ID number of the unit sending the message
...
F7H : EOX
```

The transfer of a file can be triggered either directly by the sending unit
or by the receiving unit, which in this case sends a request to the sending
unit. This request has the following form:

Dump Request

Format: F0H 7EH ddH 07H 03H ssH <type> <name>
               F7H

```
F0H         : System Exclusive ID
7EH         : category = Non-Real time
<device ID> : ID number of the unit which is being asked
              to send the dump
<sub-ID#1>  : 07H = file dump
<sub-ID#2>  : 03H = dump request
ssH         : ID number of the unit for which the dump is
              intended
<type>      : type of file extension (four ASCII bytes,
              over 7 bits)
<name>      : file name (a variable number of ASCII bytes,
              over 7 bits)
F7H         : EOX
```

Typical recommended file extensions are listed below.

‹TYPE›	RECOMMENDED FILE EXTENSION	MEANING
MIDI	MID	a MIDI file
MIEX	MEX	a MIDIEX file
ESEQ	ESQ	an ESEQ file

‹TYPE›	RECOMMENDED FILE EXTENSION	MEANING
TEXT	TXT	a text file (ASCII, 7 bits)
BIN<space>	BIN	a binary file
MAC<space>	MAC	a Macintosh file (with a MacBinary header)

The MacBinary header refers to the file data, accompanied by the information (such as the file type, the program that created the file, etc.) needed by the part of the Macintosh operating system known as the Finder.

Each of the characters in the file name (which can be of any size, with the end delimited by the F7H byte) is represented in ASCII over 7 bits. The name as a whole has to be printable (that is, it has to consist of characters between 20H and 7EH, inclusive). If a file has no name, then the receiving unit will interpret this lack as a request to send the file that's currently residing in memory. This would be the case, for example, with a request addressed directly to a piece of sequencer software on a computer, or even to a hardware sequencer without a disk reader (i.e., a sequencer that is limited to storing data in RAM), which would thereby be asked to send the "current" song.

In response to a Dump Request message, assuming that no file has the name contained in the message, or if there is no name, that no file is present in memory, then the receiving unit has the option of either interrupting the transaction (by sending a Cancel message, as described below), or asking the user to select manually the file to send. In the latter case, a Wait message (described below) is sent to the receiving unit, in order to ask the receiving unit to wait the necessary amount of time.

The transmitted file consists of a so-called "identity card" (i.e., the dump header), followed by a given number of data packets, depending on the length of the file.

The Dump Header

Format: F0H 7EH ddH 07H 01H ssH \<type> \<length>
               \<name> F7H

```
F0H          : System Exclusive ID
7EH          : category = Non-Real time
<device ID>  : ID number of the unit receiving the dump
<sub-ID#1>   : 07H = the file dump
<sub-ID#2>   : 01H = the dump header
ssH          : ID number of the unit sending the dump
<type>       : the type of file extension (four ASCII
               bytes, over 7 bits)
<length>     : the length of the file, expressed over four
               bytes (28 bits), starting with the least
               significant byte
<name>       : the file name (a variable number of ASCII
               bytes, over 7 bits)
F7H          : EOX
```

If the length is unknown (i.e., if the file is being converted on the fly), a value of zero should be transmitted.

The Data Packet

Format: F0H 7EH ddH 07H 02H \<packet #> \<byte
               count> \<data> \<checksum> F7H

```
F0H            : System Exclusive ID
7EH            : category = Non-Real time
<device ID>    : ID number of the device receiving the dump
<sub-ID#1>     : 07H = file dump
<sub-ID#2>     : 02H = data packet
<packet#>      : packet number, expressed as a byte (reset
                 to zero every 128 packets)
<byte count>   : the size of the packet, reduced by one unit
<data>         : data bytes
```

```
<checksum>   : "exclusive OR" (XOR), applied to the bytes
               from 7EH inclusive and the end of the data
               bytes
F7H          : EOX
```

Such a message can contain a total of up to 137 bytes, of which 1 to 128 can be data bytes (for a <byte count> value between 0 and 127). These bytes are transmitted in so-called "packed" form, with eight MIDI bytes (8×7 bits) transmitting seven memory bytes (7×8 bits), as shown below:

Memory bytes:

```
a7 a6 a5 a4 a3 a2 a1 a0
b7 b6 b5 b4 b3 b2 b1 b0
c7 c6 c5 c4 c3 c2 c1 c0
d7 d6 d5 d4 d3 d2 d1 d0
e7 e6 e5 e4 e3 e2 e1 e0
f7 f6 f5 f4 f3 f2 f1 f0
g7 g6 g5 g4 g3 g2 g1 g0
```

MIDI bytes:

```
0 a7 b7 c7 d7 e7 f7 g7
0 a6 a5 a4 a3 a2 a1 a0
0 b6 b5 b4 b3 b2 b1 b0
0 c6 c5 c4 c3 c2 c1 c0
0 d6 d5 d4 d3 d2 d1 d0
0 e6 e5 e4 e3 e2 e1 e0
0 f6 f5 f4 f3 f2 f1 f0
0 g6 g5 g4 g3 g2 g1 g0
```

If the total number of data bytes to be transmitted isn't a multiple of seven, the last packet will contain fewer than eight bytes. For example:

Memory bytes:

```
a7 a6 a5 a4 a3 a2 a1 a0
b7 b6 b5 b4 b3 b2 b1 b0
c7 c6 c5 c4 c3 c2 c1 c0
```

MIDI bytes:

```
0 a7 b7 c7 0  0  0  0
0 a6 a5 a4 a3 a2 a1 a0
0 b6 b5 b4 b3 b2 b1 b0
0 c6 c5 c4 c3 c2 c1 c0
```

The three preceding messages (the Dump Request, the Dump Header, and the Data Packet messages) can be followed by four so-called "handshaking" messages (i.e., the Wait, Cancel, Acknowledge, and Not Acknowledged messages), which are also used by the Sample Dump Standard. They can also be followed by a fifth, more recently implemented message, i.e., the End of File message.

ACK (acknowledge)

Format: F0H 7EH <device ID> 7FH ppH F7H

```
F0H          : System Exclusive ID
7EH          : category = Non-Real time
<device ID>  : ID number of the device receiving the dump
<sub-ID#1>   : 7FH = ACK
ppH          : the packet number
F7H          : EOX
```

This message is sent by the receiving unit to let the sending unit know that either a Data Packet message or a File Header message was received correctly, and to invite the sending unit to transmit the next packet. In a sense, this message is a notice of receipt. The contents of the ppH byte usually correspond to the number of the packet that was received—except when a response to a File Header message is involved, in which case the contents of the ppH byte don't really matter.

NAK (not acknowledged)

Format: F0H 7EH <device ID> 7EH ppH F7H

```
F0H          : System Exclusive ID
7EH          : category = Non-Real time
<device ID>  : ID number of the device receiving the dump
<sub-ID#1>   : 7EH = NAK
ppH          : the packet number
F7H          : EOX
```

This message is sent by the receiving unit to warn the sending unit that a
Data Packet message, whose number is indicated by the ppH byte, was
not received correctly (i.e., because the length or checksum was incorrect).
The sending unit should then send the same packet again. After three er-
rors in a row, the receiving unit stops sending NAK messages and sends a
Cancel message instead.

Cancel

Format: F0H 7EH <device ID> 7DH ppH F7H

```
F0H          : System Exclusive ID
7DH          : category = Non-Real time
<device ID>  : ID number of the device for which the
               message is intended
<sub-ID#1>   : 7DH = cancel
ppH          : the packet number
F7H          : EOX
```

This message ends the transaction prematurely. It can be sent by the receiving unit to the sending unit, and vice versa, as a result of an erroneous
packet number, due to an interruption of the transfer at the user's request,
because of an unknown file type, etc.

Wait

Format: F0H 7EH <device ID> 7CH ppH F7H

```
F0H          : System Exclusive ID
7EH          : category = Non-Real time
<device ID>  : the ID number of the unit for which the
               message is intended
<sub-ID#1>   : 7CH = wait
ppH          : the packet number
F7H          : EOX
```

This message is sent either by the receiving unit, after it receives a File Header message or a Data Packet message, or by the sending unit, after it receives a File Dump Request message. In the first case (i.e., in response to a File Header message), the sending unit should not send anything further until it receives an ACK or Cancel message. In the second case (i.e., in response to a Data Packet message), the sending unit should interrupt the transmission of packets until it receives an ACK, NAK, or Cancel message. In the third and last case (i.e., in response to a File Dump Request message), the receiving unit should wait until it receives a File Header or Cancel message.

End of File

Format: F0H 7EH <device ID> 7BH ppH F7H

```
F0H          : System Exclusive ID
7EH          : category = Non-Real time
<device ID>  : ID number of the unit sending the dump
<sub-ID#1>   : 7BH = end of file
ppH          : the packet number
F7H          : EOX
```

This message is transmitted by the sending unit after that unit has sent the last packet, in order to inform the receiving unit of the end of the transaction.

It should also be noted that after having sent a Dump Request message, the receiving unit waits to receive a response (either a Dump Header, a Wait message, or a Cancel message) sometime during the next 200 milliseconds. Likewise, after having sent a Dump header, the sending unit waits to receive a response (either an ACK message, a Wait message, or a Cancel message) during the same period of time. If it doesn't get any of these responses, the sending unit treats the link as unidirectional and sends the packets one after another until it reaches the end of the file, without making any attempt to continue the dialogue.

The MIDI Tuning Standard

This extension of the MIDI standard enables the exchange of microtonal scales between different instruments, and also lets the instruments be programmed in real time. Such scales are defined by the fact that each of the 128 MIDI notes they consist of (or, by default, each of the notes that the instrument uses) can be tuned. The frequency of these notes is expressed in the form of three bytes, as indicated below:

```
0xxxxxxx 0abcdefg 0hijklmn
```

xxxxxxx: the number of the MIDI note between 0 (C-2) and 127 (G8), to which a frequency, expressed in Hz, corresponds (starting with the tempered scale and with reference to A3 at a pitch of 440 Hz).

abcde-fghijklmn: the interval between 0 cents, inclusive (0), and 100 cents, exclusive (16,383), to be added to the preceding frequency. The 100 cents, which as you'll recall are equal to one semitone, are divided into 16,384 intervals of 0.0061035156 cent each (or, rounded off, 0.0061 cent each).

As a result, in order to code a given frequency, you start with the MIDI note xxxxxxx with the closest pitch in Hz (see Table 3.4 in Chapter 3) and then add the necessary number of cents (that is, from 0 to 16,383 × 0.0061 cent). Here are a few examples:

```
OOH OOH OOH =      8.1758 Hz  : the pitch of C-2 (tempered scale)
                               (the minimum frequency)
OOH OOH 01H =      8.1758 Hz  : 8,1758 Hz (C-2) + 0.0061 cent
01H OOH OOH =      8.6620 Hz  : the pitch of C#-2 (tempered scale)
OCH OOH OOH =     16.3516 Hz  : the pitch of C-1 (tempered scale)
3CH OOH OOH =    261.6256 Hz  : the pitch of C3 (tempered scale)
3DH OOH OOH =    277.1826 Hz  : the pitch of C#-3 (tempered scale)
44H 7FH 7FH =    439.9984 Hz  : 369.994 Hz (F#3) + 16,383 × 0.0061 cent
45H OOH OOH =    440.0000 Hz  : the pitch of A3 (tempered scale)
45H OOH 01H =    440.0016 Hz  : 440 Hz (A3) + 0.061 cent
78H OOH OOH =   8372.0181 Hz  : the pitch of C8 (tempered scale)
78H OOH 01H =   8372.0476 Hz  : 8,372.0181 Hz (C8) + 0.0061 cent
7FH OOH OOH = 12,543.8540 Hz  : the pitch of G8 (tempered scale)
7FH OOH 01H = 12,543.8982 Hz  : 12,543.8540 Hz (G8) + 0.0061 cent
7FH 7FH 7EH = 13,289.6567 Hz  : 12,543.8540 Hz (G8) + 16,383 × 0.0061 cent
                               (the maximum frequency)
7FH 7FH 7FH = reserved        : no change
```

The value 7FH 7FH 7FH is for the benefit of instruments that use only part of the entire MIDI tessitura from C-2 to G8. When certain tuning messages are transmitted, those instruments can warn the receiving unit about unused notes by associating these three bytes with those notes.

On the functional level, the messages in the MIDI tuning family fall into three categories:

- The transmission of microtonal scales in the form of a dump (bulk tuning dump request, bulk tuning dump);

- Modification of the pitch of two or more consecutive notes (real-time single-note tuning change); and

- Changes in the tuning program and the tuning bank, in the same way as the Program Change and Bank Select messages for sounds.

When one of these three latter types of messages (that is, a real-time single note tuning change, a tuning program change, or a tuning bank change) is received, the instrument should immediately adapt itself to the new pitches, if necessary by making a real-time change in the frequency of the notes that are being played. The instrument has the option of providing a supplementary mode in which that the pitch changes will not affect notes that are being played, but only the notes that are triggered after reception of a real-time single-note tuning change message, a tuning program message, or a tuning bank message.

Here's the syntax of the various messages:

Bulk Tuning Dump Request

Format: F0H 7EH <device ID> 08H 00H ttH F7H

Type: Universal Non-Real Time System Exclusive message

```
F0H           : System Exclusive ID
7EH           : category = Non-Real Time
<device ID>   : device ID number
08H           : sub-ID#1 = MIDI tuning standard
00H           : sub-ID#2 = bulk dump request
ttH           : number of the tuning program (0 to 127)
F7H           : EOX
```

Bulk Tuning Dump

Format: F0H 7EH <device ID> 08H 01H ttH <tuning
             name> [xxH yyH zzH] ... <checksum> F7H

```
F0H           : System Exclusive ID
7EH           : category = Non-Real Time
<device ID>   : device ID number
08H           : sub-ID#1 = MIDI tuning standard
01H           : sub-ID#2 = bulk dump reply
ttH           : number of the tuning program
```

```
<tuning name> : name, in the form of 16 characters in ASCII
[xxH yyH zzH] : frequency of MIDI note 0 (C-2)
[xxH yyH zzH] : frequency of MIDI note 1 (C#-2)
...
[xxH yyH zzH] : frequency of MIDI note 127 (G8)
<checksum>    : "exclusive OR" (XOR), applied to the data
                bytes
F7H           : EOX
```

Real-Time Single-Note Tuning Change

Format: F0H 7FH <device ID> 08H 02H ttH llH [kkH
             xxH yyH zzH] ... F7H

Type: Universal Real-Time System Exclusive message

```
F0H           : System Exclusive ID
7FH           : category = Real Time
<device ID>   : device ID number
08H           : sub-ID#1 = MIDI tuning standard
02H           : sub-ID#2 = note change
ttH           : number of the tuning program
llH           : number of notes to be modified (one modification
                = kkH xxH yyH zzH)
[kkH          : the MIDI note number, and the
xxH yyH zzH]  : frequency of the note as expressed over three
                bytes (sequence repeated llH times)
F7H           : EOX
```

The Tuning Program and the Tuning Bank

A tuning program or a tuning bank is selected through the transmittal of
the registered parameters 00H 03H and 00H 04H, respectively, followed
by either a data entry message (indicating the program number or the
bank number), or by a data increment message (requesting that the
program number or the bank number be incremented), or by a data
decrement message (requesting that the program number or the bank

number be decremented):

```
BcH (1011cccc) 65H 00H: recorded parameter number (MSB)
BcH (1011cccc) 64H 03H: recorded parameter number (LSB)
BcH (1011cccc) 06H ttH: data entry MSB (program numbers 1 to 128)

            or

BcH (1011cccc) 60H 7FH: data increment

            or

BcH (1011cccc) 61H 7FH: data decrement

BcH (1011cccc) 65H 00H: recorded parameter number (MSB)
BcH (1011cccc) 64H 04H: recorded parameter number (LSB)
BcH (1011cccc) 06H ttH: data entry MSB (bank numbers 1 to 128)

            or

BcH (1011cccc) 60H 7FH: data increment

            or

BcH (1011cccc) 61H 7FH: data decrement
```

You can get more information about microtonal scales by writing to:

The Just Intonation Network
MIDI Tuning Standard Committee
535 Stevenson Street
San Francisco, CA 94103

The MIDI Implementation Chart

A MIDI Implementation Chart is an official document designed by the MMA and the JMSC. In a sense, this chart is the instrument's "MIDI identity card." Manufacturers are required to publish the chart and to distribute it with every product they sell.

An implementation chart does not go into a great deal of detail, but rather provides the basic information you need in order to make a more in-depth study of an instrument. A typical chart is shown in Figure 4.15.

The first column indicates the function or message category for each row (Note messages, Aftertouch messages, Pitch Bend messages, etc.). There are twelve of these categories, followed at the bottom of the page by an additional optional category (the "Remarks" or "Notes" row).

The second and third columns ("Transmitted" and "Recognized") correspond respectively to the transmission and reception functions. An X at the intersection of one of these columns and one of the function rows indicates that the corresponding MIDI category is transmitted or received (in other words, implemented). Conversely, an O at the intersection of one of these columns and one of the function rows indicates that the category is not handled by the instrument. Any further details will appear in the fourth ("Remarks") column.

The make, the model, the version of the operating-system software, and the introduction date of the unit should appear in the title of the implementation chart. As a reminder, the bottom of the chart includes the meaning of the four MIDI modes, as shown below:

Mode 1   Omni On, Poly

Mode 2   Omni Off, Poly

Mode 3   Omni On, Mono

Mode 4   Omni Off, Mono

In defining the major MIDI criteria, the implementation chart displays an instrument's capabilities. For example, if you want to drive an expander through a MIDI guitar, you should first make sure that Mode 4 is implemented on the expander. Thanks to its standardized format, the chart makes it easy to compare the transmission and reception information for two (or more) MIDI instruments.

MODEL		MIDI Implementation Chart		Date: Version:

Function . . .		Transmitted	Recognized	Remarks
Basic Channel	Default Channel			
Mode	Default Messages Altered			
Note Number	True Voice			
Velocity	Note ON Note OFF			
Aftertouch	Key's Ch's			
Pitch Bender				
Control Change				
Prog Change	True #			
System Exclusive				
System Common	Song Pos Song Sel Tune			
System Real Time	Clock Commands			
Aux Messages	Local ON/OFF All Notes OFF Active Sense Reset			
Notes				

Mode 1: OMNI ON, POLY   Mode 2: OMNI ON, MONO   O: Yes
Mode 3: OMNI OFF, POLY   Mode 4: OMNI OFF, MONO   X: No

FIGURE 4.15: *A typical MIDI implementation chart*

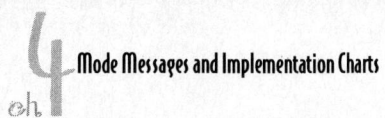

The Meanings of the Rows

Before looking at specific examples, it's worth defining the meaning of each of the twelve function rows in the MIDI implementation chart.

Basic Channel

This section contains two lines. The first line, "Default," theoretically gives the initialization value of the instrument's transmission and reception channels when the instrument is turned on. However, the interpretation of this value is linked to the "Remarks" column, which, if it's not empty, should contain a storage indication ("stored"). In practice, the notation indicates that the MIDI channels specified for transmission and reception stay stored in memory after the instrument is turned off, saving you the trouble of reprogramming these channels every time you turn on the instrument. In such a case, the "Default" line doesn't display the initialization values (generally on channel 1); instead, it shows all the channels that are available on the instrument (which should theoretically be the same as the information given in the next line).

The second line, "Channel," gives information about how to change the initialization values. This information should include a statement of the modification range. This range usually covers all 16 channels, although in some instruments, particularly the ones designed at the very beginning of the MIDI era, it doesn't.

Mode

This section contains three lines. The first line, "Default," specifies the initialization values of the modes when the device is turned on. (Here again, these values can be stored in memory.)

The second line, "Messages," indicates the Mode messages that are recognized or transmitted via MIDI. Some instruments, although they implement different modes, don't necessarily receive the corresponding messages. As a result, these modes have to be programmed manually from the instrument's front panel.

The third line, "Altered," describes how an instrument acts if it receives messages in non-implemented modes. For instance, the notation "Mode 2 → Mode 1" in the reception column indicates that an Omni On/Poly message (Mode 1) will force the instrument to switch to "Omni On/Mono" (Mode 2). In the same way, an instrument that refuses to act like a monophonic instrument could well switch into Mode 1 when M has a value other than 1, and into Mode 3 when M = 1. Such a condition would be expressed in the chart by a notation that looks something like this: "Mono (M <> 1) → Mode 1, (M = 1) → Mode 3," or "Mono (M <> 1) → Mode 1,3."

Note Number

The transmission column tells you the range of notes that an instrument can transmit. However, a keyboard that has a transposition capability can transmit a number of note numbers that's greater than the number of keys on the keyboard. During reception, the instrument distinguishes between the number of notes received and the number of different notes that can be played (*true voices*). In effect, the instrument assumes that the range of a sound generator covers seven octaves, within a range of notes from C0 (24) to C7 (108).

When some sound generators receive messages that involve notes below 24 or above 108, they simply ignore them, while other generators play them in the nearest octave in their own range. In the latter case, the implementation chart should specify the number of notes received and also the number of different notes actually played. In this example the chart would indicate "0 – 127" and "24 – 108," respectively. For the values mentioned above, this "octave folding" phenomenon would be interpreted in the following way:

NOTE RECEIVED (NOTE NUMBER)	NOTE PLAYED (NOTE NUMBER)	EFFECT
C −2 (0)	C 0 (24)	Octave folding, two octaves higher
C# −2 (1)	C# 0 (25)	Octave folding, two octaves higher
D -2 (2)	D 0 (26)	Octave folding, two octaves higher
…	…	…
…	…	…
C −1 (12)	C 0 (24)	Octave folding, one octave higher
B −1 (23)	B 0 (35)	Octave folding, one octave higher
C 0 (24)	C 0 (24)	No folding
…	…	…
C 7 (108)	C 7 (108)	No folding
C# 7 (109)	C# 6 (97)	Octave folding, one octave lower
…	…	…
…	…	…
C# 8 (121)	C# 6 (97)	Octave folding, two octaves lower
G 8 (127)	G 6 (103)	Octave folding, two octaves lower

Velocity

These two lines indicate whether the instrument is sensitive to velocity. Sometimes a notation will indicate which of the two possible transmission methods for released notes is used (Note Off, or Note On with Velocity zero). A non-dynamic instrument automatically issues a velocity equal to 64 (40H).

Aftertouch

These two lines correspond respectively to the reception and transmission of Polyphonic Key Pressure ("Key's") and Channel Aftertouch ("Ch's") messages.

Pitch Bender

The "Remarks" column may indicate the minimum-to-maximum range of variation of the pitch bend (for example, plus or minus 12 semitones), its resolution (from 7 to 14 bits), and the option of modifying the sensitivity by means of Registered Parameter Number 0.

Control Change

From the simplest (YES/NO) indication to a detailed list of continuous controllers, the interpretation of these few lines often requires reference to the user's manual. Some controllers are used in the standard way (for modulation, volume, etc.), while others can be assigned to one parameter or another (synthesis, console automation, etc.), and still others can use undefined numbers for very specific purposes. The information on the implementation chart gives only a vague idea of the richness of the implementation of continuous controllers.

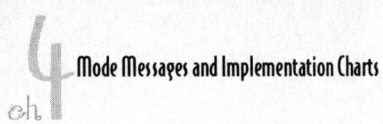
Program Change

In addition to indicating whether Program Change messages are transmitted and/or recognized, the "True #" line indicates the number of programs that the instrument contains (a concept which is analogous to the "true voices" for Note Number messages). Some fairly rare instruments use certain Program Change numbers for very specific purposes (bank selection or selection of a certain type of memory, such as cartridge, internal etc.). As much as possible, this type of information should be listed in the "Remarks" column.

System Exclusive

The only purpose of this row is to indicate whether the instrument uses System Exclusive messages.

System Common

This row includes the SPP (Song Position Pointer), Song Select, and Tune Request messages. If synchronization is extremely important to you, then, the SPP will be a determining factor, because it's what keeps different synchronized machines from re-starting from zero (i.e., from the beginning of a piece) at each new reading.

System Real Time

System Real Time messages are described in two lines. The first line, "Clock," refers to the MIDI timing clock, and the second line, "Commands," refers to the Start, Stop, and Continue commands. The names of the messages that are implemented are sometimes listed in plain text in the reception or transmission columns. Because the implementation chart was designed before the MIDI time code came into use, this protocol is often the subject of a separate note in the "Remarks" column.

Aux (Auxiliary) Messages

Auxiliary messages are grouped in four lines, dedicated respectively to Local On/Off, All Notes, Off, Active Sensing, and Reset messages. Because the All Notes Off message is implicitly included in four of the Mode messages (Omni On, Omni Off, Poly, and Mono), the Control Change numbers for these messages are sometimes listed in parentheses. In some instruments, Local mode is accessible via MIDI, even though it cannot be set manually from the front panel of the device.

Notes

This space is for remarks that have no direct bearing on the twelve preceding lines.

General Recommendations

As a general rule, you should always study the implementation chart before buying any instrument. This lets you determine at a glance whether the instrument meets the specifications on your list. Although you usually need more information than the charts contain, the charts do help. With a little practice it'll take you only a few minutes to make a broad-brush evaluation of the MIDI capabilities of any instrument. Meanwhile, for reference, Appendix E contains annotated examples of MIDI implementation charts for the Roland Alpha Juno-1 synthesizer, for the Roland D-550 expander, and for the Ensoniq VFX-SD synthesizer.

CHAPTER

5

XIII XIV XV XVI A B C D E F F G H I

Synthesis
and
Sampling Methods

THE PURPOSE OF this chapter isn't to describe in detail every possible sound-synthesis and signal-sampling method used by MIDI instruments (there are plenty of books on those subjects), but instead to review the most widely used ones.

As you know, a MIDI instrument consists of two modules: the controller and the sound generator. The controller transforms the musician's motions into Channel messages (Note On, Pitch Bend, Control Change, Aftertouch, etc.), in order to control the sound generator, which is responsible for actually producing the tone or tones. As its name indicates, the sound generator is a device that can deliver a tone, either by synthesis or by sampling. When a sound generator isn't physically connected to a keyboard, it's generally referred to as an *expander*. In any event, in accordance with the acoustic rules explained in Chapter 1, all sound generators and expanders act on the pitch, timbre, and amplitude of a waveform, using both analog and digital methods. This chapter provides a brief overview of these methods and their associated techniques.

Analog Synthesis

The term "analog" applies to any representation of a physical phenomenon by means of a continuous electrical signal, as opposed to a discontinuous (i.e., digital) signal. A typical example of this distinction is illustrated by the two clocks shown in Figure 5.1 below.

We'll just look at the basic components of an analog synthesizer: the oscillator, the filter, the envelope generator, and the low-frequency oscillator (LFO).

FIGURE 5.1: *Abstract representation of the incremental motion of the second hand by one-second intervals, with the clock with hands indicating the time in analog form (that is, with a continuous motion), and the digital clock indicating the time in numeric form (that is, with a discontinuous motion). In this example, there is no intermediate value between 12:58 and 12:59.*

The Oscillator

The oscillator is responsible for delivering the raw material—that is, for producing the raw sound that will be refined by the other modules. The oscillator is relatively limited, and only generates a few different periodic waves. The frequency of these waves is controlled by a signal from the keyboard. This signal corresponds to the pitch of the note played. Depending on whether the signal is transmitted in the form of a voltage or in the form of a piece of digitally coded information (for instance, via MIDI), an oscillator is known as a *voltage controlled oscillator* (VCO) or a *digitally controlled oscillator* (DCO). The lack of stability in the voltage control of an oscillator is responsible for slight discords, which give the tones a "thickness" that's characteristic of analog instruments.

You may recall that a periodic signal consists of a set of sinusoidal waveforms (also known as harmonics) whose frequencies are whole-number multiples of the fundamental frequency. The principle of analog synthesis (also known as "subtractive synthesis") consists of generating a rich periodic signal (that is, a signal that consists of a large number of harmonics) and then filtering the signal (that is, removing certain harmonics as desired or required).

The major waveforms that oscillators produce are listed below.

- *A sine-wave signal:* this signal consists of the fundamental, without any harmonics.

- *A sawtooth signal:* this signal, shown in Figure 5.2 below, contains all of the harmonics. The amplitude of each harmonic is inversely

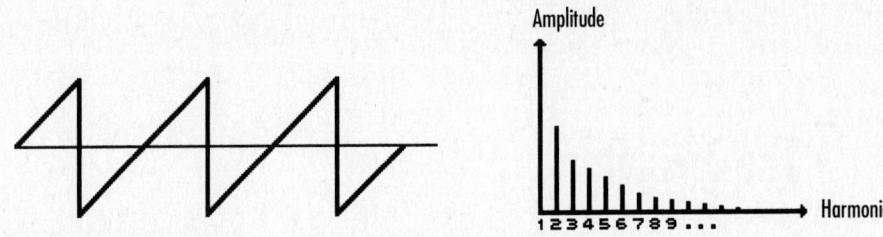

FIGURE 5.2: *The waveform of a sawtooth signal and its harmonic content*

proportional to its order (for instance, an Xth-order harmonic is equal to $1/X$). The timbre of sawtooth signals is fairly close to the timbre of string instruments.

- *A triangular signal:* this signal, shown in Figure 5.3 below, is an intermediate signal between the sawtooth and sinusoidal signals. The amplitudes of its harmonics decrease fast.

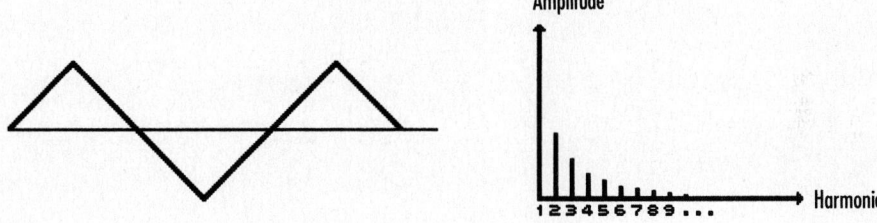

FIGURE 5.3: *The waveform of a triangular signal and its harmonic content*

- *A square signal:* this signal, shown in Figure 5.4 below, consists of all of the uneven harmonics. The amplitude of each harmonic is inversely proportional to its order. The timbre of a square signal is fairly close to the timbre of certain wind instruments.

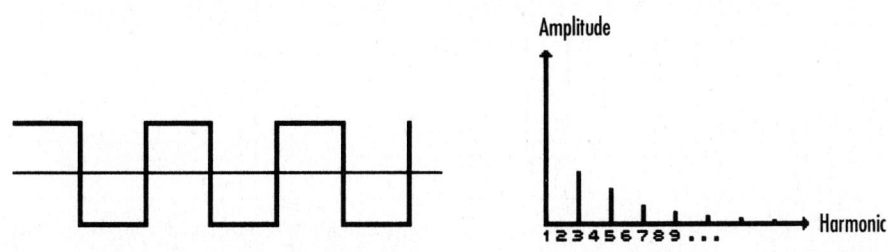

FIGURE 5.4: *The waveform of a square signal and its harmonic content*

▪ *A rectangular or pulse-width signal:* the positive half-period of the amplitude of this signal lasts from 50 percent to approximately 100 percent of a period, and the negative half-period of the amplitude lasts from 40 percent to approximately 0 percent of a period (i.e., the complementary amount of time in a single period). Generally speaking, the spectrum of a pulse-width signal at X percent (where X indicates the duration of the positive half-period of the amplitude) consists of all of the harmonics (except for the harmonics whose order is a whole-number multiple of the denominator of the X-percent fraction), converted into a fraction whose numerator is equal to 1. For example, a square signal (i.e., a 50-percent signal) includes all of the harmonics except the ones whose order is a whole-number multiple of 2 (because 50 percent is equal to 1/2). In the same way, the spectrum of a 33-percent signal includes all of the harmonics except for the ones whose order is a whole-number multiple of 3 (because 33 percent is equal to 1/3). It's also worth noting that the timbre of a pulse-width signal at X percent is equal to the timbre of a pulse-width signal at (100 − X percent), which is simply its phase opposite. As an example, the waveform of a 33-percent pulse-width signal is shown in Figure 5.5 below.

FIGURE 5.5: *The waveform of a 33-percent pulse-width signal and its harmonic content*

- *White noise:* this signal is an aperiodic signal whose spectrum consists of a large number of frequencies that can cover the entire range of the pass-band or indeed any specified frequency range, such that the amount of power at each frequency is equal to the amount of power at every other frequency. This signal is used to generate special effects (such as storms, aircraft taking off, and so on) or to simulate certain attack transients. Its pitch is generally fixed; in other words, its pitch is independent of the note played on the keyboard.

- *Pink noise:* this signal consists of an even distribution of all of the possible frequencies, such that the power within all of the octaves is equal. Pink noise is equivalent to depleted or shaped white noise.

- *Bandwidth-limited noise:* this signal, which can start as either white noise or pink noise, is a signal which has been taken through a pass-band filter in order to restrict power to specific ranges of frequencies. It's sometimes used for tuned natural or meteorological wind effects, such as wind blowing through trees.

The Filter

The filter removes harmonics from the waveform generated by the oscillator, thereby giving the waveform its final timbre. There are two major types of filters: low-pass filters and high-pass filters. Low-pass filters (LPFs) remove the high sounds, letting the low ones pass through, and high-pass filters (HPFs) remove the low sounds, letting the high ones pass through.

The frequency at which the filter goes into action is known as the cut-off frequency. The effectiveness of the filter is expressed in terms of decibels (dB) per octave. In reality, a low-pass filter doesn't remove harmonics that are higher than the cut-off frequency. Instead, it attenuates them more and more as their distance from the cut-off frequency increases. For

instance, at 12 dB per octave, the amplitude of the first, second, and third harmonics that are higher than the cut-off frequency will decrease by 12, 24, and 36 dB, respectively, as shown in Figure 5.6 below.

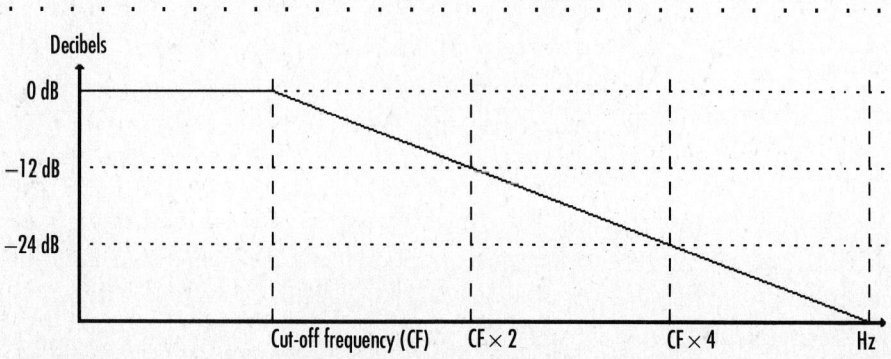

FIGURE 5.6: *The curve for a low-pass filter at 12 dB per octave*

The value of the cut-off frequency for the low-pass filter of a sound generator is relative (that is, it's measured in terms of the order of the harmonics). The value increases proportionally with the pitch of the key that's pressed, in such a way that the timbre keeps the same structure (in other words, so that the timbre consists of the same harmonics) regardless of the note that's played on the keyboard.

Depending on whether this pitch information is presented in the form of a voltage or in the form of a piece of digital information, the filter is known as a *voltage-controlled filter* (VCF) or a *digitally controlled filter* (DCF), respectively.

Finally, low-pass filters can produce a very specific effect known as *resonance*. This effect is characterized by an increase in the amplitude on either side of the cut-off frequency, as shown in Figure 5.7 below.

High-pass filters eliminate all of the bass sounds. Without exception, the cut-off frequency for these filters does not change with pitch. However,

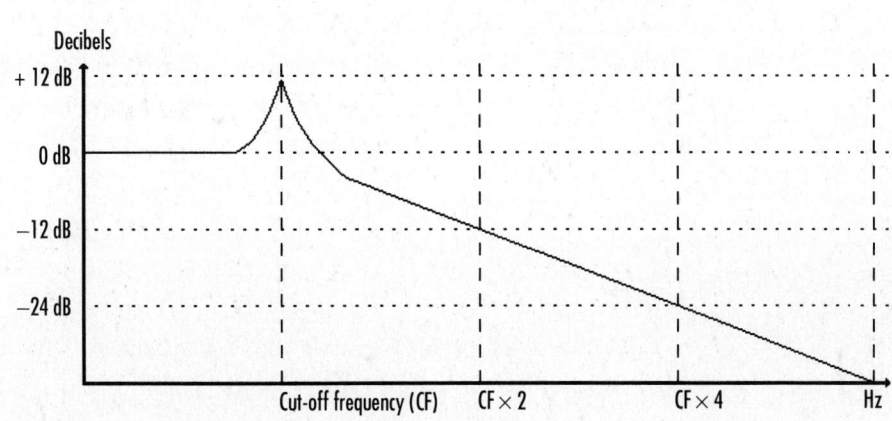

FIGURE 5.7: *The resonance effect of a low-pass filter*

in such a case, if a high-pass filter is used in conjunction with a low-pass filter, what you have is a band-pass filter.

The logical question arises: if you can have a band-pass filter, can you also have a band-elimination filter? The answer is yes, of course. However, band-elimination filters, which work in exactly the opposite way from band-pass filters, are much rarer creatures.

The Amplifier and the Envelope Generator

The amplifier uses the envelope generator (EG) to modify the volume of a sound, not in a static way (as with a simple potentiometer) but dynamically (that is, over time). Depending on whether the signal from the keyboard is in the form of a voltage or in digital form, the amplifier is known as a *voltage-controlled amplifier* (VCA) or a *digitally controlled amplifier* (DCA). Unlike the signals sent to the oscillator and the filter, the signals

the amplifier and EG work with don't involve a representation of the pitch of the note that was played. Instead, these signals indicate the status of the keys (that is, either pressed or released), in order to trigger the opening and closing of the envelope generator, which controls the change in volume over time.

In its original form, the envelope consists of four segments: the attack, the decay, the sustain, and the release—which is where the term "ADSR" comes from.

- *The attack phase* is the first segment in the envelope. It determines the speed at which the sound reaches its maximum volume. (The slope of this line is almost vertical for percussion sounds, and more gradual for the sounds of string instruments.)

- *The decay phase* represents the time the sound needs to reach the stabilization level (i.e., the sustain) once the attack phase has ended. For instance, the volume of a sound produced by a piano progresses rapidly, then decreases slowly before stabilizing.

- *The sustain phase* corresponds not to a slope but to a so- called "maintenance" level, and applies only to instruments whose sounds can be held indefinitely. For instance, the sound of an organ can be prolonged as long as the corresponding key is held down (i.e., because sustain is present), while the sound of a piano gradually fades (i.e., because sustain is absent).

- *The release phase* affects the amount of time the sound needs to stop or fade away as soon as it's no longer being held or sustained (or when the key is released).

The combination of these phases to form an envelope is shown in Figure 5.8 below.

However, the envelopes of digital synthesizers (which are examined in detail in later chapters) generally consist of a larger number of segments,

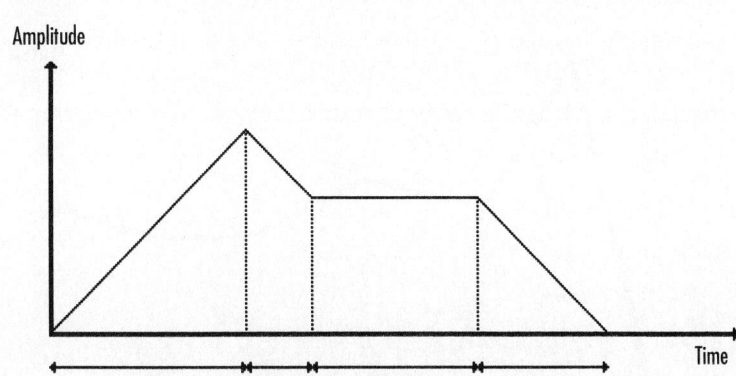

FIGURE 5.8: *A typical ADSR (attack, decay, sustain, release) envelope*

each of which is characterized by a rate (or time) and by a level. The rate (or time) and the level of a segment determine its slope, as shown in the example in Figure 5.9 below.

Most synthesizers can send the signal from the amplitude envelope generator to the filter and the oscillator, if the synthesizers don't have independent envelopes dedicated to these specific tasks. In either case, the cut-off frequency and the pitch of the oscillator have to be made to evolve over time.

The Low-Frequency Oscillator (LFO)

Like a standard oscillator, a low-frequency oscillator produces various predetermined waveforms, emitting them at frequencies ranging from several tenths to several tens of Hertz. In the same way as with envelopes, but this time in a cyclic manner, these signals are intended to cause a gradual

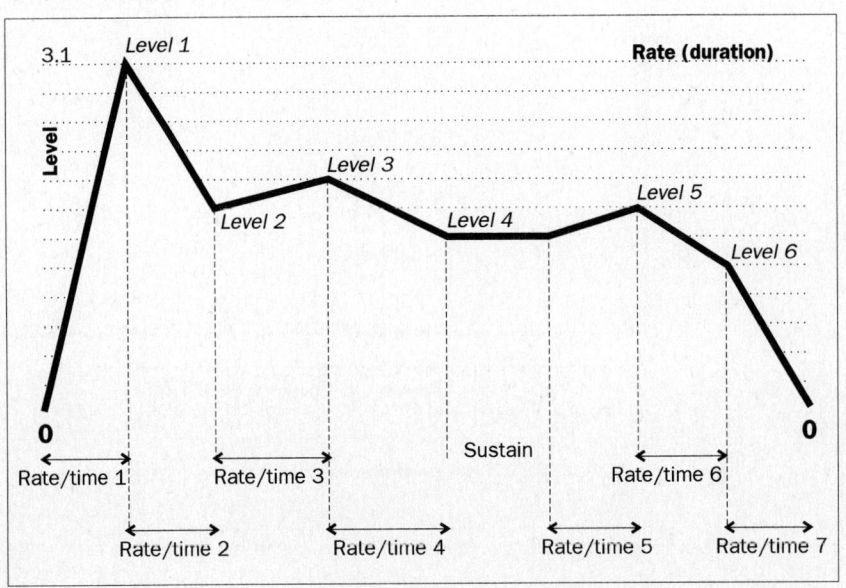

FIGURE 5.9: *The envelope of the Kawai K5 digital synthesizer has eight segments: attack (one segment), decay (three segments), sustain (one segment), and release (three segments). This synthesizer's parameters are: rate 1/level 1, rate 2/level 2, rate 3/level 3, rate 4/level 4 (the sustain level), rate 5/level 5, rate 6/level 6, and rate 7.*

change in various parameters, such as the pitch of the oscillator (for a vibrato effect), the filter cut-off frequency (for a wah-wah effect), the volume of the sound (for a tremolo effect), the pulse width of a rectangular waveform, and so on. The change is characterized by the speed (that is, the frequency) and the shape of the waveform (for instance, square, sinusoidal, sawtooth, triangular, random, etc.) of the LFO.

The Future of Analog Synthesis

With regard to timbre, the research for analog instruments is somewhat limited. In fact, apart from the restricted number of signals delivered by

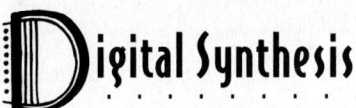

the oscillator, it's impossible to modify analog signals with any degree of precision, because the low-pass filter doesn't eliminate harmonics individually or selectively. Instead, it simply attenuates them all as they go beyond its cut-off frequency.

On the other hand—in a phenomenon that's intimately related to the imperfections and instabilities of analog electrical processing—the particular "color" of analog synthesizers is extremely tricky and hard to reproduce with digital procedures. This is why, in spite of their outdated technology, these instruments are still in widespread use. From a teaching point of view they also have the advantage of displaying, in a simple and intuitive way, some of the elementary principles that are common to all types of synthesis.

Digital Synthesis

Unlike analog synthesizers, digital synthesizers generate and process signals that aren't electrical but, as their name implies, are represented by numbers.

An example of this kind of signal generation appears in Figure 5.10 below. In this case, in order to deliver a triangular waveform, the oscillator reads, in a loop, a set of numbers corresponding to a period. Each of these numbers represents the amplitude of a sound at a particular moment (call it "t"). A change in the reading speed causes a change in the pitch of the waveform. Specifically, an increase in the reading speed raises the pitch and a decrease in the reading speed lowers the pitch. Multiplying or dividing all of the numbers by any given single value has the effect of changing the amplitude of the signal.

Set of numbers read in a loop at regular intervals by a digital oscillator:

0, 2, 4, 8, 6, 4, 2, 0, -2, -4, -6, -8, -6, -4, -2, 0

Waveform produced:

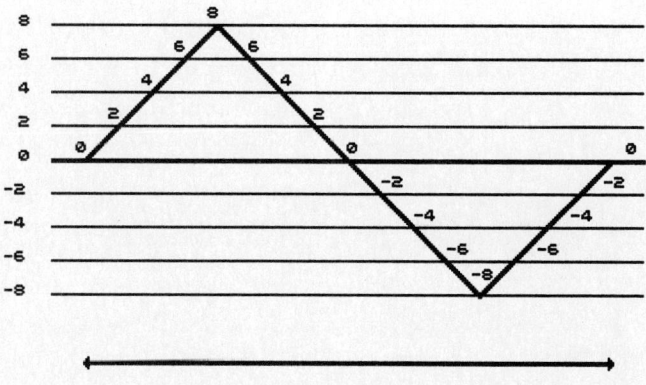

Period (the duration corresponds to the inverse of the frequency of the note played)

FIGURE 5.10: *A digital sound generator represents a waveform as a series of numbers. Each time a key is pressed, these numbers are read in a loop by the oscillator. The waveform in this example is a triangular signal.*

In digital synthesis, filters play the same role as they do in analog synthesizers. However, filtering operations with digital synthesizers involve calculation algorithms that are much too complex to study here.

Once the necessary processing has been done, the resulting numbers are converted into an electrical signal (in a step known as digital-to-analog conversion) and sent to the audio outputs of the instrument.

Subtractive Synthesis

In principle, subtractive digital synthesis is equivalent to analog subtractive synthesis. The fact that subtractive digital synthesis uses numbers instead of an electrical signal gives this method an edge in terms of precision and performance (that is, with regard to storage in memory and for editing), but at the cost of some of the "warmer" characteristics of analog circuits.

Additive Synthesis

Additive synthesis works in the opposite way from subtractive synthesis as shown in Figure 5.11 below.

This method could be characterized as rather gluttonous, because it requires as many oscillators as there are harmonics to be generated. (The usual minimum number is 32.) Under the most favorable possible

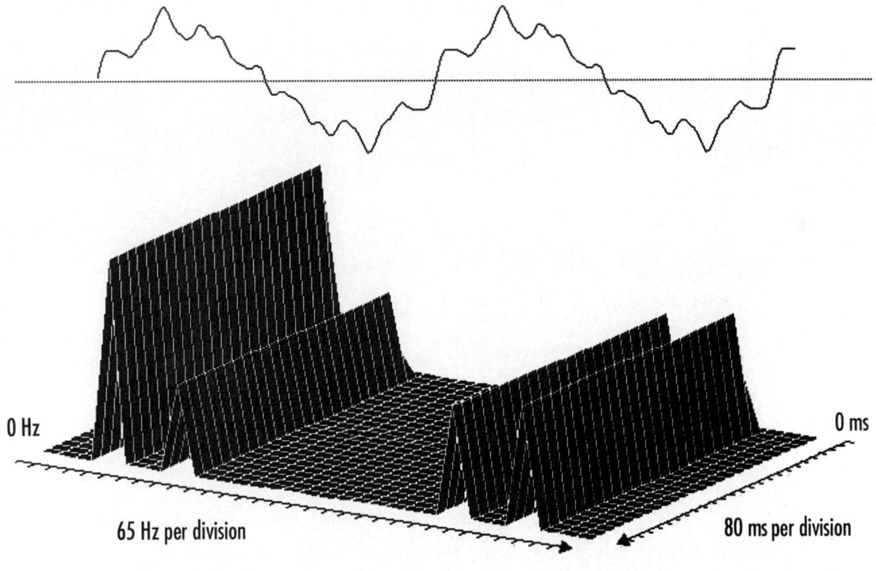

0 Hz   0 ms

65 Hz per division   80 ms per division

FIGURE 5.11: *Additive synthesis works by means of successive additions of sinusoidal waveforms. The timbre shown here (in two dimensions and also in three dimensions) contains the first, second, sixth, and seventh harmonics.*

circumstances, each oscillator has its own amplitude envelope, or even its own pitch envelope. The filter becomes somewhat less valuable, because the harmonic content is developed by the oscillator. In spite of a certain complexity in its implementation, this procedure is one of the most comprehensive available to MIDI musicians, mainly because of the way it lets you perform operations on timbre with a high degree of precision.

Phase Distortion

When a digital oscillator generates a waveform with a fixed pitch, the numbers that correspond to the period of the waveform are read in a loop at a constant speed. In other words, any two consecutive numbers are separated by the same time interval. Phase distortion consists of increasing the speed at which the first half-period of a co-sinusoidal signal is read and decreasing the speed at which the second half-period of the signal is read, but without changing the overall duration of the period. The result is shown in Figure 5.12 below. Even though the pitch of the

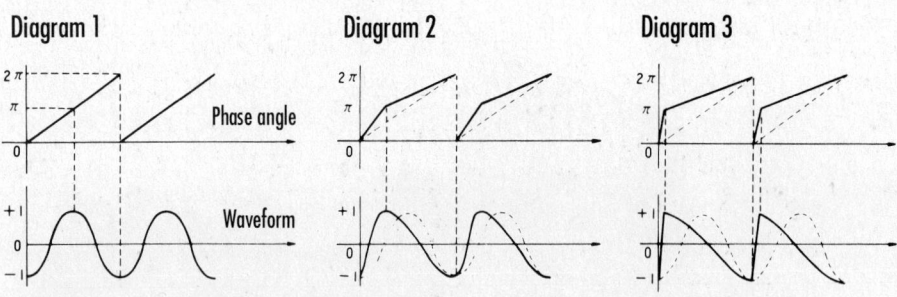

FIGURE 5.12: *The first of these three diagrams shows a co-sinusoidal waveform (that is, a sinusoidal waveform shifted by three-quarters of a period). The digits that make up the waveform are read at regular intervals. In the second diagram, the first half-period is read twice as fast, while the second half-period is read one and a half times more slowly. The resulting timbre is harmonically richer. The third diagram shows the maximum degree of distortion, with the oscillator delivering a sawtooth waveform.*

modified waveform is exactly the same as the pitch of the original signal, the shape of the modified waveform is different.

The signal produced by the oscillator is then processed by filters, envelopes, and low-frequency oscillators, and possibly by other modules.

Phase distortion is a clever way to create multiple waveforms starting with a simple oscillator. In the same way as for subtractive synthesis, its research field is more restricted than that of additive synthesis. However, the ease with which it can be programmed makes it very attractive.

Frequency Modulation Synthesis

Frequency modulation (FM) synthesis became widespread in 1983 after the appearance on the market of the Yamaha DX7 synthesizer. Instead of adding frequencies, subtracting them, or distorting them, FM synthesis simply modulated them. Although the FM procedure was harder to learn to use and program than earlier systems, it made it possible to reproduce a wide variety of waveforms with the aid of a minimal number of oscillators. Figure 5.13 below shows a typical example of FM synthesis.

When the speed of the LFO is gradually increased, the vibrato effect disappears, giving way to a change in timbre. This way, in the example given above, if the frequency of the LFO is set to 100 Hz, our ear doesn't hear a sinusoidal waveform or a cyclical variation in pitch. Instead, it hears a waveform that's increasingly richer in harmonics as the amplitude at which the LFO modulates the oscillator increases.

When the result of dividing the oscillator frequency by the frequency of the LFO (or the other way around) is a whole number, then the waveform is periodic. In the opposite case, the waveform is aperiodic.

Starting with this principle, the FM synthesis that the Yamaha DX7 uses involves six sinusoidal oscillators known as "operators." (Other Yamaha instruments only use four.) Each of these operators plays the role of

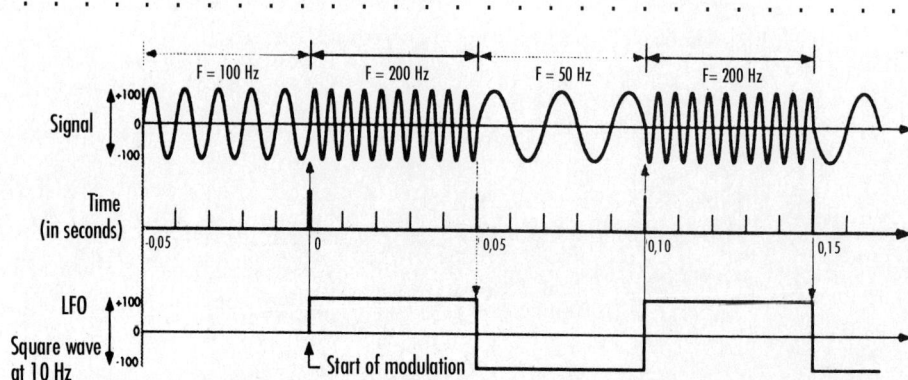

FIGURE 5.13: *In this example, the oscillator produces a sinusoidal waveform at a frequency of 100 Hz. This frequency is modulated ten times a second by a low-frequency oscillator (LFO) at a frequency of 10 Hz, so the resulting signal has a square waveform. The amplitude of the LFO is adjusted so that the frequency of the oscillator is developed over a range of plus or minus one octave. As a result, the amplitude alternates between a value of 200 Hz (which corresponds to the positive half-period of the amplitude of the LFO) and a value of 50 Hz (which corresponds to the negative half-period of the LFO).*

either a modulator (exactly the same way as an LFO) or a carrier (exactly the same way as an oscillator).

A modulator can modulate two or more carriers, and a carrier can be modulated by two or more modulators. Whether each of these six operators plays the role of a carrier or the role of a modulator is determined by the algorithm.

The DX7 synthesizer has 32 algorithms, ranging from very complex (for instance, four oscillators in series, with a first modulator modulating a second modulator, the second modulator modulating a third modulator, and the third modulator modulating the carrier) to very simple (for instance, a single carrier/modulator pair). The intermediate configurations in the DX7's algorithm collection include arrangements in which two or more modulators modulate the same carrier, or several carriers are modulated by the same modulator, and so on. Figure 5.14 below shows how one particular algorithm determines the roles played by the operators.

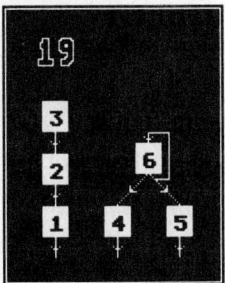

FIGURE 5.14: *Under algorithm 19 in the Yamaha DX7 synthesizer, operators 1, 4, and 5 play the role of carriers, while operators 2, 3, and 6 play the role of modulators. Operator 1 is modulated by operator 2, which in turn is modulated by operator 3. Operator 6 modulates operators 4 and 5.*

For each operator, you can set the frequency either in terms of a ratio (that is, by multiplying by this ratio the pitch of the note to be produced) or in terms of a fixed frequency (that is, a frequency which is independent of the note played). You can also specify the amplitude (that is, the general volume and also the four-segment envelope).

While the amplitude of a carrier operator has a direct effect on the volume of a sound, the volume of a modulator operator is responsible for the modulation rate—in other words, the harmonic richness of the modulated signal. A simple combination of the two sinusoidal operators (that is, one modulator plus one carrier) makes it possible to obtain an infinite number of complex waveforms. Figure 5.15 below shows how Algorithm 32 of the Yamaha DX7 lets you use additive synthesis.

. . . .

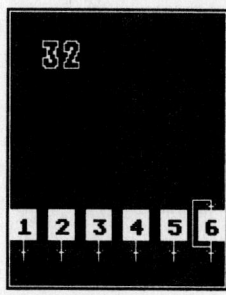

FIGURE 5.15: *Algorithm 32 of the DX7 is an exception. Thanks to its use of six sinusoidal carrier oscillators, it lets you use the additive synthesis procedure to create a sound.*

In the same way as additive synthesis, FM synthesis can manage without filters, because the harmonic content (that is, the timbre) of a sound is determined by the combination of carriers and modulators. The pitch and amplitude envelopes work exactly the same way they do in subtractive synthesis, as shown in Figure 5.16 below.

Some FM synthesizers enhance this method by offering not only sinusoidal waveforms but also more complex waveforms, as shown in Figure 5.17-A and Figure 5.17-B below.

Vector Synthesis

In vector synthesis (which is the method used in particular by the Sequential Circuits Prophet VS, the Korg WS, and the Yamaha SY22), the oscillator consists of four waveforms whose amplitude can be modified in real time. Each waveform is represented by a pole, with the position of a control handle (i.e., the joystick) determining the volume. When the joystick

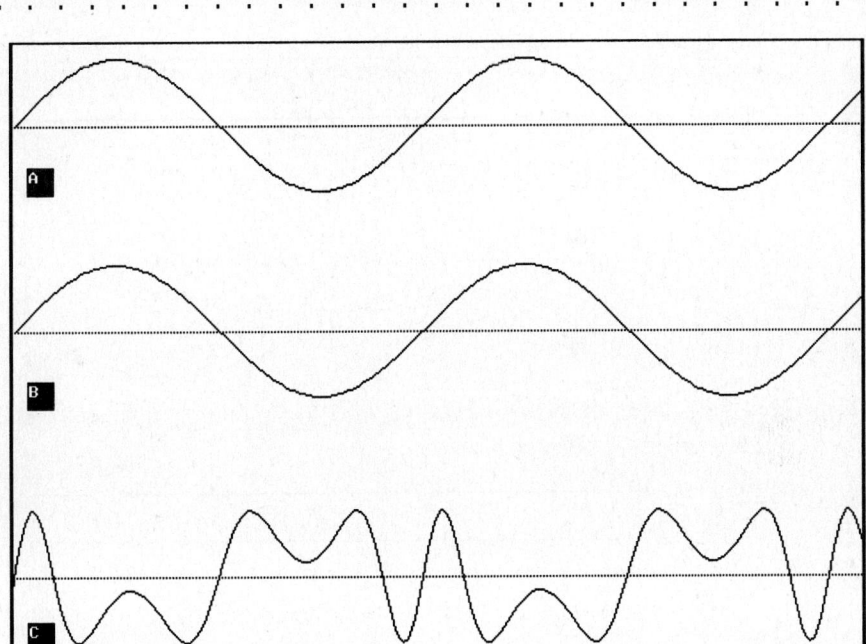

FIGURE 5.16: *Waveform C corresponds to sinusoidal waveform B, whose pitch is modulated by the amplitude of sinusoidal waveform A.*

is in the central position, the four waveforms are mixed in equal proportions, as shown in Figure 5.18 below.

The movements imparted to the joystick by the user can be stored in memory and reproduced every time a key is pressed on the keyboard.

Wave Tables

The principle behind wave tables is simply the idea that waveforms can be strung together, or concatenated, either with the close harmonics for a given played note (as in the PPG and Waldorf Microwave instruments) or without them (as in the Korg WS). This concatenation is done by

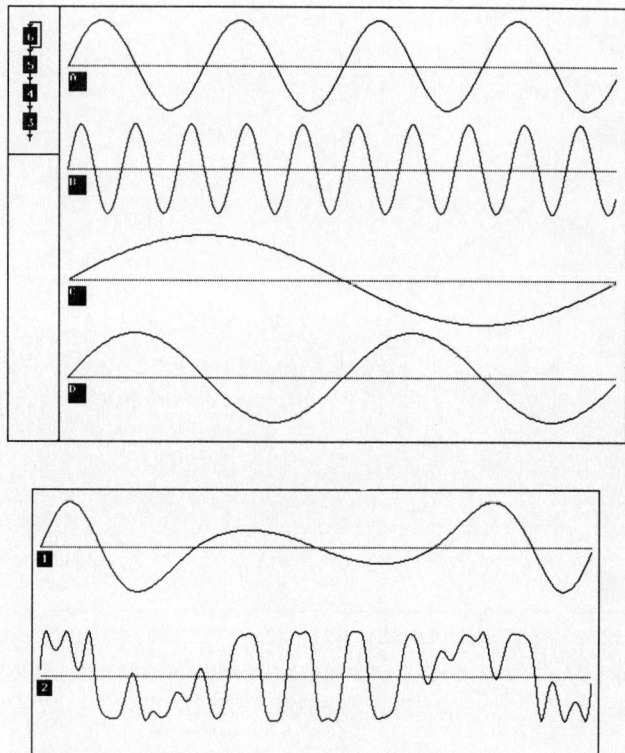

FIGURE 5.17: *This algorithm branch consists of a carrier (whose ratio is equal to 1) and three modulators (whose ratios are equal to 0.5, 5, and 2, respectively). Waveform 1 corresponds to sinusoidal waveform B, whose pitch is modulated by the amplitude of sinusoidal waveform A. Waveform 2 corresponds to sinusoidal waveform C, whose pitch is modulated by the amplitude of sinusoidal waveform 1—that is, it corresponds to waveform B as modulated by waveform A. Waveform 3, which is the final result of this algorithm, corresponds to sinusoidal waveform D, whose pitch is modulated by the amplitude of sinusoidal waveform 2—that is, it corresponds to waveform C as modulated by waveform B as modulated by waveform A.*

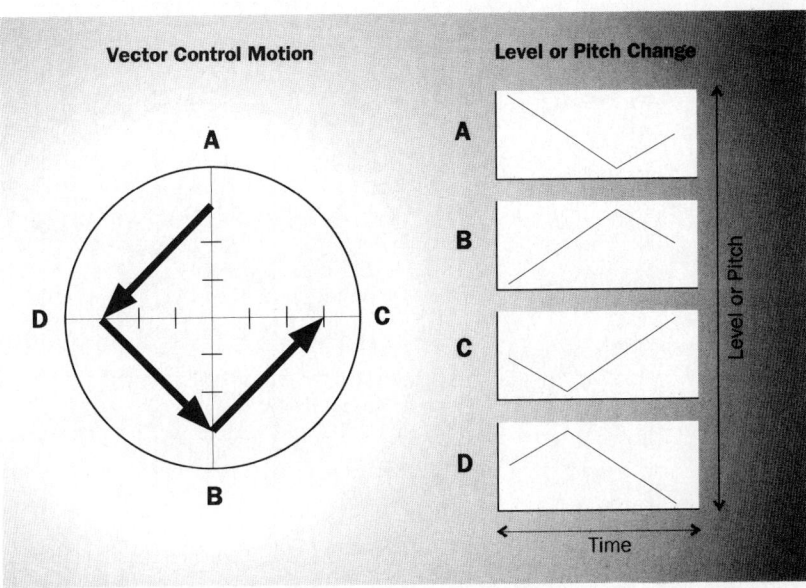

FIGURE 5.18: *In vector synthesis, the position of the joystick has a dynamic effect on the volume of the four waveforms.*

programming the duration of each of the waveforms, along with an optional *crossfade.* The wave table for the Waldorf Microwave expander is shown in Figure 5.19 below.

Sampling

Instead of synthesizing a waveform, a sampler records and stores an actual sound in memory. This procedure, which is also known as analog-to-digital conversion, relies on a module known as an ADC (analog-to-digital converter). The procedure consists of converting an audio signal

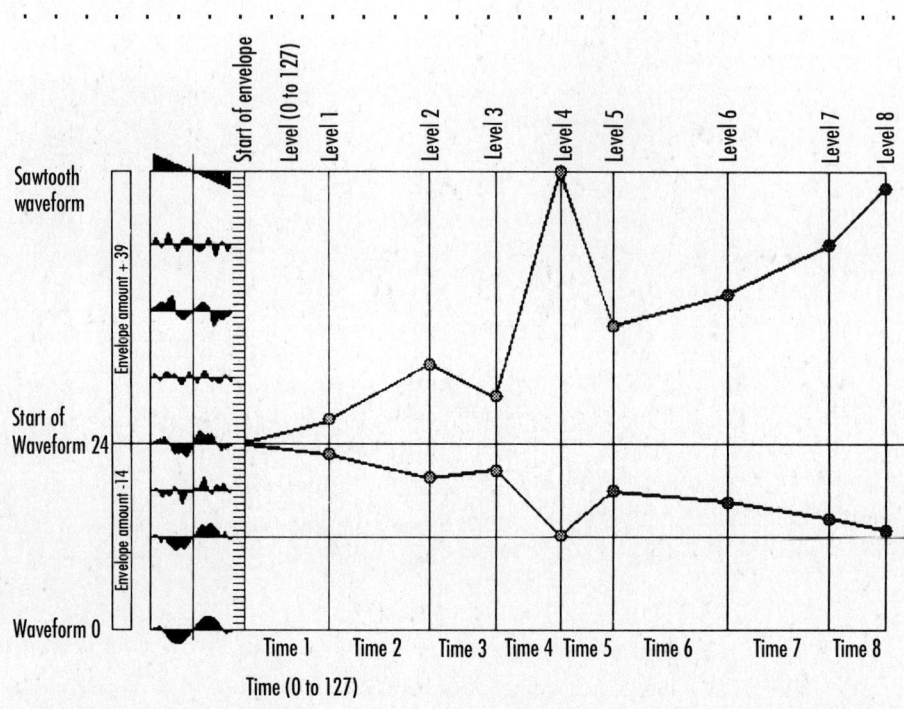

FIGURE 5.19: *The wave table for the Waldorf Microwave expander is read starting with Wave-form 24, which is then scanned as a function of an eight-segment envelope. (This figure shows two envelope curves.)*

into a series of numbers—in other words, measuring the amplitude of the signal at regular intervals. These numbers are then handled the same way as in digital synthesis. Specifically, they're read by an oscillator, processed by various modules (filters, envelope generators, LFOs, etc.), and then converted back into an analog audio signal by a DAC (digital-to-analog converter).

The Sampling Rate

The sampling rate corresponds to the number of time-slices in one second (i.e., the number of signal-amplitude measurements made in a second). For instance, a frequency of 44.1 KHz indicates that the sound is analyzed more than forty thousand times a second.

The sampling rate and the pass-band of the signal are both expressed in Hertz. These parameters are interconnected by the Nyquist theorem, which states that the analog-to-digital conversion of a sound whose highest frequency is equal to X Hz requires a sampling clock frequency of at least 2X. If this is not the case, then a phenomenon known as *folding* occurs. This phenomenon is illustrated in Figure 5.20 below.

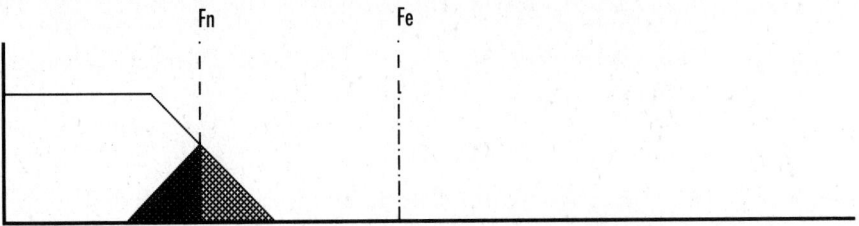

The signal to be sampled does not exceed the Nyquist frequency; therefore, no aliasing occurs.

The signal to be recorded does exceed the Nyquist frequency; therefore, an aliasing phenomenon is observed.

Fe is the sampling frequency

Fn is the Nyquist frequency (that is, half of Fe)

FIGURE 5.20: *The folding phenomenon*

For instance, for a sampling frequency of 30,000 Hz (and therefore with a Nyquist frequency of 15,000 Hz), a 16,000 Hz signal would be "folded" or converted into a 14,000 Hz signal. Likewise, a 22,000 Hz signal would be folded into an 8,000 Hz signal, and so on. This phenomenon is known as *aliasing*. As a result, in order to cover the theoretical range of frequencies which the human ear can hear (that is, from 20 Hz to 20,000 Hz), the sampling rate should be greater than 40,000 Hz.

In order to avoid aliasing, samplers use an anti-folding filter (in other words, a low-pass filter with an extremely steep slope) located upstream of the analog-to-digital converter. They also use a method known as *oversampling*. Instead of sampling at a rate of 2X, you sample at some greater multiple of X; usually a binary multiple (i.e., a power of 2). For instance, instead of sampling at 44.1 KHz, which is standard for work with compact discs, you could follow the modern practice of using a much faster converter and sampling at a higher rate.

Resolution

During each analysis (that is, during each time-slice of the selected signal), the amplitude is converted from analog form into an approximate numeric value. This value is generally known as a *sample*, although it's sometimes also referred to as a *digital word*. Figure 5.21 below shows a typical example of analog-to-digital conversion during sampling.

The precision of this conversion depends on the range of numbers available to the sampler for representing these values. Like any computer, the sampler stores these values in the form of a given number of bits (8, 12, 16, etc.).

Assume that each sample is quantified as a single 8-bit byte. In this case, the maximum amplitude would have a value of 255 (11111111), and the minimum amplitude would have a value of 0 (00000000). For the sake of simplicity, use positive and negative values, depending on whether the

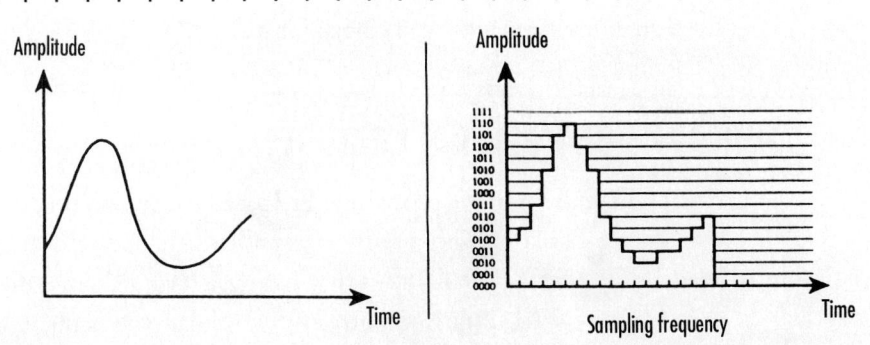

FIGURE 5.21: *During sampling, the analog signal is converted to a digital signal*

amplitude is greater than or less than zero. In such a case, the absolute values 0 (minimum amplitude) and 255 (maximum amplitude) would be represented by the relative values +127 and −127, respectively.

Now imagine that each sample is expressed in the form of 16 bits instead of 8 bits. In this case, you go from 256 values to 65,536 values. What this means is that the amplitude of a single given sample is measured over a range that runs from −32,768 to +32,768, with a correspondingly significant increase in the accuracy of the analysis.

In a sampler, the number of bits used to quantify the amplitude of a signal is known as the resolution of the signal, and each bit theoretically accounts for a dynamic increment of 6 dB. In other words, this analog-to-digital conversion converts a continuous signal, consisting of an infinite number of values, into a discontinuous signal consisting of a finite number of values. The more precise the resolution and the sampling rate are, the finer the graphing is, and the less the original signal is deformed.

The amount of memory required for digital storage of a signal is directly proportional to the accuracy of the time-slicing. For 16-bit resolution (i.e., resolution in the form of two bytes) at a sampling rate of 44,100 Hz, you'd need a

total of 88,200 bytes to store one second of sound. In other words, you'd need an entire megabyte of memory for just under 12 seconds of music.

Synthesis on Personal Computers

Because digital synthesis procedures are based solely on numerical calculations, some developers began offering synthesizers in the form of software. As a result, programs exist that can transform PCs into all kinds of synthesizers—FM, additive, subtractive, modular, you name it. Figure 5.22 shows how SoftSynth software simulates an additive or FM synthesizer.

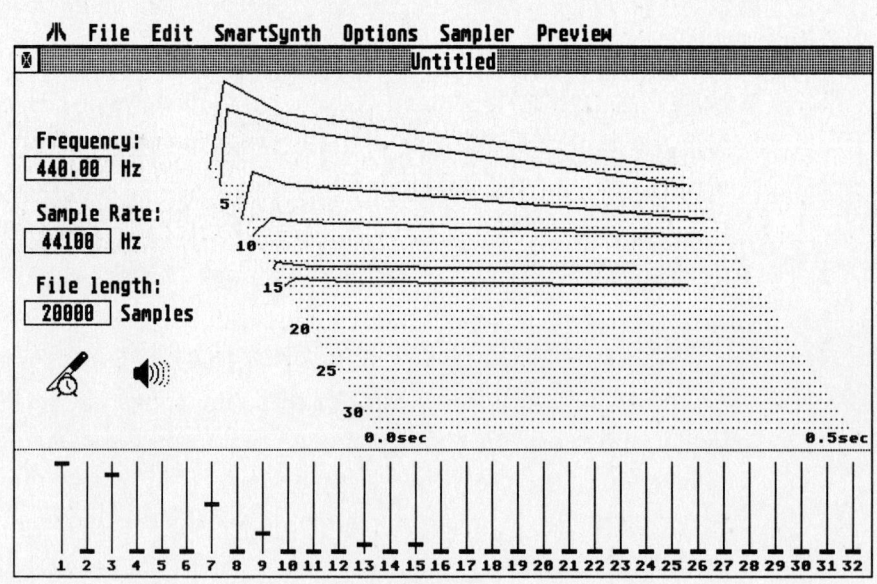

FIGURE 5.22: *The SoftSynth software simulates an additive or FM synthesizer. The result of the calculations is then sent to a sampler.*

Once a sound has been computed, it's sent via MIDI to a sampler, particularly with the help of the so-called Sample Dump Standard transfer protocol. Going in the opposite direction, this transfer makes it possible to recover through software a sample sent by the sampler, so that the sample can be used as a basic oscillator waveform in conjunction with any desired synthesis method.

Sample Readers

At present, most instruments are replacing the conventional waveforms used by digital synthesizers with sampled waveforms. A sample reader consists of read-only memory (ROM) in which a given number of previously digitized sounds are stored.

The Korg M and T series instruments (the M1, M1R, M3R, EXM1R, T1, T2, T3, et al.), the E-mu Proteus and Proteus XR, the Roland U series (U110, U220, U20, et al.), the Yamaha SY55, and the Ensoniq SQ1, VFX, and VFX-SD are examples of sample readers. In addition to their acoustic instrument sounds, most of these devices also include sampled analog waveforms (such as square-wave signals, sawtooth signals, and pulse-width signals). Some devices of this type are equipped with random-access memory (RAM), which, although it doesn't let you record your own samples, does let you transfer them, either via the Sample Dump Standard or by reading floppy disks from a sampler. (The Kurzweil 2000, which is a combined sampler and sample reader, is a notable exception to this rule.)

Hybrid Synthesis

Hybrid synthesis combines digital synthesis (the additive kind, for Roland D series instruments, and the FM kind, for Yamaha SY series instruments) and sample reading.

For example, in the case of the Roland D50 (which was one of the first instruments of this type), it's primarily the attack transients that reside in ROM, along with various "noises" and sound loops. The transients are used to reproduce the part of the sound that's the trickiest to synthesize, while the conventional waveforms (square waves, sawtooth waves, etc.) are generally effective enough to generate the stable portion of the auditory spectrum. The Yamaha SY series instruments contain a separate sample reader and an FM-synthesis sound generator in the same unit.

Resynthesis

So far you've seen on the one hand that additive synthesis was the only procedure that could deliver absolutely any sound. On the other hand, sampling made it possible to grab any given sound exactly. In a way, resynthesis combines the advantages of these two concepts, doing it in three stages:

1 ▪ Signal sampling

2 ▪ Analysis of the signal, thanks to a Fourier transform operation that makes it possible for the signal to be broken down into a set of sinusoidal waveforms

3 ▪ Restoration of the signal, with the help of as many sinusoidal oscillators as there are harmonics derived from the preceding breakdown (in the same way as in additive synthesis)

At first glance, this procedure may seem a little odd. After all, after analysis and restoration, you should theoretically get a sound that's identical to the original sample. In reality, however, all of the power of this procedure lies in the third stage, which makes it possible to edit each component (that is, each sinusoidal waveform) of the sampled signal.

Once the analytical breakdown is done, the sampled and broken-down signal can be recreated through the allocation of one sinusoidal oscillator to each harmonic. This step makes it possible for any and all necessary modifications to be performed. Figure 5.23 below shows how you can use resynthesis software to manipulate harmonic values.

In addition to the instruments dedicated to resynthesis (such as the Axcel Technos), some sample-editing software for PCs (such as the programs available from Avalon, Passport Designs, and others) offers Fourier-breakdown algorithms. After analyzing a sound from a sampler, users can tinker with each of the harmonics (by removing them, adding them, changing their amplitude, etc.). The resulting sound can then be sent to the sampler.

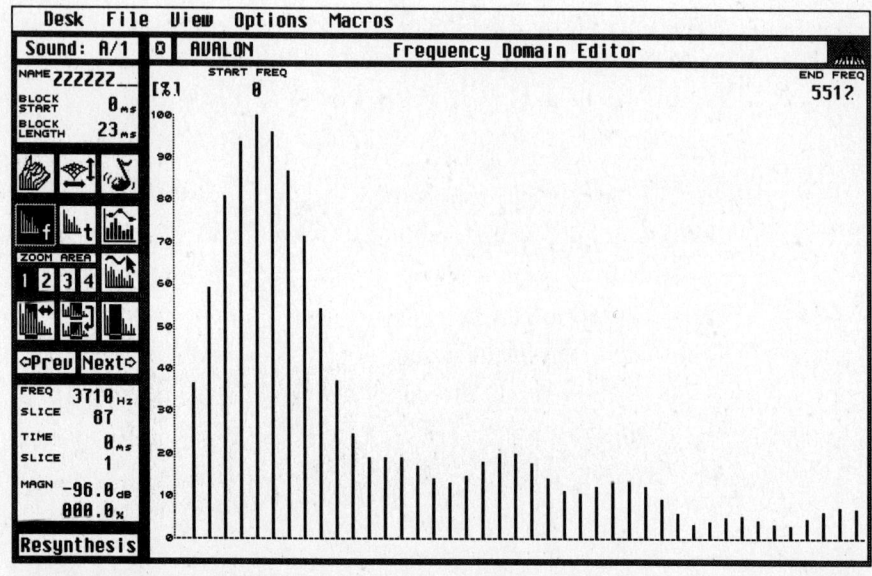

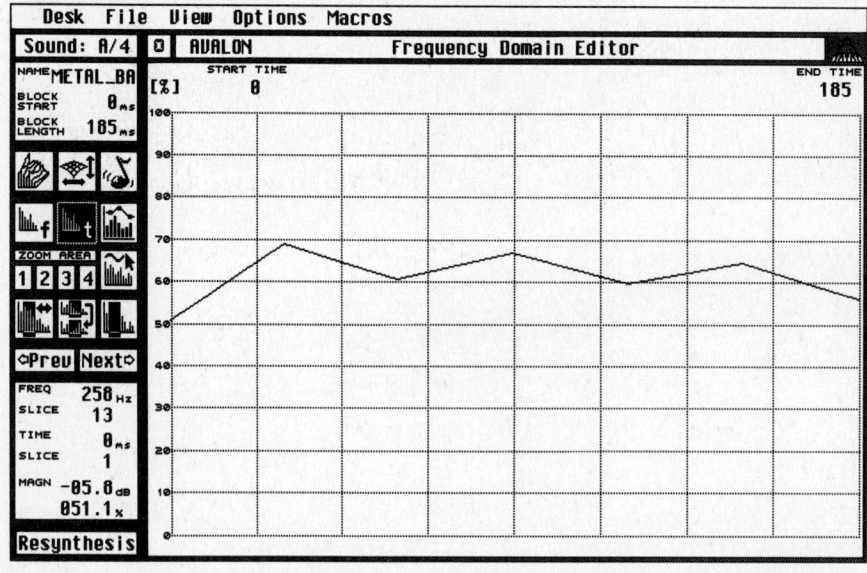

FIGURE 5.23: *After a Fourier breakdown, the resynthesis section of the Avalon sample-editing software lets you work on the development of a harmonic over time, or else on all of the harmonics of a signal at a single given time* t.

CHAPTER

6

XIII XIV XV XVI A B C D E F G H I

Sound Generators
and
Controllers

AS NOTED IN the last chapter, the controller in a MIDI instrument transforms the musician's motions into Channel messages (Note On, Pitch Bend, Control Change, Aftertouch, etc.), in order to control the sound generator, which produces the tone or tones. The interchange between controllers and sound generators is why the MIDI standard was originally created.

Typical Characteristics of Sound Generators

Like the synthesis and sampling principles discussed in Chapter 5, the topics addressed in this section provide a brief overview of some of the typical characteristics of sound generators. For further information, interested readers should consult more specialized reference tools.

Programming Synthesizers

Regardless of the sound-synthesis method used, a tone is always generated by means of parameters that act on pitch, timbre, and amplitude.
These parameters determine the harmonic content of a waveform and
also the waveform's evolution over time.

Nonprogrammable Sound Generators

Not all sound generators can be manipulated by the user. The parameter
settings for the synthesis, whose values are preprogrammed by the manufacturer and stored in ROM, are inaccessible to users.

Semi-Programmable Sound Generators

This family of instruments lets you program a limited number of parameters (such as the attack time or release time for an envelope, the cut-off
frequency of a filter, etc.). Instead of creating radically new sounds, these
instruments let you adapt existing sounds to your wishes or needs.

Programmable Sound Generators

A sound generator is said to be programmable when a user can edit the
entire set of parameters. In the earliest analog synthesizers, each parameter
was represented by a potentiometer or a switch. This way, without being
forced to turn into a sound-synthesis guru, a musician could learn how
the instrument worked, by studying the cause-and-effect relationships between the changes in parameters and the resulting sounds.

In today's sound generators, this multitude of buttons has been replaced
by a much smaller number of so-called "physical" controls associated
with a set of light-emitting diodes (LEDs) or a liquid-crystal display

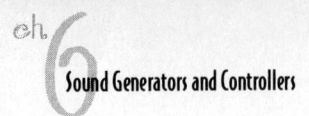

(LCD) screen. Some of these controls are dedicated to the selection of parameters (with the aid of menus), while others are meant to be used to
edit the values of parameters (for example, by means of Increment and
Decrement keys, etc.).

In spite of a less intuitive, less learning-oriented implementation, this type
of design has the advantage of increased precision (as provided for instance by the digital display of edited values). On the other hand, users
no longer have the option of experimenting quite as easily and leisurely as
before, with fast, simultaneous changes in several parameters at once.

From Monophonic to Multitimbral

The first analog synthesizers were monophonic. In other words, they let
you play only one note at a time. Furthermore, the range of the keyboard
was usually limited to three or four octaves. Among these instruments are
the Korg MS-10 and MS-20 (with 32 and 37 notes, respectively), the
Minimoog (44 notes), the Oberheim OB-1 (37 notes), the Roland SH-5
(44 notes), and the Yamaha CS-30 (44 notes). After a short transition
period with so-called duophonic systems (which let you play two notes at
once), manufacturers quickly shifted toward synthesizers that had 6-, 8-,
or 12-note polyphony (in other words, 6, 8, or 12 voices). Today, the capacity of a typical synthesizer is anywhere from 16 to 64 voices.

A synthesizer's polyphonic capability is sometimes expressed in terms of
the number of oscillators—which isn't necessarily the same as the number
of voices. For instance, the Roland D10, D110, and D20 synthesizers
have 32 oscillators; however, a single given sound (i.e., a tone) can use as
many as four of these oscillators, thereby reducing the polyphonic total
to 8 voices.

The Distribution of Polyphony

The MIDI standard clearly defines the assignment of Channel messages to the various polyphonic voices of a sound generator. However, the standard doesn't impose any rules with regard to the question of overflow (imagining, for instance, that an eight-note chord would be played by an eight-voice synthesizer, and that a ninth note would be presented before the chord was released). In fact, when an instrument receives more notes than it can play, it has the option of responding in accordance with various internal procedures, some of which are listed below.

- *Low-note priority:* in this case, the highest note is cut off.

- *High-note priority:* in this case, the lowest note is cut off.

- *Last-note priority:* in this case, the oldest note (that is, the first note that arrived) is cut off.

- *First-note priority:* in this case, the most recent note (that is, the last note that arrived) is cut off.

- *The Oberheim Xpander method:* If the number of the last note that arrives (that is, the note that's responsible for the polyphonic overflow) corresponds to the number of one of the notes that are being played, then the note that's being played is replaced by the new note.

- *The spillover or overflow method:* All of the Note On messages that are received starting with the polyphonic overflow are sent to the MIDI Out port. This way, if a second generator (the same model from the same manufacturer, with the same sound and the same MIDI channel) is connected, the polyphony of the machine will be doubled (or tripled, or quadrupled, depending on the number of sound generators in the chain).

- *The Waldorf Microwave method:* The Link mode of the Waldorf Microwave expander is an improved version of the overflow method.

The memory locations of sounds in the master unit (i.e., the buffers) are automatically collected and sent via MIDI to the slave units, along with the real-time editing changes.

- *The Kurzweil K250 method:* The Cycle mode of the K250 is a variant of the spillover method. Consider for example a setup with three K250 units: a master unit (call it "A") and two slave units ("B" and "C"). The MIDI Out port of Device A (set to MIDI Channel X) is connected to the MIDI In port of Device B (that is, Channel X + 1), and the MIDI Thru port of Device B is connected to the MIDI In port of Device C (that is, Channel X + 2). If six notes are pressed at the same time on the keyboard of Device A, then the first note will be played by Device A (via Channel X), the second note will be played by Device B (via Channel X + 1), the third note will be played by Device C (via Channel X + 2), the fourth note will be played by Device A, the fifth note will be played by Device B, and the sixth note will be played by Device C. In this mode, up to fifteen K250 units can be connected in a network.

- *The Akai S2800, S3000, S3200, and CD3000 method:* If the polyphony limit is exceeded, the sampler "steals" voices by silencing the earliest notes (i.e., by implementing last-note priority) or the slowest notes (i.e., by implementing high-velocity priority) in the lowest-priority "programs." Each "program" can be assigned to one of the following classes: "low" (i.e., minimum priority), "mid" (i.e., average priority), "high" (i.e., maximum priority), or "hold" (in which case voices can be "stolen" only on behalf of notes that are being played by the same "program").

- *The Yamaha TX802 methods:* The Yamaha TX802 expander, with 16-voice polyphony, has three reception modes:

  1. All of the Note On and Note Off messages are selected.

  2. Only the even-numbered Note On and Note Off messages are selected.

3 ▪ Only the odd-numbered Note On and Note Off messages are selected.

If two TX802 units that are set to the same sounds and that are operating on the same channels are connected, with one unit programmed to receive the even-numbered notes and the other unit programmed to receive the odd-numbered notes, the result is an instrument with 32 voice polyphony at least in the ideal case in which the even- and odd-numbered notes are equally allocated.

Multitimbral Synthesizers

In the beginning, polyphonic synthesizers didn't let you play more than one timbre at a time. In other words, these synthesizers were monotimbral. It wasn't until the first sequencers started appearing that the need to have several sonorities available at the same time on the same generator began to make itself felt. Synthesizers with this ability are called multitimbral or polytimbral.

Functionally, a multitimbral sound generator with X timbres corresponds to X independent generators. For instance, a polyphonic and multitimbral synthesizer with 16 voices and 8 timbres could be viewed as a collection of eight synthesizers with two voices each, or four synthesizers with four voices each, or one synthesizer with ten voices and another with six voices, and so on. This distribution of the various timbres and numbers of polyphonic voices depends on the allocation, as explained below.

Allocating Voices

There are two ways to distribute timbres for a given level of polyphony, namely, static allocation and dynamic allocation. In static allocation mode, the user decides at the start on the maximum number of polyphonic voices to be allotted to each sound. For instance, for a 16-voice

polyphonic instrument, you might decide to allocate eight voices for an electric piano and 8 other voices for string instruments. Operating on this principle, you can see how it would be impossible to play a nine-note piano chord, even if the strings were only using two notes.

The principle of dynamic allocation is much more subtle, in the sense that it's no longer necessary to assign arbitrarily a certain number of voices to each type of sound. In this case, the sound module is responsible for managing the real-time distribution of voices among the various selected sounds, as a function of each sound's needs, within the maximum polyphonic limits of the instrument.

Here's a summary of the major principles that are implemented by this method:

- *Static allocation:* The maximum number of voices that can be assigned to each virtual generator (that is, to each polyphonic voice) is defined beforehand by the user.

- *Dynamic allocation:* The polyphony of each virtual generator is variable, within the overall polyphonic limits of the instrument. Thanks to this so-called "floating assignment," the instrument calculates the distribution of voices in real time in order to adjust it as properly as possible among the various virtual generators being used.

- *Dynamic allocation with polyphonic reservation:* This method combines dynamic allocation with the reservation of a given number of voices (in other words, the minimum amount of polyphony that can be programmed by the user) for each of the virtual generators.

- *Dynamic allocation with priority:* If the polyphonic limit is exceeded, the generators with the lowest priority levels are affected first. For instance, in the S1000, each virtual generator (that is, each program) is associated with one of the following four priority levels: Low, Normal, High, and Hold. If the polyphonic limit is exceeded, a voice executed by the program in Hold mode can only be removed by a new voice intended for that same program.

The MIDI Channels

Each virtual generator in a multitimbral instrument can be programmed to receive messages on its own channel. This capability is indispensable if you want to use a sequencer. Remember, the management of the reception of Voice messages as a function of MIDI channels and polyphony is governed by Mode messages.

Horizontal Mapping

In addition to allocating a MIDI channel number, you can also set the response of each virtual generator in a multitimbral instrument as a function of the note range. To do that, each virtual generator has to be assigned the two MIDI note numbers that correspond to the lower and upper limits of the interval within which that generator should recognize and accept Voice messages.

For instance, in programming a piano sound and a violin sound in such a way that they responded in the range from C0 to B2 and from C3 to G8 respectively, with both sounds responding over the same MIDI channel, you'd control first one sound and then the other as a function of the note number played on the keyboard. This procedure gives you different timbres distributed over different, possibly overlapping zones.

Vertical Mapping

Some multitimbral instruments let you set the response of each virtual generator as a function of a velocity zone. To do that, each virtual generator has to be assigned the two Velocity values that correspond to the

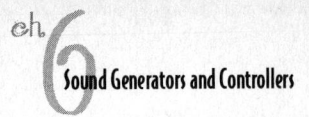

lower and upper limits of the interval within which that generator should recognize and accept Voice messages.

For instance, in deciding that a piano sound should respond in the velocity range from 1 to 63, and a violin sound in the velocity range from 64 (described in Chapter 8) to 127, with both sounds responding over the same MIDI channel, you would control first one sound and then the other as a function of the striking speed of the note played on the keyboard. This method gives you access to timbres distributed over different, optionally overlapping vertical zones.

Outputs

Almost all monotimbral instruments have stereophonic outputs. The sound is first enlarged, thanks to any of a large group of procedures (Chorus, Effects Processor, etc.), before being sent simultaneously to the left and right outputs. One of these two outputs is usually indicated as a mono output. This means that starting at the moment when the instrument physically detects the fact that no jack is connected to the other output, the left and right signals are added in order to be sent to this mono output. This feature gives you the choice of working equally easily in mono or in stereo.

Multitimbral instruments also have one of these so-called global stereo outputs. The output of each and any virtual generator can be directed toward this output if the pan and the volume of the generator in question is programmed beforehand. Furthermore, many multitimbral instruments have supplementary outputs that let each virtual generator be handled independently from a mixing console. These outputs can be in the form of mono outputs (known as "separate outputs," because each one is linked to one of the virtual generators) or supplementary stereo outputs that are used the same way as the global stereo outputs.

MIDI Expressiveness

Regardless of a sound generator's performance parameters, there's nothing (except possibly an exhaustive study of the operating manual) that indicates beforehand the way in which the various MIDI messages can have a real-time effect on the way a sound behaves. In fact, although Pitch Bend, Aftertouch, and other Control Changes offer enormously broad possibilities with regard to how the dynamic evolution of a sound can be controlled, each manufacturer uses these parameters as it sees fit.

These characteristics, which aren't easy to find (the fact that they're indicated on the MIDI implementation chart doesn't really describe the role they play!), nevertheless do constitute selection criteria that can be decisive when it comes to buying an instrument. Appendix F describes how various instruments, such as the Ensoniq VFX-SD, use MIDI messages to control the parameters of a sound.

Test Procedures

The operating system of most MIDI devices includes hidden functions, such as reinitializations, the display of version numbers, test procedures (including diagnostic aids for use in case of failures—the role of these aids is to verify the modules currently in use, such as memory, the LCD screen, input and outputs, converters, etc.), and other functions.

Appendix G explains how some of these procedures, which aren't often documented in users' manuals, are launched. (In most cases all you have to do is press certain keys simultaneously, sometimes while turning on the device.) Handle them with all due care if you want to avoid unpleasant surprises!

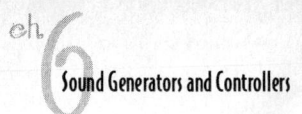
Controllers

By definition, a controller is an interface whose job is to convert a musician's gestures and movements into MIDI messages in order to drive sound generators. By extension, this job also includes various other energy sources, such as lights and images. In their latest form, controllers look a lot like keyboards. There are several reasons for this, including the fact that keyboard instruments are among the most widely used instruments; the fact that they are still fairly easy to use, because pressure on a key is sufficient to produce the proper note; and the fact that the harmonic structure of a keyboard is linear (i.e., a series of semitones). All of these considerations make a keyboard a tool that's ideally well suited to composition and orchestration work, as well as to other musical tasks.

MIDI Keyboards

In the beginning, each sound generator had its own control keyboard. This isn't necessary today, because MIDI makes it possible to drive several generators from a single controller. Hence the success of expanders, which represent a clear savings in terms of space and also in terms of money. As a result, many manufacturers are selling sound generators in both keyboard and expander versions. In fact, some machines are available only in the expander version.

Conversely, master keyboards have recently appeared. These devices have no sound generators and therefore are mute. As a result, their performance (with regard to touch and also with regard to their MIDI characteristics) is generally far superior to that of keyboards that are equipped with sound generators.

Here, then, is a brief overview of some of the functions and features of sound-generator keyboards and master keyboards.

Sound-Generator Keyboards

The functions and features of this type of keyboard, which is primarily dedicated to controlling its internal sound generator, are necessarily more limited than those of a master keyboard, which by definition is better adapted to driving a MIDI network.

The current range of a MIDI keyboard is 61 notes, or five octaves (from C1 to C6). Although wildly narrower than the overall MIDI range (which consists of 127 notes), this range is still broad enough to be expressive. However, in order to gain access to a broader MIDI range, some keyboards are transposable. There are also smaller ones (such as the Roland Juno 1, with 49 keys over four octaves), and of course much larger ones (such as the Yamaha DX5 and the Roland D70, with 76 notes over six and a half octaves).

With just a few exceptions, the touch of this type of keyboard is very light. This indicates that—unlike the keys on a master keyboard—the keys on a sound-generator keyboard aren't weighted. Likewise with regard to the keys, there are two expression parameters: Velocity (that is, the pressing speed, and optionally the release speed), and Aftertouch (that is, either Channel Aftertouch or Polyphonic Key Pressure). A keyboard that's sensitive to pressure velocity (in other words, the speed with which pressure is applied to a key) is said to be "dynamic." If this is not the case, then the keyboard invariably emits a constant value that's equal to 64 (40H). With regard to Aftertouch, this feature (if present) is usually monophonic (per channel).

In addition to the expression parameters triggered by notes, so-called integrated keyboards offer at least one modulation wheel, one Pitch Bend wheel, and a Sustain pedal. Some keyboards provide additional functions and features that more properly belong in the domain of master keyboards (for instance, split zones per channel during transmission, potentiometers that can be assigned to various different messages, etc.).

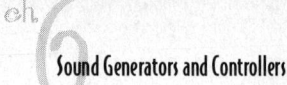

Master Keyboards

Master keyboards, which are also known as *control keyboards* or *command keyboards,* have the particular feature of not producing any sounds at all. On the other hand, these keyboards often have a weighted touch, and include quite a few functions and features designed to let them drive a network of MIDI expanders efficiently and effectively. These features and functions make master keyboards particularly well suited to stage work or for use by musicians who want the benefit of MIDI but the feel of an acoustic piano.

One of the usual major advantages of a master keyboard is that it's a lot like a piano. It has a range of 76 or 88 notes and, depending on the model, its keys are to some extent weighted. So that users can adapt themselves accurately to how each master keyboard works, the velocity response curve of these instruments is usually programmable (either logarithmically or in a linear manner), as is the aftertouch response curve (which may optionally be polyphonic).

Apart from modulation and pitch-bend wheels, some master keyboards give you access to various pedals (for volume control, incrementation of configuration memory spaces, etc.), along with definable potentiometers or faders that can make any given parameter evolve in real time (as is the case with Control Change messages) and switches that can transmit different message strings (such as Program Change messages, for reconfiguring a network, System Exclusive (SysEx) messages previously received and stored in a memory location reserved for that purpose, etc.). In order to drive sequencers and drum machines, master keyboards sometimes include an internal MIDI clock, with tempo settings that can be coordinated with the Start, Stop, and Continue keys.

Keyboard Mapping

Any master keyboard worthy of the name should be able to drive several sound generators in real time. To do that, the master keyboard has to be divided geographically into as many zones as there are expanders to be controlled. Each of these zones is characterized by an upper limit (that is, its highest note), a lower limit (that is, its lowest note), and a transmission channel (over which the appropriate Voice messages for this zone can be sent). This technique is known as *mapping*.

For example, imagine that a keyboard transmits on Channel 1 between notes C0 and B2, on Channel 2 between notes C3 and B3, on Channel 4 between notes C4 and G4, and so on. The notes that mark the boundaries between zones (in this example, C3 and G4) are known as separation points or split points.

In addition to mapping (that is, horizontal separations), such divisions are sometimes made according to velocity (in which case they're referred to as vertical separations, or velocity splits). So you can imagine that a keyboard transmits on Channel 1 between velocities 1 and 40, on Channel 2 between velocities 41 and 64, on Channel 3 between velocities 65 and 127, and so on. These two methods can even be combined, and the various zones can be allowed to overlap (in a technique known as *crossfading*). Yet further, if the master keyboard is equipped with several MIDI outputs, you can assign any particular zone to any particular output.

Other Controllers and Acoustic Instruments

Many manufacturers have tried, with varying degrees of success, to sell controllers that imitate the character and style of other conventional instruments (such as MIDI guitars, MIDI brasses and woodwinds, etc.), in order to let as many musicians as possible drive sound generators with the skills and techniques of their respective instruments.

In a similar way, some manufacturers have oriented their marketing and sales efforts toward the MIDIfication of acoustic instruments. This approach has the advantage of preserving the physical contact that musicians are used to, as opposed to what happens with an imitation of an instrument realized in a synthetic material, which necessarily involves changing and adapting your playing style. The superior touch qualities of an acoustic instrument are derived directly from the physical structure of the instrument; so, no matter how refined it may become, a master keyboard will (probably!) never be the equal of a real piano, for the good and simple reason that the weighted touch of a real piano is a direct result of the way the instrument works (with keys that trigger the action of hammers, which in turn strike the strings, and so on).

Action Conversion and Pitch Conversion

In any event, two very different methods make it possible to convert an instrumentalist's actions into MIDI messages. The first method directly transforms an action into the equivalent message, and the second method works by means of pitch conversion. Assume that a musician presses a C on a keyboard. The conversion method analyzes the pitch of the note as captured by a microphone, while the first method (which is much easier to implement) detects the application of pressure to the C key by means of a mechanical contact-sensing device. In each case, the corresponding MIDI message is sent.

The choice of which method to use is dictated by the way the instrument works. It's necessary to distinguish the instruments (such as pianos and accordions) on which it's physically possible to create a contact as a result of a generated note from the instruments whose physical structure is incompatible with this method. Naturally, this second group of instruments includes all of the unfretted instruments (such as violins, cellos, and basses) for which the pitch depends on the position of the player's fingers on the neck of the instrument. It also includes the instruments that, once a note has been produced, let the performer modify the pitch (by changing the position of his or her fingers in a direction perpendicular to the neck of the instrument).

CHAPTER 7

XIII XIV XV XVI A B C D E F G H I

MIDI Recording:

The Basics

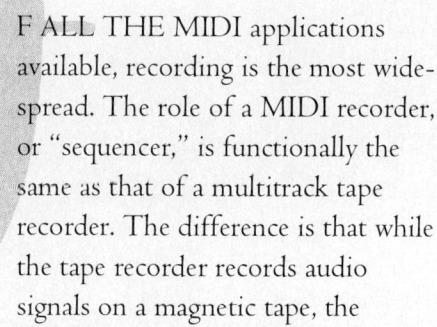

F ALL THE MIDI applications available, recording is the most widespread. The role of a MIDI recorder, or "sequencer," is functionally the same as that of a multitrack tape recorder. The difference is that while the tape recorder records audio signals on a magnetic tape, the sequencer records MIDI messages. When you make a recording with a tape recorder, the sound that comes from the instrument is recorded on the tape so that later it can be sent through an amplification system and out to speakers. But when you make a recording with the help of a sequencer, the MIDI messages that come from the instrument are stored in memory so that during the reading stage, they can be sent to sound generators.

Multitrack Recorders and Sequencers

A multitrack tape recorder can have anywhere from 3 to 64 tracks. Multitrack tape recorders let you record instruments on separate tracks, either simultaneously or successively. Successive recording makes it possible to develop a musical production track by track. For instance, the drummer can start recording on Track 1, then the bass player can start recording on Track 2 while listening to Track 1, then the keyboard player can record on Track 3 while listening to Track 1 and Track 2, and so on.

As a result, if one of the three players makes a mistake, there's no reason why he or she can't re-record that track, without requiring the other two musicians to play their parts again. In a similar way, with the help of sound generators, a single musician can take the place of the different instrumentalists and build a complete musical piece, track by track, without any collaboration from any other musicians.

The fact that sequencers record MIDI messages instead of sound has several advantages. For instance, there's no signal degradation, because, by definition, the signal isn't what's recorded. The problems having to do with the quality of reproduction that are inherent in the physical characteristics of magnetic media (tape hiss, the loss of dynamics and of the analog pass-band, and unrecoverable losses of digital data) don't exist in MIDI. In addition, sequencers let you edit a performance after the fact. This editing capability is the major advantage of sequencers.

The Two Main Kinds of Sequencers

There are two kinds of sequencers: *software sequencers* and *hardware sequencers*.

Software sequencers are programs that run on computers equipped with MIDI interfaces. These sequencers take advantage of a computer's large screen and graphic environment that are especially well suited to editing.

Hardware sequencers are boxes dedicated exclusively to MIDI recording. When it comes to editing, these devices are relatively unfriendly, because their tiny LCD screens can't display enough information to give users an overall view of what's going on. On the other hand, however, hardware sequencers have the advantage of portability.

In this category, drum machines (also called "rhythm boxes") combine a sound generator that replicates percussion instruments and a hardware sequencer that, although relatively primitive, is perfectly adequate for this kind of application. Finally, some manufacturers combine hardware sequencers with multitimbral synthesizers. This kind of all-in-one product is known as a *workstation*.

To make the editing process easier, sequencers try to incorporate the various elements of a tape recorder, such as tracks, transport commands (Record, Play, Stop, Wind, Rewind, etc.), VU meters, and other functions (Mute, Solo, etc.) into the interface.

Real-Time and Step Mode Recording

Sequencers offer two ways to record MIDI messages: in real time and step mode.

In real-time recording, the sequencer acts like a tape recorder. It directly records the messages it receives at its MIDI In port from a keyboard or from any other MIDI controller. This is the most commonly used method.

In step mode recording, the "performance" is built gradually. With the help of the computer (that is, via the keyboard, mouse, etc.), the user "enters" the MIDI events one after another with the help of an editing screen. Each event is characterized by a position, a type (i.e., a status), and by one or more values (i.e., data). If the event is a note, it's also characterized by a duration.

More efficient, although reserved for note messages, is the so-called "mixed" step mode method, which combines manual data entry (that is, the acquisition of positions and duration from the computer) and data entry via MIDI (that is, the acquisition of pitches and velocities from a keyboard or from any other controller). Step mode recording generally uses the same tools that are used when a real-time recording is edited.

There are hundreds of hardware and software sequencers, which is why this chapter doesn't presume to compile an exhaustive list of the functions and features that each of them implements. Instead, the intention of the following sections is to provide an overview of the options that are available in MIDI recording.

Basic Principles

Regardless of how it's put together, a MIDI sequencer consists of a set of functions that can be divided into three distinctly different categories, namely, *recording*, *editing*, and *playback*. Before examining these categories, however, it's worthwhile first to take a look at how MIDI messages are stored in computer memory, and in doing so consider the concepts of tempo, time signature, clock, and resolution.

The Data Format

Assume that the MIDI Out port of a keyboard is connected to the MIDI In port of a sequencer. Assume further that you set the sequencer to Record mode and play the notes C3, D3, and E3 one after the other. The sequencer's job is to memorize these messages and the time intervals that separate them. For example:

35 milliseconds	The interval between the start of recording and the C3 Note On message
90H 3CH 40H	C3 Note On/Channel 1/Velocity 64

500 milliseconds	The interval separating the C3 Note On message from the C3 Note Off message
90H 3CH 00H	C3 Note Off message/Channel 1
59 milliseconds	The interval separating the C3 Note Off message from the D3 Note On message
90H 3EH 40H	D3 Note On message/Channel 1/Velocity 64
450 milliseconds	The interval separating the D3 Note On message from the D3 Note Off message
90H 3EH 00H	D3 Note Off message/Channel 1
72 milliseconds	The interval separating the D3 Note Off message from the E3 Note On message
90H 40H 40H	E3 Note On message/Channel 1/Velocity 64
512 milliseconds	The interval separating the E3 Note On message from the E3 Note Off message
90H 40H 00H	E3 Note Off message/Channel 1

Once recorded, the sequencer can play back the passage by sending the data to the Out port, which is connected to the MIDI In port of a sound generator. The sequencer observes the time intervals separating each of these notes from the other notes.

Tempo and Time Signature

In actuality, the sequencer doesn't count the intervals between two messages in terms of milliseconds. Instead, it reckons time in terms of the number of pulses per quarter-note, as expressed in the form of *ticks* or ppq. The range and accuracy of tempo settings vary from one sequencer to another. Generally speaking, however, the average range is from 40 to 240 quarter-notes per minute, accurate to the unit (40, 41, 42, ..., 239, 240). Some sequencers offer faster or slower metronome speeds, and also finer subdivisions, which are especially well suited to applications with demanding synchronization requirements (for instance, the needs of frame-related music, or the slaving of the sequencer's tempo to an external source, etc.). These subdivisions can be as small as a thousandth of a unit (for a tempo of 120,579 quarter-notes per minute!).

Thanks to this method of counting in terms of ticks, sequencers aren't bound by an absolute time reference. Users can modify the tempo (for instance, in order to perform a tricky passage more slowly) during play back as well as while the piece is being recorded.

In addition to the tempo, the *time signature*, which indicates how many beats there are in a measure and what kind of note gets one beat, also has to be set. Some sequencers are limited to simple time signatures, such as 2/4, 4/4, 6/8, etc., while other sequencers handle odd meters, such as 5/4, 7/8, 13/2, (and mixed meters). Furthermore, you can use tempo changes and signature changes within the same piece, either manually (by acquiring values and positions) or (and this applies only to tempo) in real time, by using a mouse to modify the tempo value as displayed onscreen, or by keeping time by means of a MIDI keyboard, etc.

Resolution

Resolution refers to the division of a quarter-note into a given number of ticks. A tick is the unit the sequencer uses to count the interval that separates two MIDI messages that it receives successively. The greater the resolution, the more faithful the rhythmic reconstruction of the recorded data.

In the same way as for the range and accuracy of the tempo, resolution is different with each sequencer. The most popular values are 48, 96, 192,

384, and 768 subdivisions of the quarter-note. Table 7.1 below summarizes the minimum time intervals that a sequencer can detect at different tempos and at different resolutions.

TABLE 7.1: *Minimum Detectable Time Intervals at Various Tempos and Resolutions (in milliseconds)*

QUARTER-NOTE RESOLUTION	TEMPO, IN QUARTER-NOTES PER SECOND	DURATION OF A QUARTER-NOTE	DURATION OF A TICK
48	60	1000 ms	20.83 ms
	120	500 ms	10.42 ms
	240	250 ms	5.21 ms
96	60	1000 ms	10.42 ms
	120	500 ms	5.21 ms
	240	250 ms	2.60 ms
192	60	1000 ms	5.21 ms
	120	500 ms	2.60 ms
	240	250 ms	1.30 ms
384	60	1000 ms	2.60 ms
	120	500 ms	1.30 ms
	240	250 ms	0.65 ms
768	60	1000 ms	1.30 ms
	120	500 ms	0.65 ms
	240	250 ms	0.33 ms

At a tempo of 120 and resolution of 192 ticks to the quarter-note, the first example above would be transformed in the following way:

13 ticks	The interval between the start of recording and the C3 Note On message
90H 3CH 40H	C3 Note On/Channel 1/Velocity 64
192 ticks	The interval separating the C3 Note On message from the C3 Note Off message
90H 3CH 00H	C3 Note Off message/Channel 1
23 ticks	The interval separating the C3 Note Off message from the D3 Note On message
90H 3EH 40H	D3 Note On message/Channel 1/Velocity 64
173 ticks	The interval separating the D3 Note On message from the D3 Note Off message
90H 3EH 00H	D3 Note Off message/Channel 1
28 ticks	The interval separating the D3 Note Off message from the E3 Note On message
90H 40H 40H	E3 Note On message/Channel 1/Velocity 64
197 ticks	The interval separating the E3 Note On message from the E3 Note Off message
90H 40H 00H	E3 Note Off message/Channel 1

Of course, each time interval is rounded to the nearest tick. This error, which is known as the "quantization error," becomes more significant as the resolution decreases. Therefore, the degree of so-called "rhythmic" accuracy at which a sequence is recorded depends on this resolution.

The number of ticks separating MIDI messages from one another is stored in the sequencer's memory in the form of bytes. As a result, the higher the resolution, the faster the sequencer's memory fills up. While a total of 8 bits is enough to represent an interval of a little more than five quarter-notes at a resolution of 48 ticks (i.e., $4 \times 48 = 240$), a total of 12 bytes would be necessary to represent this same interval at a resolution of 768 ticks (i.e., $5 \times 768 = 3,940$). This calculation increases exponentially with the length of the time period separating any two given messages.

Connections

Once a musician has assimilated the principles of MIDI recording, the next thing he or she usually faces is a series of connection problems—usually without having any concrete ideas about how to connect the various instruments to the sequencer. The following examples use the term "Play mode" to refer to the training or practicing session that precedes the recording stage, in order to be able to tell the two stages apart.

The examples start with a minimal configuration consisting of a sequencer and a keyboard that includes a sound generator, as shown in Figure 7.1 below.

To make a MIDI recording, you connect the keyboard's MIDI Out port to the sequencer's MIDI In port. Once that connection has been made, messages are sent from the keyboard simultaneously to the sequencer, via the MIDI link (in order to be recorded), and to the sound generator (in order to be listened to as the keys are pressed, either in Record mode or

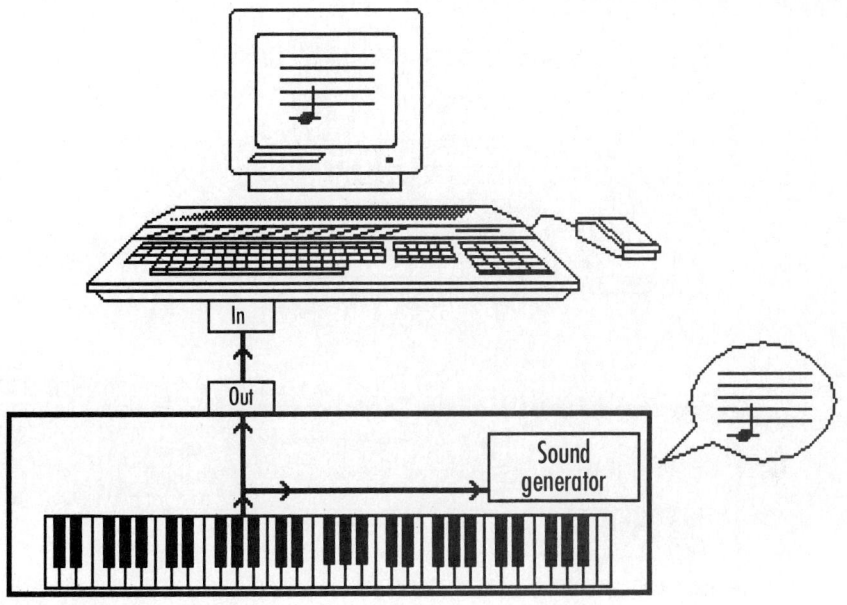

FIGURE 7.1: *In Record mode or in Play mode, the messages sent from the keyboard are transmitted simultaneously to the sound generator (via the internal link) and to the sequencer (via the MIDI link).*

in Play mode). During playback, as shown in Figure 7.2 below, the sequencer's MIDI Out port is connected to the instrument's MIDI In port so that messages recorded earlier can be replayed.

Next is a more complicated configuration. This one replaces the sound-generator-and-keyboard combination in the previous example with a master keyboard (that is, a mute keyboard), which controls a sound generator in the form of an expander, as shown in Figure 7.3 and Figure 7.4 below.

After connecting the master keyboard's MIDI Out port to the sequencer's MIDI In port (in order to record messages) and connecting the

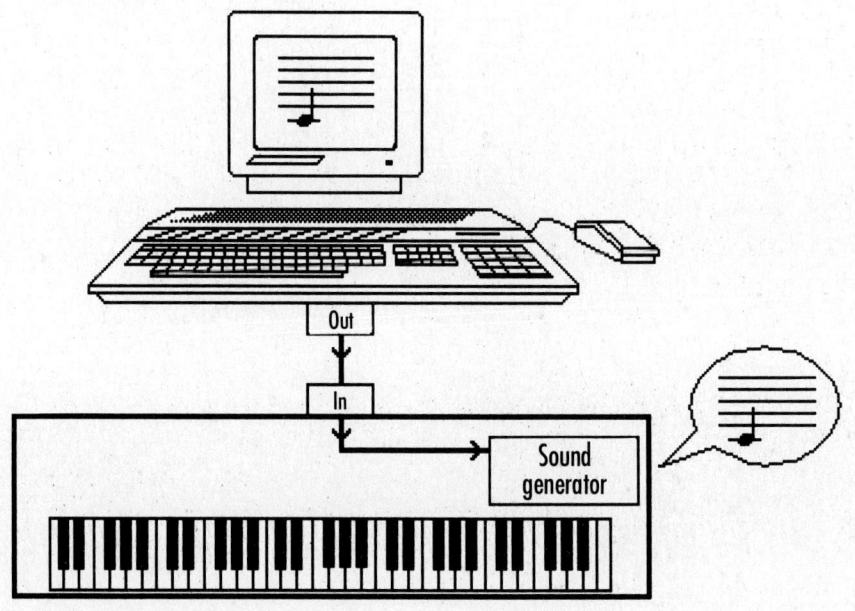

FIGURE 7.2: *In Play mode, the messages recorded by the sequencer are transmitted to the sound generator.*

sequencer's MIDI Out port to the expander's MIDI In port, you find that the expander produces no sound when the keys of the master keyboard are pressed. What's happening here is that although messages are being sent from the keyboard to the sequencer, the messages are not being transmitted to the expander. However, during the playback stage, and in spite of this so-called "mute" recording, the sequencer correctly reconstitutes the messages intended for the expander.

In order to get around this difficulty, every sequencer has a so-called "pass-through" function (known as MIDI Thru) that can be enabled or disabled and whose role is to pass along to the MIDI Out port the information that comes from the MIDI In port. This way, messages sent from

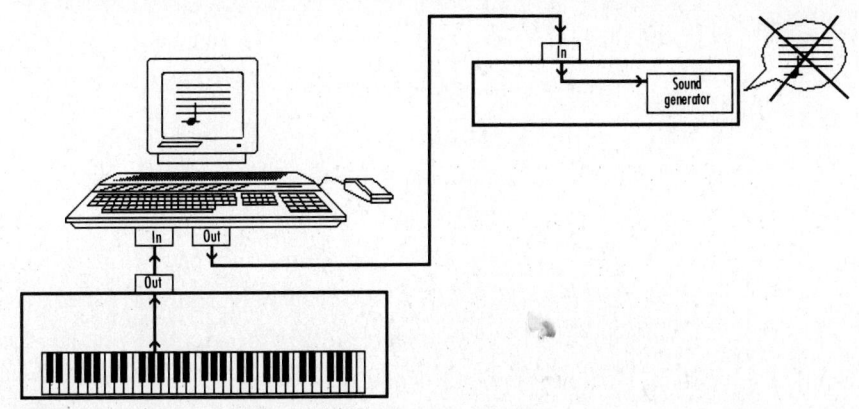

FIGURE 7.3: *In Record mode, the messages sent from the keyboard are transmitted to the sequencer. The expander stays mute.*

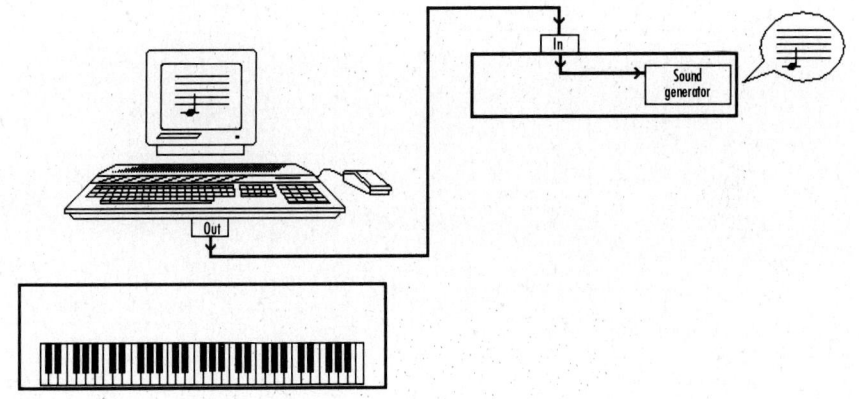

FIGURE 7.4: *In Play mode, the messages recorded by the sequencer are properly transmitted to the expander.*

the keyboard to the sequencer in either Record mode or Play mode are si-multaneously retransmitted to the expander by means of the Thru func-tion, as shown in Figure 7.5 below.

Thanks to this function, the expander is driven from the keyboard. In other words, the sequencer's MIDI Out port plays a dual role: on the one hand, it transmits the messages recorded to the expander (a task that theo-retically belongs to the MIDI Out port), and, on the other hand, it passes along to the expander the messages received from the keyboard in either Record mode or Play mode (a task that theoretically belongs to the MIDI Thru port). In short, the MIDI port at the output of a sequencer combines the functions of a MIDI Out port and a MIDI Thru port.

The next arrangement keeps the expander but replaces the master key-board with the keyboard in the first example described above (that is, the keyboard that includes a sound generator). This configuration puts you in position to record two tracks successively, with each track containing the musical material provided by one of these two instruments. In this

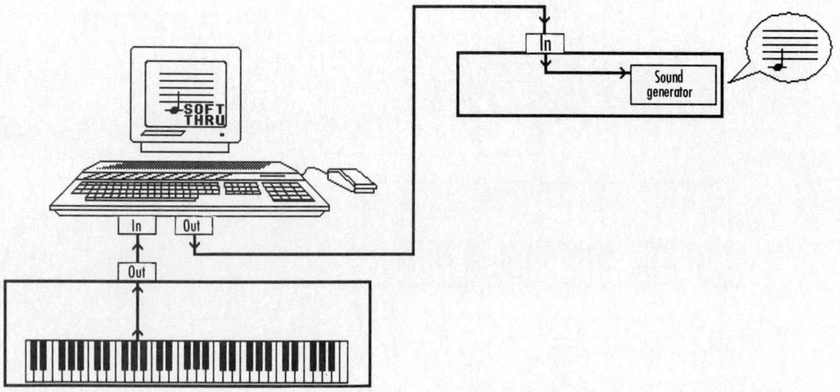

FIGURE 7.5: *In Record mode or in Play mode, the messages sent from the keyboard are transmit-ted to the sequencer, which is responsible for passing them along to the expander by means of the MIDI Thru function.*

case, the Thru function makes it possible to use two different connection arrangements, as shown in Figure 7.6 and Figure 7.7 below.

These two arrangements, which are functionally equivalent, make it possible for the keyboard's sound generator and the expander's sound generator to receive messages from the sequencer's MIDI Out port (in Play mode or Record mode).

In Record mode or in Play mode, the sequencer's Thru function has to be enabled in order for the messages sent from the keyboard to be passed along to the expander. However, the Thru function presents a size problem, because the keyboard's sound generator, which is in Record mode or Play mode, receives the same information twice.

What's happening here is that the messages sent from the keyboard are transmitted on the one hand to the sound generator via the internal link, and on the other hand to the sequencer via the MIDI link. Via the Thru

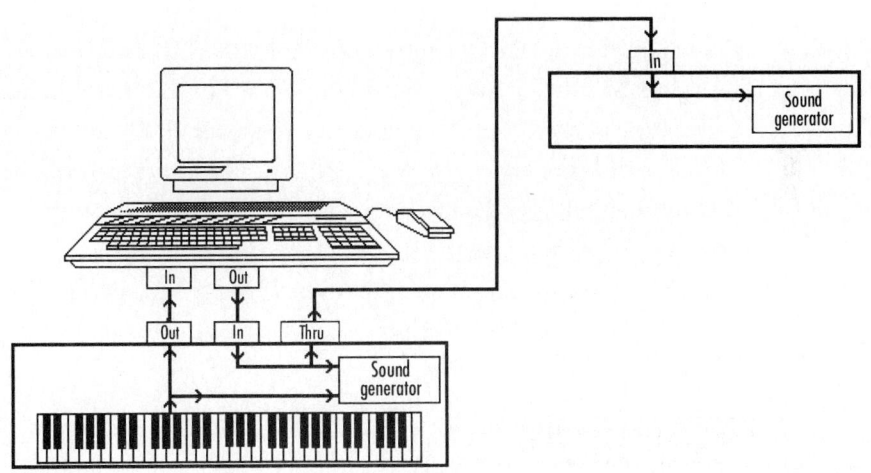

FIGURE 7.6: *The sequencer's MIDI Out port is connected to the MIDI In port of the keyboard or sound generator, whose MIDI Thru port is connected to the MIDI In port of the expander.*

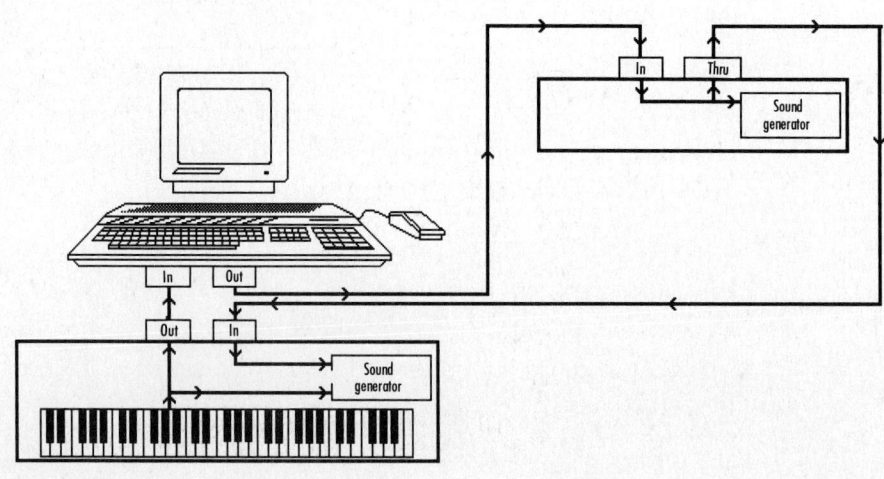

FIGURE 7.7: *The MIDI Out port of the sequencer is connected to the MIDI In port of the expander, whose MIDI Thru port is connected to the MIDI In port of the keyboard or sound generator.*

function, the sequencer is responsible for passing these messages along toward its MIDI Out port, which is connected to the MIDI In port to which the keyboard's sound generator responds. This way, the generator receives the same messages twice, either nearly simultaneously (when the Thru function operates fast enough), or several milliseconds apart (when the Thru function causes a slight delay). In this latter case, the time lapse separating two identical Note On messages received successively by the keyboard's sound generator produces an undesirable phase effect, as shown in Figure 7.8 below.

However, the major disadvantage of this duplicated reception lies in the fact that it reduces the polyphony of the instrument by half. In other

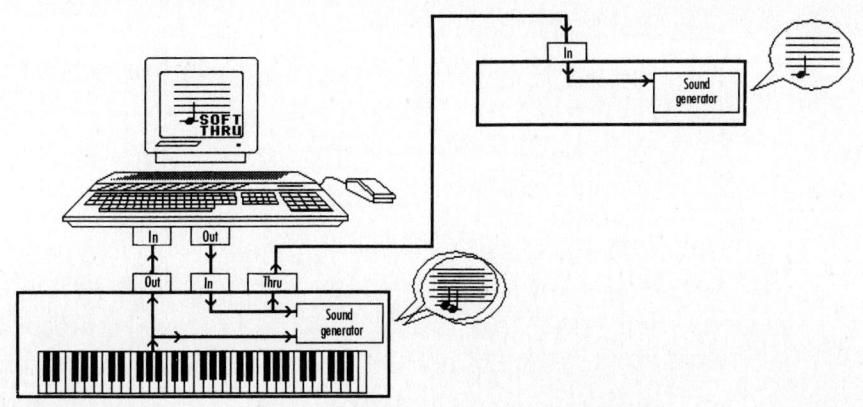

FIGURE 7.8: *In Record mode or in Play mode, the messages sent from the keyboard are transmitted to the sequencer, which is responsible for passing them along to the expander and to the keyboard's sound generator by means of the Thru function. However, there's a problem, because this generator receives the messages twice (once from the keyboard and once from the sequencer). As a result, the generator's polyphony is reduced by half, and some slight phasing effects could occur.*

words, when an arpeggiated chord consisting of four notes (for instance, C2, C3, E3, and G3) is played on the keyboard of a six-voice polyphonic instrument, the integrated sound generator will actually receive 4×2 messages (namely, C2, C2, C3, C3, E3, E3, G3, and G3), and therefore will not be able to respond to the last two notes. However, the sequencer will record only the four notes of the chord, and will reconstitute them properly by means of the sound generator in Play mode. In other words, the reduction in polyphony only occurs in Record mode or in Play mode.

At first glance, the solution would appear to lie in enabling the Thru function during recording operations that involve the expander's sound generator and disabling the Thru function during recording operations that involve the keyboard's sound generator. Fortunately, however, most of the keyboards associated with a sound generator have a Local Off mode that can be disabled, as shown in Figure 7.9 below. This step solves the problem much more elegantly, because it avoids the need for continual enabling and disabling of the Thru function. You'll see later on that Local Off mode has other advantages as well.

If the instrument being used doesn't have a Local mode, then, as mentioned above, you have to disable the sequencer's Thru function during recording operations that involve the keyboard's sound generator and re-enable the Thru function during recording operations that involve the expander's sound generator. However, during recording operations that involve the expander, the keyboard's generator goes on playing, because of the internal link. To solve this problem, you can record the expander on a first track while manually setting the volume of the keyboard's sound generator to zero, in order later on to record this sound generator on a second track (taking care, of course, to readjust the volume level). You can't do it the opposite way, because if you start by recording the

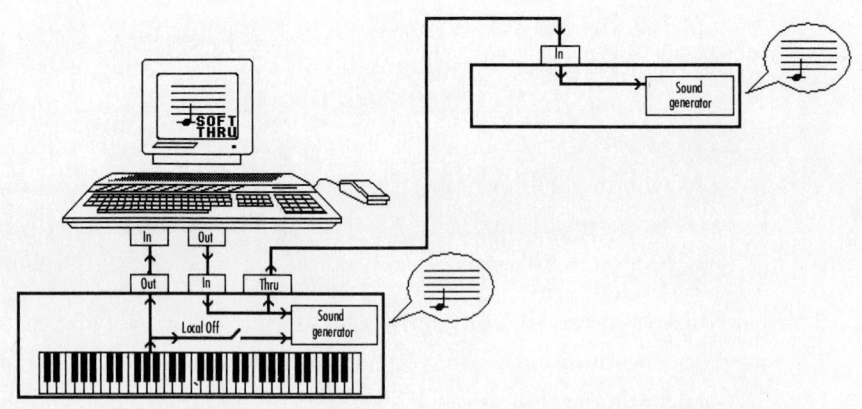

FIGURE 7.9: *In Record mode or in Play mode, the keyboard's sound generator (placed in Local Off mode) only receives messages once, by means of the sequencer's Thru function.*

first track with the help of the keyboard's sound generator, the act of lowering the volume of the first track while recording the expander on the second track will keep you from hearing the first track.

You can create more elaborate configurations by connecting several sound generators (either keyboards or expanders, provided that only the keyboard connected to the sequencer's MIDI In port is used for recording) at the output of the sequencer, either cascade-style (that is, in a daisy-chain link) or in a star network. Either way, the principles you've just learned will still apply.

The MIDI Channels

Up till now, for the sake of simplicity, this examination of the Thru function and Local Off mode has ignored the MIDI channels. However, if you look again at the last configuration in the preceding section, you can see that the sequencer sends exactly the same messages to the expander and to the keyboard's sound generator. In order for track X to address only the expander and in order for track Y to address only the keyboard's sound generator, you have to set the MIDI channels appropriately.

To proceed with the successive recording of two tracks, you start by setting the keyboard's sound generator, with Local Mode off, to a channel X (for instance, Channel 1), and setting the expander's sound generator, with Local Mode off, to a channel Y (for instance, Channel 2). In order to practice (that is, to work in Play mode) without recording, all you have to do is set the keyboard's sending channel to Channel 1 or Channel 2. This step lets you hear the keyboard's own sound generator or the expander's sound generator, respectively, courtesy of the sequencer's Thru function.

Assume further that the instruments used in the following examples receive MIDI information in Omni Off mode, which means that the instruments respond only to the messages whose channels are the same as their own receiving channels, as illustrated in Figure 7.10 and Figure 7.11 below.

In short, then, here are the steps you have to perform in order to record on two tracks:

1 • Make the connections as described in the section earlier in this chapter entitled "Connections."

2 • Enable the Thru function of the sequencer.

3 • Set the keyboard/sound generator link to Local Mode off.

4 • Set the keyboard's sound generators and the expander's sound generator to Omni Off.

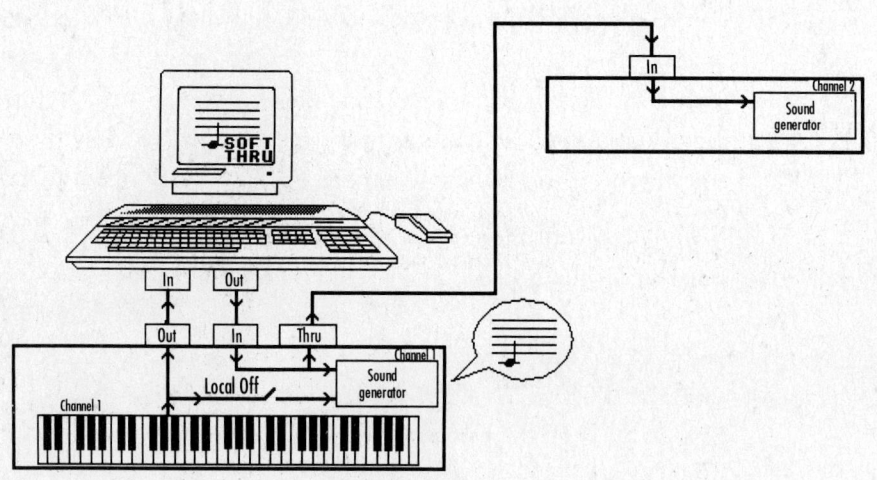

FIGURE 7.10: *The keyboard's sending channel is set to Channel 1. In Record mode or in Play mode, in spite of the fact that the two sound generators receive the same messages by means of the sequencer's Thru function, only the sound generator whose receiving channel corresponds to Channel 1 (in this example, the keyboard's sound generator) produces a sound.*

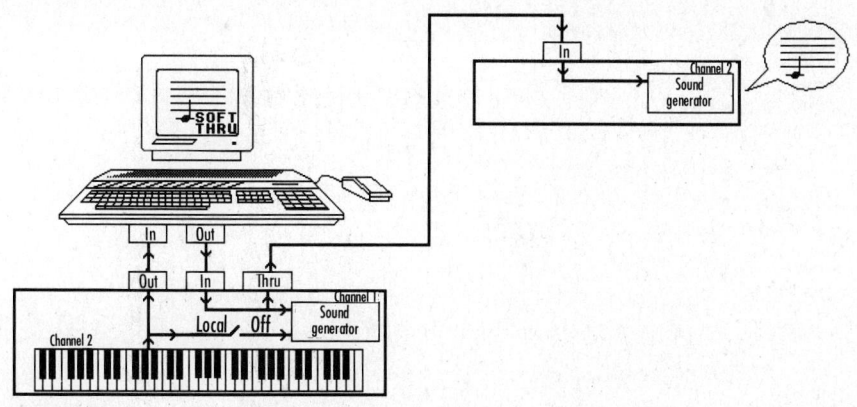

FIGURE 7.11: *The keyboard's sending channel is set to Channel 2. In Record mode or in Play mode, in spite of the fact that the two sound generators receive the same messages by means of the sequencer's Thru function, only the sound generator whose receiving channel corresponds to Channel 2 (in this example, the expander's sound generator) produces a sound.*

5 ▪ Set the receiving channel of the keyboard's sound generator.

6 ▪ Set the receiving channel of the expander to any number, provided that this channel number is different from the channel number that the keyboard's sound generator is set to.

7 ▪ Select any sequencer track, for instance Track 1.

8 ▪ Set the keyboard's sending channel to the number that corresponds to the receiving channel of the instrument to be recorded— in this example, to Channel 1 (that is, the receiving channel of the keyboard's sound generator).

9 ▪ Record Track 1.

10 ▪ Select another sequencer track.

11 ▪ Set the keyboard's sending channel to the number that corresponds to the receiving channel of the instrument to be recorded—

in this example, to Channel 1 (that is, the receiving channel of the expander).

12 • Record Track 2, while the sequencer drives the keyboard's sound generator by simultaneously reading Track 1.

Figures 7.12 and 7.13 below show how MIDI messages travel when you record on two tracks.

Most sequencers let users assign a channel number to each track. During reading, the channel number of the recorded messages (that is, the keyboard's channel number) is replaced by the number of the selected track. In the above example, once the tracks have been recorded, all you have to do is assign Channel 2 to Track 1 and Channel 1 to Track 2 in order for

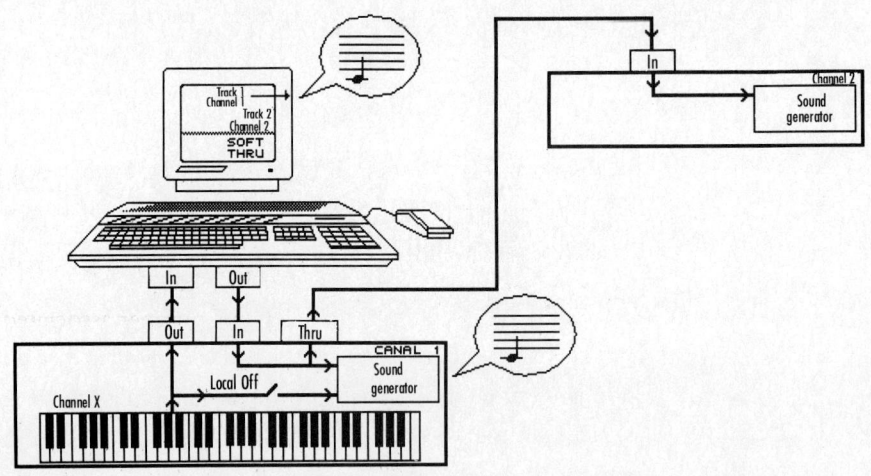

FIGURE 7.12: *When Track 1 is recorded, the keyboard messages, as sent via Channel 1, are simultaneously stored in the sequencer's memory and transmitted to the two instruments by means of the Thru function. Only the keyboard's sound generator, which is set to the same channel number, responds to the messages.*

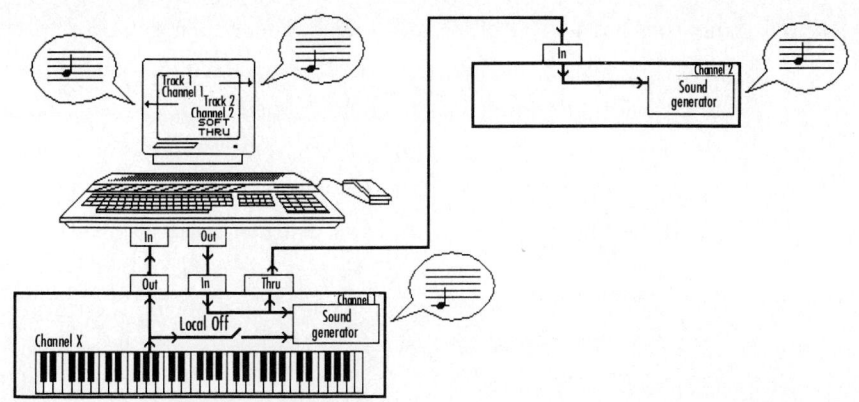

FIGURE 7.13: *When Track 2 is recorded, the messages from the keyboard, sent via Channel 2, are simultaneously stored in the sequencer's memory and transmitted to the two instruments by means of the Thru function. Only the expander, which is set to the same channel number, responds to the messages. Likewise, the messages recorded on Track 1 via Channel 1 are also read in order to be transmitted to the two instruments. Only the keyboard's sound generator, which is set to the same channel number, responds to the messages.*

the expander to reproduce the track originally intended for the keyboard's sound generator, and vice versa (that is, for the keyboard's sound generator to reproduce the track originally intended for the expander).

Together with the Thru function, the channel number associated with each track plays a crucial role. In Record mode or in Play mode, the number of the sending channel to which the keyboard is set makes no difference, because the Thru function automatically substitutes the number of the selected track. This method is known as *rechannelization*, which simplifies steps 8 and 11 in the procedure described above:

   8 ▪ Set Track 1 to Channel 1.

  11 ▪ Set Track 2 to Channel 2.

This procedure keeps you from having to make frequent changes in the number of the keyboard's sending channel depending on the sound generator they want to address, and also lets you change the channel number of a track that was recorded earlier, in such a way that that track can control a different sound generator. However, this rechannelization is done in real time, and therefore doesn't affect the channel number of the recorded messages, which is the same as the keyboard's channel number. In this regard, most sequencers let you set one track not only to a given channel, but to the original channel that was used during the recording operation. Figure 7.14 below shows an example of channel number assignments for tracks.

The concept of rechannelization leads to an improvement in the Thru function for instruments that don't have a Local mode. In some sequencers, this function can even be programmed in such a way as to be

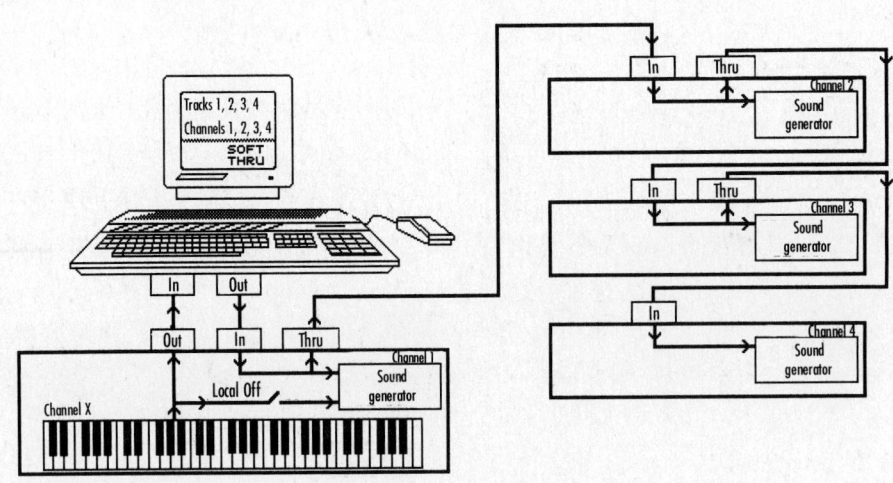

FIGURE 7.14: *Assuming that three expanders are set to channels 2, 3, and 4, it's sufficient to assign these same channels to three tracks, as desired, so that simply selecting one of the channels makes it possible to drive the corresponding expander from the keyboard.*

operational on all but one of the channels (under the circumstances, the channel of the keyboard's sound generator). Even though you're still faced with the problem of manually setting the volume, as noted earlier, you no longer have to disable the Thru function during a recording operation that involves the keyboard's sound generator.

In the absence of Local mode, and if the instrument allows it, the ideal solution would be to assign different numbers to the keyboard's sending channel and the channel(s) of the integrated sound generators.

To close this section, Figures 7.15, 7.16, and 7.17 show examples of more complex configurations:

To conclude this discussion of tracks and channels, you should note that the number of tracks in a sequencer is often greater than the number of MIDI channels (that is, sixteen). This characteristic can be useful if you want to record the same instrument on different tracks assigned to the

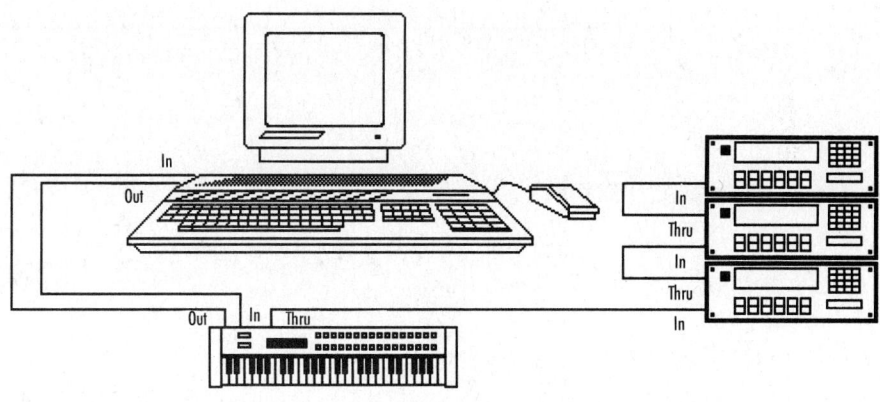

FIGURE 7.15: *A configuration with a keyboard and three expanders*

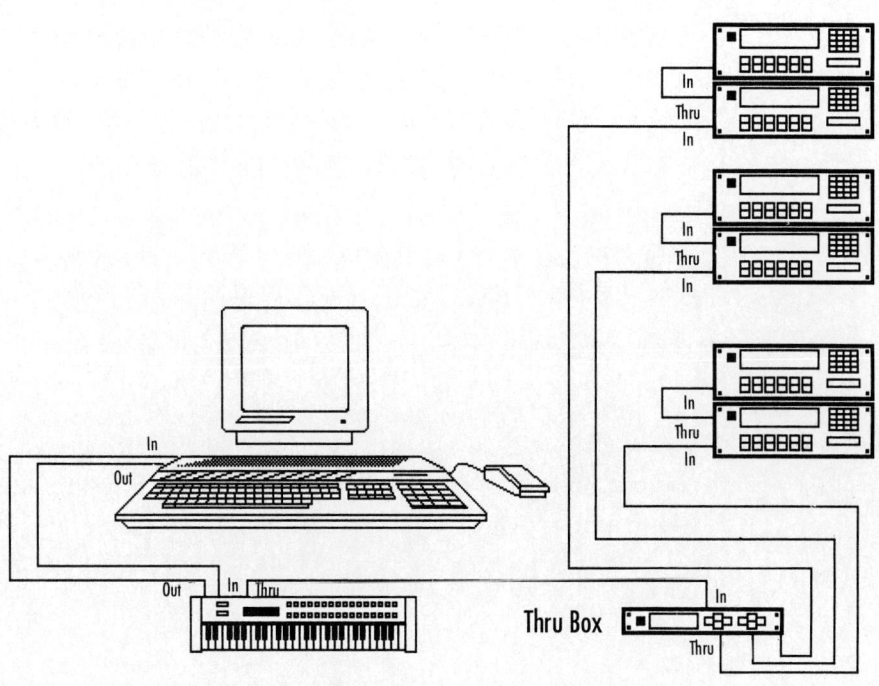

FIGURE 7.16: *A configuration with a keyboard and six expanders connected in groups of two via the outputs of a MIDI Thru Box*

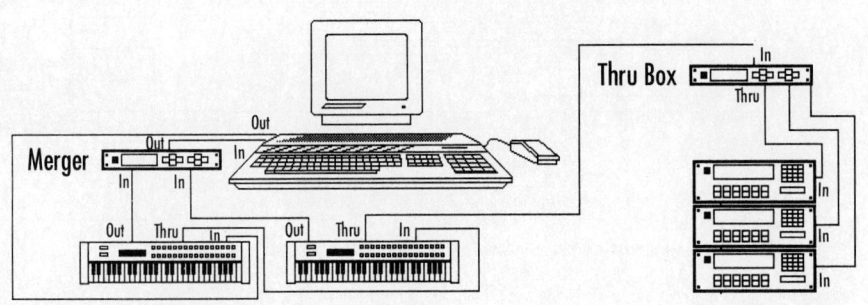

FIGURE 7.17: *A configuration that makes it possible to record from two keyboards connected to a sequencer by means of a MIDI Merge Box*

same channel, whether to simplify the musician's job (with the right-hand piano part on one track and the left-hand part on another, with the notes of a bass part on one track and the Pitch Bend information on a second track, etc.), to facilitate the handling of the various drum and percussion elements (each one on one track), or to store several versions of the same part, etc.

Furthermore, some sequencers have several independent MIDI outputs. In such a case, in addition to transmitting information over such and such a channel, each track can be directed toward one of these outputs, as desired. For instance, you can envision a situation in which Track 1, via Channel 1, drives a sound generator connected to Output A, and in which Track 2, also via Channel 1, drives another sound generator connected to Output B. This way, a sequencer with four MIDI Out ports would offer no fewer than 64 channels (4 × 16), and would have at least 64 tracks available.

Editing

Now that you're acquainted with the concepts of connection, MIDI channels, and tracks, it's time to look at the ways in which recorded data can be handled. To work with recorded information, you need to be familiar with two different types of editing: the *editing of structures* and the *editing of events*.

Editing Structures

Sequencers make it possible to divide a track into several sections, each one recorded independently of the others. These sections—which can be of different lengths and which are characterized by their starting and ending positions as expressed in terms of time signatures, measures or bars, beats, and ticks—are known as *patterns*. For instance, a given track can be recorded not only in its entirety, but also and particularly in terms of its component parts (for instance, a four-bar introduction, followed by two eight-bar phrases, then a six-bar chorus, etc.).

In addition to representing the different tape-recorder-style transport commands, tempo and time-signature settings, and the channels associated with each track, etc., the main screen of a sequencer represents the patterns that have been recorded in one way or another.

Starting with this breakdown into tracks and patterns, musicians have access to a set of functions they can manipulate in order to modify and organize the structure of a piece. Among these functions are copying, insertion, shifting, deletion, and repetition.

Editing Events

Sequencers make it possible to edit, with a high degree of accuracy, MIDI events that have been recorded. Before examining some of these editing functions, here's a look at how certain sequencers represent MIDI events onscreen, starting with Cubase shown in Figure 7.18 below.

The Score

For users who are familiar with conventional musical notation, the score is initially the most intuitive data-visualization method, because of the way it shows one musical staff per track. The main drawback of this method is that it deals only with note messages, to the exclusion of all other kinds of messages (continuous controllers and Pitch Bend, Aftertouch, and SysEx messages, etc.). Sometimes a track can be broken down

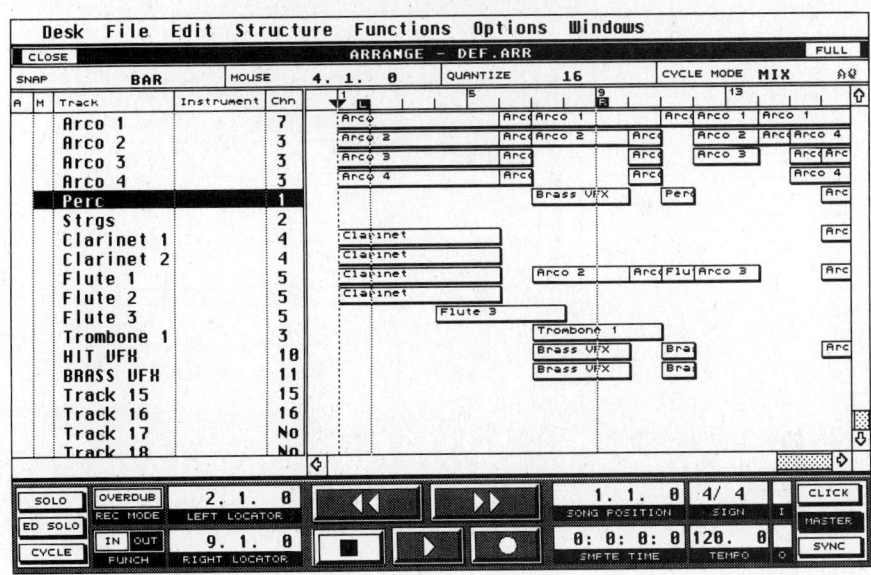

FIGURE 7.18: *The main screen of Cubase. The vertical axis indicates the tracks, and the horizontal axis indicates the time. The patterns are shown by rectangles whose length is a function of their duration.*

into two staves, one on either side of a given note. This function, which is very useful in representing a piano score (which uses the F-clef and the G-clef), is known as *splitting*.

In addition to the individual editing of notes, you'll also run into other specific functions, such as key changes and changes from one tonality to another with clef changes.

For reasons of readability, some sequencers quantify a score when they display it but leave the actual recording unchanged, as shown in Figure 7.19 below.

FIGURE 7.19: *The first staff shows the interpretation of four quarter-notes as they were played, while the second staff, for reasons of readability, is quantized by quarter-notes.*

This type of representation is generally associated with the printing of a score. As a result, some options (such as the ability to name staves and to combine them, and to position the various symbols, such as repetitions, crescendos and decrescendos, organ points etc.) are found in all score editors, as illustrated in Figure 7.20 below.

The Editing Grid

The editing grid looks like a checkerboard pattern in which each event is represented by a horizontal rectangle whose length (that is, for note messages) corresponds to its duration. Furthermore, vertical bars indicate the time signature in accordance with more or less fine divisions (eighth-notes, sixteenth-notes, etc.). Opposite the grid is a listing of various pieces of information about the events: the starting position, the status, the data associated with the status, etc. A typical editing grid, in this case that of the Pro 24 III sequencer, is shown in Figure 7.21 below.

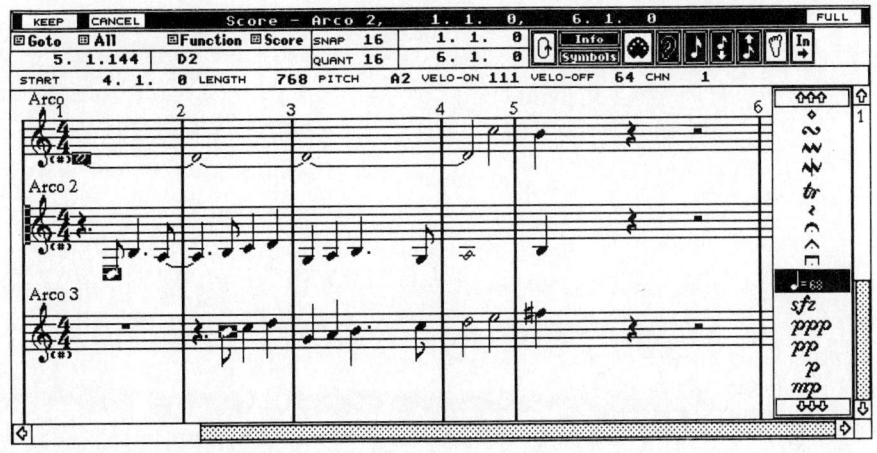

FIGURE 7.20: *A score formatted by the Score Edit screen of Cubase*

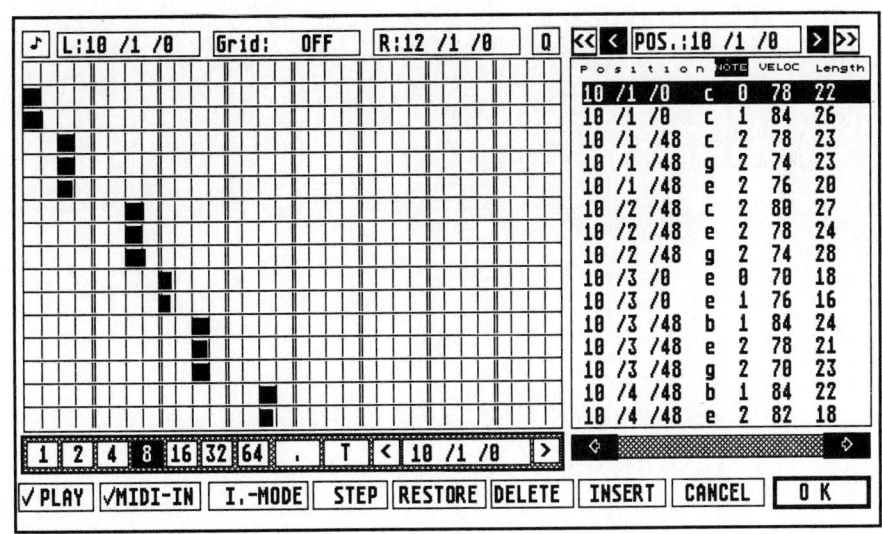

FIGURE 7.21: *The grid screen of the Pro 24 III sequencer*

The Piano-Roll Display

The piano-roll display looks like the wheel of a barrel organ or street organ. The left-hand side of the screen represents a vertical keyboard, and the notes are indicated by horizontal lines that are more or less dark depending on their velocity. Vertical bars indicate the time signature in more or less fine divisions. Like the score-type displays, this screen generally shows only note information. The Key Edit screen of Cubase, shown in Figure 7.22 below, is a good example of this kind of display.

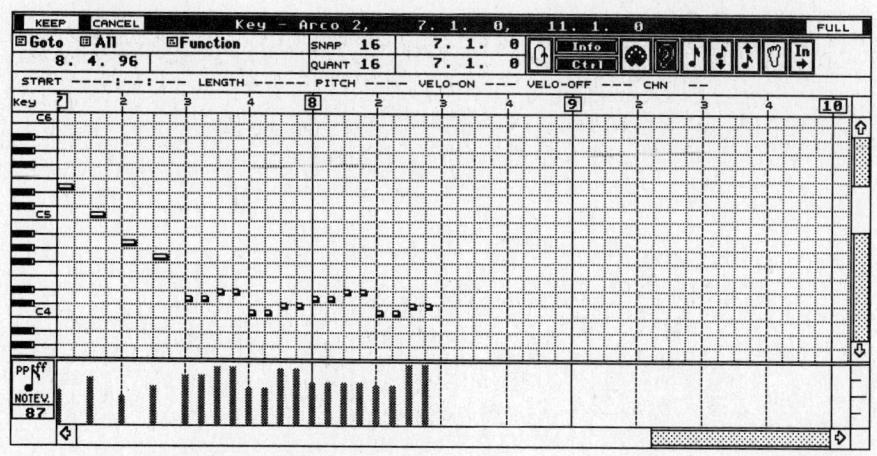

FIGURE 7.22: *The Key Edit screen of Cubase.*

The Percussion Instrument Display

The display for percussion instruments was inspired by the displays for the programming grids of drum machines. Here again, vertical bars indicate the time signature in more or less fine divisions, and each instrument is named at the left-hand side of the screen. Facing these instruments, the notes are represented by different symbols, which can be darker or lighter depending on the velocity of each note. The Drum Edit screen of the Pro 24 III sequencer, shown in Figure 7.23 below, is a good example of this kind of display.

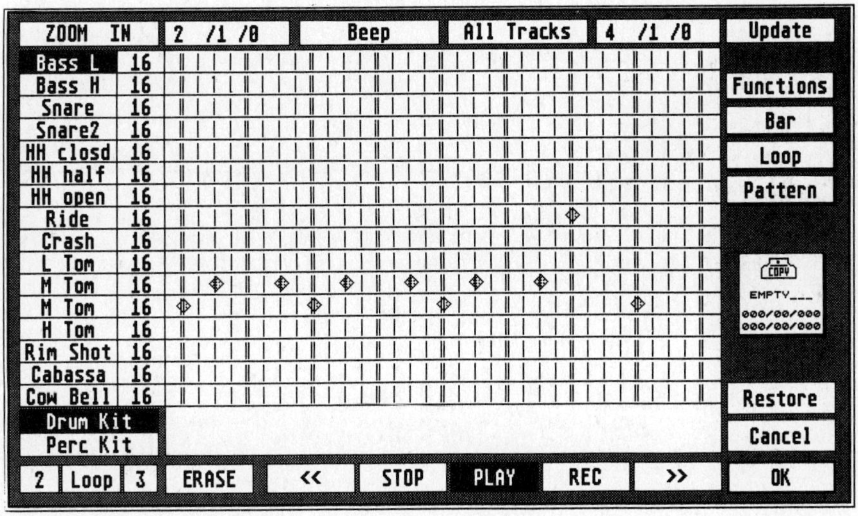

FIGURE 7.23: *The Drum Edit screen of the Pro 24 III sequencer*

The Representation of Velocity

Together with the four types of display described above, velocity is sometimes represented by horizontal or vertical lines, whose length depends on the value of the note. Figure 7.24 below shows how velocities are represented on the Edit Grid screen of Cubase.

START-POS	LENGTH	VAL1	VAL2	VAL3	STATUS
7. 1. 0	48	E5	72	64	Note
7. 1. 96	48	C5	96	64	Note
7. 2. 0	48	A4	61	64	Note
7. 2. 96	48	G4	81	64	Note
7. 3. 0	24	D4	102	64	Note
7. 3. 48	24	D4	102	64	Note
7. 3. 96	24	D#4	120	64	Note
7. 3.144	24	D#4	120	64	Note
7. 4. 0	24	C4	77	64	Note
7. 4. 48	24	C4	77	64	Note
7. 4. 96	24	C#4	117	64	Note
7. 4.144	24	C#4	117	64	Note
8. 1. 0	24	D4	89	64	Note
8. 1. 48	24	D4	89	64	Note

FIGURE 7.24: *The representation of velocities, as shown on the right side of the Edit Grid screen of Cubase*

Representation of the Controllers

None of the methods described above is really suitable for displaying MIDI controllers (continuous controllers and Pitch Bend and Aftertouch messages, etc.). Some sequencers use a two-dimensional display (with the time shown along the abscissa and the value of each message along the ordinate), with each message being represented by a horizontal line whose height is determined by the length of the message. As an example, Figure 7.25 below shows how Cubase represents the Pitch Bend controller.

Multi-Windowing

Multi-windowing, as shown in Figure 7.26 below, simultaneously combines several of the preceding types of screens when the same section is

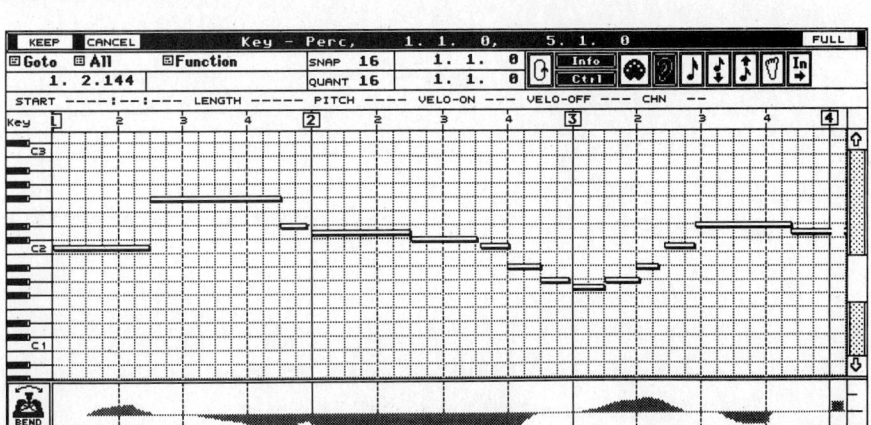

FIGURE 7.25: *The graphic representation of the controllers (in this example, Pitch Bend) below the Key Edit screen of Cubase*

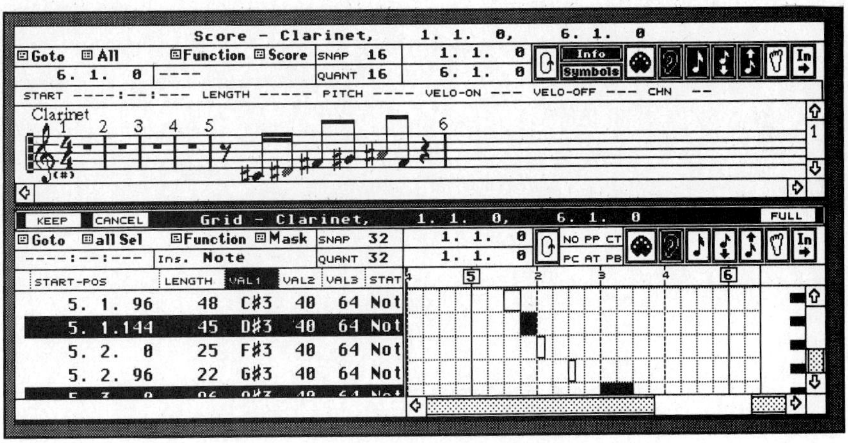

FIGURE 7.26: *Simultaneous display of the editing grid and the score in Cubase*

being edited. This feature lets you use different methods at once: a score for the notes, the editing grid for Program Change messages, and so on. The modification of an event in one of the windows is passed along in real time to the other windows.

Absolute Metrical or Temporal Position

In the editing grids that display positions, each position is described in terms of the measure in which it appears, its temporal position within the measure, and its tick with regard to the temporal position: in other words, its *bar*, *beat*, and *tick* parameters. However, some sequencers, such as Cubase, offer the option of converting each position into SMPTE code, as shown in Figure 7.27 below.

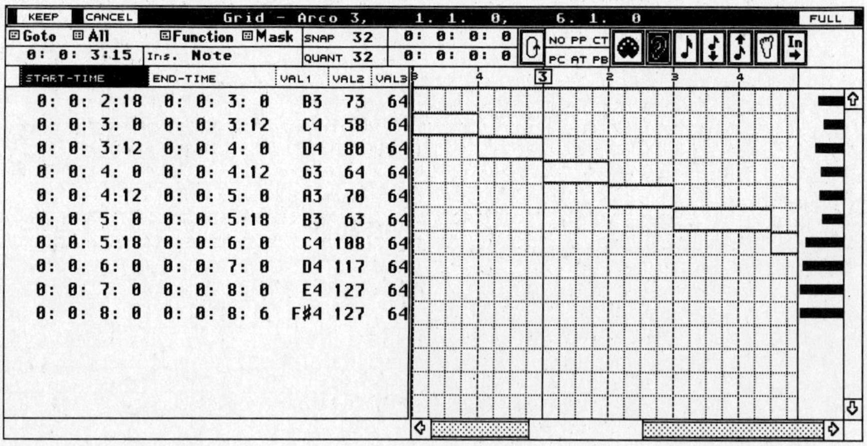

FIGURE 7.27: *The Edit Grid screen of Cubase. The note positions are represented in accordance with SMPTE time code.*

Various Kinds of Processing

After a recording is made, the sequencer lets users edit the recording, particularly thanks to the different types of displays listed above. Before applying any kind of treatment to MIDI events, it's useful first to select the events you want to work with. You can make this selection according to the track, pattern, block, or status (Pitch Bend, Aftertouch, Notes, Program Change, Control Change, etc.).

It's pointless to try to list all of the editing functions that sequencers implement, because these functions are so numerous and vary so much from one sequencer to another. With regard to editing, it's enough to note that every MIDI recording can be modified as desired, either structurally or in terms of the messages it contains.

Although hardly exhaustive, the following section provides a more detailed description of one of the more subtle processing operations (namely, quantization). The next chapter continues with advanced software editing and a look at various applications designed to let you simulate audio effects with the aid of a sequencer.

 **uantization** •

Quantization is a procedure that's intended to correct the rhythmic errors in a recording by rounding off the note positions (that is, the positions of MIDI Note On and Note Off messages) or, more precisely, by readjusting the note positions to a value that is a multiple of a boundary of a predetermined rhythmic value (such as a quarter-note, an eighth-note, etc.).

In a concrete example, suppose you've just recorded a measure in 4/4 time that contains four quarter-notes. If the resolution is 96 ticks to the quarter-note (indicated as values from 0 to 95) and if your interpretation is perfectly accurate, you'd get the following messages and intervals. (Remember, an interval corresponds to the number of ticks separating two successive MIDI messages.)

POSITION IN TERMS OF BARS, BEATS, AND TICKS	MEMORY EVENT
1/1/0	Note On message for the first quarter-note Interval of 96 ticks
1/2/0	Note Off message for the first quarter-note
1/2/0	Note On message for the second quarter-note Interval of 96 ticks
1/3/0	Note Off message for the second quarter-note
1/3/0	Note On message for the third quarter-note Interval of 96 ticks
1/4/0	Note Off message for the third quarter-note
1/4/0	Note On message for the fourth quarter-note Interval of 96 ticks
2/1/0	Note Off message for the fourth quarter-note

As you see, each quarter-note lasts for 96 ticks (which is the interval between the Note On and Note Off messages), and each note's position coincides with a quarter-note boundary (1/1/0, 1/2/0, 1/3/0, and 1/4/0). Because of its precision, the existence of any such recording in real time is purely theoretical. It's obvious that in reality the result would contain slight imperfections, such as the ones shown below:

POSITION IN TERMS OF BARS, BEATS, AND TICKS	MEMORY EVENT
1/1/2	Note On message for the first quarter-note Interval of 83 ticks

POSITION IN TERMS OF BARS, BEATS, AND TICKS	MEMORY EVENT
1/1/85	Note Off message for the first quarter-note Interval of 16 ticks
1/2/5	Note On message for the second quarter-note Interval of 85 ticks
1/2/90	Note Off message for the second quarter-note Interval of 6 ticks
1/3/0	Note On message for the third quarter-note Interval of 84 ticks
1/3/84	Note On message for the fourth quarter-note Interval of 1 tick
1/3/85	Note Off message for the third quarter-note Interval of 97 ticks
1/4/86	Note Off message for the fourth quarter-note

With regard to the strong beats (1/1/0, 1/2/0, 1/3/0, and 1/4/0), you can see that the first note is 2 ticks behind and the second note is 5 ticks behind; the third note is "on time"; and the fourth note is 12 ticks ahead. You can also see that all the notes except for the fourth one are slightly shorter than a quarter-note should be, and that the fourth note was pressed before the third note was released.

The sequencer works with rhythmic figures: whole notes, half-notes, quarter-notes, eighth-notes, sixteenth-notes, thirty-second notes, dotted notes, and so on. For instance, after the recording described above was quantized to the quarter-note, the Note On and Note Off messages that needed to be tweaked were readjusted to the border of the nearest quarter-note (that is, to a position characterized by the following format: bar/beat/0, or $b_1/b_2/0$). This procedure gives you this result (with the values in parentheses corresponding to the positions prior to quantization):

POSITION IN TERMS OF BARS, BEATS, AND TICKS	MEMORY EVENT
1/1/0 (1/1/2)	Note On message for the first quarter-note Interval of 96 ticks
1/2/0 (1/1/85)	Note Off message for the first quarter-note
1/2/0 (1/2/5)	Note On message for the second quarter-note Interval of 96 ticks
1/3/0 (1/2/90)	Note Off message for the second quarter-note
1/3/0 (1/3/0)	Note On message for the third quarter-note Interval of 96 ticks
1/4/0 (1/3/84)	Note On message for the fourth quarter-note
1/4/0 (1/3/85)	Note Off message for the third quarter-note Interval of 96 ticks
2/1/0 (1/4/86)	Note Off message for the fourth quarter-note

More generally speaking, where b_1, b_2, and x correspond respectively to the bar number, the beat number within the bar, and the tick number within the beat, you can describe the procedure numerically:

POSITION BEFORE QUANTIZATION	POSITION AFTER QUANTIZATION
$b_1/b_2/x$ (where x is less than 48)	$b_1/b_2/0$
$b_1/b_2/x$ (where x is greater than 48)	$b_1/b_2 + 1/0$

For x = 48, the sequencer has the option of rounding the position either to the next beat or to the last beat (that is, of either advancing the position or retarding it).

In short, you can see that the quantization of a sequencer, stored as a series of interval counts and MIDI messages, is simply a mathematical procedure applied to the value of the counters associated with the Note On and Note Off messages in order to readjust the position of these notes as a function of the selected quantization value.

Table 7.2 below shows the positions to which note messages can be adjusted as a function of the various rhythmic figures and the various resolutions to the quarter-note:

TABLE 7.2: *Positions to Which Note Messages Are Adjusted, Depending on Rhythmic Figures and Resolutions*

RESOLUTION:	48	96	192	384
Quarter-note	$b_1/b_2/0$	$b_1/b_2/0$	$b_1/b_2/0$	$b_1/b_2/0$
Eighth-note	$b_1/b_2/0$	$b_1/b_2/0$	$b_1/b_2/0$	$b_1/b_2/0$
	$b_1/b_2/24$	$b_1/b_2/48$	$b_1/b_2/96$	$b_1/b_2/192$
Eighth-note triplet	$b_1/b_2/0$	$b_1/b_2/0$	$b_1/b_2/0$	$b_1/b_2/0$
	$b_1/b_2/16$	$b_1/b_2/32$	$b_1/b_2/64$	$b_1/b_2/128$
	$b_1/b_2/32$	$b_1/b_2/64$	$b_1/b_2/128$	$b_1/b_2/256$
Sixteenth-note	$b_1/b_2/0$	$b_1/b_2/0$	$b_1/b_2/0$	$b_1/b_2/0$
	$b_1/b_2/12$	$b_1/b_2/24$	$b_1/b_2/48$	$b_1/b_2/96$
	$b_1/b_2/24$	$b_1/b_2/48$	$b_1/b_2/9$	$b_1/b_2/192$
	$b_1/b_2/36$	$b_1/b_2/72$	$b_1/b_2/14$	$b_1/b_2/288$

TABLE 7.2: *Positions to Which Note Messages Are Adjusted, Depending on Rhythmic Figures and Resolutions (continued)*

RESOLUTION:	48	96	192	384
Sixteenth-note triplet	$b_1/b_2/8$	$b_1/b_2/16$	$b_1/b_2/3$	$b_1/b_2/64$
	$b_1/b_2/16$	$b_1/b_2/32$	$b_1/b_2/6$	$b_1/b_2/128$
	$b_1/b_2/24$	$b_1/b_2/48$	$b_1/b_2/9$	$b_1/b_2/192$
	$b_1/b_2/32$	$b_1/b_2/64$	$b_1/b_2/12$	$b_1/b_2/256$
	$b_1/b_2/40$	$b_1/b_2/80$	$b_1/b_2/16$	$b_1/b_2/320$
Thirty-second note	$b_1/b_2/0$	$b_1/b_2/0$	$b_1/b_2/0$	$b_1/b_2/0$
	$b_1/b_2/0$	$b_1/b_2/0$	$b_1/b_2/0$	$b_1/b_2/0$
	$b_1/b_2/6$	$b_1/b_2/12$	$b_1/b_2/2$	$b_1/b_2/48$
	$b_1/b_2/12$	$b_1/b_2/24$	$b_1/b_2/4$	$b_1/b_2/96$
	$b_1/b_2/18$	$b_1/b_2/36$	$b_1/b_2/7$	$b_1/b_2/144$
	$b_1/b_2/24$	$b_1/b_2/48$	$b_1/b_2/96$	$b_1/b_2/192$
	$b_1/b_2/30$	$b_1/b_2/60$	$b_1/b_2/120$	$b_1/b_2/240$
	$b_1/b_2/36$	$b_1/b_2/72$	$b_1/b_2/144$	$b_1/b_2/288$
	$b_1/b_2/42$	$b_1/b_2/84$	$b_1/b_2/168$	$b_1/b_2/336$

Every sequencer manufacturer implements quantization differently. Here are some of the approaches they take.

The Quantization of Note On Messages

As its name indicates, this type of quantization does not affect Note Off messages.

The Quantization of Note On Messages with Length Readjustments

This type of quantization preserves the lengths of the notes (that is, the number of ticks separating each Note On message from the corresponding Note Off message). This way, when a Note On message is quantized (that is, when it's shifted by plus or minus X ticks), the corresponding Note Off message is shifted by the same number of ticks.

Note On/Note Off Quantization

As its name indicates, this type of quantization readjusts both Note on and Note Off messages.

When a sequencer processes the Note On and Note Off messages at the same time, there's a potential disadvantage—namely the fact that if the length of the note is less than the quantized value, both of the messages are readjusted to the same point—that is, to the same beat.

Generally speaking, Note On/Note Off quantization is relatively strict. However, it has the advantage of clarifying the display of a score (for printing directly from the sequencer, or for importing a file into a particular piece of software), because in addition to performing a temporal readjustment of the notes it also changes their durations, converting them into whole-number multiples of the quantization unit.

Incremental Quantization

This procedure is rather like a gradual "magnetization" of Note On messages. Each time this function is triggered, the notes are shifted by half the distance that they would normally be shifted in order to reach their quantized position (with this distance being rounded, of course, if the number of ticks is an odd number). Thanks to this method, the recording retains its original character, because it undergoes a more or less subtle re-adjustment (depending on the number of processing steps performed) as opposed to the more mechanistic simple quantization operation. In short, you don't lose the feel.

Incremental Quantization with Regulated Attraction

In the last example, each increment was equal to half the distance the note had to travel in order to be properly quantized. Now you can qualify this quantization procedure in terms of 50-percent increments (that is, half the distance in question). By imposing parameters on the attraction of each increment, you can quantify the "magnetization," as it were, in a much more flexible way.

Zone Quantization

This procedure consists of defining, around each quantization position (for instance, around every eighth-note), a zone expressed in terms of a greater or lesser number of ticks (that is, a given number of ticks in front of or behind the selected unit) within which notes will be quantized in the usual way. Outside this zone, the messages will not be readjusted at all. In the same way as with incremental quantization (the two methods can sometimes be combined), the result you get has the advantage of being more musical than it would have under simple quantization.

Quantization by Modeling

All of the quantization procedures described up till now rely on mathematical manipulations. Quantization by modeling acts differently in that it lets users decide what the readjustment positions should be, either by defining them or by basing them on a previously recorded track.

Assume that a drum track and a bass track, each of which is one measure long, have been recorded in the following way:

The Drum Track

1/1/2	Note On, bass drum
1/1/93	Note On, snare drum
1/3/3	Note On, bass drum
1/13/92	Note On, snare drum

The Bass Track

1/1/0	Note On, C2
1/1/49	Note On, G2
1/2/1	Note On, C2
1/2/42	Note On, G2
1/3/6	Note On, F2
1/3/47	Note On, C3
1/3/88	Note On, F2
1/4/48	Note On, C3

If the bass is quantized in accordance with the drum track, the notes near the bass drum and the snare drum will be readjusted to the corresponding beats, while the positions of the other notes, which are too far from the drum notes to be quantized, remain unchanged. The quantized messages are shown in boldface type.

1/1/2	Note On, C2
1/1/49	Note On, G2
1/1/93	Note On, C2
1/2/42	Note On, G2
1/3/3	Note On, F2
1/3/47	Note On, C3
1/3/92	Note On, F2
1/4/48	Note On, C3

Instead of starting with previously recorded tracks, some quantization methods let you program the various models for themselves. In such cases, you decide which positions should be used as bases for the quantization of your recording. These programmable models can be saved on disk, thereby letting you build up a bank or library of so-called "quantization models" adapted to your particular needs.

Figure 7.28 below shows how Cubase uses its Groove Quantize window to let you model your own quantization scheme.

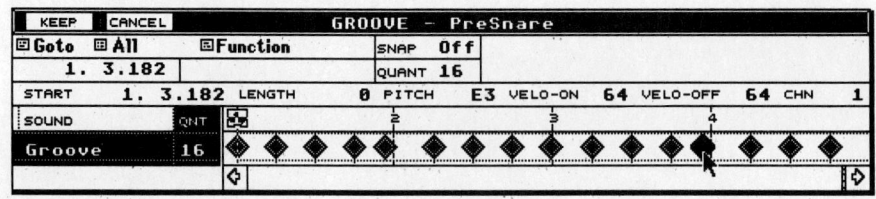

FIGURE 7.28: *Modeling as viewed by Cubase's Groove Quantize window*

Intelligent Quantization

Some so-called "intelligent quantization" procedures can be adapted to a musician's performing style. For instance, after a recording has been analyzed, and provided that a majority of the notes are located either "ahead of" or "behind" a particular location or position, the quantization method will respect and reflect this interpretive style instead of treating these shifts as rhythmic errors. Likewise, a section consisting of binary and ternary passages will be quantized with respect to the musician's playing style.

Reversible Quantization

In performing quantization operations, a very few sequencers systematically store in memory the unprocessed version of the recording. Although this method has the disadvantage of taking up twice as much memory space (and, when the recording is saved, twice as much disk space), it also lets users work backward at any time by recovering the original version. The act of "freezing" the quantized version—that is, irreversibly destroying the duplicate of the original version of the recording—makes it possible to free up memory space as soon as the quantization is deemed correct and definitive.

Quantization Before, During, or After

As a general rule, most sequencers carry out quantization operations during the editing stage, although some sequencers also offer quantization as an option while recording. With quantization during recording, the software immediately readjusts the note messages it receives at the MIDI In port. This procedure represents a significant time savings for anyone who wants to process all of the sequences systematically. However, unlike quantization during reading, which doesn't change the recorded data, this method is irreversible, inasmuch as it operates in real time by transmitting the messages on the desired beats. On the other hand, this procedure requires software that's powerful enough to handle the MIDI inputs and outputs while performing the quantization at the same time.

Fixed Length

In addition to performing time-based readjustments, sequencers can also work on the lengths of notes—that is, on the number of ticks that separate a Note On message from the corresponding Note Off message. For instance, a sequencer can use the Fixed Length function to allocate a given length (such as a quarter-note, an eighth-note, a predetermined number of ticks, etc.) to each note. Each Note Off message is then shifted by a greater or lesser amount, depending on whether the distance separating the message from the corresponding Note On messages is less than or greater than the value of the selected length.

Minimum and Maximum Lengths

The so-called "Minimum Length" function lengthens all the notes whose duration is less than a predetermined rhythmic value, in such a way as to assign that predetermined value to all of those notes. Notes whose duration is greater than or equal to the predetermined value are not affected. Conversely, the so-called "Maximum Length" function shortens all the notes whose duration is greater than a predetermined rhythmic value, in such a way as to assign that predetermined value to all of those notes. Notes whose duration is less than or equal to the predetermined value are not affected.

This overview of the various time-based readjustment procedures for Note On and Note Off messages gives you some idea of the processing power that sequencers can offer.

CHAPTER

8

XIII XIV XV XVI A B C D E F G H I

MIDI Recording:

Advanced Techniques

N THE LAST chapter you got acquainted with the basic procedures for
MIDI recording. Now it's time to move
on to more sophisticated techniques,
starting with logical or mathematical operations and effects simulation, and ending with ways to handle delay problems
and store the sequences you've created.

Logical Manipulations

Logical manipulations are mathematical operations applied to MIDI messages. They consist essentially of additions, subtractions, divisions, multi-
plications, and conditional operations. Although they're not very
intuitive, these tools can be extremely effective. For example, take a look
at the Logical Edit screen of Cubase, shown in Figure 8.1 below.

The Logical Edit screen lets you select MIDI bytes before applying
various processing operations to them. The Event block in the upper

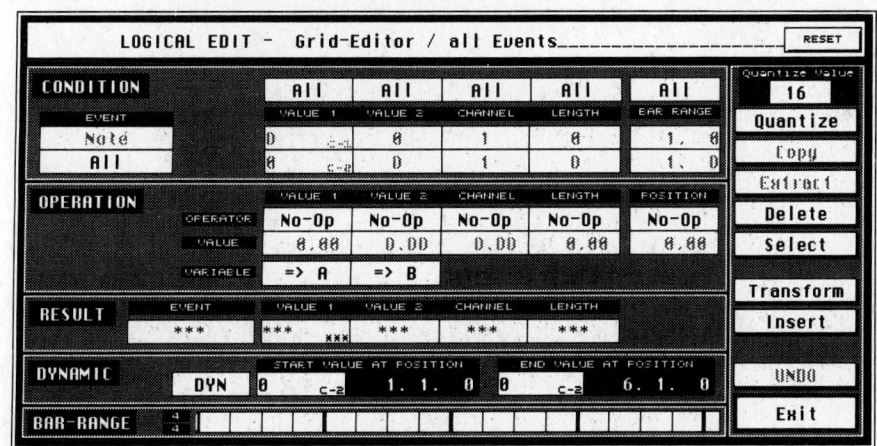

FIGURE 8.1: *The Logical Edit screen of Cubase*

left-hand corner of the screen determines the type or types of events (that is, status) to be taken into consideration. The upper line lets you select the events from among the seven existing channel messages (Note On, Note Off, Polyphonic Key Pressure, Control Change, Program Change, Channel Pressure, and Pitch Bend), while the bottom line lets you select the events in accordance with the following criteria:

- "all": taking into consideration all status types
- "equal": taking into consideration selected status types
- "unequal": taking into consideration all status types, except the selected event
- "higher": taking into consideration all strictly higher status types (i.e., bits 4 to 6, with the exclusion of the channel) without a selected status type

- "lower": taking into consideration all strictly lower status types (i.e., bits 4 to 6, with the exclusion of the channel) or a selected status type

Here are a few examples of typical settings:

- To work with all status types except for Program Change messages:

```
program change
unequal
```

- To work only with Aftertouch messages:

```
channel pressure
equal
```

- To work with notes, Polyphonic Key Pressure messages, Program Change messages, and Control Change messages:

```
channel pressure
lower
```

Starting with this first selection, the five columns to the right enable the display of the type of processing within each type of event.

The column headed "Value 1" corresponds to the first data byte, the column headed "Value 2" corresponds to the second byte (which doesn't exist for Program Change messages and Channel Aftertouch messages), the column headed "Channel" corresponds to the channel, the column headed "length" corresponds to the length (but only when notes are involved), and the column headed "bar range" corresponds to the position within the measure (for instance, all of the messages located on either side of the fourth beat, etc.). This last column is represented in the form of an interactive graphic located at the bottom of the screen.

The first line governs the selection for each column (All, Equal, Unequal, Higher, Lower, Inside, or Outside). The second line indicates the value at which the selection will be implemented. The "inside" and "outside" parameters refer to the second and third lines, which delimit the minimum and maximum intervals within (Inside) and beyond (Outside) which the selection will be implemented.

For example, Figure 8.2 below shows the parameters you have to implement if you want to select the note messages on Channel 5, Channel 6, and Channel 7, within a pitch interval from C2 to C3, for a velocity greater than 64, for a length less than a quarter-note, and for a position between the second and third beats:

At this stage in the operation, you can quantify the specified events (by means of the Quantize command), remove them (by means of the Delete command), reproduce them in a different pattern (by means of the Copy command), extract them (by deleting them and then copying them in a different pattern), or select them for further treatment in an editing grid (by means of the Select command).

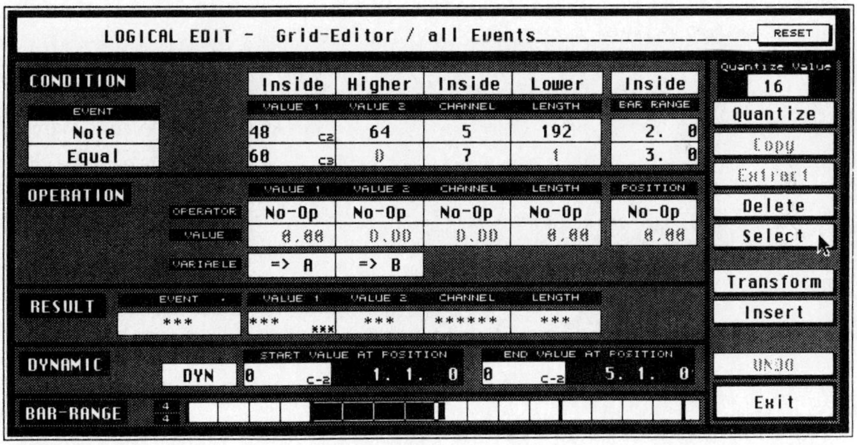

FIGURE 8.2: *Parameter settings for the note messages, pitch interval, velocity, duration, and position described in the text*

In addition to these operations, the logical processing (Operation) line mathematically converts the so-called "operands" in the five preceding columns in accordance with the following criteria:

- "No-Op": no effect

- "Plus": addition of an offset

- "Minus": removal of an offset

- "Mul": the multiplication factor

- "Div": the division factor

The lower line ("value") specifies the offset or the factor to be applied in the foregoing operations.

The Result line is divided into five blocks: "Event," "Value 1," "Value 2," "Channel," and "Length." The "Event" block is somewhat special in that it lets you modify the status of the MIDI channel message according to any of the seven possible options, provided that the contents of this block are something other than "***". With regard to the other four blocks, you can choose between a fixed value to be acquired directly, and the result of the operation performed with regard to the corresponding column ("***").

The variables "=> A" and "=> B" form a mini-patch. By using the mouse to drag "=> A" to the "Value 2" results block, the modifications made in the "Value 1" column are applied (that is, patched) to the "Value 2" results block. In the same way, by dragging "=> B" to the "Value 1" results block, the modifications made in the "value 2" column are applied to the "Value 1" results block.

Furthermore, after a starting value and an ending value have been specified, the act of dragging the dynamic symbol ("DYN") to one of the results blocks creates a linear progression between the value of the first message for the pattern(s) to be processed and the value of the last message. The conversion ("Transform") and insertion ("Insert") options involve the modification and insertion, respectively, of the selected and treated events.

In conclusion, and to help you familiarize yourself with software editing grids, here are a few practical examples.

Assume that a keyboard which is sensitive to Channel Aftertouch is sending via Channel 5, and that the reverberation time of an effects processor set to Channel 10 reacts to Control Change 11 (0BH, the Expression controller). In order to have an effect on the reverb time directly from the keyboard, you have to convert the previously recorded aftertouch messages into a controller expression and replace Channel 5 with Channel 10, as shown in Figure 8.3 below.

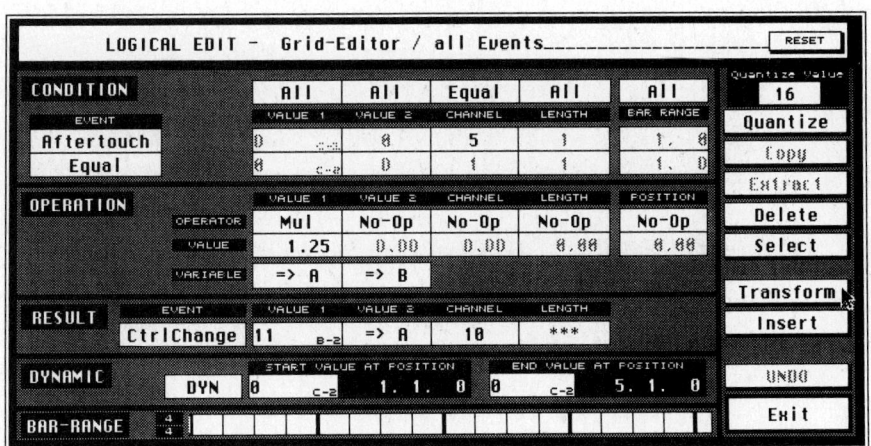

FIGURE 8.3: *Conversion of Aftertouch on Channel 5 to Control Change 11 on Channel 10*

The "=> A" option in the "Value 2" results block has the effect of patching the Channel Aftertouch value (that is, the second byte of a message that only uses two bytes) to the value of the Control Change (that is, the third byte of the messages). If you want to improve and refine the effectiveness of this message, there's no reason not to program a multiplication factor or a division factor in the "Value 1" column.

Now assume that a snare drum programmed on a sound generator set to Channel 2 is causing an excessive amount of background noise, and that a mixing console is equipped with an automatic mute (that is, a voice cut-off) command driven by Control Change message 68 on Channel 3. (The values 127 and 0, respectively, trigger the opening and closing of the snare-drum voice.) For each note message, the maneuver consists of inserting a voice-opening message at a position several ticks earlier, and then a track-closing message located as many ticks later as required by the duration of the sound of the snare drum, as shown in Figure 8.4 and

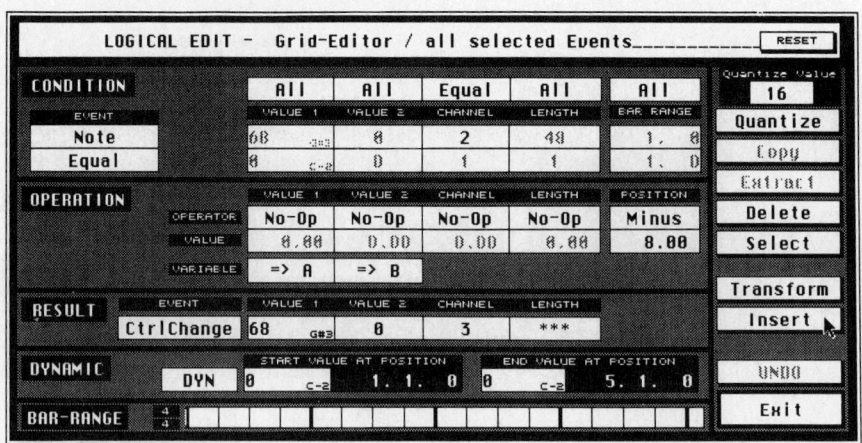

FIGURE 8.4: *Insertion of a voice-opening ("unmute") message triggered a few instants before each snare drum message*

Figure 8.5 below. Then, by controlling the console voice assigned to re-turn a reverb programmed for the snare drum, you can get a so-called "gate" reverb effect.

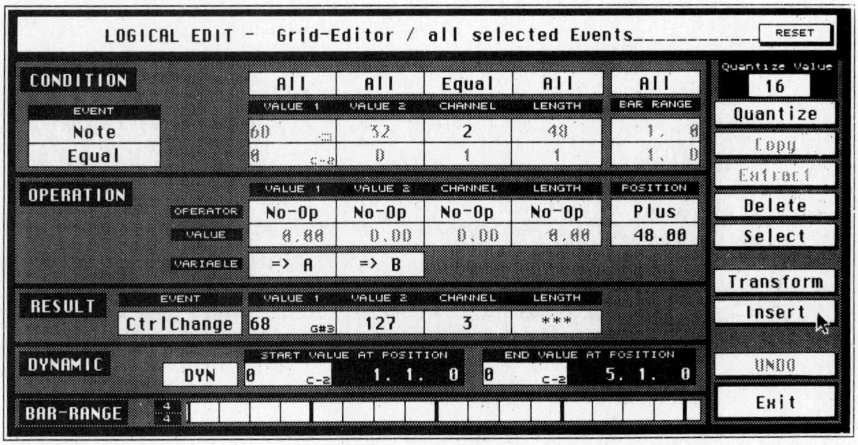

FIGURE 8.5: *Insertion of a voice-closure ("mute") message triggered a few instants after each snare drum*

In a third and last example, a sequence programmed on a sound generator set to Channel 8 triggers an eighth-note echo on a second sound gener-ator, this one set to Channel 9. This slightly odd echo occurs only on notes located within an interval of one quarter-note centered on the fourth beat of each measure, and transposes these notes by an interval based on a multiplication factor of 1.20, as shown in Figure 8.6 below. The velocity is decreased by half and the notes are decreased by one-quarter of their length.

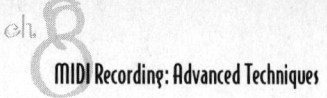

LOGICAL EDIT - Grid-Editor / all Events_____					RESET	

CONDITION

	All	All	Equal	All	Inside	Quantize Value: 16
EVENT	VALUE 1	VALUE 2	CHANNEL	LENGTH	BAR RANGE	Quantize
Note	60	32	8	48	3. 96	Copy
Equal	0 c-2	0	1	1	4. 96	Extract

OPERATION

	VALUE 1	VALUE 2	CHANNEL	LENGTH	POSITION	Delete
OPERATOR	Mul	Div	Plus	Div	Plus	Select
VALUE	1.20	0.50	1.00	0.75	96.00	
VARIABLE	=> A	=> B				Transform

RESULT

EVENT	VALUE 1	VALUE 2	CHANNEL	LENGTH		Insert
***	*** xxx	***	***	***		

DYNAMIC

	START VALUE AT POSITION		END VALUE AT POSITION		UNDO
DYN	0 c-2 1. 1. 0		0 c-2 5. 1. 0		Exit

BAR-RANGE 4/4

FIGURE 8.6: *Parameter settings that trigger an eighth-note echo on a second sound generator*

The Simulation of Effects

Now that you've examined logical or software processing, it's time to take a look at several practical exercises for editing MIDI events. These exercises are intended to simulate some of the treatments that an effects processor can apply to an audio signal and that can most easily be reproduced by a sequencer.

Delay and Echo

The delay and echo effects impose one or more repetitions on a sound, at time intervals ranging from a few milliseconds to several seconds. In order to simulate this process in MIDI, you have to copy the tracks to be processed onto a free track—that is, a track that's set to the same channel number—while advancing this copy by a certain number of ticks, depending on the duration of the desired effect.

For example, with the help of a sequencer at a resolution of 96 ticks to the quarter-note, the act of copying Track A to Track B while advancing the copy by 48 ticks is the same as applying an eighth-note delay to Track A. By repeating this procedure (that is, by copying Track B to Track C, copying Track C to Track D, and so on), you get several successive repetitions, without forcing them to be spaced the same number of ticks apart. This way, there's no reason why you couldn't shift Track C by, say, 96 ticks with regard to Track B, and Track D by, say, 24 ticks with regard to Track C. In this case the echoes would come at a distance of one eighth-note, one dotted quarter-note (that is, a quarter-note plus an eighth-note), and one double-dotted quarter-note (that is, a quarter-note plus an eighth-note plus a sixteenth-note) from the notes on Track A.

Compared to any conventional procedure, the MIDI echo has the advantage of letting you use as many different sounds as there are successive repetitions (because to do that, all you have to do is assign a different channel number to each track that you copy). However, the MIDI echo also has the disadvantage of multiplying the number of tracks and therefore the number of polyphonic voices required (which doubles with each repetition).

At base, the volume of a natural echo has a tendency to decrease with the number of repetitions. In order to reproduce this acoustical characteristic, you have a choice. You can decrease the velocity of each copy (provided that the velocity has an effect on the amplitude of the sound), or you can program a decrescendo of the MIDI volume (provided that your copies are assigned to different channels).

Some sequencers, such as the Cubase software shown in Figure 8.7 below, go so far as to incorporate a module dedicated to the MIDI echo effect. This effects processor acts either upon input (that is, at the MIDI In port) or upon output (that is, at the MIDI Out port), letting you hear

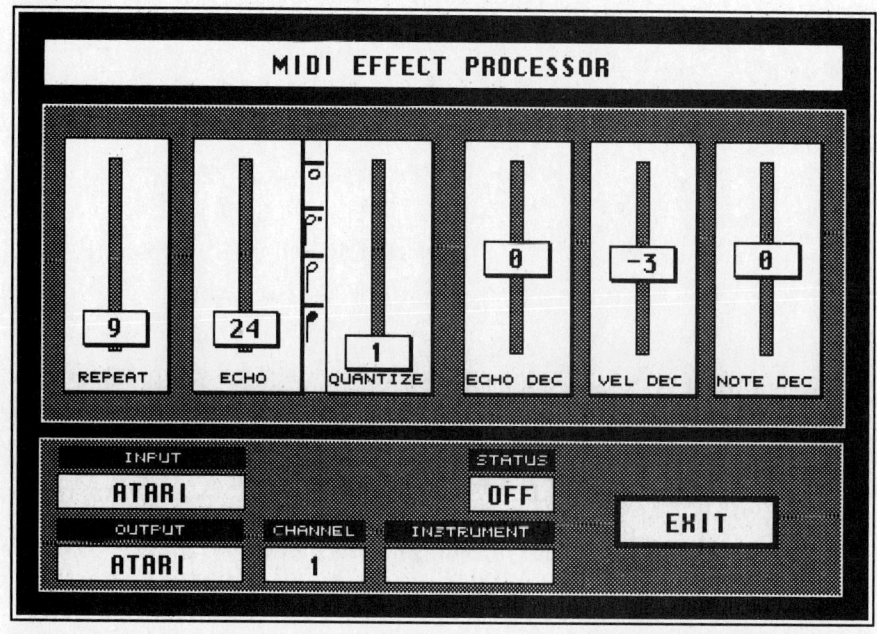

FIGURE 8.7: *The MIDI Processor window of Cubase*

the effect in real time (to the extent that the interpretation allows it), record it directly on a track, or trigger it only during reading. The number, spacing, and quantification of these repetitions are programmable, because each repetition is associated with a positive or negative shift-offset of the echo time, the velocity, and the transposition.

The Harmonizer

A harmonizer produces an effect that duplicates a signal at a certain pitch interval (for instance, a third, a fifth, etc.). To reproduce this effect with a sequencer, all you have to do is copy the desired track before transposing this copy by a greater or lesser given number of semitones. In the same way as for the MIDI echo effect, there's no reason why you can't program a tone-doubling sound that's different from the original (provided that another MIDI channel is available).

How Dynamics Are Handled

The dynamic range of a signal, as expressed in decibels (dB), measures the extent of the volume of the signal from its minimum level to its maximum level. In audio, this dynamic range lends itself to a variety of treatments. The most widely used of these treatments are compression, limitation, and expansion. All of these effects can be simulated by means of a sequencer, provided the sequencer is capable of performing operations on velocity (by addition, subtraction, multiplication, and division), and provided the velocity has an effect on the volume of the sound that's being processed.

The Compressor

Compressing an audio signal consists of attenuating it by a certain percentage when its level is greater than a given threshold value. This percentage, which is known as the *ratio*, is expressed in the form "A:1". If you let X represent the compression threshold, let Y represent the level of the signal at the input of the compressor, and let Z represent the level of the signal at the output of the compressor, then the following treatments can be applied:

- When Y is less than or equal to X:

  $$Z = Y$$

- When Y is greater than X:

  $$Z = X + ((Y - X) / A) = X + Y:A - X:A$$

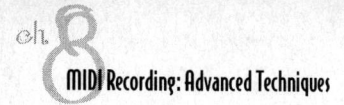
For example, for a compression ratio of 2:1 and a threshold value of 80 dB, as shown in Figure 8.8 below, the signals whose levels are higher (for instance, 90 dB, 100 dB, 110 dB, etc.) will be decreased by an amplitude equal to half the distance between these values and the threshold value (for instance, 85 dB, 90 dB, 95 dB, etc.).

In order to obtain an equivalent result with a sequencer, the sequencer should be capable of operating selectively on the velocities that are greater than the threshold value. (In this case the sequencer has to divide these velocities by the value of A, add the value of X, and then deduct the value of X/A.) If this is not the case, then you can approximate the desired result by dividing the entire set of velocities by A (which is equivalent to working with a null threshold), then adding a constant to the set of divided velocities (with the constant being small enough that the result is never greater than 127), in such a way as to raise the general level of the dynamic range that has been compressed in this manner.

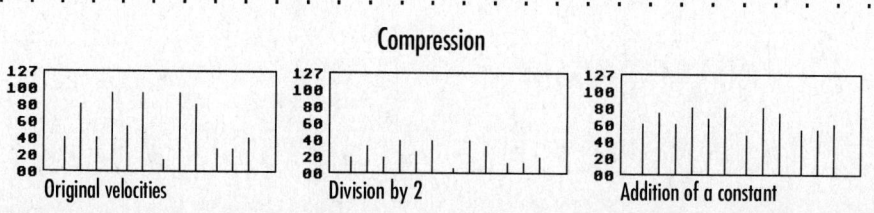

FIGURE 8.8: *Compression of all the velocities with a ratio of 2:1, followed by the addition of a constant (in this case, 40)*

The Expander

Expansion, which is the opposite of compression, consists of increasing or extending an audio signal by a certain percentage when its level is greater than a given threshold value. This percentage, which is also known as the ratio, is expressed in the form "A:1". If you let X represent the expansion threshold, let Y represent the level of the signal at the input of the expander, and let Z represent the level of the signal at the output of the expander, then the following treatments can be applied:

- When Y is less than or equal to X:

  Z = Y

- When Y is greater than X:

  Z = X + ((Y − X) x A) = X + X × A − X x A

For example, for an expansion ration of 4:1 and a threshold value of 20 dB, as shown in Figure 8.9 below, the signals whose level is higher (for instance, 30 dB, 35 dB, 40 dB, etc.) will be increased with regard to the threshold value by an amplitude equal to four times the distance between these levels and the threshold value (that is, for the signals listed above, 60 dB, 80 dB, 100 dB, etc.).

In order to obtain an equivalent result with the aid of a sequencer, the sequencer should be capable of operating selectively on the velocities that are greater than the threshold value. (In this case the sequencer has to multiply these velocities by the value of A, add the value of X, and then deduct the value of X × A.) If this is not the case, then you can approximate the desired result by multiplying the entire set of velocities by A (which is equivalent to working with a null threshold). Either way, you should make sure that the result of these operations does not exceed 127.

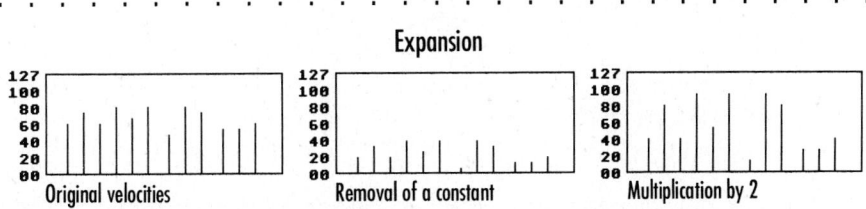

Expansion

FIGURE 8.9: *Expansion of velocities whose value is greater than a threshold value of 20 dB with a ratio of 4:1*

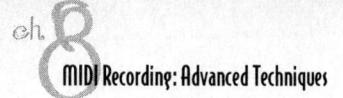
The Limiter

Limiting an audio signal is the equivalent of compressing the signal with a maximum ratio (from + infinity:1)—in other words, keeping the signal from going beyond the threshold. If you let X represent the limitation threshold, let Y represent the level of the signal at the input of the limiter, and let Z represent the level of the signal at the output of the limiter, then the following treatments can be applied:

- When Y is less than or equal to X:

  Z = Y

- When Y is greater than or equal to X:

  Z = X

To obtain an equivalent result with the aid of a sequencer, you would start by setting a velocity threshold value X that should not be exceeded, and then add to the set of velocities in the sequence the difference W between this threshold value and the maximum value that the velocity can accept (in other words, W = 127 −X). This operation has the effect of bringing all velocities that are greater than or equal to X to a value of 127, while increasing by W the velocities that are strictly less than X. Then you can remove the value W (still operating on the entire set of velocities), to bring back to their original values those values that initially didn't exceed the value of X, and to force the other values to X (that is, 127 − W). This way, all of the velocities are between 1 and X, as shown for example in Figure 8.10 below.

It's easy to see how the opposite operation can be performed (that is, with a minimum threshold value beyond which none of the velocities should fall). This latter operation can be useful when the volume of certain notes in a recording is too low.

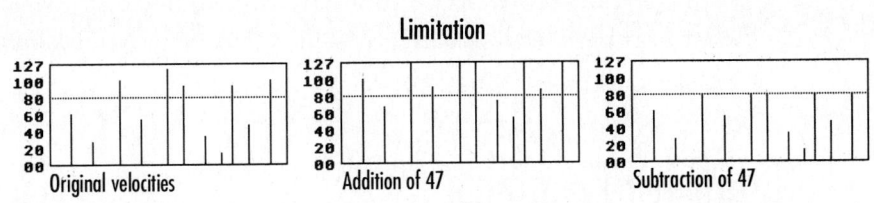

Limitation

| Original velocities | Addition of 47 | Subtraction of 47 |

FIGURE 8.10: *Removal of a constant (in this case, 40), followed by the expansion of all the velocities with a ratio of 2:1*

These operations—compression, expansion, and limitation—can be applied to other types of status (such as aftertouch and modulation), and can sometimes lead to unexpected results.

The Modulation Effects

Commonly known as the "modulation effects," the chorus, vibrato, and other phase-based effects are intended to "thicken" a sound. They add one or more quasi-identical signals to the original tone, with slight cyclic fluctuations in pitch, often delayed by several milliseconds. This type of effect is harder to achieve with a sequencer.

To do so, first you have to select a controller that has a moderate effect on the pitch of a sound (preferably by modulation or aftertouch, as opposed to Pitch Bend), and then get access to a multitimbral expander on which you can set two identical timbres on two different MIDI channels. After recording one track on the first channel, you can duplicate this track by assigning the second channel to the copy, in order to record slight pitch variations, with the aid of the controller, on a third track. This third track is programmed on either of the other two channels. (A small number of bars is sufficient, as long as they're repeated throughout the length of the track.) The variations in pitch applied by this controller

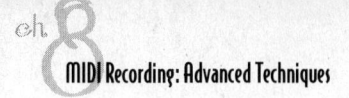

cause vibratory phenomena identical to those created by the vibrato, chorus, or phase effects. This procedure can be improved by shifting either of the first two tracts by several ticks.

Automatic Panorama

The automatic pan, or auto-pan, effect consists of dynamically shifting a signal in stereophonic space. This effect can be simulated with the aid of Control Change number 10 (0AH). Starting with a window that provides a graphic representation of the controllers, you can, for example, use the mouse to draw the desired curve.

Chorus, Auto-Pan, and the MIDI Harmonizer

This section, which ranges farther afield from sequencers, discusses how to obtain effects that are equivalent to the ones you've just been looking at, but this time in real time, with the help of a few lines of code written in BASIC. The listing shown below represents a MIDI program that can generate three effects simultaneously—namely, Chorus, Auto-Pan, and Harmonizer.

In this example, a keyboard sending over Channel 1 is connected to the computer, whose output is directed toward a sound generator (optionally the sound generator of the same keyboard, with Local Mode off). Two identical tones are programmed on Channel 1 and Channel 2, in order to be sent to the right-hand and left-hand outputs of the sound generator.

When the program receives a Note On message via Channel 1, it calculates three random numbers. The first two numbers create a discord between Sound 1 and Sound 2 by sending Pitch Bend messages, while the third number sets the pan effect for Sound 1 (with Sound 2 being set the opposite way). Once these various settings have been established, the note that was received is retransmitted, twice, via MIDI Channel 1 and MIDI Channel 2 (as are the messages indicating that the note has been released). Furthermore, the value 12 is added to the note number on Channel 2, thereby creating an octave harmony. The other MIDI bytes are sent unchanged (via the Thru function). For the sake of simplicity, messages other than the note messages are not reduplicated. As a result, an action such as the application of pressure to a sustain pedal or the shifting of a modulation wheel will be effective only on Channel 1.

The following program was written and implemented in the T-BASIC language provided by Dr. T's Music Software.

A MIDI Multi-Effect: Chorus, Panorama, and Harmonizer

```
10 CLS

20 MIDIOUT &HB0:MIDIOUT 123:MIDIOUT 0:        All Notes Off Channel 1

30 MIDIOUT &HB1:MIDIOUT 123:MIDIOUT 0:        All Notes Off Channel 2

40 LOOP:                                      main loop

50 GOSUB MIDI_IN:                             reception of a byte

60 IF BYTE = &H90 THEN GOTO NOTE_ON:          is it a Note On?

70 IF BYTE = &H80 THEN GOTO NOTE_OFF:         is it a Note Off?

80 IF BYTE < 128 AND N = 1 THEN GOTO 150:     Running Status Note On

90 IF BYTE < 128 AND N = 2 THEN GOTO 250:     Running Status Note Off

100 N = 0:MIDIOUT BYTE:GOTO LOOP:             MIDI Thru

110 '

120 NOTE_ON:

130 N = 1:                                    pointer set to 1

140 GOSUB MIDI_IN:                            reception of Note Number
```

```
150 NOTE = BYTE:                                      storage in NOTE

160 GOSUB MIDI_IN:                                    reception of velocity

170 GOSUB PAN_BEND:                                   chorus/auto-pan subroutine

180 MIDIOUT &H90:MIDIOUT NOTE:MIDIOUT BYTE:           send Note On Channel 1

186 FOR X = 1 TO (P2*5):NEXT:                          random delay

190 MIDIOUT &H91:MIDIOUT (NOTE + 12):                 send Note On...

196 MIDIOUT BYTE:                                     ...Channel 2

200 GOTO LOOP:                                        return to the loop

210 '

220 NOTE_OFF:

230 N = 2 :                                           pointer at 2

240 GOSUB MIDI_IN:                                    reception of Note Number

250 NOTE = BYTE:                                      storage in NOTE

260 GOSUB MIDI_IN:                                    reception of velocity

270 MIDIOUT &H80:MIDIOUT NOTE: MIDIOUT BYTE:          send Note Off Channel 1

280 MIDIOUT &H81:MIDIOUT (NOTE + 12):                 send Note Off...

286 MIDIOUT BYTE:                                     ...Channel 2

290 GOTO LOOP:                                        return to the loop

300 '

310 PAN_BEND:

320 P0 = INT ((RND(1)*8) + 1):                        random between 1 and 8

330 P1 = INT ((RND(1)*9) - 8):                        random between 0 and - 8

340 P2 = INT ((RND(1)*127) + 1):                      random between 0 and 127

350 P3 = 128 - P2:                                    complement to 127
```

```
360 MIDIOUT &HEO: MIDIOUT O:MIDIOUT (64 + PO): Pitch Bend Channel 1

370 MIDIOUT &HE1: MIDIOUT O:MIDIOUT (64 + P1): Pitch Bend Channel 2

380 MIDIOUT &HBO: MIDIOUT &HOA:MIDIOUT P2:      Pan Channel 1

390 MIDIOUT &HB1: MIDIOUT &HOA:MIDIOUT P3:      Pan Channel 2

400 RETURN

410 '

420 MIDI_IN:                             reception of a byte

430 S=INP(-3): IF S=0 THEN GOTO MIDI_IN

440 BYTE=INP(3): RETURN
```

The Programmable Harmonizer

This second program simulates a harmonizer. However, unlike a conventional harmonizer, the transposition interval can be programmed independently for each degree of the scale (that is, for each of the twelve semitones). For instance, by associating the notes C, D, E, F, G, A, and B with the intervals +4 (E), +3 (F), +3 (G), +4 (A), +4 (B), +3 (C), and +3 (D), you get a so-called "tonal" harmonizer with so-called "variable" thirds (that is, minor or major thirds, as necessary, but always in the key of C major).

```
10 DIM TRA(132)
20 DATA C, C#, D, D#, E, F, F#, G, G#, A, A#, B
30 FOR X = 0 TO 11
40 READ NOTE$
50 CLS
60 PRINT NOTE$;: INPUT " TRANSPOSITION "; T
70 IF T > 12 OR T < -12 THEN GOTO 50
80 Z = X
90 FOR Y = 1 TO 11
100 TRA(Z) = Z + T
110 IF Y = 1 AND (Z + T) < 0 THEN TRA(Z) = TRA(Z) + 12
```

```
120 IF Y = 11 AND (Z + T) > 127 THEN TRA(Z) = TRA(Z) - 12
130 Z = Z + 12
140 NEXT Y
150 NEXT X
160 MIDIOUT &HB0:MIDIOUT 123:MIDIOUT 0
170 MIDIOUT &HB1:MIDIOUT 123:MIDIOUT 0
180 CLS
190 '
200 LOOP:
210 GOSUB MIDI_IN
220 IF BYTE = &H90 THEN GOTO NOTE_ON
230 IF BYTE = &H80 THEN GOTO NOTE_OFF
240 IF BYTE < 128 AND N = 1 THEN GOTO 310
250 IF BYTE < 128 AND N = 2 THEN GOTO 410
260 N = 0:MIDIOUT BYTE:GOTO LOOP
270 '
280 NOTE_ON:
290 N = 1
300 GOSUB MIDI_IN
310 NOTE = BYTE
320 GOSUB MIDI_IN
340 MIDIOUT &H90:MIDIOUT NOTE:MIDIOUT BYTE
350 MIDIOUT &H90:MIDIOUT TRA(NOTE):MIDIOUT BYTE
360 GOTO LOOP
370 '
380 NOTE_OFF:
390 N = 2
400 GOSUB MIDI_IN
410 NOTE = BYTE
420 GOSUB MIDI_IN
430 MIDIOUT &H80:MIDIOUT NOTE: MIDIOUT BYTE
440 MIDIOUT &H80:MIDIOUT TRA(NOTE): MIDIOUT BYTE
450 GOTO LOOP
460 '
470 MIDI_IN:
480 S=INP(-3):IF S=0 THEN GOTO MIDI_IN
490 BYTE=INP(3):RETURN
```

MIDI Recording and Delay Problems

Despite their attractiveness, sequencers can leave MIDI without a leg to stand on, because they let musicians record an astonishing number of tracks—in other words, transmit message at a high density. This section addresses the delays that sequencers and MIDI in general can cause.

MIDI's speed, which is set at 31,250 bits per second, allows the transmission of approximately 3000 bytes per second. No application, not even the densest sequence, requires the continuous sending of this many messages. In fact, the delay problems arise partly because of the fact that MIDI, thanks to its serial nature, can't send more than one piece of information at a time.

As a result, when a musician plays five notes at the same time on a keyboard, the corresponding Note On messages are sent not in a single bunch but sequentially, one after another. At a rate of 0.32 millisecond per byte, two consecutive Note On messages are separated by an interval of 0.96 millisecond (because each Note On message consists of three bytes). Therefore, a period of exactly 4.8 milliseconds elapses between the first and the last of these five messages. For the human ear, this delay is virtually imperceptible. However, this delay phenomenon is more discernible with a sequencer when several instruments are playing at the same time.

Furthermore, the distribution of messages over time is far from uniform. Instead of being apportioned in equal amounts throughout the length of a piece, notes have a tendency to pile up. Beyond a certain limit, these concentrations cause audible delays.

Suppose, for example, that on the first beat of a measure, a sequencer transmits four notes over each of the sixteen MIDI channels, at a rate of one track per channel (a circumstance which is fairly unlikely). In such a

case, you would have no fewer than 192 simultaneous MIDI bytes (that is, 4 × 16 Note On messages). Of course, the Running Status is responsible for partially reducing the number of these messages, even though it acts only on the consecutive status indicators of the same type and the same channel. In such a case, the Running Status would process each track, i.e., each channel, independently. As a result, you'd have 144 bytes instead of 192 bytes for the entire set of 16 tracks.

An interval of 46.08 milliseconds (i.e., 144 × 0.32), or an interval of 61.44 milliseconds (i.e., 192 × 0.32) separates the sending of the last note from the sending of the first note. This delay is clearly perceptible, and denser messages (such as Pitch Bend, Aftertouch, and continuous controllers) can make it even more noticeable. Although purely theoretical, this example shows the limitations of MIDI transmission speed.

Paradoxically, quantization is sometimes responsible for delay problems. Imagine, for instance, that a sequence consisting of five non-quantized tracks (piano, strings, melody, bass, and drums) contains a high density of messages clustered around the third beat of the first measure, as shown below.

Track 1 (piano)

1/2/90	Note On C1
1/2/94	Note On C2
1/2/95	Note On E3
1/3/3	Note On G3
1/3/3	Note On B3

Track 2 (strings)

1/2/94	Note On B3
1/3/1	Note On C4
1/3/1	Note On G4

Track 3 (melody)

1/3/5	Note On B4

Track 4 (bass)

1/2/95	Note On C1

Track 5 (drums)

1/2/94	Note On (bass drum)
1/3/1	Note On (closed charley)

Naturally, the few notes located at the same position (1/2/94 and 1/1/95, and 1/3/1 and 1/3/3) will be transmitted by the MIDI port one after another. In other words, at 1/2/94, only the first of the three notes will keep its original position. The other two notes will appear 0.96 and 1.92 milliseconds later, respectively, at the sequencer's MIDI Out port. (This delay could be reduced to 0.64 and 1.28 milliseconds, respectively, if Running Status were activated.). Either way, these delays are nontrivial.

A quantization operation performed on the five tracks of the sequence will readjust the foregoing thirteen notes to the same position (that is, to 1/3/0). As a result, the last note will be sent 11.52 (that is, 0.96×12)

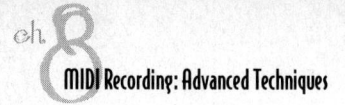
milliseconds later than the first note. (As before, this delay can be reduced to 7.68 milliseconds by using Running Status.) Although this shift is still acceptable with a string sound (whose attack is slow), it is unacceptable for instruments with a fast attack.

Generally speaking, there are a few procedures that make it possible to reduce these delays in a satisfactory manner.

Priorities

From the sequencer's point of view, not all messages have the same degree of priority. As a result, in order to ensure perfect synchronization between the different devices in a network, the MIDI clock signal takes precedence over the other status indicators. (The MIDI clock signal can even interrupt a MIDI message in the middle.) Furthermore, apart from the clock signal, a properly designed sequencer will give priority to transmitted notes, for which delays are more damaging than they are for the other messages.

Filtering

Because of their high transmission density, the aftertouch messages (either Polyphonic Key Pressure or Channel Aftertouch) the Pitch Bend message, and Modulation are among the three main parameters responsible for MIDI traffic jams. Although most of the continuous controllers (such as volume, balance, and panorama) are just as greedy, it's these three types of messages that are most often to blame, because of their physical implementation on most instruments. Although Pitch Bend and Modulation messages are transmitted when the musician repositions the corresponding wheels, the aftertouch messages are often generated without the musician's knowledge, if the keyboard is a little too sensitive to pressure. This is why, when (as often happens) a sound doesn't use aftertouch, this type of message should usually be filtered, either during recording or during reading. This second option offers the advantage of keeping these messages in the sequencer's memory, so that transmission of them can be re-enabled if the need to do so should arise.

Density

Pitch Bend messages, monophonic and channel-wise aftertouch messages, and the set of continuous controllers are sent at a given rate, depending on the instrument being used. This rate is sometimes too high for the desired result. Consequently, while accuracy on the order of thirty messages per second may be enough to convey the motion that the musician imparts to the modulation wheel, the keyboard may have issued fifty or a hundred messages. In order to reduce this kind of clogging of the MIDI network (and therefore the delay problems), along with the amount of memory space occupied by the messages, some sequencers let users reduce the density of these messages after recording them.

Channel Priorities

It's obvious that delays penalize first the sounds whose attacks are rapid, and particularly percussive sounds. As a result, unlike a track of sustained sounds (strings, etc.), a drum track or a bass track can't tolerate delays. This is why some sequencers give output priority to a particular channel. In the event of a conflict (that is, the emission of several different notes simultaneously over different channels), the messages on the priority channel will be transmitted first. Therefore, it's useful to allocate the most sensitive instruments to this channel.

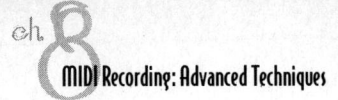
Track Priorities

At the data-processing level, the different messages located at the same position are read by the sequencer track by track, from first to last. As a result, looking again at the example at the beginning of this section with regard to the delays caused by quantization, the drums will suffer a maximum degree of delay (because they're recorded on the last track), and the piano is spared any delays at all (because it's recorded on the first track). Therefore it's advisable to operate in the opposite direction, assigning to the first tracks the sounds that are the most sensitive to delays—that is, the sounds whose attacks are the most rapid.

The Concept of Multiple Outputs

Even though they provide a partial solution, the procedures described above aren't miracle cures for MIDI bottlenecks. The multiple-output solution, which consists of using several MIDI Out ports, as shown in Figure 8.11 below, is by far the most effective answer. This method makes it possible to gather the instruments to be driven into several clusters, each of which is connected to one of the sequencer's MIDI Out ports. Thanks to a port addressing system, the sequencer can assign any given track to any given output. Delays are reduced accordingly.

Some hardware sequencers include several MIDI Out ports. In the absence of multiple outputs, it is also possible to make several synchronized MIDI sequencers, each of which has one or more outputs, run in parallel, as shown in Figure 8.12 below.

In addition to alleviating possible MIDI delay problems, multiple outputs increase the number of usable channels (for instance, 4 outputs = 16 × 4 = 64 channels). This procedure can be indispensable when you're using several multitimbral sound generators at once.

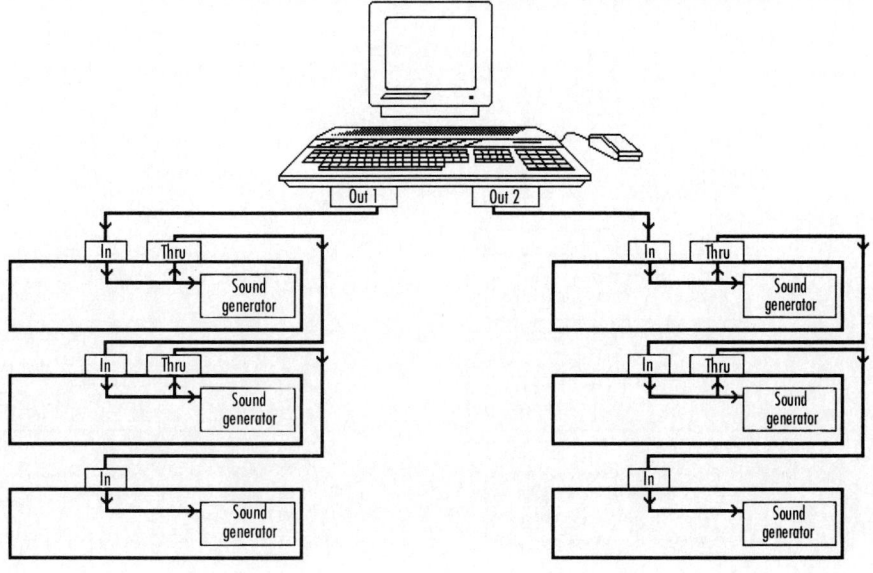

FIGURE 8.11: *A sequencer with multiple outputs, each of which addresses a network of expanders*

These various methods, which can be used in conjunction with one another, let you solve most of the MIDI delay problems. However, the noticeable density of the data generated by a sequencer isn't the only reason these problems exist.

Sound-Generator Response Times

Even if MIDI events are transmitted to sound generators on time, there's still no guarantee that the sound generators will react instantaneously. The response time varies from one instrument to another, ranging from one millisecond to as many as 20 milliseconds or more in the worst

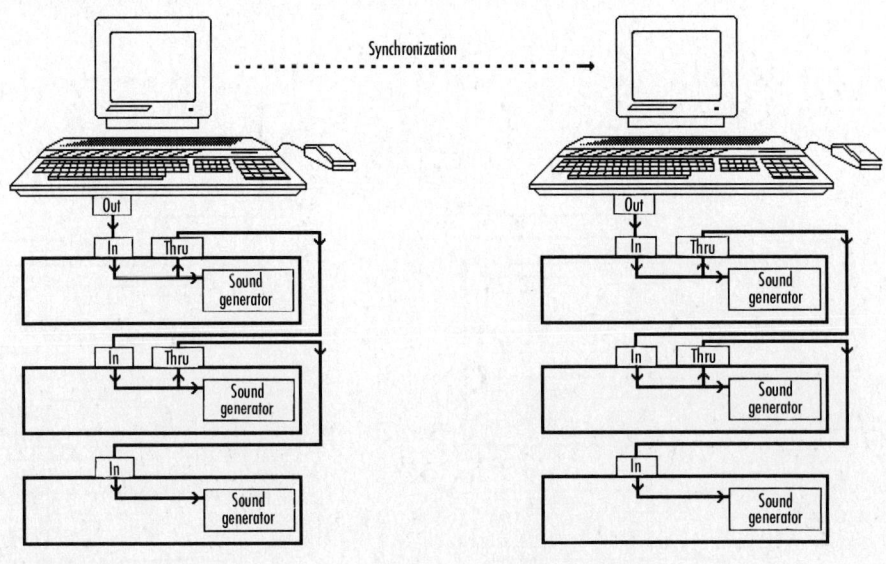

FIGURE 8.12: *Synchronization of several sequencers, each of which addresses a network of expanders*

case—a delay that's clearly discernible for sounds with a rapid attack. However, with the help of a stereo sampler, there's an easy way to evaluate these response times.

Suppose you begin by selecting a percussive sound with a maximum attack on the sound generator to be tested, taking care to initialize all of the control parameters for the envelope (such as the response to velocity and aftertouch, the weighting curves, etc.). Then you record a note with the help of a sequencer, positioning the note on a strong beat (for instance, at the beginning of a bar). When the sequence is read, all you have to do is sample the sound generator at one of the stereo inputs simultaneously with the metronome click at the other stereo input in order to deduce the response time from the conversion into milliseconds of the number of periods separating the start of each of the signals. (At a sampling frequency of 44,100 Hz, one sampling period is equal to 0.0226757 millisecond, and one millisecond is equal to slightly more than 44 periods.) Because this type of delay increases with polyphony and multitimbrality, it's worthwhile to repeat this experiment, recording increasing numbers of notes located at the same position over different channels (i.e., timbres).

A simplified version of this method lets you work with a monaural sampler, provided that the sampler is able to trigger a sample when it receives a MIDI Note On message, which replaces the metronome click. The calculation is even simpler, because in this case all you have to do is count the number of periods separating the beginning of the sample from the beginning of the sound. However, this procedure is less reliable than the stereo version, because you can't assume that the triggering of the sampler via MIDI will happen exactly the same way every time.

These different measurements, taken for each of the sound generators, help make it possible to solve delay problems. To do that, you have to compensate for each generator's response time by advancing the corresponding track by an appropriate amount (or else by delaying all the other tracks), either with the help of a delay function or by shifting the track.

Exclusive Messages

Having examined the performance of sound generators with regard to response times, this section ends with a study of their reactions to the transmission and reception of Exclusive messages. Once again, its extent can be measured with the help of a sequencer.

The size of Exclusive messages is currently on the order of several thousand bytes. To optimize the transmission of these messages, the sending

device should theoretically make maximum use of the MIDI pass-band—in other words, send the data at a rate of 3,125 bytes per second. But even if data is transmitted at a speed of 31,250 bits per second, the standard doesn't provide any way to regulate the time interval between any two of these bytes. As a result, some MIDI instruments may be happy sending data at a rate of only 2000 bytes per second, i.e., using only about 64 percent of the available MIDI pass-band.

The MIDI Buffer

The job of the MIDI receiving buffer (not to be confused with the editing buffer) is to keep the instrument from losing the bytes it receives while it's attending to other tasks. This buffer temporarily stores the messages the instrument receives, in order to give the instrument time it may need to process other messages it received earlier.

Nevertheless, when the number of messages to be stored exceeds the capacity of the buffer, the buffer overflows, and any subsequent incoming information is lost.

It's worth emphasizing that it is possible to test the limits of an instrument's buffer with the help of a sequencer by sending MIDI events to the sequencer continuously and at maximum density while waiting for the sequencer to display an overflow message, hang up, or freeze.

Storing Sequences

At the beginning of this section, you saw that sequencers don't record just MIDI messages, but also temporal references, expressed in the form of ticks, intended to measure the duration of the periods between

MIDI messages. Both of these quantities (that is, the durations and the MIDI messages), which can differ in size, are stored together in the computer's memory in the same form—that is, as bytes. In order not to confuse these two types of information (for instance, how can you tell whether the value 90H/144 indicates a note-pressed status on Channel 1, or an interval of 144 ticks?), sequencers use appropriate storage formats. Because they aren't governed by any standards, these formats are generally different from one device to another. Here's an example.

Korg M1 Format

The Korg M1 sequencer, whose resolution is 48 to the quarter-note, stores MIDI events in the form of four bytes, as shown below:

Note On/Note Off

1vvv vvvt tttt tttt kkkk kkkl llll llll

- Bit 31, which is set to 1, characterizes a note event.

- vvvvvv: the velocity, truncated to 6 bits. In other words, because only bits 1 to 6 are retained, the quantification of the velocity is divided by two with regard to its original value.

- ttttttttt: a temporal event (i.e., a time interval separating two messages) expressed in the form of 9 bits, in terms of the number of ticks

- lllllllll: the length of the event expressed in the form of 9 bits in terms of the number of ticks. The Korg M1 sequencer stores the information in the form of a Note On/duration message. Once this duration has elapsed, the corresponding Note Off message is automatically sent (excluding any consideration of the release speed).

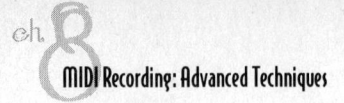

The types of time signatures that the M1 accepts are the following: 2/4, 3/4, 4/4, 5/4, and 6/4. In this last case, there are 288 ticks per bar. In general, of course, bits llllllll (whose value is from 0 to 511) can't represent intervals with a duration of 11 signals (because 11 × 48 ticks = 528 ticks). This is why Korg has developed the following approach: When the end of a note exceeds the measure within which the note began, bits llllllll no longer represent the length of the note, but rather signal the fact that the note is continuing beyond the end of the measure in question. In such a case these bits take on the value 1FEH. A new event is created in the next measure, for which bits tttttttt also take on the value 1FEH, in order to signal that the note began in the preceding measure. In other words, with regard to the length of an event as well as to its temporal position, the value 1FHE indicates a link or bond.

- kkkkkkk: the MIDI note number

Pitch Bend

`0001000t 0vvvvvvv 0vvvvvvv tttttttt`

- 0001: the Pitch Bend message identifier
- vvvvvvvvvvvvvv: the value

Channel Aftertouch

`0010000t 0vvvvvvv 00000000 tttttttt`

- 0010: the Aftertouch message identifier
- vvvvvvv: the value

Program Change

```
0011000t pppppppp 00000000 tttttttt
```

- 0011: the Program Change message identifier

- PPPPPPPP:
  - 0 to 199 / I00 to C99 (allocation of 100 programs and 100 combinations)
  - 0 to 49, 100 to 149 / I00 to 49, C00 to 49 (50 programs and 50 combinations)

Control Change

```
0100000t 0ccccccc 0vvvvvvv tttttttt
```

- 0100: the Control Change message identifier

- vvvvvvv: the value

- ccccccc: the MIDI control number, from 00 to 65 and from 66 to 6B for events specific to the M1

- 66H: an assignable pedal

- 67H: effect 1 on or off

- 68H: effect 2 on or off

- 69H: balance of effect 1

- 6AH: balance of effect 2

- 6BH: tempo

End of Track

`0111000t tttttttt 00000000 00000000`

- 0111: the end-of-track identifier

- tttttttt: temporal position expressed in the form of 9 bits, in terms of the number of ticks

Start of Bar

`01100000 bbbbbbbb xx000000 0ppppppp`

- 0110: the start-of-bar identifier

- bbbbbbbb: the bar number

- xx: the type of bar

    xx = 00:   the bar does not use any of the 100 patterns of the M1

    xx = 10:   the pattern occurs within this bar

    xx = 11:   the pattern starts with this bar

- ppppppp: the pattern number

In addition to the conversion of a Note On/Note Off pair into a Note On/duration pair (whereas the Pro 24 stores Note On and Note Off messages separately), one of the other peculiarities of the storage format used by the Korg M1 is the fact that it doesn't store the MIDI channel number. Instead, this information is calculated directly from a reading of the channel number as programmed for each track of the sequencer.

Advantages and Limitations of MIDI Files

The standard MIDI file format allows you to exchange sequences created on different sequencer programs. The fact that a single given file can be read by most sequencers has several advantages. In addition to making it easier for companies to sell sequences on disk without having to convert the sequences to the various different existing formats specific to each piece of software, MIDI Files compatibility lets several users exchange a file without having to own or use the same sequencers. This compatibility also lets a single individual work on a piece with the help of different software, such as a sequencer X that performs especially well for recording, a sequencer Y that's better suited to editing, software Z that specializes in printing stores, and so on.

However, MIDI Files compatibility is limited by formatting compatibility. In point of fact, computers are *a priori* incapable of reading disks whose format is different from their own unless they use the services of a specialized utility, as is the case with the Apple File Exchange utility for the Macintosh. This utility was designed to read and write MS-DOS disks (that is, disks that can be read and written by IBM PCs and PS systems), which in turn are recognized by Atari ST, STE, and TT systems. Without exception (particularly at Roland), and always because of formatting constraints and requirements, most hardware sequencers are not compatible with MIDI Files. In microcomputer-based data processing, another method—remote loading—lets you get around the problem by transferring files between two different computers via a modem or a simple RS-232 port, with the help of suitable telecommunications software.

The Concept of Real Time: Delta Times

MIDI Files, and more generally speaking all sequence files, are different from other types of MIDI files (such as SysEx files, Sample Dump Standard files, etc.) because they incorporate the concept of real time, with two consecutive MIDI messages being separated by a given number of metronome pulses. As a result, the role of the Standard MIDI Files Version 1.0 consists of enabling the exchange of temporally related data between different pieces of software.

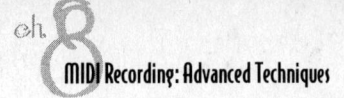

As you saw earlier, each MIDI message recorded by a sequencer is stored along with a piece of temporal data indicating the "time" at which the message arrived (or, more accurately, the number of ticks separating the message in question from the next one). Hence the terms "temporally referenced data" and "time-stamped data." In the MIDI Files vocabulary, the time interval between two MIDI events is expressed with the help of data known as *delta times*. In order to optimize file sizes, these delta times are compressed, thanks to a representation procedure that allows variable sizes. Because of the amount of calculation time these operations require, the MIDI Files format is unsuitable for the storage of data in a sequencer's memory. In fact, when performed in real time, during recording and during reading, respectively, the compression and decompression operations would slow the software by a corresponding amount of time. Therefore the sequencers store ticks and MIDI messages in memory in their own format, converting them into MIDI Files when a file needs to be saved, and performing the opposite operation when a file is loaded.

The Compression of Temporal Data

Before embarking on a detailed description of the MIDI Files language, it's advisable to start by examining the variable-size representation method used by the delta times. When a sequencer receives two successive Note On messages at an interval of one quarter-note, a piece of temporal data is stored which indicates that X ticks have elapsed between the reception of the first note and the reception of the second note. Remember, resolution has a direct effect on the memory location occupied by the temporal data, because the number of bits required to store an interval (as expressed in the form of ticks) increases proportionally with the duration of the interval.

This is why the Standard MIDI Files rely on a variable-size format, which optimizes the size of the delta times to the nearest byte. The ticks are indicated as accurately as possible in terms of 1, 2, 3, or 4 bytes, in order to use no more than the amount of space necessary to store a duration.

Delta Times

Suppose you have available only numbers whose size is fixed and which consist of four digits which we're constrained to use in order to express numeric values. For instance, the values 1, 25, 167, and 8371 would be indicated by 0001, 0025, 0167, and 8371, respectively. Now, suppose you agree never to use the digit zero when it isn't functional (that is, when it appears to the left of another, non-zero digit). Without knowing it, you're intuitively using a variable-size format that represents only the necessary information.

Conversely, computers can't perform this kind of reasoning, because they can't tell whether the digits in a binary number are useful or useless in representing a number. For instance, whether it's a matter of expressing the values 2, 16, or 255 (that is, 10, 10000, and 11111111, respectively, in binary notation), the numeric information is coded in the form of an 8-bit byte (that is, as 00000010, 00010000, and 11111111, respectively).

However, thanks to the delta-time method, the duration of an interval expressed in the form of ticks can be stored in the form of a variable number of bytes ranging from 1 to 4. In order to be able to detect whether the interval in question occupies 1, 2, 3, or 4 bytes, the most significant bit in each byte is set to zero (0) when the byte is the last byte of a delta time; otherwise, this byte is set to one (1). Therefore only seven bits per byte can be used to store information, and as a result you have a total of 7, 14, 21, or 28 bits available, depending on the number of bytes in the delta-time message (1, 2, 3, or 4, respectively).

In order to familiarize ourselves with this concept of variable size, here are a few practical examples designed to convert into delta time a number

of ticks expressed in the form of four bytes (or, more precisely, in the form of 28 bits, which is the maximum allowed by delta time). By convention, the bits that are shifted to the left after compression, as a result of the length-identification function of bit 7, are underlined.

Before Compression

```
Hexadecimal          Binary

00H 00H 00H 00H      00000000 00000000 00000000 00000000
00H 00H 00H 40H      00000000 00000000 00000000 01000000
00H 00H 00H 64H      00000000 00000000 00000000 01100100
00H 00H 00H 7FH      00000000 00000000 00000000 01111111
00H 00H 00H 80H      00000000 00000000 00000000 10000000
00H 00H 00H 82H      00000000 00000000 00000000 10000010
00H 00H 20H 00H      00000000 00000000 00100000 00000000
00H 00H 21H 45H      00000000 00000000 00100001 01000101
00H 00H 3FH FFH      00000000 00000000 00111111 11111111
00H 00H 40H 00H      00000000 00000000 01000000 00000000
00H 10H 00H 00H      00000000 00010000 00000000 00000000
00H 1FH FFH FFH      00000000 00011111 11111111 11111111
00H 20H 00H 00H      00000000 00100000 00000000 00000000
08H 00H 00H 00H      00001000 00000000 00000000 00000000
0FH FFH FFH FFH      00001111 11111111 11111111 11111111
```

Remember, bit 7 of a delta-time byte (shown in boldface type in the following listing) is set to zero when that byte is the last byte. Otherwise, this bit is set to 1.

After Compression

```
Hexadecimal          Binary

            00H                          00000000
            40H                          01000000
            64H                          01100100
            7FH                          01111111
```

```
        81H  00H                                    10000001 00000000
        81H  02H                                    10000001 00000010
        C0H  00H                                    11000000 00000000
        C2H  45H                                    11000010 01000101
        FFH  7FH                                    11111111 01111111
   81H  80H  00H                          10000001 10000000 00000000
   C0H  80H  00H                          11000000 10000000 00000000
   FFH  FFH  7FH                          11111111 11111111 01111111
81H 80H  80H  00H                10000001 10000000 10000000 00000000
C0H 80H  80H  00H                11000000 10000000 10000000 00000000
FFH FFH  FFH  7FH                11111111 11111111 11111111 01111111
```

The values shown in terms of bytes by a number of useful bits from 0 to 7 (that is, from 00000000 to 01111111), from 8 to 14 (that is, from 10000000 to 00111111 11111111), from 15 to 21 (that is, from 01000000 00000000 to 00011111 11111111 11111111), and from 22 to 28 (that is, from 00100000 00000000 00000000 to 00001111 11111111 11111111 11111111) are coded respectively over 1, 2, 3, or 4 delta-time bytes. Here is how the operations should be carried out for each of these four categories:

- For values that can be represented by a number of useful bits from 0 to 7 (that is, values from 0 to 127):

Before Compression

```
minimum value: 00000000 (00H)
maximum value: 01111111 (7FH)
```

After Compression

```
minimum value: 00000000 (00H)
maximum value: 01111111 (7FH)
```

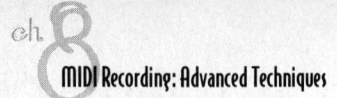

Procedure to Follow:

- Set bit 7 to zero.

- For values that can be represented by a number of useful bits from 8 to 14 (that is, values from 128 to 16,383):

Before Compression

```
minimum value:           10000000 (80H)
maximum value: 00111111 11111111 (3FH FFH)
```

After Compression

```
minimum value: 10000001 00000000 (81H 00H)
maximum value: 11111111 01111111 (FFH 7FH)
```

Procedure to Follow:

- Shift bits 7 to 13 one position to the left.

- Set bit 7 of the least significant byte to zero (0).

- Set bit 7 of the other bytes to one (1).

- For values that can be represented by a number of useful bits from 15 to 21 (that is, values from 16,384 to 2,097,151):

Before Compression

```
minimum value:           01000000 00000000     (40H 00H)
maximum value: 00011111 11111111 11111111 (1FH FFH FFH)
```

After Compression

```
minimum value: 10000001 10000000 00000000 (81H 80H 00H)
maximum value: 11111111 11111111 01111111 (FFH FFH 7FH)
```

Procedure to Follow:

- Shift bits 7 to 13 one position to the left.

- Shift bits 14 to 20 two positions to the left.

- Set bit 7 of the least significant byte to zero (0).

- Set bit 7 of the other bytes to one (1).

- For values that can be represented by a number of useful bits from 22 to 28 (that is, values from 2,097,152 to 268,435,455):

Before Compression

```
minimum value:          00100000 00000000 00000000
                        (20H 00H 00H)
maximum value: 00001111 11111111 11111111 11111111
               (0FH FFH FFH FFH)
```

After Compression

```
minimum value: 00000001 10000000 10000000 00000000
               (81H 80H 80H 00H)
maximum value: 11111111 11111111 11111111 01111111
               (FFH FFH FFH 7FH)
```

Procedure to Follow:

- Shift bits 7 to 13 one position to the left.

- Shift bits 14 to 20 two positions to the left.

- Shift bits 21 to 27 three positions to the left.

- Set bit 7 of the least significant byte to zero.

- Set bit 7 of the other bytes to 1.

So, for the maximum value as represented by 28 bits (i.e., 268,435,455), the number of ticks that elapse at a tempo of 120 quarter-notes to the

minute and at a resolution of 96 ticks to the quarter-note corresponds to a duration of approximately 16 days.

The Composition of MIDI Files: Chunks

MIDI Files are structured in the form of a given number of chunks. Each chunk is identified by a string of four ASCII characters (the name of the chunk) followed by four bytes, whose function is to determine the length of the chunk in terms of bytes, without including in the length the eight identification bytes (that is, the bytes that indicate the name and length of the chunk). There are two kinds of chunks: *header chunks* and *track chunks*. MIDI Files consist of a header chunk (which contains information of a general nature) followed by one or more track chunks.

The Header Chunk

The format of a header chunk is shown below:

```
<header chunk> = <chunk type> <length> <format> <ntrks>
<division>
```

- chunk type: specifies the type of chunk, in the form of 4 bytes in ASCII (for example, "MThd", 4DH 54H 68H 64H for the header chunk).

- length: specifies the length of the chunk in the form of 4 bytes (the length of a header chunk is in the form of 6 bytes), for example: 00H 00H 00H 06H.

- format: specifies the type of format in the form of 2 bytes whose value is currently limited to 0, 1, or 2 (and whose meanings are explained in the next section).

- ntrks: specifies, in the form of 2 bytes, the number of tracks (that is, the number of track chunks) used by the file.

- division: specifies, in the form of 2 bytes, the unit used by the delta times.

The delta times can be expressed not only with the help of a metric format, as you've done up till now (in terms of ticks, whose duration is a function of the resolution and of the tempo), but also with the help of a temporal format (with frame subdivision, in accordance with a SMPTE or MTC time code whose duration is a function of the number of subdivisions per frame, as well as a function of the number of frames per second). Bit 15 of the so-called "division" word is responsible for indicating whether the temporal format is a relative metrical reference (as it is if this bit is set to zero) or an absolute temporal reference (as it is if this bit is set to 1).

- Format of the metrical division:

```
0xxxxxxx xxxxxxxx
```

- xxxxxxx xxxxxxxx corresponds to the number of ticks per quarter-note (that is, the sequencer's resolution), among the 32,768 possible values. For a resolution of 192 ticks to the quarter-note, you would get the following result:

```
0000000 11000000 (00H C0H)
```

In other words, the duration of a delta time, at a rate of 192 to the quarter-note, depends on the tempo.

- Format of the temporal division:

```
1yyyyyyy xxxxxxxx
```

- yyyyyyy: the number of frames per second, in terms of negative values (for instance, −24, −25, −29, −30 (where the value of −29 characterizes the 30 drop-frame format, with 29.97 frames per second)). These negative values are expressed in terms of the two's complement, which means you have to invert all of the bits of the

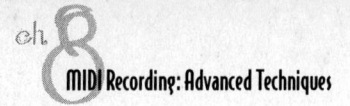

byte or bytes and then add 1. (Positive numbers aren't affected by this procedure.) For instance, with this method, a byte represents the values from −128 to +127, instead of the values from 0 to 255. To take an example, the number −29 is converted into its two's complement in the following way:

```
29 in binary:  0011101 (expressed over a 7-bit field)
bit inversion: 1100010
             +       1
               -------
               1100011
```

- xxxxxxxx: the number of subdivisions per frame (4 with the MIDI time code, and usually 8, 10, 80, or 100 with SMPTE code). With a time code with 25 frames per second and 40 subdivisions per frame, you get the following result:

```
11100111 00101000 (E7H 28H)
```

In the example shown in Figure 8.13 below, the duration of a delta time is equal to 1 millisecond.

Type 0, Type 1, and Type 2 Formats

The Type 0 format, which consists of a header chunk followed by a single track chunk, combines all of the tracks of a sequence into a single track. This format is intended essentially for software that can import sequences for monitoring purposes (which is the case with many library editors, which can generally read a so-called "single-track" sequence in such a way that you can listen in real time to the changes that are made in a sound).

The Type 1 format, which consists of a header chunk followed by one or more track chunks, involves most sequencers, because it is a multitrack format. Its architecture is vertical, with the various tracks being read simultaneously.

360

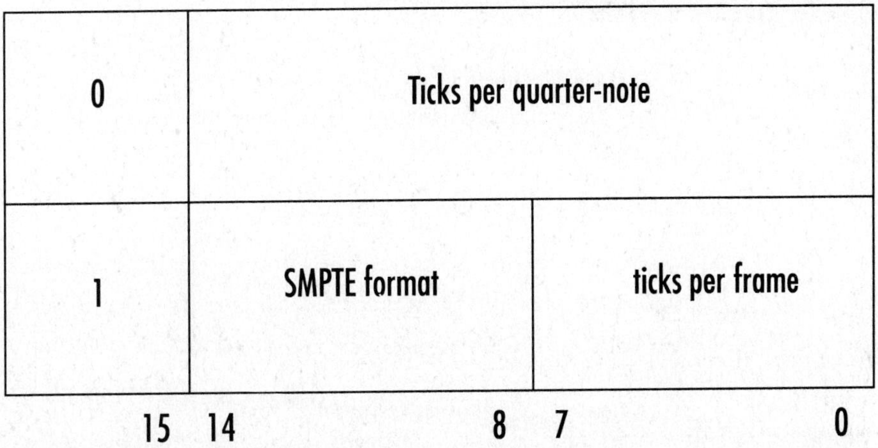

0	Ticks per quarter-note	
1	SMPTE format	ticks per frame

15   14   8   7   0

FIGURE 8.13: *Delta time units, in terms of the number of ticks (with quarter-note resolution), or in terms of the number of frame divisions*

Like the Type 1 format, the Type 2 format is a multitrack format consisting of a header chunk followed by one or more track chunks. However, its architecture is horizontal, and the various tracks are read sequentially (one after another, the same way the patterns in rhythm boxes are read).

Regardless of which format is used, each track can contain multichannel information.

The Track Chunk and Types of Events

The format of a track chunk is shown below:

```
<track chunk> = <chunk type> <length> <MTrk event 1> ...
<MTrk event n>
```

- chunk type: specifies the type of chunk ("MTrk", 4DH 54H 72H 6BH for a track chunk), in ASCII in the form of 4 bytes.

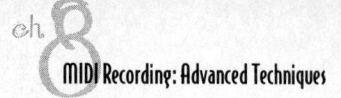
- length: specifies the length of the chunk (which can vary, depending on the number of events) in the form of 4 bytes.

A track chunk is only a series of events, each of which consists of a delta time that is associated with either a MIDI event or a non-MIDI event, as shown below:

```
<MTrk event> = <delta time> <event>
```

As you saw earlier, the delta times are stored with the help of a variable-length format. Even if the value of the delta times is null (such as at the start of a track, or for simultaneous events), the delta times must still be present.

Three types of events are associated with the delta times:

```
<event> = <MIDI event> or <SysEx event> or <meta event>
```

MIDI Events

MIDI events consist of channel messages (at the rate of one message per event). Running Status is accepted, even though it may be cancelled by a SysEx event or a Meta event.

SysEx Events

There are three types of formats for SysEx events. The first type of format, identified by F0H, consists of a string of exclusive MIDI bytes, as shown below:

```
<SysEx event> = F0H <length> <bytes to be transmitted
after F0H>
```

The length of the message (not including F0H and the length indicator) specifies the number of bytes to be transmitted. Unlike the length for a header chunk or a track chunk, this one is stored in variable-length form, just as it is for delta times. For example, the Exclusive message F0H 43H

20H 00H F7H (which happens to be the attention request in the DX7 synthesizer) is indicated in the following way:

```
F0H 04H (length) 43H 20H 00H F7H
```

The presence of the F7H End of Exclusive (EOX) status message is mandatory. Its purpose is to mark the end of the SysEx event.

The second SysEx format applies to System Exclusive messages that are divided into two or more packets separated by some interval of time. (Roland is one of the manufacturers that have adopted this approach.) For example, suppose that instead of sending a single message containing the following bytes:

```
F0H 41H 00H 16H 11H 03H 00H 00H 00H 00H 7FH 7EH F7H
```

the instrument did this:

```
F0H 41H 00H 16H
interval of 100 ticks
11H 03H 00H 00H 00H
interval of 200 ticks
00H 7FH 7EH F7H
```

Translated into MIDI File language, this kind of parcelling-out implies some knowledge of where the message starts and stops. To provide that information, the first packet starts with F0H (as in the previous format), while F7H is substituted for the following packets. Here again, it's essential that the last packet end with F7H, to indicate the end of the Exclusive message. The final product looks like this:

```
F0H 03H (length) 41H 00H 16H
64H (delta time, 100 ticks)
F7H 05H (length) 11H 03H 00H 00H 00H
81H 48H (delta time, 200 ticks)
F7H 04H (length) 00H 7FH 7EH F7H
```

The third format for a SysEx event, identified by F7H, takes the form shown below:

```
<SysEx event> = F7H <length> <bytes to be transmitted>
```

The purpose of this message is to authorize and enable the transmission of so-called "special" messages, such as System messages and Real Time messages (SPP, MTC, Song Select messages, etc.).

Meta Events

Meta events communicate information other than information couched in the MIDI language, as indicated below:

`<meta event> = FFH <type> <length> <bytes>`

- type: specifies the type of Meta event (only 15 of which are currently defined).

- length: indicates the length of the message in bytes (excluding the FFH, <type> and <length> parameters), expressed with the help of a variable-length format identical to the one used by delta times.

Descriptions of the fifteen Meta events appear below:

`sequence number: FFH 00H 02H ssH ssH`

This Meta event specifies, in the form of two bytes (ssH ssH), the pattern number for each track chunk in Type 2 format. It specifies the number of a sequence in Type 0 or Type 1 format, doing so on the first track chunk. When used, this number appears at the beginning of the track, ahead of any MIDI event or non-null delta times.

`text event: FFH 01H length, text`

The text is of variable length and can be used freely (for example, to describe a track, etc.). This event is usually coded in ASCII, although extended character sets can also be used without causing any problems.

`copyright notice: FFH 02H length, text`

This event contains the © character, the year, and the author's name (in ASCII). When used, this event appears at the beginning of the first track chunk, ahead of any non-null delta times.

`sequence/track name: FFH 03H length, text`

This event specifies the sequence name (in a Type 0 format, or else on the first track of a Type 1 format); otherwise, it indicates the track name. This event is expressed in ASCII.

`instrument name: FFH 04H length, text`

This event describes the type of instrument. It can be used in conjunction with the MIDI Channel Prefix Meta event.

`lyric: FFH 05H length, text`

This event indicates sung text, generally represented in the form of syllables (one per note).

`marker: FFH 06H length, text`

This event expresses information about the structure of a piece (couplet, refrain, repetition, etc.). It is generally found in a Type 0 format or else on the first track of a Type 1 format.

`cue point: FFH 07H length, text`

This event describes an occurrence of some sort (noise, music, etc.).

`MIDI channel prefix: FFH 20H 01H ccH`

This event specifies the MIDI channel associated with the following set of data. Its effect is cancelled by the MIDI Channel Prefix or by the next MIDI event.

`end of track: FFH 2FH 00H`

This event indicates the end of the track (a mandatory Meta event).

`set tempo: FFH 51H 03H ttH ttH ttH`

This event specifies a change in tempo, as expressed in terms of microseconds per quarter-note in the form of three bytes, generally positioned in such a way as to operate simultaneously with a MIDI clock message.

`SMPTE offset: FFH 54H 05H hrH mnH seH frH ffH`

This event specifies a SMPTE starting point or shift point for a track, in terms of hours, minutes, seconds, frames per second, and frame subdivisions, expressed in terms of hundredths of a frame (regardless of the subdivision of the header chunk). When used, this event appears at the beginning of a track, ahead of any non-null delta times. Furthermore, in a Type 1 file, this event is stored together with the tempo chart. The format used to represent the time is identical to the format of the MIDI time code, namely:

hrH	hour
mnH	minute
seH	second
frH	frames per second
ffH	subdivisions per frame

`hrH = 0 yy zzzzz`

yy	number of frames per second
yy = 00	24 frames per second
yy = 01	25 frames per second
yy = 10	30 frames per second (drop frame)
yy = 11	30 frames per second (non-drop frame)
zzzzz	number of hours (from 0 to 23)

`time signature: FFH 58H 04H nnH ddH ccH bbH`

This event specifies the time signature of the piece. The nnH and ddH bytes correspond respectively to the numerator and the denominator. The numerator is represented in its own right, while the denominator is equal to the power to which the digit 2 has to be raised in order to reach the number of rhythmic subdivisions per whole note: for instance, 0 for a whole note (one whole note per whole note: $2^0 = 1$); 1 for a half-note (two half-notes per whole note: $2^1 = 2$); 2 for a quarter-note (four quarter-notes per whole note: $2^2 = 4$); 3 for an eighth-note (eight eighth-notes per whole note: $2^3 = 8$), and so on. The cc parameter indicates the number of MIDI clock signals (at a rate of 24 per quarter-note) per metronome pulse, and the bb parameter indicates the number of thirty-second notes per MIDI quarter-note (i.e., per 24 MIDI clock signals).

For example, in the case of a measure in 6/8 time and a dotted quarter-note metronome pulse, you would get the following result:

`FFH 58H 04H 06H 03H 24H 08H`

Here, the number 24H (36 in decimal) indicates that the metronome is issuing a pulse every three eighth-notes (that is, every dotted quarter-note), because 36 MIDI clock signals are transmitted during this period. The number 08H indicates that a MIDI quarter-note contains eight thirty-second notes (which, no surprise, is usually the case).

`key signature: FFH 59H 02H sfH miH`

This event specifies the key (that is, the tonality) and also the type of scale (either major or minor).

> sfH = −7   7 flats (C-flat major or A-flat minor)
>
> ... ...
>
> sfH = −1   1 flat (F major or D minor)
>
> sfH = 0   no changes (C major or A minor)
>
> sfH = 1   1 sharp (G major or E minor)
>
> ... ...
>
> sfH = 7   7 sharps (C-sharp major or A-sharp minor)
>
> miH = 0   a major key
>
> miH = 1   a minor key

```
sequencer specific: FFH 7FH length, data
```

The sequencer-specific Meta event is to MIDI Files what a SysEx message is to MIDI. In other words, the data corresponds to the manufacturer's identification message (as expressed in the form of a byte, or even in the form of three bytes, when the first byte is equal to zero), followed by messages whose meaning, which is proprietary to each manufacturer, should be published in the user's manual.

A Few Remarks

When MIDI Files don't specify the tempo or time signature, the default values of 120 and 4/4 are assumed. On the other hand, if the tempo and time signature are present, these events should appear at the beginning of the track (and, for a Type 1 format, at the beginning of the first track), ahead of any non-null delta times. Of course, with regard to the Type 2 format, each track can contain its own tempo and time-signature information. Some sequencers allow the programming of a tempo-and-time-signature chart throughout the length of a piece. With a Type 1 format, the corresponding events are the object of a separate track (namely, the first track).

A piece of software that doesn't implement certain Meta events, and which therefore ignores these events, must necessarily take their length into consideration in order to be in position to read subsequent events properly. On another level, a piece of reading software that doesn't recognize the format type of the header chunk (i.e., Type 0, Type 1, or Type 2) can still read the track chunks, whose reorganization is the user's responsibility.

Some software imports and exports Type 0 and Type 1 MIDI Files, as desired. Therefore, these programs can be used to convert into Type 0 format MIDI Files that were saved with software that only exports files in Type 1 format. (The opposite procedure works only if the conversion software incorporates a channel un-mixing feature that lets you "explode" a single-track Type 0 file into a multitrack Type 1 file.)

Intelligent management of MIDI Files imports should theoretically let you select this or that track, or one or another import channel, and let you do it at any particular position. With this as a starting point, you can envision mixing different tracks or sequences from different programs. Furthermore, some specialized programs for frame-based music can develop complex tempo-and-time-signature charts for synchronization purposes. The ability to save these charts on a separate track (namely, the first track in the Type 1 format) makes it possible to export this information independently to sequencing software.

Translating a Score

As implemented under the Pro 24 III as shown in Figure 8.14 below, the two-track recording, which is two measures long, should give you a better understanding of how MIDI events are converted into the MIDI Files format. Two types of saving have been performed: one into the Type 0 format (after mixing on a single track), and the other into the Type 1 format. Track 1 of the Pro 24 was recorded on Channel 1, and contains a Program Change message at the beginning of the recording. Track 2 was handled the same way, except it was recorded on Channel 3. The tempo and time-signature values for the piece were 122 and 4/4, respectively.

As you can see, the Type 1 format leads to the use of a third track, namely, the tempo track. Saved separately, in this example this track contains two Meta events. The first Meta event, which consists of three bytes, specifies the tempo in terms of milliseconds per quarter-note, while the second event is allocated to the time signature (indicating the numerator, the denominator, the number of MIDI clock signals per metronome pulse, and the number of thirty-second notes per MIDI quarter-note).

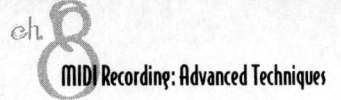

FIGURE 8.14: *The score as presented by the Pro 24*

However, the Pro 24 doesn't save Meta events such as the names of tracks, changes in tempo, etc.

In this example, the only compressed intervals correspond to the values C0H (11000000) and 01H 80H (00000001 10000000), which are equal to 192 and 384 in decimal, respectively (that is, a half-note and a quarter-note at a resolution of 96 ticks to the quarter-note), and which are converted into 81H 40H (10000001 01000000) and into 83H 00H (10000011 00000000) after compression. The other intervals (which are equivalent to an eighth-note, namely 30H, or 48 in decimal) are less than 7FH and therefore are not modified.

Type 0 (Single-Track) MIDI Files

The syntax and contents of Type 0 MIDI Files messages are shown below.

The Header Chunk

4DH 54H 68H 64H	MThd (ASCII)
00H 00H 00H 06H	Chunk length
00H 00H	Type 0 format

00H 01H		One track
00H 60H		Resolution of the Pro 24(96 ticks to the quarter-note)

The Track Chunk

DELTA TIME	EVENT	TYPE
	4DH 54H 72H 6BH	MTrk (ASCII)
	00H 00H 00H 44H	Chunk length
00H	C0H 0BH	Program Change 12/Channel 1
00H	90H 45H 35H	A3 Note On/Channel 1
00H	C2H 01H	Program Change 2/Channel 3
00H	92H 35H 33H	F2 Note On/Channel 3
81H 40H	90H 45H 00H	A3 Note Off/Channel 1
00H	90H 47H 3DH	B3 Note On/Channel 1
00H	92H 35H 00H	F2 Note Off/Channel 3
00H	92H 2BH 37H	G1 Note On/Channel 3
30H	90H 47H 00H	B3 Note Off/Channel 1
30H	90H 43H 39H	G3 Note On/Channel 1
30H	90H 43H 00H	G3 Note Off/Channel 1
30H	90H 48H 35H	C4 Note On/Channel 1
00H	92H 2BH 00H	G1 Note Off/Channel 3
00H	92H 30H 31H	C2 Note On/Channel 3
83H 00H	90H 48H 00H	C4 Note Off/Channel 1

DELTA TIME	EVENT	TYPE
00H	92H 30H 00H	C2 Note Off/Channel 3
00H	FFH 2FH 00H	Meta event: End of Track

Type 1 MIDI Files (Three Tracks)

The syntax and contents of Type 1 MIDI Files messages are shown below.

The Header Chunk

DELTA TIME	EVENT	TYPE
4DH 54H 68H 64H	MThd (ASCII)	
00H 00H 00H 06H	Chunk length	
00H 00H	Type 1 format	
00H 03H	Three tracks	
00H 60H	Resolution of the Pro 24 (96 ticks to the quarter-note)	

Track Chunk 1 (The Tempo and Time-Signature Track)

DELTA TIME	EVENT	TYPE
	4DH 54H 72H 6BH	MTrk (ASCII)
	00H 00H 00H 13H	Chunk length
00H	FFH 51H 03H	Meta event 51 (tempo)
	07H 81H 1BH	491,803 microseconds per quarter-note
00H	FFH 58H 04H	Meta event 58 (time signature)

	04H 02H 18H 08H	Measure in 4/4 time, plus metronome
00H	FFH 2FH 00H	Meta event: end of track

Track Chunk 2 (Channel 1)

DELTA TIME	EVENT	TYPE
	4DH 54H 72H 6BH	MTrk (ASCII)
	00H 00H 00H 29H	Chunk length
00H	C0H 0BH	Program Change 12/ Channel 1
00H	90H 45H 35H	A3 Note On/Channel 1
81H 40H	90H 45H 00H	A3 Note Off/Channel 1
00H	90H 47H 3DH	B3 Note On/Channel 1
30H	90H 47H 00H	B3 Note Off/Channel 1
30H	90H 43H 39H	G3 Note On/Channel 1
30H	90H 43H 00H	G3 Note Off/Channel 1
30H	90H 48H 35H	C4 Note On/Channel 1
83H 00H	90H 48H 00H	C4 Note Off/Channel 1
00H	FFH2 FH 00H	Meta event: end of track

Track Chunk 3 (Channel 3)

DELTA TIME	EVENT	TYPE
	4DH 54H 72H 6BH	MTrk (ASCII)
	00H 00H 00H 22H	Chunk length

DELTA TIME	EVENT	TYPE
00H	C2H 01H	Program Change 2/ Channel 3
00H	92H 35H 33H	F2 Note On/Channel 3
81H 40H	92H 35H 00H	F2 Note Off/Channel 3
00H	92H 2BH 37H	G1 Note On/Channel 3
81H 40H	92H 2BH 00H	G1 Note Off/Channel 3
00H	92H 30H 31H	C2 Note On/Channel 3
83H 00H	92H 30H 00H	C2 Note Off/Channel 3
00H	FFH 2FH 00H	Meta event: end of track

CHAPTER 9

Recording
and
Synchronization

HETHER IT involves MIDI, audio, or video, synchronization lets you make any number of separate machines (sequencers, tape recorders, videotape recorders, etc.) run in accordance with a single and unique timing reference signal: namely, the clock signal. Depending on the kind of application, the clock signal is derived either from the tempo (in which case it's a relative timing signal) or from an actual clock (in which case it's an absolute timing signal).

The distinction between these two time-division methods is a basic one. For instance, for a given duration X (for example, one minute), the time calculated by a clock and the time expressed in terms of the number of quarter-notes that pass in a minute will be different, depending on the tempo (for example, 120 quarter-notes for a tempo of 120, 60 quarter-notes for a tempo of 60, and so on). In relative timing you're dealing with a unit that depends on the tempo, as opposed to an absolute unit that depends on the amount of time that has elapsed (as measured in terms of hours, minutes, seconds, milliseconds, etc.).

In a configuration of synchronized machines, one of the machines plays the role of master by transmitting a reference clock signal to the other machines—the slave machines—so as to force them to run at the same speed at which the master machine is running.

From a synchronization point of view, there are two major kinds of recorders:

- *Physical recorders,* which are based on a mechanical running system. This group includes tape recorders (audiotape recorders, or ATRs) and videotape recorders (VTRs); and

- *Logical recorders.* Although this group consists mainly of sequencers, it also includes Direct to Disk systems.

Beyond this first classification, there are four different synchronization procedures:

1 ▪ *The slaving of one or more logical recorders to another logical recorder.* The time code can be either absolute or relative. The clock signal is sent directly from the master machine to the slave machine or machines, which run at the speed imposed by the metronome pulses or clock-signal pulses that they receive.

2 ▪ *The slaving of one or more logical recorders to a physical recorder.* The time code can be either absolute or relative. After having optionally been formatted by a converter (for instance, when its physical characteristics are incompatible with direct-to-tape recording), the clock signal is first recorded on one of the tracks of the physical recorder so that the logical recorder or recorders can be synchronized with it. (If necessary, the converter can also provide the formatting in the opposite direction.)

3 ▪ *The slaving of one or more physical recorders to another physical recorder or to a synchronizer.* In this case, the time code is absolute. The clock-signal tracks are recorded in the way described above. These tracks are then read by a synchronizer so that they can be compared against a reference clock signal provided by a master machine or

by the synchronizer itself, so that the synchronizer can set the speed of the slave machines. The synchronizer does that through specialized interfaces that let it gain mechanical control of the running speed.

4 ▪ *The slaving of one or more physical recorders to a logical recorder.* In this case, the time code is absolute. The principle behind this approach is exactly the same as the principle outlined in item 3 above, except that the master clock signal (i.e., the reference clock signal) is sent to the synchronizer from the sequencer.

For a single type of master clock, procedures 1 and 4 or procedures 2 and 3 can be combined.

These four principles, along with the applications derived from them, are the subject of the following sections. However, there are already two types of units that can be used for synchronization purposes, namely, converters and synchronizers. Converters turn a logical clock signal into a signal that can be recorded, and vice versa, while synchronizers control the so-called "rotating equipment" through specialized interfaces.

There are two standards for absolute clock signals: the SMPTE (the standard originally developed by the Society of Motion Picture and Television Engineers, pronounced "SIMP-ty") standard and the MIDI Time Code. Depending on whether the clock signal is recorded on an audio track or incorporated directly into a video frame, you'll be dealing with SMPTE LTC code or SMPTE VITC code, respectively.

There are also only two standards for relative clock signals: PPQN, or pulses per quarter-note, and the MIDI Timing Clock, which is sometimes associated with SPP (Song Position Pointer) messages. FSK (Frequency-Shift Keying), which is well known to MIDI users, isn't strictly speaking a clock signal. Instead, it's a way to convert a relative clock signal into recordable form.

So much for generalities. It's time now to take a look at logical synchronization—that is, the synchronization of sequencers with one another—before going on to integrating the sequencers into an audio/video environment (in other words, slaving the sequencers to tape recorders and videotape recorders).

Synchronizing Sequencers

In Chapter 4 you learned the MIDI synchronization messages: Timing Clock, Start, Stop, Continue, and SPP. The Timing Clock message comes straight from the tempo, and leads directly to the following two applications:

- Sequencer-to-sequencer synchronization (MIDI/MIDI or analog/MIDI); and
- Synchronization between a physical recorder and a sequencer.

Sequencer-to-Sequencer MIDI Synchronization

Assume that a sequencer is the basic instrument being used to record all the elements of a piece except for the percussion, which is being programmed directly from an independent drum machine that's being treated as a second sequencer. In order for these two units to run at the same speed—in other words, for them to start, stop, and start again at the same time, one of them (the master unit) has to be able to send commands and provide a continuous time signal to the other unit (the slave unit). This synchronous operation is ensured by the Timing Clock messages, while the start (at the beginning of the piece), the stop, and the restart (from the previous stopping point) are controlled by the Start, Stop, and Continue messages, respectively.

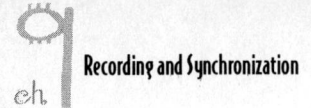

The Timing Clock messages are sent from the MIDI Out port of the master unit to the MIDI In port of the slave unit. Because these messages are transmitted at a rate of 24 per quarter-note, their transmission density is a function of the tempo.

Generally speaking, any MIDI sequencer can serve as a master unit or a slave unit. In the case at hand, the trick is first to set the sequencer to master mode so that it can transmit the clock signal to the drum machine, and then to set the drum machine to slave mode so that it can adjust itself when it receives the clock signal (i.e., in External or MIDI mode).

The Advantage of Song Position Pointer Messages

Thanks to the MIDI Timing Clock messages, the drum machine is now running at the same speed as the sequencer. However, the drum machine is running blind, because it doesn't know where it is in the piece. Of course, that doesn't keep the synchronization from happening properly, because the Start command makes the sequencer and the drum machine start at the beginning of the piece, and the Continue command orders them to restart at the point at which they were stopped by the Stop message. As a result, the position of the drum machine in the piece is exactly the same as the position of the sequencer—so far.

But now suppose you've pressed the Stop key on the sequencer at the beginning of bar 15, and that the next thing you want to do is to skip straight to bar 49. When you position the sequencer at bar 49 in order to switch into Read mode, the sequencer will send the drum machine a Continue message followed by a Timing Clock message. The drum machine, all unaware of the change in position, perfectly naturally and understandably will start up again where it had been stopped—namely, at bar 15. The upshot of course is that even though the drum machine and the sequencer are running at the same tempo, they're running 34 bars apart. In other words, the MIDI clock signal can't synchronize two units that are positioned at different locations.

The Song Position Pointer message, which expresses a position in terms of the number of sixteenth-notes that have elapsed since the beginning of the piece, has the job of telling the slave sequencer which location to start from, in sync with the Timing Clock messages, after the slave sequencer receives a Continue message. So, in resuming at bar 49 of a piece in 4/4 time, the master sequencer will send an SPP message having a value of 784 (that is, 49 × 16) before it sends the Continue message. The binary and hexadecimal equivalents of this SPP message are 11110010 00000110 00001111 and F2H 06H 0FH, respectively. (After distributing the two data bytes 06H and 0FH over 14 bits you get 03H and 0FH, which correspond to 783.)

Because software sequencers usually don't come with implementation charts, it's advisable to contact the vendor for information about how, and whether, a particular device handles SPP messages.

MIDI/Audio-Video Synchronization

This section explains the principles of logical synchronization and then describes in detail how to synchronize MIDI sequencers and tape-based machines (i.e., tape recorders and videotape recorders).

The two major applications of this type of synchronization are:

- Mixed sequencer/tape-recorder multitrack recording, and
- The synchronization of sound with pictures (or in general post-production audio work)

General Information

As every musician knows all too well, multitrack recording on an analog tape recorder degrades the signal. Hiss or background noise is added, and the pass-band and the dynamics are reduced. Of course, digital tape recorders do a lot to solve these problems. However, as soon as a production stops using acoustic instruments and starts working exclusively with sound generators, sequencers start displaying many advantages over their tape-based analogues. These advantages include instantaneous repositioning to any point in the piece and the option of editing recordings right up to the very last minute. When performances are exclusively MIDI based, multitrack tape recorders may not be needed at all, because the products of the sound generators will be mixed directly without having to be recorded beforehand.

Synchronization Codes in Use

There are currently three very different ways to slave a sequencer to a tape-based recording device:

1. • *Use of a relative code.* In the same way as for sequencer-to-sequencer synchronization, tape-recorder-to-sequencer synchronization based on the use of a relative code relies on MIDI Real Time messages (clock signals, SPP messages, etc.). Because of their digital content, these messages can't be recorded directly on tape. Therefore, a conversion step is necessary for both writing and reading.

2. • *Conversion of an absolute code into a relative code.* An absolute synchronization code (such as a SMPTE code) is recorded on the tape and is then converted into a relative synchronization code that's sent to the sequencer (in the form of clock signals, SPP messages, etc.).

3. • *Use of an absolute code.* An absolute synchronization code (such as a SMPTE code) is recorded on tape and is then converted into another absolute synchronization code that's MIDI compatible. This code, which is the one that's sent to the sequencer, is known as the MIDI Time Code.

Before making a detailed study of the major codes that are currently being used and the ways in which they're implemented, it's worth taking a moment to review the caveats that you should be aware of when you're recording a synchronization signal.

How Codes Are Recorded

Because of the information they carry, synchronization codes are extremely sensitive to crosstalk (i.e., signal overflow between two adjacent tracks in a tape recorder). That's why it's worth taking the trouble to record these codes on relatively isolated tracks (such as tracks 1 and 8 on an 8-track tape recorder, track 1 or track 24 on a 24-track machine, and so on), so as to reduce the number of immediately neighboring tracks to one instead of two.

To minimize the amount of crosstalk within the single neighboring track, it's advisable for that track not to contain recorded sounds with high transients (i.e., sudden attacks) or very high gain levels. The ideal procedure, of course, would be to have an interval consisting of an empty track separating the synchronization codes from any instrumental recordings.

To avoid changing the synchronization signal, you should take care not to subject the signal to any processing steps (corrections, effects, noise-reduction procedures, etc.), or to any writing or reading. As if that weren't enough, because of the often weak performance of their erasing heads, some tape recorders don't take kindly at all to the re-recording of a code on any particular given track.

The last problem involves the adjustment of the recording level. An excessively high level poses the risk of saturating the code and thereby deforming it, while an excessively low level poses the risk of making the code impossible to read. One good way to make the adjustment is to measure the level at which break-up occurs during reading or playing and then set the recording level a few decibels below that level.

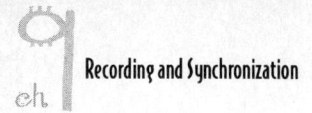

PPQN and MIDI/FSK

PPQN and FSK are the two ways to code a tempo (with relative reference) in a signal that can be recorded on tape. PPQN involves only analog sequencers, while FSK works with MIDI.

PPQN (Pulses Per Quarter Note) Synchronization

As you saw in Chapter 1, PPQN is a low-frequency electrical signal (at 24 Hz, 48 Hz, 96 Hz, etc.) issued by the analog sequencers. The role of this signal is exactly the same as the role of the Timing Clock message. On the other hand, it is recorded as-is on a tape-recorder track, and directly drives the sequencer for reading or playing. Because of its analog component, this signal doesn't need to be converted in either direction. However, its low frequency makes it extremely vulnerable to magnetic recording. This method is entirely obsolete, and is almost never used anymore.

Frequency-Shift Keying (FSK) Synchronization

The MIDI/FSK converter is a bidirectional conversion module that turns MIDI clock messages into an equivalent signal whose major special feature is that it can be recorded on tape. Physically, this signal alternates between two different frequencies at the speed of the MIDI clock (i.e., 24 pulses per quarter-note). This dual-frequency coding system has the advantage over PPQN of being located in a pass-band that is clearly much better suited to magnetic recording. Some MIDI/FSK converters are incorporated right into sequencers and drum machines, while others are packaged as independent boxes.

Because the FSK signal depends on the tempo, you can start by connecting the MIDI Out port of the sequencer to the MIDI In port of the MIDI/FSK converter. This connection gives the converter a relative timing reference. When it receives clock-signal messages from the sequencer, which has been placed in Read mode (and for which the sending of timing-clock signals has been enabled), the converter generates the FSK code intended for the tape recorder, which has been placed in Record mode.

If no clock-signal messages are present, the converter issues a sort of test tone (i.e., a constant frequency), which has to be recorded for a good ten seconds or so on the tape recorder before the read key of the sequencer can be pressed. The test tone then serves as a mark that the converter can use to find the beginning of the piece. Although it's not consistent with the MIDI standard, some sequencers don't give absolute priority to clock-signal messages. To make sure these messages are sent with the proper regularity, it's worthwhile to disconnect all the tracks (by using the Mute function) before doing any FSK recording.

Once the recording operation is complete there's no way to tinker with the tempo of the piece, which has now been definitively fixed—cast in concrete, you might say—on the tape. On the other hand, to the extent that the sequencer allows it, there's nothing keeping you from programming a tempo-change chart during the piece. You can get away with this, provided of course that you do it before the conversion operation begins, because FSK is simply a faithful reflection of the MIDI clock.

In addition to a margin of safety at the end of the piece, which you can get by recording a minute or two of additional code with a view toward a possible extension of the piece, it's also worthwhile to provide a few bars of white noise at the beginning of the sequence, so as not to be prevented at some later time from adding a longer introduction or a metronome count for musicians to use.

During reading, after the MIDI Out port of the converter has been connected to the MIDI In port of the sequencer, the conversion takes place in the opposite direction. The purpose of this conversion is to transform the FSK signals from the code track into mobile MIDI clock signals, and also to send a Start signal at the beginning of the piece (i.e., at the end of the test tone), along with a Stop signal whenever the tape recorder is stopped.

When the sequencer is slaved to the tape recorder, the MIDI Out port of a keyboard can be slaved to the MIDI In port of the converter. In this arrangement, the messages from the converter will be mixed (that is, merged) with the clock signals produced by the FSK/MIDI conversion before being sent from the MIDI Out port of the keyboard to the MIDI In port of the sequencer. This function, which is absolutely indispensable, lets you record a sequence while you listen to tracks that were recorded earlier on the tape recorder.

The problem with MIDI/FSK conversion is the same one you run into with MIDI/MIDI synchronization. If no SPP messages are present, then each new reading forces you to start again at the beginning of the tape. What's worse is that even the slightest change in the recorded FSK signal is fatal, because the slave sequencer has no way to evaluate the resulting delay.

MIDI/SMPTE Synchronization

The SMPTE standard is to audio/video synchronization what the MIDI standard is to musical data processing: namely, a single and unique universal standard. Unlike the codes you've learned so far in this chapter, which have been characterized by a relative timing reference (i.e., tempo), SMPTE provides an absolute timing reference in terms of the number of hours, minutes, seconds, and frames per second.

The Evolution of SMPTE

In the beginning, the four codes that are gathered under the umbrella term "SMPTE" were designed to synchronize visual signals on film and on videotape. The codes were gradually extended to include the synchronization of audio signals for tape recorders and the synchronization of MIDI signals for sequencers.

In the film and video world, time is measured not according to tempo, but in terms of the number of frames per second. This is why all the audio/video synchronization codes work with the number of hours, minutes, seconds, and frames per second. The number of frames per second varies, depending on requirements and also on the countries involved (particularly because of AC electrical power, whose frequency in Europe is 50 Hz, as opposed to the standard U.S. frequency of 60 Hz).

The first synchronization standard goes back to 1970. Its name, "SMPTE," comes from the initials of the organization that contributed to its implementation: i.e., the Society of Motion Picture and Television Engineers. In force primarily in the United States, Canada, and Asia, this standard is based on NTSC (National Television Standards Committee (sometimes known as Never Twice the Same Color!) video coding, which, for esoteric technical reasons of compatibility between black and white and color, is referenced to 30 frames per second in black and white and to 29.97 frames per second in color. These two SMPTE codes are known respectively as "30" and "30 drop frame." The term "drop frame" comes from the fact that this code is the same as a 30-frame-per-second code that skips two frames per minute except at every tenth minute, or six times per hour (i.e., $29.97 \times 3600 = (30 \times 3600) - (2 \times 54)$).

In Europe, the video standards (PAL and SECAM) that are currently in effect are both referenced to 25 frames per second. In 1972 the European Broadcasting Union (EBU) adopted this synchronization code. Apart from the fact that it's referenced to a rate of 25 frames per second, this standard is physically exactly the same as its elder sibling, SMPTE. Finally, for reasons relating to the film industry, there's a fourth standard. This one is referenced to 24 frames per second.

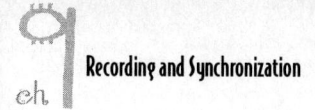

These four codes are often grouped indiscriminately under the overall name "SMPTE." To prevent confusion, it's worth taking the trouble to associate each of these codes with the number of frames per second that it uses. Incidentally, the duration of a frame at 24 frames per second is 41.67 ms. At 25 frames per second it's 40 ms; at 30 frames per second it's 33.33 ms; and at 30 drop frame it's 33.37 ms.

VITC and LTC

Physically, there are two ways to lay down a code on a videotape recorder. The first one, known as the Longitudinal Time Code (LTC), makes the recording on an audio track. The second method, which is known as the Vertical Interval Time Code (VITC), records the code directly in an invisible area at the top of the frame. The part of the videotape that lets the VITC code be written without affecting the image corresponds to the period of time during which the vertical scanning passes from the extreme right at the bottom of the screen to the extreme left at the top of the screen (hence the term "vertical interval").

This procedure has nothing to do with *burn-in*, which, for practical reasons, consists of superimposing the SMPTE time on each frame. In such cases, the time is usually placed in the lower portion of the screen, so as not to interfere with the display. In fact, as far as the LCD display of an independent synchronizer is concerned, burn-in makes it easier to follow the time code.

The Structure of SMPTE LTC Code

The SMPTE LTC code is a so-called "dual-phase" electrical signal whose purpose is to code a digital signal on tape. The signal consists of 80 bits (10 bytes) per frame. The signal density is 2000 bits per second (25×80) for EBU code and 2400 bits per second (30×80) for SMPTE code. The meaning of each of the 80 bits is listed in Table 9.1 below.

TABLE 9.1: *Meaning of the Bits in SMPTE LTC Code*

BITS	MEANING
uuuubbbb	uuuu = the ones digit (from 0 to 9) for the frames, and bbbb = the user bits
ddfcbbbb	dd = the tens digit (from 0 to 2) for the frames, f = the drop-frame flag, c = the color frame flag , and bbbb = the user bits
uuuubbbb	uuuu = the ones digit (from 0 to 9) for the seconds, and bbbb = the user bits
dddgbbbb	ddd = the tens digit (from 0 to 5) for the seconds, g = the binary group flag, and bbbb = the user bits
uuuubbbb	uuuu = the ones digit (from 0 to 9) for the minutes, and bbbb = the user bits
dddgbbbb	ddd = the tens digit (from 0 to 5) for the minutes, g = the binary group flag, and bbbb = the user bits
uuuubbbb	uuuu = the ones digit (from 0 to 9) for the hours, and bbbb = the user bits
ddipbbbb	dd = the tens digit (from 0 to 2) for the hours, i = unassigned, p = the phase-correction bit, and bbbb = the user bits
00111111	Synchronization word
11111101	Synchronization word

In short, this gives you:

- 32 bits that are free for use
- 16 synchronization bits
- 26 timing address bits

- 5 flag bits (including the phase-correction bit)
- 1 unassigned bit (forced to zero)

Bits 27 and 43, which are the flags for the binary groups, indicate the standard that was used to encode the characters for the user bits, as shown below:

	Bit 27	Bit 43
Set of unassigned characters	0	0
Type of character set (the ISO-646 and ISO-2022 standards)	1	0
Unassigned	0	1
Unassigned	1	1

Note that in the above list, under no circumstances should the unassigned combinations be used.

In an LTC frame, each bit (known as a *subframe*) lasts 520.8 microseconds at 25 frames per second, 500 microseconds at 25 frames per second, 416.7 microseconds at 30 frames per second, and 417.1 microseconds at 30 frames per second (drop frame). The breakdown of a SMPTE LTC frame is shown in Figure 9.1 below.

The dual-phase nature of SMPTE LTC code is shown in Figure 9.2 below.

Figure 9.3 below shows the waveform of the LTC signal.

The Structure of SMPTE VITC Code

VITC data isn't encoded in accordance with the dual-phase method. Instead, it's encoded under the NRZ (Non Return to Zero) scheme. This

80 bits per frame

32 bits free for use

16 synchronization bits

26 timing address bits

4 flag bits

2 unassigned bits

All of the unassigned
bits are set to zero.
These bits can be
assigned only by the Unit
Equipment Register (UER)

Timing address	Bit weighting	Bit number	Beginning of the code word
Frame ones	1	0	
	2	1	
	4	2	
	8	3	
		4	
		5	Binary group No. 1
		6	
		7	
Frame tens	1	8	
	2	9	
		10	Unassigned bit
		11	Color flag bit
		12	
		13	Binary group No. 2
		14	
		15	
Seconds ones	1	16	
	2	17	
	4	18	
	8	19	
		20	
		21	Binary group No. 3
		22	
		23	
Seconds tens	1	24	
	2	25	
	4	26	
		27	Binary group flag bit
		28	
		29	Binary group No. 4
		30	
		31	
Minutes ones	1	32	
	2	33	
	4	34	
	8	35	
		36	
		37	Binary group No. 5
		38	
		39	
Minutes tens	1	40	
	2	41	
	4	42	
		43	Binary group flag bit
		44	
		45	Binary group No. 6
		46	
		47	
Hours ones	1	48	
	2	49	
	4	50	
	8	51	
		52	
		53	Binary group No. 7
		54	
		55	
Hours tens	1	56	
	2	57	
		58	Unassigned bit
		59	Phase correction bit
		60	
		61	Binary group No. 8
		62	
		63	
		64	0
		65	0
		66	1
		67	1
		68	1
		69	1
		70	1
		71	1
		72	1 Synchronization word
		73	1
		74	1
		75	1
		76	1
		77	1
		78	0
		79	1

Frame time format:
HH:MM:SS.FF
23:59:59:29

FIGURE 9.1: *Breakdown of a SMPTE LTC frame. (Bit 10 is actually a frame-jump flag.)
The frame is read starting with Bit 79, which is transmitted first.*

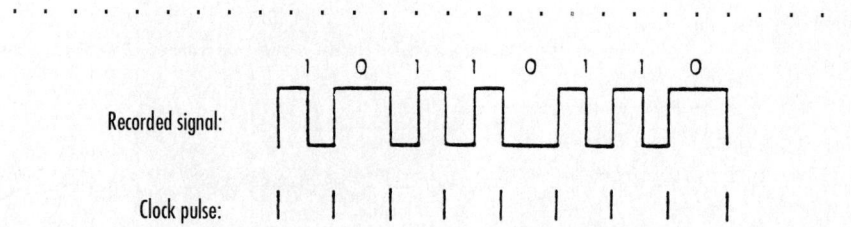

Recorded signal:

Clock pulse:

FIGURE 9.2: *In the dual-phase system, each clock signal causes a change in voltage. On the other hand, unlike what happens with zero, the coding of the digit 1 causes an additional change in voltage—but this time between two clock pulses.*

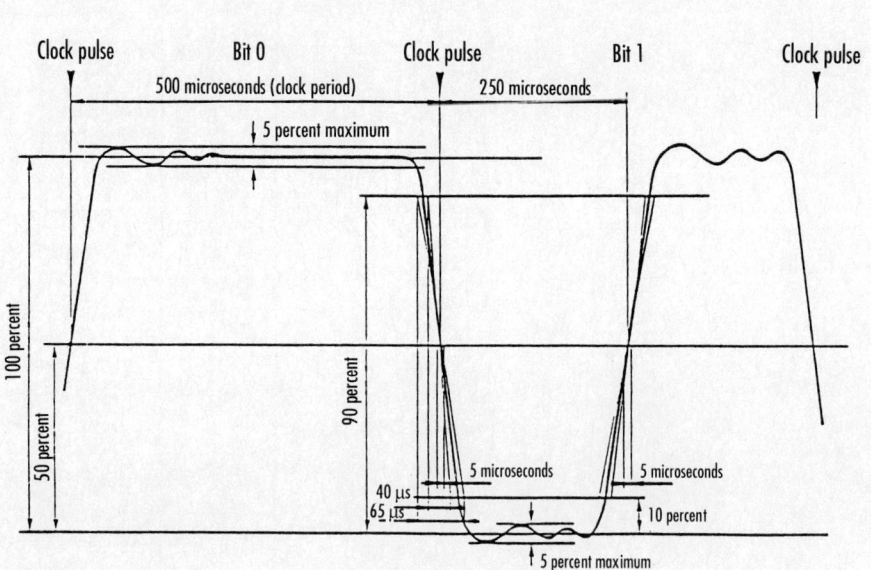

FIGURE 9.3: *The waveform of the LTC signal*

arrangement requires ten bits more than LTC code does. The additional ten-bit groups are assigned as shown in Table 9.2 below:

TABLE 9.2: *Meaning of the Bits in SMPTE LTC Code*

BIT GROUP NUMBER	SYNTAX
1	xx uuuubbbb
2	xx dddgbbbb
3	xx uuuubbbb
4	xx ddfcbbbb
5	xx uuuubbbb
6	xx dddgbbbb
7	xx uuuubbbb
8	xx ddipuuuu
9	xx yyyyyyyy

xx = Synchronization bits

yyyyyyyy = The correction code (i.e., a CRC or cyclic redundancy check code)

· ·

As you saw earlier, the use of VITC is limited to videotape recorders, because the code, instead of being recorded on an audio track, is integrated directly into the image. Some converters can transform VITC code into LTC code in order, for instance, to make a working copy from a one-inch master videotape or a Beta SP videotape for use with a U-Matic or VHS videotape recorder. (Simultaneously with the frame copy, the VITC code on the master tape is converted into LTC code in order to be laid down on one of the audio tracks of the U-Matic or VHS tape.)

However, most of these converters only go so far as to record VITC data in LTC form, without filtering the ten bits of additional information. This is why most SMPTE/MIDI converters refuse to read LTC code that's derived from VITC code. Only a few converters try to do the trick, by eliminating the additional bits when they make the copy. Nevertheless, the unprecedented and entirely unexpected growth of the post-production industry is leading more and more manufacturers to incorporate direct VITC inputs into their sequencers, along with Direct to Disk ports, etc.

The main advantage of VITC code lies in the fact that it can be read at very slow speed, even in stop-frame mode—something LTC code can't do. (In magnetic recording, the tape has to be shifted past the read heads.) Conversely, VITC code can't operate at high speed, whereas a multitrack tape recorder that's equipped to handle very high frequencies can read LTC code at running speeds that are up to 3 to 5 times higher than the nominal reading speed. (Any faster than that, and the tape flies away from the heads.) See Figures 9.4, 9.5A and B, 9.6, and 9.7 below.

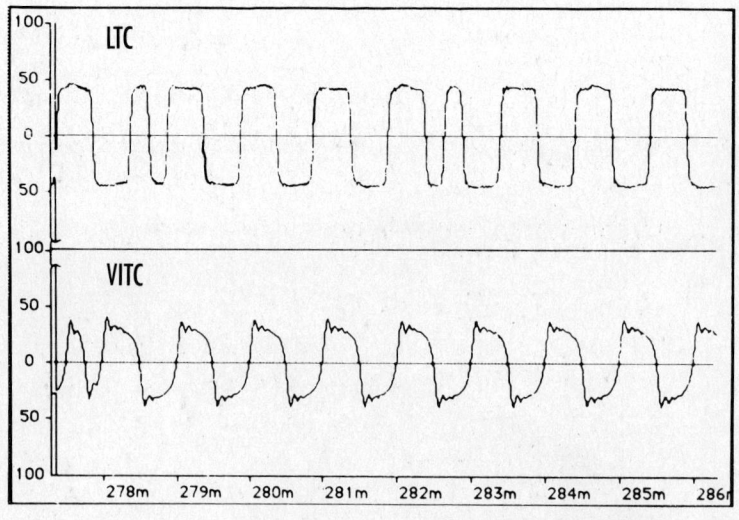

FIGURE 9.4: *The difference between the waveforms of LTC and VITC codes*

VITC ... **LTC**

VITC Bit No.					LTC Bit No.
0	"1"	Synchronization bits			
1	"0"	Synchronization bits			Bit No.
2		1	Frame ones	1	0
3		2		2	1
4		4		4	2
5		8		8	3
6					4
7			First binary group		5
8					6
9					7
10	"1"	Synchronization bits			
11	"0"	Synchronization bits			
12		10	Frame tens	10	8
13		20		20	9
14			Unassigned bit		10
15			Color-lock flag bit		11
16					12
17			Second binary group		13
18					14
19					15
20	"1"	Synchronization bits			
21	"0"	Synchronization bits			
22		1	Seconds ones	1	16
23		2		2	17
24		4		4	18
25		8		8	19
26					20
27			Third binary group		21
28					22
29					23
30	"1"	Synchronization bits			
31	"0"	Synchronization bits			
32		10	Seconds tens	10	24
33		20		20	25
34		40		40	26
35			Binary group flag bit		27
36					28
37			Fourth binary group		29
38					30
39					31
40	"1"	Synchronization bits			
41	"0"	Synchronization bits			
42		1	Minutes ones	1	32
43		2		2	33
44		4		4	34
45		8		8	35
46					36
47			Fifth binary group		37
48					38
49					39
50	"1"	Synchronization bits			
51	"0"	Synchronization bits			
52		10	Minutes tens	10	40
53		20		20	41
54		40		40	42
55			Binary group flag bit		43
56					44
57			Sixth binary group		45
58					46
59					47

FIGURE 9.5A: *The difference between the contents of LTC and VITC codes. (Bit 10 is actually a frame-jump flag.)*

60 "1"	Synchronization bits			
61 "0"	Synchronization bits			
62	1	Hours ones	1	48
63	2		2	49
64	4		4	50
65	8		8	51
66				52
67		Seventh binary group		53
68				54
69				55
70 "1"	Synchronization bits			
71 "0"	Synchronization bits			
72	10	Hours tens	10	56
73	20		20	57
74		Unassigned bit		58
75		Pattern identification | Phase-correction bit		59
76				60
77		Eighth binary group		61
78				62
79				63
80 "1"	Synchronization bits			
81 "0"	Synchronization bits			
82				64
83				65
84		Cyclic control code | Synchronization word		.
85				.
86				.
87				
88				78
89				79

FIGURE 9.5B: *The difference between the contents of LTC and VITC codes. (Bit 10 is actually a frame-jump flag.)*

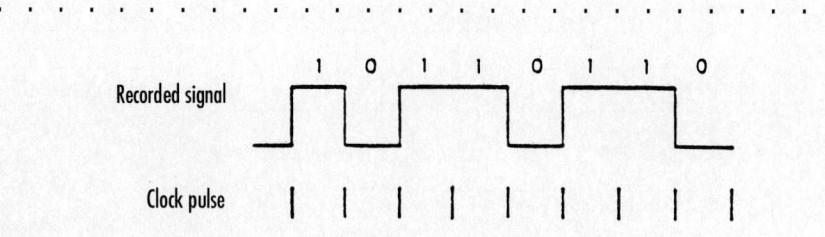

FIGURE 9.6: *The NRZ system produces a transition from one level to another only when a change occurs in the binary state (i.e., when a change from bit 0 to bit 1 occurs, or vice versa).*

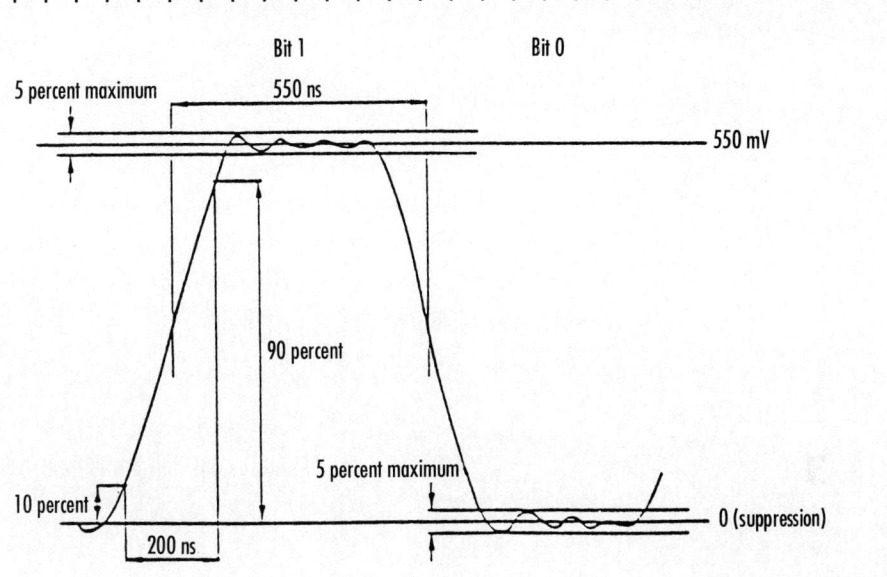

FIGURE 9.7: *The waveform of the VITC signal*

SMPTE in Practice

At first glance it's hard to see how hours, minutes, seconds, and frames per second could communicate with Pulses Per Quarter-Note and Song Position Pointer messages. At the very least, in order to converse in SMPTE code, a sequencer has to have a MIDI/SMPTE interface—in other words, a converter. This interface manages two very different functions: writing the SMPTE code on the tape (a function that's separate and independent from the MIDI/FSK converter, to which the sequencer would send a MIDI clock signal), and, during reading, converting the code into MIDI synchronization events (e.g., Timing Clock, Start, Stop, Continue, and Song Position Pointer messages). In this second phase, it's up to the user to program certain parameters, such as the starting time for

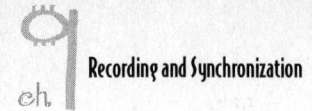

the piece, the tempo, and the initial time signature (4/4, 6/8, etc.), along with any tempo or bar changes within the sequence.

The three stages of SMPTE/MIDI synchronization are summarized below:

1 ▪ *Writing the SMPTE code on tape:* select the starting time and the type of code (for example, 2 hours 0 minutes 0 seconds 0 frames, at 25 frames per second). For the sake of simplicity, it's advisable to "time-code" the tape throughout its length.

2 ▪ *Programming the starting time for the piece and the tempo/bar chart.* For instance:

SMPTE	TEMPO	TIME SIGNATURE	POSITION (BY BAR, BEAT, AND TICK)
02.00.30.00	120	4/4	1/1/0
	126	5/4	12/1/0
	118	6/8	20/1/0
	120	4/4	25/1/0

You should always take care to provide a margin or blank space between the start of the code on the tape and the starting time for the sequence. (In this example, the space is 30 seconds long.) This space leaves you room to add an introduction ahead of the beginning of the piece after one or more tracks have been laid down on tape. In fact, if you wanted to add a two-bar introduction at a tempo of 120 to the quarter-note, all you'd have to do is program the sequencer to start four seconds earlier: that is, at 02.00.26.00.

3 ▪ *Reading the SMPTE code and conversion into MIDI,* in accordance with the previously programmed chart.

Thanks to this information, the converter can send the MIDI Timing Clock messages to the sequencer, along with the SPP messages, which it will calculate from the tempo/bar chart. When the tape is read, when the code reaches the starting time for the piece (02.00.30.00) the converter sends a Start message to the sequencer, followed by a Timing Clock message in the rhythm of the programmed tempo (which in this example is 120).

If you assume the tape recorder will start right in the middle of the piece, for instance at 02.01.00.00, then the converter will calculate the value of the corresponding SPP message from the tempo/bar chart, as explained below.

The piece starts at time 02.00.30.00, at a tempo of 120 beats per minute and a time signature of 4/4 (that is, 4 beats to the bar, with a quarter-note getting one beat). As shown in the table, the first tempo change happens at the beginning of bar 12. This means you have 11 bars, at four quarter-notes or 16 sixteenth-notes per bar, before the first tempo change—in other words, 176 sixteenth-notes between the beginning of the piece and the beginning of bar 12. At a tempo of 120 each quarter-note lasts 500 ms, and each sixteenth-note is 125 ms long. In other words, these 11 bars occupy 22 seconds of real time.

At 02.00.52.00—that is, 8 seconds before the desired continuation point (i.e., the time at which the tape recorder will start)—the tempo increases to 126 beats per minute and the time signature changes to 5/4. Using the same technique as above, you can calculate that the interval to the next tempo change (that is, the change to 118 beats per minute) is 336 sixteenth-notes, or a little more than 19 seconds (actually, 19.048 seconds). That number tells you that the continuation point lies within this interval.

At a tempo of 126, each quarter-note lasts 476.19 ms, and each sixteenth-note is 119.047 ms long. By dividing 119.047 into 8 seconds, you find that there are 67.2 sixteenth-notes between the tempo change at the start of bar 12 and the continuation point. So as not to have to deal with backing up the tape, you round the figure of 67.2 up to 68 sixteenth-notes.

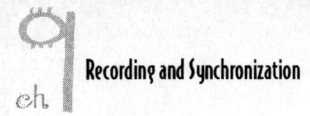

Therefore, the converter sends an SPP that has a value of 244 (that is, 176 sixteenth-notes in the first 11 bars + 68 sixteenth-notes, as calculated above). The converter then sends a Continue message 95.2 ms after the tape recorder passes 02.01.00.00. This delay is necessary because 68 sixteenth-notes at a tempo of 126 quarter-notes to the minute result in a time of 8.0952 seconds, which is 95.2 ms longer than 8 seconds. The converter then sends Timing Clock messages at the corresponding tempo of 126 beats per minute, i.e., with a message every 119.047 ms.

The enormous advantage of SMPTE code is that it's independent of the tempo of a piece. If you want to change the tempo after you've recorded the code, all you have to do is reprogram the chart. You don't have to lay down the code again on the tape, as you would with FSK.

In the same way as with MIDI/FSK, the presence of a MIDI In port in the converter lets you send to the input of the sequencer a mix consisting of the clock signals from the SMPTE/MIDI conversion and the signals from a control keyboard connected to this MIDI In port. This combined input, known as the Merge function, lets you record a sequence while simultaneously listening to tracks that were laid down earlier on tape.

As with all audio recording, the recording of a SMPTE code isn't impervious to imperfections in the magnetic tape. As a result, a SMPTE/MIDI converter will "break up" if the tape has a defect, erasure, or blank spot that lasts more than a few fractions of a second. However, some converters go on generating clock-signal messages at the current tempo until the code recovers from the mishap.

There are two major kinds of SMPTE/MIDI converters: independent converters and converters that are connected directly to a particular sequencer.

Independent SMPTE/MIDI Converters

Independent converters have a minimum of two SMPTE ports (In and Out) that let you record and read code on the tape. These converters also have a MIDI Out port, which they use to send clock-signal messages and SPP messages to the sequencer. The tempo/bar chart is programmed directly on the converter. However, it's not at all unusual for only one of these charts to be accepted and allowed to reside in memory. In the best of all possible cases, such a chart would be stored and saved on magnetic media (such as a floppy disk), or even by means of a System Exclusive message.

SMPTE/MIDI Converters Connected to Sequencers

Converters connected to sequencers are directly linked to one of the input/output (I/O) ports of the computer. The role of this kind of converter is limited to reading and writing the code on tape. The job of converting the SMPTE code into clock-signal messages and into SPP messages, and also the task of programming the tempo/bar chart, are done directly by the software. (In such a case, of course, the chart can be stored in the same file as the processed piece.) As a result, the only task this family of converters has to deal with is the task of providing a SMPTE interface for the computer. Because they're more flexible and cost less, converters that are integrated into sequencers are more desirable than universal converters. On the other hand, their operation depends on the operation of the software they work with.

A Few Typical Applications

Without going into the gory details of all the applications that use SMPTE (other than the simple slaving of a sequencer), the following

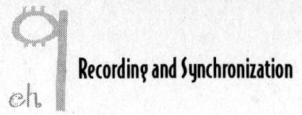
sections present a brief overview of audio post-production and the synchronization of tape recorders and videotape recorders, concluding with a short discussion of human synchronization.

MIDI in Audio Post-Production

Audio post-production covers all of the work that deals with the addition of sounds—noises, voice overs or voices off, conversations, the environmental sounds, original music, and so on—to an image. The job of the post-production studio or auditorium is only to adjust and mix all these elements with the image (which they can do, thanks to the synchronization methods that tape-based machines use with one another). Ever since MIDI environments got into the act, musicians have had the option of taking charge of some of this work by synchronizing sequencers with videotape recorders. The most widely used way to do this is described below.

To begin with, the master film or videotape (which in most cases is in one-inch or Beta SP format) is copied onto a U-Matic or VHS tape, depending on the type of videotape recorder the musician is using. The original time code (either VITC or LTC) is recorded on one of the audio tracks (LTC). For easier handling, this code is also burned into the frame. Of course, if the tape delivered by the post-production studio isn't time-coded, and if the VHS or U-Matic equipment includes a dubbing function (that is, if it can record an audio track without erasing the image), then you can use the SMPTE/MIDI converter to record your own SMPTE code.

The presence of the converter means that during reading, the videotape recorder can control an entire MIDI environment—an environment that's especially well suited to this kind of work, with the music and sounds being provided by a sequencer that drives several different sound generators. In return, the musician delivers the mixed product on a two-track tape recorder: for instance, on analog tape or on synchronizable digital audio tape (DAT).

Furthermore, if the tape recorder (synchronizable DAT, or a tape recorder that has a central track reserved for the time code) allows it, simultaneously with the mixing you can record a regenerated copy of the SMPTE code from the tape recorder. This procedure simplifies the work of the post-production studio, because (except during dubbing) the same timing reference is preserved throughout the series of steps. This regeneration function is linked to the fact that the LTC code, which is a square-wave signal, doesn't work well with direct recopying, because recopying has a strong tendency to round off the leading and trailing edges of the signal. This is why converters exist that let you regenerate the signal by writing a "new" code when they read the original. This procedure prevents any signal degradation.

Some sequencers are better suited to post-production work than others. In any event, any sequencer that's used in this environment should be capable of displaying the position of each MIDI event not only in accordance with the bar/beat/tick system but also in terms of SMPTE time, in order to allow accurate synchronization with the frames. More refined functions let you program a list of SMPTE times (the so-called *cue list*) in order to link the triggering of notes or patterns with the frames. These functions also let you calculate the tempo that's best suited to a given visual sequence within which certain points (that is, certain SMPTE times) need to be emphasized by a strong beat, and so on.

Nevertheless, sequencers become inadequate as soon as you have to synchronize acoustic elements, such as human verbal conversations or the sounds of instruments, with a frame (unless of course you use a Direct to Disk recorder or a sampler that has enough RAM). This need is met by multitrack tape recorders that are synchronized with videotape recorders.

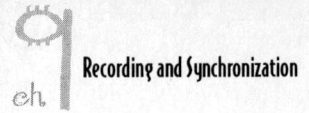

Synchronizing the Rotating Equipment

Synchronizing tape recorders and videotape recorders is an extremely complex operation. It's no longer a matter of controlling a simple piece of computer software by using a SMPTE code to send MIDI synchronization messages, but rather of interacting in real time with the way the running speed of a motor (that is, the motor that controls the capstan of the recording device) is set. In other words, what you have here is the slaving of a mechanical device. This is why the SMPTE interfaces that are responsible for this kind of slaving are known as synchronizers rather than converters.

Generally speaking, the same SMPTE code (that is, the same time) is recorded on all of the tape recorders and videotape recorders that need to be synchronized. If this is not the case (in other words, if the starting time for an audio and/or video sequence to be synchronized differs from one machine to another), you have to tell the synchronizer about it. You do that by programming the proper offset (that is, the clock difference, plus or minus, with regard to a reference code) for each machine.

During reading, this SMPTE reference code, which controls the entire set of machines, comes either directly from one of the machines (the master device) or from an independent synchronizer that generates the code according to its own internal clock. Regardless of which of these approaches you use, the synchronizer reads the SMPTE time of the tape recorders and videotape recorders in order to compare them continually against the time indicated by the reference code. Depending on the differences it finds, the synchronizer sends orders to each of the machines (via as many specialized interfaces as there are devices), telling them to speed up or slow down in order to adjust their running speed to the SMPTE reference code, so that all the codes coincide perfectly.

During rapid running (that is, during fast forward or rewinding), the read heads are no longer pressed against the tape, which means the codes can't be read. To preserve synchronicity, the tape recorders and videotape recorders switch into a mode in which they send specific information (i.e., tachometry and direction) that gives the synchronizer an indication of their approximate position, more or less, in the absence of the SMPTE code.

Synchronizers for tape-based machines are different from simple MIDI/SMPTE converters (even though they sometimes include the same functions) in that they maintain a continuous dialogue with the motor of the tape recorder, in accordance with a protocol that's specific to each manufacturer. Apart from its use in synchronizing tape recorders and videotape recorders in post-production, this principle is very widespread in the audio world. It even lets two tape recorders be slaved to one another in such a way as to increase the number of tracks available. Under this scheme, two 24-track tape recorders turn into a single 46-track tape recorder (48 tracks less the two that are reserved for recording of the SMPTE codes). Figure 9.8 below shows one example of a flexible and sophisticated configuration.

In the example the synchronizer is the master device. The SMPTE code that it generates from its internal clock is compared against the clock signals from the videotape recorder, the multi-track tape recorder, and the two-track tape recorder reserved for mixing. These three physical units are thereby slaved. The synchronizer also plays the role of a converter by transforming the SMPTE code into MIDI messages in order to drive a sequencer in parallel.

Human Synchronization and Its Various Applications

"Human synchronization" is a concept that lets you slave a sequencer not to a computer-generated clock signal but to the rhythm produced by a

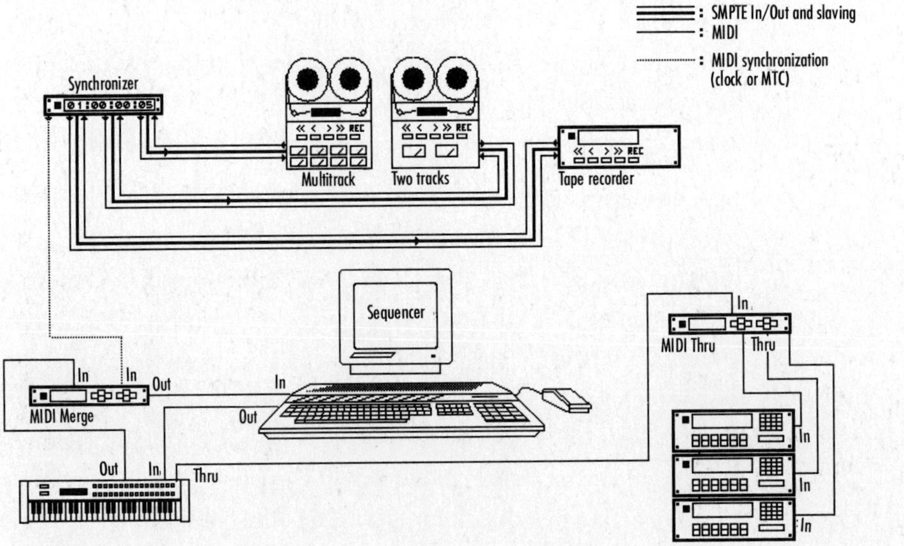

FIGURE 9.8: *A configuration that includes MIDI, audio, and video.*

musician (or to any other external source). This procedure introduces slight fluctuations in tempo that tend to make a recording sound more human. It's also used to resynchronize tapes that don't carry a time code.

Consider for instance the Human Sync function of Cubase. The purpose of this function is to let the tempo evolve in accordance with the input frequency of the MIDI notes. The result is that the rhythm can be marked on a simple keyboard so that the metronome speed of a piece can be regulated in real time, in much the same way that an orchestra conductor controls the speed at which a composition is played. These variations in tempo can also be recorded in the sequencer, as indicated in Figure 9.9 below.

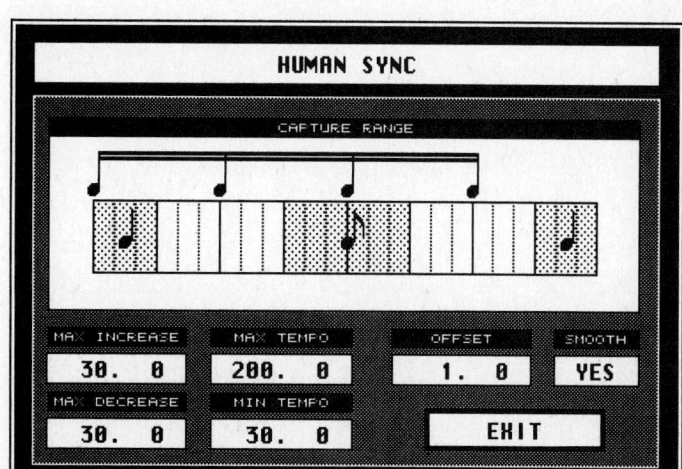

FIGURE 9.9: *The Human Sync function of Cubase*

The upper portion of the screen represents sixteen subdivisions of a quar-ter-note. It's up to you, the user, to set the zones within which the notes you play will be handled when the tempo is modified. Depending on the effect you want, these zones can be programmed to be advanced or de-layed in terms of quarter-notes, eighth-notes, and sixteenth-notes. The larger the zones, the more the changes in tempo can be shifted (provided, of course, that the shifts stay within the limits set for the "max increase" and "max decrease" parameters and for the tempo range). To prevent un-necessarily sudden fluctuations, the Smooth option automatically calcu-lates the average of the variation in the current tempo and the previous value.

Because of the increasing difficulty of reproducing under live concert con-ditions the studio version of an arrangement of a piece, it isn't unusual for musicians onstage to play directly on top of the sequences. Human synchronization lets any of the human performers drive the sequencer

---

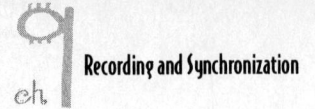
tempo in real time. In most cases, this job is done by the percussionist, whose playing is converted into MIDI notes by means of devices such as pads or triggers.

In the studio, tapes that have no time codes on them need to be re-worked—for instance, by being remixed with the addition of MIDI sequences that are synchronized with a tape recorder, etc. Although the after-the-fact recording of a SMPTE track presents no problems, the track has to be converted into a tempo chart in order to be able to drive the sequencer in perfect sync with the recorded music.

To do that, you have to use a MIDI/SMPTE converter which, starting with an audio input instead of with a MIDI input, can perform a task that's identical to the one performed by the Human Sync function discussed above. So you'd start by selecting one or more appropriate rhythm tracks (percussion elements, bass, etc.) and then send the output to the corresponding input of the synchronizer, which then calculates the tempo chart in real time while reading the SMPTE code from the tape.

Another approach is to use an audio/MIDI converter to convert the audio output directly into MIDI notes, in such a way as to describe the metronomic evolution of the piece to a sequencer that has a function which is equivalent to the Human Sync function. If a converter isn't available, there's always the option of beating out the tempo by ear on a MIDI keyboard.

Regardless of the procedure you use to lay down a time code on a previously recorded tape, none of the procedures has any way of knowing what the starting tempo is without being told. Audio/tempo or MIDI/tempo converters generally need to be informed as accurately as possible about the initial tempo, so that they can avoid sudden accelerations or slow-downs at the beginning of the piece.

Some older tapes are "time-coded" with PPQN or FSK signals, or even with other kinds of signals. In the same way as the audio/MIDI converters in the application discussed above, some synchronizers offer the option of converting these signals into a tempo chart—provided that a SMPTE reference code has been recorded on one of the tracks of the tape recorder.

The Direct Time Lock

To wrap up this discussion of SMPTE, you should be aware of the existence of a hybrid synchronization code known as Direct Time Lock (DTL). In principle, the method consists of converting the first SMPTE time indicator that's read on the tape into an Exclusive message (similar to MIDI Time Code messages) that's sent to the sequencer, and then issuing a timing-clock signal at a rate of 30 pulses per frame. Starting with this information and its own tempo/bar chart, the sequencer adapts itself to the SMPTE code. On the other hand, if the code on the tape happens to suffer a small erasure, synchronization will definitely be lost, because instead of being sent continuously the SMPTE time signal is sent only once (i.e., when the tape recorder is turned on).

The MIDI Time Code

In 1986 a few members of the MMA decided to integrate a new synchronization code into the MIDI standard. They prepared a rough draft of what in April 1987 became the MIDI Time Code (MTC).

The SMPTE/MIDI conversion process lets you slave a sequencer to a tape-based machine such as an audiotape recorder or a videotape recorder, by transforming an absolute timing reference (the SMPTE time signal) into a relative timing reference (the MIDI clock signal). The basic principle of the MIDI Time Code involves the direct conversion of the

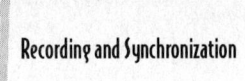

SMPTE code from a master device in the form of MIDI messages. This way, an entire network can take advantage of a single unique reference timing signal without having to deal with the conversion into clock-signal messages.

An MTC configuration consists of a device (a tape recorder, a videotape recorder, or a synchronizer) that generates SMPTE code, a SMPTE/MTC converter, and various devices (sequencers, drum machines, tape recorders, etc.) that are slaved to the MTC standard. As you'll see, the applications of the MIDI Time Code go well beyond simple synchronization. But first, here's a look at the basic language.

SMPTE/MIDI Conversion: Timing Messages

Three messages are used to convert SMPTE data into MIDI data in real time. The first one is the MIDI Time Code Quarter Frame message. It consists of a status byte (F1H in the System Common message category) followed by a data byte. Its format is shown below:

Format:	11110001 (F1H) 0nnndddd
Type:	System Common message

The MTC Quarter Frame message is a simultaneous real-time conversion of some of the information in a SMPTE message, namely the hours, minutes, and seconds, and the number of frames per second. Therefore, the conversion into binary of the value of each of these four categories of SMPTE data occupies 5 bits (that is, 24 values, from 0 to 23, for the hours), 2 × 6 bits (60 values, from 0 to 59, for the minutes and the seconds), and 5 bits (from 24 to 30 values for the frames, depending on the standard that the code is following). As a result, the conversion of a single and unique SMPTE message needs several MTC Quarter Frame messages. To keep the format consistent, each of these four categories of SMPTE information is coded over 8 bits, in the form of two half-bytes or nybbles, even if some of the bits aren't used. (A single data bit, which by definition consists of 7 useful bits, isn't enough to transmit any of these four categories, each of which consists of 8 bits.)

The data byte for an MTC Quarter Frame message (which, like all MIDI data, consists of 7 useful bits), is broken down into two groups of bits: nnn and dddd. Bits 0 to 3 (dddd) represent half of one of the four categories of SMPTE information (hours, minutes, seconds, or the number of frames per second), while bits 4 to 6 (nnn) indicate the category and the half involved. The meaning of the nnn bits is shown in Table 9.3 below.

TABLE 9.3: *Category and Significance Indicators in MTC Quarter-Frame Data Byte Messages*

INDICATOR	MEANING
nnn = 000	the least significant portion of the frames-per-second indicator (Frame Count LS Nybble)
nnn = 001	the most significant portion of the frames-per-second indicator (Frame Count MS Nybble)
nnn = 010	the least significant portion of the seconds indicator (Seconds Count LS Nybble)
nnn = 011	the most significant portion of the seconds indicator (Seconds Count MS Nybble)
nnn = 100	the least significant portion of the minutes indicator (Minutes Count LS Nybble)
nnn = 101	the most significant portion of the minutes indicator (Minutes Count MS Nybble)
nnn = 110	the least significant portion of the hours indicator (Hours Count LS Nybble)
nnn = 111	the most significant portion of the seconds indicator (Seconds Count MS Nybble)

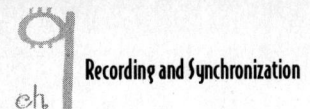

TABLE 9.3: *Category and Significance Indicators in MTC Quarter-Frame Data Byte Messages (continued)*

INDICATOR	MEANING
nnn = 111	the most significant portion of the hour indicator and the type of SMPTE code (Hours Count MS Nybble and SMPTE Type)
LS Nybble	the least significant half-byte
MS Nybble	the most significant half-byte

. . . .

By combining the most significant and least significant half-bytes, you get eight significant bits per SMPTE information category, as shown below:

Frames per Second

xxx yyyyy (0001xxxy + 0000yyyy)

    xxx   reserved for later use. The sending unit should force these bits to zero, and the receiving unit should ignore them.

    yyyyy   frames from 00000 (0) to 11101 (29)

Seconds

xx yyyyyy (0011xxyy + 0010yyyy)

    xx   reserved for later use. The sending unit should force these bits to zero, and the receiving unit should ignore them.

    yyyyyy   seconds from 000000 (0) to 111011 (59)

Minutes

`xx yyyyyy (0101xxyy + 0100yyyy)`

xx   reserved for later use. The sending unit should force these bits to zero, and the receiving unit should ignore them.

yyyyyy   minutes from 000000 (0) to 111011 (59)

The Hours and the Type of SMPTE Code

`x yy zzzzz (0111xyyz + 0110zzzz)`

x   reserved for later use. The sending unit should force this bit to zero, and the receiving unit should ignore it.

yy   the type of SMPTE code

00 = 24 frames per second

01 = 25 frames per second

10 = 30 frames per second (with drop frame)

11 = 30 frames per second (with non-drop frame)

zzzzz = hours from 00000 (0) to 10111 (23)

For example, the SMPTE message "08:51:21:12" at 25 frames per second would be represented as shown in Table 9.4 below:

TABLE 9.4: *Syntax of a Typical SMPTE Message*

TIME DIVISION	SYNTAX
For the number of hours:	zzzzz = 01000 (08), yy = 01 (25 frames per second), and x = 0
	MS dddd + LS dddd = xyyzzzzz = 00101000

TABLE 9.4: *Syntax of a Typical SMPTE Message (continued)*

TIME DIVISION	SYNTAX
	MS dddd = 0010
	LS dddd = 1000
	Hours Count MS Nybble and SMPTE Type = 01110010
	Hours Count LS Nybble and SMPTE Type = 01101000
For the number of minutes:	yyyyyy = 110011 (51), and xx = 00
	MS dddd + LS dddd = xxyyyyyy = 00110011
	MS dddd = 0011
	LS dddd = 0011
	Minutes Count MS Nybble: 01010011
	Minutes Count LS Nybble: 01000011
For the number of seconds:	yyyyyy = 010101 (21), and xx = 00
	MS dddd + LS dddd = xxyyyyyy = 00010101
	MS dddd = 0001
	LS dddd = 0101
	Seconds Count MS Nybble: 00110001
	Seconds Count LS Nybble: 00100101
For the number of frames:	yyyyy = 01100 (12), and xxx = 000
	MS dddd + LS dddd = xxxyyyyy = 00001100

. . . .

TABLE 9.4: *Syntax of a Typical SMPTE Message (continued)*

TIME DIVISION	SYNTAX
	MS dddd = 0000
	LS dddd = 1100
	Frame Count MS Nybble: 00010000
	Frame Count LS Nybble: 00001100

· ·

From which the following eight MTC Quarter Frame messages are derived:

```
F1H 00001100 (0CH): frame/least significant nybble
F1H 00010000 (10H): frame/most significant nybble
F1H 00100101 (25H): second/least significant nybble
F1H 00110001 (31H): second/most significant nybble
F1H 01000011 (43H): minute/least significant nybble
F1H 01010011 (53H): minute/most significant nybble
F1H 01101000 (68H): hour/least significant nybble
F1H 01110010 (72H): hour/most significant nybble + type of
                    SMPTE code
```

When the SMPTE code is read in the forward operating direction, these eight messages are sent at regular intervals, as shown below:

```
F1H 0XH
F1H 1XH
F1H 2XH
F1H 3XH
F1H 4XH
F1H 5XH
F1H 6XH
F1H 7XH
```

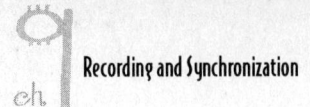

Under reverse operation, the order of these messages is inverted:

```
F1H 7XH
F1H 6XH
F1H 5XH
F1H 4XH
F1H 3XH
F1H 2XH
F1H 1XH
F1H 0XH
```

With regard to the intervals at which the MTC Quarter Frame messages are sent, you know that you need eight of these messages in order to code a SMPTE frame. So, in theory, you should be able to get a density of 200 messages per second (8 × 25) for a code that's set to run at 25 frames per second. In actuality, though, the density is cut by half (that is, to 100, or one message every ten milliseconds at 25 frames per second). A moment's thought explains why: as its name indicates, the MTC Quarter Frame message is sent at every quarter, not at every eighth, of a frame. As a result, two SMPTE frames will pass while the MTC is transmitting one message.

At speeds of 24 or 30 frames per second the MIDI Time Code represents the even-numbered frames, while at a speed of 25 frames per second the MTC alternates once a second between the even-numbered frames and the odd-numbered frames.

Therefore, in the following example, frames 08:51:21:13 and 08:51:21:15 are not converted into MTC messages:

SMPTE	MTC QUARTER FRAME
08:51:21:12 and 0 hundredths of a frame	F1H 0CH
08:51:21:12 and 25 hundredths of a frame	F1H 10H (0CH = 12 frames)

SMPTE	MTC QUARTER FRAME
08:51:21:12 and 50 hundredths of a frame	F1H 25H
08:51:21:12 and 75 hundredths of a frame	F1H 31H (15H = 21 seconds)
08:51:21:13 and 0 hundredths of a frame	F1H 43H
08:51:21:13 and 25 hundredths of a frame	F1H 53H (33H = 51 minutes)
08:51:21:13 and 50 hundredths of a frame	F1H 68H (8H = 8 hours)
08:51:21:13 and 75 hundredths of a frame	F1H 72H (28H = 8 hours, 25 frames per second)
08:51:21:14 and 0 hundredths of a frame	F1H 0EH
08:51:21:14 and 25 hundredths of a frame	F1H 10H (0EH = 14 frames)
08:51:21:14 and 50 hundredths of a frame	F1H 25H
08:51:21:14 and 75 hundredths of a frame	F1H 31H (15H = 21 seconds)
08:51:21:15 and 0 hundredths of a frame	F1H 43H
08:51:21:15 and 25 hundredths of a frame	F1H 53H (33H = 51 minutes)
08:51:21:15 and 50 hundredths of a frame	F1H 68H

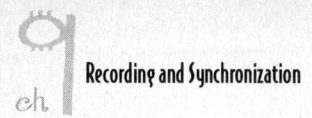
SMPTE	MTC QUARTER FRAME
08:51:21:15 and	F1H 72H (28H = 8 hours,
75 hundredths of a frame	25 frames per second)

In any event, messages F1H 0XH and F1H 4XH correspond to a change in the SMPTE frame. In order for a MIDI unit connected to the output of a SMPTE/MTC converter to be able to display an entire SMPTE message, the unit has to read a complete sequence of eight MTC messages. The first MTC Quarter Frame message (F1H 0XH), like the first bit in the 80 subframes of the SMPTE code, physically falls at a boundary at the start of the frame. It's important to note that at the exact instant the SMPTE/MTC converter receives the last of the eight quarter-frame messages, the information converted into MTC is actually two frames behind with regard to the SMPTE position of the tape. The converter compensates for this delay.

As far as network loading goes, the MIDI Time Code isn't very greedy at all. Its maximum density corresponds to the conversion of a SMPTE code at 30 frame per second, for a total of 240 bytes per second (30 divided by 2 and multiplied by 8 × 2 bytes), or less than 8 percent of the MIDI pass-band. This transmission-capacity limit also explains why it's impossible to send quarter-frame messages during fast-forwarding or high-speed rewinding.

This is where the second MTC timing message, known as the Full Message, comes in handy. This message, whose purpose is to encode an entire SMPTE time signal all at once, is used in any mode other than Read mode (e.g., during fast-forwarding, rewinding, locating, etc.). It belongs to the Real Time category of Exclusive messages. The role it plays will become clearer when you look at the MTC-1 Fostex interface.

Format:	F0H 7FH <channel> 01H <sub-ID#2>
	hrH mnH scH frH F7H

Type:	System Exclusive Real Time message
F0H	Exclusive message status
7FH	Category = Real Time
\<channel\> = 7FH	indicates that the message should be received and handled by the entire network
\<sub-ID#1\> = 01H	MTC message identifier
\<sub-ID#2\> = 01H	identifies the type of MTC message (full message)
hrH	the hour and the type of SMPTE code (0 yy zzzzz)
	yy = 00: 24 frames per second
	yy = 01: 25 frames per second
	yy = 10: 30 frames per second (drop frame)
	yy = 11: 30 frames per second (non-drop frame)
	zzzz = hours
mnH	minutes
scH	seconds
frH	frames per second
F7H	EOX (End of Exclusive)

The third MTC timing message, or *user bits*, is responsible for converting the 32 SMPTE bits that are available to the user. These bits, which aren't used very often, code information such as a tape number, a recording date, etc.

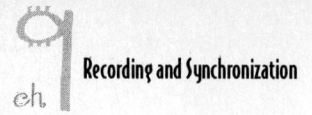

Format:	F0H 7FH <channel> 01H <sub-ID#2> u1H u2H u3H u4H u5H u6H u7H u8H u9H F7H
Type:	System Exclusive message
F0H	Exclusive message status
7FH	Category = Real Time
<channel> = 7FH	indicates that the message should be received and handled by the entire network
<sub-ID#1> = 01H	MTC Cueing message identifier
<sub-ID#2> = 02H	identifies the type of MTC message (User Bits)
	u1H = 0000aaaa
	u2H = 0000bbbb
	u3H = 0000cccc
	u4H = 0000dddd
	u5H = 0000eeee
	u6H = 0000ffff
	u7H = 0000gggg
	u8H = 0000hhhh
	u9H = 000000ji
F7H	EOX (End of Exclusive)

The nybbles u1H to u8H, along with bits "j" and "i", respectively encode the binary groups from 1 to 8 as well as bits 59 and 43 of a

SMPTE frame. When information is represented in the form of a whole byte, the eight binary groups are read in the following order:

```
hhhhgggg ffffeeee ddddcccc bbbbaaaa
```

When a time has to be represented in BDC (Binary Decimal Code) format, the eighth group corresponds to the number of digits that indicate the units in the frame number, the seventh group corresponds to the tens digit in the frame number, and so on through the first group, which corresponds to the tens digit in the number of hours. The following table shows how BDC works to code the digits from 0 to 9:

BINARY	BDC SYMBOL
0000	0
0001	1
0010	2
0011	3
0100	4
0101	5
0110	6
0111	7
1000	8
1001	9
1010	- not used -
1011	- not used -
1010	- not used -
1101	- not used -

BINARY	BDC SYMBOL
1110	- not used -
1111	- not used -

So, the SMPTE time 01.21.12.23 would be represented this way:

hhhh = 0000

gggg = 0001

ffff = 0010

eeee = 0001

dddd = 0001

cccc = 0010

bbbb = 0010

aaaa = 0011

The three messages described above ensure the faithful conversion of the SMPTE standard, and enrich MIDI by giving it a synchronization code that's based on an absolute timing reference. But the applications that the MIDI Time Code makes possible go much further than the simple slaving of a MIDI environment, audio, and video to a common clock reference signal. MTC can automate any given number of procedures by sending a series of orders to compatible intelligent MTC devices (sequencers, tape recorders, etc.). In such a case each order in the series is accompanied by its own SMPTE execution time.

Set-Up Messages (MTC Cueing)

Now, consider again the configuration you started with: the one in which a master device distributes the SMPTE code to a SMPTE/MTC converter, which in turn distributes the MTC code to a series of slave units.

Assume there are three slave units, A, B, and C. Now add a computer, D, that can program and send, via MIDI, a series of orders to these three units. For instance, you could program this computer D to issue orders x1, x2, y, and z, which are to be executed by units A, A, B, and C, respectively, at the times shown below:

```
x1: 01.10.17.06
x2: 01.10.19.04
 y: 01.10.03.22
 z: 01.11.00.00
```

These orders are sent from the computer D to the memories of devices A, B, and C before the MTC code is read. When the MTC code is sent, devices A, B, and C continually compare the time signal they receive against the specified execution time for each order. If there's a conflict, the order in question is carried out immediately. The entire set of orders stored by a peripheral MTC device is known as the insertion list, or *cue list*. These orders are implemented by means of MTC Set Up messages (i.e., implementation messages), which in this example would be sent from the computer D to devices A, B, and C. These messages belong to the Non-Real Time category of System Exclusive messages.

Format:	F0H 7EH \<channel\> 04H \<sub-ID#2\> hrH mnH scH frH ffH slH smH \<add. info\> F7H
Type:	System Exclusive Non-Real Time message
F0H	Exclusive message status
7EH	Category = Non-Real Time
\<channel\>	channel number
\<sub-ID#1\>	04H: MTC message identifier
\<sub-ID#2\>	type of set-up (i.e., the kind of order)
	00H = special

01H = Punch In Point

02H = Punch Out Point

03H = Delete Punch In Point

04H = Delete Punch Out Point

05H = Event Start Point

06H = Event Stop Point

07H = Event Start Point with additional info

08H = Event Stop Point with additional info

09H = Delete Event Start Point

0AH = Delete Event Stop Point

0BH = Cue Point

0CH = Cue Point with additional info

0DH = Delete Cue Point

0EH = Event Name in additional info

hrH	the hour and the type of SMPTE code (0 yy zzzzz)
	yy = 00: 24 frames per second
	yy = 01: 25 frames per second
	yy = 10: 30 frames per second (drop frame)
	yy = 11: 30 frames per second (non-drop frame)
	zzzz = hours
mnH	minutes
scH	seconds

frH	the number of frames per second
ffH	fractions of a frame (from 00 to 99)
slH	Event Number LSB
smH	Event Number MSB
\<add. info\>	additional information
F7H	EOX (End of Exclusive)

Among the 128 set-up messages that are theoretically usable (\<sub-ID#2\>), only fifteen are currently defined by the standard. Their meanings are described in detail below.

ooH Special

Unlike the fourteen following messages, which address a specific portion of the receiving unit (a track, etc.), the Special message involves the entire unit in question as a whole. Six of these messages are currently defined; their number is specified by the event number (slH/smH). However, messages 01H 00H to 04H 00H do not take into consideration the clock reference signal (i.e., the hrH, mnH, scH, frH, and ffH bytes).

slH/smH = ooH ooH: Time Code Offset

Suppose, for instance, you want to synchronize an audio tape read by a slave MTC device (starting at 01.06.58.07) with a frame read by a master SMPTE device (starting at 01.02.54.03). In this case, you'd have to shift the synchronization of the slave device by a total of 4 minutes, 4 seconds, and 4 frames (i.e., because 01.02.54.03 + 00.04.04.04 = 01.06.58.07). This shift, known as the *offset*, is encoded in the hrH, mnH, scH, and frH bytes.

slH/smH = 01H 00H: Enable Event List

This message orders the receiving unit to execute the events on the insertion list when it receives the corresponding MTC time. In a way, this message enables the list.

slH/smH = 02H 00H: Disable Event List

This message orders the receiving unit to ignore the events on the insertion list, but without erasing them from its memory.

slH/smH = 03H 00H: Clear Event List

This message orders the receiving unit to erase from its memory the events on the insertion list.

slH/smH = 04H 00H: System Stop

This message orders the receiving unit to stop.

slH/smH = 05H 00H: Event List Request

When the master unit transmits this message over a channel that's the same as the channel of a receiving unit, the receiving unit sends its insertion list to the master unit, starting with the event whose time is specified by the hrH, mnH, scH, frH, and ffH bytes.

01H/02H: Punch-In/Punch-Out

These messages order the receiving unit to start or stop recording on one of the tracks at the time specified by the hrH, mnH, scH, frH, and ffH bytes. The track number is coded in the slH/smH (Event Number) bytes. Several messages of this type can be sent at different times.

03H/04H: Delete Punch-In/Punch-Out

These messages order the receiving unit to erase from its memory one of the preceding messages, provided that the time specified by the hrH, mnH, scH, frH, and ffH bytes matches the track number coded in the slH/smH bytes, and vice versa.

05H/06H: Event Start/Event Stop

These messages order the receiving unit to activate or deactivate a continuous event (such as the reading of a sample, a potentiometer movement, etc.) at the time specified by the hrH, mnH, scH, frH, and ffH bytes. The event number is coded in the slH/smH (Event Number) bytes. Several messages of this type can be sent at different times.

07H/08H: Event Start/Event Stop with Additional Information

These messages are exactly the same as the preceding messages, except that they include a supplementary description of an event corresponding to a variable number of bytes under the <add. info> heading.

09H/0AH: Delete Event Start/Event Stop

These messages order the receiving unit to erase from its memory one of the preceding four messages, provided that the time specified by the hrH, mnH, scH, frH, and ffH bytes matches the event number coded in the slH/smH bytes, and vice versa.

0BH: Cue Point

Unlike the Event Start/Event Stop messages, this message orders the receiving unit to activate an event promptly at the time specified by the hrH, mnH, scH, frH, and ffH bytes. The event number is coded in the

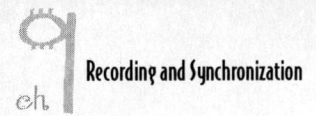

slH/smH (event number) bytes. Several messages of this type can be sent at different times.

0CH: Cue Point with Additional Information

This message is exactly the same as the preceding message, except that it includes a supplementary description of an event corresponding to a variable number of bytes under the <add. info> heading.

0DH: Delete Cue Point

These messages order the receiving unit to erase from its memory one of the preceding two types of messages (0BH, 0CH), provided that the time specified by the hrH, mnH, scH, frH, and ffH bytes matches the event number coded in the slH/smH bytes, and vice versa.

0EH: Event Name in Additional Information

This message makes it possible to use ASCII code to name an event, with the help of the Additional Information bytes. The bytes in the additional information area represent the MIDI messages and the ASCII codes in the form of half-bytes or nybbles. For instance, to code MIDI information over three bytes, as shown below:

```
9FH 64H 00H (E6 released)
```

you'd use three groups of two bytes of additional information, in the form LSB/MSB:

```
0FH 09H 04H 06H 00H 00H
```

Most of the Set Up messages described above exist in a second form, in the Real Time System Exclusive category. As a result, a device that receives these messages should immediately carry out the orders that the messages contain (punch-in or punch-out on the fly, etc.). This explains why the time disappears, and also the following types of Set Up messages: 00H (special), with slH/smH = 00H 00H (Time Code Off-set); 01H 00H (Enable Event List); 02H 00H (Disable Event List); 03H 00H (Clear Event List); and 05H 00H (Event List Request), as well as 03H (Delete Punch In Point); 04H (Delete Punch Out Point); 09H (Delete Event Start Point); 0AH (Delete Event Stop Point), and 0DH (Delete Cue Point).

Format:	F0H 7FH <channel> 05H <sub-ID#2> slH smH <add. info> F7H
Type:	System Exclusive Real Time message
F0H	Exclusive message status
7FH	Category = Real Time
<channel>	channel number
<sub-ID#1>	05H: MTC Cueing Message identifier
<sub-ID#2>	type of Set Up (i.e., type of command)
	00H = special (only the Event Number 04H 00H is used)
	01H = Punch In Point
	02H = Punch Out Point
	03H = reserved
	04H = reserved
	05H = Event Start Point
	06H = Event Stop Point
	07H = Event Start Point with additional info
	08H = Event Stop Point with additional info
	09H = reserved

0AH = reserved

0BH = Cue Point

0CH = Cue Point with additional info

0DH = reserved

0EH = Event Name in additional info

slH	LSB of the Event Number
slH	MSB of the Event Number
<add. info>	additional information
F7H	EOX (End of Exclusive)

So much for the Set Up messages. Now here's a summary of how the various synchronization modes (that is, the various timing messages) operate, in this instance under an MTC configuration:

- A master unit (tape recorder, videotape recorder, sequencer, etc.) issues a SMPTE code to the SMPTE/MTC converter.

- The SMPTE/MTC converter converts the SMPTE code into timing messages (Quarter Frame or Full Message messages) in order to send them to the peripheral MTC devices (sequencers, etc.) so that the peripheral devices will be synchronized. The principle is exactly the same as the principle behind the Timing Clock and SPP messages, except for the fact that the MTC works in terms of an absolute timing reference signal instead of a relative timing reference signal, with all of the advantages that this kind of operation provides.

- When the master unit is in Read mode, the converter sends the MTC Quarter Frame messages.

- When the master unit is in a high-speed mode (such as fast forward, rewind, shuttle, etc.), the converter sends Full Message data, roughly indicating the position of the tape. This information is generally derived from the tachometry and direction signals (explained in detail below) as soon as the time-code track becomes unreadable (that is, as soon as the tape loses contact with the heads).

- When the master unit is in an editing mode (such as Cue mode, or when the tape is being turned by hand in one direction or the other), the converter sends Quarter Frame messages.

- If the peripheral devices are intelligent (that is, if they can accept an insertion list or event list), then when they receive the MTC code the actions that correspond to the Non-Real Time Set Up messages that were previously programmed or transmitted via MIDI by a specific unit will be triggered at the specified time, whereas with Real Time Set Up messages, the actions will be performed immediately.

At present, intelligent MTC peripherals (that is, ones that can interpret Set Up messages) are still fairly rare. On the other hand, some sequencers can receive and send synchronization timing messages (i.e., Quarter Frame or Full Message messages).

To conclude this look at these various different synchronization methods, here's a description of how Cubase does the job.

Fundamentally, Cubase uses an absolute timing reference signal—in other words, a time code—for all of its operations. This time code can be generated internally by a computer, from the MIDI In port by means of the MIDI Time Code, or from a dedicated converter (such as the SMP/24, Timelock, or MIDEX+), in SMPTE form. Independently of these three settings, the tempo can be generated internally or can come from Human Sync mode, or even from the MIDI In port (via the Timing Clock and SPP messages), as shown in Figure 9.10 below.

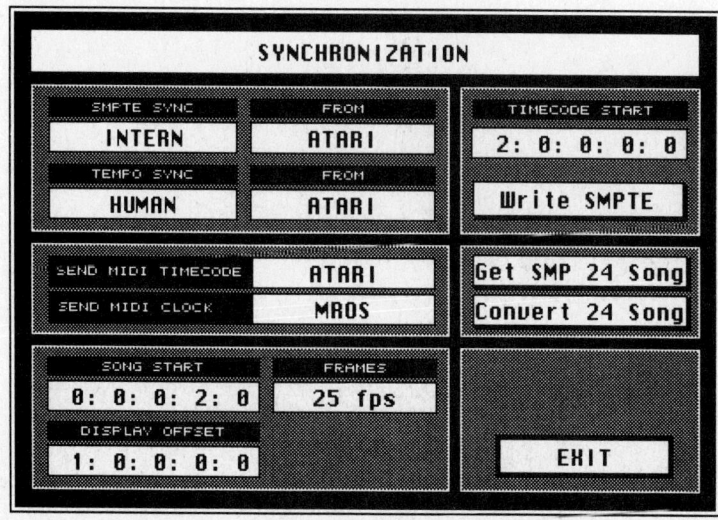

FIGURE 9.10: *The synchronization settings of Cubase*

With regard to transmission, even if it's synchronized under a different
format, Cubase can transmit both types of MIDI synchronization (via
Timing Clock messages plus SPP messages, or via the MIDI Time Code)
and can generate the four types of SMPTE code by using the converters
mentioned above. In a word, this implementation covers all the bases.

CHAPTER

10

XIII XIV XV XVI A B C D E F G H I

Working with MIDI Devices: *Memory,*
Dump Messages,
and Data Formats

T HE FIRST MAJOR family of MIDI applications involves sequencer-type applications and the extensions to MIDI-and-audio/video synchronization. The second major family of MIDI applications involves managing and editing instrument memories. These applications are the subject of this chapter.

The information stored in MIDI devices is edited and exchanged with the outside world by means of Exclusive messages. These messages have given rise to various types of programs, such as dump utilities, librarians, and editors. Chapter 12 examines the roles these programs play; but first, this chapter takes a detailed look at how this information is stored and transmitted.

ROM and RAM

Functionally speaking, there are two kinds of memory. As its name implies, ROM, or read-only memory, can be read but not written to. RAM, or random-access memory, can be both read and written to. ROM and

RAM are to data processing what disks and cassettes are to music. Disks only let you listen (i.e., "read" the data), while cassettes also let you record (i.e., "write" the data).

For that matter, in this context the word "random" really has nothing whatever to do with chance or accident. All it means is that RAM (but also ROM) allows direct access to any memory location, whether it's a question of reading data (from RAM or from ROM) or of writing data (only to RAM), as opposed to sequential access, in which the entire memory has to be searched before the desired location is found. This procedure is analogous to what happens with a cassette tape, which you have to fast-forward if you want to listen to a piece that's located in the middle of the tape.

The Operating System and Updates

As noted above, the memory of a data-processing system is divided into two parts: one for the program and one for the data. In the case of a synthesizer, the program (or operating system) monitors the keyboard in order to detect an action, such as the pressing or releasing of a key, a Pitch Bend instruction, a modulation, etc. The program also manages the MIDI ports and the user interface that lets you program sounds, and calculates and sends the digital signal to the converters, etc. In short, the operating system lies at the functional core of the synthesizer.

When a user wants to update his or her instrument, either of the following two conditions will occur:

1 • The operating system resides in ROM, in which case the component has to be replaced. This procedure generally involves taking the device to a specialized after-market service office.

2 • The operating system resides in RAM, in which case the new version is provided in the form of a program on a floppy disk, which

simply has to be loaded into the device. When an instrument is the subject of frequent updates, this second method has the advantage of being much more flexible. On the other hand, it means that a floppy has to be read every time the device is turned on.

This is why some MIDI units offer a mixed loading procedure that combines the advantages of both of these methods. In this case, even though the operating system resides in RAM, when the unit is turned on the OS is loaded and duplicates itself in ROM. In point of fact, this ROM is only a storage memory—a sort of permanent fast-access program disk. When a new version of the OS comes out, either the ROM can be replaced physically (in which case it will copy itself into RAM every time the unit is turned on), or a disk can be inserted that contains an exact copy of the information stored in ROM. The disk has a higher OS version number than the ROM, and therefore takes priority over the ROM. As a result, the contents of the disk will be installed directly into RAM. This is the update procedure that's used by the Akai S-1000 sampler.

The kinds of memory you'll be looking at in the following sections don't involve programs. Instead, they deal with the data that these programs handle. You'll be working with the data by means of System Exclusive messages. As with operating systems, some of this information resides in ROM and therefore can't be programmed by users, while some of it resides in RAM and therefore can be programmed by users. Furthermore, most MIDI instruments are built to receive extension cards or boards. This ability makes it possible to increase the memory capacity of the instruments, in terms of ROM and also in terms of RAM. Extension cards can be either internal (i.e., mounted inside the instrument) or external (i.e., inserted into separate slots provided for the purpose). Specific examples will help you gain a detailed understanding of the functional role of the data memories of MIDI instruments.

How Memory Is Organized

The simplest case is that of a programmable synthesizer with a given number of sounds (such as for example 128). The memory of this kind of synthesizer is divided into as many locations as there are sounds, with each location consisting of as many bytes as are necessary to store all of the parameters for the sound. Such a synthesizer is said to be "programmable" as soon as these parameters exist in storable form and are stored in a readable and writable memory (i.e., in RAM).

It's worth noting that because the number of bytes in a sound varies depending on the structure of the sound, some rare instruments divide their memory into different-sized areas. This is the case, for instance, with the Yamaha SY-99, SY-77, and TG-77.

In certain synthesizers, some of the sounds are programmed in ROM to start with. This means that users won't be able to edit these sounds. In such a case, it's easy to see how memory could be divided into two blocks of 4096 bytes (64 × 64), with the first block with its 64 non-programmable sounds residing in ROM and the second block with its 64 programmable sounds residing in RAM. However, there's no reason why you can't select a sound from ROM, tinker with it or tweak it as you please, and then store the edited version in RAM. One advantage of storing non-programmable sounds in ROM is that it gives you a number of additional sounds at negligible cost.

The Edit Buffer

Regardless of whether a sound resides in ROM or in RAM, when the sound is selected on a synthesizer or on an expander, the contents of the corresponding memory location are immediately copied into a supplementary memory known as an *edit buffer*. It's only by means of this buffer that the user can program a sound. As a result, the business of editing the parameters of sounds takes place in real time in this temporary memory area. Once the sound has been edited, all that's left to do is store it in final form in one of the locations in RAM—in other words, by writing the information to memory.

Some systems have two edit buffers—or, more precisely, one storage buffer and one edit buffer. As soon as a sound is selected, the storage buffer receives the contents of the edit buffer. As soon as any attempt is made to edit the sound in question, the contents of the storage buffer are copied into the edit buffer. The edit buffer then becomes the current buffer and also the site of all the changes the user makes in the sound.

By alternating between these two buffers with the help of a specific key (such as Compare, Edit/Recall, etc.), it's easy to compare the original sound and the edited sound, or to compare the edited sound and a new sound that's been selected (and therefore transferred into the storage buffer). As soon as the results of the editing procedure are satisfactory, all that's left to do is to store the edited sound in memory in order for it to fill the first buffer again. This method has the advantage of letting you edit a sound by successive stages, safe in the knowledge that at any time you can go back to the most recently stored version of the sound).

The problem gets more complicated with multitimbral machines in which several sounds can be produced at the same time. Some devices, such as the Yamaha TX-802 and the Roland D-10, D-20, and D-110, have one storage buffer and/or edit buffer per multitimbral voice. Others, such as the Korg M1 and WS, have one storage buffer and/or one edit buffer for the entire set of voices. This second arrangement limits the transfer options, in ways that will be described in later chapters.

While first-generation MIDI devices contained only a single type of data—that is, sound data—current instruments are completely different. The next few sections of this chapter take a closer look at the memory structure of three of these instruments, to give you a clearer under-standing of how the programmable information is distributed. These three devices will serve as the basis for the next chapter's examination of System Exclusive messages.

The Memory of the Yamaha TX802

The Yamaha TX802 is a multitimbral expander that operates according to the principle of frequency-modulation (FM) synthesis. The instrument is delivered with 128 factory-installed sounds in ROM. The sounds are allocated among two memory banks, A and B, each of which contains 64 sounds. The sounds are numbered from A01 to A64 and from B01 to B64. The TX802 also has 64 sounds resident in RAM. These sounds are numbered from I01 to I64 (with "I" as in "internal"). In the TX802, the term "voice" is used to designate a sound.

The TX802 has 16 polyphonic voices and 8 multitimbral sounds. The business of programming the allocation of these eight sounds is known as "performance." There are 64 performance memories in RAM, numbered from INT01 to INT64 (with "INT" as in "internal"). In addition to a double edit buffer reserved for performances, each voice has its own double edit buffer (for a total of eight double buffers or sixteen individual buffers).

The TX802 lets you program microtonal scales—in other words, assign any desired pitch to each MIDI note that's received. This feature lets you program a tempered scale, quarter-tones, eighth-tones, and indeed any other frequencies you might want to use. Eleven scales are pre-programmed in the TX802's ROM, while two other scales that reside in RAM can be edited. In this case, the edit buffer is a single buffer.

In addition to the three categories described above, there's also *fractional weighting*. This procedure lets you regulate the volume that applies to each voice, for each operator and for each group of three notes. Although this part of memory is integral to the double buffers for the voices, it's still independent with regard to System Exclusive MIDI transmissions, which you'll be looking at later on.

This look at the TX802's memories closes with a glance at the instrument's system memory. This memory contains various global parameters, such as the MIDI channels that correspond to the reception of various categories of messages, the reassignment of controllers, memory protection, and the reassignment table for Program Change messages. It doesn't have an edit buffer.

This overview gives you a general idea of how the RAM of a sound generator is organized. However, the TX802 is also designed to receive a RAM card that's divided into a maximum of 16 memory locations, each of which contains 64 voices (numbered from C01 to C64), 64 performances (numbered from CRT01 to CRT64), fractional weighting data, and 63 microtonal scales, as indicated in Figure 10.1 below.

The Memory of the Roland D-50 and D-550

The Roland D-50 and D-550 are sound generators based on the principle of linear arithmetic (L/A) synthesis. The D-50 is the keyboard version of the instrument and the D-550 is the rack-mounted version. These sound generators aren't multitimbral; however, they do contain different types of memories.

As in the Yamaha TX-802, the edit buffer in each of these Rolands is a double buffer with a comparison system. However, if a new sound is selected there's no way to recall a sound from the second buffer. In the beginning, the D-50 and the D-550 had 64 sounds, known as *patches*, in internal RAM. In accordance with Roland's proprietary system, these sounds were numbered from I11 to I88 (in series from I11 to I18, I21 to I28, I31 to I38, and so on). However, thanks to a ROM or RAM card

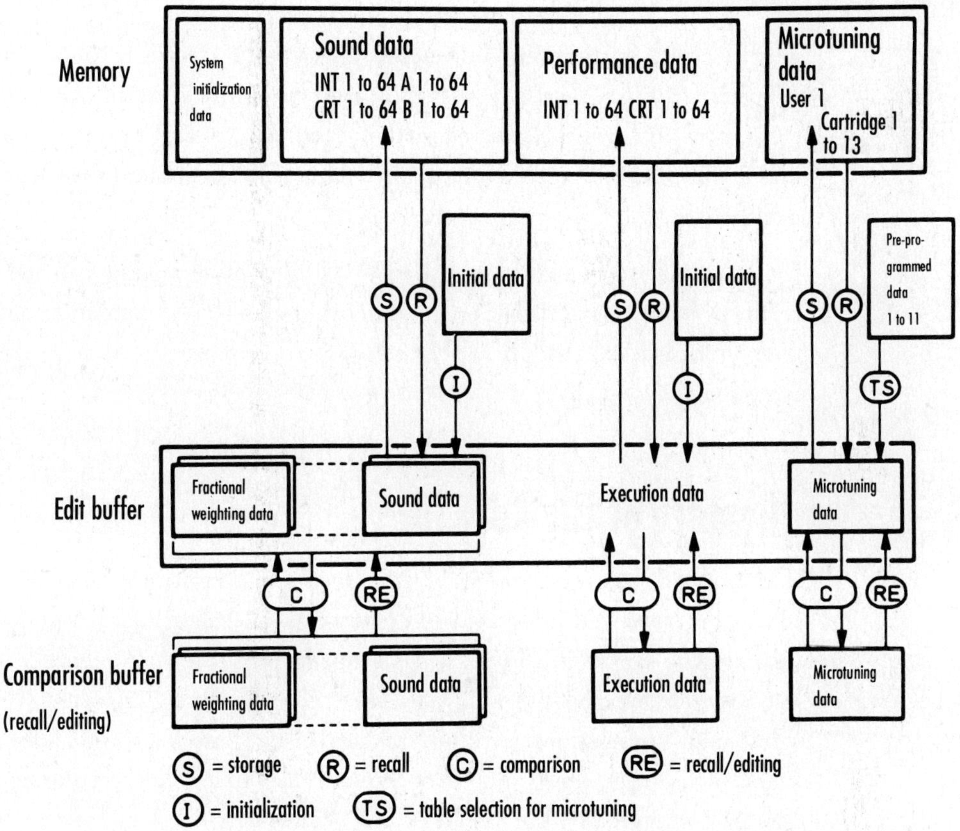

Memory

| System initialization data | Sound data
INT 1 to 64 A 1 to 64
CRT 1 to 64 B 1 to 64 | Performance data
INT 1 to 64 CRT 1 to 64 | Microtuning data
User 1
Cartridge 1 to 13 |

Initial data   Initial data   Pre-pro-grammed data 1 to 11

(S)(R)   (S)(R)   (S)(R)

(I)   (I)   (TS)

Edit buffer

| Fractional weighting data | Sound data | Execution data | Microtuning data |

(C) (RE)   (C) (RE)   (C) (RE)

Comparison buffer

(recall/editing)

| Fractional weighting data | Sound data | Execution data | Microtuning data |

(S) = storage   (R) = recall   (C) = comparison   (RE) = recall/editing

(I) = initialization   (TS) = table selection for microtuning

FIGURE 10.1: *The memory allocation map for the Yamaha TX802*

that can be plugged into the front panel, another 64 patches (numbered from C11 to C88) can be added.

The D-50 and the D-550 have 32 effects (reverb, echo, chorus, etc.). The first 16 effects (numbered from 1 to 16) reside in ROM, while the next 16 (numbered from 17 to 32) live in RAM, thereby providing the option of writing effects from a card. However, the effects aren't accompanied by an edit buffer.

The D-550 has a third and last memory area that's accessible to users. This is the system area, which lets you automate the operation of writing to the edit buffer at the selected memory address. As with most monotimbral sound generators, the memory structure of the D-50 and the D-550 is fairly easy to grasp.

On another level, the D-50 and the D-550 are sample-reading instruments. What this means is that they incorporate a ROM containing pulse code modulations, or PCMs. This memory isn't accessible to users (at least not intentionally).

The Memory of the Korg M1

The Korg M1 is a workstation which consists of a multitimbral generator (that uses Advanced Integrated (AI) synthesis) and a keyboard. The M1 also has two effects processors and a sequencer. In this instrument, sounds are referred to as "programs" and include effects parameters, while multitimbral configurations are known as "combinations." The special thing about memory allocation in the M1 is that it can to some extent be configured by the user. You can choose to use 100 programs, 100 combinations, and a sequencer with a capacity of about 4400 notes, or else 50 programs, 50 combinations, and a sequencer with a capacity of about 7700 notes.

Like the Roland D-50 and unlike the Yamaha TX-802, all of the sounds and internal multitimbral performances in the Korg M1 reside in RAM. The device's memory can be extended by means of a RAM card or a ROM card. The ROM card contains only programs and combinations, while the RAM card is configured exactly the same way as the M1's internal memory. The M1's system memory is known as the set of so-called "global parameters" (such as the microtonal scale, the mapping of percussion instruments, the overall MIDI channel, and so on). As a result, there are two edit buffers: one for combinations and the other for programs.

What you should remember from this overview is that the ROM or RAM memories of MIDI instruments are generally subdivided into as many categories as there are different types of objects. Furthermore, each of these categories contains from 1 to *n* equal-sized locations. This explanation will help give you a better understanding of how MIDI System Exclusive messages are handled.

The MIDI Dump

Because the memories of MIDI instruments are different in terms of size and contents, it's hard to draw up a universal standard for data transfers that use a single MIDI protocol. Dumps carry information as varied as a single synthesis parameter (the cut-off frequency, the envelope, etc.), a sound (a voice, a patch, a preset, etc.), a set of sounds (bulk), a rhythm-box pattern, an automated mixing-board configuration, a Program Change assignment table, microtuning data, and so on.

This is why the Dump function is managed by the only set of messages that's proprietary to each manufacturer, namely, the System Exclusive (SysEx) messages. When you think about it, it's obvious: for instance, an L/A synthesizer isn't concerned with the parameters for an FM synthesizer, and vice versa. As a result, each manufacturer uses MIDI to send SysEx messages that contain the data peculiar to each device.

By definition, a Dump is an Exclusive message that contains all or part of the data for a MIDI instrument. When data is being transferred from the instrument to an external unit (i.e., when the data is being saved), a Dump message travels from the MIDI Out port of the instrument to the

MIDI In port of the storage device (which can be a microcomputer, a second instrument of the same type, etc.). Going in the opposite direction, from the external unit to the instrument (i.e., when the data is being loaded), the Dump message travels from the MIDI Out port of the storage unit to the MIDI In port of the instrument.

The Dump Request

When a request is sent to most MIDI devices that have RAM, the devices return the corresponding data in the form of a Dump. The initial request is known as a Dump Request, and has several advantages.

There are two ways to transmit a Dump from an instrument to a storage device. The first is to trigger the Dump directly from the instrument by means of the appropriate function. The second way uses the Exclusive Dump Request message. This message, when transmitted by the storage unit to the instrument, orders the instrument to empty its memory areas—or, more precisely, to send an exact copy of the contents of its memory areas to the MIDI Out port. This is an automated or remotely controlled data-transfer procedure. It's worth noting that some MIDI instruments can only implement one or the other of these two methods.

The MIDI Rules

According to the MIDI standard, every Exclusive message has to start with F0H and end with F7H. But between these two status bytes you can have an unlimited number of data bytes. Only Real Time messages (such as MIDI Clock messages or MTC Quarter Frame messages) are allowed to position themselves between two bytes in an Exclusive message—for instance, in order to preserve perfect synchronization. If any other status byte is issued, the transaction will be interrupted.

When the byte that follows F0H is less than 125 (7DH), it indicates which manufacturer built the device (see also the discussion at the end of Chapter 4). In such a case, this byte is known as the "manufacturer's ID." To allow for increasing numbers of potential manufacturers, a value of zero represents a special case indicating that the identifier uses two additional bytes, for a total of 14 useful bits or 16,384 possible combinations. However, there are three other values that are exceptions to this rule: 7D, for non-commercial use (universities, schools, research centers, etc.), 7E, for Non-Real Time links (e.g., the Sample Dump Standard), and 7F, for Real Time links (MTC messages, etc.). These are the only "musts" the MIDI standard imposes with regard to System Exclusive messages. Beyond them, each manufacturer can use these messages as it sees fit.

Experience has shown that the headers of Dump and Dump Request messages contain certain pieces of information that are more or less common to most instruments, to wit:

- Identification of the type of instrument and/or the family the instrument belongs to

- The MIDI channel

- The type of message (Dump, Dump Request, etc.)

- The portion of the memory contents to be dumped (the address, the size, etc.)

In practical terms, Exclusive messages let you use a computer and appropriate software (Dump utilities, librarians, editors, etc.) to work with the data stored in the memory of a MIDI instrument, with all of the attendant advantages a computer provides (ergonomics, inexpensive storage media, and so on).

Sometimes, however, you'll want to handle Exclusive messages yourself. You can do that by using the procedure mentioned above, by directly ordering the instrument to empty its memory contents to an external device. You'd send this order by pressing the appropriate keys (if the instrument has them). Or else you can automate the procedure by sending a Dump Request message. This second solution, which is by far the more elegant one, orders the unit in question to transmit (i.e., to duplicate) all or part of its data to the MIDI Out port.

In the following sections you'll review the general considerations. The following Exclusive codes are given only as illustrations, in order to show the syntax of the Dump and Dump Request messages. The practical implementation of these messages is the subject of Chapter 14, which describes them in greater detail.

The Roland Method

The SysEx transmission methods that Roland uses have been common to all of the company's products for several years now. The methods use two types of exchanges: *one-way mode* and *handshake mode*. In this section you'll take a look at the one-way mode. A much more detailed description of the Roland protocol appears at the end of this chapter.

Naturally, the Exclusive messages start with F0H, which is followed by 41H (the value that corresponds to the manufacturer's ID number). The next byte, the Device ID, indicates the MIDI channel number (which can range from 00H to 0FH), or the unit number (which can range from 10H to 1FH). The advantages of having a unit number are that it doesn't depend on the concept of channels (for instance, in configurations in which several identical devices are set to the same channels) and that it allows access to so-called "protected" data (that is, information that can't be reached through the channel number). Next comes the Model ID number, which indicates the name of the product or the family of products (for instance, the D-10, D-20, or D-110 series), and the Command ID, which specifies the type of message: either 11H for a Dump Request in one-way mode (RQ1/Request Data 1), or 41H for its equivalent in handshake mode (RQD/Request Data), etc.

As far as Dump Request messages are concerned, the major advantage of this method lies in the meaning of the next six bytes. The first three bytes in this group indicate the memory address of the data to go and get, and the last three bytes indicate the size of the data. Roland's user manuals automatically include a table of the memory addresses of the device. The checksum and EOX (End of Exclusive) bytes conclude the operation.

Going the other way, with Dump messages, the RQ1 and RQD identifiers are replaced with DT1 (12H/Data Set 1) and DAT (42H/Data Set). The information is located between the address bytes and the checksum. In short, then, the superiority of the method developed by Roland lies in the fact that messages and data are independent from one another. For instance, the same message can empty either all or part of memory, from its entire contents down to a single parameter (discussed in more detail below). However, some of the more recent Roland devices, such as the Juno-1, Juno-2, and the MKS-50 family, which implement the one-way and handshake modes, have yet to adopt this procedure.

A One-Way Dump Request

```
F0H (11110000): Exclusive message status byte
41H (01000001): identification (Roland)
aaH:(0aaaaaaa): MIDI channel or unit number (device ID)
bbH (0bbbbbbb): model or family (model ID)
11H (00010001): RQ1 code (one-way request)
ddH (0ddddddd): address (start)
eeH (0eeeeeee): address (continued)
ffH (0fffffff): address (end)
ggH (0ggggggg): size (start)
hhH (0hhhhhhh): size (continued)
iiH (0iiiiiii): size (end)
ccH (0ccccccc): checksum
F7H (11110111): EOX
```

A One-Way Dump

```
F0H (11110000): Exclusive message status byte
41H (01000001): identification (Roland)
aaH:(0aaaaaaa): MIDI channel or unit number (device ID)
bbH (0bbbbbbb): model or family (model ID)
12H (00010010): DT1 code (one-way dump)
ddH (0ddddddd): address (start)
eeH (0eeeeeee): address (continuation)
ffH (0fffffff): address (end)
xxH (0xxxxxxx): data
...
ccH (0ccccccc): checksum
F7H (11110111): EOX
```

Whether at Roland, at Yamaha, or among other manufacturers, dump procedures developed empirically toward a sort of standardization as users' needs evolved.

Data-Storage and Data-Transmission Formats

In addition to its header (which contains F0H, the manufacturer's ID, the instrument ID, the MIDI channel, etc.) and its suffix (which contains the checksum, F7H, etc.), Dump messages contain a certain amount of MIDI data. However, this information consists of bytes in which only bits 0 to 6 are significant, because bit 7 in a MIDI byte is always equal to zero. Given that the memories of MIDI instruments are also filled with bytes, there's no reason why manufacturers can't store 8-bit values in those bytes. If that were the case, if you wanted to transmit an eight-bit memory byte, you'd need two MIDI bytes (or, more precisely, one byte and one bit). In other words, the storage format isn't necessarily the same as the transmission format that the Exclusive messages use. Now, with the help of specific examples, here's a closer look at the most widely used ways of storing and transferring dumps.

Compressed Storage

On the Sequential Circuits Prophet 600, each sound consists of 16 bytes, for a total of 38 programmable parameters. In fact, some bytes represent several parameters. This principle, which you'll run into again with many manufacturers' instruments, makes it possible to optimize the way memory space is allocated and used. Table 10.1 below shows how the memory of the Prophet 600 is organized.

TABLE 10.1: *The Memory Organization of the Prophet 600*

BYTE	BIT	BIT 6	BIT 5	BIT 4	BIT 3	BIT 2	BIT 1	BIT 0
00	B0	A6	A5	A4	A3	A2	A1	A0
01	D0	C3	C2	C1	C0	B3	B2	B1
02	E1	E0	D6	D5	D4	D3	D2	D1
03	F4	F3	F2	F1	F0	E4	E3	E2
04	H0	G5	G4	G3	G2	G1	G0	F5
05	I1	I0	H6	H5	H4	H3	H2	H1
06	J3	J2	J1	J0	I5	I4	I3	I2
07	K4	K3	K2	K1	K0	J6	J5	J4
08	M2	M1	M0	L3	L2	L1	L0	K5
09	O2	O1	O0	N3	N2	N1	N0	M3
10	Q2	Q1	Q0	P3	P2	P1	P0	O3
11	S2	S1	S0	R3	R2	R1	R0	Q3
12	U2	U1	U0	T3	T2	T1	T0	S3
13	V6	V5	V4	V3	V2	V1	V0	U3
14	Z7	Z6	Z5	Z4	Z3	Z2	Z1	Z0
15	Z15	Z14	Z13	Z12	Z11	Z10	Z9	Z8

Except for the sixteen parameters from Z0 to Z15 (each of which occupies only one bit), each letter corresponds to one of the parameters of the Prophet 600. The number associated with the letter indicates the position of the bit. As you know, each of these parameters is coded over a certain number of bits, depending on the required range of values: 7 bits for a parameter that needs from 65 to 128 values, 6 bits for a parameter that needs from 33 to 64 values, 5 bits for a parameter that needs 17 to 32 values, and so on. The meanings of these parameters are listed in detail in Table 10.2 below.

TABLE 10.2: *The Meaning of the Parameters in the Prophet 600*

LETTER AND PARAMETER	MEANING
A (7 bits: A6 A5 A4 A3 A2 A1 A0)	Osc A PW
B (4 bits: B3 B2 B1 B0)	Pmod Fil Env
C (4 bits: C3 C2 C1 C0)	Lfo Freq
D (7 bits: D6 D5 D4 D3 D2 D1 D0)	Pmod Osc B
E (5 bits: E4 E3 E2 E1 E0)	Lfo Amt
F (6 bits: F5 F4 F3 F2 F1 F0)	Osc B Freq
G (6 bits: G5 G4 G3 G2 G1 G0)	Osc A Freq
H (7 bits: H6 H5 H4 H3 H2 H1 H0)	Osc Fine
I (6 bits: I5 I4 I3 I2 I1 I0)	Mixer
J (7 bits: J6 J5 J4 J3 J2 J1 J0)	Filter Cutoff
K (6 bits: K5 K4 K3 K2 K1 K0)	Resonance
L (4 bits: L3 L2 L1 L0)	Fil Env Amt
M (4 bits: M3 M2 M1 M0)	Fil Res
N (4 bits: N3 N2 N1 N0)	Fil Sus
O (4 bits: O3 O2 O1 O0)	Fil Dec

. . . .

TABLE 10.2: *The Meaning of the Parameters in the Prophet 600 (continued)*

LETTER AND PARAMETER	MEANING
P (4 bits: P3 P2 P1 P0)	Fil Atk
Q (4 bits: Q3 Q2 Q1 Q0)	Amp Rel
R (4 bits: R3 R2 R1 R0)	Amp Sus
S (4 bits: S3 S2 S1 S0)	Amp Dec
T (4 bits: T3 T2 T1 T0)	Amp Atk
U (4 bits: U3 U2 U1 U0)	Glide
V (7 bits: V6 V5 V4 V3 V2 V1 V0)	Osc B PW
Z0 (1 bit)	Osc A Pulse
Z1 (1 bit)	Osc B Pulse
Z2 (1 bit)	Fil Kbd Full
Z3 (1 bit)	Fil Kbd 1/2
Z4 (1 bit)	Lfo Shape
Z5 (1 bit)	Lfo Freq
Z6 (1 bit)	Lfo PW
Z7 (1 bit)	Lfo Fil
Z8 (1 bit)	Osc A Saw
Z9 (1 bit)	Osc A Tri
Z10 (1 bit)	Osc A Sync
Z11 (1 bit)	Osc B Saw
Z12 (1 bit)	Osc B Tri
Z13 (1 bit)	Pmod Freq A
Z14 (1 bit)	Pmod Fil
Z15 (1 bit)	Unison

As you see, this instrument uses memory as efficiently as possible, and no bits are lost. If you'd wanted to represent each parameter by an entire byte (for a total of 38 bytes), you'd have wasted 22 bytes ($38 - 16 = 22$).

Transmission by Nybbles

With the Prophet 600, information is transmitted via MIDI in groups of half-bytes, or *nybbles*. Each of the 16 memory bytes is divided in two and sent in the form of two MIDI bytes, with the least significant nybble (that is, bits 0 to 3) being sent first. In the MIDI bytes, these nybbles are justified to the right. This way, the dump contains twice as many MIDI bytes as memory bytes—in other words, a total of 32 MIDI bytes.

When the least significant nybble (sometimes referred to as the "low" nybble) is transmitted before the most significant ("high") nybble, the transmission is known as a "L/H nybble," and "L/H nybblize" is what you're said to have done to the transmission. Some MIDI instruments, such as the Lexicon PCM-70, do it the other way, sending the most significant ("high") nybble before the least significant ("low") nybble. This type of transmission is a "H/L nybble," and the procedure can be said to have been "H/L nybblized."

The information stored in the memory of instruments such as the E-mu Proteus is expressed in terms of two bytes rather than one. Of these two bytes, only the 14 least significant bits are used, which is why two MIDI bytes are necessary in order to transmit the data—first bits 0 to 6, and then bits 7 to 13.

"7 plus 1" Transmission

In addition to transmission by nybbles, as described above for the Prophet 600, some instruments, such as the Alesis Midiverb III, divide each memory byte in two in order to send it over two MIDI bytes, with bits 0 to 6 going first, followed by bit 7, a conversion known as "7 plus 1."

Uncompressed Storage

Assume you have a Yamaha TX802 in multitimbral configuration. The MIDI Data Format for this instrument indicates the meaning of each byte in the performance edit buffer, in the form of a list that looks a lot like the contents of Table 10.3 below:

TABLE 10.3: *The Meaning of the Bytes in the Performance Edit Buffer of the Yamaha TX802*

BYTE NUMBER	PARAMETER	DESCRIPTION	RANGE OF VALUES
0 to 7	VCHOFS	Voice Channel Offset	0 to 7
8 to 15	RXCH	Receive Channel (16 = omni)	0 to 16
16 to 23	VNUM	Voice Number (0 to 63: internal) (64 to 127: cartridge) (128 to 191: preset A) (192 to 255: preset B)	0 to 255
24 to 31	DETUNE	Detune (7: center)	0 to 14
32 to 39	OUTVOL	Output Volume	0 to 99
40 to 47	OUTCH	Output assign (0: Off, 1: I)	0 to 3

· ·

TABLE 10.3: *The Meaning of the Bytes in the Performance Edit Buffer of the Yamaha TX802* *(continued)*

BYTE NUMBER	PARAMETER	DESCRIPTION	RANGE OF VALUES
		(2: II, 3: I + II)	
48 to 55	NLMTL	Note limit low (C-2 to G8)	0 to 127
56 to 63	NLMTH	Note limit high (C-2 to G8)	0 to 127
64 to 71	NSHFT	Note Shift (24: center) (+/− 2 octaves)	0 to 48
72 to 79	FDAMP	EG forced damp (0: off, 1: on)	0 to 1
80 to 87	KASG	Key assign group	0 to 1
88 to 95	MTTNUM	Micro tuning table	0 to 254
96 to 115	PNAM	Performance name	

The TX802 is an eight-voice multitimbral instrument. For a total of twelve parameters per voice, each parameter is duplicated eight times ($8 \times 12 = 96$). The last ten bytes indicate the name of the performance. Unlike data storage in the Prophet 600, data storage in the TX802 isn't optimized. Regardless of the number of values each parameter needs (i.e., from 2 to 256), all of the values are represented by eight bits.

ASCII Transmission

Here again, the 116 bytes in the performance buffer of the TX802 are broken down into two nybbles for transmission via MIDI. As a result, in this case you have a total of 232 bytes. However, these bytes aren't represented as bytes. Instead, they're converted into ASCII, in accordance with their value as expressed in hexadecimal notation, as shown in Table 10.4 below.

TABLE 10.4: *ASCII Representation of the Nybbles in the Performance Buffer of the Yamaha TX802*

NYBBLE, IN BINARY	HEXADECIMAL VALUE	ASCII REPRESENTATION OF THE HEX VALUE
0000	0	30H
0001	1	31H
0010	2	32H
0011	3	33H
0100	4	34H
0101	5	35H
0110	6	36H
0111	7	37H
1000	8	38H
1001	9	39H
1010	A	41H
1011	B	42H
1100	C	43H
1101	D	44H
1110	E	45H
1111	F	46H

Suppose you want to send the following eight bytes:

```
01111111    7FH
01010000    50H
00010001    11H
10001000    88H
11111111    FFH
00000001    01H
00001000    08H
01100110    66H
```

In this case, you'd first have to break them down into nybbles in hex, with the least significant nybble leading, this way:

F 7 0 5 1 1 8 8 F F 1 0 8 0 6 6

in order to convert them into hex-coded ASCII, this way:

46H 37H 30H 35H 31H 31H 38H 38H 46H 46H 31H 30H 38H 30H 36H 36H

which gives you the following binary code:

```
01000110
00110111
00110000
00110101
00110001
00110001
00111000
00111000
01000110
01000110
00110001
00110000
00111000
00110000
00110110
00110110
```

Mixed Storage

In some cases, mixed storage compresses several parameters into the same byte—without however achieving 100 percent optimal use of all the bits. What this gives you is a mixture of compressed and uncompressed storage. The Korg M1 operates this way.

Packed Transmission

Unlike nybble-based transmission methods, packed transmission uses the seven bits in a MIDI data byte. As a result, you need a total of eight MIDI bytes (7 bits × 8) to transmit seven memory bytes (8 bits × 7). The following code fragments show how the Korg M1 does the conversion:

Memory Bytes

```
a7 a6 a5 a4 a3 a2 a1 a0
b7 b6 b5 b4 b3 b2 b1 b0
c7 c6 c5 c4 c3 c2 c1 c0
d7 d6 d5 d4 d3 d2 d1 d0
e7 e6 e5 e4 e3 e2 e1 e0
f7 f6 f5 f4 f3 f2 f1 f0
g7 g6 g5 g4 g3 g2 g1 g0
```

MIDI Bytes

```
0 g7 f7 e7 d7 c7 b7 a7
0 a6 a5 a4 a3 a2 a1 a0
0 b6 b5 b4 b3 b2 b1 b0
0 c6 c5 c4 c3 c2 c1 c0
0 d6 d5 d4 d3 d2 d1 d0
0 e6 e5 e4 e3 e2 e1 e0
0 f6 f5 f4 f3 f2 f1 f0
0 g6 g5 g4 g3 g2 g1 g0
```

Some instruments send the byte containing the most significant bits last, instead of first, as shown below:

MIDI Bytes

```
0 a6 a5 a4 a3 a2 a1 a0
0 b6 b5 b4 b3 b2 b1 b0
0 c6 c5 c4 c3 c2 c1 c0
0 d6 d5 d4 d3 d2 d1 d0
0 e6 e5 e4 e3 e2 e1 e0
0 f6 f5 f4 f3 f2 f1 f0
0 g6 g5 g4 g3 g2 g1 g0
0 g7 f7 e7 d7 c7 b7 a7
```

The principle described above is the one that's most widely used in connection with packed formats. However, a few rare variants also exist. For instance, the Kurzweil K-2000 lets any number of memory bytes be transmitted, not just packets of seven bytes. For example, the following four memory bytes:

Hexadecimal	Binary (8 bits)
4FH	01001111 (a7 a6 a5 a4 a3 a2 a1 a0)
D8H	11011000 (b7 b6 b5 b4 b3 b2 b1 b0)
01H	00000001 (c7 c6 c5 c4 c3 c2 c1 c0)
29H	00101001 (d7 d6 d5 d4 d3 d2 d1 d0)

are transmitted over five MIDI bytes, in the following way:

Hexadecimal	Binary (7 bits)
27H	0100111 (a7 a6 a5 a4 a3 a2 a1)
76H	1110110 (a0 b7 b6 b5 b4 b3 b2)
00H	0000000 (b1 b0 c7 c6 c5 c4 c3)
12H	0010010 (c2 c1 c0 d7 d6 d5 d4)
48H	1001000 (d3 d2 d1 d0 0 0 0)

instead of over eight MIDI bytes, as the previous method would require:

Hexadecimal	Binary (7 bits)
02H	0000010 (g7 f7 e7 d7 c7 b7 a7)
4FH	1001111 (a6 a5 a4 a3 a2 a1 a0)
58H	1011000 (b6 b5 b4 b3 b2 b1 b0)

```
01H            0000001 (c6 c5 c4 c3 c2 c1 c0)
29H            0010001 (d6 d5 d4 d3 d2 d1 d0)
00H            0000000 (e6 e5 e4 e3 e2 e1 e0)
00H            0000000 (f6 f5 f4 f3 f2 f1 f0)
00H            0000000 (g6 g5 g4 g3 g2 g1 g0)
```

In practice, when the number of memory bytes to be transmitted isn't a multiple of 7, the Korg method completes the last packet with additional bytes that are equal to zero. In contrast, the Kurzweil method sends a variable number of MIDI bytes (that is, exactly as many bytes as necessary), of which only the unused bits in the last byte are forced to zero.

Standard Transmission

The Roland D-50 and D-550 store information in memory at the rate of one byte per parameter, without compression. Furthermore, some bytes are reserved for future extensions and don't always have any particular meaning right now. For instance, out of 468 bytes per patch, 93 are still unused. Because none of these 468 parameters exceeds the value 127, each of them can be transmitted in its current form via MIDI. As a result, if you wanted to empty a patch memory, a total of only 468 MIDI bytes would do the trick.

The Various Formats in Brief

In summary, then, there are three main ways to store data:

- Compressed storage, in which all of the bits are used

- Uncompressed storage, which allocates one byte for each parameter

- Mixed storage, which is essentially the same as compressed storage, except that it's not optimized

—and six main ways to send data via MIDI:

- Transmission by nybbles with two MIDI bytes for each memory byte

- Transmission of a memory word (14 bits) in the form of two MIDI bytes

- So-called "7 plus 1" transmission, with two MIDI bytes for every memory byte

- Transmission by nybbles in ASCII format

- Packed transmission, with eight MIDI bytes for every seven memory bytes

- Standard transmission, with one MIDI byte for every memory byte

Displayed Values and Real Values

Sometimes the value of a parameter as displayed on the LCD screen of an instrument is different from the actual value of the parameter as stored in memory. This difference usually involves parameters whose values range over positive and negative scales. For instance, in the Korg M1, some parameters range from a value of +99 to a value of −99 (for a total of 199 possible values). In memory, these parameters are coded over a byte in the form of the numbers 63H (+99) to 9DH (−99). Sure, 63H is equal to 99 decimal; but 9DH is equal to 157, not −99. In actuality, the negative numbers are represented by their one's complement—that is, by the number that's created when each bit in the byte is inverted (i.e., when every zero becomes a 1, and every 1 becomes a zero), as shown below:

```
+99  =  01100011
−99  =  10011100

+01  =  00000001
−01  =  11111110
```

However, Roland doesn't use the one's-complement method. Consider for example the address of the second Partial Parameter (01H, or WG Pitch Fine). You can see that for a range whose actual value is from 0 to 100 (in hex, from 00H to 64H), the displayed value can be anything from −50 (00H) to +50 (64H).

Generally speaking, there are many ways to represent parameters. There's no need to go into exhaustive detail about all of the methods currently in use. You should simply keep in mind that a value stored in memory isn't always the same as the corresponding number displayed on the screen of the instrument.

The Representation of Alphanumeric Characters

For representing alphanumeric characters, ASCII format is by far the most widely used method. However, a few instruments are exceptions to the rule. Two of them are the Roland D-50 and D-550.

The character-representation format used by the Akai S-1000 sampler is described in detail in Chapter 12.

Individual Parameter Messages

In addition to Dump messages and Dump Request messages, there's another group of messages that are dedicated to editing the memory contents of MIDI devices. These are the individual parameter messages (which you learned in passing above in the discussion of the Roland method). When they're sent to an instrument (even if they aren't implemented on all MIDI devices) these messages let you change the value of an individual parameter inside the edit buffer. On the other hand, on some machines, the act of editing a parameter manually from the front panel of an instrument causes the corresponding individual parameter message to be sent to the MIDI Out port. The usefulness of these messages will become more clear in connection with Chapter 12's discussion of editing programs. How these messages are implemented is the subject of the following chapters, which deal with setting up an editor/librarian for the Yamaha SY-55, converting a Roland PG-300 into a MIDI console, and using FM synthesis to simulate a Hammond organ with FM synthesis.

Data Integrity

In any information network, the interface techniques (that is, the procedures that let data be exchanged between two systems) pose the problem of data integrity. Information can be affected by various factors (cables that are too long, electrical interference, etc.). Happily, though, the problem can be at least partly solved by error-detection and error-correction codes. MIDI is no exception to the rule: checksums, handshakes, acknowledgments, rejections, and other items described in the user manuals help contribute to the reliability of transmissions.

Error-Detection and Error-Correction Codes

An error is any change in the smallest unit of digital information, namely a bit, that occurs when the bit travels through the interface. But because a bit can only have two states (either 0 or 1), any change means a conversion from the 0 state to the 1 state, or from the 1 state to the 0 state. As a result, an error that occurs because a bit is set to 1 can be corrected by setting that bit to 0, and vice versa. In short, if an error can be found, it can be corrected. Logically, then, error-related codes fall into two categories: error-detection codes and error-correction codes (which first determine that an error has occurred and then find out where it happened).

An error-detection code is a way of supplementing the useful information with a piece of redundant information that complies with a known rule that applies to both the transmitter and the receiver. Before sending data, the transmitter applies a calculation (i.e., the rule) to the data, and the result of this calculation is also transmitted. When the data is received, the receiver applies the same calculation to the same data, and compares the results of this calculation against the result of the calculation that was performed by the transmitter. If there's a difference, the receiver announces that an error has occurred. For instance, assume that the transmitter sends the data 2, 9, 4, 1, and that the detection rule is in the form of a simple summation. In this case, the data frame that's sent will look like this:

```
2-9-4-1-16 (where 2 + 9 + 4 + 1 = 16)
```

Now suppose the third piece of information was changed during the transfer—for instance, from a value of 4 to a value of 5. In this case, what the receiver will see is the following frame:

```
2-9-5-1-16
```

If you add the first four items (2 + 9 + 5 + 1 = 17), you'll find that the result is different from the result calculated by the transmitter (namely, 16). As a result, the receiver will infer, correctly, that a transmission error occurred.

So far, so good. But all a detection code tells you is that an error has occurred. It doesn't tell you *where* the error is. There's nothing to indicate which data byte is affected by the change, or indeed whether the change involves the useful data or the result of the calculation. After an error has been found, the receiver has the option of either displaying a message and interrupting the transaction, or, if it's programmed to do so, requesting that the frame affected by the error be transmitted again.

In the binary system, the parity bit is one of the codes most frequently used in error detection. In a serial link, when a byte is transmitted the transmitter adds an extra bit so as to provide an even number of ones (i.e., even parity). (Parity always refers to the number of bits that are set to 1. The number of bits set to zero doesn't affect parity either way.) Then the receiver calculates the parity of the byte it receives, in order to compare it with the result obtained by the transmitter (i.e., the ninth bit transmitted).

However, this procedure is handicapped by the fact that it can't detect an even number of errors. In the following example, the transmitter sends a byte followed by a parity bit calculated in such a way as to obtain an odd number of bits set to zero:

```
10100011 0 (for a total of five bits set to zero)
```

Now suppose that a double transmission error occurs and that both bit 0 and bit 7 are affected (in other words, that their value is changed from 1 to 0). In this case, the parity system will conclude that no changes occurred, because the number of bits set to zero is still odd, as shown below:

```
00100010 0 (for a total of seven bits set to zero; in
spite of the double error, the parity is still correct)
```

Error-correction codes are more sophisticated. After an error is detected, these codes can locate and therefore correct the changed bits. Because of their ability to locate errors, these codes, which are used particularly in digital audio, take up a large number of redundant bytes.

Without going into too much detail, here's an example of a simple correction code that, in addition to a simple calculation of horizontal parity for each byte, adds a vertical parity calculation after every eighth byte that's sent:

TRANSMISSION	RECEPTION ERROR, AND DETERMINATION OF ITS LOCATION
11001101 1	11001101 1
01010000 0	01010000 0
00001111 0	00001111 0
01010001 1	0101 7001 0
11101010 1	11101010 1

TRANSMISSION	RECEPTION ERROR, AND DETERMINATION OF ITS LOCATION
01000101 1	01000101 1
00100010 0	00100010 0
00011110 0	00011110 0
01010000	0101*1*000

This matrix-style parity calculation makes it possible to pinpoint the location of the error at the intersection of the horizontal and vertical parity errors. The error can be corrected immediately by changing the value of the affected bit.

The MIDI Solution: The Checksum

As specified, the MIDI standard primarily carries real-time messages that are shorter than 4 bytes. Therefore, it's not possible to implement a simple detection system, because the fact of sending messages in real time as a function of what a musician is playing isn't compatible with requests for re-transmission of erroneous messages. Error-correction systems would uselessly overload the MIDI network, especially in view of the fact that typical short MIDI messages statistically aren't subject to change. Furthermore, some status messages (All Notes Off, Reset All Controllers, and System Reset) are provided in order to prevent or reduce the effect of any blocking errors that may occur.

On the other hand, the length of Exclusive messages (i.e., Dump messages) seems to grow in direct proportion to technological progress. That's why you need an error-detection system, or even an error-correction system. Except for the Sample Dump Standard, whose exchange protocol is defined by the MIDI standard, each manufacturer enjoys complete freedom when it comes to checking and verifying the integrity of data.

Up till now, the only error-detection technique that's been used is the checksum. The checksum is a piece of information (in the form of one or more bytes) that corresponds to the result of a calculation performed on all of the data in an Exclusive message, usually with the exception of the header bytes (e.g., the channel number, the instrument ID, and so on). Without drawing up a tediously exhaustive list, here are the major types of checksums—that is, the major types of calculations—in use today:

Standard Checksums

This method, used by the E-mu Proteus, among others, is equal to the seven least significant bits in the sum of the data bytes.

The "Two's Complement" Checksum

Used by Yamaha and Roland, among other manufacturers, this checksum is equal to the so-called "two's complement" of the seven least significant bits in the sum of the data bytes. This method, which is used in data processing to represent negative data, consists of inverting all of the bits in a byte, a word, or any other unit of information, and then adding the number 1 to the result.

The "One's Complement" Checksum

This approach, used by the MIDI DMC MX-8 patch, among other instruments, is equal to the one's complement of the seven least significant bits in the sum of the data bytes. Popular among data-processing programmers, this method consists of inverting all of the bits of a byte, of a word, etc.

The Checksum with a Shift

This method, used by Kurzweil, among other manufacturers, is equal to the seven least significant bits in the sum of the data bytes. This addition is performed on a 16-bit word, which prior to each new addition is rotated to the left. (In other words, bit 0 is replaced by bit 15, and each subsequent bit is shifted one position to the left.)

The "Nybble" Checksum (over seven bits)

This method, which is used by the Oberheim Matrix 1000, is equivalent to the one's complement of the seven least significant bits in the sum of the data bytes (rather than the sum of the nybbles, even though in this instance the information is being transmitted via MIDI in the form of nybbles).

The "Nybble" Checksum (in the form of two times four bits)

This method, used by some of the older Korg synthesizers, among others, is equivalent to the one's complement of the eight least significant bits in the sum of the data bytes (rather than the sum of the nybbles, even though in this instance the information is being transmitted via MIDI in the form of nybbles).

The Checksum of the Kawai K5

This checksum is calculated on the basis of the 16 least significant bits in the sum of the data. This value is derived neither from nybbles (even though in this instance the information is being transmitted via MIDI in the form of nybbles) nor from bytes, but instead from words (that is, groups of 16 bits). By adding the checksum, which itself is also expressed in terms of a word, to this sum of the data, the result should be equal to

5A3CH (or possibly to 15A3CH, in the event that the 16 least significant bits in the sum exceed the value of 5A3CH).

Handshaking, Roland Style

During data exchanges (i.e., dumps) between two units, a certain number of control messages (similar to a dialog) can be included in order to regulate the transmission flow. These messages indicate whether a transmission was received properly or received incorrectly, whether an error occurred, whether a message should be re-transmitted, and so on. Depending on the kind of interface, this control logic is implemented either in hardware or in software. For instance, the EIA/TIA-232E interface (formerly known as the RS-232 interface) has a given number of pins (i.e., lines) dedicated to this task. In a case like this, what you're dealing with is *handshaking hardware.*

To set up an artificial bidirectional link between two units in order to exchange Exclusive messages, the MIDI interface uses two unidirectional links (one per line, from the MIDI Out port of the sender to the MIDI In port of the receiver, and vice versa). Because each line carries only one piece of information at a time (i.e., because the link is a serial link), only one software handshaking protocol can be implemented.

The Roland communications protocol, which is valid for all of the company's more recent instruments, was designed to increase the reliability of data-exchange operations. This protocol, whose use is by no means obligatory, is known as the "handshake" protocol. In point of fact, the same data can be exchanged in a more conventional way simply by transmitting Dump and Dump Request messages (using the one-way mode, which you learned earlier in this chapter). In the explanations that appear below, the unit that's transmitting the Dump messages is referred to as the *sender,* while the unit that receives the Dump messages (and that sends the Dump Request messages) is referred to as the *receiver.*

One-Way Mode

One-way mode is easier to implement than handshake mode, but it's less efficient. One-way mode consists of two messages: a request (the Dump Request message) and a reply (the Dump message). The receiver transmits the Dump Request to the sender, which in return sends back the contents of its memory. Naturally, this exchange requires a bidirectional link between the sender and the receiver, from the sender's MIDI Out port to the receiver's MIDI In port and vice versa.

However, there's no reason why you can't initiate the transmission of data from the sender directly, by pressing the corresponding keys on the instrument. In this case all you have to do is install a unidirectional link between the MIDI Out port of the sender and the MIDI In port of the receiver. In either case, the two messages that are used in one-way mode are the following ones:

Request: RQ1 (Request Data 1)

The RQ1 message is transmitted from the receiver to the sender. The message instructs the sender to send a group of data whose starting memory address and whose size in bytes are indicated by the following message:

Reply: DT1 (Data Set 1)

When an RQ1 message is received or when the user initiates it (by applying manual pressure to the Dump Send keys of the instrument), the sender transmits the data. Some instruments, such as the MT-32 expander, can send data only when they receive an RQ1 message. (The instrument doesn't have any keys that are dedicated to sending dumps.) Roland's D-50 and D-550 synthesizers are also an exception to the rule, in the sense that the RQ1 message only works with the data in the edit buffer. In order to do a complete memory dump (that is, 64 patches), you'd have to manipulate the instrument's keys directly.

A DT1 message can be up to 256 bytes long. This length limit keeps DT1 messages from slowing down or otherwise interfering with the circulation of non-priority MIDI messages (that is, MIDI messages other than Real Time messages) in MIDI Merge or Soft Thru configurations. If a dump is bigger than 256 bytes, several DT1 messages will follow one another at a minimum interval of 20 milliseconds (ms). Error-detection works very simply in one-way mode, thanks to the inclusion of a checksum byte at the end of the DT1 message. As a result, it's not possible to do any error-correction. All the receiver can do is interrupt the transaction and display an error message.

Example of a Dialogue-Type Transfer

This type of transfer includes the use of a Dump Request message.

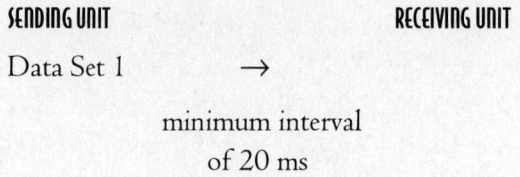

SENDING UNIT		RECEIVING UNIT
	←	Request Data 1
Data Set 1	→	
	minimum interval of 20 ms	
Data Set 1	→	
…	…	…

Example of a Manual-Type Transfer

SENDING UNIT		RECEIVING UNIT
Data Set 1	→	
	minimum interval of 20 ms	

SENDING UNIT		RECEIVING UNIT
Data Set 1	→	
...	...	...

Handshake Mode

Handshake mode consists of seven messages, described below:

RQD (Request Data)

This message is equivalent to the RQ1 message in one-way mode.

DAT (Data Set)

This message is equivalent to the DT1 message in one-way mode.

WSD (Want to Send Data)

The sender uses this message to notify the receiver that the sender wants to open a dialog with the receiver in order to send a dump. The size and starting address of the dump are included in the notification message. Then the sender waits to receive either an ACK (Acknowledge) message, which lets the sender send the first DAT, or an RJC (Rejection) message, which orders the sender to suspend the transaction.

ACK (Acknowledge)

The receiver uses this message to notify the sender that a WSD, DAT, or EOD message has been received properly. After any of these three messages has been sent, the sender waits to receive an ACK before continuing with the transaction. In this sense the ACK message serves as a receipt, confirming that the incoming message has arrived properly.

EOD (End of Data)

The sender uses this message to inform the receiver that the last data packet has just been sent (in other words, that no more data packets remain to be sent). Then the sender waits to receive an ACK before closing the dialog.

ERR (Communication Error)

The receiver uses this message to inform the sender that a reception error has occurred (as detected for instance by a checksum). The sender has the option of either abandoning the transaction or re-sending the erroneous message. (The latter case shows why handshaking is such a useful and worthwhile procedure.)

RJC (Rejection)

A Rejection message is sent to the sender by the receiver under any of several circumstances, such as when a WSD message or an RQD message contains an illegal address or size, when the device isn't ready to communicate, when the user manually interrupts the transmission (for instance, by pressing the Cancel key), or when any other transaction error occurs.

Example of a Transfer Requested by the Receiver

SENDING UNIT		RECEIVING UNIT
	←	Request Data
Data Set	→	
	←	Acknowledge
Data Set	→	
	←	Acknowledge
…	…	…
End of Data	→	
	←	Acknowledge

Example of a Transfer Initiated by the Sender

SENDING UNIT		RECEIVING UNIT
Want to Send Data	→	
	←	Acknowledge
Data Set	→	
	←	Acknowledge
Data Set	→	
	←	Acknowledge
…	…	…
End Of Data	→	
	←	Acknowledge

Example of a Transfer Initiated by the Sender, with Error Correction

SENDING UNIT		RECEIVING UNIT
Want to Send Data	→	
	←	Acknowledge
Data Set	→	
	←	Acknowledge
Data Set	→	(checksum error)
	←	Communication Error
Data Set (the same)	→	
	←	Acknowledge
…	…	…

SENDING UNIT		RECEIVING UNIT
End Of Data	→	
	←	Acknowledge

Example of a Transfer Initiated by the Sender, with Error Detection and Abandonment of the Transfer

SENDING UNIT		RECEIVING UNIT
Want to Send Data	→	
	←	Acknowledge
Data Set	→	
	←	Acknowledge
Data Set	→	(checksum error)
	←	Communication Error
Data Set (the same)	→	(checksum error)
(Quit)	←	Rejection

—Or else:

SENDING UNIT		RECEIVING UNIT
Want to Send Data	→	
	←	Acknowledge
Data Set	→	
	←	Acknowledge
Data Set	→	(checksum error)
(Quit)	←	Rejection

In conclusion, here's a summary of the features and characteristics of the Roland communications protocol. Except for the ACK, EOD, ERR, and RJC messages, which strictly speaking don't include data bytes, all of the other messages (RQ1, DT1, RQ2, DT2) use a checksum. Remember, the checksum determines whether an ACK message or an ERR message will be sent—an ACK message when no errors have been detected, and an ERR message when an error has been detected. The RQ1, RQD, and WSD messages specify the starting address and the memory size of the data to be transferred. The DT1 and DAT messages contain the starting address followed by the data itself. (The size of the chunk of data can vary, as long as it doesn't exceed 256 bytes.) Finally, two other procedures make it possible to launch a data transfer:

- Initiation by the user, by manually pressing the Dump Send keys on the sending device. (In handshake mode, this operation causes a WSD message to be sent; in one-way mode, it causes a given number of DT1 messages to be sent.)

- Request by the receiver (which can be the Dump program, the editing program, another instrument of the same type, etc.). In this case, a Dump Request message (RQ1 in one-way mode or RQD in handshake mode) is sent.

The usefulness of handshake mode lies in its ability to re-send (and therefore to correct) the erroneous data once an error has been detected.

The Format of Roland Messages

Now here's a detailed look at the hex formats of these nine Exclusive messages, as mentioned in the preceding section. Of course, each of these messages starts with F0H, followed by the manufacturer's ID (which for Roland is 41H), the device ID (i.e., the channel or device number), the model ID (i.e., the type or family the device belongs to), the command (i.e., one of the nine dialog phrases), and, finally, the body of the message (whose length and contents can vary depending on the type of command). The entire collection ends with the EOX (End of Exclusive) status byte.

Request Data 1 (RQ1/11H)

```
F0H: Exclusive message status byte
41H: identification (Roland)
DEV: MIDI channel or unit number
MDL: model or family of models
11H: RQ1 code
a1H: address 1 (most significant byte)
a2H: address 2 (averagely significant byte)
a3H: address 3 (least significant byte)
t1H: size 1 (most significant byte)
t2H: size 2 (averagely significant byte)
t3H: size 3 (least significant byte)
CSH: checksum including the data between a1H and t3H
F7H: EOX
```

Data Set 1 (DT1/12H)

```
F0H: Exclusive message status byte
41H: identification (Roland)
DEV: MIDI channel or unit number
MDL: model or family of models
12H: DT1 code
a1H: address 1 (most significant byte)
a2H: address 2 (averagely significant byte)
a3H: address 3 (least significant byte)
ddH: body of data (for a maximum of 256 bytes)
...
CSH: checksum including the data between a1H and ddH
F7H: EOX
```

Want to Send Data (WSD/40H)

```
F0H: Exclusive message status byte
41H: identification (Roland)
DEV: MIDI channel or unit number
```

```
MDL: model or family of models
40H: WSD code
a1H: address 1 (most significant byte)
a2H: address 2 (averagely significant byte)
a3H: address 3 (least significant byte)
t1H: size 1 (most significant byte)
t2H: size 2 (averagely significant byte)
t3H: size 3 (least significant byte)
CSH: checksum including the data between a1H and t3H
F7H: EOX
```

Request Data (RQD/41H)

```
F0H: Exclusive message status byte
41H: identification (Roland)
DEV: MIDI channel or unit number
MDL: model or family of models
41H: RQD code
a1H: address 1 (most significant byte)
a2H: address 2 (averagely significant byte)
a3H: address 3 (least significant byte)
t1H: size 1 (most significant byte)
t2H: size 2 (averagely significant byte)
t3H: size 3 (least significant byte)
CSH: checksum including the data between a1H and t3H
F7H: EOX
```

Data Set (DAT/42H)

```
F0H: Exclusive message status byte
41H: identification (Roland)
DEV: MIDI channel or unit number
MDL: model or family of models
42H: code DAT
a1H: address 1 (most significant byte)
a2H: address 2 (averagely significant byte)
a3H: address 3 (least significant byte)
ddH: body of data (for a maximum of 256 bytes)
...
CSH: checksum including the data between a1H and ddH
F7H: EOX
```

Acknowledge (ACK/43H)

```
F0H: Exclusive message status byte
41H: identification (Roland)
DEV: MIDI channel or unit number
MDL: model or family of models
43H: ACK code
F7H: EOX
```

End Of Data (EOD/45H)

```
F0H: Exclusive message status byte
41H: identification (Roland)
DEV: MIDI channel or unit number
MDL: model or family of models
45H: EOD code
F7H: EOX
```

Communication Error (ERR/4EH)

```
F0H: Exclusive message status byte
41H: identification (Roland)
DEV: MIDI channel or unit number
MDL: model or family of models
4EH: ERR code
F7H: EOX
```

Rejection (RJC/4FH)

```
F0H: Exclusive message status byte
41H: identification (Roland)
DEV: MIDI channel or unit number
MDL: model or family of models
4FH: RJC code
F7H: EOX
```

The handshaking principle, which is currently being used in data processing by a number of interfaces, will probably be extended gradually to apply to MIDI exchanges that involve major amounts of data. The implementation of the principle in the Sample Dump Standard (which generally carries several kilobytes of data) is living proof of this trend.

CHAPTER

11

XIII XIV XV XVI A B C D E F G H I

Working with MIDI Devices:

Managing SysEx Messages

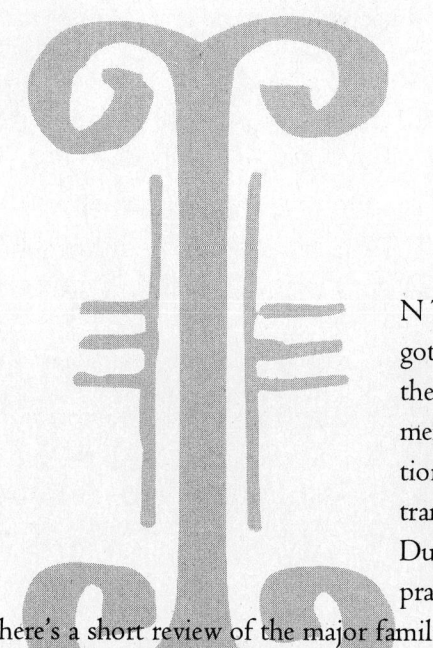

N THE PRECEDING chapters you got acquainted with the structure and the memory contents of MIDI instruments, along with the communications protocols that are used to transfer this data in the form of Dumps. Now, before getting into practical programming examples, here's a short review of the major families of software applications that use Exclusive messages. The general information in the first four sections of this chapter will familiarize you with the possibilities offered by Dump utilities, librarians, and sound editors. The section after that contains a detailed description of the MIDI Sample Dump Standard, which is the protocol that governs the exchange of samples.

The Dump Utilities

Dump programs are archival utilities that let you store part or all of the contents of the memory of MIDI instruments on media such as floppy disks or hard disks before sending the memory contents somewhere else later on. Dump programs give you a sizable data base for sounds, etc. at a very low cost.

In practice, all Dump software includes at least one receive function and one send function:

- The *receive function* issues a request in the form of a Dump Request message that tells the MIDI instrument to send the program the contents of all or part of its memory in the form of a Dump message, so that those contents can be stored on disk. If the instrument doesn't accept a Dump Request message (as is the case with the 64-sound RAM of the Roland D-50 and D-550), you have to start the data transfer manually from the front panel of the instrument.

- The *send function* reads the information to disk and resends it to the instrument in the form of a Dump message. Before this operation can be carried out, it's sometimes necessary to de-protect the instrument's memory or to enable the reception of Exclusive messages, etc.

A dialog between the computer and the instrument can begin only if the two devices are connected in handshake mode, with the MIDI Out port of the computer connected to the MIDI In port of the instrument, so that Dump Request messages (if implemented) can be sent, and vice versa so that Dumps can be received. A typical arrangement is shown in Figure 11.1 below.

The MIDI instruments this chapter deals with have two kinds of Dump programs: non-programmable universal Dump utilities and programmable universal Dump utilities.

Non-programmable universal programs, such as the one shown in Figure 11.2 below, can take part in dialogues with a wide variety of instruments whose language (that is, the Request to Send Dump messages) the

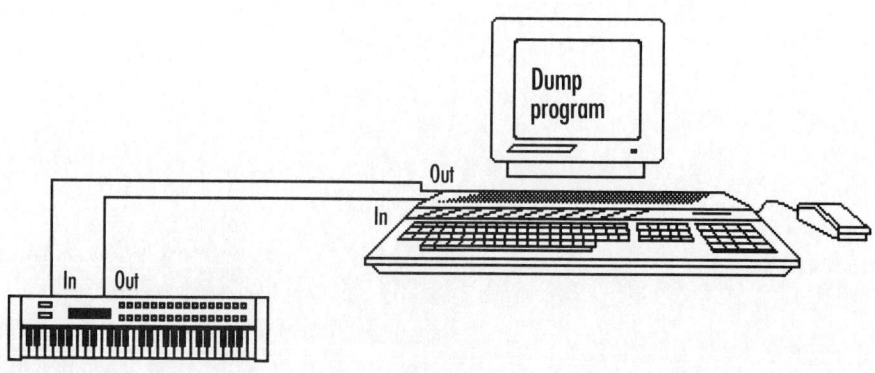

FIGURE 11.1: *The connection between a MIDI instrument and a dump program running on a microcomputer.*

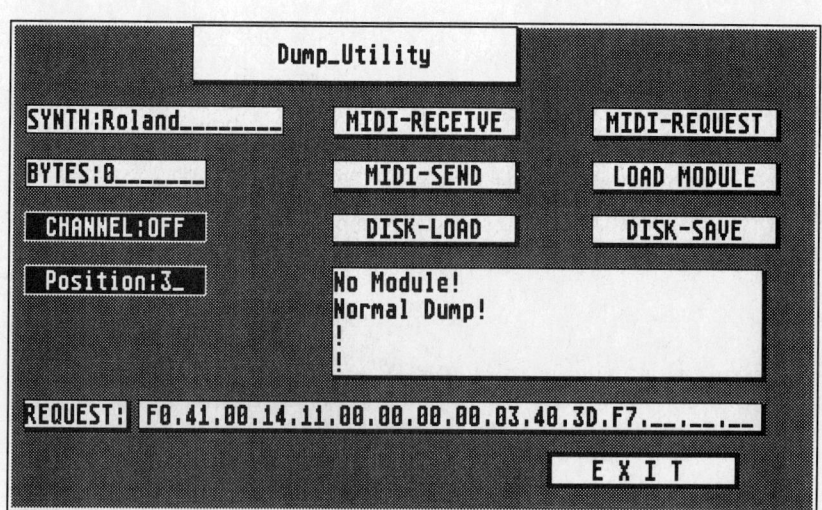

FIGURE 11.2: *The Dump Utility option of the Pro 24 sequencer embodies the functions of a non-programmable universal dump program.*

programs are already familiar with. Continual updates make these programs compatible with new instruments (depending to some extent on how widely the instruments are marketed).

However, none of these programs is 100 percent inclusive. That's why there's a third kind of program—the programmable universal programs—that lets you write your own Exclusive messages, in accordance with the instruments that need to be managed. The Satellite accessory shown in Figure 11.3 below is typical of these programs. Although this class of programs is by far the most efficient and effective of the three, it requires advanced knowledge of how SysEx (System Exclusive) messages are programmed.

Finally, some hardware units, such as the Alesis Datadisk, are dedicated to Dump storage. These devices, which are equipped with a disk reader, can store SysEx messages sent from any MIDI unit.

```
                   UNIVERSAL DUMP UTILITY

                         ┌─ MODE: ─┐
                        WAIT FOR DUMP
    RECEIVE             SEND REQUEST              TRANSMIT

   ┌─┐   nr 12      Request: TX802 PERF      Channel Pos.: 3
   │↑│  ┌────────────────────────────────────────────────┐
   │↓│  │ F0,43,20,7E,4C,4D,20,20,38,39,35,32,50,4D,F7│
        └────────────────────────────────────────────────┘
              SAVE SETTINGS              EXIT
```

FIGURE 11.3: *The Satellite accessory is a programmable universal dump program that allows the writing of up to 32 Dump Request messages. This figure shows the Satellite accessory for the 64-performance Yamaha TX802.*

Dumps and the MIDI Channel

Very roughly speaking, the Dump and Dump Request messages have the following structure:

- The Dump Request Message

    ```
    F0H <dump request> F7H
    ```

- The Dump Message

    ```
    F0H <dump header> <memory data> <optional checksum> F7H
    ```

The Dump Request and the header for the Dump messages automatically contain a channel number (or, in some rare instances, a unit number, as is the case with certain Roland instruments). What this means is that, on the one hand, the Dump Request should be transmitted over the same channel being used by the instrument in question, and, on the other hand, that the instrument should not recognize or receive a Dump unless the Dump channel is the same as the channel indicated in the header.

At the operational level, when the instrument responds to a Dump Request message by sending data to the Dump utility, there are three options:

1 - Storing the entire contents of the dump on disk:

    ```
    F0H <dump header> <memory data> <checksum> F7H
    ```

2 - Storing only part of the contents of the dump:

    ```
    <dump header> <memory data> <checksum>
    ```

3 - Storing only the strictly necessary data:

    ```
    <memory data>
    ```

In cases 2 and 3, the program should be able to add the missing bytes when the Dump is sent back to the instrument. If the header is stored, then by implication the channel number is stored, too. Unless the utility allows changes in the dump before transmission, the dump will be transmitted with its original channel number, which won't necessarily still correspond to the channel number of the instrument. In such a case, when a utility doesn't let you change the number of the sending channel for a Dump message, it's wise to make a note of the number—for example, by making it part of the file name.

Librarians

Librarians are special-purpose Dump programs. In addition to authorizing the transfer of sound banks between a MIDI instrument and a computer, they can also organize the contents of the sound banks.

Librarians are connected to instruments in essentially the same way as dump programs. Figure 11.4 below shows a typical connection between

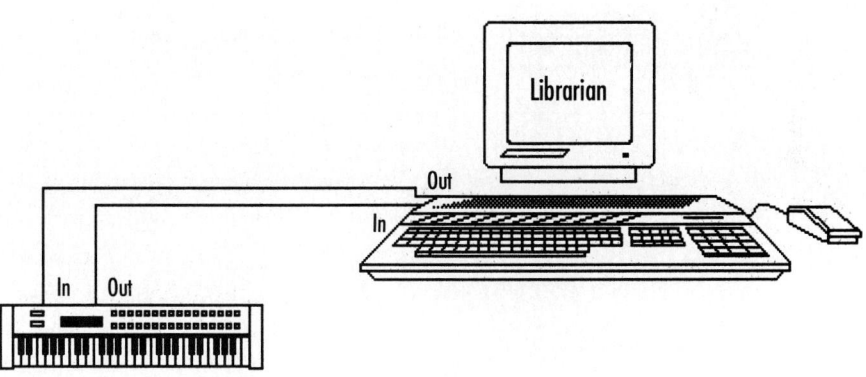

FIGURE 11.4: *The handshake connection between a keyboard instrument and a librarian: from the MIDI Out port of the instrument to the MIDI In port of the microcomputer, and vice versa.*

an instrument and a librarian, and Figure 11.5 below shows a typical connection between an expander and a librarian.

In the connection between an expander and a librarian, the handshake link is dedicated to the transfer of Dump messages and Dump Request messages, and the second link lets you hear the sounds that are transferred. In order for the sounds to be audible, the MIDI Merge box mixes the output of the microcomputer with the output of the keyboard and then sends the combined output to the MIDI In port of the expander.

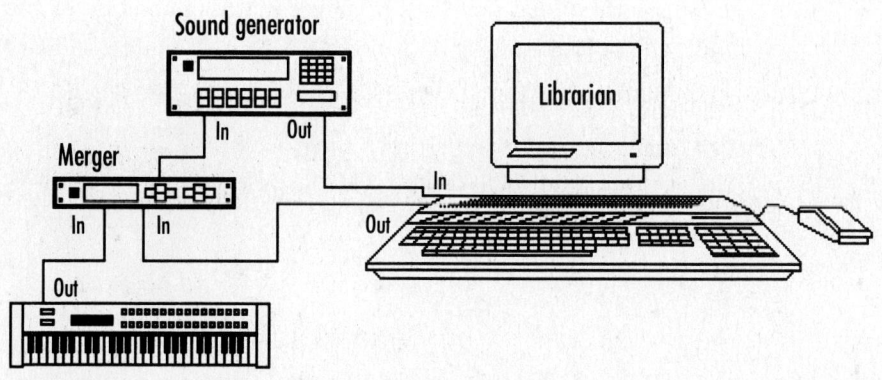

FIGURE 11.5: *The connection between an expander and a librarian requires first a handshake link (dedicated to the transfer of Dump messages and Dump Request messages) between the two units, and then a link (dedicated to letting users hear the sounds that are transferred) between the MIDI Out port of a keyboard and the MIDI In port of the expander.*

Librarians come in three flavors: those that are dedicated to particular instruments, non-programmable universal librarians, and programmable universal librarians. Examples of these types of librarians are shown in Figures 11.6, 11.7, and 11.8 below.

```
┌─────────────────────────────────────────────────────────────────────┐
│ 1) Bank 1      2) Bank 2            Your command?                      │
│ 3) Receive     4) Transmit      5) Copy    6) Load    7) Save   8) Quit│
│ 11:  Acoustic Glass Pik   36:  Female Breath      63:  Nice Synth -4 vel│
│ 12:  Afterthought 2       37:  Flute Atmosphere   64:  Overtn Divergence│
│ 13:  Afterthought 3       38:  Flutish Brass Ster 65:  Pick -n- Brass 2 │
│ 14:  Afterthought Ensmb   41:  Gals Pik           66:  Pipe Swap u1---12 │
│ 15:  Arco Fantasy         42:  Gated Elec Bass 1  67:  RingPiano Guitar 2│
│ 16:  Autopan Horns        43:  Glass Horns        68:  Simple PCM        │
│ 17:  Blue Vibes           44:  Guitar b-w Sweep   71:  Space Flute       │
│ 18:  Bubbleized 1         45:  Gals Pik           72:  Space Piano       │
│ 21:  Bubblsynth aftrtch   46:  Gated Elec Bass 1  73:  Spacious Pik      │
│ 22:  Chiff-Voices         47:  Glass Horns        74:  Spacious Voice    │
│ 23:  Digi-Choir Pik       48:  Guitar b-w Sweep   75:  Syn Harp Piano    │
│ 24:  Digital Sweeper      51:  Nice Breathy Sound 76:  Syn Horns Combo 1 │
│ 25:  E- Bass 1 Flanged    52:  Nice Breathy -2    77:  SynHorn Piano     │
│ 26:  E-Guitar Vibes       53:  Nice Female        78:  SynHorn Pi U1-L2  │
│ 27:  Elec Bass2 w-Wah     54:  Nice Synth -1      81:  Vibe Voice 2      │
│ 28:  Elec Bass 1 and 2    55:  Nice Breathy Sound 82:  Violin  Loop Organ│
│ 31:  Elec-Ensemble 1      56:  Nice Breathy -2    83:  Wah Horns Attack 1 │
│ 32:  Ensemble2-Voices     57:  Nice Female        84:  Wah Trumpets      │
│ 33:  Fantasy Lips         58:  Nice Synth -1      85:  Wah Trumpt w-violn │
│ 34:  Fantasy-Voices       61:  Nice Synth -2      86:  Wah Trumpt w-guitr │
│ 35:  Fantasy-Voices Dbl   62:  Nice Synth -3      87:  Wire String Pik   │
│                                                   88:  X Polinated Horn 2 │
└─────────────────────────────────────────────────────────────────────┘
```

FIGURE 11.6: *The Bankloader program: a librarian for the Roland D-50 and D-550*

After receiving a sound bank from an instrument, or after having loaded a sound bank from disk, the librarian displays onscreen as many locations as there are sounds in the bank (for instance, 32 locations for the 32 voices of a Yamaha DX7, 100 locations for the 100 programs of a Korg M1, 64 locations for the 64 patches of a Roland D-50, etc.). Most of the time, the act of selecting one of these locations has the effect of automatically transferring the contents of the location to the Edit buffer of the MIDI instrument. Sometimes this kind of program lets you send Note messages to the instrument (with the help of the mouse, a virtual keyboard, a mini-sequencer, etc.), so that you can hear the sound being transferred without having to leave the computer.

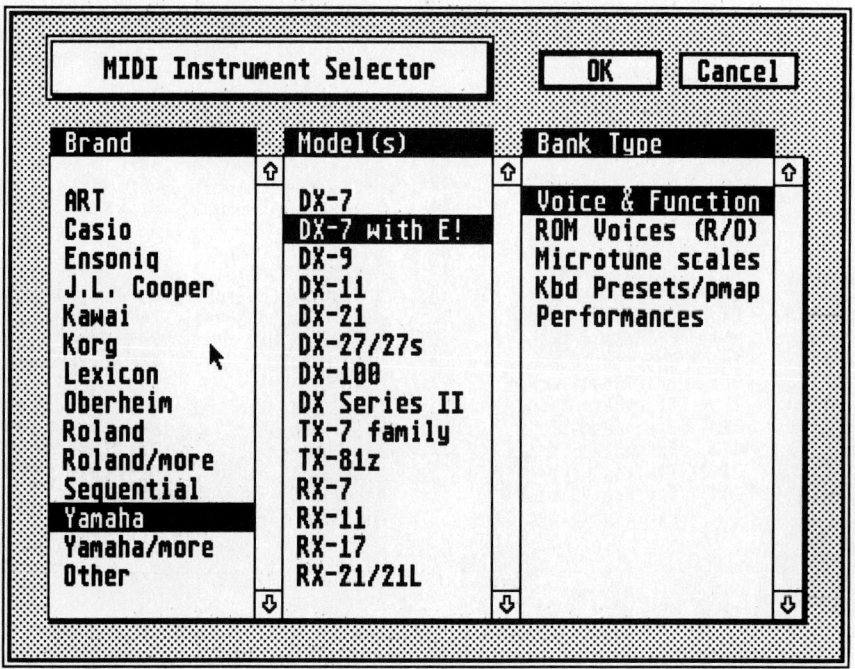

FIGURE 11.7: *The Omnibanker program: a non-programmable universal librarian*

Librarians offer various different ways to organize and arrange information, such as:

- Copying the contents of a location to another space

- Copying the contents of a block consisting of several locations (either contiguous or separated from one another) to another block of locations (either contiguous or non-contiguous)

- Inserting an empty location

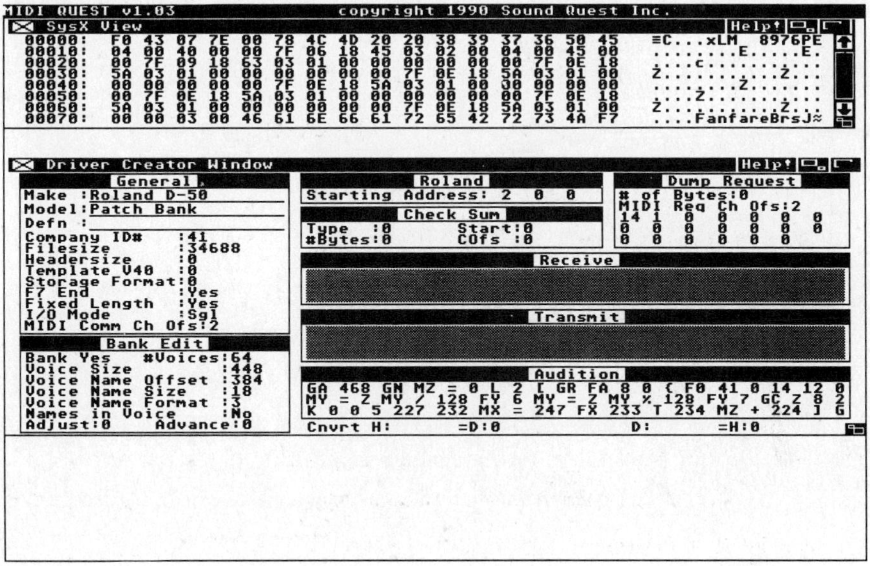

FIGURE 11.8: *The SoundQuest MIDI Quest program: a programmable universal librarian*

- Copying the contents of a location, with an insertion, to the destination location

- Exchanging the contents of two locations (i.e., swapping their contents)

- Exchanging the contents of two blocks of locations (either contiguous or separated from one another)

- Erasing the contents of a location

- Erasing the contents of a location, with a shift (with each of the following locations being moved toward the next lower location, and so on until the end of the bank, with the last location being either identical to the preceding location or initialized)

- Erasing the contents of a block of locations (either contiguous or separated from one another)

- Erasing the contents of a block of locations, with shifting

- Alphabetical sorting of all of the locations in a bank

- Rotating the location in a block (in one direction or the other)

- Detecting duplicated locations (the entire bank is scanned and the duplicates are erased)

- Detecting duplicated locations with parameter masking. (Some of the parameters of the sound, such as the name of the sound, are not taken into consideration during detection. In this case, masking the name of the sound makes it possible to detect two sounds that are identical but have different names.)

For the sake of efficiency, most librarians let you load several of the same kind of banks into memory. Some of the operations listed above will apply to one bank or another. In any event, this type of program makes it much easier to organize and store MIDI instrument data banks.

The Library Concept

The bank is limited to reflecting strictly the memory contents of the instrument. It's quite otherwise with the library (also known as the data base). Theoretically, the size of the library is limited only by the amount of memory in the computer, or by the capacity of mass memory. (In the latter case, a library can be loaded as needed, and not necessarily in its entirety.) For instance, with the Yamaha DX7, although a simple librarian can load only a limited number of 32-sound banks (with each bank consisting of 4,096 bytes, or 128 bytes per sound), a librarian that includes a

library can contain many more banks (with up to approximately 7,000 sounds per megabyte of RAM).

Unlike the banks of a librarian, which are an exact reflection of the memory contents of the instrument (e.g., 32 voices for the Yamaha DX7, 100 programs for the Korg M1, etc.), the size of a library is much larger. That's why transfers between this library and the instrument use banks instead of being done directly. (Transfers of individual sounds, which use the Edit buffer, are an exception to this rule.) For instance, if you wanted to fill the memory of a Yamaha DX7 with the best 32 sounds in a library, you'd first have to copy the sounds from the library into a bank in the librarian and then send the bank to the DX7.

The library concept is generally accompanied by features and functions that are similar to those of a conventional data base. You can use these features to create links between several elements, in order to find them again more easily. The semantic search criteria used by the Steinberg company's Synthworks programs are a perfect illustration of this principle. Each sound can be associated with a certain number of adjectives that you can program. These adjectives are in the form of the names of families of instruments (bass, piano, strings, special effects, etc.), various qualifiers ("brilliant," "soft," "aggressive," etc.), and so on. In order to recover all of the "aggressive bass" sounds at some later time, all you have to do is select these two criteria in conjunction with one another. Because they're so complex and hard to implement, libraries are generally reserved for editing programs dedicated to a particular instrument.

Editors

Editors, also known as *editors/librarians*, are librarians that, in addition to allowing the archiving and classification of banks, let you extract a sound so that it can be edited and then put back into the bank. Like librarians, there are three flavors of editors: those that are dedicated to specific instruments, non-programmable universal editors, and programmable universal editors. Examples of these types of editors are shown in Figures 11.9, 11.10, and 11.11 below.

As you saw earlier, synthesizers and expanders let you edit the different parameters of a sound one by one on their LCD screens. Editors let you do the same thing, but with all of the power of the graphic user interface (GUI) of the computer with which they're associated. When the parameters (the envelope, the filter, the amplitude, etc.) are appropriate, the editor can show them in the form of objects (e.g., graphic envelopes, curves, rotating and linear potentiometers, etc.) that can be manipulated with a

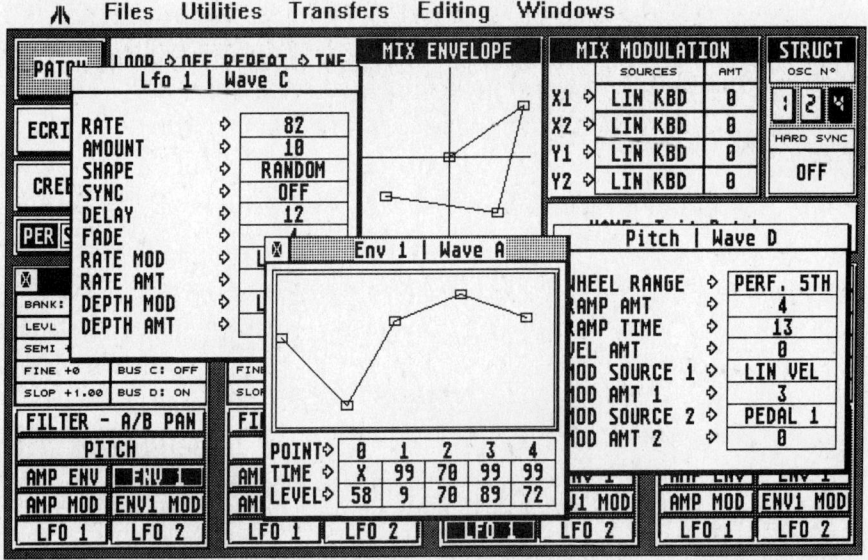

FIGURE 11.9: *The ACS editor for the Korg WS*

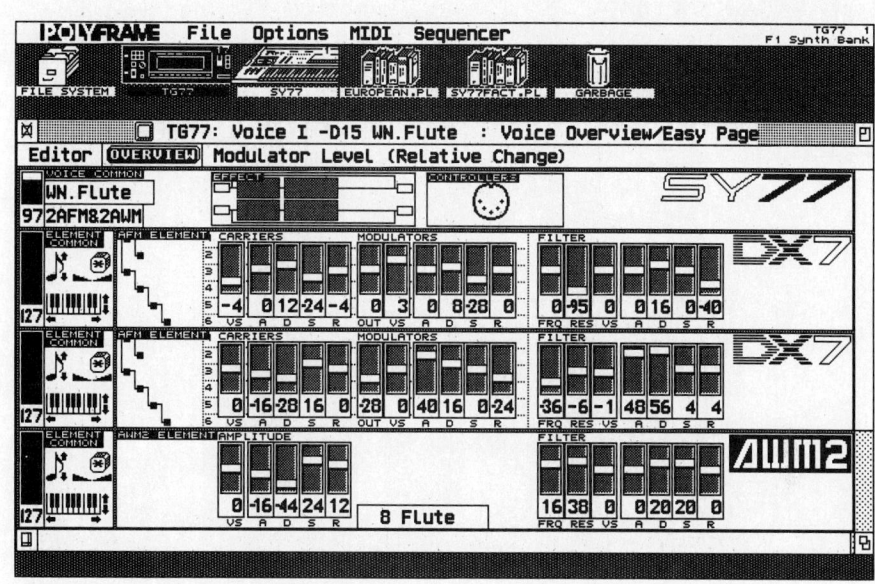

FIGURE 11.10: *The SoundQuest MIDI Quest program: a non-programmable universal editor*

mouse. Furthermore, the fact that all of the parameters are displayed on
one or more screen pages gives you a good overview of what's going on.

This family of programs is virtually indispensable for anyone who wants
to program an instrument to the full extent of its capabilities. In addition
to offering ease of use through graphics, editors provide a number of supplementary functions, such as random creation, as illustrated in Figure 11.12. Some programs let you define a *mask* (that is, select the
parameters of a sound that will be affected by the random creation).
Other programs mix several sounds from a single bank in order to create
a new sound, and so on.

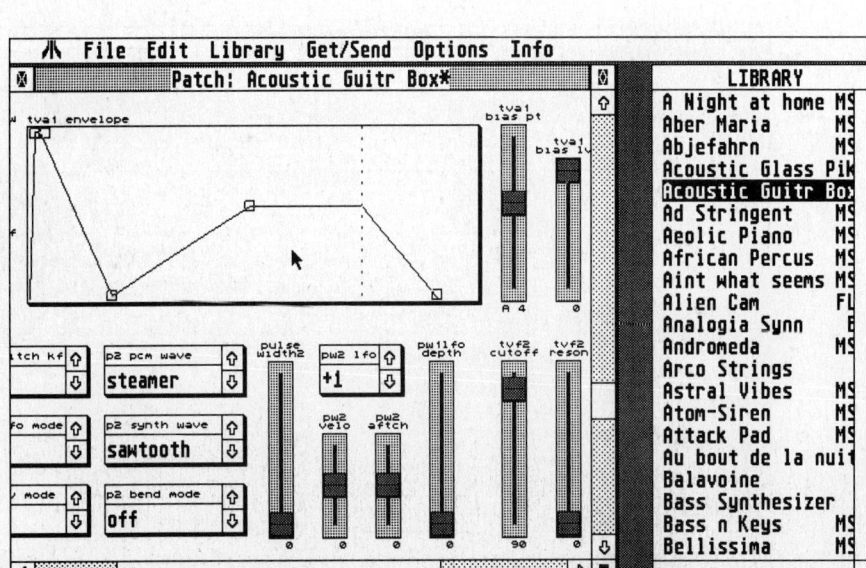

FIGURE 11.11: *The Dr. T's X-oR program: a programmable universal editor*

On the MIDI level, when an instrument implements Exclusive messages for individual parameters, these parameters are sent to the Edit buffer by the software as soon as a parameter is modified onscreen. On the other hand, if the instrument doesn't implement Exclusive messages for individual parameters, the entire contents of the Edit buffer are transferred after each editing operation, with the result that an unnecessary burden is placed on the MIDI network.

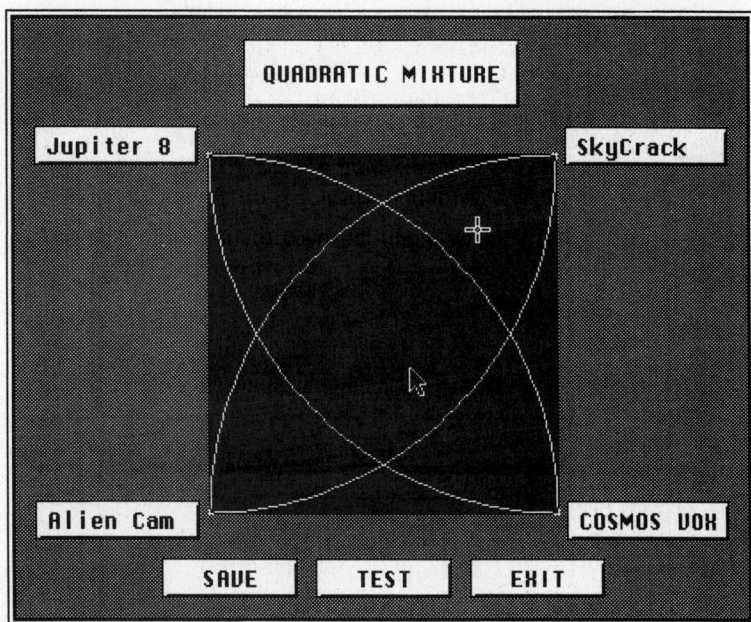

FIGURE 11.12: *Random creation. The position of the mouse determines the proportions in which the four sounds will be mixed in order to generate a new sound.*

Universal Programs

Universal programs, whether they're Dump utilities, librarians, or editors, are in a sense molds or matrices. They contain the code that's necessary for their overall operation (i.e., managing the user interface and disk access operations, etc.), up to but not including the routines that handle the

Exclusive MIDI messages that are specific to each instrument. These routines are programmed by the user.

Consider for example a so-called "minimum" Dump utility: that is, one that can fetch the memory contents of a MIDI instrument and store them on disk, and vice-versa. The only things that will be different from one instrument to another are the Dump Request message and the reception and sending of the dump itself. The procedures for storing and loading the data to disk and the procedures for managing the user interface (i.e., the set of commands that make it possible to manipulate the software: scrolling menus, dialog boxes, etc.) stay the same. In short, the purpose of a universal Dump utility is to provide the entire software infrastructure that's common to the set of instruments, while giving you the means for writing the few lines of program code (known as the "configuration") that are specific to each of these instruments. The same principle applies to librarians and editors.

The concept of universality has two main advantages. First, a universal program lets you deal with an entire MIDI environment; and, second, a universal program is theoretically protected from obsolescence, because it can be updated as new instruments appear on the market. In order to save users the task of having to program the configurations, the companies that develop universal programs also provide a number of configurations for the most widely used MIDI devices.

Sampling Editors

You've already taken a look at the structure and contents of the memory of a sound generator and seen how the contents of memory are transferred via MIDI. You've also reviewed some of the applications derived from these operations. Now it's time to consider the specific case represented by the sampling editors.

The Two Types of Memory in a Sampler

Schematically speaking, a sampler is just a sound generator whose oscillators produce waveforms that you can record on your own, or load from and/or store in mass memory (floppy disks, hard disks, magneto-optical disks, etc.). These waveforms are known as "samples." In terms of memory structure, there are two very different kinds of data: first, the data corresponding to the parameters of the samples (e.g., the filter, the envelopes, the LFO, the geographic assignment to the keyboard, the MIDI channels, etc.), and then the data corresponding to the samples themselves. In addition to being storable in mass memory that's a part of the sampler, the contents of these two types of RAM can be transmitted via MIDI by means of Exclusive messages (e.g., Dump and Dump Request messages).

Transferring the Parameters of Samples

Information about the parameters of samples is transferred via MIDI by means of Dump and Dump Request messages that are specific to each manufacturer. However, unlike the situation with a simple synthesizer, which has a fixed number of sounds, the number of sounds that can reside within a sampler is variable, because you can create them or load them as needed. This is why, in addition to the conventional Dump and Dump Request messages, you'll run into Exclusive messages whose job is to give information about the state of the sampler's memory to the unit that's talking to the sampler. (After receiving this request, the sampler returns the number of samples present in memory and optionally indicates their names, or responds by indicating that the sample number that has been asked for doesn't exist, and so on.)

For the sake of illustration, here's a description of the Dump and Dump Request procedures that the samplers in the Akai S1000 family use to exchange the data corresponding to the sample parameters. Keep in mind that several programs can be active at the same time and that each program consists of a variable number of keygroups, with each keygroup containing from one to four samples.

- Format of the RPLIST (Request List of Resident Program Names) Message

```
F0H (11110000): Exclusive message status byte
47H (01000111): Akai ID
ccH (0ccccccc): Exclusive channel (0 to 127)
02H (00000010): RPLIST
48H (01001000): S1000 family ID
F7H (11110111): EOX
```

This request is transmitted to the S1000, which, as soon as it receives it, returns the list of programs residing in memory. This list is sent in the following form:

- Format of the PLIST (List of Resident Program Names) Message

```
F0H (11110000): Exclusive message status byte
47H (01000111): Akai ID
ccH (0ccccccc): Exclusive channel (0 to 127)
03H (00000011): PLIST
48H (01001000): S1000 family ID
ppH (0ppppppp): program number (LSB)
ppH (0ppppppp): program number (MSB)
nnH (0nnnnnnn): 12 bytes per program name
...
F7H (11110111): EOX
```

Instead of being transmitted in ASCII, the names are sent in the format shown in Table 11.1 below.

TABLE 11.1: *The Name-Transmission Format for the PLIST Message*

BYTE	CHARACTER
0 (00H)	"0"
1 (01H)	"1"
2 (02H)	"2"
3 (03H)	"3"
4 (04H)	"4"
5 (05H)	"5"
6 (06H)	"6"
7 (07H)	"7"
8 (08H)	"8"
9 (09H)	"9"
10 (0AH)	" "
11 (0BH)	"A"
12 (0CH)	"B"
13 (0DH)	"C"
14 (0EH)	"D"
15 (0FH)	"E"
16 (10H)	"F"
17 (11H)	"G"
18 (12H)	"H"
19 (13H)	"I"
20 (14H)	"J"
21 (15H)	"K"

TABLE 11.1: *The Name-Transmission Format for the PLIST Message (continued)*

BYTE	CHARACTER
22 (16H)	"L"
23 (17H)	"M"
24 (18H)	"N"
25 (19H)	"O"
26 (1AH)	"P"
27 (1BH)	"Q"
28 (1CH)	"R"
29 (1DH)	"S"
30 (1EH)	"T"
31 (1FH)	"U"
32 (20H)	"V"
33 (21H)	"W"
34 (22H)	"X"
35 (23H)	"Y"
36 (24H)	"Z"
37 (25H)	"#"
38 (26H)	"+"
39 (27H)	"-"
40 (28H)	"."

- Format of the RSLIST (Request List of Resident Sample Names)
  Message

```
F0H (11110000): Exclusive message status byte
47H (01000111): Akai ID
ccH (0ccccccc): Exclusive channel (0 to 127)
04H (00000100): RSLIST
48H (01001000): S1000 family ID
F7H (11110111): EOX
```

This request is sent to the S1000, which, as soon as it receives it, sends back the list of the samples that are resident in memory, in the following form:

- Format of the SLIST (List of Resident Sample Names) Message

```
F0H (11110000): Exclusive message status byte
47H (01000111): Akai ID
ccH (0ccccccc): Exclusive channel (0 to 127)
05H (00000101): SLIST
48H (01001000): S1000 family ID
ppH (0ppppppp): number of samples (LSB)
ppH (0ppppppp): number of samples (MSB)
nnH (0nnnnnnn): 12 bytes per sample name
...
F7H (11110111): EOX
```

- Format of the RPDATA (Request Program Common Data)
  Message

```
F0H (11110000): Exclusive message status byte
47H (01000111): Akai ID
ccH (0ccccccc): Exclusive channel (0 to 127)
06H (00000110): RPDATA
48H (01001000): S1000 family ID
ppH (0ppppppp): program number (LSB)
ppH (0ppppppp): program number (MSB)
F7H (11110111): EOX
```

This request is sent to the S1000, which, as soon as it receives it, sends back the data for the corresponding program (if one exists), in the following form:

- Format of the PDATA (Program Common Data) Message

```
F0H (11110000): Exclusive message status byte
47H (01000111): Akai ID
ccH (0ccccccc): Exclusive channel
07H (00000111): PDATA
48H (01001000): S1000 family ID
ppH (0ppppppp): program number (LSB)
ppH (0ppppppp): program number (MSB)
nnH (0nnnnnnn): X data bytes
...
F7H (11110111): EOX
```

This message is bidirectional. When it's sent to the S1000, and if the program number doesn't exist in its memory, then a new program is created (provided of course that the S1000's memory has enough unallocated space for the new program). The contents of the keygroups (see below) should then be sent to the S1000 by means of KDATA messages. When an existing program has the same name, that name is removed before the messages are sent.

When the program number matches the number of an existing program, the existing program is replaced by the contents of the PDATA message, provided that the number of keygroups (as specified in the body of the PDATA message) is the same.

- Format of the RKDATA (Request Keygroup Data) Message

```
F0H (11110000): Exclusive message status byte
47H (01000111): Akai ID
ccH (0ccccccc): Exclusive channel (0 to 127)
08H (00001000): RKDATA
48H (01001000): S1000 family ID
```

```
ppH (0ppppppp): program number (LSB)
ppH (0ppppppp): program number (MSB)
kkH (0kkkkkkk): keygroup number
F7H (11110111): EOX
```

This request is sent to the S1000, which, as soon as it receives it, sends back the data for the corresponding keygroup (if one exists), in the following form:

- Format of the KDATA (Keygroup Data) Message

```
F0H (11110000): Exclusive message status byte
47H (01000111): Akai ID
ccH (0ccccccc): Exclusive channel (0 to 127)
09H (00001001): KDATA
48H (01001000): S1000 family ID
ppH (0ppppppp): program number (LSB)
ppH (0ppppppp): program number (MSB)
kkH (0kkkkkkk): keygroup number
nnH (0nnnnnnn): X data bytes
...
F7H (11110111): EOX
```

This message is bidirectional. When it's sent to the S1000, and if the keygroup number doesn't exist in its memory, then a new keygroup is created (provided of course the S1000's memory has enough unallocated space for the new keygroup). When the program number is set to 255, the KDATA messages will address a program that was previously created by means of a PDATA message. (This trick gets around the chore of having to send an RPLIST request in order to find out the program number.)

- Format of the DELP (Delete Program and its Keygroups) Message

```
F0H (11110000): Exclusive message status byte
47H (01000111): Akai ID
ccH (0ccccccc): Exclusive channel (0 to 127)
12H (00010010): DELP
48H (01001000): S1000 family ID
```

```
ppH (Opppppppp): program number (LSB)
ppH (Opppppppp): program number (MSB)
F7H (11110111): EOX
```

As soon as it receives this message the S1000 erases the corresponding program from its memory, along with the keygroups associated with the program.

- Format of the DELK (Delete Keygroup) Message

```
F0H (11110000): Exclusive message status byte
47H (01000111): Akai ID
ccH (0ccccccc): Exclusive channel (0 to 127)
13H (00010011): DELK
48H (01001000): S1000 family ID
ppH (0ppppppp): program number (LSB)
ppH (0ppppppp): program number (MSB)
kkH (0kkkkkkk): keygroup number
F7H (11110111): EOX
```

As soon as it receives this message the S1000 erases from its memory the keygroup of the corresponding program. (The number of this keygroup is the one specified in the kkH byte.)

- Format of the REPLY (Reply) Message

```
F0H (11110000): Exclusive message status byte
47H (01000111): Akai ID
ccH (0ccccccc): Exclusive channel (0 to 127)
16H (00010110): REPLY
48H (01001000): S1000 family ID
rrH (0rrrrrrr): response (0 = OK, 1 = error)
F7H (11110111): EOX
```

Assume that an error message is sent by the S1000 when the S1000 receives a program request or a keygroup request that addresses a non-existent memory address (i.e., a non-existent number). For example, an "OK" message is sent by the S1000 after a program or a keygroup has been successfully written.

The PDATA and KDATA messages send the data in the form of half-bytes (nybbles) in the following way:

The S1000 memory byte (symbolized by bits d0 to d7):

d7 d6 d5 d4 d3 d2 d1 d0

MIDI transmission:

0 0 0 0 d3 d2 d1 d0

followed by:

0 0 0 0 d7 d6 d5 d4

The format of these two data groups as they appear in the S1000's memory (that is, before the bytes have been broken down into nybbles for transmission) is shown in Table 11.2 and Table 11.3 below:

- PDATA

TABLE 11.2: *Data-Group Formats for PDATA Messages in Akai S1000 Samplers*

NUMBER OF BYTES	NAME	MEANING
1	PRIDENT	1 = program header block identifier
2	KGPR1	First keygroup block address (internal use)
12	PRNAME	Name
1	PRGNUM	MIDI program number (0 to 127)
1	PMCHAN	MIDI channel (0 to 15, FFH = omni)
1	POLYPH	Polyphony (1 to 16)
1	PRIORT	Priority (0 = low, 1 = normal, 2 = high, 3 = hold)
1	PLAYLO	Play range low (24 to 127 = C0 to G8)
1	PLAYHI	Play range high (24 to 127 = C0 to G8)

TABLE 11.2: *Data-Group Formats for PDATA Messages in Akai S1000 Samplers (continued)*

NUMBER OF BYTES	NAME	MEANING
1	OSHIFT	Play octave (keyboards) shift $(+/-2)$
1	OUTPUT	Output number (0 to 7, FFH = off)
1	STEREO	Left and right level (0 to 99)
1	PANPOS	Left/right balance $(+/-50)$
1	PRLOUD	Basic loudness (0 to 99)
1	V_LOUD	Velocity loudness $(+/-50)$
1	K_LOUD	Key loudness $(+/-50)$
1	P_LOUD	Pressure loudness $(+/-50)$
1	PANRAT	Pan LFO rate (0 to 99)
1	PANDEP	Pan depth (0 to 99)
1	RANDOM	Pan LFO delay (0 to 99)
1	K_PANP	Key pan position $(+/-50)$
1	LFORAT	LFO speed (0 to 99)
1	LFODEP	LFO fixed depth (0 to 99)
1	LFODEL	LFO delay (0 to 99)
1	MWLDEP	Modwheel LFO depth (0 to 99)
1	PRSDEP	Pressure LFO depth (0 to 99)
1	VELDEP	Velocity LFO depth (0 to 99)
1	B_PTCH	Bendwheel pitch (0 to 12 semitones)
1	P_PTCH	Pressure pitch (0 to 12 semitones)
1	KXFADE	Keygroup crossfade (0 = off, 1 = on)
1	GROUPS	Number of keygroups (0 to 99)

TABLE 11.2: *Data-Group Formats for PDATA Messages in Akai S1000 Samplers (continued)*

NUMBER OF BYTES	NAME	MEANING
1	TPNUM	Temporary program number (internal use)
12	TEMPER	Key tempering (+/−25 cents): C, C#, D, D#, E, F, F#, G, G#, A, A#, B
1	ECHOUT	Echo out level (0 = off, 1 = on)
1	MW_PAN	Modwheel pan amount (+/−50)
1	COHERE	Sample start coherence (0 = off, 1 = on)
1	DESYNC	LFO de-sync (0 = off, 1 = on)
1	PALW	Pitch law (0 = linear)

- KDATA

TABLE 11.3: *Data-Group Formats for KDATA Messages in Akai S1000 Samplers*

NUMBER OF BYTES	NAME	MEANING
	KEYGROUP COMMON	
1	KGIDENT	1 = program header block identifier
2	NXTKG	Next keygroup block address (internal use)
1	LONOTE	Key range low (24 to 127 = C0 to G8)
1	HINOTE	Key range high (24 to 127 = C0 to G8)
2	KGTUNO	Tune offset cent: semi (+/−50.00 fraction is binary)
1	FILFRQ	Basic filter frequency (0 to 99)

TABLE 11.3: *Data-Group Formats for KDATA Messages in Akai S1000 Samplers (continued)*

NUMBER OF BYTES	NAME	MEANING
1	K_FREQ	Key filter frequency (+/−24 semitones/octave)
1	V_FREQ	Velocity filter frequency (+/−50)
1	P_FREQ	Pressure filter frequency (+/−50)
1	F_FREQ	Envelope filter frequency (+/−50)
1	ATTAK1	Amplitude attack (0 to 99)
1	DECAY1	Amplitude decay (0 to 99)
1	SUSTN1	Amplitude sustain level (0 to 99)
1	RELSE1	Amplitude release (0 to 99)
1	V_ATT1	Velocity amplitude attack (+/−50)
1	V_REL1	Velocity amplitude release (+/−50)
1	O_REL1	Off velocity amplitude release (+/−50)
1	K_DAR1	Key decay and release (+/−50)
1	ATTAK2	Filter attack (0 to 99)
1	DECAY2	Filter decay (0 to 99)
1	SUSTN2	Filter sustain level (0 to 99)
1	RELSE2	Filter release (0 to 99)
1	V_ATT2	Velocity filter attack (+/−50)
1	V_REL2	Velocity filter release (+/−50)
1	O_REL2	Off velocity filter release (+/−50)
1	K_DAR2	Key decay and release (+/−50)
1	V_ENV2	Velocity filter envelope output (+/−50)

TABLE 11.3: *Data-Group Formats for KDATA Messages in Akai S1000 Samplers (continued)*

NUMBER OF BYTES	NAME	MEANING
1	E_PTCH	Envelope pitch (+/−50)
1	VXFADE	Velocity zone crossfade (0 = off, 1 = on)
1	VZONES	Number of velocity zones in use (not used)
1	LKXF	Calculated left key crossfade factor (internal)
1	RKXF	Calculated right key crossfade factor (internal)
	VELOCITY ZONE 1	
12	SNAME	Sample name
1	LOVEL	Velocity range low (0 to 127)
1	HIVEL	Velocity range high (0 to 127)
2	VTUNO	Tune offset (+/−50.00 fraction is in binary form)
1	VLOUD	Loudness offset (+/−50)
1	VFREQ	Filter frequency offset (+/−50)
1	VPANO	Pan offset (+/−50)
1	LIREL	Loop in release (0 = as sample, 1 = off, 2 = on)
1	LVFX	Low velocity crossfade factor (internal use)
1	HVFX	High velocity crossfade factor (internal use)
2	SBADD	Calculated factor header block address (internal)

TABLE 11.3: *Data-Group Formats for PDATA Messages in Akai S1000 Samplers (continued)*

NUMBER OF BYTES	NAME	MEANING
		VELOCITY ZONE 2, 3, 4 (IDENTICAL TO ZONE 1)
		MORE KEYGROUP COMMON
1	KBEAT	Fixed-rate detune (byte)
1	AHOLD	Attack hold until loop
		MORE VELOCITY ZONE ITEMS
1	CP1	
1	CP2	
1	CP3	Constant pitch for each velocity zone
1	CP4	(0 = track, 1 = cons)
1	VZOUT1	
1	VZOUT2	
1	VZOUT3	
1	VZOUT4	output number offset for each velocity zone (0 to 7)

· ·

Because its memory size is variable, the data-exchange protocols are more complex to implement with a sampler than with simple synthesizers or expanders that only need two Exclusive messages (namely, the Dump and Dump Request messages).

Transferring Samples

Data corresponding to samples is transferred via MIDI, either by means of Dump and Dump Request messages that are proprietary to each manufacturer or by means of the Sample Dump Standard (i.e., the standardized protocol for the transfer samples), which you'll meet in the next section.

With a synthesizer, data transfers involve no more than several tens of kilobytes. With sample exchanges it's completely different. For instance, at a data rate of 31,250 bits per second (that is, 3,125 bytes per second, because each byte is framed by the two additional Start and Stop bits), MIDI needs more than 28 seconds to transmit one second's worth of sampling at a resolution of 16 bits and at a sampling frequency of 44,100 Hz (i.e., 88,200 bytes per second of sound).

As an example, here's a description of the Dump and Dump Request procedures used by the S1000 family of Akai samplers to exchange sample data.

- The Format of the RSDATA (Request Sample Header Data) Message

```
F0H (11110000): Exclusive message status byte
47H (01000111): Akai ID
ccH (0ccccccc): Exclusive channel (0 to 127)
0AH (00001010): RSDATA
48H (01001000): S1000 family ID
ppH (0ppppppp): sample number (LSB)
ppH (0ppppppp): sample number (MSB)
F7H (11110111): EOX
```

This request is sent to the S1000, which, as soon as it receives it, sends back the header for the corresponding sample (if one exists), in the following form:

- Format of the SDATA (Sample Header Data) Message

```
F0H (11110000): Exclusive message status byte
47H (01000111): Akai ID
ccH (0ccccccc): Exclusive channel (0 to 127)
0BH (00001011): SDATA
48H (01001000): S1000 family ID
ppH (0ppppppp): sample number (LSB)
ppH (0ppppppp): sample number (MSB)
nnH (0nnnnnnn): X data bytes
...
F7H (11110111): EOX
```

This message is bidirectional. When it's sent to the S1000, and if the sample number doesn't exist in the S1000's memory, then a new sample is created (provided the S1000 has enough unallocated memory space for the new sample). Once this message has been received, the sample should be sent (in accordance with the Sample Dump Standard protocol). When an existing sample has the same name, that name is removed before the new sample is sent.

When the sample number matches the number of an existing sample, the existing sample is replaced by the contents of the SDATA message, provided that the length of the sample (SLNGTH, as indicated in the body of the message) is the same.

When the S1000 receives an SDATA message whose purpose is to create a new sample, it behaves exactly the same way it would if it had received a header under the Sample Dump Standard protocol. As a result, the S1000 waits to receive the data packets that correspond to the sample itself. Optionally, an ASPACK (see below) message can be sent to the S1000. In this case, the S1000 issues a receipt (in the form of a Sample Dump Standard ACK message), provided that the S1000 is ready to receive the packets that correspond to the sample. (In the opposite case, an error message is transmitted.)

The format of the sample header data as it appears in the memory of the S1000 (that is, before the bytes have been broken down into nybbles for transmission) is shown in Table 11.4 below:

- SDATA

TABLE 11.4: *Data-Group Formats for SDATA Messages in Akai S1000 Samplers*

NUMBER OF BYTES	NAME	MEANING
1	SHIDENT	3 = sample header block identifier
1	SBANDW	Bandwidth (0 = 10 kHz, 1 = 20 kHz)
1	SPITCH	Original pitch (24 to 127, C0 to G8)
12	SHNAME	Name
1		Spare byte
1	SLOOPS	Number of loops (internal use)
1	SALOOP	First active loop (internal use)
1		Spare byte
1	SPTYPE	Playback type*
2	STUNO	Tune offset cent: semi (+/−50.00)
4	SLOCAT	Data absolute start address
4	SLNGTH	Data length (number of samples)
4	SSTART	Play relative start address
4	SMPEND	Play relative end address

TABLE 11.4: *Data-Group Formats for SDATA Messages in Akai S1000 Samplers (continued)*

NUMBER OF BYTES	NAME	MEANING
		FIRST LOOP
4	LOOPAT	Relative loop point (bits 0 to 5 are treated as 1)
6	LLNGTH	Loop length (binary) fraction: int.low: int.high
2	LDWELL	DWELL time (0 = no loop, 1 to 9998 = ms, 9999 = hold)
		LOOPS 2 THROUGH 8 (SAME AS LOOP 1)
2	SSPARE	Spare bytes used internally
2	SSPAIR	Address of stereo partner (internal use)

* Playback type:
0 = normal looping
1 = loop until release
2 = no looping
3 = play to sample end

- The Format of the RSPACK (Request Sample Data Packet) Message

```
F0H (11110000)
47H (01000111)
ccH (0ccccccc)
0BH (00001011): RSPACK
48H (01001000)
ppH (0ppppppp): sample number (LSB)
ppH (0ppppppp): sample number (MSB)
```

```
a1H (Oaaaaaaa): address offset in relation to the start of the
                sample (LSB)
a2H (Oaaaaaaa): address offset in relation to the start of the
                sample
a3H (Oaaaaaaa): address offset in relation to the start of the
                sample
a4H (Oaaaaaaa): address offset in relation to the start of the
                sample (MSB)
n1H (Onnnnnnn): number of samples requested (LSB)
n2H (Onnnnnnn): number of samples requested
n3H (Onnnnnnn): number of samples requested
n4H (Onnnnnnn): number of samples requested (MSB)
iiH (Oiiiiiii): interval between the samples
ffH (Offfffff): type of interval*
F7H (11110111): EOX
```

This request is sent to the S1000, which, as soon as it receives it, sends back the sample packets (provided the sample number exists in the S1000's memory) in the form of messages that comply with the Sample Dump Standard.

*NOTE: When an interval, X, that's greater than 1 is specified in iiH, then a single sample is transmitted for each group of X samples in the S1000's memory. The value of a transmitted sample matches the value of the first sample in the group (a single sample, when the value of ffH = 0), the average of all of the samples in the group (when the value of ffH = 1), or the value of the sample in the group having the greatest amplitude (peak, when the value of ffH = 2).

- The Format of the ASPACK (Accept Sample Data Packet) Message

```
F0H (11110000)
47H (01000111)
ccH (Occccccc)
0CH (00001100): ASPACK
48H (01001000)
ppH (Oppppppp): sample number (LSB)
ppH (Oppppppp): sample number (MSB)
```

```
a1H (Oaaaaaaa): address offset in relation to the start of the
                sample (LSB)
a2H (Oaaaaaaa): address offset in relation to the start of the
                sample
a3H (Oaaaaaaa): address offset in relation to the start of the
                sample
a4H (Oaaaaaaa): address offset in relation to the start of the
                sample (MSB)
n1H (Onnnnnnn): number of samples requested (LSB)
n2H (Onnnnnnn): number of samples requested
n3H (Onnnnnnn): number of samples requested
n4H (Onnnnnnn): number of samples requested (MSB)
F7H (11110111): EOX
```

The time it takes to transfer a sample via MIDI is so prohibitively long that Dump utilities or librarians lose their fundamental reason for existing, despite the fact that a sampler automatically includes a mass memory storage device. On the other hand, sample-editing programs offer nontrivial advantages.

Sample Editors

Sample editors that are dedicated to a specific instrument use the two types of Exclusive messages described above: the transfer of sample parameters and the transfer of the sample itself (either through messages that are proprietary to each manufacturer, or through the Sample Dump Standard). For parameter messages, the editor behaves the same way it does with a conventional sound generator (with the digital and/or graphic display of the various parameters, which can be edited from the computer keyboard or with the aid of a mouse, etc.). For editing the samples themselves, the editor displays the samples onscreen, the way the Steinberg Soundworks sample editor does in Figure 11.13 below. The editor also lets you work directly on the corresponding waveforms, performing operations that have a direct effect on the sound (copying, removing and/or inserting blocks, changing the volume, filtering, resynthesis, etc.),

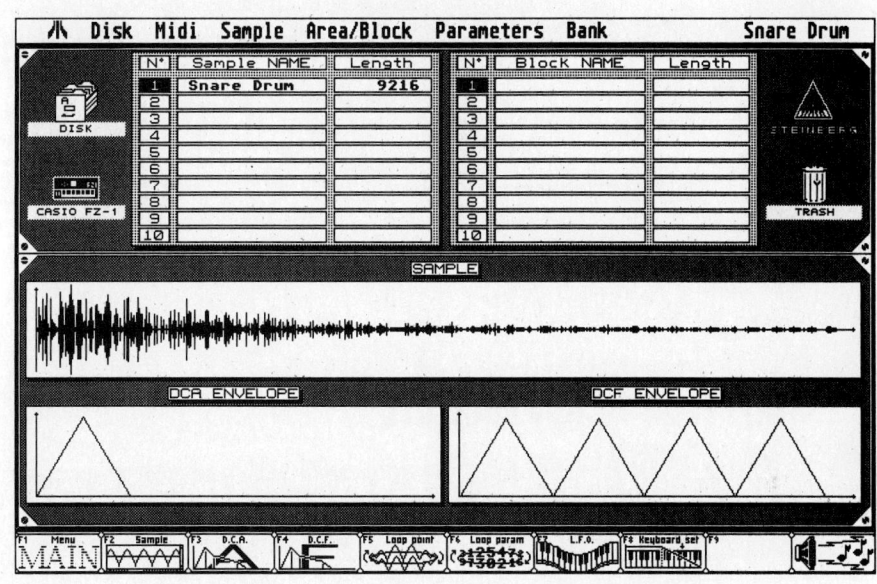

FIGURE 11.13: *The Steinberg Soundworks sample editor for the Casio FZ1 sampler*

involving the programming of loop points with the help of sophisticated algorithms, and so on (with the proviso that these operations can't always be performed from the sampler).

Except for operations that don't have a direct effect on the sound (as is the case with loop points, which can be transferred from the program to the sampler via MIDI, either by means of Exclusive messages involving individual parameters or by means of the Sample Dump Standard), all of the other functions (such as block manipulations, filtering, and changes in amplitude) involve sending back the entire sample, with all of the slowness that this operation entails, in order to be able to hear the results of the processing that has been done. This is why some programs let you do a test hearing of the edited sample, by converting the sample either from the computer (in most instances, in the form of eight bits) or from an external card. This digital-to-analog conversion makes it possible to do so-called "sketchpad monitoring" of the various editing stages, so that the entire sample is transferred only once, after the desired result has been obtained.

For performance reasons, SCSI (the Small Computer System Interface, which was designed primarily to manage mass memory) is sometimes used instead of MIDI to exchange the samples at high speed between the editing program and the sampler.

Universal Sample Editors

Universal sample editors are concerned with samples rather than with their parameters (which differ from one instrument to another). These editors, typified by the Avalon program shown in Figure 11.14 below, can open a dialog with any given number of samplers. In other words, they can receive and transmit samples in the format that's specific to each machine (in terms of resolution and sampling frequency), either by means of the messages that are proprietary to each manufacturer or by means of the Sample Dump Standard—or even sometimes via SCSI, if the instruments are SCSI compatible. The sample can then be processed in the same ways as the samples described above.

Even though a sample consists of a set of values that represent, in digital form, the waveform of an audio signal, the resolution and the sampling frequency are different from one instrument to the next. Some universal editors can receive a sample from an instrument whose resolution is equal to A and whose sampling frequency is equal to B, in order to convert the sample and transmit it to a sampler whose resolution is equal to C and whose sampling frequency is equal to D. Viewed in terms of interfaces,

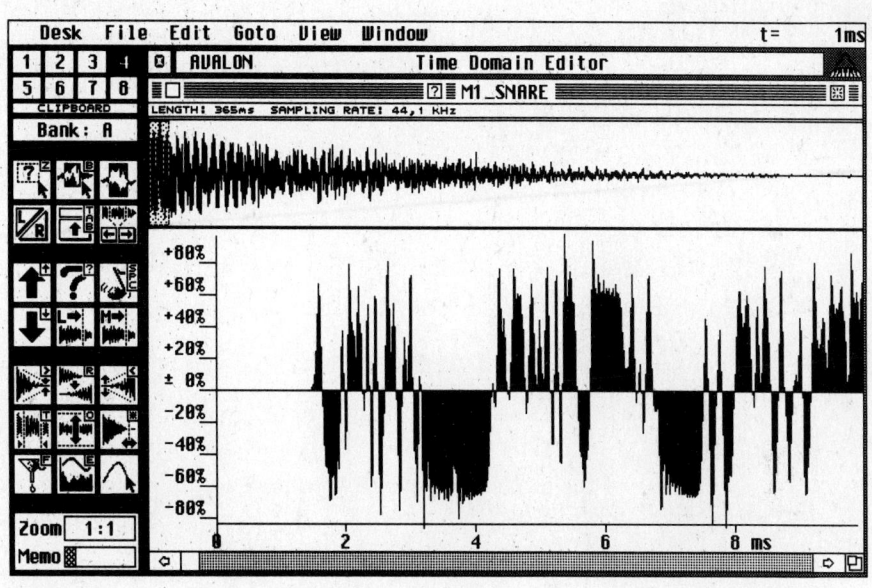

FIGURE 11.14: *Avalon, a universal sample editing program*

these kinds of universal editors can transfer sample banks between several instruments with different characteristics. On the other hand, in such cases the set of parameters (i.e., the filter, the envelope, the LFO, the geographic keyboard assignment, the MIDI channels, etc.) would have to be reprogrammed, because these factors are independent of the sample and proprietary to each instrument. However, even if the sampling parameters are different from one instrument to another, the instruments still have a certain number of constants in common, such as mapping (i.e., the geographic allocation on the keyboard), etc. A few editors (such as Alchemy) let you convert a program (that is, the set of samples associated with the mapping of sounds, etc.) from one sampler to another.

The Sample Dump Standard

Thanks to the Sample Dump Standard, samplers now have the ability to transfer their samples in a universal way via MIDI networks. In principle, the protocol is similar to the one used by instruments to exchange the contents of their memory (i.e., Dump and Dump Request messages). The difference in this case is that the protocol is standardized, even though it is officially part of the MIDI System Exclusive message group (in category 7EH, the so-called Non-Real Time category).

The sample is transferred either by means of a one-way (unidirectional) link from the MIDI Out port of the sender to the MIDI In port of the receiver, or by means of a handshake (bidirectional) link from the MIDI Out port of the sender to the MIDI In port of the receiver and vice-versa. The Sample Dump Standard (SDS) refers to these links as "open loop" and "closed loop," respectively. The second procedure is clearly more efficient, because it allows the exchanges to be managed intelligently through a specific dialog, in much the same way as the handshake protocol developed by Roland.

The SDS exchange protocol uses a total of nine messages, described in detail below:

Data Packet

```
F0H 7EH ccH 02H kkH <data> llH F7H
```

where:

F0H	= the System Exclusive identifier
7EH	= the Non-Real Time category indicator

ccH	= the channel number
<sub-ID#1>: 02H	= the data packet
kkH	= the packet number
<data>	= 120 bytes
llH	= the checksum, calculated for the bytes between 7EH, inclusive, and the end of the data
F7H	= EOX

In order to avoid saturating the MIDI lines and exceeding the buffer capacity of the receiving machine, the SDS transfers the data in the form of packets of 127 bytes. As with the set of MIDI data, only bits 0 to 6 are used, because bit 7 is always set to zero. If the size of the sample to be transferred is not a whole-number multiple of 120 bytes, then the unused bytes in the last packet are filled with zeros. When the size of the sample exceeds 128 packets (that is, when the value of kkH is greater than 127), then the number of the 129th packet (kkH) is reset to zero, and so on, in much the same way that a three-place mileage indicator in a car or motorcycle turns from 999 to 000.

The use of data bytes is not optimized. In fact, one, two, three, or four data bytes are needed to transmit a sample whose resolution is from 1 to 7 bits, from 8 to 14 bits, from 15 to 21 bits, or from 22 to 28 bits (which is the maximum allowed by the SDS).

Dump Request

F0H 7EH ccH 03H ssH ssH 7FH

where:

F0H	= the System Exclusive identifier
7EH	= the Non-Real Time category indicator
ccH	= the channel number
<sub-ID#1>: 03H	= the dump request
ssH ssH	= the sample number (LSB/MSB)
F7H	= EOX

When such a message is received, the sending unit (i.e., the sampler) starts the transfer of the sample, provided that the number (ssH ssH) matches one of the numbers that are present in memory. If not, then the message is ignored.

ACK (Acknowledge)

F0H 7EH ccH 7FH ppH F7H

where:

F0H	= the System Exclusive identifier
7EH	= the Non-Real Time category indicator
ccH	= the channel number
<sub-ID#1>: 7FH	= acknowledge
ppH	= the packet number
F7H	= EOX

This message is used by the receiving unit in a closed-loop configuration, and serves as a kind of receipt for the last packet received. As soon as this message is received, the sending unit sends the next packet.

NAK (Not Acknowledge)

FOH 7EH ccH 7EH ppH F7H

where:

FOH	= the System Exclusive identifier
7EH	= the Non-Real Time category indicator
ccH	= the channel number
<sub-ID#1>: 7EH	= not acknowledged
ppH	= the packet number
F7H	= EOX

Likewise in the closed-loop configuration, the receiving unit notifies the sending unit that the last packet was not received properly (a conclusion usually reached after an erroneous checksum is detected), and asks the sender to transmit the packet again.

Cancel

FOH 7EH ccH 7DH ppH F7H

where:

FOH	= the System Exclusive identifier
7EH	= the Non-Real Time category indicator
ccH	= the channel number

                       <sub-ID#1>: 7DH   = cancel

                       ppH   = the packet number

                       F7H   = EOX

This message, which requests the cancellation of the dump, is initiated by the receiving unit in a closed-loop configuration.

Wait

```
F0H 7EH ccH 7CH ppH F7H
```

where:

        F0H   = the System Exclusive identifier

        7EH   = the Non-Real Time category indicator

        ccH   = the channel number

        <sub-ID#1>: 7CH   = wait

        ppH   = the packet number

        F7H   = EOX

The receiving unit uses this message to ask the sending unit not to send any more packets until otherwise instructed. For instance, when the receiving unit processes each packet it receives in real time, as is the case when packets are stored immediately in mass memory, a certain delay is necessary so that a packet can be stored after it's received and before the next packet is received. This is where the Wait message comes in handy. An ACK message (i.e., a request to send the next packet) indicates resumption of the dialog, while a Cancel message ends the dialog.

Dump Header

```
F0H 7EH ccH 01H ssH ssH eeH ffH ffH ffH ggH ggH ggH hhH
hhH hhH iiH iiH iiH jjH F7H
```

where:

F0H	= the System Exclusive identifier
7EH	= the Non-Real Time category indicator
ccH	= the channel number
\<sub-ID#1\>: 01H	= the dump header
ssH ssH	= the sample number
eeH	= the resolution of the sample as expressed in terms of the number of bits (from 8 to 28, which of course is equivalent to 08H to 1CH)
ffH ffH ffH	= the period of the sample as expressed in nanoseconds (i.e., 10^{-9}, or billionths of a second)
ggH ggH ggH	= the length of the sample as expressed in terms of the number of words (with one word corresponding to the number of bits that make up a sample, i.e., to the number of bits of resolution)
hhH hhH hhH	= the starting point of the loop (expressed in terms of the number of words)
iiH iiH iiH	= the end point of the loop (expressed in terms of the number of words)

jjH	= the type of loop (00 for a forward loop, 01 for a forward/backward loop, and 7F for an inactive loop (i.e., a loop that's off))
F7H	= EOX

In all of the quantities described above, the least significant byte (LSByte) is at the head or front and the most significant byte (MSByte) is at the end.

Here's an example of how a piece of data represented in terms of 3 bytes with 7 useful bits each (i.e., with bit 7 in each byte set to zero) is converted into a decimal or hexadecimal number.

Suppose the three MIDI data bytes are the following three bytes:

01001001 01110100 01100011 (49H 74H 63H)

If you number the bytes in increasing order and from left to right (that is, from byte 1 (the LSByte) to byte 2 to byte 3 (the MSByte)), then bits 0 to 6 of byte 1 correspond respectively to the powers of 2 from 0 to 6, as shown below:

$$01001001 = 1 \times 2^0 + 0 \times 2^1 + 0 \times 2^2 + 1 \times 2^3 + 0 \times 2^4 + 0 \times 2^5 + 1 \times 2^6$$
$$= 1 \quad\quad + 0 \quad\quad + 0 \quad\quad + 8 \quad\quad + 0 \quad\quad + 0 \quad\quad + 64$$
$$= 73 \ (49H)$$

Bits 0 to 6 of byte 2 correspond respectively to the powers of 2 from 7 to 13 (or, if you prefer, to the powers of 2 from 0 to 6, with the whole being multiplied by 2^7, which works because $2^x \times 2^y = 2^{x+y}$):

$$01110100 = (0 \times 2^0 + 0 \times 2^1 + 1 \times 2^2 + 0 \times 2^3 + 1 \times 2^4 + 1 \times 2^5 + 1 \times 2^6) \times 2^7$$
$$= (0 \quad\quad + 0 \quad\quad + 4 \quad\quad + 0 \quad\quad + 16 \quad + 32 \quad + 64) \times 128$$
$$= 116 \times 128 = 74H \times 80H = 14{,}848$$

Bits 0 to 6 of byte 3 correspond respectively to the powers of 2 from 14 to 120 (or, if you prefer, to the powers of 2 from 0 to 6, with the whole being multiplied by 2^{14}, because $2^x \times 2^y = 2^{x+y}$):

```
01100011 = (1 × 2⁰ + 1 × 2¹ + 0 × 2² + 0 × 2³ + 0 × 2⁴ + 1 × 2⁵ + 1 × 2⁶) × 2¹⁴
         = (1      + 2      + 0      + 0      + 0      + 32     + 64) × 16,384
         = 99 × 16,384 = 63H × 80H × 80H = 1,622,016
```

—for an overall result of 1,622,016 + 14,848 + 73, or 1,636,937, which in hex is:

```
1,636,937 divided by 16 = 102,308 with a remainder of 9
  102,308 divided by 16 =   6,394 with a remainder of 4
    6,394 divided by 16 =     399 with a remainder of 10 (AH)
      399 divided by 16 =      24 with a remainder of 15 (FH)
       24 divided by 16 =       1 with a remainder of 8
        1 divided by 16 =       0 with a remainder of 1
```

These operations yield a result of 1,636,937, or 18FA49H.

Incidentally, the largest number that can be expressed in terms of 21 bits (that is, over three MIDI bytes) is 2,097,151 (*01111111 01111111 01111111*).

The following header identifies the so-called "square" factory sample (i.e., the sample whose form is that of a square wave) for an Akai S1000 sampler:

```
F0H 7EH 00H 01H 03H 00H 10H 14H 31H 01H 00H 02H 00H 18H
00H 00H 40H 01H 00H 00H F7H
```

- The transfer channel is channel 1 (byte 3 = 00H).

- The sample in question is sample number 3 (bytes 5 and 6 = 03H and 00H).

- The resolution of the sample is 16 bits (byte 7 = 10H = 16 decimal).

- The period of the sample is equal to $22,676 \times 10^{-9}$ seconds (bytes 8, 9, and 10 = 14H 31H 01H = 01H × 80H × 80X + 31H × 80H + 14H = 1 × 128 × 128 + 49 × 128 + 20 = 22,676), which corresponds to a sampling frequency of 44,100 Hz, because $1/44,100 = 22,676 \times 10^{-9}$.

- The length of the sample is 256 words (bytes 11, 12, and 13 = 00H 02H 00H = 00H × 80H × 80H + 02H × 80H + 00H = $0 \times 128 \times 128 + 2 \times 128 + 0 = 256$).

- The sustain loop starts at word 24 (bytes 14, 15, and 16 = 18H 00H 00H = 00H × 80H × 80H + 00H × 80H + 18H = $0 \times 128 \times 128 + 0 \times 128 + 24 = 24$).

- The sustain loop ends at word 192 (bytes 17, 18, and 19 = 40H 01H 00H = 00H × 80H × 80H + 01H × 80H + 40H = $0 \times 128 \times 128 + 1 \times 128 + 64 = 192$).

- The sustain loop is a forward loop (byte 20 = 00H).

Two messages were added later to the Sample Dump Standard in order to enable the transmission of 16,383 loop points.

Loop Point Transmission

```
F0H 7EH ccH 05H 01H ssH ssH bbH bbH ccH ddH ddH ddH eeH
eeH eeH F7H
```

where:

F0H	= the System Exclusive identifier
7EH	= the Non-Real Time category indicator
ccH	= the channel number
<sub-ID#1>: 05H	= additional information about the loops
<sub-ID#2>: 01H	= multiple-loop message indicator

ssH ssH	= the sample number
bbH bbH	= the loop number (when bbH bbH = 7FH 7FH, the receiving unit removes all of the loops in the current sample)
ccH	= the type of loop (00 for a forward loop, 01 for a forward/backward loop, and 7F for an inactive loop (i.e., a loop that's off))
ddH ddH ddH	=the starting point for the loop (expressed in terms of the number of words)
eeH eeH eeH	= the end point for the loop (expressed in terms of the number of words)
F7H	= EOX

Loop Point Request

F0H 7EH ccH 05H 02H ssH ssH bbH bbH F7H

where:

F0H	= the System Exclusive identifier
7EH	= the Non-Real Time category indicator
ccH	= the channel number
<sub-ID#1>: 05H	= additional information about the loops
<sub-ID#2>: 02H	= loop-transmission request message
ssH ssH	= the sample number

bbH bbH	= the loop number (when bbH bbH = 7FH 7FH, the request involves all of the loops in the current sample)
F7H	= EOX

Thanks to these two messages (particularly in conjunction with an editing program), you don't have to resend the sample in its entirety in order to make a simple change in a loop.

Implementation of the Transfer Protocol

With the Sample Dump Standard, a sample is sent either by starting the transmission manually from the front-panel keys of the sampler, or by starting it externally by sending a Dump Request message. In both of these cases, and if in the second case the request is valid (i.e., if the sample number is good), then the sending unit starts by sending a Dump Header message in order to display the identity card, as it were, of the sample in question.

The receiving unit analyzes the header in order to make sure the sample is compatible with its own characteristics. Depending on the result of this analysis, the receiving unit decides to either accept or reject the transfer. It can decide to reject the transfer for any number of reasons: saturated memory in the receiving unit, different resolutions, etc. If the receiving unit decides to reject the transfer, it sends a Cancel message; otherwise, to indicate its acceptance of the transfer, it sends an ACK message.

This direct response via MIDI requires a handshake (i.e., a closed-loop) connection. This is why, if the sender of the sample doesn't receive a response within two seconds after the sample is sent, the sender infers that the connection is an open-loop connection. In this case, the sender starts transmitting packets one after another without waiting for any messages in return. In the opposite case, with a closed-loop connection, the reception of a Cancel message immediately causes the sending unit to interrupt the transaction, whereas the reception of an ACK message triggers the sending of the first packet.

Once the first packet has been sent, the sending unit waits for the receiving unit to notify it of the outcome of the reception by sending back either an ACK ("packet received OK") message, which authorizes the sending unit to send the second packet, or an NAK message (requesting that the packet be sent again) in the event that an error has occurred (as detected through the checksum, etc.). If the sending unit can't resend the erroneous message (because of a bad packet number, a function that the program can't handle, etc.), then the exchange continues as though nothing had happened. Under this protocol, when the sending unit receives a Wait message it should wait until it also receives an ACK message before it sends the next packet.

1 ▪ Normal transmission at the initiative of the sender:

Sender		Receiver
	←	Dump Request
Dump Header	→	
	←	ACK
Data Packet 1	→	
	←	ACK
...	...	...
Data Packet n	→	
	←	ACK

2 ▪ Transmission with erroneous reception of the first packet, followed by retransmission:

Sender		Receiver
	←	Dump Request
Dump Header	→	
	←	ACK

Data Packet 1	→	
	←	NAK
Data Packet 1	→	
	←	ACK
...	...	...
Data Packet n	→	
	←	ACK

3 ▪ Transmission with immediate cancellation:

Sender		Receiver
		Receiver
	←	Dump Request
Dump Header	→	
	←	Cancel

To conclude this review of the Sample Dump Standard, here's an application. This one's for the transfer of samples in SDS format (with Dump and Dump Request messages), as programmed with the help of the GenEdit universal editor/librarian.

The RECEIVE Segment

```
OpenWindow                 : open a window
PAT = InputPatch 0 0 PAT: user acquisition of the sample number
Transmit $F0 $7E $00 $03: send the Dump Request message via
                           channel 1
TransmitVar PAT            : send a sample number as a byte
Transmit $00 $F7           : second byte of the number is 0; end
                             of message
Receive $F0 $7E $00 $01  : receive the header
ReceiveAny 1               : receive and eliminate the sample
                             number (so as to be able to send it
                             back with another number)
ReceiveData 15 $F7 1       : body and end of header
Receive $F7
Transmit $F0 $7E $00 $7F: send an Acknowledge message
Transmit $00 $F7           : packet number set to zero
```

```
Loop 0                    : while there is data
  ReceiveData 127 $F7 1 : receive data packets
  Transmit $F0 $7E $00  : send an Acknowledge message
  Transmit $7F $00 $F7
EndLoop
```

The TRANSMIT Segment

```
OpenWindow              : open a window
PAT = InputPatch 0 0 PAT: user acquisition of the sample number
Transmit $F0 $7E $00 $01: send a header message
TransmitVar PAT         : sample number as a byte
TransmitData 15 $F7 1   : contents of the header
Transmit $F7            : end of header
Receive $F0 $7E $00     : presumptive reception of an
                          Acknowledge message
ReceiveAny 2            : the program does not verify the
                          message; it ignores the handshake
                          and assumes that the transaction is
                          proceeding properly
Receive $F7             : end of message
Loop 0                  : while data remains to be sent
  TransmitData 127 $F7 1: send data packets
  Receive $F0 $7E $00   : presumptive reception of an
                          Acknowledge message
  ReceiveAny 2          : the same principle as above
  Receive $F7           : end of Acknowledge message
EndLoop
```

CHAPTER

12

XIII XIV XV XVI A B C D E F G H I

Using
GenEdit

THIS CHAPTER GOES beyond the
simple practical operations you can
perform with the universal GenEdit
software. In it, you'll learn how to
program dump utilities, libraries, and
editors—a set of procedures that can
help everyone who wants to be able
to develop these kinds of programs
themselves. By way of introduction, here's some general information
about GenEdit. This information is limited to the software functions
you'll need to know about in order to understand the examples in this
chapter.

General Information: Configurations and More

As you'll recall, a universal program such as GenEdit provides all the infrastructure you need in order to manage and edit the memories of MIDI
instruments, except for a few lines of code that are particular to each instrument. These lines are grouped in segments (a lot like mini-programs
dedicated to very specific tasks), and the groups themselves are arranged
in sets called *configurations*. Depending on whether you want to use

GenEdit as a dump utility, a library, or an editor, you'll use the filing configuration, the organizing configuration, or the editing configuration. Figure 12.1 and the list below summarize the respective roles of these three configurations.

- *The filing configuration*: In this mode, the program receives a dump from an instrument and saves the dump on disk. Going in the other direction, it loads a dump from disk and sends the dump to the instrument.

- *The organizing configuration*: This mode uses the same principle as the filing configuration, but with dumps that contain several identical elements (such as banks of patches, to borrow a phrase from GenEdit terminology, which will be used throughout this chapter).

```
                    Configurations: AUTOLOAD.CNX

          ▮ Some Editing          Some Organizing        Some Filing
            Configurations:       Configurations:        Configurations:

  🗑  🖨     TX802/DX7IIvoicesT2V  SPX90 II effects  SPX  User Dump 1       US1
            TX81Z voices     TZV                         User Dump Many    USM
  🗔  🗔     DX7 voices       DX7  PX+ master (bank)PXM   Akai S900         AK9
 📋  ALL                                                 P2000sample parmsP2P
            U220 128 timbres U2T  M3 programs      M3P   Linn Drum data    LNN
            D110 64 tones    D1T
            D50 full         D50  K5 int singles   K5S   ***************

            Matrix-6 patches M6P  VFX-SD programs  VFP   These are copies
                                                         of SOME of the
            K4 single bank   K4S  CZ101/1000 voicesC10   configurations
            K1 single bank   K1S                         supplied on the
                                                         CONFIGURATIONS
            Proteus/1   RAM  PRA                         Disk; additional
                                                         configurations
  [ Exit ]  M1 programs      M1P                         are found in the
                                                         .CNX files on
            HR-16 Kits       NRK                         that disk.
```

FIGURE 12.1: *Selecting a configuration from among the sixty-three possible options that GenEdit's memory can hold*

As shown in Figure 12.2 below, two windows are dedicated to the management of these banks. Each window can receive, send, save, and load banks. More importantly, however, each window can organize banks. That is, it lets you display and edit the names of patches, copy patches, and send individual patches to the instrument (i.e., to the instrument's edit buffer).

- *The editing configuration*: In association with the organizing configuration, this mode lets you program a given number of editing screens, so that you can graphically or digitally modify each parameter of a patch in a bank and send the result to the instrument (i.e., to the instrument's edit buffer) (see the example in Figure 12.3 below).

```
 Desk  File  Edit  Windows  MIDI
```

	FROMMIDI.VFP			FROMMIDI.VFP
0:1	ITS-A-SYNTH		7:1	SWELLSTRNGS
0:2	ZIRCONIUM		7:2	PIZZICATO
0:3	FAT-BRASS		7:3	LUSH-STRNGS
0:4	STAR-DRIVE		7:4	GOLDEN-HARP
0:5	WONDERS		7:5	REZ-STRINGS
0:6	SAW-O-LIFE		7:6	ORCH+SOLO
1:1	DIGIPIANO-1		8:1	REEL-STEEL
1:2	NEW-PLANET		8:2	SUN-N-MOON
1:3	DANGEROUS	**Edit**	8:3	FLANG-CLEAN
1:4	FUNKYCLAV		8:4	FUZZ-LEAD
1:5	WARM-TINES	**Randomize**	8:5	SPANISH-GTR
1:6	METAL-TINES		8:6	12-STRING
2:1	BIG-PIANO	**Distort**	9:1	KITCHN-SINK
2:2	BRIGHT-PNO2		9:2	PERCUSSION
2:3	SYN-PIANO	**Name**	9:3	FUSION-KIT
2:4	TRANS-PIANO		9:4	BALLAD-KIT
2:5	CLASSIC-PNO	**Average**	9:5	SYNTH-KIT
2:6	HARPSICHORD		9:6	ROCKIN-KIT
3:1	DOUBLE-REED			

FIGURE 12.2: *The two bank windows. In this example they're dedicated to organizing the patches for a Roland D-50 synthesizer.*

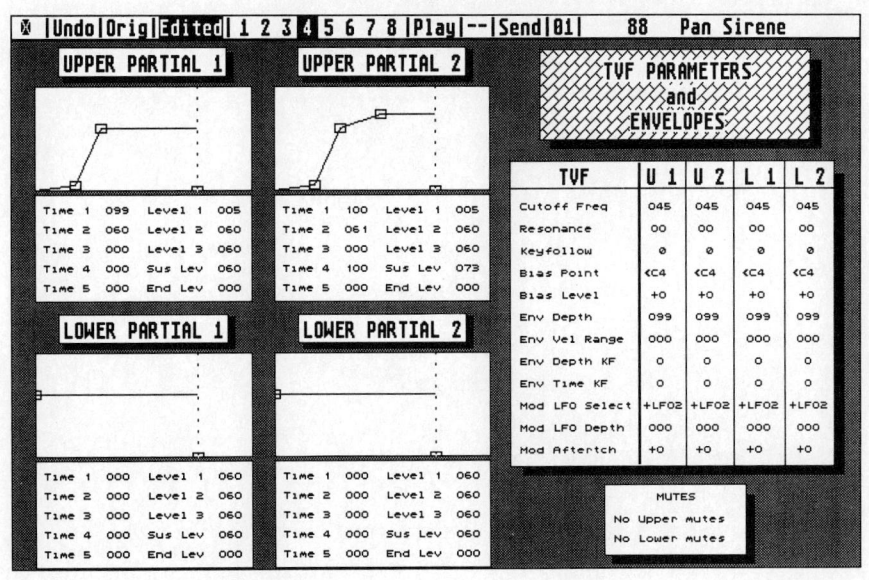

TVF	U 1	U 2	L 1	L 2
Cutoff Freq	045	045	045	045
Resonance	00	00	00	00
Keyfollow	∅	∅	∅	∅
Bias Point	<C4	<C4	<C4	<C4
Bias Level	+0	+0	+0	+0
Env Depth	099	099	099	099
Env Vel Range	000	000	000	000
Env Depth KF	0	0	0	0
Env Time KF	0	0	0	0
Mod LFO Select	+LFO2	+LFO2	+LFO2	+LFO2
Mod LFO Depth	000	000	000	000
Mod Aftertch	+0	+0	+0	+0

FIGURE 12.3: *An editing screen for the Korg M1*

Segments

The implementation of a configuration involves programming the related segments. The purpose of these segments, which are built in a language that is specific to GenEdit, is to manage the transfers (i.e., filing), organization, and editing of the data contained in one or another of the types of memory in a MIDI instrument. The editor also makes use of a so-called "template" that defines the graphical and numeric objects that correspond to the parameters of the instrument to be edited. (The implementation of the template is the subject of the following sections.) Before describing in detail how these various segments work, it's worth reviewing a few general fundamental concepts.

Data Formats

Functionally speaking, at the level of the exclusive MIDI data that the segments deal with, there are five types of formats:

1 ▪ The format for storage of a bank in an instrument (e.g., compressed, uncompressed, mixed, etc.).

2 ▪ The format for storage in the edit buffer in an instrument (e.g., compressed, uncompressed, mixed, etc.).

3 ▪ The MIDI transmission format for a bank (e.g., standard dump, by nybbles, packed, etc.).

4 ▪ The MIDI transmission format for the edit buffer (e.g., standard dump, by nybbles, packed, etc.).

5 ▪ The GenEdit editing format, known as "EBDT" (for "Edit Buffer Definition Table"), which consists of not storing more than one parameter per byte.

The Data Buffer

The MIDI data received from an instrument in the form of a dump is stored by GenEdit in a portion of the computer's memory known as the *data buffer*. If the dump utility is a simple one, the data buffer is usually happy to store the exclusive data in the same format as the transmission format. Conversely, but also at the data-buffer level, for the sake of organization a librarian or an editor works exclusively in a format that's similar to the format in which the data is stored in the instrument. What this means is that when the data-transmission format is different from the data-storage format (e.g., packed transmission, transmission by nybbles, etc.), GenEdit has to reconvert the data from the transmission format into the storage format after it receives a dump, and make the conversion in the opposite direction before it sends a dump.

The Edit Buffer

The edit buffer is a memory area dedicated to the temporary storage of a patch from the bank. The librarian uses the edit buffer to:

- Display and edit the name of a patch;
- Transfer a patch to the clipboard (which is a temporary storage area whose job is to make copy operations easier);
- Transfer a patch to the edit buffer in the instrument.

The editor uses the edit buffer to:

- Edit a patch; and
- Transfer the edited patch to the edit buffer in the instrument.

When you're using the librarian section of GenEdit, the format of the patch in the edit buffer is the same as the format of the patch in the data buffer (i.e., in a simple transfer of the patch between these two buffers). However, when you're using the editor section, a patch is stored in the edit buffer in EBDT format (in a ratio of one or more bytes per parameter, which is the fundamental requirement for editing). If the format of the patch in the data buffer doesn't meet this requirement (i.e., when the data buffer is compressed, with several parameters per byte), decompression operations will have to be performed in order for the patch to be transferred from the data buffer (i.e., in compressed format) to the edit buffer (i.e., in EBDT format), and conversely (i.e., with compression operations so that a patch can be transferred from the edit buffer to the data buffer).

What's more, in order to transfer a patch from the edit buffer to the instrument, either from the librarian section (in which the format of the patch in the edit buffer is the same as the format of the patch in the data buffer) or from the editor section (i.e., in EBDT format), you first have

to convert the patch from edit-buffer format to storage format and then to the proper format for transmission to the instrument.

Segments in the Filing Configuration

The dump utility requests the Send and Receive segments, which play the following roles:

- The Receive segment sends a Dump Request message to the instrument, then receives the corresponding dump and stores it in the data buffer.

- The Send segment sends the dump from the data buffer to the instrument.

Segments in the Organizing Configuration

The librarian requests the Receive, Transmit, Initialize, Get Patch, Put Patch, Make Edit, Unmake Edit, Send Edit, and Common segments, which play the roles described below:

- *The Receive segment:* This segment is identical to the one in the filing configuration, and is present in this configuration simply because a utility for converting received data from the transmission format for a bank to the storage format for a bank is necessary when these two formats are different.

- *The Transmit segment:* This segment is identical to the one in the filing configuration, and is present in this configuration simply because a utility for converting outgoing data from the storage format for a bank to the transmission format for a bank is necessary when these two formats are different.

- *The Initialize segment:* This segment determines the number of patches per bank, the way in which the names of the patches will be displayed in the window (e.g., I01 to I32 on the Yamaha TX81Z; I11 to I18 and I21 to I28 on the Roland D50 and 550, etc.), the size of the edit buffer (which therefore will contain a patch extracted from the data buffer, with that patch having the same format as the data buffer if the librarian section is being used, and an EBDT-type format if the editor section is being used), the address at which the patch name starts inside the edit buffer, the size of the patch (in terms of the number of characters), etc.

- *The Get Patch segment:* This segment copies a patch from the data buffer to the edit buffer without doing any format conversion (for instance, in order to display the name of the patch in the bank window, or to copy the patch from one location to another, by executing the Put Patch segment immediately afterward). When the name of a patch doesn't use standard ASCII (which is the case with instruments such as the Roland D50 and 550 and the Akai S900), the translation has to be performed.

- *The Put Patch segment:* This segment copies a patch from the edit buffer to the data buffer without doing any format conversion (for instance, in order to store a patch after the patch has been renamed, or after a Get Patch segment has been executed when a copy operation is being performed). When the Put Patch segment translates the name of a patch into ASCII, the conversion in the opposite direction has to be performed.

- *The Make Edit segment:* This segment copies a patch from the data buffer to the edit buffer, either to transfer the patch from a bank to the clipboard or to send the patch via MIDI by executing the Send Edit segment immediately afterward. If you're dealing only with a librarian, the Make Edit segment is always exactly identical to the Get Patch segment.

- *The Unmake Edit segment:* This segment copies a patch from the edit buffer to the data buffer, to transfer the patch from the clipboard to a bank. If you're dealing only with a librarian, the Unmake Edit segment is always exactly identical to the Put Patch segment.

- *The Send Edit segment:* This segment sends a patch from the edit buffer to the edit buffer in the instrument after the patch has been transferred from the data buffer to the edit buffer by the Make Edit segment. When the formats are different, the outgoing data has to be converted from the storage format for a patch in the edit buffer (which is identical to the format for a patch in the data buffer) to the format for storage and transmission that's being used by the edit buffer of the instrument.

- *The Common segment:* This segment, which usually consists of conversion tables, can be called by any other segment. It is used particularly by the Get Patch and Put Patch segments when names are being converted from a particular format to ASCII and vice versa.

Segments in the Editing Configuration

In addition to creating a template, the editor requests the same segments that are used in the organizing section (with the Make Edit and Unmake Edit segments usually being somewhat more highly developed). The editor also uses the Validate segment. The roles of these segments are summarized below:

- *The Make Edit segment:* This segment copies a patch from the data buffer to the edit buffer for the same reasons given above, but also and particularly (and this is its major role) to convert the patch from the storage format of the data buffer to EBDT format, so that the patch can be manipulated by the various editing screens.

- *The Unmake Edit segment:* This segment copies a patch from the edit buffer to the data buffer for the same reasons given above, but also and particularly to convert the patch from EBDT format to the storage format of the data buffer in order to be able to pass along the editing manipulations to the bank.

- *The Validate segment:* When a patch is edited, certain modifications may not be authorized (such as the effect of a change in one parameter on the value of another parameter, etc.). The Validate segment manages these constraints and interactions.

- *The Send Edit segment:* This segment sends a patch (from the edit buffer) to the edit buffer of the instrument, either directly from the editor or, as indicated above, from the librarian, after execution of the Make Edit segment. When these formats are different, it's necessary to convert the outgoing data from the storage format for a patch in the edit buffer (that is, EBDT) to the storage and transmission format used by the edit buffer in the instrument.

Summary of Operations

The conversions mentioned below are performed only when needed (i.e., if different formats are involved).

- *Initialize:* The general parameters for a configuration.

- *Receive:* The reception of a dump from the instrument in the data buffer (i.e., the conversion from the transmission format to the storage format for an editor configuration or a librarian configuration).

- *Transmit:* The transmission of a dump from the data buffer to the instrument (i.e., the conversion from the storage format to the transmission format for an editor configuration or a librarian configuration).

- *Get Patch:* Copying a patch from a data buffer to the edit buffer (with the conversion of the name from the individual format that's peculiar to the instrument into ASCII format).

- *Put Patch:* Copying a patch from the edit buffer to the data buffer (with the conversion of the name from ASCII format to the individual format that's peculiar to the instrument).

- *Make Edit:* Copying a patch from a data buffer to the edit buffer (i.e., recopying the Get Patch segment for a librarian configuration, or conversion from storage format to EBDT format for an editor configuration).

- *Unmake Edit:* Copying a patch from the edit buffer to the data buffer (i.e., recopying the Put Patch segment for a librarian configuration, or conversion from EBDT format to storage format for an editor configuration).

- *Send Edit:* Transmitting a patch created by the Make Edit segment to the edit buffer in an instrument (i.e., the conversion from the format of the edit buffer, namely, from the format of the data buffer from the librarian, and from an EBDT formation from the editor, into the storage and transmission format that's peculiar to the edit buffer of the instrument).

- *Validate:* Conditional operations involving the editing of parameters.

- *Common:* Tables that are accessible to all of the segments.

Manipulations

The following list summarizes the principal manipulations that GenEdit authorizes, showing each manipulation associated with the segments that are activated.

MANIPULATION	SEGMENT(S)
Reception and saving of a dump on disk	Receive
Loading and sending a dump to an instrument	Transmit
Receiving a dump from a bank into a bank window	Receive
Displaying the names of patches in a bank window	Initialize, Get Patch (for each patch in the bank)
Sending a dump from a bank window to the instrument	Transmit
Copying a patch from one location to another in the bank windows	Get Patch, Put Patch
Sending a patch from a bank window to the instrument	Make Edit, Send Edit
Copying a patch from a bank window to the clipboard	Make Edit
Copying a patch from the clipboard to a bank window	Unmake Edit
Editing a patch	Make Edit
Sending a patch from the editor to the instrument	Send Edit

The GenEdit Language

The GenEdit language has the advantage of being one of the most readily understandable languages available on the market today. It doesn't require

any special programming knowledge or experience. (NOTE: Only the instructions used in this book are described in detail in Appendix G, *GenEdit Commands at a Glance.*) Of course, the following examples can easily be transferred to other universal dump utilities, such as Dr. T's X-Or and SoundQuest's MIDI Quest, and can also serve as the basis for true programs written in BASIC, C, or other high-level languages. Before getting into practical example, though, there's one more important point to make. It involves the PTR and PAT variables, which are crucially important.

In the overall group of segments, the PTR variable points to the address of the data buffer—except in the Send Edit segment, where it points to the address of the edit buffer. Unless a specific value has been assigned to it, this variable is initialized to zero at the beginning of the segment. Its address at the end of the segment determines the upper limit of the data buffer, i.e., the size of the amount of data that will be stored on disk.

The PAT variable corresponds to the number of the patch in the bank. As soon as you select a patch from the screen, this variable is sent to the activated segments. Then, when the names of the patches in a bank are displayed, the Get Patch segment is activated as many times as there are patches in that bank, and the PAT variable increments itself by one unit each time the segment is activated.

Programming Dump Utilities

This section is based on examples that have been prepared with the help of various MIDI devices. It analyzes the way a program uses Exclusive Dump and Dump Request messages during dialogues between the computer and the instrument. In other words, this section deals with writing the Receive and Transmit segments without worrying about format conversions.

The Yamaha TX81Z

The four-operator synthesizers in the Yamaha TX81Z series accept the following dump requests. (The language of these requests was described in Chapter 10.)

General Syntax

1 ▪ The Voice Edit Buffer dump request (VCED, for "VoiCe EDit buffer"):

```
F0H (11110000): start of Exclusive message
43H (01000011): Yamaha ID
2nH (0010nnnn): type of message (2 = request, n = channel)
03H (00000100): type of request (edit buffer for one voice)
F7H (11110111): EOX
```

2 ▪ The 32-voice dump request (VMEM, for "Voices MEMory"):

```
F0H (11110000): start of Exclusive message
43H (01000011): Yamaha ID
2nH (0010nnnn): type of message (2 = request, n = channel)
04H (00000100): type of request (32 voices)
F7H (11110111): EOX
```

3 ▪ The Performance Edit buffer dump request (PCED, for "PerformanCe EDit buffer"):

```
F0H (11110000): start of Exclusive message
43H (01000011): Yamaha ID
2nH (0010nnnn): type of message (2 = request, n = channel)
7EH (01111110): type of format
4CH (01001100): "L" (ASCII)
4DH (01001101): "M" (ASCII)
20H (00100000): " " (ASCII)
20H (00100000): " " (ASCII)
38H (00111000): "8" (ASCII)
39H (00111001): "9" (ASCII)
37H (00110111): "7" (ASCII)
36H (00110110): "6" (ASCII)
```

```
50H (01010000): "P" (ASCII for Performance)
45H (01000101): "E" (ASCII for Edit buffer)
F7H (11110111): EOX
```

4 ▪ The twenty-four-performance dump request (PMEM, for "Performance MEMory"):

```
F0H (11110000): start of Exclusive message
43H (01000011): Yamaha ID
2nH (0010nnnn): type of message (2 = request, n = channel)
7EH (01111110): type of format
4CH (01001100): "L" (ASCII)
4DH (01001101): "M" (ASCII)
20H (00100000): " " (ASCII)
20H (00100000): " " (ASCII)
38H (00111000): "8" (ASCII)
39H (00111001): "9" (ASCII)
37H (00110111): "7" (ASCII)
36H (00110110): "6" (ASCII)
50H (01010000): "P" (ASCII for Performance)
4DH (01001101): "M" (ASCII for Memory)
F7H (11110111): EOX
```

5 ▪ The Voice Edit buffer dump request (VCED), together with an Additional Parameters Edit buffer dump request (ACED):

```
F0H (11110000): start of Exclusive message
43H (01000011): Yamaha ID
2nH (0010nnnn): type of message (2 = request, n = channel)
7EH (01111110): type of format
4CH (01001100): "L" (ASCII)
4DH (01001101): "M" (ASCII)
20H (00100000): " " (ASCII)
20H (00100000): " " (ASCII)
38H (00111000): "8" (ASCII)
39H (00111001): "9" (ASCII)
37H (00110111): "7" (ASCII)
36H (00110110): "6" (ASCII)
41H (01010000): "A" (ASCII for Additional)
45H (01000101): "E" (ASCII for Edit buffer)
F7H (11110111): EOX
```

6 ▪ The dump request for System Category 0 data (SYS0, for system data):

```
F0H (11110000): start of Exclusive message
43H (01000011): Yamaha ID
2nH (0010nnnn): type of message (2 = request, n = channel)
7EH (01111110): type of format
4CH (01001100): "L" (ASCII)
4DH (01001101): "M" (ASCII)
20H (00100000): " " (ASCII)
20H (00100000): " " (ASCII)
38H (00111000): "8" (ASCII)
39H (00111001): "9" (ASCII)
37H (00110111): "7" (ASCII)
36H (00110110): "6" (ASCII)
53H (01010011): "S" (ASCII for System)
30H (00110000): "0" (ASCII for category 0)
F7H (11110111): EOX
```

7 ▪ The dump request for System Category 1 data (SYS1, for the program-change reassignment table):

```
F0H (11110000): start of Exclusive message
43H (01000011): Yamaha ID
2nH (0010nnnn): type of message (2 = request, n = channel)
7EH (01111110): type of format
4CH (01001100): "L" (ASCII)
4DH (01001101): "M" (ASCII)
20H (00100000): " " (ASCII)
20H (00100000): " " (ASCII)
38H (00111000): "8" (ASCII)
39H (00111001): "9" (ASCII)
37H (00110111): "7" (ASCII)
36H (00110110): "6" (ASCII)
53H (01010011): "S" (ASCII for System)
31H (00110001): "1" (ASCII for category 1)
F7H (11110111): EOX
```

8 ▪ The dump request for System Category 2 data (SYS2, for effects):

```
F0H (11110000): start of Exclusive message
43H (01000011): Yamaha ID
2nH (0010nnnn): type of message (2 = request, n = channel)
7EH (01111110): type of format
4CH (01001100): "L" (ASCII)
4DH (01001101): "M" (ASCII)
20H (00100000): " " (ASCII)
20H (00100000): " " (ASCII)
38H (00111000): "8" (ASCII)
39H (00111001): "9" (ASCII)
37H (00110111): "7" (ASCII)
36H (00110110): "6" (ASCII)
53H (01010011): "S" (ASCII for System)
31H (00110010): "2" (ASCII for category 2)
F7H (11110111): EOX
```

9 ▪ The dump request for the special range for an octave (microtuning 1):

```
F0H (11110000): start of Exclusive message
43H (01000011): Yamaha ID
2nH (0010nnnn): type of message (2 = request, n = channel)
7EH (01111110): type of format
4CH (01001100): "L" (ASCII)
4DH (01001101): "M" (ASCII)
20H (00100000): " " (ASCII)
20H (00100000): " " (ASCII)
4DH (01001101): "M" (ASCII)
43H (01010011): "C" (ASCII)
52H (01010010): "R" (ASCII)
54H (01010100): "T" (ASCII)
45H (01000101): "E" (ASCII)
30H (00110000): "0" (ASCII)
F7H (11110111): EOX
```

10 ▪ The dump request for the special range covering the entire range of the keyboard (microtuning 2):

```
F0H (11110000): start of Exclusive message
43H (01000011): Yamaha ID
2nH (0010nnnn): type of message (2 = request, n = channel)
7EH (01111110): type of format
4CH (01001100): "L" (ASCII)
4DH (01001101): "M" (ASCII)
20H (00100000): " " (ASCII)
20H (00100000): " " (ASCII)
4DH (01001101): "M" (ASCII)
43H (01010011): "C" (ASCII)
52H (01010010): "R" (ASCII)
54H (01010100): "T" (ASCII)
45H (01000101): "E" (ASCII)
31H (00110001): "1" (ASCII)
F7H (11110111): EOX
```

In return, the following dump messages are sent. (The checksum is calculated on the basis of the entire set of data following the two size bytes.)

1 ▪ The Voice Edit Buffer dump (VCED, for "VoiCe EDit buffer"):

```
F0H (11110000): start of Exclusive message
43H (01000011): Yamaha ID
0nH (0000nnnn): type of message (0 = dump, n = channel)
03H (00000011): type of dump (edit buffer for one voice)
00H (00000000): data size (most significant byte)
5DH (01011101): data size (least significant byte, 5DH = 93)
ddH (0ddddddd): data (93 bytes)
...
ccH (0ccccccc): checksum
F7H (11110111): EOX
```

The two size bytes correspond to the 93 data bytes.

2 ▪ The 32-voice dump (VMEM, for "Voices MEMory"):

```
F0H (11110000): start of Exclusive message
43H (01000011): Yamaha ID
```

```
OnH (0000nnnn): type of message (0 = dump, n = channel)
04H (00000100): type of dump (32 voice)
20H (00100000): data size (most significant byte)
00H (00000000): data size (least significant byte)
ddH (0ddddddd): data (4,096 bytes)
...
ccH (0ccccccc): checksum
F7H (11110111): EOX
```

The two size bytes (in the form 0xxxxxxy 0yyyyyyy), distributed over two eight-bit bytes (in the form 00xxxxxx xyyyyyyy), correspond to the hexadecimal value 1000H, which is the same as 4,096 in decimal notation.

3 • The Performance Edit buffer dump (PCED, for "PerformanCe EDit buffer"):

```
F0H (11110000): start of Exclusive message
43H (01000011): Yamaha ID
OnH (0010nnnn): type of message (0 = dump, n = channel)
7EH (01111110): type of format
00H (00000000): data size (most significant byte)
78H (01111000): data size (least significant byte, 78H = 120)
4CH (01001100): "L" (ASCII)
4DH (01001101): "M" (ASCII)
20H (00100000): " " (ASCII)
20H (00100000): " " (ASCII)
38H (00111000): "8" (ASCII)
39H (00111001): "9" (ASCII)
37H (00110111): "7" (ASCII)
36H (00110110): "6" (ASCII)
50H (01010000): "P" (ASCII for Performance)
45H (01000101): "E" (ASCII for Edit buffer)
ddH (0ddddddd): data (110 bytes)
...
ccH (0ccccccc): checksum
F7H (11110111): EOX
```

The two size bytes correspond to the 110 data bytes, to which the ten ASCII header bytes should be added.

4 ▪ The twenty-four-performance dump (PMEM, for "Performance MEMory"):

```
FOH (11110000): start of Exclusive message
43H (01000011): Yamaha ID
OnH (0000nnnn): type of message (0 = dump, n = channel)
7EH (01111110): type of format
13H (00010011): data size (most significant byte)
OAH (00001010): data size (least significant byte)
4CH (01001100): "L" (ASCII)
4DH (01001101): "M" (ASCII)
20H (00100000): " " (ASCII)
20H (00100000): " " (ASCII)
38H (00111000): "8" (ASCII)
39H (00111001): "9" (ASCII)
37H (00110111): "7" (ASCII)
36H (00110110): "6" (ASCII)
50H (01010000): "P" (ASCII for Performance)
4DH (01001101): "M" (ASCII for Memory)
ddH (0ddddddd): data (2.432 bytes)
...
ccH (0ccccccc): checksum
F7H (11110111): EOX
```

The two size bytes (in the form 0xxxxxxy 0yyyyyyy), distributed over two eight-bit bytes (in the form 00xxxxxx xyyyyyyy), correspond to the hexadecimal value 098AH, which is the same as 2,442 in decimal notation (that is, 2,432 data bytes plus 10 ASCII header bytes).

5 ▪ The Voice Edit buffer dump (VCED), together with an Additional Parameters Edit buffer dump (ACED):

```
FOH (11110000): start of Exclusive message
43H (01000011): Yamaha ID
OnH (0000nnnn): type of message (0 = dump, n = channel)
7EH (01111110): type of format
OOH (00000000): data size (most significant byte)
21H (00100001): data size (least significant byte, 21H = 33)
4CH (01001100): "L" (ASCII)
4DH (01001101): "M" (ASCII)
```

```
20H (00100000): " " (ASCII)
20H (00100000): " " (ASCII)
38H (00111000): "8" (ASCII)
39H (00111001): "9" (ASCII)
37H (00110111): "7" (ASCII)
36H (00110110): "6" (ASCII)
41H (01010000): "A" (ASCII for Additional)
45H (01000101): "E" (ASCII for Edit buffer)
ddH (0ddddddd): data (23 bytes)
...
ccH (0ccccccc): checksum
F7H (11110111): EOX
```

The two size bytes correspond to the 23 data bytes, to which the ten
ASCII header bytes should be added.

The following message (VCED) is transmitted after the preceding message (SCED):

```
F0H (11110000): start of Exclusive message
43H (01000011): Yamaha ID
0nH (0000nnnn): type of message (0 = dump, n = channel)
03H (00000011): type of dump (edit buffer for one voice)
00H (00000000): data size (most significant byte)
5DH (01011101): data size (least significant byte, 5DH = 93)
ddH (0ddddddd): data (93 bytes)
...
ccH (0ccccccc): checksum
F7H (11110111): EOX
```

The two size bytes correspond to the 93 data bytes.

6 ▪ The System Category 0 data dump (SYS0, for system data):

```
F0H (11110000): start of Exclusive message
43H (01000011): Yamaha ID
0nH (0000nnnn): type of message (0 = dump, n = channel)
7EH (01111110): type of format
00H (00000000): data size (most significant byte)
25H (00100101): data size (least significant byte, 25H = 37)
4CH (01001100): "L" (ASCII)
```

```
4DH (01001101): "M" (ASCII)
20H (00100000): " " (ASCII)
20H (00100000): " " (ASCII)
38H (00111000): "8" (ASCII)
39H (00111001): "9" (ASCII)
37H (00110111): "7" (ASCII)
36H (00110110): "6" (ASCII)
53H (01010011): "S" (ASCII for System)
30H (00110000): "0" (ASCII for category 0)
ddH (0ddddddd): data (27 bytes)
...
ccH (0ccccccc): checksum
F7H (11110111): EOX
```

The two size bytes correspond to the 27 data bytes, to which the ten ASCII header bytes should be added.

7 • The System Category 1 data dump (SYS1, for the program-change reassignment table):

```
F0H (11110000): start of Exclusive message
43H (01000011): Yamaha ID
0nH (0000nnnn): type of message (0 = dump, n = channel)
7EH (01111110): type of format
02H (00000010): data size (most significant byte)
0AH (00001010): data size (least significant byte)
4CH (01001100): "L" (ASCII)
4DH (01001101): "M" (ASCII)
20H (00100000): " " (ASCII)
20H (00100000): " " (ASCII)
38H (00111000): "8" (ASCII)
39H (00111001): "9" (ASCII)
37H (00110111): "7" (ASCII)
36H (00110110): "6" (ASCII)
53H (01010011): "S" (ASCII for System)
31H (00110001): "1" (ASCII for category 1)
ddH (0ddddddd): data (256 bytes)
...
ccH (0ccccccc): checksum
F7H (11110111): EOX
```

The two size bytes (in the form 0xxxxxxy 0yyyyyyy), distributed over two eight-bit bytes (in the form 00xxxxxx xyyyyyyy), correspond to the hexadecimal value 010AH, which is the same as 266 in decimal notation (that is, 256 data bytes plus 10 ASCII header bytes).

8 ▪ The System Category 2 data dump (SYS2, for effects):

```
F0H (11110000): start of Exclusive message
43H (01000011): Yamaha ID
0nH (0000nnnn): type of message (0 = dump, n = channel)
7EH (01111110): type of format
00H (00000000): data size (most significant byte)
41H (01000001): data size (least significant byte, 41H = 65)
4CH (01001100): "L" (ASCII)
4DH (01001101): "M" (ASCII)
20H (00100000): " " (ASCII)
20H (00100000): " " (ASCII)
38H (00111000): "8" (ASCII)
39H (00111001): "9" (ASCII)
37H (00110111): "7" (ASCII)
36H (00110110): "6" (ASCII)
53H (01010011): "S" (ASCII for System)
31H (00110010): "2" (ASCII for category 2)
ddH (0ddddddd): data (55 bytes)
...
ccH (0ccccccc): checksum
F7H (11110111): EOX
```

The two size bytes correspond to the 55 data bytes, to which the ten ASCII header bytes should be added.

9 ▪ The dump for the special range for an octave (microtuning 1):

```
F0H (11110000): start of Exclusive message
43H (01000011): Yamaha ID
0nH (0000nnnn): type of message (0 = dump, n = channel)
7EH (01111110): type of format
00H (00000000): data size (most significant byte)
22H (00100010): data size (least significant byte, 22H = 34)
4CH (01001100): "L" (ASCII)
```

```
4DH (01001101): "M" (ASCII)
20H (00100000): " " (ASCII)
20H (00100000): " " (ASCII)
4DH (01001101): "M" (ASCII)
43H (01010011): "C" (ASCII)
52H (01010010): "R" (ASCII)
54H (01010100): "T" (ASCII)
45H (01000101): "E" (ASCII)
30H (00110000): "O" (ASCII)
ddH (0ddddddd): data (24 bytes)
...
ccH (0ccccccc): checksum
F7H (11110111): EOX
```

The two size bytes correspond to the 24 data bytes, to which the ten ASCII header bytes should be added.

10 ▪ Dump for the special range covering the entire range of the keyboard (microtuning 2):

```
F0H (11110000): start of Exclusive message
43H (01000011): Yamaha ID
0nH (0000nnnn): type of message (0 = dump, n = channel)
7EH (01111110): type of format
02H (00000010): data size (most significant byte)
0AH (00001010): data size (least significant byte)
4CH (01001100): "L" (ASCII)
4DH (01001101): "M" (ASCII)
20H (00100000): " " (ASCII)
20H (00100000): " " (ASCII)
4DH (01001101): "M" (ASCII)
43H (01010011): "C" (ASCII)
52H (01010010): "R" (ASCII)
54H (01010100): "T" (ASCII)
45H (01000101): "E" (ASCII)
31H (00110001): "1" (ASCII)
ddH (0ddddddd): data (256 bytes)
...
ccH (0ccccccc): checksum
F7H (11110111): EOX
```

The two size bytes (in the form 0xxxxxxy 0yyyyyyy), distributed over two eight-bit bytes (in the form 00xxxxxx xyyyyyyy), correspond to the hexa-decimal value 010AH, which is the same as 266 in decimal notation (that is, 256 data bytes plus 10 ASCII header bytes).

Dumping All of Memory

In this next example, the different data categories in the memory of the TX81Z are received and transmitted one after another, except for the edit buffers (VCED, ACED, and PCED). The checksum is stored in memory when it's received (that is, it's stored on disk after the data). This way, the checksum doesn't have to be recalculated before the categories are transmitted.

The Receive Segment

```
;
; acquisition of the MIDI channel
;
OpenWindow                            : open the window
CHN = InputChannel 0 0 CHN            : acquisition of the channel
CloseWindow                           : close the window
V00 = $20 | CHN                       : V00 = 2cH, with c = CHN
;
; transmission of dump request messages + reception of data
;
; 1) 32 voices (VMEM)
;
Transmit $F0 $43                      : start of Exclusive + Yamaha ID
TransmitVar V00                       : sub-status request (2) + channel
Transmit $04                          : request 32 voices
Transmit $F7                          : EOX
Receive $F0 $43                       : start of Exclusive + Yamaha ID
Receive $00                           : sub-status dump (0) + channel 1 (0)
Receive $04                           : ID, 32 voices
Receive $20 $00                       : data size (4,096 bytes)
```

```
ReceiveData 4097 $F7 1              : store 4,096 data bytes + checksum
Receive $F7                         : EOX
;
; 2) 24 performances (PMEM)
;
Transmit $F0 $43                    : start of Exclusive + Yamaha ID
TransmitVar V00                     : sub-status request (2) + channel
Transmit $7E                        : format number
Transmit $4C $4D $20 $20            : TX81Z ID
Transmit $38 $39 $37 $36            : ID, continued
Transmit $50 $4D                    : request for 24 performances
Transmit $F7                        : EOX
Receive $F0 $43                     : start of Exclusive + Yamaha ID
Receive $00                         : sub-status dump (0) + channel 1 (0)
Receive $7E                         : format number
Receive $13 $0A                     : data size (2,442)
Receive $4C $4D $20 $20             : TX81Z ID
Receive $38 $39 $37 $36             : continued
Receive $50 $4D                     : ID, 24 performances
ReceiveData 2433 $F7 1              : store 2,432 data bytes + checksum
Receive $F7                         : EOX
;
; 3) system data (SYS0)
;
Transmit $F0 $43                    : start of Exclusive + Yamaha ID
TransmitVar V00                     : sub-status request (2) + channel
Transmit $7E                        : format number
Transmit $4C $4D $20 $20            : TX81Z ID
Transmit $38 $39 $37 $36            : ID, continued
Transmit $53 $30                    : request for system data
Transmit $F7                        : EOX
Receive $F0 $43                     : start of Exclusive + Yamaha ID
Receive $00                         : sub-status dump (0) + channel 1 (0)
Receive $7E                         : format number
Receive $00 $25                     : data size (37)
Receive $4C $4D $20 $20             : TX81Z ID
Receive $38 $39 $37 $36             : continued
Receive $53 $30                     : system data ID
ReceiveData 28 $F7 1                : store 27 data bytes + checksum
Receive $F7                         : EOX
```

```
;
; 4) program change table (SYS1)
;
Transmit $F0 $43                : start of Exclusive + Yamaha ID
TransmitVar V00                 : sub-status request (2) + channel
Transmit $7E                    : format number
Transmit $4C $4D $20 $20        : TX81Z ID
Transmit $38 $39 $37 $36        : ID, continued
Transmit $53 $31                : request for reassignment table
Transmit $F7                    : EOX
Receive $F0 $43                 : start of Exclusive + Yamaha ID
Receive $00                     : sub-status dump (0) + channel 1 (0)
Receive $7E                     : format number
Receive $02 $0A                 : data size (266)
Receive $4C $4D $20 $20         : TX81Z ID
Receive $38 $39 $37 $36         : continued
Receive $53 $31                 : reassignment table ID
ReceiveData 257 $F7 1           : store 256 data bytes + checksum
Receive $F7                     : EOX
;
; 5) effects (SYS2)
;
Transmit $F0 $43                : start of Exclusive + Yamaha ID
TransmitVar V00                 : sub-status request (2) + channel
Transmit $7E                    : format number
Transmit $4C $4D $20 $20        : TX81Z ID
Transmit $38 $39 $37 $36        : ID, continued
Transmit $53 $32                : request for effects data
Transmit $F7                    : EOX
Receive $F0 $43                 : start of Exclusive + Yamaha ID
Receive $00                     : sub-status dump (0) + channel 1 (0)
Receive $7E                     : format number
Receive $00 $41                 : data size (65)
Receive $4C $4D $20 $20         : TX81Z ID
Receive $38 $39 $37 $36         : continued
Receive $53 $32                 : effects ID
ReceiveData 56 $F7 1            : store 55 data bytes + checksum
Receive $F7                     : EOX
;
; 6) microtuning 1
```

```
;
Transmit $F0 $43                  : start of Exclusive + Yamaha ID
TransmitVar V00                   : sub-status request (2) + channel
Transmit $7E                      : format number
Transmit $4C $4D $20 $20          : TX81Z ID
Transmit $4D $43 $52 $54          : ID, continued
Transmit $45 $30                  : request for microtuning
Transmit $F7                      : EOX
Receive $F0 $43                   : start of Exclusive + Yamaha ID
Receive $00                       : sub-status dump (0) + channel 1 (0)
Receive $7E                       : format number
Receive $00 $22                   : data size (34)
Receive $4C $4D $20 $20           : TX81Z ID
Receive $4D $43 $52 $54           : continued
Receive $45 $30                   : microtuning 1 ID
ReceiveData 25 $F7 1              : store 24 data bytes + checksum
Receive $F7                       : EOX
;
; 7) microtuning 2
;
Transmit $F0 $43                  : start of Exclusive + Yamaha ID
TransmitVar V00                   : sub-status request (2) + channel
Transmit $7E                      : format number
Transmit $4C $4D $20 $20          : TX81Z ID
Transmit $4D $43 $52 $54          : ID, continued
Transmit $45 $31                  : request for microtuning (continued)
Transmit $F7                      : EOX
Receive $F0 $43                   : start of Exclusive + Yamaha ID
Receive $00                       : sub-status dump (0) + channel 1 (0)
Receive $7E                       : format number
Receive $02 $0A                   : data size (266)
Receive $4C $4D $20 $20           : TX81Z ID
Receive $4D $43 $52 $54           : continued
Receive $45 $31                   : microtuning 2 ID
ReceiveData 257 $F7 1            : store 256 data bytes + checksum
Receive $F7                       : EOX
```

The Transmit Segment

```
;
; acquisition of the MIDI channel
;
OpenWindow                        : open the window
CHN = InputChannel 0 0 CHN        : acquisition of the channel
CloseWindow                       : close the window
V00 = CHN                         : V00 = 0cH, with c = CHN
;
; transmission of dump messages
;
; 1) 32 voices (VMEM)
;
Transmit $F0 $43                  : start of Exclusive + Yamaha ID
TransmitVar V00                   : sub-status dump (0) + channel
Transmit $04                      : ID, 32 voices
Transmit $20 $00                  : data size (4,096 bytes)
TransmitData 4097 $F7 1           : transmit 4,096 data bytes + checksum
Transmit $F7                      : EOX
Wait 4                            : wait 200 ms
;
; 2) 24 performances (PMEM)
;
Transmit $F0 $43                  : start of Exclusive + Yamaha ID
TransmitVar V00                   : sub-status dump (0) + channel
Transmit $7E                      : format number
Transmit $13 $0A                  : data size (2432)
Transmit $4C $4D $20 $20          : TX81Z ID
Transmit $38 $39 $37 $36          : continued
Transmit $50 $4D                  : ID, 24 performances
TransmitData 2433 $F7 1           : transmit 2432 data bytes + checksum
Transmit $F7                      : EOX
Wait 4                            : wait 200 ms
;
; 3) system data (SYS0)
;
Transmit $F0 $43                  : start of Exclusive + Yamaha ID
TransmitVar V00                   : sub-status dump (0) + channel
Transmit $7E                      : format number
```

```
Transmit $00 $25                    : data size (37)
Transmit $4C $4D $20 $20            : TX81Z ID
Transmit $38 $39 $37 $36            : continued
Transmit $53 $30                    : system ID
TransmitData 28 $F7 1               : transmit 27 data bytes + checksum
Transmit $F7                        : EOX
Wait 4                              : wait 200 ms
;
; 4) program change table (SYS1)
;
Transmit $F0 $43                    : start of Exclusive + Yamaha ID
TransmitVar V00                     : sub-status dump (0) + channel
Transmit $7E                        : format number
Transmit $02 $2A                    : data size (266)
Transmit $4C $4D $20 $20            : TX81Z ID
Transmit $38 $39 $37 $36            : continued
Transmit $53 $31                    : table ID
TransmitData 257 $F7 1              : transmit 256 data bytes + checksum
Transmit $F7                        : EOX
Wait 4                              : wait 200 ms
;
; 5) effects (SYS2)
;
Transmit $F0 $43                    : start of Exclusive + Yamaha ID
TransmitVar V00                     : sub-status dump (0) + channel
Transmit $7E                        : format number
Transmit $00 $41                    : data size (65)
Transmit $4C $4D $20 $20            : TX81Z ID
Transmit $38 $39 $37 $36            : continued
Transmit $53 $32                    : table ID
TransmitData 56 $F7 1               : transmit 55 data bytes + checksum
Transmit $F7                        : EOX
Wait 4                              : wait 200 ms
;
; 6) microtuning 1
;
Transmit $F0 $43                    : start of Exclusive + Yamaha ID
TransmitVar V00                     : sub-status dump (0) + channel
Transmit $7E                        : format number
Transmit $00 $22                    : data size (34)
```

```
Transmit $4C $4D $20 $20        : TX81Z ID
Transmit $4D $43 $52 $54        : continued
Transmit $45 $30                : microtuning ID 1
TransmitData 25 $F7 1           : transmit 24 data bytes + checksum
Transmit $F7                    : EOX
Wait 4                          : wait 200 ms
;
; 7) microtuning 2
;
Transmit $F0 $43                : start of Exclusive + Yamaha ID
TransmitVar V00                 : sub-status dump (0) + channel
Transmit $7E                    : format number
Transmit $02 $2A                : data size (266)
Transmit $4C $4D $20 $20        : TX81Z ID
Transmit $4D $43 $52 $54        : continued
Transmit $45 $31                : microtuning ID 1
TransmitData 257 $F7 1          : transmit 256 data bytes + checksum
Transmit $F7                    : EOX
Wait 4                          : wait 200 ms
```

The Korg M1

All of the Exclusive messages of the Korg M1 have the following format:

General Syntax

```
F0H (11110000): Exclusive message status byte
42H (01000010): manufacturer's ID (42H = Korg)
3cH (0011cccc): 3 = type of message, c = channel
19H (00011001): instrument ID (19H = M1/M1R)
xxH (0xxxxxxx): meaning of the message
...
...
...
F7H (11110111): EOX
```

The memory of the M1 is divided into a certain number of programs (i.e., sounds), combinations (i.e., multitimbral groupings and arrangements of sounds), and sequences. As described in the preceding sections, the following combinations are available, depending on the partitioning method you select:

- 100 programs (numbered from I00 to I99), plus 100 combinations (also numbered from I00 to I99), plus a certain number of sequences, for a total overall maximum capacity of about 4,200 MIDI events, or

- 50 programs (numbered from I00 to I49), plus 50 combinations (also numbered from I00 to I49), plus a certain number of sequences, for a total overall maximum capacity of about 7,700 MIDI events.

You can double the amount of internal memory by adding a board or card. In this case you end up with the same structure described above, except that the "I"s are replaced by "C"s.

Starting from there, the following request messages relating to programs and combinations apply:

1 ▪ Program parameter dump request:

```
F0H 42H 3cH 19H 10H F7H
12H: the code for the program parameter dump request
```

This message invites the M1 to send the contents of the current program located in the edit buffer. (In spite of the eight-voice multitimbrality, this is a single request.) The following message is sent in return:

```
F0H 42H 3cH 19H 40H <data> F7H
```

The fifth byte (40H) corresponds to the transmission of the program buffer, which occupies 164 data bytes.

2 • Combination parameter dump request:

```
F0H 42H 3cH 19H 19H F7H
19H: code for the combination parameter dump request
```

This message invites the M1 to send the contents of the current combination located in the edit buffer. The following message is sent in return:

```
F0H 42H 3cH 19H 49H <data> F7H
```

The fifth byte (49H) corresponds to the transmission of the combination buffer, which occupies 142 data bytes.

3 • All program parameter dump request:

```
F0H 42H 3cH 19H 1CH 0000000c F7H
1CH: the all program parameter dump request
0000000c: the type of memory (c = 0, internal; c = 1,
board)
```

This message invites the M1 to send the contents of all of the programs (either 50 or 100, depending on the partitioning). The following message is sent in return:

```
F0H 42H 3cH 19H 4CH <data> F7H
000000mc: partitioning and type of memory
(m = 0, 100 programs; m = 1, 50 programs; c = 0, internal;
c = 1, board)
```

The fifth byte (4CH) corresponds to the transmission of the entire set of programs, which occupies either 16,343 bytes (for 100 programs) or 8172 bytes (for 50 programs).

4 • All combination parameter dump request:

```
F0H 42H 3cH 19H 1DH 0000000c F7H
1DH: the all combination parameter dump request
```

This message invites the M1 to send the contents of all of the combinations (either 50 or 100). The following message is sent in return:

```
F0H 42H 3cH 19H 4DH <data> F7H
```

The fifth byte (4DH) corresponds to the transmission of the entire set of combinations, which occupies either 14,172 bytes (for 100 combinations) or 7,086 bytes (for 50 combinations).

A Dump of 50 Internal Combinations

The Receive Segment

```
OpenWindow                     : open the window
CHN = InputChannel 0 0 CHN     : acquisition of the MIDI channel in CHN
CloseWindow                    : close the window
Transmit $F0                   : start of Exclusive
Transmit $42                   : Korg identifier
V00 = CHN | $30                : V00 = $3c, with c = CHN
TransmitVar V00                : type of message + channel
Transmit $19                   : M1/M1R ID
Transmit $1D                   : request for dump combinations
Transmit $00                   : internal memory
Transmit $F7                   : end of exclusive
ReceiveAny 6                   : $F0 $42 $3c $19 $4D %000000mc
ReceiveData 7086 $F7 1         : store 7086 data bytes
Receive $F7                    : EOX
```

The Transmit Segment

```
OpenWindow                     : open the window
CHN = InputChannel 0 0 CHN     : acquisition of the MIDI channel in CHN
CloseWindow                    : close the window
Transmit $F0 $42               : start of SysEx + Korg ID
V00 = CHN | $30                : V00 = $3c, with c = CHN
TransmitVar V00                : type of message + channel
Transmit $19                   : M1 ID
Transmit $4D                   : dump combinations
Transmit $02                   : 50 combinations, internal memory
TransmitData 7086 $F7 1        : data
Transmit $F7                   : EOX
```

A Dump of 50 Programs on Cartridge

The Receive Segment

```
OpenWindow                        : open the window
CHN = InputChannel 0 0 CHN        : acquisition of the MIDI channel in CHN
CloseWindow                       : close the window
Transmit $F0                      : start of Exclusive
Transmit $42                      : Korg identifier
V00 = CHN | $30                   : V00 = $3c, with c = CHN
TransmitVar V00                   : type of message + channel
Transmit $19                      : M1/M1R ID
Transmit $1C                      : request for program dump
Transmit $01                      : 50 programs on the memory card
Transmit $F7                      : EOX
ReceiveAny 6                      : $F0 $42 $3c $19 $4C %000000mc
ReceiveData 8172 $F7 1            : store 8172 data bytes
Receive $F7                       : EOX
```

The Transmit Segment

```
OpenWindow                        : open the window
CHN = InputChannel 0 0 CHN        : acquisition of the MIDI channel in CHN
CloseWindow                       : close the window
Transmit $F0 $42                  : start of SysEx + Korg ID
V00 = CHN | $30                   : V00 = $3c, with c = CHN
TransmitVar V00                   : type of message + channel
Transmit $19                      : M1 ID
Transmit $4C                      : dump programs
Transmit $03                      : 50 programs on the memory card
TransmitData 8172 $F7 1           : data
Transmit $F7                      : EOX
```

The Yamaha FM Synthesizers with Six Operators

General Syntax

The six-operator Yamaha DX series synthesizers accept the following dump requests (which were examined briefly in Chapter 10):

```
F0H (11110000): Exclusive message status byte
43H (01000011): manufacturer's ID (43H = Yamaha)
2nH (0010nnnn): type of message (2 = request, n = channel)
ffH (0fffffff): type of request
F7H (11110111): EOX
fffffff = 0: request for voice buffer
fffffff = 1: request for performance buffer
fffffff = 2: request for 64 performances
fffffff = 9: request for 32 voices
```

In return, the following messages are sent:

1 ▪ The voice buffer:

```
F0H (11110000): Exclusive message status byte
43H (01000011): manufacturer's ID (43H = Yamaha)
0nH (0000nnnn): 0 = dump, c = channel
00H (00000000): voice buffer (f = 0)
01H (00000001): data size (most significant byte)
1BH (00011011): data size (least significant byte)
ddH (0ddddddd): data (155 bytes)
...
ccH (0ccccccc): checksum
F7H (11110111): EOX
```

The two size bytes (in the form 0xxxxxxy 0yyyyyyy), distributed over two eight-bit bytes (in the form 00xxxxxx xyyyyyyy), correspond to the hexadecimal value 009BH, which is the same as 155 in decimal notation.

2 ▪ The performance buffer:

```
F0H (11110000): Exclusive message status byte
43H (01000011): manufacturer's ID (43H = Yamaha)
```

```
OnH (0000nnnn): 0 = dump, c = channel
01H (00000001): performance buffer (f = 1)
00H (00000000): data size (most significant byte)
5EH (00011011): data size (least significant byte, 5EH = 94)
ddH (0ddddddd): data (94 bytes)
...
ccH (0ccccccc): checksum
F7H (11110111): EOX
```

3 ▪ Sixty-four performances:

```
FOH (11110000): Exclusive message status byte
43H (01000011): manufacturer's ID (43H = Yamaha)
OnH (0000nnnn): 0 = dump, c = channel
02H (00000010): 64 performances (f = 2)
20H (00100000): data size (most significant byte)
00H (00000000): data size (least significant byte)
ddH (0ddddddd): data (4,096 bytes)
...
ccH (0ccccccc): checksum
F7H (11110111): EOX
```

The two size bytes (in the form 0xxxxxxy 0yyyyyyy), distributed over two eight-bit bytes (in the form 00xxxxxx xyyyyyyy), correspond to the hexadecimal value 1000H, which is the same as 4,096 in decimal notation.

4 ▪ Thirty-two voices:

```
FOH (11110000): Exclusive message status byte
43H (01000011): manufacturer's ID (43H = Yamaha)
OnH (0000nnnn): 0 = dump, c = channel
09H (00001001): 32 voices (f = 9)
20H (00100000): data size (most significant byte)
00H (00000000): data size (least significant byte)
ddH (0ddddddd): data (4,096 bytes)
...
ccH (0ccccccc): checksum
F7H (11110111): EOX
```

The two size bytes (in the form 0xxxxxxy 0yyyyyyy), distributed over two eight-bit bytes (in the form 00xxxxxx xyyyyyyy), correspond to the hexa-decimal value 1000H, which is the same as 4,096 in decimal notation.

A Dump of the 32 Voices of a TX-7

The Receive Segment

```
OpenWindow                      : open the window
CHN = InputChannel 0 0 CHN      : acquisition of the channel
CloseWindow                     : close the window
V00 = $20 | CHN                 : V00 = 2cH, with c = CHN
Transmit $F0 $43                : start of Exclusive + Yamaha ID
TransmitVar V00                 : sub-status request (2) + channel
Transmit $09                    : ID, 32 voices
Transmit $F7                    : EOX
Receive $F0 $43                 : start of Exclusive + Yamaha ID
ReceiveAny 1                    : sub-status dump (0) + channel 1 (0)
Receive $09                     : ID, 32 voices
Receive $20 $00                 : data size (4,096 bytes)
ReceiveData 4097 $F7 1          : reception of 4,096 data bytes + checksum
Receive $F7                     : EOX
```

The Transmit Segment

```
OpenWindow                      : open the window
CHN = InputChannel 0 0 CHN      : acquisition of the channel
CloseWindow                     : close the window
V00 = CHN                       : V00 = 0cH, with c = CHN
Transmit $F0 $43                : start of Exclusive + Yamaha ID
TransmitVar V00                 : sub-status dump (0) + channel
Transmit $09                    : ID, 32 voices
Transmit $20 $00                : data size (4,096 bytes)
TransmitData 4097 $F7 1         : transmission of 4,096 bytes + checksum
Transmit $F7                    : EOX
```

A Dump of the 64 Performances of a TX-7

The Receive Segment

```
OpenWindow                      : open the window
CHN = InputChannel 0 0 CHN      : acquisition of the channel
CloseWindow                     : close the window
VOO = $20 | CHN                 : VOO = 2cH, with c = CHN
Transmit $FO $43                : start of Exclusive + Yamaha ID
TransmitVar VOO                 : sub-status request (2) + channel
Transmit $02                    : ID, 64 performances
Transmit $F7                    : EOX
Receive $FO $43                 : start of Exclusive + Yamaha ID
ReceiveAny 1                    : sub-status dump (0) + channel 1 (0)
Receive $02                     : ID, 64 performances
Receive $20 $00                 : data size (4,096 bytes)
ReceiveData 4097 $F7 1          : reception of 4,096 data bytes + checksum
Receive $F7                     : EOX
```

The Transmit Segment

```
OpenWindow                      : open the window
CHN = InputChannel 0 0 CHN      : acquisition of the channel
CloseWindow                     : close the window
VOO = CHN                       : VOO = 0cH, with c = CHN
Transmit $FO $43                : start of Exclusive + Yamaha ID
TransmitVar VOO                 : sub-status dump (0) + channel
Transmit $02                    : ID, 64 performances
Transmit $20 $00                : data size (4,096 bytes)
TransmitData 4097 $F7 1         : transmission of 4,096 bytes + checksum
Transmit $F7                    : EOX
```

The Roland MT-32

This section will not repeat the syntax of the Dump and Dump Request messages that Roland products use, since those messages were covered in detail in Chapter 10. Instead, this example shows how the dialogue (i.e., handshake) protocol is used. And instead of the channel number, the unit or device number is set to 16 (10H).

As shown in Figure 12.4 below, the patch memories start at 05H 00H 00H (patch memory location 1), and the starting address of the last patch is located at 05H 07H 78H (patch memory location 128). Because a patch consists of 8 bytes, it can logically be inferred that 128 patches are equal to 128 × 8 byte, or 1,024 bytes. In hex, 1024 is 0400H, or, distributed over three 7-bit MIDI bytes, 00H 08H 00H. At a rate of 256 useful data bytes per data-set packet (with the 261 bytes received and stored by the REceiveData instruction corresponding to 3 bytes for the address, 256 bytes for the data, one byte for the checksum, and one byte for the EOX), the total is 4 packets (4 × 256 = 1,024).

A Dump of 128 Patches

The Receive Segment

```
Transmit $F0 $41                      : start of Exclusive + ID Roland
Transmit $10                          : device number (instead of the channel
                                        number)
Transmit $16                          : MT32 identifier
Transmit $41                          : request for data (handshake mode)
Transmit $05 $00 $00                  : address of the first patch
Transmit $00 $08 $00                  : size of the 128 patches
Transmit $73                          : checksum
Transmit $F7                          : EOX
Loop 4                                : start of loop (4 iterations)
   Receive $F0 $41 $10 $16 $42        : message data set
   ReceiveData 261 $F7 1              : 261 bytes (address/data/checksum)
   Transmit $F0 $41 $10 $16 $43 $F7:  ACK message
EndLoop                               : end of loop
Receive $F0 $41 $10 $16 $45 $F7       : end-of-data message
Transmit $F0 $41 $10 $16 $43 $F7      : ACK message
```

- **Parameter base address**

Temporary area (accessible on each basic channel)

Start address	Description	
00 00 00	Patch Temp Area (part)	
01 00 00	Setup Temp Area (rhythm part)	
02 00 00	Timbre Temp Area (part)	*4-1

Whole part (accessible on UNIT #)

Start address	Description	
03 00 00	Patch Temp Area (part 1)	
03 00 10	Patch Temp Area (part 2)	
. . .	. . .	
03 00 60	Patch Temp Area (part 7)	
03 00 70	Patch Temp Area (part 8)	
03 01 00	Patch Temp Area (rhythm part)	
03 01 10	Setup Temp Area (rhythm part)	
04 00 00	Timbre Temp Area (part 1)	*4-1
04 01 76	Timbre Temp Area (part 2)	*4-1
. . .	. . .	
04 0B 44	Timbre Temp Area (part 7)	*4-1
04 0D 3A	Timbre Temp Area (part 8)	*4-1
05 00 00	Patch Memory #1	
05 00 08	Patch Memory #2	
. . .	. . .	
05 07 70	Patch Memory #127	
05 07 78	Patch Memory #128	
08 00 00	Timbre Memory #1	*4-1
08 02 00	Timbre Memory #2	*4-1
. . .	. . .	
08 7C 00	Timbre Memory #63	*4-1
08 7E 00	Timbre Memory #64	*4-1
10 00 00	System area	
20 00 00	Display	*4-2
7F xx xx	All parameter reset	*4-3

FIGURE 12.4: *The memory-address chart for the Roland MT-32*

■ Patch Memory

Offset address		Description	
00 00H	0000 00aa	TIMBRE GROUP (GROUP A, GROUP B, MEMORY, RHYTHM)	0–3
00 01H	00aa aaaa	TIMBRE NUMBER	0–63
00 02H	00aa aaaa	KEY SHIFT	0–48 (-24 to +24)
00 03H	0aaa aaaa	FINE TUNE	0–100 (-50 to +50)
00 04H	000a aaaa	BENDER RANGE	0–24
00 05H	0000 00aa	ASSIGN MODE (POLY 1, POLY2, POLY3, POLY4)	0–3
00 06H	0000 000a	REVERB SWITCH	0–1 (OFF, ON)
00 07H	0xxx xxxx	dummy	
Total size		00 00 08H	

FIGURE 12.4: *The memory-address chart for the Roland MT-32 (continued)*

The Transmit Segment

```
Transmit $FO $41                      : start of Exclusive + ID Roland
Transmit $10                          : device number (instead of the channel
                                        number)
Transmit $16                          : MT32 identifier
Transmit $40                          : want-to-send-data message
Transmit $05 $00 $00                  : address of the first patch
Transmit $00 $08 $00                  : size of the 128 patches
Transmit $73                          : checksum
Transmit $F7                          : EOX
Wait 1                                : 20 ms pause
Loop 4                                : start of loop (4 iterations)
  Transmit $FO $41 $10 $16 $42        : data set message
  TransmitData 261 $F7 1              : 261 bytes (address/data/checksum)
  Wait 1                              : 20 ms pause
EndLoop                               : end of the loop
Transmit $FO $41 $10 $16 $45 $F7      : end-of-data message
```

The Roland D-110

In this example, the protocol is a dialog-type or handshake protocol, and the unit number (instead of the channel number) is set to 16 (10H). Figure 12.5 below shows the memory-address chart for the D-110.

Syntax

The memory addresses for timbres start at 05H 00H 00H (timbre memory location 1), and the starting address of the last timbre is located at 05H 07H 78H (timbre memory location 128). Because a timbre consists of 8 bytes, you can logically infer that 128 patches are equal to 128×8 byte, or 1,024 bytes. In hex, 1,024 is equal to 0400H, or, distributed over three 7-bit MIDI bytes, 00H 08H 00H. At a rate of 256 useful data bytes per data-set packet (with the 261 bytes received and stored by the REceiveData instruction corresponding to 3 bytes for the address, 256 bytes for the data, one byte for the checksum, and one byte for the EOX), the total is 4 packets ($4 \times 256 = 1,024$).

Tone memories start at 08H 00H 00H (tone memory location 1), and the starting address of the last tone is located at 08H 7EH 00H (tone memory location 64). Because a tone consists of 256 bytes (of which 246 are useful; 14 bytes are for the common parameter portion, and each of the four partials takes 58 bytes), it can logically be inferred that the size—64 tones—is equal to 64×256 bytes or 16,384 bytes. In hex, 16,384 is equal to 4000H, or, distributed over three 7-bit MIDI bytes, 01H 00H 00H. Thus, the total is 64 packets ($64 \times 1256 = 16,384$).

The memory in the system area starts at 10H 00H 00H, for a total size of 22 bytes. In hex, 22 is equal to 16H or, distributed over three 7-bit MIDI bytes, 00H 00H 16H. The result here is a single packet consisting of 22 bytes.

■ **Parameter base address**

Temporary area (accessed through each basic channel)

Start address	Description	
02 00 00	Tone Temporary Area (synth part)	*5-1

Whole part (accessible on UNIT #)

Start address	Description	
03 00 00	Timbre Temporary Area (part 1)	*5-2
03 00 10	Timbre Temporary Area (part 2)	
. . .	. . .	
03 00 60	Timbre Temporary Area (part 7)	
03 00 70	Timbre Temporary Area (part 8)	
03 01 00	Timbre Temporary Area (rhythm part)	
03 01 10	Rhythm Setup Temporary Area	*5-3
04 00 00	Tone Temporary Area (part 1)	*5-1
04 01 76	Tone Temporary Area (part 2)	
. . .		
04 0B 44	Tone Temporary Area (part 7)	
04 0D 3A	Tone Temporary Area (part 8)	
05 00 00	Timbre Memory #1	*5-4
05 00 08	Timbre Memory #2	
. . .	. . .	
05 07 70	Timbre Memory #127	
05 07 78	Timbre Memory #128	
06 00 00	Patch Memory #1	*5-5
06 01 00	Patch Memory #2	
. . .	. . .	
06 3E 00	Patch Memory #63	
06 3F 00	Patch Memory #64	
08 00 00	Tone Memory #1	*5-1
08 02 00	Tone Memory #2	
. . .	. . .	
08 7C 00	Tone Memory #63	
08 7E 00	Tone Memory #64	
10 00 00	System Area	*5-6
20 00 00	Display	*5-7
40 00 00	Write Request	*5-8

FIGURE 12.5: *The memory-address chart for the Roland D-110*

Notes...

*5-1   **Tone temporary area / Tone memory**

Offset address	Description	
00 00 00	Common parameter	*5-1-1
00 00 0E	Partial parameter (for Partial #1)	*5-1-2
00 00 48	Partial parameter (for Partial #2)	
00 01 02	Partial parameter (for Partial #3)	
00 01 3C	Partial parameter (for Partial #4)	

*5-1-1   **Common parameter**

Offset address		Description	
00	0aaa aaaa	TONE NAME 1	32–127
...	...	...	(ASCII)
09	0aaa aaaa	TONE NAME 10	
0A	0000 aaaa	Structure of Partial #1 & 2	0–12 (1–13)
0B	0000 aaaa	Structure of Partial #3 & 4	0–12 (1–13)
0C	0000 aaaa	PARTIAL MUTE	0–15 (0000–1111)
0D	0000 000a	ENV MODE	0–1 (normal, no sustain)
	Total size	00 00 0E	

FIGURE 12.5: *The memory-address chart for the Roland D-110 (continued)*

*5-1-2   **Partial parameter**

Offset address			Description	
00 00	0aaa	aaaa	WG PITCH COARSE	0–96 (C1, C#1, –C9)
00 01	0aaa	aaaa	WG PITCH FINE	0–100 (-50 to +50)
00 02	0000	aaaa	WG PITCH KEYFOLLOW	0–16 (-1, -1/2, -1/4, 0, 1/8, 1/4, 3/8, 1/2, 5/8, 3/4, 7/8, 1, 5/4, 3/2, 2, s1, s2)
00 03	0000	000a	WG PITCH BENDER SW	0–1 (OFF, ON)
00 04	0000	000a	WG WAVEFORM/PCM BANK	0–3 (SQU/1, SAW/1, SQU/2, SAW/2)
00 05	0aaa	aaaa	WG PCM WAVE #	0–127 (1–128)
00 06	0aaa	aaaa	WG PULSE WIDTH	0–100
00 07	0000	aaaa	WG PV VELO SENS	0–14 (-7 to +7)
00 08	0000	aaaa	P-ENV DEPTH	0–10
00 09	0aaa	aaaa	P-ENV VELO SENS	0–100
00 0A	0000	0aaa	P-ENV TIME KEYF	0–4
00 0B	0aaa	aaaa	P-ENV TIME 1	0–100
00 0C	0aaa	aaaa	P-ENV TIME 2	0–100
00 0D	0aaa	aaaa	P-ENV TIME 3	0–100
00 0E	0aaa	aaaa	P-ENV TIME 4	0–100
00 0F	0aaa	aaaa	P-ENV LEVEL 0	0–100 (-50 to +50)
00 10	0aaa	aaaa	P-ENV LEVEL 1	0–100 (-50 to +50)
00 11	0aaa	aaaa	P-ENV LEVEL 2	0–100 (-50 to +50)
00 12	0xxx	xxxx	P-ENV SUSTAIN LEVEL	50 (always 0)
00 13	0aaa	aaaa	END LEVEL	0–100 (-50 to +50)
00 14	0aaa	aaaa	P-LFO RATE	0–100
00 15	0aaa	aaaa	P-LFO DEPTH	0–100
00 16	0aaa	aaaa	P-LFO MOD SENS	0–100

FIGURE 12.5: *The memory-address chart for the Roland D-110 (continued)*

00 17	0aaa aaaa	TVF CUTOFF FREQ	0–100	
00 18	000a aaaa	TVF RESONANCE	0–30	
00 19	0000 aaaa	TVF KEYFOLLOW	0–14	
			(-1, -1/2, -1/4, 0, 1/8, 1/4, 3/8, 1/2, 5/8, 3/4, 7/8, 1, 5/4, 3/2, 2)	
00 1A	0aaa aaaa	TVF BIAS POINT/DIR	0–127 (<1A–<7C >1A–>7C)	
00 1B	0000 aaaa	TVF BIAS LEVEL	0–14 (-7 to +7)	
00 1C	0aaa aaaa	TVF ENV DEPTH	0–100	
00 1D	0aaa aaaa	TVF ENV VELO SENS	0–100	
00 1E	0000 0aaa	TVF ENV DEPTH KEYF	0–4	
00 1F	0000 0aaa	TVF ENV TIME KEYF	0–4	
00 20	0aaa aaaa	TVF ENV TIME 1	0–100	
00 21	0aaa aaaa	TVF ENV TIME 2	0–100	
00 22	0aaa aaaa	TVF ENV TIME 3	0–100	
00 23	0aaa aaaa	TVF ENV TIME 4	0–100	
00 24	0aaa aaaa	TVF ENV TIME 5	0–100	
00 25	0aaa aaaa	TVF ENV LEVEL 1	0–100	
00 26	0aaa aaaa	TVF ENV LEVEL 2	0–100	
00 27	0aaa aaaa	TVF ENV LEVEL 3	0–100	
00 28	0aaa aaaa	TVF ENV SUSTAIN LEVEL	0–100	
00 29	0aaa aaaa	TVA LEVEL	0–100	
00 2A	0aaa aaaa	TVA VELO SENS	0–100 (-50 to +50)	
00 2B	0aaa aaaa	TVA BIAS POINT 1	0–127 (<1A–<7C >1A–>7C)	
00 2C	0000 aaaa	TVA BIAS LEVEL 1	0–12 (-12–0)	
00 2D	0aaa aaaa	TVA BIAS POINT 2	0–127 (<1A–<7C >1A–>7C)	
00 2E	0000 aaaa	TVA BIAS LEVEL 2	0–12 (-12–0)	
00 2F	0000 0aaa	TVA ENV TIME KEYF	0–4	
00 30	0000 0aaa	TVA ENV TIME V_FOLLOW	0–4	
00 31	0aaa aaaa	TVA ENV TIME 1	0–100	
00 32	0aaa aaaa	TVA ENV TIME 2	0–100	
00 33	0aaa aaaa	TVA ENV TIME 3	0–100	
00 34	0aaa aaaa	TVA ENV TIME 4	0–100	
00 35	0aaa aaaa	TVA ENV TIME 5	0–100	
00 36	0aaa aaaa	TVA ENV LEVEL 1	0–100	
00 37	0aaa aaaa	TVA ENV LEVEL 2	0–100	
00 38	0aaa aaaa	TVA ENV LEVEL 3	0–100	
00 39	0aaa aaaa	TVA ENV SUSTAIN LEVEL	0–100	
	Total size	00 00 3A		

FIGURE 12.5: *The memory-address chart for the Roland D-110 (continued)*

Example of RQ1 and DT1 application – 1
Assuming that D-110 sets Unit # to 17, obtain Part 2 tone data from the temporary area by sending the following messages: F0 41 10 16 11 04 01 76 00 01 76 0E F7

*5-2   Timbre temporary area

Offset address			Description	
00 00	0000	0aaa	TONE GROUP	0–3 (a, b, i/c, r)
00 01	00aa	aaaa	TONE NUMBER	0–63 (1–64)
00 02	00aa	aaaa	KEY SHIFT	0–48 (-24 to +24)
00 03	0aaa	aaaa	FINE TUNE	0–100 (-50 to +50)
00 04	000a	aaaa	BENDER RANGE	0–24
00 05	0000	00aa	ASSIGN MODE	0–3 (POLY 1, POLY 2, POLY3, POLY 4)
00 06	0000	0aaa	OUTPUT ASSIGN	0–7 (MIX, MIX, MULTI 1, 2, 3, 4, 5, 6)
00 07	0xxx	xxxx	dummy	
00 08	0aaa	aaaa	OUTPUT LEVEL	0–100
00 09	0000	aaaa	PANPOT	0–14 (L–R)
00 0A	0aaa	aaaa	KEY RANGE LOWER	0–127
00 0B	0aaa	aaaa	KEY RANGE UPPER	0–127
00 0C	0xxx	xxxx	dummy	
...	...		...	
00 0F	0xxx	xxxx	dummy	
	Total size	00 00 10		

*5-3   Rhythm part setup area

Offset address	Description	
00 00 00	Rhythm Setup (for Key #24)	*5-3-1
00 00 04	Rhythm Setup (for Key #25)	
00 00 08	Rhythm Setup (for Key #26)	
00 00 0C	Rhythm Setup (for Key #27)	
00 00 10	Rhythm Setup (for Key #28)	
...	...	
00 02 4C	Rhythm Setup (for Key #107)	
00 02 50	Rhythm Setup (for Key #108)	

FIGURE 12.5: *The memory-address chart for the Roland D-110 (continued)*

. . . .

*5-3-1   Rhythm setup (for each Key #)

Offset address			Description	
00 00	0aaa	aaaa	TONE	0–127 (i01–i64, r01–r64)
00 01	0aaa	aaaa	OUTPUT LEVEL	0–100
00 02	0000	aaaa	PANPOT	0–14 (L–R)
00 03	0000	0aaa	OUTPUT ASSIGN	0–7 (MIX, MIX, MULTI 1, 2, 3, 4, 5, 6)
	Total size	00 00 04		

*5-4   Timbre memory

Offset address			Description	
00 00	0000	0aaa	TONE GROUP	0–3 (a, b, i/c, r)
00 01	00aa	aaaa	TONE NUMBER	0–63
00 02	00aa	aaaa	KEY SHIFT	0–48 (-24 to +24)
00 03	0aaa	aaaa	FINE TUNE	0–100 (-50 to +50)
00 04	000a	aaaa	BENDER RANGE	0–24
00 05	0000	00aa	ASSIGN MODE	0–3 (POLY 1, POLY 2, POLY3, POLY 4)
00 06	0000	0aaa	OUTPUT ASSIGN	0–7 (MIX, MIX, MULTI 1, 2, 3, 4, 5, 6)
00 07	0xxx	xxxx	dummy	
	Total size	00 00 08		

FIGURE 12.5: *The memory-address chart for the Roland D-110 (continued)*

*5-5   **Patch memory**

The total number of Partial reserves for 9 parts must be 32 or less.
All Partial reserves must be sent as a package of 9 parts.

Offset address		Description	
00	0aaa aaaa	PATCH NAME 1	32–127
...	...	...	(ASCII)
09	0aaa aaaa	PATCH NAME 1	
00 0A	0000 00aa	REVERB MODE	0–8 (Room 1/2, Hall 1/2, Plate, Tap delay 1/2/3, OFF)
00 0B	0000 0aaa	REVERB TIME	0–7 (1–8)
00 0C	0000 0aaa	REVERB LEVEL	0–7
00 0D	00aa aaaa	PARTIAL RESERVE (Part 1)	0–32
00 0E	00aa aaaa	PARTIAL RESERVE (Part 2)	0–32
00 0F	00aa aaaa	PARTIAL RESERVE (Part 3)	0–32
00 10	00aa aaaa	PARTIAL RESERVE (Part 4)	0–32
00 11	00aa aaaa	PARTIAL RESERVE (Part 5)	0–32
00 12	00aa aaaa	PARTIAL RESERVE (Part 6)	0–32
00 13	00aa aaaa	PARTIAL RESERVE (Part 7)	0–32
00 14	00aa aaaa	PARTIAL RESERVE (Part 8)	0–32
00 15	00aa aaaa	PARTIAL RESERVE (Part R)	0–32
00 16	000a aaaa	MIDI CHANNEL (Part 1)	0–16 (1–16, OFF)
00 17	000a aaaa	MIDI CHANNEL (Part 2)	0–16
00 18	000a aaaa	MIDI CHANNEL (Part 3)	0–16
00 19	000a aaaa	MIDI CHANNEL (Part 4)	0–16
00 1A	000a aaaa	MIDI CHANNEL (Part 5)	0–16
00 1B	000a aaaa	MIDI CHANNEL (Part 6)	0–16
00 1C	000a aaaa	MIDI CHANNEL (Part 7)	0–16
00 1D	000a aaaa	MIDI CHANNEL (Part 8)	0–16
00 1E	000a aaaa	MIDI CHANNEL (Part R)	0–16
00 1F		PATCH PARAMETERS (Part 1)	*5-5-1
00 2B		PATCH PARAMETERS (Part 2)	
00 37		PATCH PARAMETERS (Part 3)	
00 43		PATCH PARAMETERS (Part 4)	
00 4F		PATCH PARAMETERS (Part 5)	
00 5B		PATCH PARAMETERS (Part 6)	
00 67		PATCH PARAMETERS (Part 7)	
00 73		PATCH PARAMETERS (Part 8)	
00 7F	0aaa aaaa	OUTPUT LEVEL (Rhythm Part)	0–100
	Total size	00 01 00	

FIGURE 12.5: *The memory-address chart for the Roland D-110 (continued)*

*5-5-1   Patch parameters (for each part)

Offset address			Description	
00 00	0000 00aa		TONE GROUP	0–4
00 01	00aa aaaa		TONE NUMBER	0–63
00 02	00aa aaaa		KEY SHIFT	0–48 (-24 to +24)
00 03	0aaa aaaa		FINE TUNE	0–100 (-50 to +50)
00 04	000a aaaa		BENDER RANGE	0–24
00 05	0000 00aa		ASSIGN MODE	0–3
00 06	0aaa aaaa		OUTPUT ASSIGN	0–7
00 07	0xxx xxxx		dummy	
00 08	0aaa aaaa		OUTPUT LEVEL	0–100
00 09	0000 aaaa		PANPOT	0–14 (L–R)
00 0A	0aaa aaaa		KEY RANGE LOWER	0–127
00 0B	0aaa aaaa		KEY RANGE UPPER	0–127
	Total size		00 00 0C	

*5-6   System area

The total number of Partial reserves for 9 parts must be 32 or less.
All Partial reserves must be sent as a package of 9 parts.

Offset address			Description	
00 00	0aaa aaaa		MASTER TUNE	0–127 (432.1 Hz–457.6 Hz)
00 01	0000 00aa		REVERB MODE	0–8 (Room 1/2, Hall 1/2, Plate, Tap delay 1/2/3, OFF)
00 02	0000 0aaa		REVERB TIME	0–7 (1–8)
00 03	0000 0aaa		REVERB LEVEL	0–7
00 04	00aa aaaa		PARTIAL RESERVE (Part 1)	0–32
00 05	00aa aaaa		PARTIAL RESERVE (Part 2)	0–32
00 06	00aa aaaa		PARTIAL RESERVE (Part 3)	0–32
00 07	00aa aaaa		PARTIAL RESERVE (Part 4)	0–32
00 08	00aa aaaa		PARTIAL RESERVE (Part 5)	0–32
00 09	00aa aaaa		PARTIAL RESERVE (Part 6)	0–32
00 0A	00aa aaaa		PARTIAL RESERVE (Part 7)	0–32
00 0B	00aa aaaa		PARTIAL RESERVE (Part 8)	0–32
00 0C	00aa aaaa		PARTIAL RESERVE (Part R)	0–32

FIGURE 12.5: *The memory-address chart for the Roland D-110 (continued)*

00 0D	000a aaaa	MIDI CHANNEL (Part 1)	0–16 (1–16, OFF)
00 0E	000a aaaa	MIDI CHANNEL (Part 2)	0–16 (1–16, OFF)
00 0F	000a aaaa	MIDI CHANNEL (Part 3)	0–16 (1–16, OFF)
00 10	000a aaaa	MIDI CHANNEL (Part 4)	0–16 (1–16, OFF)
00 11	000a aaaa	MIDI CHANNEL (Part 5)	0–16 (1–16, OFF)
00 12	000a aaaa	MIDI CHANNEL (Part 6)	0–16 (1–16, OFF)
00 13	000a aaaa	MIDI CHANNEL (Part 7)	0–16 (1–16, OFF)
00 14	000a aaaa	MIDI CHANNEL (Part 8)	0–16 (1–16, OFF)
00 15	000a aaaa	MIDI CHANNEL (Part R)	0–16 (1–16, OFF)
00 16	0xxx xxxx	dummy	
00 17	0aaa aaaa	PATCH NAME 1	32–127
...	...	...	(ASCII)
00 20	0aaa aaaa	PATCH NAME 10	
	Total size	00	

Example of RQ1 and DT1 application – 2

Assuming that D-110 sets Unit # to 17, set Partial reserve to each part as follows by sending the byte string listed below: F0 41 10 16 12 10 00 04 08 0A 00 00 00 00 00 00 08 66 F7

Part 1 8		Parts 3 through 8 0	
Part 2 10		Rhythm part 0	

*5-7   Display

D-110 deciphers incoming data and sends them to the LCD as a string of ASCII code characters (in Play mode).

Fiddling D-110 panel switches or sending Display reset address data to D-110 returns the display to the normal reading.

No display data in this area can be brought to the outside world by the use of RQ1 and RQD.

Offset address		Description	
00 00	0aaa aaaa	DISPLAYED LETTER	32–127
...	...	...	(ASCII)
00 1F	0aaa aaaa	DISPLAYED LETTER	
01 00	0xxx xxxx	DISPLAY RESET	
	Total size	00 00 21	

FIGURE 12.5: *The memory-address chart for the Roland D-110 (continued)*

*5-8   **Write request**

This message simulates write switch on D-110; that is, D-110 writes data of each part in the temporary area into internal memory or memory card. (Memory must be specified by two bytes addresses.) D-110 will inform back of the writing result.

No data in the temporary area can be brought outside world through MIDI exclusive message such as RQ1 and RQD.

Offset address		Description	
00 00	00aa aaaa	Tone Write (Part 1)	0–63 (01–64)
00 01	0000 000a		0, 1
			(Internal, Card)
00 02	00aa aaaa	Tone Write	
00 03	0000 000a	(Part 2)	
...	...	...	
00 0E	00aa aaaa	Tone Write	
00 0F	0000 000a	(Part 8)	
	...		
01 00	0aaa aaaa	Timbre Write (Part 1)	0–127 (A11–B88)
01 01	0000 000a		0, 1
			(Internal, Card)
01 02	0aaa aaaa	Timbre Write	
01 03	0000 000a	(Part 2)	
...	...	...	
01 0E	0aaa aaaa	Timbre Write	
01 0F	0000 000a	(Part 8)	
...	...	...	
02 00	00aa aaaa	Patch Write	0–63 (11–88)
02 01	0000 000a		0, 1
			(Internal, Card)
10 00	0000 00aa	Result	0–3
			0 = Function Completed
			1 = Card Not Ready
			2 = Write Protected
			3 = Incorrect Mode

FIGURE 12.5: *The memory-address chart for the Roland D-110 (continued)*

Patch memories start at 06H 00H 00H (patch memory location 1), and the starting address of the last patch is located at 06H 3FH 00H (patch memory location 64). Because a patch is equal to 128 bytes, it can logically be inferred that the size of 64 patches is equal to 64×128 bytes or 8,192 bytes. In hex, 8192 is equal to 2000H, or, distributed over three 7-bit MIDI bytes, 00H 40H 00H. Thus, the total is 32 packets ($32 \times 256 = 8,192$).

The rhythm setup temporary area starts at 03H 01H 10H, with a size equal to 340 bytes (4 bytes $\times$ 85 notes, whose numbers range from 24 to 108). In hex, 340 is equal to 0154H, or, distributed over three 7-bit MIDI bytes, 00H 02H 54H. Thus, the total is two packets: the first consisting of 256 bytes and the second consisting of 84 bytes.

The Receive Segment

```
;
; 1) 128 timbres
;
Transmit $F0 $41                      : start of Exclusive + ID Roland
Transmit $10                          : device number (instead of the
                                        channel number)
Transmit $16                          : D10 identifier (MT32-compatible)
Transmit $41                          : request for data
Transmit $05 $00 $00                  : address of the first timbre
Transmit $00 $08 $00                  : size of the 128 timbres
Transmit $73                          : checksum
Transmit $F7                          : EOX
Loop 4                                : start of loop (64 iterations)
  Receive $F0 $41 $10 $16 $42         : data set message
  ReceiveData 261 $F7 1               : 261 bytes (address/data/checksum)
  Transmit $F0 $41 $10 $16 $43 $F7:   ACK message
EndLoop                               : end of loop
Receive $F0 $41 $10 $16 $45 $F7       : end of data
Transmit $F0 $41 $10 $16 $43 $F7      : ACK
;
; 2) 64 tones (i1-i64)
;
```

```
Transmit $F0 $41                         : start of Exclusive + ID Roland
Transmit $10                             : device number (instead of the
                                           channel number)

Transmit $16                             : D10 identifier (MT32-compatible)
Transmit $41                             : request for data
Transmit $08 $00 $00                     : address of the first tone
Transmit $01 $00 $00                     : size of the 64 tones
Transmit $77                             : checksum
Transmit $F7                             : EOX
Loop 64                                  : start of loop (64 iterations)
  Receive $F0 $41 $10 $16 $42            : data set message
  ReceiveData 261 $F7 1                  : 261 bytes (address/data/checksum)
    Transmit $F0 $41 $10 $16 $43 $F7: ACK message
EndLoop                                  : end of loop
Receive $F0 $41 $10 $16 $45 $F7          : end-of-data message
Transmit $F0 $41 $10 $16 $43 $F7         : ACK message
;
; 3) System setup
;
Transmit $F0 $41                         : start of Exclusive + ID Roland
Transmit $10                             : device number (instead of the
                                           channel number)

Transmit $16                             : D10 identifier (MT32-compatible)
Transmit $41                             : request for data
Transmit $10 $00 $00                     : address of the system setup
Transmit $00 $00 $16                     : size of the system setup
Transmit $5A                             : checksum
Transmit $F7                             : EOX
Receive $F0 $41 $10 $16 $42              : data set message
ReceiveData 27 $F7 1                     : 27 bytes (address/data/checksum)
Transmit $F0 $41 $10 $16 $43 $F7         : ACK message
Receive $F0 $41 $10 $16 $45 $F7          : end-of-data message
Transmit $F0 $41 $10 $16 $43 $F7         : ACK message
;
; 4) 64 patches
;
Transmit $F0 $41                         : start of Exclusive + ID Roland
Transmit $10                             : device number (instead of the
                                           channel number)

Transmit $16                             : D10 identifier (MT32-compatible)
```

```
Transmit $41                          : request for data
Transmit $06 $00 $00                  : address of the first patch
Transmit $00 $40 $00                  : size of the patches
Transmit $3A                          : checksum
Transmit $F7                          : EOX
Loop 32                               : start of the loop (32 iterations)
  Receive $F0 $41 $10 $16 $42         : data set message
  ReceiveData 261 $F7 1               : 261 bytes (address/data/checksum)
  Transmit $F0 $41 $10 $16 $43 $F7:   ACK message
EndLoop                               : end of the loop
Receive $F0 $41 $10 $16 $45 $F7       : end-of-data message
Transmit $F0 $41 $10 $16 $43 $F7      : ACK message
;
; 5) rhythm setup (temporary area)
;
Transmit $F0 $41                      : start of Exclusive + ID Roland
Transmit $10                          : device number (instead of the
                                        channel number)
Transmit $16                          : D10 identifier (MT32-compatible)
Transmit $41                          : request for data
Transmit $03 $01 $10                  : address of the rhythm setup
Transmit $00 $02 $54                  : size of the rhythm setup
Transmit $16                          : checksum
Transmit $F7                          : EOX
Receive $F0 $41 $10 $16 $42           : data set message
ReceiveData 261 $F7 1                 : 261 bytes (address/data/checksum)
Transmit $F0 $41 $10 $16 $43 $F7      : ACK message
Receive $F0 $41 $10 $16 $42           : data set message
ReceiveData 89 $F7 1                  : 89 bytes (address/data/checksum)
Transmit $F0 $41 $10 $16 $43 $F7      : ACK message
Receive $F0 $41 $10 $16 $45 $F7       : end-of-data message
Transmit $F0 $41 $10 $16 $43 $F7      : ACK message
```

The Transmit Segment

```
;
; 1) 128 timbres
;
Transmit $F0 $41                      : start of Exclusive + ID Roland
Transmit $10                          : device number (instead of the
                                        channel number)
```

```
Transmit $16                    : MT32 identifier
Transmit $40                    : want-to-send-data message
Transmit $05 $00 $00            : address of the first timbre
Transmit $00 $08 $00            : size of the 128 timbres
Transmit $73                    : checksum
Transmit $F7                    : EOX
Wait 1                          : 20 ms pause
Loop 4                          : start of the loop (4 iterations)
  Transmit $F0 $41 $10 $16 $42  : data set message
  TransmitData 261 $F7 1        : 261 bytes (address/data/checksum)
  Wait 1                        : 20 ms pause
EndLoop                         : end of the loop
Transmit $F0 $41 $10 $16 $45 $F7 : end-of-data message
Wait 1                          : 20 ms pause
;
; 2) 64 tones
;
Transmit $F0 $41                : start of Exclusive + ID Roland
Transmit $10                    : device number (instead of the
                                  channel number)
Transmit $16                    : MT32 identifier
Transmit $40                    : want-to-send-data message
Transmit $08 $00 $00            : address of the first tone
Transmit $01 $00 $00            : size of the 64 tones
Transmit $77                    : checksum
Transmit $F7                    : EOX
Wait 1                          : 20 ms pause
Loop 64                         : start of the loop (64 iterations)
  Transmit $F0 $41 $10 $16 $42  : data set message
  TransmitData 261 $F7 1        : 261 bytes (address/data/checksum)
  Wait 1                        : 20 ms pause
EndLoop                         : end of the loop
Transmit $F0 $41 $10 $16 $45 $F7 : end-of-data message
Wait 1                          : 20 ms pause
;
; 3) system setup
;
Transmit $F0 $41                : start of Exclusive + ID Roland
Transmit $10                    : device number (instead of the
                                  channel number)
```

598

```
Transmit $16                          : MT32 identifier
Transmit $40                          : want-to-send-data message
Transmit $10 $00 $00                  : system setup address
Transmit $00 $00 $16                  : system setup size
Transmit $5A                          : checksum
Transmit $F7                          : EOX
Wait 1                                : 20 ms pause
Transmit $F0 $41 $10 $16 $42          : data set message
TransmitData 27 $F7 1                 : 27 bytes (address/data/checksum)
Wait 1
Transmit $F0 $41 $10 $16 $45 $F7      : end-of-data message
Wait 1                                : 20 ms pause
;
; 4) patches
;
Transmit $F0 $41                      : start of Exclusive + ID Roland
Transmit $10                          : device number (instead of the
                                        channel number)
Transmit $16                          : MT32 identifier
Transmit $40                          : want-to-send-data message
Transmit $06 $00 $00                  : address of the first patch
Transmit $00 $40 $00                  : size of the 128 patches
Transmit $3A                          : checksum
Transmit $F7                          : EOX
Wait 1                                : 20 ms pause
Loop 32                               : start of the loop (32 iterations)
   Transmit $F0 $41 $10 $16 $42       : data set message
   TransmitData 261 $F7 1             : 261 bytes (address/data/checksum)
   Wait 1                             : 20 ms pause
EndLoop                               : end of the loop
Transmit $F0 $41 $10 $16 $45 $F7      : end-of-data message
Wait 1                                : 20 ms pause
;
; 5) rhythm setup
;
Transmit $F0 $41                      : start of Exclusive + ID Roland
Transmit $10                          : device number (instead of the
                                        channel number)
Transmit $16                          : MT32 identifier
Transmit $40                          : want-to-send-data message
```

```
Transmit $03 $01 $10            : address of the rhythm setup
Transmit $00 $02 $54            : size of the rhythm setup
Transmit $16                    : checksum
Transmit $F7                    : EOX
Wait 1                          : 20 ms pause
Transmit $F0 $41 $10 $16 $42    : data set message
TransmitData 261 $F7 1          : 261 bytes (address/data/checksum)
Wait 1                          : 20 ms pause
Transmit $F0 $41 $10 $16 $42    : data set message
TransmitData 89 $F7 1           : 89 bytes (address/data/checksum)
Wait 1                          : 20 ms pause
Transmit $F0 $41 $10 $16 $45 $F7  : end-of-data message
Wait 1                          : 20 ms pause
```

The Yamaha SPX-90 Multieffect

Syntax

1 ▪ A program dump request:

```
F0H (11110000): Exclusive message status byte
43H (01000011): Yamaha ID
2nH (0010nnnn): type of message (2 = request, n = channel)
7EH (01111110): type of format
4CH (01001100): "L" (ASCII)
4DH (01001101): "M" (ASCII)
20H (00100000): " " (ASCII)
20H (00100000): " " (ASCII)
38H (00111000): "8" (ASCII)
33H (00110011): "3" (ASCII)
33H (00110011): "3" (ASCII)
32H (00110010): "2" (ASCII)
4DH (01001101): "M" (ASCII for Memory)
ppH (0ppppppp): program number
F7H (11110111): EOX
```

2 ▪ A program dump:

```
F0H (11110000): Exclusive message status byte
43H (01000011): Yamaha ID
0nH (0000nnnn): type of message (0 = dump, n = channel)
7EH (01111110): type of format
00H (00000000): data size (most significant byte)
58H (01011000): data size (least significant byte, 58H = 88)
4CH (01001100): "L" (ASCII)
4DH (01001101): "M" (ASCII)
20H (00100000): " " (ASCII)
20H (00100000): " " (ASCII)
38H (00111000): "8" (ASCII)
33H (00110011): "3" (ASCII)
33H (00110011): "3" (ASCII)
32H (00110010): "2" (ASCII)
4DH (01001101): "M" (ASCII for Memory)
ppH (0ppppppp): program number
ddH (0ddddddd): data (78 bytes)
...
ccH (0ccccccc): checksum
F7H (11110111): EOX
```

A Program Dump

In this example, the channel is fixed and equal to 1.

The Receive Segment

```
OpenWindow                      : open the window
PAT = InputPatch 0 0 PAT        : acquisition of the program number
CloseWindow                     : close the window
Transmit $F0                    : start of Exclusive
Transmit $43                    : Yamaha identifier
Transmit $20                    : sub-status request (2) + channel (1)
Transmit $7E                    : format number
Transmit $4C $4D $20 $20        : identification SPX90
Transmit $38 $33 $33 $32        : continued
Transmit $4D                    : program request
```

```
TransmitVar PAT                        : program number
Transmit $F7                           : EOX
Receive $F0 $43                        : start of Exclusive + Yamaha ID
Receive $00                            : sub-status dump (0) + channel (1)
Receive $7E                            : format number
Receive $00 $58                        : data size (88)
Receive $4C $4D $20 $20                : SPX90 ID
Receive $38 $33 $32 $32                : continued
Receive $4D                            : ID ("M" for memory)
ReceiveData 80 $F7 1                   : 80 bytes (PAT/data/checksum)
Receive $F7                            : EOX
```

The Transmit Segment

```
Le segment transmit
Transmit $F0                           : start of Exclusive
Transmit $43                           : Yamaha identifier
Transmit $00                           : sub-status dump (0) + channel (1)
Transmit $7E                           : format number
Transmit $00 $58                       : data size (88)
Transmit $4C $4D $20 $20               : identification SPX90
Transmit $38 $33 $33 $32               : continued
Transmit $4D                           : program request
TransmitData 80 $F7 1                  : 80 bytes (PAT/data/checksum)
Transmit $F7                           : EOX
```

The Casio CZ-1

The instruments in the Casio CZ series work via handshakes, using an exclusive procedure that doesn't conform to the MIDI standard. This noncompliance is the result of the fact that certain messages don't have the Start of Exclusive (F0H) status and/or the End of Exclusive (EOX) (F7H) status.

The General Syntax of the CZ Family

Here are the details of the dialog protocol that are common to the entire set of Casio synthesizers when a timbre transfer takes place:

The Send Request

```
F0H (11110000): Exclusive message status byte
44H (01000100): Casio ID
00H (00000000): sub ID 1 (the CZ family)
00H (00000000): sub ID 2 (the CZ family)
7nH (0111nnnn): n = channel
ccH (0ccccccc): operation code (send request)
ttH (0ttttttt): timbre number
```

When it receives one of these messages, the CZ sends back the timbre whose number is equal to the value of ttH.

The Receive Request

```
F0H (11110000): Exclusive message status byte
44H (01000100): Casio ID
00H (00000000): sub ID 1 (the CZ family)
00H (00000000): sub ID 2 (the CZ family)
7nH (0111nnnn): n = channel
ccH (0ccccccc): operation code (receive request)
ttH (0ttttttt): timbre number
```

This message is used to send a timbre to the CZ, which stores it directly in the memory area whose number is equal to the value of ttH.

Data Block/Block End

```
ddH (0ddddddd): timbre data (X bytes)
7nH (0111nnnn): n = channel
32H (00110010): operation code (block end)
```

The transmission of large amounts of data is broken down into packets. This message indicates the end of a packet while also specifying that the packet in question isn't the last packet.

Last Data Block/EOX

```
ddH (0ddddddd): timbre data (X bytes)
F7H (11110111): EOX
```

This message identifies the last packet in the transmission.

Ready 1

```
F0H (11110000): Exclusive message status byte
44H (01000100): Casio ID
00H (00000000): sub ID 1 (the CZ family)
00H (00000000): sub ID 2 (the CZ family)
7nH (0111nnnn): n = channel
30H (00110000): operation code (ready 1)
```

This message is sent from the Casio to the outside world following a dump request (i.e., a send request), to indicate that the Casio is ready to send the packets.

Continue

```
7nH (0111nnnn): n = channel
31H (00110001): operation code (continue)
```

This message is sent to the Casio after the Casio has sent a block of data, in order to tell the Casio to send the next block of data.

Ready 2

```
7nH (0111nnnn): n = channel
30H (00110000): operation code (ready 2)
```

This message is sent from the Casio to the outside world after the Casio has received a block of data, in order to acknowledge that the Casio has received the block in question.

The transactions for these seven take place as shown below:

1 ▪ Transfer of data from the Casio to the dump software:

DUMP SOFTWARE		CASIO
Send request	→	
	←	Ready 1
Continue	→	
	←	Data block/block end
Continue	→	
	←	Data block/block end
...		
...		
	←	Last data block/EOX
EOX	→	

2 ▪ Transfer of data from the dump software to the Casio:

DUMP SOFTWARE		CASIO
Receive request	→	
	←	Ready 1
Data block/block end	→	
	←	Ready 2
Data block/block end	→	
	←	Ready 3
...		
...		
Last data block/EOX	→	
	→	EOX

The Send Request 1 (10H) and Receive Request 1 (20H) messages deal with only one timbre at a time. These messages are compatible with the entire CZ synthesizer family (i.e., the CZ-1, the CZ-101, the CZ-300, the CZ-500, the CZ-230, and the CZ-6500). On the other hand, the Send Request 2 (11H) and Receive Request 2 (21H) messages exclusively address the CZ-1. The CA family is one of the rare ones within

which sounds are transferred not by banks but one by one, without going through an edit buffer. Because the data in a CZ-1 timbre doesn't need to be broken into two or more blocks, the Data Block/EOX message isn't used.

The Receive Segment

```
OpenWindow                      : open the window
CHN = InputChannel 0 0 CHN      : acquisition of the channel
CloseWindow                     : close the window
VO1 = $00                       : initialize the timbre number
VOO = CHN | $70                 : VOO = 7cH, with c = channel
Loop 64                         : start of loop (64 iterations)
   Transmit $FO                 : start of Exclusive
   Transmit $44                 : Casio identifier
   Transmit $00 $00             : sub ID 1, sub ID 2
   TransmitVar VOO              : 7cH, with c = channel
   Transmit $11                 : send request 2
   TransmitVar VO1              : timbre number
   VO1 = VO1 + 1                : increment the timbre number
   ReceiveAny 6                 : ready 1 ($FO $44 $00 $00 $7c $30)
   TransmitVar VOO              : sub-status (7) + channel (CHN)
   Transmit $31                 : continue
   ReceiveData 288 $F7 1        : store data (data block)
   Receive $F7                  : EOX
   Transmit $F7                 : EOX
EndLoop                         : end of loop
```

The Transmit Segment

```
OpenWindow                      : open the window
CHN = InputChannel 0 0 CHN      : acquisition of the channel
CloseWindow                     : close the window
VO1 = $00                       : initialize the timbre number
VOO = CHN | $70                 : VOO = 7cH, with c = channel
Loop 64                         : start of the loop (64 iterations)
   Transmit $FO                 : start of Exclusive
   Transmit $44                 : Casio identifier
   Transmit $00 $00             : sub ID 1, sub ID 2
   TransmitVar VOO              : 7cH, with c = channel
```

```
   Transmit $21                        : receive request 2
   TransmitVar VO1                     : timbre number
   VO1 = VO1 + 1                       : increment the timbre number
   TransmitData 288 $F7 1              : data block
   Transmit $F7                        : EOX
   Wait 1                              : 20 ms pause
EndLoop                                : end of the loop
```

I   II   III   IV   V   VI   VII   VIII   IX   X   XI   XII

CHAPTER

13

XIV XV XVI A B C D E F G H I

An Editor/Librarian

for the

Yamaha TX81Z

THIS CHAPTER DESCRIBES the implementation of an editor/librarian dedicated to the 32 voices, stored in RAM, of the Yamaha TX81Z expander. The corresponding segments (which were created by Philip Galanter and Tom Bajoras for Hybrid Arts) are intended above all to show the main programming principles for Exclusive messages, so as to illustrate the internal operation of management programs and editing programs for MIDI memories.

The Storage and Transmission Formats for a 32-Voice Dump

The dump in question (known as VMEM, for "Voice MEMory" or "voice bulk data format") consists of 32 voices of 128 bytes, for a total of 4,096 bytes. The transmission format is identical to the format for memory storage in the TX81Z (which only uses bits 0 to 6 of the bytes). As a result, the Transmit segment and the Receive segment don't have to do any conversions.

At the format level, each of the voices appears as shown in Table 13.1 below:

TABLE 13.1: *Format of the Voices in a 32-Voice Dump for the Yamaha TX81Z*

ADDRESS	BITS	MEANING
0	000xxxxx	(xxxxx = AR) operator 4
1	000xxxxx	(xxxxx = D1R) operator 4
2	000xxxxx	(xxxxx = D2R) operator 4
3	0000xxxx	(xxxx = RR) operator 4
4	0000xxxx	(xxxx = D1L) operator 4
5	0xxxxxxx	(xxxxxx = LS) operator 4
6	0xyyyzzz	(x = AME, y = EBS, z = KVS) operator 4
7	0xxxxxxx	(xxxxxx = OUT) operator 4
8	00xxxxxx	(xxxxxx = CRS) operator 4
9	000xxyyy	(xx = RS, yyy = DET) operator 4
10 to 19	the same as operator 3	
20 to 29	the same as operator 2	
30 to 39	the same as operator 1	
40	0xyyyzzz	(x = Sync, y = Feedback, z = ALG)
41	0xxxxxxx	(xxxxxx = Speed)
42	0xxxxxxx	(xxxxxx = Delay)
43	0xxxxxxx	(xxxxxx = P Mod Depth)
44	0xxxxxxx	(xxxxxx = A Mod Depth)
45	0xxxyyzz	(xxx = P Mod Sens, yy = AMS, zz = Wave)
46	00xxxxxx	(xxxxxx = Middle C)

TABLE 13.1: *Format of the Voices in a 32-Voice Dump for the Yamaha TX81Z (continued)*

ADDRESS	BITS	MEANING
47	000xxxxx	(xxxxx = P Bend Range)
48	000abcde	(a = Chorus, b = Poly Mode, c = Sustain, d = Portamento, e = Full Time Porta)
49	0xxxxxxx	(xxxxxxx = Porta Time)
50	0xxxxxxx	(xxxxxxx = FC Volume)
51	0xxxxxxx	(xxxxxxx = MW Pitch)
52	0xxxxxxx	(xxxxxxx = MW Amplitude)
53	0xxxxxxx	(xxxxxxx = BC Pitch)
54	0xxxxxxx	(xxxxxxx = BC Amplitude)
55	0xxxxxxx	(xxxxxxx = BC Pitch Bias)
56	0xxxxxxx	(xxxxxxx = BC EG Bias)
57	0xxxxxxx	(xxxxxxx = Voice char 1)
58	0xxxxxxx	(xxxxxxx = Voice char 2)
59	0xxxxxxx	(xxxxxxx = Voice char 3)
60	0xxxxxxx	(xxxxxxx = Voice char 4)
61	0xxxxxxx	(xxxxxxx = Voice char 5)
62	0xxxxxxx	(xxxxxxx = Voice char 6)
63	0xxxxxxx	(xxxxxxx = Voice char 7)
64	0xxxxxxx	(xxxxxxx = Voice char 8)
65	0xxxxxxx	(xxxxxxx = Voice char 9)
66	0xxxxxxx	(xxxxxxx = Voice char 10)
67 to 72	not used	(reserved for the DX21)
73	00xxyzzz	(xx = EG Shift, y = FIX, zzz = Fix Range) op 4

TABLE 13.1: *Format of the Voices in a 32-Voice Dump for the Yamaha TX81Z (continued)*

ADDRESS	BITS	MEANING
74	0xxxyyyy	(xxx = OSW, yyyy = FIN) op 4
75 to 76	the same as op 3	
77 to 78	the same as op 2	
79 to 80	the same as op 1	
81	00000xxx	(xxx = Reverb Rate)
82	0xxxxxxx	(xxxxxxx = FC Pitch)
83	0xxxxxxx	(xxxxxxx = FC Amplitude)
84 to 127	—not used—	

The Receive and Transmit Segments

Purely as a matter of convenience, the channel that is acquired in the Receive segment is stored on disk after the data. This lets the Transmit segment display the value of the channel by default in the window dedicated to the acquisition of the channel number for the sending of the dump. Likewise for the sake of convenience, when the Transmit or Receive segments are activated several times in a row (such as to transmit or receive successively several 32-voice banks), only the first activation is accompanied by a request from the user for acquisition of a channel number.

The Transmit segment has to calculate the checksum during transmission. Although this calculation, which is included here as an example, has no practical value in the context of a simple dump utility, it is essential to the proper functioning of an editor or of a librarian, since any change in one or more pieces of data (such as the editing of a parameter or a patch name) automatically causes a change in the checksum.

The Receive Segment

```
;
; acquisition of the MIDI channel by the user
;
V22 = 1
GoSub L90
V21 = $20 | CHN              : V21 = 2cH, with c = CHN
;
; data reception address (V00) and channel storage address (V01)
;
V00 = 0
V01 = 4,096
;
PTR = V00                    : data buffer address (for data reception)
Transmit $F0 $43             : start of Exclusive, and Yamaha ID
TransmitVar V21              : sub-status request (2) + channel
Transmit $04                 : request for 32 voices
Transmit $F7                 : EOX
Receive $F0 $43              : start of Exclusive, and Yamaha ID
ReceiveAny 1                 : sub-status dump (0) + channel
Receive $04                  : ID for 32 voices
Receive $20 $00              : data size (4,096 bytes)
ReceiveData 4,096 $F7 1      : store 4,096 data bytes + checksum
Receive Any 1                : checksum
Receive $F7                  : EOX
;
; storage of the channel number at the end of the dump
;
PTR = PTR + 2                : PTR = 4,098 (number of bytes to save)
V11 = V01
PokeData V11 CHN B           : storage of channel
V11 = V11 + 1
PokeData V11 V22 B           : storage of channel flag
Stop
```

```
;
; subroutine for MIDI channel acquisition
;
L90
V99 = CHN LT 16          : the first time, CHN is set to FFFFFFFFH
If V99 GoTo L91          : the channel is acquired only on the first pass
;
OpenWindow               : open a window for channel acquisition
CHN = InputChannel 0 0 0 : channel verification (CHN < 17) is
V22 = 0                  : done automatically by GenEdit
CloseWindow              : close the window
;
L91
Return
```

The Transmit Segment

```
;
; address for data reception (V00) and channel storage (V01)
;
V00 = 0
V01 = 4,096
;
; channel acquisition, and transfer to variable V21
;
GoSub L90
V21 = CHN
;
; transmission of the dump, and on-the-fly checksum calculation (V25)
;
V10 = V00
V25 = 0
Transmit $F0 $43         : start of Exclusive, and Yamaha ID
TransmitVar 21           : sub-status dump (0) + channel
Transmit $04             : ID for 32 voices
Transmit $20 $00         : data size (4,096 bytes)
Loop 4,096
  V30 = PeekData V10 B
  TransmitVar V30        : transmission of data bytes, one by one
  V25 = V30 + V25        : addition of data bytes for the checksum
```

```
   V10 = V10 + 1
EndLoop
V25 = NEG V25
V25 = V25 & %01111111
TransmitVar V25          : checksum
Transmit $F7             : EOX
Stop
;
; channel-acquisition subroutine
;
L90
V99 = CHN LT 16          : la first time, CHN is set to FFFFFFFFH
If V99 GoTo L91          : the channel is acquired only on the first pass
;
; recovery of the channel stored with the dump file
; for display by default
;
CHN = PeekData V01 B
OpenWindow
CHN = InputChannel 0 0 CHN
CloseWindow
;
L91
Return
```

The Initialize Segment

The Initialize segment indicates how big the edit buffer is (upon receiving a voice from the data buffer, either by a simple copy made by means of the Get Patch segment, or by conversion into EBDT format by means of the Make Edit segment), tells it the number and type of voice numbering (32, and from I01 to I32), and also tells it the position and length of the name within a voice (as transferred into the edit buffer by the Get Patch segment).

```
EBL = 128                : the number of bytes in the edit buffer
NMO = 57                 : the position of the name of a voice within the
```

```
                         : buffer
NML = 10                 : the length of the name
FormatBank 'I' 32 1      : the number of sounds (32, from I01 to I32)
```

The Get Patch and Put Patch Segments

Based on this information, the names of the 32 voices in the bank are displayed onscreen in the window that was selected upon reception, as shown in Figure 13.1 below, by means of successive copyings of these voices from the data buffer into the edit buffer (using the Get Patch segment). The Put Patch segment functions in conjunction with the Get

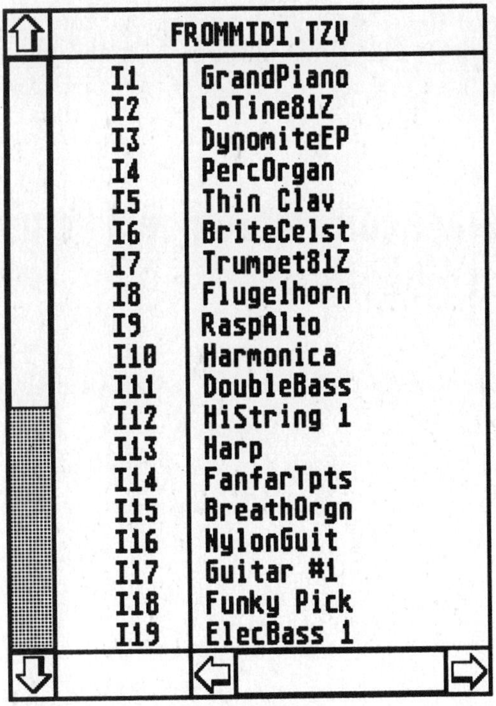

```
        FROMMIDI.TZV
   I1   GrandPiano
   I2   LoTine81Z
   I3   DynomiteEP
   I4   PercOrgan
   I5   Thin Clav
   I6   BriteCelst
   I7   Trumpet81Z
   I8   Flugelhorn
   I9   RaspAlto
   I10  Harmonica
   I11  DoubleBass
   I12  HiString 1
   I13  Harp
   I14  FanfarTpts
   I15  BreathOrgn
   I16  NylonGuit
   I17  Guitar #1
   I18  Funky Pick
   I19  ElecBass 1
```

FIGURE 13.1: *The 32-voice bank in the Yamaha TX81Z*

Patch segment when copies are manipulated. Because the names of the voices in the TX81Z are coded in ASCII, no translation is necessary.

The Get Patch Segment

```
;
V30 = PAT * 128            : PAT corresponds to the voice number, V30, at
                             the address of the voice in the data buffer
CopyDtoE V30 0 128 B       : copy a voice from the data buffer to the edit
                             buffer
```

The Put Patch Segment

```
;
V30 = PAT * 128            : PAT corresponds to the voice number, V30,
                             at the address of the voice in the data buffer
CopyEtoD 0 V30 128 B       : copy a voice from the edit buffer to the data
                             buffer
```

The Storage and Transmission Formats for the Edit Buffer

By examining the syntax of the Exclusive messages of the TX81Z, you can see that the format for the storage of any of the 32 voices in a TX81Z bank (i.e., the VMEM dump) is different from the format in which the voice is stored in the edit buffer. For reasons having to do with compatibility with other four-operator synthesizers made by Yamaha, this edit buffer is divided into two sections: VCED for Voice EDit parameters, and ACED for voiCe EDit Additional parameters, as indicated in Table 13.2 and Table 13.3 below.

TABLE 13.2: *The Structure of VCED Data (93 Bytes)*

ADDRESS	PARAMETER	ABBREVIATION	VALUE
0	Attack Rate (op 4)	AR	0 to 31
1	Decay 1 Rate (op 4)	D1R	0 to 31
2	Decay 2 Rate (op 4)	D2R	0 to 31
3	Release Rate (op 4)	RR	0 to 15
4	Decay 1 Level (op 4)	D1L	0 to 15
5	Level Scaling (op 4)	LS	0 to 99
6	Rate Scaling (op 4)	RS	0 to 3
7	EG Bias Sensitivity (op 4)	EBS	0 to 7
8	Amplitude Modulation Enable (op 4)	AME	0 to 1
9	Key Velocity Sensitivity (op 4)	KVS	0 to 7
10	Operator Output Level (op 4)	OUT	0 to 99
11	Frequency (op 4)	CRS	0 to 63
12	Detune (op 4)	DET	0 to 6
13 to 25	the same as op 3		
26 to 38	the same as op 2		
39 to 51	the same as op 1		
52	Algorithm	ALG	0 to 7
53	Feedback	Feedback	0 to 7
54	LFO Speed	Speed	0 to 99
55	LFO Delay	Delay	0 to 99
56	Pitch Modulation Depth	P Mod Depth	0 to 99
57	Amplitude Modulation Depth	A Mod Depth	0 to 99

TABLE 13.2: *The Structure of VCED Data (93 Bytes) (continued)*

ADDRESS	PARAMETER	ABBREVIATION	VALUE
58	LFO Sync	Sync	0 to 1
59	LFO Wave	Wave	0 to 3
60	Pitch Modulation Sensitivity	P Mod Sens	0 to 7
61	Amplitude Modulation Sensitivity	AMS	0 to 3
62	Transpose	Middle C =	0 to 48
63	Poly/Mono	Poly Mode	0 to 1
64	Pitch Bend Range	P Bend Range	0 to 12
65	Portamento Mode	Full Time Porta	0 to 1
66	Portamento Time	Porta Time	0 to 99
67	Foot Control Volume	FC Volume	0 to 99
68	Sustain		0 to 1
69	Portamento		0 to 1
70	Chorus		0 to 1
71	Modulation Wheel Pitch	MW Pitch	0 to 99
72	Modulation Wheel Amplitude	MW Amplitude	0 to 99
73	Breath Control Pitch	BC Pitch	0 to 99
74	Breath Control Amplitude	BC Amplitude	0 to 99
75	Breath Control Pitch Bias	BC Pitch Bias	0 to 99
76	Breath Control EG Bias	BC EG Bias	0 to 99
77	Voice Name char 1		32 to 127
78	Voice Name char 2		32 to 127

TABLE 13.2: *The Structure of VCED Data (93 Bytes) (continued)*

ADDRESS	PARAMETER	ABBREVIATION	VALUE
79	Voice Name char 3		32 to 127
80	Voice Name char 4		32 to 127
81	Voice Name char 5		32 to 127
82	Voice Name char 6		32 to 127
83	Voice Name char 7		32 to 127
84	Voice Name char 8		32 to 127
85	Voice Name char 9		32 to 127
86	Voice Name char 10		32 to 127
87 to 92	—not used—		

. . . .

TABLE 13.3: *The Structure of ACED Data (23 Bytes)*

ADDRESS	PARAMETER	ABBREVIATION	VALUE
0	Fixed Frequency (op 4)	FIX	0 to 1
1	Fixed Frequency Range (op 4)	Fix Range	0 to 7
2	Frequency Range Fine (op 4)	FIN	0 to 15
3	Operator Waveform (op 4)	OSW	0 to 7
4	EG Shift (op 4)	SHFT	0 to 3
5 to 9	the same as op 3		
10 to 14	the same as op 2		
15 to 19	the same as op 1		
20	Reverb Rate	Reverb rate	0 to 7
21	Foot Controller Pitch	FC Pitch	0 to 99
22	Foot Controller Amplitude	FC Amplitude	0 to 99

. . . .

The Made Edit and Unmake Edit Segments

While the VMEM format uses certain bytes to code several parameters for a voice, the VCED + ACED format stores only one parameter per byte. What this means is that the VMEM format corresponds exactly to the definition of the EBDT format that's used in the implementation of the editor. As a result, the Make Edit segment does the conversion between the VMEM format for a voice in the data buffer (i.e., 128 bytes) and the VCED + ACED format of the edit buffer (i.e., 116 bytes), while the Unmake Edit segment does the conversion in the opposite direction.

The Make Edit Segment

```
;
V10 = PAT * 128          : pointer to the data buffer (format VMEM)
V09 = 0                  : convert operator 4 from VMEM to VCED
GoSub L10
V09 = 13                 : convert operator 3 from VMEM to VCED
GoSub L10
V09 = 26                 : convert operator 2 from VMEM to VCED
GoSub L10
V09 = 39                 : convert operator 1 from VMEM to VCED
V09 = 39
GoSub L10
;
V09 = 0
; decompress and copy Sync, Feedback, ALG
;
V51 = %01000000
V61 = 6
V71 = 58
V52 = %00111000
V62 = 3
V72 = 53
V53 = %00000111
V63 = 0
V73 = 52
GoSub L40
```

```
;
; copy Speed, Delay, P Mod Depth, A Mod Depth
;
V50 = 4
V70 = 54
GoSub L50
;
; decompress and copy P Mod Sens, AMS, Wave
;
V50 = 3
V51 = %01110000
V61 = 4
V71 = 60
V52 = %00001100
V62 = 2
V72 = 61
V53 = %00000011
V63 = 0
V73 = 59
GoSub L40
;
; copy Transpose
;
V50 = 1
V70 = 62
GoSub L50
;
; copy P Bend Range
;
V50 = 1
V70 = 64
GoSub L50
;
; decompress and copy Chorus, Poly Mode, Sustain, Portamento, Full
;
; Time Porta
;
V50 = 5
V51 = %00010000
V61 = 4
```

```
V71 = 70
V52 = %00001000
V62 = 3
V72 = 63
V53 = %00000100
V63 = 2
V73 = 68
V54 = %00000010
V64 = 1
V74 = 69
V55 = %00000001
V65 = 0
V75 = 65
GoSub L40
;
; copy Porta Time, FC Volume
;
V50 = 2
V70 = 66
GoSub L50
;
; copy MW Pitch, MW Amplitude, BC Pitch, BC Amplitude,
; BC Pitch Bias, BC EG Bias
;
V50 = 22
V70 = 71
GoSub L50
V09 = 93                    : copy operator 4 from VMEM to ACED
GoSub L20
V09 = 98                    : copy operator 3 from VMEM to ACED
GoSub L20
V09 = 103                   : copy operator 2 from VMEM to ACED
GoSub L20
V09 = 108                   : copy operator 1 from VMEM to ACED
GoSub L20
;
V09 = 0
; copy Reverb Rate, FC Pitch, FC Amplitude
;
V50 = 3
```

```
V70 = 113
GoSub L50
;
Stop
;
; subroutine for decompressing and copying the operator from VMEM to VCED
;
L10
;
; decompress and copy AR DR1 DR2 RR D1L LS
;
V50 = 6
V70 = 0
GoSub L50
;
; decompress and copy AME EBS KVS
;
V50 = 3
V51 = %01000000
V61 = 6
V71 = 8
V52 = %00111000
V62 = 3
V72 = 7
V53 = %00000111
V63 = 0
V73 = 9
GoSub L40
;
; copy OUT CRS
;
V50 = 2
V70 = 10
GoSub L50
;
; decompress and copy RS DET
;
V50 = 2
V51 = %00011000
V61 = 3
```

```
V71 = 6
V52 = %00000111
V62 = 0
V72 = 12
GoSub L40
Return
;
; subroutine for decompressing the operator from VMEM to ACED
;
L20
;
; decompress and copy SHFT, Fix, Fix Range
;
V50 = 3
V51 = %00110000
V61 = 4
V71 = 4
V52 = %00001000
V62 = 3
V72 = 0
V53 = %00000111
V63 = 0
V73 = 1
GoSub L40
;
; decompress and copy OSW, FIN
;
V50 = 2
V51 = %01110000
V61 = 4
V71 = 3
V52 = %00001111
V62 = 0
V72 = 2
GoSub L40
Return
;
; decompression subroutine intended to create as many VCED or
; ACED bytes as there are parameters in several bits in a VMEM byte
;
```

```
;         V10 - VMEM pointer (data buffer)
;         V09 - VCED or ACED pointer (edit buffer)
;         V50 - number of parameters in the VMEM byte
; V51 - V58 - mask for each of these parameters
; V61 - V68 - rightward shift for each of these parameters
; V71 - V78 - VCED/ACED storage offset in relation to V09
;
L40
V30 = PeekData V10 B
V10 = V10 + 1
;
; field 1
;
V31 = V30 & V51
V31 = V31 >> V61
V19 = V09 + V71
PokeEdit V19 V31 B
;
; field 2
;
V99 = V50 LT 2
If V99 GoTo L42
V31 = V30 & V52
V31 = V31 >> V62
V19 = V09 + V72
PokeEdit V19 V31 B
;
; field 3
;
V99 = V50 LT 3
If V99 GoTo L42
V31 = V30 & V53
V31 = V31 >> V63
V19 = V09 + V73
PokeEdit V19 V31 B
;
; field 4
;
V99 = V50 LT 4
If V99 GoTo L42
```

```
V31 = V30 & V54
V31 = V31 >> V64
V19 = V09 + V74
PokeEdit V19 V31 B
;
; field 5
;
V99 = V50 LT 5
If V99 GoTo L42
V31 = V30 & V55
V31 = V31 >> V65
V19 = V09 + V75
PokeEdit V19 V31 B
;
; field 6
;
V99 = V50 LT 6
If V99 GoTo L42
V31 = V30 & V56
V31 = V31 >> V66
V19 = V09 + V76
PokeEdit V19 V31 B
;
; field 7
;
V99 = V50 LT 7
If V99 GoTo L42
V31 = V30 & V57
V31 = V31 >> V67
V19 = V09 + V77
PokeEdit V19 V31 B
;
; field 8
;
V99 = V50 LT 8
If V99 GoTo L42
V31 = V30 & V58
V31 = V31 >> V68
V19 = V09 + V78
PokeEdit V19 V31 B
```

```
;
L42
Return
;
; subroutine to copy a certain number of VMEM into VCED or
; ACED format
;
; V10 - VMEM pointer (data buffer)
; V09 - VCED/ACED pointer (edit buffer)
; V50 - number of bytes to shift
; V70 - copy offset in relation to V09
;
L50
V19 = V09 + V70
CopyDtoE V10 V19 V50 B
V10 = V10 + V50
Return
```

The Unmake Edit Segment

```
;
V10 = PAT * 128          : pointer to the data buffer (VMEM format)
V09 = 0                  : convert operator 4 from VCED to VMEM
GoSub L10
V09 = 13                 : convert operator 3 from VCED to VMEM
GoSub L10
V09 = 26                 : convert operator 2 from VCED to VMEM
GoSub L10
V09 = 39                 : convert operator 1 from VCED to VMEM
GoSub L10
;
V09 = 0
;
; compress and copy Sync, Feedback, ALG
;
V50 = 3
V61 = 6
V71 = 58
V62 = 3
V72 = 53
V63 = 0
```

```
V73 = 52
GoSub L40
;
; copy Speed, Delay, P Mod Depth, A Mod Depth
;
V50 = 4
V70 = 54
GoSub L50
;
; compress and copy P Mod Sens, AMS, Wave
;
V50 = 3
V61 = 4
V71 = 60
V62 = 2
V72 = 61
V63 = 0
V73 = 59
GoSub L40
;
; copy Transpose
;
V50 = 1
V70 = 62
GoSub L50
; copy P Bend Range
V50 = 1
V70 = 64
GoSub L50
; compress and copy Chorus, Poly Mode, Sustain, Portamento, Full
; Time Porta
;
V50 = 5
V61 = 4
V71 = 70
V62 = 3
V72 = 63
V63 = 2
V73 = 68
V64 = 1
```

```
V74 = 69
V65 = 0
V75 = 65
GoSub L40
;
; copy Porta Time, FC Volume
;
V50 = 2
V70 = 66
GoSub L50
;
; copy MW Pitch, MW Amplitude, BC Pitch, BC Amplitude,
; BC Pitch Bias, BC EG Bias
;
V50 = 22
V70 = 71
GoSub L50
V09 = 93                    : copy operator 4 from ACED to VMEM
GoSub L20
V09 = 98                    : copy operator 3 from ACED to VMEM
GoSub L20
V09 = 103                   : copy operator 2 from ACED to VMEM
GoSub L20
V09 = 108                   : copy operator 1 from ACED to VMEM
GoSub L20
;
V09 = 0
;
; copy Reverb Rate, FC Pitch, FC Amplitude
;
V50 = 3
V70 = 113
GoSub L50
;
Stop
;
; subroutine to decompress and copy the VCED operator in VMEM
;
L10
;
```

```
; compress and copy AR DR1 DR2 RR D1L LS
;
V50 = 6
V70 = 0
GoSub L50
;
; compress and copy AME EBS KVS
;
V50 = 3
V61 = 6
V71 = 8
V62 = 3
V72 = 7
V63 = 0
V73 = 9
GoSub L40
;
; compress and copy OUT CRS
;
V50 = 2
V70 = 10
GoSub L50
;
; compress and copy RS DET
;
V50 = 2
V61 = 3
V71 = 6
V62 = 0
V72 = 12
GoSub L40
Return
;
; subroutine to decompress the ACED operator in VMEM
;
L20
;
; compress and copy SHFT, Fix, Fix Range
;
V50 = 3
```

```
V61 = 4
V71 = 4
V62 = 3
V72 = 0
V63 = 0
V73 = 1
GoSub L40
;
; decompress and copy OSW, FIN
;
V50 = 2
V61 = 4
V71 = 3
V62 = 0
V72 = 2
GoSub L40
Return
;
; compression subroutine to create a VMEM byte from
; parameters contained in certain bits of VCED or ACED bytes
;
;        V10 - VMEM pointer (data buffer)
;        V09 - VCED or ACED pointer (edit buffer)
;        V50 - number of parameters to store in the VMEM byte
; V61 - V68 - leftward shift for each of these parameters
; V71 - V78 - VCED/ACED parameter offset in relation to V09
;
L40
V31 = %00000000
;
; field 1
;
V19 = V09 + V71
V30 = PeekEdit V19 B
V30 = V30 << V61
V31 = V31 | V30
;
; field 2
;
V99 = V50 LT 2
```

```
If V99 GoTo L42
V19 = V09 + V72
V30 = PeekEdit V19 B
V30 = V30 << V62
V31 = V31 | V30
;
; field 3
;
V99 = V50 LT 3
If V99 GoTo L42
V19 = V09 + V73
V30 = PeekEdit V19 B
V30 = V30 << V63
V31 = V31 | V30
;
; field 4
;
V99 = V50 LT 4
If V99 GoTo L42
V19 = V09 + V74
V30 = PeekEdit V19 B
V30 = V30 << V64
V31 = V31 | V30
;
; field 5
;
V99 = V50 LT 5
If V99 GoTo L42
V19 = V09 + V75
V30 = PeekEdit V19 B
V30 = V30 << V65
V31 = V31 | V30
;
; field 6
;
V99 = V50 LT 6
If V99 GoTo L42
V19 = V09 + V76
V30 = PeekEdit V19 B
V30 = V30 << V66
```

```
V31 = V31 | V30
;
; field 7
;
V99 = V50 LT 7
If V99 GoTo L42
V19 = V09 + V77
V30 = PeekEdit V19 B
V30 = V30 << V67
V31 = V31 | V30
;
; field 8
;
V99 = V50 LT 8
If V99 GoTo L42
V19 = V09 + V78
V30 = PeekEdit V19 B
V30 = V30 << V68
V31 = V31 | V30
L42
PokeData V10 V31 B
V10 = V10 + 1
Return
;
; subroutine to copy a certain number of VCED or ACED
; bytes into VMEM format
;
; V10 - VMEM pointer (data buffer)
; V09 - CED/ACED pointer (edit buffer)
; V50 - number of bytes to shift
; V70 - copy offset in relation to V09
;
L50
V19 = V09 + V70
CopyEtoD V19 V10 V50 B
V10 = V10 + V50
Return
if V32 B
V43 = PeekEdit V33 B
V42 = 31 - V42
```

```
V42 = V42 * V43
V42 = V42 / 31
PokeEdit V31 V42 B
Return
```

Transmitting a Voice to the Yamaha TX81Z

The Send Edit segment simply takes the result of the decompression performed by the Make Edit segment (i.e., from the VMEM format for a single voice in the data buffer to the VCED + ACED format of the edit buffer) and sends it to the edit buffer of the instrument.

The Send Edit Segment

```
;
V09 = 0                     : pointer to the edit buffer
;
GoSub L90                   : acquisition of the MIDI channel
GoSub L40                   : transmit ACED from the edit buffer
GoSub L30                   : transmit VCED from the edit buffer
Stop                        : end of segment
;
L30                         : transmit VCED and calculate the checksum (V25)
V19 = V09 + 0
V25 = 0
Transmit $F0 $43
TransmitVar CHN
Transmit $03 $00 $5D
Loop 93
  V30 = PeekEdit V19 B
  TransmitVar V30
  V25 = V30 + V25
  V19 = V19 + 1
EndLoop
V25 = NEG V25
V25 = V25 & %01111111
TransmitVar V25
Transmit $F7
Return
```

```
;
L40                        : transmit ACED and calculate the checksum (V25)
;                          : initialize to 573 ("LM  8976AE")
V19 = V09 + 93
V25 = 573
Transmit $F0 $43
TransmitVar CHN
Transmit $7E $00 $21 $4C $4D $20 $20 $38 $39 $37 $36 $41 $45
Loop 23
  V30 = PeekEdit V19 B
  TransmitVar V30
  V25 = V30 + V25
  V19 = V19 + 1
EndLoop
V25 = NEG V25
V25 = V25 & %01111111
TransmitVar V25
Transmit $F7
Return
;
L90                        : acquisition of the MIDI channel
V99 = CHN LT 16
If V99 GoTo L91
OpenWindow
CHN = InputChannel 0 0 0
CloseWindow
;
L91
Return
```

The Editor's Objects and EBDT Format

Each object in the editor is characterized by a range of minimum to maximum values and by the address of the corresponding parameter in the edit buffer. This is what lets GenEdit distribute the change when an object is manipulated. The programming of the address in the edit buffer and the programming of the range of values for each object are done by means of the EBDT format, as shown in Table 13.4 below.

TABLE 13.4: *The EBDT Format*

PARAMETER NAME AND ABBREVIATION	NUMBER OF BYTES	ADDRESS OF THE EDIT BUFFER	MINIMUM VALUE	MAXIMUM VALUE
Op 4 Attack Rate AR	1	00000	+00000	+00031
Op 4 Decay 1 Rate D1R	1	00001	+00000	+00031
Op 4 Decay 2 Rate D2R	1	00002	+00000	+00031
Op 4 Release Rate RR	1	00003	+00001	+00015
Op 4 Decay 1 Level D1L	1	00004	+00000	+00015
Op 4 Level Scaling RS	1	00005	+00000	+00099
Op 4 Rate Scaling RS	1	00006	+00000	+00003
Op 4 EG Bias Sensitiv. EBS	1	00007	+00000	+00007
Op 4 Ampli. Mod Enable AME	1	00008	+00000	+00001
Op 4 Key Velocity Sens.KVS	1	00009	+00000	+00007
Op 4 Oper. Output Lvl. OUT	1	00010	+00000	+00099
Op 4 Frequency CRS/F	1	00011	+00000	+00063
Op 4 Detune DET/DBT	1	00012	+00000	+0 to 00006
Op 3 Attack Rate AR	1	00013	+00000	+0 to 00031
Op 3 Decay 1 Rate D1R	1	00014	+00000	+0 to 00031
Op 3 Decay 2 Rate D2R	1	00015	+00000	+0 to 00031
Op 3 Release Rate RR	1	00016	+00001	+00015

• •

TABLE 13.4: *The EBDT Format (continued)*

PARAMETER NAME AND ABBREVIATION	NUMBER OF BYTES	ADDRESS OF THE EDIT BUFFER	MINIMUM VALUE	MAXIMUM VALUE
Op 3 Decay 1 Level D1L	1	00017	+00000	+0 to 00015
Op 3 Level Scaling RS	1	00018	+00000	+0 to 00099
Op 3 Rate Scaling RS	1	00019	+00000	+0 to 00003
Op 3 EG Bias Sensitiv. EBS	1	00020	+00000	+0 to 00007
Op 3 Ampli. Mod Enable AME	1	00021	+00000	+0 to 00001
Op 3 Key Velocity Sens.KVS	1	00022	+00000	+0 to 00007
Op 3 Oper. Output Lvl. OUT	1	00023	+00000	+0 to 00099
Op 3 Frequency CRS/F	1	00024	+00000	+0 to 00063
Op 3 Detune DET/DBT	1	00025	+00000	+0 to 00006
Op 2 Attack Rate AR	1	00026	+00000	+0 to 00031
Op 2 Decay 1 Rate D1R	1	00027	+00000	+0 to 00031
Op 2 Decay 2 Rate D2R	1	00028	+00000	+0 to 00031
Op 2 Release Rate RR	1	00029	+00001	+00015

TABLE 13.4: *The EBDT Format (continued)*

PARAMETER NAME AND ABBREVIATION	NUMBER OF BYTES	ADDRESS OF THE EDIT BUFFER	MINIMUM VALUE	MAXIMUM VALUE
Op 2 Decay 1 Level D1L	1	00030	+00000	+0 to 00015
Op 2 Level Scaling RS	1	00031	+00000	+0 to 00099
Op 2 Rate Scaling RS	1	00032	+00000	+0 to 00003
Op 2 EG Bias Sensitiv. EBS	1	00033	+00000	+0 to 00007
Op 2 Ampli. Mod Enable AME	1	00034	+00000	+0 to 00001
Op 2 Key Velocity Sens.KVS	1	00035	+00000	+0 to 00007
Op 2 Oper. Output Lvl. OUT	1	00036	+00000	+0 to 00099
Op 2 Frequency CRS/F	1	00037	+00000	+0 to 00063
Op 2 Detune DET/DBT	1	00038	+00000	+0 to 00006
Op 1 Attack Rate AR	1	00039	+00000	+0 to 00031
Op 1 Decay 1 Rate D1R	1	00040	+00000	+0 to 00031
Op 1 Decay 2 Rate D2R	1	00041	+00000	+0 to 00031
Op 1 Release Rate RR	1	00042	+00001	+00015

TABLE 13.4: *The EBDT Format (continued)*

PARAMETER NAME AND ABBREVIATION	NUMBER OF BYTES	ADDRESS OF THE EDIT BUFFER	MINIMUM VALUE	MAXIMUM VALUE
Op 1 Decay 1 Level D1L	1	00043	+00000	+0 to 00015
Op 1 Level Scaling RS	1	00044	+00000	+0 to 00099
Op 1 Rate Scaling RS	1	00045	+00000	+0 to 00003
Op 1 EG Bias Sensitiv. EBS	1	00046	+00000	+0 to 00007
Op 1 Ampli. Mod En-able AME	1	00047	+00000	+0 to 00001
Op 1 Key Velocity Sens.KVS	1	00048	+00000	+0 to 00007
Op 1 Oper. Output Lvl. OUT	1	00049	+00000	+0 to 00099
Op 1 Frequency CRS/F	1	00050	+00000	+0 to 00063
Op 1 Detune DET/DBT	1	00051	+00000	+0 to 00006
Algorithm ALG	1	00052	+00000	+0 to 00007
Feedback /FBL	1	00053	+00000	+0 to 00007
LFO Speed /LFS	1	00054	+00000	+0 to 00099
LFO Delay /LFD	1	00055	+00000	+0 to 00099

TABLE 13.4: *The EBDT Format (continued)*

PARAMETER NAME AND ABBREVIATION	NUMBER OF BYTES	ADDRESS OF THE EDIT BUFFER	MINIMUM VALUE	MAXIMUM VALUE
Pitch Modul. Depth /PMD	1	00056	+00000	+0 to 00099
Amplitude. Mod. Depth /AMD	1	00057	+00000	+0 to 00099
LFO Sync /SY	1	00058	+00000	+0 to 00001
LFO Wave /LFW	1	00059	+00000	+0 to 00003
Pitch Mod. Sens. /PMS	1	00060	+00000	+0 to 00007
Ampli. Mod. Sens. AMS/AMS	1	00061	+00000	+0 to 00003
Transpose (Middle C=) /TRPS	1	00062	+00000	+0 to 00048
Poly/Mono Poly Mode /PMO	1	00063	+00000	+0 to 00001
Pitch Bend Range /PBR	1	00064	+00000	+0 to 00012
Portamento Mode /PMO	1	00065	+00000	+0 to 00001
Portamento Time /PORT	1	00066	+00000	+0 to 00099
Foot Control Volume /FC VOL	1	00067	+00000	+0 to 00099
Sustain (not used) /SU	1	00068	+00000	+0 to 00001

TABLE 13.4: *The EBDT Format (continued)*

PARAMETER NAME AND ABBREVIATION	NUMBER OF BYTES	ADDRESS OF THE EDIT BUFFER	MINIMUM VALUE	MAXIMUM VALUE
Portamento (not used) /PO	1	00069	+00000	+0 to 00001
Chorus (not used) /CH	1	00070	+00000	+0 to 00001
Modulation Wheel Pitch	1	00071	+00000	+0 to 00099
Modulation Wheel Amplitude	1	00072	+00000	+0 to 00099
Breath Control Pitch	1	00073	+00000	+0 to 00099
Breath Control Amplitude	1	00074	+00000	+0 to 00099
Breath Control Pitch Bias	1	00075	+00000	+0 to 00099
Breath Control EG Bias	1	00076	+00000	+0 to 00099
Voice Name Char 1	1	00077	+00032	+00127
Voice Name Char 2	1	00078	+00032	+00127
Voice Name Char 3	1	00079	+00032	+00127
Voice Name Char 4	1	00080	+00032	+00127
Voice Name Char 5	1	00081	+00032	+00127
Voice Name Char 6	1	00082	+00032	+00127
Voice Name Char 7	1	00083	+00032	+00127
Voice Name Char 8	1	00084	+00032	+00127
Voice Name Char 9	1	00085	+00032	+00127

TABLE 13.4: *The EBDT Format* (continued)

PARAMETER NAME AND ABBREVIATION	NUMBER OF BYTES	ADDRESS OF THE EDIT BUFFER	MINIMUM VALUE	MAXIMUM VALUE
Voice Name Char 10	1	00086	+00032	+00127
—not used—	1	00087	+00000	+0 to 00127
—not used—	1	00088	+00000	+0 to 00127
—not used—	1	00089	+00000	+0 to 00127
—not used—	1	00090	+00000	+0 to 00127
—not used—	1	00091	+00000	+0 to 00127
—not used—	1	00092	+00000	+0 to 00127
Op 4 Fixed Frequency	1	00093	+00000	+0 to 00001
Op 4 Fixed Fq. Range /FIXRG	1	00094	+00000	+0 to 00007
Op 4 Freq. Range Fine /FINE	1	00095	+00000	+0 to 00015
Op 4 Oper. Wave OSW/OPW	1	00096	+00000	+0 to 00007
Op 4 EG Shift SHFT/EGSFT	1	00097	+00000	+0 to 00003
Op 3 Fixed Frequency	1	00098	+00000	+0 to 00001

TABLE 13.4: *The EBDT Format (continued)*

PARAMETER NAME AND ABBREVIATION	NUMBER OF BYTES	ADDRESS OF THE EDIT BUFFER	MINIMUM VALUE	MAXIMUM VALUE
Op 3 Fixed Fq. Range /FIXRG	1	00099	+00000	+0 to 00007
Op 3 Freq. Range Fine /FINE	1	00100	+00000	+0 to 00015
Op 3 Oper. Wave OSW/OPW	1	00101	+00000	+0 to 00007
Op 3 EG Shift SHFT/EGSFT	1	00102	+00000	+0 to 00003
Op 2 Fixed Frequency	1	00103	+00000	+0 to 00001
Op 2 Fixed Fq. Range /FIXRG	1	00104	+00000	+0 to 00007
Op 2 Freq. Range Fine /FINE	1	00105	+00000	+0 to 00015
Op 2 Oper. Wave OSW/OPW	1	00106	+00000	+0 to 00007
Op 2 EG Shift SHFT/EGSFT	1	00107	+00000	+0 to 00003
Op 1 Fixed Frequency	1	00108	+00000	+0 to 00001
Op 1 Fixed Fq. Range/FIXRG	1	00109	+00000	+0 to 00007
Op 1 Freq. Range Fine /FINE	1	00110	+00000	+0 to 00015
Op 1 Oper. Wave OSW/OPW	1	00111	+00000	+0 to 00007

TABLE 13.4: *The EBDT Format (continued)*

PARAMETER NAME AND ABBREVIATION	NUMBER OF BYTES	ADDRESS OF THE EDIT BUFFER	MINIMUM VALUE	MAXIMUM VALUE
Op 1 EG Shift SHFT/EGSFT	1	00112	+00000	+0 to 00003
Reverb Rate /REV	1	00113	+00000	+0 to 00007
Foot Controller Pitch /FCP	1	00114	+00000	+00099
Foot Controller Ampli./FCA	1	00115	+00000	+0 to 00099

Displayed Values and Real Values

In some instances it's useful if the value of an object onscreen can be different from the actual value of the corresponding parameter in the edit buffer. Assume, for example, that a synthesizer allows an overall detuning of plus or minus 50 hundreds (which are the values displayed on the synth's LCD screen) which are stored in its memory (and therefore in GenEdit's memory) in the form of a byte whose range of values is from 00H to 64H (i.e., from 0 = −50 to 100 = +50). In order for GenEdit to be able to display onscreen the same value that's stored in the synthesizer, each object has to have a programmed range of values (as defined by a minimum and a maximum) that are different from the actual value of the corresponding byte, provided that the displayed range does not exceed the real range (see Figure 13.2 below). Along these same lines, it's also possible to create a text-based correspondence between each displayed value and each real value (such as OFF = a byte set to 0, ON = a byte set to 1, and so on).

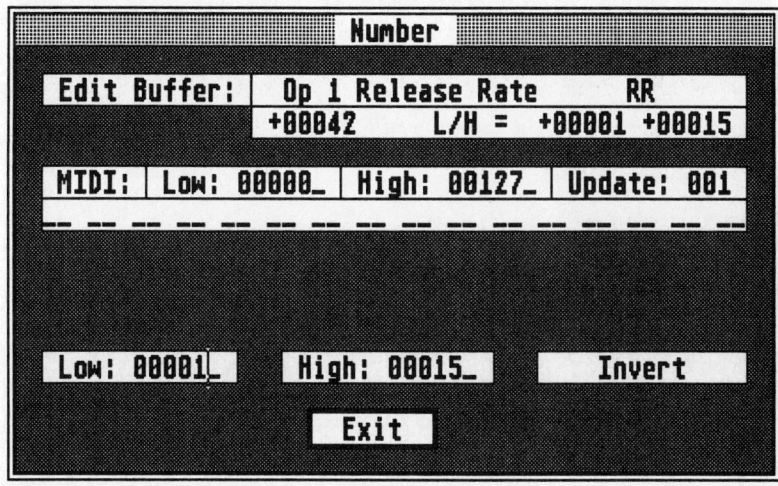

FIGURE 13.2: *An object is characterized by a range of real values and display values (defined by a minimum and a maximum), and also by an address in the edit buffer.*

How Objects Interact

The Validate segment, which is enabled whenever an object is manipulated (with the address of the object in the edit buffer being stored by the LPO variable), performs its operations within the edit buffer. If necessary, this segment performs various verification operations and creates interactions between certain parameters of a sound (assuming, for instance, that a change in parameter X automatically causes a change in parameter Y, or is incompatible with such and such a value of parameter Z, and so on).

The results of the operations performed by the Validate segment are applied to the corresponding objects being displayed onscreen. In the current example, the Validate segment converts the value of parameters for fixed frequencies and ratio-based frequencies into their uncoded equivalents (i.e., hertz and the ratio), in order to display them in the same way as on the LCD screen of the TX81Z. These operations require a few clarifications.

On the TX81Z, the following three parameters determine the fixed frequency of an operator:

- The Fixed Frequency Range (Fix Range, whose values are from 0 to 7);
- The Coarse Frequency Range (CRS, whose values are from 0 to 63); and
- The Fine Frequency Range (FIN, whose values are from 0 to 15).

The LDC screen of the TX81Z doesn't display the values of each of these three parameters. Instead, it displays the corresponding values in hertz (within a range from 8 to 32,640 Hz). In order to simulate this phenomenon on the GenEdit editing screen, it is necessary to create a fourth object, intended not to be manipulated but instead to display the frequency deduced from the value of the three preceding objects (i.e., Fix Range, CRS, and FIN). The calculation of the value in hertz of this fourth object is performed in the following way (with the result being distributed over two bytes):

- Addition of one unit to the CRS (Coarse Frequency Range) parameter
- Whole division of this value by 4
- Multiplication by 16
- Addition of the FIN (Fine Frequency) parameter
- Multiplication by 2 of the power of the Fix Range (Fixed Frequency Range) parameter

The parameter that corresponds to this fourth object takes its place in the edit buffer, following the 116 useful bytes for a voice.

The same principle is applied to ratio-based frequencies, which aren't expressed in hertz but rather in the form XX.YY (within the range from 0.50 to 27.57), as a function of the following parameters:

- The Coarse Frequency Range (CRS, whose values are from 0 to 63); and
- The Fine Frequency Range (FIN, whose values are from 0 to 15)

Because no algorithm can deduce the corresponding ratio, the ratio is looked up in a table (written inside the Common segment), in accordance with the following procedure:

- Multiplication by 16 of the CRS (Coarse Frequency Range) parameter
- Addition of the FIN (Fine Frequency) parameter
- Multiplication by 2
- Looking up at the address of the preceding result in the table in the Common segment

The parameters corresponding to these two objects (i.e., XX and YY) take their place in the edit buffer, after the preceding bytes.

The last operation performed by the Validate segment calculates a graphic envelope slope (which can't be modified with the mouse) in relation to the first level (Decay Level 1) and in relation to the second decay slope (Decay 2 Rate). The whole thing happens this way:

- Subtraction of the value of the Decay 2 Rate from 31
- Multiplication of the result by the value of the Decay 1 Level

- "Whole" division of the result by 21 (with the result being expressed in terms of one byte)

As a result, a total of five new bytes reserved for displays are created for each operator (for a total of 20 new bytes) within the edit buffer. Naturally, the size of the edit buffer increases, from 116 to 136 bytes, as indicated below in Table 13.5:

TABLE 13.5: *How the Creation of New Display Bytes Increases the Size of the Edit Buffer*

ADDRESS	MEANING
0 to 92	93 bytes VCED
93 to 115	23 bytes ACED
116	Fixed Frequency op 4 (in hertz)
118	Fixed Frequency op 3 (in hertz)
120	Fixed Frequency op 2 (in hertz)
122	Fixed Frequency op 1 (in hertz)
124	Ratio-based Frequency op 4 (XX.YY)
126	Ratio-based Frequency op 3 (XX.YY)
128	Ratio-based Frequency op 2 (XX.YY)
130	Ratio-based Frequency op 1 (XX.YY)
132	Envelope segment D2L op 4
133	Envelope segment D2L op 3
134	Envelope segment D2L op 2
135	Envelope segment D2L op 1

It's also handy to be able to modify the EBL variable of the Initialize segment, as shown below:

```
EBL = 136              : number of bytes in the edit buffer
NMO = 57               : position of the name of the sound in the buffer
NML = 10               : the length of the name
FormatBank 'I' 32 1    : displaying 32 sounds (of the type I01 to I32)
```

The following lines should be added to the end of the EBDT:

```
"Op 4 FF macro (in hertz)"    2    00116    +00000    +32767
"Op 3 FF macro (in hertz)"    2    00118    +00000    +32767
"Op 2 FF macro (in hertz)"    2    00120    +00000    +32767
"Op 1 FF macro (in hertz)"    2    00122    +00000    +32767
"Op 4 RTO macro (msb)"        1    00124    +00000    +00100
"Op 3 RTO macro (msb)"        1    00125    +00000    +00100
"Op 2 RTO macro (msb)"        1    00126    +00000    +00100
"Op 1 RTO macro (msb)"        1    00127    +00000    +00100
"Op 4 RTO macro (lsb)"        1    00128    +00000    +00100
"Op 3 RTO macro (lsb)"        1    00129    +00000    +00100
"Op 2 RTO macro (lsb)"        1    00130    +00000    +00100
"Op 1 RTO macro (lsb)"        1    00131    +00000    +00100
"Op 4 D2L"                    1    00132    +00000    +00015
"Op 3 D2L"                    1    00133    +00000    +00015
"Op 2 D2L"                    1    00134    +00000    +00015
"Op 1 D2L"                    1    00135    +00000    +00015
```

The Validate Segment

```
;
GoSub L60              : build fixed-frequency macros
GoSub L70              : build ratio-based frequency macros
GoSub L80              : build D2L macros
Stop
;
; subroutine for fixed-frequency macros
;
L60
V30 = 94               : edit-buffer pointer, ACED Fix Range (op 4)
V31 = 11               : edit-buffer pointer, VCED CRS (op 4)
V32 = 95               : edit-buffer pointer, VCED (FIN)
```

```
GoSub L66
PokeEdit 58 V00 W          : write 16 bits at address 106 (58×2)
V30 = 104                  : the same as operator 3
V31 = 37
V32 = 105
GoSub L66
PokeEdit 59 V00 W
V30 = 99                   : the same as operator 2
V31 = 24
V32 = 100
GoSub L66
PokeEdit 60 V00 W
V30 = 109                  : the same as operator 3
V31 = 50
V32 = 110
GoSub L66
PokeEdit 61 V00 W
Return
;
; subroutine to calculate the fixed frequency (uncoded) over
; 16 bits in V00 = 2**FR * (8*max(1,2*(FC/4)+FRF))
;
L66
V00 = PeekEdit V30 B
V01 = PeekEdit V31 B
V02 = PeekEdit V32 B
V01 = V01 / 4
V01 = V01 * 2
If V01 GoTo L67
V01 = 1
L67
V01 = 8 * V01
V01 = V01 + V02
GoSub L68
V00 = V00 * V01
Return
L68
If V00 GoTo L69
V00 = 1
Return
```

```
L69
V99 = V00
V00 = 1
Loop V99
  V00 = 2 * V00
EndLoop
Return
;
; subroutine for ratio-based frequency macros
;
L70
V30 = 94
V31 = 11
V32 = 95
V33 = 93
GoSub L77
PokeEdit 124 V00 B
PokeEdit 128 V01 B
V30 = 104
V31 = 37
V32 = 105
V33 = 103
GoSub L77
PokeEdit 125 V00 B
PokeEdit 129 V01 B
V30 = 99
V31 = 24
V32 = 100
V33 = 98
GoSub L77
PokeEdit 126 V00 B
PokeEdit 130 V01 B
V30 = 109
V31 = 50
V32 = 110
V33 = 108
GoSub L77
PokeEdit 127 V00 B
PokeEdit 131 V01 B
Return
```

```
;
; subroutine to calculate the ratio-based frequency (uncoded) over
; 16 bits in V00 (8 bits) and V01 (8 bits), on the basis of the
; common segment table
;
L77
V00 = 100
V01 = 100
V33 = PeekEdit V33 B
If V33 GoTo L78
V31 = PeekEdit V31 B
V32 = PeekEdit V32 B
V99 = 16 * V31
V99 = V99 + V32
V98 = V99 * 2
V00 = PeekTable 1 V98
V98 = V98 + 1
V01 = PeekTable 1 V98
L78
Return
;
; subroutine to generate D2L
;
L80
V31 = 148
V32 = 2
V33 = 4
GoSub L81
V31 = 149
V32 = 28
V33 = 30
GoSub L81
V31 = 150
V32 = 15
V33 = 17
GoSub L81
V31 = 151
V32 = 41
V33 = 43
GoSub L81
```

```
Return
;
L81
V42 = PeekEdit V32 B
V43 = PeekEdit V33 B
V42 = 31 - V42
V42 = V42 * V43
V42 = V42 / 31
PokeEdit V31 V42 B
Return
```

The Common Segment

Generally speaking, the Common segment is reserved for the writing of tables that are accessible from any other segment. In this example the Common segment corresponds to the conversion table for the frequencies used by the Validate segment.

```
; frequency table
;
BuildTable 1 00 50 00 56 00 62 00 68 00 75 00 81 00 87 00 93
BuildTable 1 01 00 01 06 01 12 01 18 01 25 01 31 01 37 01 43
BuildTable 1 00 71 00 79 00 88 00 96 01 05 01 14 01 23 01 32
BuildTable 1 01 41 01 49 01 58 01 67 01 76 01 85 01 93 02 02
BuildTable 1 00 78 00 88 00 98 01 07 01 17 01 27 01 37 01 47
BuildTable 1 01 57 01 66 01 76 01 86 01 96 02 06 02 15 02 25
BuildTable 1 00 87 00 97 01 08 01 18 01 29 01 40 01 51 01 62
BuildTable 1 01 73 01 83 01 94 02 05 02 16 02 27 02 37 02 48
BuildTable 1 01 00 01 06 01 12 01 18 01 25 01 31 01 37 01 43
BuildTable 1 01 50 01 56 01 62 01 68 01 75 01 81 01 87 01 93
BuildTable 1 01 41 01 49 01 58 01 67 01 76 01 85 01 93 02 02
BuildTable 1 02 11 02 20 02 29 02 37 02 46 02 55 02 64 02 73
BuildTable 1 01 57 01 66 01 76 01 86 01 96 02 06 02 15 02 25
BuildTable 1 02 35 02 45 02 55 02 64 02 74 02 84 02 94 03 04
BuildTable 1 01 73 01 83 01 94 02 05 02 16 02 27 02 37 02 48
BuildTable 1 02 59 02 70 02 81 02 91 03 02 03 13 03 24 03 35
BuildTable 1 02 00 02 06 02 12 02 18 02 25 02 31 02 37 02 43
BuildTable 1 02 50 02 56 02 62 02 68 02 75 02 81 02 87 02 93
BuildTable 1 02 82 02 90 02 99 03 08 03 17 03 26 03 34 03 43
```

```
BuildTable 1 03 52 03 61 03 70 03 78 03 87 03 96 04 05 04 14
BuildTable 1 03 00 03 06 03 12 03 18 03 25 03 31 03 37 03 43
BuildTable 1 03 50 03 56 03 62 03 68 03 75 03 81 03 87 03 93
BuildTable 1 03 14 03 23 03 33 03 43 03 53 03 63 03 72 03 82
BuildTable 1 03 92 04 02 04 12 04 21 04 31 04 41 04 51 04 61
BuildTable 1 03 46 03 56 03 67 03 78 03 89 04 00 04 10 04 21
BuildTable 1 04 32 04 43 04 54 04 64 04 75 04 86 04 97 05 08
BuildTable 1 04 00 04 06 04 12 04 18 04 25 04 31 04 37 04 43
BuildTable 1 04 50 04 56 04 62 04 68 04 75 04 81 04 87 04 93
BuildTable 1 04 24 04 31 04 40 04 49 04 58 04 67 04 75 04 84
BuildTable 1 04 93 05 02 05 11 05 19 05 28 05 37 05 46 05 55
BuildTable 1 04 71 04 80 04 90 05 00 05 10 05 20 05 29 05 39
BuildTable 1 05 49 05 59 05 69 05 78 05 88 05 98 06 08 06 18
BuildTable 1 05 00 05 06 05 12 05 18 05 25 05 31 05 37 05 43
BuildTable 1 05 50 05 56 05 62 05 68 05 75 05 81 05 87 05 93
BuildTable 1 05 19 05 29 05 40 05 51 05 62 05 73 05 83 05 94
BuildTable 1 06 05 06 16 06 27 06 37 06 48 06 59 06 70 06 81
BuildTable 1 05 65 05 72 05 81 05 90 05 99 06 08 06 16 06 25
BuildTable 1 06 34 06 43 06 52 06 60 06 69 06 78 06 87 06 96
BuildTable 1 06 00 06 06 06 12 06 18 06 25 06 31 06 37 06 43
BuildTable 1 06 50 06 56 06 62 06 68 06 75 06 81 06 87 06 93
BuildTable 1 06 28 06 37 06 47 06 57 06 67 06 77 06 86 06 96
BuildTable 1 07 06 07 16 07 26 07 35 07 45 07 55 07 65 07 75
BuildTable 1 06 92 07 02 07 13 07 24 07 35 07 46 07 56 07 67
BuildTable 1 07 78 07 89 08 00 08 10 08 21 08 32 08 43 08 54
BuildTable 1 07 00 07 06 07 12 07 18 07 25 07 31 07 37 07 43
BuildTable 1 07 50 07 56 07 62 07 68 07 75 07 81 07 87 07 93
BuildTable 1 07 07 07 13 07 22 07 31 07 40 07 49 07 57 07 66
BuildTable 1 07 75 07 84 07 93 08 01 08 10 08 19 08 28 08 37
BuildTable 1 07 85 07 94 08 04 08 14 08 24 08 34 08 43 08 53
BuildTable 1 08 63 08 73 08 83 08 92 09 02 09 12 09 22 09 32
BuildTable 1 08 00 08 06 08 12 08 18 08 25 08 31 08 37 08 43
BuildTable 1 08 50 08 56 08 62 08 68 08 75 08 81 08 87 08 93
BuildTable 1 08 48 08 54 08 63 08 72 08 81 08 90 08 98 09 07
BuildTable 1 09 16 09 25 09 34 09 42 09 51 09 60 09 69 09 78
BuildTable 1 08 65 08 75 08 86 08 97 09 08 09 19 09 29 09 40
BuildTable 1 09 51 09 62 09 73 09 83 09 94 10 05 10 16 10 27
BuildTable 1 09 00 09 06 09 12 09 18 09 25 09 31 09 37 09 43
BuildTable 1 09 50 09 56 09 62 09 68 09 75 09 81 09 87 09 93
BuildTable 1 09 42 09 51 09 61 09 71 09 81 09 91 10 00 10 10
```

```
BuildTable 1 10 20 10 30 10 40 10 49 10 59 10 69 10 79 10 89
BuildTable 1 09 89 09 95 10 04 10 13 10 22 10 31 10 39 10 48
BuildTable 1 10 57 10 66 10 75 10 83 10 92 11 01 11 10 11 19
BuildTable 1 10 00 10 06 10 12 10 18 10 25 10 31 10 37 10 43
BuildTable 1 10 50 10 56 10 62 10 68 10 75 10 81 10 87 10 93
BuildTable 1 10 38 10 48 10 59 10 70 10 81 10 92 11 02 11 13
BuildTable 1 11 24 11 35 11 46 11 56 11 67 11 78 11 89 12 00
BuildTable 1 10 99 11 08 11 18 11 28 11 38 11 48 11 57 11 67
BuildTable 1 11 77 11 87 11 97 12 06 12 16 12 26 12 36 12 46
BuildTable 1 11 00 11 06 11 12 11 18 11 25 11 31 11 37 11 43
BuildTable 1 11 50 11 56 11 62 11 68 11 75 11 81 11 87 11 93
BuildTable 1 11 30 11 36 11 45 11 54 11 63 11 72 11 80 11 89
BuildTable 1 11 98 12 07 12 16 12 24 12 33 12 42 12 51 12 60
BuildTable 1 12 00 12 06 12 12 12 18 12 25 12 31 12 37 12 43
BuildTable 1 12 50 12 56 12 62 12 68 12 75 12 81 12 87 12 93
BuildTable 1 12 11 12 21 12 32 12 43 12 54 12 65 12 75 12 86
BuildTable 1 12 97 13 08 13 19 13 29 13 40 13 51 13 62 13 73
BuildTable 1 12 56 12 65 12 75 12 85 12 95 13 05 13 14 13 24
BuildTable 1 13 34 13 44 13 54 13 63 13 73 13 83 13 93 14 03
BuildTable 1 12 72 12 77 12 86 12 95 13 04 13 13 13 21 13 30
BuildTable 1 13 39 13 48 13 57 13 65 13 74 13 83 13 92 14 01
BuildTable 1 13 00 13 06 13 12 13 18 13 25 13 31 13 37 13 43
BuildTable 1 13 50 13 56 13 62 13 68 13 75 13 81 13 87 13 93
BuildTable 1 13 84 13 94 14 05 14 16 14 27 14 38 14 48 14 59
BuildTable 1 14 70 14 81 14 92 15 02 15 13 15 24 15 35 15 46
BuildTable 1 14 00 14 06 14 12 14 18 14 25 14 31 14 37 14 43
BuildTable 1 14 50 15 56 14 62 14 68 14 75 14 81 14 87 14 93
BuildTable 1 14 10 14 18 14 27 14 36 14 45 14 54 14 62 14 71
BuildTable 1 14 80 14 89 14 98 15 06 15 15 15 24 15 33 15 42
BuildTable 1 14 13 14 22 14 32 14 42 14 52 14 62 14 71 14 81
BuildTable 1 14 91 15 01 15 11 15 20 15 30 15 40 15 50 15 60
BuildTable 1 15 00 15 06 15 12 12 18 15 25 15 31 15 37 15 43
BuildTable 1 15 50 15 56 15 62 15 68 15 75 15 81 15 87 15 93
BuildTable 1 15 55 15 59 15 68 15 77 15 86 15 95 16 03 16 12
BuildTable 1 16 21 16 30 16 39 16 47 16 56 16 65 16 74 16 83
BuildTable 1 15 57 15 67 15 78 15 89 16 00 16 11 16 21 16 32
BuildTable 1 16 43 16 54 16 65 16 75 16 86 16 97 17 08 17 19
BuildTable 1 15 70 15 79 15 89 15 99 16 09 16 19 16 28 16 38
BuildTable 1 16 48 16 58 16 68 16 77 16 87 16 97 17 07 17 17
BuildTable 1 16 96 17 00 17 09 17 18 17 27 17 36 17 44 17 53
```

```
BuildTable 1 17 62 17 71 17 80 17 88 17 97 18 06 18 15 18 24
BuildTable 1 17 27 17 36 17 46 17 56 17 66 17 76 17 85 17 95
BuildTable 1 18 05 18 15 18 25 18 34 18 44 18 54 18 64 18 74
BuildTable 1 17 30 17 40 17 51 17 62 17 73 17 84 17 94 18 05
BuildTable 1 18 16 18 27 18 38 18 48 18 59 18 70 18 81 18 92
BuildTable 1 18 37 18 41 18 50 18 59 18 68 18 77 18 85 18 94
BuildTable 1 19 03 19 12 19 21 19 29 19 38 19 47 19 56 19 65
BuildTable 1 18 84 18 93 19 03 19 13 19 23 19 33 19 42 19 52
BuildTable 1 19 62 19 72 19 82 19 91 20 01 20 11 20 21 20 31
BuildTable 1 19 03 19 13 19 24 19 35 19 46 19 57 19 67 19 78
BuildTable 1 19 89 20 00 20 11 20 21 20 32 20 43 20 54 20 65
BuildTable 1 19 78 19 82 19 91 20 00 20 09 20 18 20 26 20 35
BuildTable 1 20 44 20 53 20 62 20 70 20 79 20 88 20 97 21 06
BuildTable 1 20 41 20 50 20 60 20 70 20 80 20 90 20 99 21 09
BuildTable 1 21 19 21 29 21 39 21 48 21 58 21 68 21 78 21 88
BuildTable 1 20 76 20 86 20 97 21 08 21 19 21 30 21 40 21 51
BuildTable 1 21 62 21 73 21 84 21 94 22 05 22 16 22 27 22 38
BuildTable 1 21 20 21 23 21 32 21 41 21 50 21 59 21 67 21 76
BuildTable 1 21 85 21 94 22 03 22 11 22 20 22 29 22 38 22 47
BuildTable 1 21 98 22 07 22 17 22 27 22 37 22 47 22 56 22 66
BuildTable 1 22 76 22 86 22 96 23 05 23 15 23 25 23 35 23 45
BuildTable 1 22 49 22 59 22 70 22 81 22 92 23 03 23 13 23 24
BuildTable 1 23 35 23 46 23 57 23 67 23 78 23 89 24 00 24 11
BuildTable 1 23 55 23 64 23 74 23 84 23 94 24 04 24 13 24 23
BuildTable 1 24 33 24 43 24 53 24 62 24 72 24 82 24 92 25 02
BuildTable 1 24 22 24 32 24 43 24 54 24 65 24 76 24 86 24 97
BuildTable 1 25 08 25 19 25 30 25 40 25 51 25 62 25 73 25 84
BuildTable 1 25 95 26 05 26 16 26 27 26 38 26 49 26 59 26 70
BuildTable 1 26 81 26 92 27 03 27 13 27 24 27 35 27 46 27 57
```

The Make Edit Segment

At the end of the Make Edit segment, just ahead of the Stop instruction, it's worthwhile to add the whole Validate segment, in such a way as to trigger the execution of the macros that enable the display of the corresponding parameters when the editing of a patch is requested (in other words, when a patch is transferred from the data buffer to the edit buffer by means of the Make Edit segment).

An Editor/Librarian for the Yamaha SY55

This next example is an original program that illustrates the implementation of an editor/librarian dedicated to the memories of multitimbral configurations (known as "multis") in the Yamaha SY55 synthesizer. The librarian screen appears in Figure 13.3 below; Figure 13.4 shows the editing screen.

```
 Desk  File  Edit  Windows  MIDI

⬆      FACTORY.55M                         ⬆      FACTORY.55M
       1    POP                                   1    POP
       2    ROCK 1                                2    ROCK 1
       3    JAZZ 1                                3    JAZZ 1
       4    JAZZ 2                                4    JAZZ 2
       5    CHAMBER                               5    CHAMBER
       6    ROCK 2                                6    ROCK 2
       7    FOLK                                  7    FOLK
       8    JAZZ 3                                8    JAZZ 3
       9    CHOIRS              [  Edit  ]        9    CHOIRS
       10   FUNK                                  10   FUNK
       11   FLEXIBLE           [Randomize]        11   FLEXIBLE
       12   NOSTALGIA                             12   NOSTALGIA
       13   Pf&STRINGS          [ Distort ]       13   Pf&STRINGS
       14   MoonRock                              14   MoonRock
       15   MinuteRice           [  Name  ]       15   MinuteRice
       16   Theater                               16   Theater
                               [ Average ]
⬇     ⬅            ➡                      ⬇     ⬅            ➡
```

FIGURE 13.3: *The librarian screen of the Yamaha SY55*

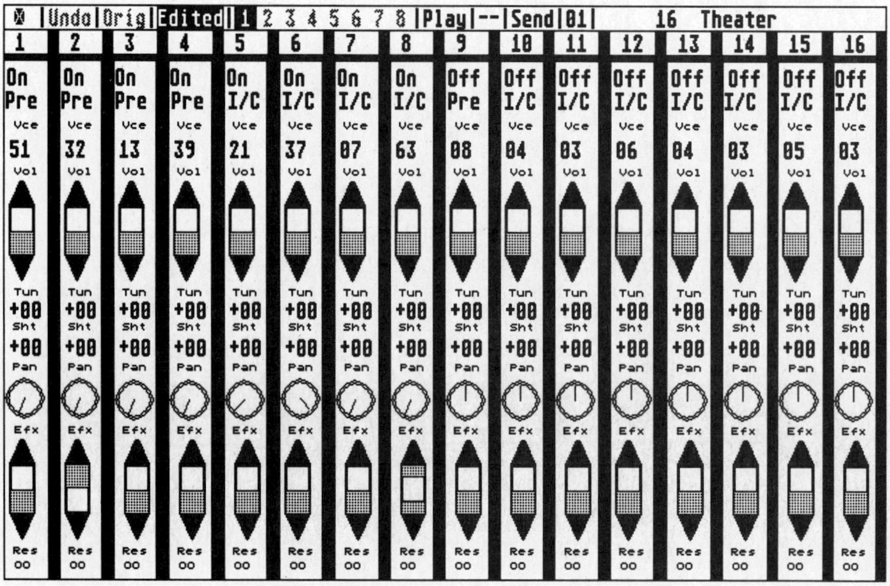

FIGURE 13.4: *The editing screen of the Yamaha SY55*

Syntax of the Exclusive Messages

Here's the syntax for the Exclusive messages that are used in this code listing. For more information about the format of the SysEx messages, and particularly about the format of individual parameter change messages, see the Yamaha document entitled "The SY55 MIDI Data Format."

A Request for a "Multi" (MU) Dump

```
F0H (11110000) : Exclusive message status byte
43H (01000011) : manufacturer's ID (43H = Yamaha)
2nH (0010nnnn) : sub-status/channel (2 = dump request, n = channel)
7AH (01111010) : type of format
```

```
4CH (01001100) : first header byte ("L" in ASCII)
4DH (01001101) : second header byte ("M" in ASCII)
20H (00100000) : third header byte (" " in ASCII)
20H (00100000) : fourth header byte (" " in ASCII)
38H (00111000) : first byte for the type of instrument ("8" in ASCII)
31H (00110001) : second byte for the type of instrument ("1" in ASCII)
30H (00110000) : third byte for the type of instrument ("0" in ASCII)
33H (00110011) : fourth byte for the type of instrument ("3" in ASCII)
4DH (01001101) : first byte of the data format ("M" in ASCII)
55H (01010101) : second byte of the data format ("U" in ASCII)
iiH (0iiiiiii) : additional 14-byte header (set to zero)
...
jjH (0jjjjjjj) : type of memory *
kkH (0kkkkkkk) : memory number
F7H (11110111) : EOX
```

*NOTE: A value of jjH = 00H indicates internal memory (RAM); a value of jjH = 02H indicates memory presets (ROM).

A "Multi" (MU) Dump

```
F0H (11110000) : Exclusive message status byte
43H (01000011) : manufacturer's ID (43H = Yamaha)
0nH (0000nnnn) : sub-status/channel (0 = dump request, n = channel)
7AH (01111010) : type of format
eeH (0eeeeeee) : MSB counter for the number of data bytes
ffH (0fffffff) : LSB counter for the number of data bytes
4CH (01001100) : first header byte ("L" in ASCII)
4DH (01001101) : second header byte ("M" in ASCII)
20H (00100000) : third header byte (" " in ASCII)
20H (00100000) : fourth header byte (" " in ASCII)
38H (00111000) : first byte for the type of instrument ("8" in ASCII)
31H (00110001) : second byte for the type of instrument ("1" in ASCII)
30H (00110000) : third byte for the type of instrument ("0" in ASCII)
33H (00110011) : fourth byte for the type of instrument ("3" in ASCII)
4DH (01001101) : first byte of the data format ("M" in ASCII)
55H (01010101) : second byte of the data format ("U" in ASCII)
iiH (0iiiiiii) : additionnal 14-byte header (set to zero)
...
jjH (0jjjjjjj) : type of memory *
```

```
kkH (0kkkkkkk) : memory number
ddH (0ddddddd) : data
...
ccH (0ccccccc) : checksum
F7H (11110111) : EOX
```

The General Format of a Parameter-Change Message

```
F0H (11110000) : Exclusive message status byte
43H (01000011) : Yamaha ID
1nH (0001nnnn) : type of message (1 = individual parameter, n = channel)
35H (00110101) : group number
ssH (0sssssss) : MSB structure number
ssH (0sssssss) : LSB structure number
ppH (0ppppppp) : MSB parameter number
ppH (0ppppppp) : LSB parameter number
vvH (0vvvvvvv) : value of the MSB parameter
vvH (0vvvvvvv) : value of the LSB parameter
F7H (11110111) : EOX
```

This listing uses the following parameter-change messages:

A Parameter-Change Message (for the Name of a Multi)

```
F0H (11110000) : Exclusive message status byte
43H (01000011) : Yamaha ID
1nH (0001nnnn) : type of message (1 = individual parameter, n = channel)
35H (00110101) : group number
00H (00000000) : MSB structure number (name of a multi)
00H (00000000) : LSB structure number (name of a multi)
00H (00000000) : MSB parameter number
ppH (0ppppppp) : LSB parameter number (number of a letter from 00H to 09H)
00H (00000000) : value of the MSB parameter
vvH (0vvvvvvv) : value of the LSB parameter (ASCII value from 20 to 127)
F7H (11110111) : EOX
```

A Parameter-Change Message (for Each Voice of a Multi)

```
F0H (11110000) : Exclusive message status byte
43H (01000011) : Yamaha ID
1nH (0001nnnn) : type of message (1 = individual parameter, n = channel)
35H (00110101) : group number
01H (00000001) : MSB structure number (each voice of a multi)
0sH (0000ssss) : LSB structure number (voice number for a multi) *
00H (00000000) : MSB parameter number
0pH (0ppppppp) : LSB parameter number
00H (00000000) : value of the MSB parameter
vvH (0vvvvvvv) : value of the LSB parameter
F7H (11110111) : EOX
```

* NOTE: The variable "s" covers a range of values from 0H to 7H.

Table 13.6 below shows the parameter numbers for each value of "s":

TABLE 13.6: *Parameter Numbers for Each Value of the "s" Variable*

PARAMETER NUMBER	PARAMETER	ABSOLUTE VALUE	DISPLAYED VALUE
00H	Voice on/off	0 to 1	off (0), on (1)
01H	Voice memory select	0 to 1	int/crd (0), pre (1)
02H	Voice number	0 to 63	
03H	Volume	0 to 127	
04H	Tuning	0 to 127	−64/+63
05H	Note shift	0 to 127	−64/+63
06H	Multi static pan	0 to 63	voice (0), −31/+31 (0 to 63)
07H	Effect level	0 to 100	
08H	Reserve note	0 to 16	

· · · · · · · · · · ·

A Parameter-Change Message (Remote Control of the Multi Key)

```
F0H (11110000) : Exclusive message status byte
43H (01000011) : Yamaha ID
1nH (0001nnnn) : type of message (1 = individual parameter, n = channel)
35H (00110101) : group number
0DH (00001101) : MSB structure number (key remote control)
00H (00000000) : LSB structure number (key remote control)
00H (00000000) : MSB parameter number
11H (00010001) : LSB parameter number(key number 11H = multi)
00H (00000000) : value of the MSB parameter
vvH (0vvvvvvv) : value of the LSB parameter (00H-3FH off, 40H-7FH on)
F7H (11110111) : EOX
```

A Parameter-Change Message (System: Memory Protection On/Off)

```
F0H (11110000) : Exclusive message status byte
43H (01000011) : Yamaha ID
1nH (0001nnnn) : type of message (1 = individual parameter, n = channel)
35H (00110101) : group number
0FH (00001111) : MSB structure number (system message)
00H (00000000) : LSB structure number (system message)
00H (00000000) : MSB parameter number
07H (00000111) : LSB parameter number (07H = memory protection)
00H (00000000) : value of the MSB parameter
vvH (0vvvvvvv) : value of the LSB parameter (00H off, 01H on)
F7H (11110111) : EOX
```

The Receive Segment

```
;
; acquisition of the channel number
;
OpenWindow
CHN = InputChannel 0 0 CHN
V00 = CHN | $20
V02 = CHN | $10
CloseWindow
```

```
;
; acquisition of the type of memory to be dumped (internal
; or preset)
;
L07
OpenWindow
V06 = InputVar 0 0 0 B "0/Internal 1/Preset"
CloseWindow
V07 = V06 GT 1
If V07 GoTo L07
V08 = V06 EQ 1
;
; memory de-protection
;
Transmit $F0 $43
TransmitVar V02
Transmit $35 $0F $00 $00 $07 $00 $00 $F7
If V08 GoSub L05
;
; request for the 16 multis
;
V01 = 0
Loop 16
  Transmit $F0 $43
  TransmitVar V00
  Transmit $7A $4C $4D $20 $20 $38 $31 $30 $33 $4D $55
  Transmit $00 $00 $00 $00 $00 $00 $00 $00 $00 $00 $00 $00 $00 $00
  TransmitVar V06
  TransmitVar V01
  Transmit $F7
  Receive $F0 $43
  ReceiveAny 1
  Receive $7A
  ReceiveAny 2
  Receive $4C $4D $20 $20 $38 $31 $30 $33 $4D $55
  Receive $00 $00 $00 $00 $00 $00 $00 $00 $00 $00 $00 $00 $00 $00
  ReceiveAny 2
  ReceiveData 160 $F7 1
  ReceiveAny 1
  Receive $F7
```

```
    VO1 = VO1 + 1
EndLoop
;
; simulate pressure on the multi key
;
Transmit $FO $43
TransmitVar VO2
Transmit $35 $0D $00 $00 $11 $00 $7F $F7
;
; send "GenEdit" in the multi buffer (just as a style exercise)
;
Transmit $FO $43
TransmitVar VO2
Transmit $35 $00 $00 $00 $00 $00 $42 $F7
Transmit $FO $43
TransmitVar VO2
Transmit $35 $00 $00 $00 $01 $00 $79 $F7
Transmit $FO $43
TransmitVar VO2
Transmit $35 $00 $00 $00 $02 $00 $20 $F7
Transmit $FO $43
TransmitVar VO2
Transmit $35 $00 $00 $00 $03 $00 $47 $F7
Transmit $FO $43
TransmitVar VO2
Transmit $35 $00 $00 $00 $04 $00 $65 $F7
Transmit $FO $43
TransmitVar VO2
Transmit $35 $00 $00 $00 $05 $00 $6E $F7
Transmit $FO $43
TransmitVar VO2
Transmit $35 $00 $00 $00 $06 $00 $45 $F7
Transmit $FO $43
TransmitVar VO2
Transmit $35 $00 $00 $00 $07 $00 $64 $F7
Transmit $FO $43
TransmitVar VO2
Transmit $35 $00 $00 $00 $08 $00 $69 $F7
Transmit $FO $43
TransmitVar VO2
```

```
Transmit $35 $00 $00 $00 $09 $00 $74 $F7
Stop
;
; offset for a preset dump
;
L05
V06 = 2
Return
```

The Transmit Segment

```
;
; acquisition of the channel number
;
OpenWindow
CHN = InputChannel 0 0 CHN
V00 = CHN
V09 = V00 | $10
CloseWindow
V01 = 0
;
; memory de-protection
;
Transmit $F0 $43
TransmitVar V09
Transmit $35 $0F $00 $00 $07 $00 $00 $F7
;
; transmit the 16 multis
;
Loop 16
  V02 = 583
  V04 = V01 * 160
  Transmit $F0 $43
  TransmitVar V00
  Transmit $7A $01 $3A
  Transmit $4C $4D $20 $20 $38 $31 $30 $33 $4D $55
  Transmit $00 $00 $00 $00 $00 $00 $00 $00 $00 $00 $00 $00 $00 $00
  Transmit $00
  TransmitVar V01
  V02 = V02 + V01
```

```
   Loop 160
     VO3 = PeekData VO4 B
     TransmitVar VO3
     VO2 = VO2 + VO3
     VO4 = VO4 + 1
   EndLoop
   VO2 = NEG VO2
   VO2 = VO2 & %01111111
   TransmitVar VO2
   Transmit $F7
   VO1 = VO1 + 1
EndLoop
;
; simulate pressure on the multi key
;
Transmit $F0 $43
TransmitVar VO9
Transmit $35 $0D $00 $00 $11 $00 $7F $F7
;
; send "GenEdit" in the multi buffer (just as a style exercise)
;
Transmit $F0 $43
TransmitVar VO9
Transmit $35 $00 $00 $00 $00 $00 $42 $F7
Transmit $F0 $43
TransmitVar VO9
Transmit $35 $00 $00 $00 $01 $00 $79 $F7
Transmit $F0 $43
TransmitVar VO9
Transmit $35 $00 $00 $00 $02 $00 $20 $F7
Transmit $F0 $43
TransmitVar VO9
Transmit $35 $00 $00 $00 $03 $00 $47 $F7
Transmit $F0 $43
TransmitVar VO9
Transmit $35 $00 $00 $00 $04 $00 $65 $F7
Transmit $F0 $43
TransmitVar VO9
Transmit $35 $00 $00 $00 $05 $00 $6E $F7
Transmit $F0 $43
```

```
TransmitVar V09
Transmit $35 $00 $00 $00 $06 $00 $45 $F7
Transmit $F0 $43
TransmitVar V09
Transmit $35 $00 $00 $00 $07 $00 $64 $F7
Transmit $F0 $43
TransmitVar V09
Transmit $35 $00 $00 $00 $08 $00 $69 $F7
Transmit $F0 $43
TransmitVar V09
Transmit $35 $00 $00 $00 $09 $00 $74 $F7
```

The Initialize Segment

```
;
EBL = 160
NMO = 0
NML = 10
;
FormatBank ' ' 16 1
```

The Get Patch Segment

```
;
V30 = PAT * 160
CopyEtoD V30 0 160 B
```

The Put Patch Segment

```
;
V30 = PAT * 160
CopyEtoD 0 V30 160 B
```

The Make Edit Segment

```
;
V30 = PAT * 160
CopyDtoE V30 0 160 B
```

The Unmake Edit Segment

```
;
V30 = PAT * 160
CopyEtoD 0 V30 160 B
```

The Send Edit Segment

```
;
OpenWindow
CHN = InputChannel 0 0 CHN
V00 = CHN
V06 = CHN | $10
Transmit $F0 $43
TransmitVar V06
Transmit $35 $0D $00 $00 $11 $00 $7F $F7
CloseWindow
V02 = 583
V04 = 0
Transmit $F0 $43
TransmitVar V00
Transmit $7A $01 $3A
Transmit $4C $4D $20 $20 $38 $31 $30 $33 $4D $55
Transmit $00 $00 $00 $00 $00 $00 $00 $00 $00 $00 $00 $00 $00 $00
Transmit $7F $00
V02 = V02 + $7F
Loop 160
  V03 = PeekEdit V04 B
  TransmitVar V03
  V02 = V02 + V03
  V04 = V04 + 1
EndLoop
V02 = NEG V02
V02 = V02 & %01111111
TransmitVar V02
Transmit $F7
Transmit $F0 $43
TransmitVar V06
Transmit $35 $0D $00 $00 $11 $00 $7F $F7
```

The Validate Segment

```
;
V80 = LPO
V70 = 18
V71 = 24
;
; select voice number ==> voice on
;
Loop 16
  V81 = V80 EQ V70
  If V81 GoSub L01
  V70 = V70 + 9
EndLoop
V86 = 0
;
; verify that the "voice reserve" total is less than 16
;
Loop 16
  V81 = V80 EQ V71
  If V81 GoSub L02
  V71 = V71 + 9
  V86 = V86 + 1
EndLoop
Stop
L01
V82 = V80 - 2
PokeEdit V82 64 B
Return
L02
V73 = 0
V71 = 24
Loop 16
  V72 = PeekEdit V71 B
  V73 = V73 + V72
  V71 = V71 + 9
EndLoop
V73 = V73 GT 16
If V73 GoSub L03
Return
L03
```

```
V85 = PeekEdit V80 B
V85 = V85 - 1
PokeEdit V80 V85 B
V87 = CHN | $10
Transmit $F0 $43
TransmitVar V87
Transmit $35 $01
TransmitVar V86
Transmit $00 $08 $00
TransmitVar V85
Transmit $F7
Return
```

EBDT

Appendix I summarizes the characteristics of the parameters relating to the edit buffer.

The Edit Buffer and Individual Parameters

The act of sending all of a multi to the edit buffer of the SY55 by means of the Send Edit segment each time a parameter is modified has the effect of clogging the MIDI network for no good reason. Therefore, in view of the fact that most instruments implement Exclusive messages for individual parameters, these messages can be sent directly each time an object is manipulated. This way, in addition to being stored in the GenEdit data buffer by means of the Unmake Edit segment, the values that result from these manipulations are transmitted directly to the edit buffer of the instrument by means of the Exclusive messages for individual parameters, as shown in Figure 13.5 below.

In addition to its EBDT definition and the range of values displayed, each object can issue an Exclusive individual parameter message each time it is manipulated.

```
┌────────────────────────────────────────────┐
│                    Knob                      │
│  ┌─────────────┐ ┌─────────────────────────┐│
│  │ Edit Buffer:│ │ PAN 9                    ││
│  └─────────────┘ │ +00094     L/H = +00000 +00064 ││
│                  └─────────────────────────┘│
│  ┌──────┬──────────────┬──────────┬────────┐│
│  │ MIDI:│ Low: 00000_  │ High: 00063_ │ Update: 001 ││
│  └──────┴──────────────┴──────────┴────────┘│
│  F0 43 1n 35 01 08 00 06 00 yz F7 __ __ __ __ __ │
│                                              │
│  ┌──────────────┐ ┌──────────────┐ ┌────────┐│
│  │ Low: -00032│ │ │ High: 00031_ │ │ Invert ││
│  └──────────────┘ └──────────────┘ └────────┘│
│           ┌──────┐                           │
│           │ Exit │                           │
│           └──────┘                           │
└────────────────────────────────────────────┘
```

FIGURE 13.5: *Values for individual parameters, as transmitted by Exclusive messages*

Here's the list of messages associated with each object in the editor. In the string of hex codes in this table, the value "yz" corresponds to the current position of the object.

```
VOICE ON/OFF 1           F0H 43H 1nH 35H 01H 00H 00H 00H 00H yz F7H
VOICE MEMORY SELECT      F0H 43H 1nH 35H 01H 00H 00H 01H 00H yz F7H
VOICE NUMBER 1           F0H 43H 1nH 35H 01H 00H 00H 02H 00H yz F7H
VOLUME 1                 F0H 43H 1nH 35H 01H 00H 00H 03H 00H yz F7H
TUNING 1                 F0H 43H 1nH 35H 01H 00H 00H 04H 00H yz F7H
NOTE SHIFT 1             F0H 43H 1nH 35H 01H 00H 00H 05H 00H yz F7H
PAN 1                    F0H 43H 1nH 35H 01H 00H 00H 06H 00H yz F7H
EFFECT LEVEL 1           F0H 43H 1nH 35H 01H 00H 00H 07H 00H yz F7H
RESERVE NOTE 1           F0H 43H 1nH 35H 01H 00H 00H 08H 00H yz F7H
VOICE ON/OFF 2           F0H 43H 1nH 35H 01H 01H 00H 00H 00H yz F7H
VOICE MEMORY SELECT 2    F0H 43H 1nH 35H 01H 01H 00H 01H 00H yz F7H
VOICE NUMBER 2           F0H 43H 1nH 35H 01H 01H 00H 02H 00H yz F7H
VOLUME 2                 F0H 43H 1nH 35H 01H 01H 00H 03H 00H yz F7H
TUNING 2                 F0H 43H 1nH 35H 01H 01H 00H 04H 00H yz F7H
```

```
NOTE SHIFT 2            F0H 43H 1nH 35H 01H 01H 00H 05H 00H yz F7H
PAN 2                   F0H 43H 1nH 35H 01H 01H 00H 06H 00H yz F7H
EFFECT LEVEL 2          F0H 43H 1nH 35H 01H 01H 00H 07H 00H yz F7H
RESERVE NOTE 2          F0H 43H 1nH 35H 01H 01H 00H 08H 00H yz F7H
VOICE ON/OFF 3          F0H 43H 1nH 35H 01H 02H 00H 00H 00H yz F7H
VOICE MEMORY SELECT 3   F0H 43H 1nH 35H 01H 02H 00H 01H 00H yz F7H
VOICE NUMBER 3          F0H 43H 1nH 35H 01H 02H 00H 02H 00H yz F7H
VOLUME 3                F0H 43H 1nH 35H 01H 02H 00H 03H 00H yz F7H
TUNING 3                F0H 43H 1nH 35H 01H 02H 00H 04H 00H yz F7H
NOTE SHIFT 3            F0H 43H 1nH 35H 01H 02H 00H 05H 00H yz F7H
PAN 3                   F0H 43H 1nH 35H 01H 02H 00H 06H 00H yz F7H
EFFECT LEVEL 3          F0H 43H 1nH 35H 01H 02H 00H 07H 00H yz F7H
RESERVE NOTE 3          F0H 43H 1nH 35H 01H 02H 00H 08H 00H yz F7H
VOICE ON/OFF 4          F0H 43H 1nH 35H 01H 03H 00H 00H 00H yz F7H
VOICE MEMORY SELECT 4   F0H 43H 1nH 35H 01H 03H 00H 01H 00H yz F7H
VOICE NUMBER 4          F0H 43H 1nH 35H 01H 03H 00H 02H 00H yz F7H
VOLUME 4                F0H 43H 1nH 35H 01H 03H 00H 03H 00H yz F7H
TUNING 4                F0H 43H 1nH 35H 01H 03H 00H 04H 00H yz F7H
NOTE SHIFT 4            F0H 43H 1nH 35H 01H 03H 00H 05H 00H yz F7H
PAN 4                   F0H 43H 1nH 35H 01H 03H 00H 06H 00H yz F7H
EFFECT LEVEL 4          F0H 43H 1nH 35H 01H 03H 00H 07H 00H yz F7H
RESERVE NOTE 4          F0H 43H 1nH 35H 01H 03H 00H 08H 00H yz F7H
VOICE ON/OFF 5          F0H 43H 1nH 35H 01H 04H 00H 00H 00H yz F7H
VOICE MEMORY SELECT 5   F0H 43H 1nH 35H 01H 04H 00H 01H 00H yz F7H
VOICE NUMBER 5          F0H 43H 1nH 35H 01H 04H 00H 02H 00H yz F7H
VOLUME 5                F0H 43H 1nH 35H 01H 04H 00H 03H 00H yz F7H
TUNING 5                F0H 43H 1nH 35H 01H 04H 00H 04H 00H yz F7H
NOTE SHIFT 5            F0H 43H 1nH 35H 01H 04H 00H 05H 00H yz F7H
PAN 5                   F0H 43H 1nH 35H 01H 04H 00H 06H 00H yz F7H
EFFECT LEVEL 5          F0H 43H 1nH 35H 01H 04H 00H 07H 00H yz F7H
RESERVE NOTE 5          F0H 43H 1nH 35H 01H 04H 00H 08H 00H yz F7H
VOICE ON/OFF 6          F0H 43H 1nH 35H 01H 05H 00H 00H 00H yz F7H
VOICE MEMORY SELECT     F0H 43H 1nH 35H 01H 05H 00H 01H 00H yz F7H
VOICE NUMBER 6          F0H 43H 1nH 35H 01H 05H 00H 02H 00H yz F7H
VOLUME 6                F0H 43H 1nH 35H 01H 05H 00H 03H 00H yz F7H
TUNING 6                F0H 43H 1nH 35H 01H 05H 00H 04H 00H yz F7H
NOTE SHIFT 6            F0H 43H 1nH 35H 01H 05H 00H 05H 00H yz F7H
PAN 6                   F0H 43H 1nH 35H 01H 05H 00H 06H 00H yz F7H
EFFECT LEVEL 6          F0H 43H 1nH 35H 01H 05H 00H 07H 00H yz F7H
RESERVE NOTE 6          F0H 43H 1nH 35H 01H 05H 00H 08H 00H yz F7H
```

```
VOICE ON/OFF 7          F0H 43H 1nH 35H 01H 06H 00H 00H 00H yz F7H
VOICE MEMORY SELECT     F0H 43H 1nH 35H 01H 06H 00H 01H 00H yz F7H
VOICE NUMBER 7          F0H 43H 1nH 35H 01H 06H 00H 02H 00H yz F7H
VOLUME 7                F0H 43H 1nH 35H 01H 06H 00H 03H 00H yz F7H
TUNING 7                F0H 43H 1nH 35H 01H 06H 00H 04H 00H yz F7H
NOTE SHIFT 7            F0H 43H 1nH 35H 01H 06H 00H 05H 00H yz F7H
PAN 7                   F0H 43H 1nH 35H 01H 06H 00H 06H 00H yz F7H
EFFECT LEVEL 7          F0H 43H 1nH 35H 01H 06H 00H 07H 00H yz F7H
RESERVE NOTE 7          F0H 43H 1nH 35H 01H 06H 00H 08H 00H yz F7H
VOICE ON/OFF 8          F0H 43H 1nH 35H 01H 07H 00H 00H 00H yz F7H
VOICE MEMORY SELECT 8   F0H 43H 1nH 35H 01H 07H 00H 01H 00H yz F7H
VOICE NUMBER 8          F0H 43H 1nH 35H 01H 07H 00H 02H 00H yz F7H
VOLUME 8                F0H 43H 1nH 35H 01H 07H 00H 03H 00H yz F7H
TUNING 8                F0H 43H 1nH 35H 01H 07H 00H 04H 00H yz F7H
NOTE SHIFT 8            F0H 43H 1nH 35H 01H 07H 00H 05H 00H yz F7H
PAN 8                   F0H 43H 1nH 35H 01H 07H 00H 06H 00H yz F7H
EFFECT LEVEL 8          F0H 43H 1nH 35H 01H 07H 00H 07H 00H yz F7H
RESERVE NOTE 8          F0H 43H 1nH 35H 01H 07H 00H 08H 00H yz F7H
VOICE ON/OFF 9          F0H 43H 1nH 35H 01H 00H 00H 00H 00H yz F7H
VOICE MEMORY SELECT 9   F0H 43H 1nH 35H 01H 00H 00H 01H 00H yz F7H
VOICE NUMBER 9          F0H 43H 1nH 35H 01H 00H 00H 02H 00H yz F7H
VOLUME 9                F0H 43H 1nH 35H 01H 00H 00H 03H 00H yz F7H
TUNING 9                F0H 43H 1nH 35H 01H 00H 00H 04H 00H yz F7H
NOTE SHIFT 9            F0H 43H 1nH 35H 01H 00H 00H 05H 00H yz F7H
PAN 9                   F0H 43H 1nH 35H 01H 00H 00H 06H 00H yz F7H
EFFECT LEVEL 9          F0H 43H 1nH 35H 01H 00H 00H 07H 00H yz F7H
RESERVE NOTE 9          F0H 43H 1nH 35H 01H 00H 00H 08H 00H yz F7H
VOICE ON/OFF 10         F0H 43H 1nH 35H 01H 0FH 00H 00H 00H yz F7H
VOICE MEMORY SELECT 1   F0H 43H 1nH 35H 01H 0FH 00H 01H 00H yz F7H
VOICE NUMBER 10         F0H 43H 1nH 35H 01H 0FH 00H 02H 00H yz F7H
VOLUME 10               F0H 43H 1nH 35H 01H 0FH 00H 03H 00H yz F7H
TUNING 10               F0H 43H 1nH 35H 01H 0FH 00H 04H 00H yz F7H
NOTE SHIFT 10           F0H 43H 1nH 35H 01H 0FH 00H 05H 00H yz F7H
PAN 10                  F0H 43H 1nH 35H 01H 0FH 00H 06H 00H yz F7H
EFFECT LEVEL 10         F0H 43H 1nH 35H 01H 0FH 00H 07H 00H yz F7H
RESERVE NOTE 10         F0H 43H 1nH 35H 01H 0FH 00H 08H 00H yz F7H
VOICE ON/OFF 11         F0H 43H 1nH 35H 01H 09H 00H 00H 00H yz F7H
VOICE MEMORY SELECT     F0H 43H 1nH 35H 01H 09H 00H 01H 00H yz F7H
VOICE NUMBER 11         F0H 43H 1nH 35H 01H 09H 00H 02H 00H yz F7H
VOLUME 11               F0H 43H 1nH 35H 01H 09H 00H 03H 00H yz F7H
```

```
TUNING 11                     F0H 43H 1nH 35H 01H 09H 00H 04H 00H yz F7H
NOTE SHIFT 11                 F0H 43H 1nH 35H 01H 09H 00H 05H 00H yz F7H
PAN 11                        F0H 43H 1nH 35H 01H 09H 00H 06H 00H yz F7H
EFFECT LEVEL 11               F0H 43H 1nH 35H 01H 09H 00H 07H 00H yz F7H
RESERVE NOTE 11               F0H 43H 1nH 35H 01H 09H 00H 08H 00H yz F7H
VOICE ON/OFF 12               F0H 43H 1nH 35H 01H 0AH 00H 00H 00H yz F7H
VOICE MEMORY SELECT 12 F0H 43H 1nH 35H 01H 0AH 00H 01H 00H yz F7H
VOICE NUMBER 12               F0H 43H 1nH 35H 01H 0AH 00H 02H 00H yz F7H
VOLUME 12                     F0H 43H 1nH 35H 01H 0AH 00H 03H 00H yz F7H
TUNING 12                     F0H 43H 1nH 35H 01H 0AH 00H 04H 00H yz F7H
NOTE SHIFT 12                 F0H 43H 1nH 35H 01H 0AH 00H 05H 00H yz F7H
PAN 12                        F0H 43H 1nH 35H 01H 0AH 00H 06H 00H yz F7H
EFFECT LEVEL 12               F0H 43H 1nH 35H 01H 0AH 00H 07H 00H yz F7H
RESERVE NOTE 12               F0H 43H 1nH 35H 01H 0AH 00H 08H 00H yz F7H
VOICE ON/OFF 13               F0H 43H 1nH 35H 01H 0BH 00H 00H 00H yz F7H
VOICE MEMORY SELECT 13 F0H 43H 1nH 35H 01H 0BH 00H 01H 00H yz F7H
VOICE NUMBER 13               F0H 43H 1nH 35H 01H 0BH 00H 02H 00H yz F7H
VOLUME 13                     F0H 43H 1nH 35H 01H 0BH 00H 03H 00H yz F7H
TUNING 13                     F0H 43H 1nH 35H 01H 0BH 00H 04H 00H yz F7H
NOTE SHIFT 13                 F0H 43H 1nH 35H 01H 0BH 00H 05H 00H yz F7H
PAN 13                        F0H 43H 1nH 35H 01H 0BH 00H 06H 00H yz F7H
EFFECT LEVEL 13               F0H 43H 1nH 35H 01H 0BH 00H 07H 00H yz F7H
RESERVE NOTE 13               F0H 43H 1nH 35H 01H 0BH 00H 08H 00H yz F7H
VOICE ON/OFF 14               F0H 43H 1nH 35H 01H 0CH 00H 00H 00H yz F7H
VOICE MEMORY SELECT 1  F0H 43H 1nH 35H 01H 0CH 00H 01H 00H yz F7H
VOICE NUMBER 14               F0H 43H 1nH 35H 01H 0CH 00H 02H 00H yz F7H
VOLUME 14                     F0H 43H 1nH 35H 01H 0CH 00H 03H 00H yz F7H
TUNING 14                     F0H 43H 1nH 35H 01H 0CH 00H 04H 00H yz F7H
NOTE SHIFT 14                 F0H 43H 1nH 35H 01H 0CH 00H 05H 00H yz F7H
PAN 14                        F0H 43H 1nH 35H 01H 0CH 00H 06H 00H yz F7H
EFFECT LEVEL 14               F0H 43H 1nH 35H 01H 0CH 00H 07H 00H yz F7H
RESERVE NOTE 14               F0H 43H 1nH 35H 01H 0CH 00H 08H 00H yz F7H
VOICE ON/OFF 15               F0H 43H 1nH 35H 01H 0DH 00H 00H 00H yz F7H
VOICE MEMORY SELECT 15 F0H 43H 1nH 35H 01H 0DH 00H 01H 00H yz F7H
VOICE NUMBER 15               F0H 43H 1nH 35H 01H 0DH 00H 02H 00H yz F7H
VOLUME 15                     F0H 43H 1nH 35H 01H 0DH 00H 03H 00H yz F7H
TUNING 15                     F0H 43H 1nH 35H 01H 0DH 00H 04H 00H yz F7H
NOTE SHIFT 15                 F0H 43H 1nH 35H 01H 0DH 00H 05H 00H yz F7H
PAN 15                        F0H 43H 1nH 35H 01H 0DH 00H 06H 00H yz F7H
EFFECT LEVEL 15               F0H 43H 1nH 35H 01H 0DH 00H 07H 00H yz F7H
```

```
RESERVE NOTE 15            F0H 43H 1nH 35H 01H 0DH 00H 08H 00H yz F7H
VOICE ON/OFF 16            F0H 43H 1nH 35H 01H 0EH 00H 00H 00H yz F7H
VOICE MEMORY SELECT 16 F0H 43H 1nH 35H 01H 0EH 00H 01H 00H yz F7H
VOICE NUMBER 16            F0H 43H 1nH 35H 01H 0EH 00H 02H 00H yz F7H
VOLUME 16                  F0H 43H 1nH 35H 01H 0EH 00H 03H 00H yz F7H
TUNING 16                  F0H 43H 1nH 35H 01H 0EH 00H 04H 00H yz F7H
NOTE SHIFT 16              F0H 43H 1nH 35H 01H 0EH 00H 05H 00H yz F7H
PAN 16                     F0H 43H 1nH 35H 01H 0EH 00H 06H 00H yz F7H
EFFECT LEVEL 16            F0H 43H 1nH 35H 01H 0EH 00H 07H 00H yz F7H
RESERVE NOTE 16            F0H 43H 1nH 35H 01H 0EH 00H 08H 00H yz F7H
```

I II III IV V VI VII VIII IX X XI XII

CHAPTER

14

XIII XV XVI A B C D E F G H I

Recent Extensions:

General MIDI
and MIDI Show Control

OST INTERFACES ARE developed on the initiative of an individual manufacturer and are adopted later by other makers. MIDI is an exception to this general rule. The development of this standard is a result of a continuing dialogue between the major manufacturers involved. Thanks to the various associations that are involved (the IMA, the MMA, and the JMSC), the yearly meetings of the NAMM and other conferences, and online services such as the Performing Arts Network (PAN), the development of MIDI is the fruit of virtually daily efforts and coordination. For the first time in the history of interfaces, users are enjoying the benefit of devices that talk to each other with the help of a single, unique language that provides a universal communications protocol.

Originally designed with the single goal of standardizing the exchange of information between keyboards and sound generators, thereby putting an end to the anarchy and instability of the various analogous standards that were in effect at the time, the MIDI interface has gradually been modified to perform many other tasks. For instance, there are the Sample Dump Standard (for the transfer of samples), MIDI Files (for the transfer of sequences), and the MIDI Time Code (for synchronization), to name just a few. Who, back at the beginning, could have imagined that the MIDI standard would attract and handle such immense amounts of data?

Although MIDI's fixed hardware requirements, which are the essential condition for its compatibility, are also its major limitation with regard to unidirectional communications as well as with regard to the pass-band and the number of channels, its open software capabilities are an enormous advantage. It is these capabilities that have let MIDI continue unceasingly to adapt itself to users' needs and to technological advances. As a result, new messages, new applications, and new products are continuously appearing. This chapter examines two of the most recent extensions of the standard:

- General MIDI (including GS format, which is the Roland analog of General MIDI), and

- MIDI Show Control.

The General MIDI Standard

When a piece of music is developed on a synthesizer, you, the composer, are responsible for configuring your MIDI network in accordance with the requirements of the piece. In creating the configuration, you decide to assign this or that channel to this or that part of the arrangement (on this or that track); to send this or that Program Change message over this or that channel; and to adjust the sensitivity of each instrument with regard to this or that controller (such as the Pitch Bend, modulation, volume, aftertouch, etc.).

Consider for instance the example of a sequence that consists of a piano track on Channel 1, an acoustic bass track on Channel 2, and a drum track on Channel 10. Further assume that memory 23 of an expander (call it "A") corresponds to a piano sound whose volume is controlled by velocity; that memory 2 of a second expander (call it "B") corresponds to an acoustic bass sound whose pitch is controlled by aftertouch; and that memory 55 of a third expander (call it "C") corresponds to a drum kit whose bass drum and snare drum are assigned to C1 and E1, respectively.

If this sequence is moved to another MIDI environment, chances are good that the result will be different even though the messages that make up the sequence remain the same. For instance, memory 23 and memory 2 of the expanders set to Channel 1 and Channel 2 may correspond respectively to a violin sound whose filter cut-off frequency is controlled by velocity and to a synthetic bass sound whose LFO speed is controlled by aftertouch. It could also turn out that the charley and the cymbals are assigned to notes C1 and E1 on Channel 10, and so on. In short, in spite of their MIDI compatibility, you can move a sequence from one environment to another only if the configurations of the environments are exactly the same.

Major public applications, such as sequences on disk, instructional software, and MIDI on CD, are the first to suffer from this kind of incompatibility, because the user, who may not be very familiar with MIDI to begin with, is constrained to adapt the response of each of his or her instruments (sounds, channels, drum-kit mapping, and so on). This is why the new extension known as the General MIDI (GM) standard was developed.

This standard was developed on the initiative of two members of the MMA—Stanley Jungleib (who was one of the editors of the recently defunct journal of the association) and Dave Kusek (president of Passport Designs)—in order to standardize the behavior of sound generators and as a result to simplify their implementation.

A General MIDI sound generator is multitimbral and has 24 voices with dynamic allocation. It should also include a minimum of 16 timbre families (such as pianos, organs, and basses), with each family including 8 sounds (for instance, grand piano, electric piano, honky-tonk piano, and so on for the piano family). Regardless of the instrument—and this is where the value of the system resides—each of these 128 sounds is characterized by the same Program Change number (for instance, program number 1 for the grand piano, program number 33 for the acoustic bass, and so on). The mapping of the various elements of a drum kit and the response to the controllers, etc., are also standardized. As a result, a sequence written in accordance with the General MIDI standard correctly drives any compatible sound generator without needing any adjustments beforehand. Here are the specifications for a minimum configuration as described by the standard.

Type of Synthesis

Whatever the manufacturer selects.

Voices

At least 24 voices are allocated dynamically at the same time for melodic sounds and for the drum/percussion kit, or else 16 voices are allocated dynamically for melodic sounds and 8 other voices are allocated for the drum/percussion kit.

Channels

All 16 channels are supported. Each channel is polyphonic and can produce a variable number of voices. Each channel can produce a different sound. The drum/percussion kit responds to messages sent over Channel 10.

Instruments

Multitimbrality, with at least 16 timbres (that is, 16 different sounds) and a minimum of 128 sounds (i.e., 128 MIDI program numbers).

Other Characteristics

- An overall volume potentiometer
- A MIDI In port, with optional MIDI Out and MIDI Thru connectors
- Left and right audio outputs
- A headset port

The Families of Sounds

TABLE 14.1: *Families of Sounds, Grouped According to Program Numbers*

PROGRAM NUMBERS (DECIMAL)	PROGRAM NUMBERS (HEX)	FAMILY
1 to 8	(00H to 07H)	Piano
9 to 16	(08H to 0FH)	Chromatic percussion
17 to 24	(10H to 17H)	Organ
25 to 32	(18H to 1FH)	Guitar
33 to 40	(20H to 27H)	Bass
41 to 48	(28H to 2FH)	Strings
49 to 56	(30H to 37H)	Ensemble
57 to 64	(38H to 3FH)	Brass
65 to 72	(40H to 47H)	Reeds
73 to 80	(48H to 4FH)	Pipes

TABLE 14.1: *Families of Sounds, Grouped According to Program Numbers (continued)*

PROGRAM NUMBERS (DECIMAL)	PROGRAM NUMBERS (HEX)	FAMILY
81 to 88	(50H to 57H)	Synth lead
89 to 96	(58H to 5FH)	Synth pad
97 to 104	(60H to 67H)	Synth effects
105 to 112	(68H to 6FH)	Ethnic
113 to 120	(70H to 77H)	Percussive
121 to 128	(78H to 7FH)	Sound effects

The Sounds

TABLE 14.2: *Individual Sounds, Grouped According to Program Numbers*

PROGRAM NUMBERS (DECIMAL)	PROGRAM NUMBERS (HEX)	INSTRUMENT OR EFFECT
	PIANO	
1	(00H)	Acoustic grand piano
2	(01H)	Bright acoustic piano
3	(02H)	Electric grand piano
4	(03H)	Honky-tonk piano
5	(04H)	Electric piano 1
6	(05H)	Electric piano 2
7	(06H)	Harpsichord
8	(07H)	Clavi

TABLE 14.2: *Individual Sounds, Grouped According to Program Numbers (continued)*

PROGRAM NUMBERS (DECIMAL)	PROGRAM NUMBERS (HEX)	INSTRUMENT OR EFFECT
CHROMATIC PERCUSSION		
9	(08H)	Celesta
10	(09H)	Glockenspiel
11	(0AH)	Music box
12	(0BH)	Vibraphone
13	(0CH)	Marimba
14	(0DH)	Xylophone
15	(0EH)	Tubular bells
16	(0FH)	Dulcimer
ORGAN		
17	(10H)	Drawbar organ
18	(11H)	Percussive organ
19	(12H)	Rock organ
20	(13H)	Church organ
21	(14H)	Reed organ
22	(15H)	Accordion
23	(16H)	Harmonica
24	(17H)	Tango accordion
GUITAR		
25	(18H)	Acoustic guitar (nylon)
26	(19H)	Acoustic guitar (steel)
27	(1AH)	Electric guitar (jazz)
28	(1BH)	Electric guitar (clean)

TABLE 14.2: *Individual Sounds, Grouped According to Program Numbers (continued)*

PROGRAM NUMBERS (DECIMAL)	PROGRAM NUMBERS (HEX)	INSTRUMENT OR EFFECT
29	(1CH)	Electric guitar (muted)
30	(1DH)	Overdriven guitar
31	(1EH)	Distortion guitar
32	(1FH)	Guitar harmonics
BASS		
33	(20H)	Acoustic bass
34	(21H)	Electric bass (finger)
35	(22H)	Electric bass (pick)
36	(23H)	Fretless bass
37	(24H)	Slap bass 1
38	(25H)	Slap bass 2
39	(26H)	Synth bass 1
40	(27H)	Synth bass 2
STRINGS		
41	(28H)	Violin
42	(29H)	Viola
43	(2AH)	Cello
44	(2BH)	Contrabass
45	(2CH)	Tremolo strings
46	(2DH)	Pizzicato strings
47	(2EH)	Orchestral harp
48	(2FH)	Tympani

TABLE 14.2: *Individual Sounds, Grouped According to Program Numbers (continued)*

PROGRAM NUMBERS (DECIMAL)	PROGRAM NUMBERS (HEX)	INSTRUMENT OR EFFECT
ENSEMBLE		
49	(30H)	String ensemble 1
50	(31H)	String ensemble 2
51	(32H)	Synth strings 1
52	(33H)	Synth strings 2
53	(34H)	Choir aahs
54	(35H)	Voice oohs
55	(36H)	Synth voice
56	(37H)	Orchestra hit
BRASS		
57	(38H)	Trumpet
58	(39H)	Trombone
59	(3AH)	Tuba
60	(3BH)	Muted trumpet
61	(3CH)	French horn
62	(3DH)	Brass section
63	(3EH)	Synth brass 1
64	(3FH)	Synth brass 2
Reeds		
65	(40H)	Soprano sax
66	(41H)	Alto sax
67	(42H)	Tenor sax
68	(43H)	Baritone sax

TABLE 14.2: *Individual Sounds, Grouped According to Program Numbers (continued)*

PROGRAM NUMBERS (DECIMAL)	PROGRAM NUMBERS (HEX)	INSTRUMENT OR EFFECT
69	(44H)	Oboe
70	(45H)	English horn
71	(46H)	Bassoon
72	(47H)	Clarinet
PIPES		
73	(48H)	Piccolo
74	(49H)	Flute
75	(4AH)	Recorder
76	(4BH)	Pan flute
77	(4CH)	Blown bottle
78	(4DH)	Shakuhachi
79	(4EH)	Whistle
80	(4FH)	Ocarina
SYNTH LEAD		
81	(50H)	Lead 1 (square)
82	(51H)	Lead 2 (sawtooth)
83	(52H)	Lead 3 (calliope)
84	(53H)	Lead 4 (chiff)
85	(54H)	Lead 5 (charang)
86	(55H)	Lead 6 (voice)
87	(56H)	Lead 7 (fifths)
88	(57H)	Lead 8 (bass + lead)

TABLE 14.2: *Individual Sounds, Grouped According to Program Numbers (continued)*

PROGRAM NUMBERS (DECIMAL)	PROGRAM NUMBERS (HEX)	INSTRUMENT OR EFFECT
	SYNTH PAD	
89	(58H)	Pad 1 (new age)
90	(59H)	Pad 2 (warm)
91	(5AH)	Pad 3 (polysynth)
92	(5BH)	Pad 4 (choir)
93	(5CH)	Pad 5 (bowed)
94	(5DH)	Pad 6 (metallic)
95	(5EH)	Pad 7 (halo)
96	(5FH)	Pad 8 (sweep)
	SYNTH EFFECTS	
97	(60H)	FX 1 (rain)
98	(61H)	FX 2 (soundtrack)
99	(62H)	FX 3 (crystal)
100	(63H)	FX 4 (atmosphere)
101	(64H)	FX 5 (brightness)
102	(65H)	FX 6 (goblins)
103	(66H)	FX 7 (echoes)
104	(67H)	FX 8 (sci-fi)
	ETHNIC	
105	(68H)	Sitar
106	(69H)	Banjo
107	(6AH)	Shamisen
108	(6BH)	Koto

TABLE 14.2: *Individual Sounds, Grouped According to Program Numbers (continued)*

PROGRAM NUMBERS (DECIMAL)	PROGRAM NUMBERS (HEX)	INSTRUMENT OR EFFECT
109	(6CH)	Kalimba
110	(6DH)	Bagpipe
111	(6EH)	Fiddle
112	(6FH)	Shanai

PERCUSSIVE

113	(70H)	Tinkle bell
114	(71H)	Agogo
115	(72H)	Steel drums
116	(73H)	Woodblock
117	(74H)	Taiko drum
118	(75H)	Melodic tom
119	(76H)	Synth drum
120	(77H)	Reverse cymbal

SOUND EFFECTS

121	(78H)	Guitar-fret noise
122	(79H)	Breath noise
123	(7AH)	Seashore
124	(7BH)	Bird tweet
125	(7CH)	Telephone ring
126	(7DH)	Helicopter
127	(7EH)	Applause
128	(7FH)	Gunshot

The Mapping of the Drum/Percussion Kit (Channel 10)

TABLE 14.3: *Drum Kit and Percussion Mapping (Channel 10)*

NOTE NUMBERS (DECIMAL)	NOTE NUMBERS (HEX)	NOTE NAME	INSTRUMENT OR EFFECT
35	(23H)	B0	Acoustic bass drum
36	(24H)	C1	Bass drum 1
37	(25H)	C#1	Side stick
38	(26H)	D1	Acoustic snare
39	(27H)	D#1	Hand clap
40	(28H)	E1	Electric snare
41	(29H)	F1	Low-floor tom
42	(2AH)	F#1	Closed hi-hat
43	(2BH)	G1	High-floor tom
44	(2CH)	G#1	Pedal hi-hat
45	(2DH)	A1	Low tom
46	(2EH)	A#1	Open hi-hat
47	(2FH)	B1	Low-middle tom
48	(30H)	C2	High-middle tom
49	(31H)	C#2	Crash cymbal 1
50	(32H)	D2	High tom
51	(33H)	D#2	Ride cymbal 1
52	(34H)	E2	Chinese cymbal
53	(35H)	F2	Ride bell
54	(36H)	F#2	Tambourine

TABLE 14.3: *Drum Kit and Percussion Mapping (Channel 10) (continued)*

NOTE NUMBERS (DECIMAL)	NOTE NUMBERS (HEX)	NOTE NAME	INSTRUMENT OR EFFECT
55	(37H)	G2	Splash cymbal
56	(38H)	G#2	Cowbell
57	(39H)	A2)	Crash cymbal 2
58	(3AH)	A#2	Vibraslap
59	(3BH)	B2	Ride cymbal 2
60	(3CH)	C3	High bongo
61	(3DH)	C#3	Low bongo
62	(3EH)	D3	Mute high conga
63	(3FH)	D#3	Open high conga
64	(40H)	E3	Low conga
65	(41H)	F3	High timbale
66	(42H)	F#3	Low timbale
67	(43H)	G3	High agogo
68	(44H)	G#3	Low agogo
69	(45H)	A3	Cabasa
70	(46H)	A#3	Maracas
71	(47H)	B3	Short whistle
72	(48H)	C4	Long whistle
73	(49H)	C#4	Short guiro
74	(4AH)	D4	Long guiro
75	(4BH)	D#4	Claves
76	(4CH)	E4	High woodblock
77	(4DH)	F4	Low woodblock

TABLE 14.3: *Drum Kit and Percussion Mapping (Channel 10) (continued)*

NOTE NUMBERS (DECIMAL)	NOTE NUMBERS (HEX)	NOTE NAME	INSTRUMENT OR EFFECT
78	(4EH)	F#4	Mute cuica
79	(4FH)	G4	Open cuica
80	(50H)	G#4	Mute triangle
81	(51H)	A4	Open triangle

The Minimum MIDI Implementation

Note On and Note Off

The C at the middle of the keyboard is the same as note number 60 (3CH). All of the voices, including the ones in the drum/percussion kit, are sensitive to velocity. The allocation of the voices is dynamic; that is, when a note is produced, a second note having the same number can be superimposed on the first note through the use of a free or unassigned voice.

Controllers

```
  1 (01H): modulation
  7 (07H): general volume
 10 (0AH): panorama
 11 (0BH): expression
 64 (40H): sustain
121 (79H): reset all controllers
123 (7BH): all notes off
```

Registered Parameters

```
0 (00H): Pitch Bend sensitivity
1 (01H): fine tuning
2 (02H): coarse tuning
```

Other Channel Messages

- Channel Aftertouch

- Pitch Bend (with a default range of plus or minus 2 semitones)

- All-channel response to volume messages

- The default values that are in effect when the sound generator is turned on: Bend = 0, Volume = 100, with the controllers in their normal position

MIDI Messages that Let You Activate and Deactivate General MIDI Mode for a Sound Generator

Activation

```
F0H: Exclusive Message status byte
7EH: "non real time" category
<device ID>: identification (7FH = all)
09H: sub ID #1 = General MIDI message
01H: sub ID #2 = General MIDI On
F7H: EOX
```

Deactivation

```
Deactivation
F0H: Exclusive Message status byte
7EH: "non real time" category
<device ID>: identification (7FH = all)
```

```
09H: sub ID #1 = General MIDI message
02H: sub ID #2 = General MIDI Off
F7H: EOX
```

The GS Format

When the Frankfurt meeting was held in 1991, before the General MIDI standard was approved, Roland published a preliminary version of the GS format. In terms of design this standard is similar to General MIDI and is compatible with it in several areas. However, the GS format is somewhat more advanced, because it deals exclusively with the products of a single manufacturer. This section describes the contents of version 0.94 of the GS Standard document, as published on December 8, 1990.

Basic Characteristics

A GS sound generator is polyphonic over 24 voices, for a resulting multitimbrality of 16 "parts." Table 14.4 below shows the correspondence between the MIDI channel numbers and the roles that are assigned to these channels within an arrangement. (This table assumes that each *tone*—that is, each sound, in Roland's terminology—consists only of a single partial.)

TABLE 14.4: *MIDI Channels and Polyphony in a 24-Voice GS Sound Generator*

CHANNEL	ROLE	NUMBER OF PARTIALS RESERVED
10	rhythm (drums)	2
1	piano	6
2	bass	2
3	strings	2
4	melody	2

TABLE 14.4: *MIDI Channels and Polyphony in a 24-Voice GS Sound Generator (continued)*

CHANNEL	ROLE	NUMBER OF PARTIALS RESERVED
5	strings: "sub"-strings	2
6	melody: "sub"-melody	2
7	("lower" part)	2
8	(harmonic part)	2
9	(melodic part)	2
11	percussion keyboard	—
12	—undefined—	
13	—undefined—	
14	—undefined—	
15	—undefined—	
16	—undefined—	

Channel 10 and channels 1 to 6 are treated as the major channels. They have priority with regard to the allocation of partials. Of course, you can have more partials on one channel or another, provided you don't exceed the total of 24 polyphonic voices.

Assigning Sounds

The so-called "tone map" defines a certain number of sounds (tones), each of which is associated with its Program Change number. The tone map is divided into 128 banks, with each bank consisting of 128 sounds ($128 \times 128 = 16,384$ sounds). The first 64 banks (from 00H to 3FH) are standardized by the GS format ($64 \times 128 = 8,192$ sounds), while the next 63 banks (from 40H to 7EH) are reserved for the user ($63 \times 128 = 8,0643$ sounds), and therefore automatically correspond to the addresses in RAM. Finally, the last bank (7EH) is compatible with the factory-installed sounds of the Roland MT-32.

Each of these 16,384 sounds is accessible by means of a Bank Select message followed by a Program Change message (i.e., the message that selects the sound within the bank). However, only the most significant byte (MSB) of the Bank Select message is used. This byte corresponds to the continuous controller 00H. (The continuous controller 20H, which is the least significant byte (LSB) of the Bank Select message, is ignored.)

The 128 sounds in the first bank (bank 00H), which are compatible with the General MIDI standard, as known as the *capital tones*. For a given location in the bank (that is, for a given Program Change number), each sound in the seven following banks (that is, banks 01H to 07H) corresponds to a slight variation in the sound of the capital tone (in terms of the envelope, brilliance, and other parameters). However, because of the very limited degree of difference between these sounds and the original sound, these variants have the same name as the sound in the capital tone bank.

The seven banks (08H, 10H, 18H, 20H, 28H, 30H, and 38H) for the so-called *sub-capital tones* contain sounds that, for a given location (that is, for a given Program Change message), correspond to variants that are different enough from the capital tones to need different names. For instance, the sub-capital tone for the Italian accordion (bank 08H, Program Change 15H) is only a variant of the capital sound of the French accordion (bank 00H, Program Change 15H).

In the same way, the seven banks that follow each sub-capital tone (that is, banks 09H to 0FH for bank 08H, banks 11H to 17H for bank 10H, and so on) contain sounds that, for a given location (that is, for a given Program Change message) correspond to variants of the sub-capital tones. These various bank allocations are shown graphically in Figure 14.1 below.

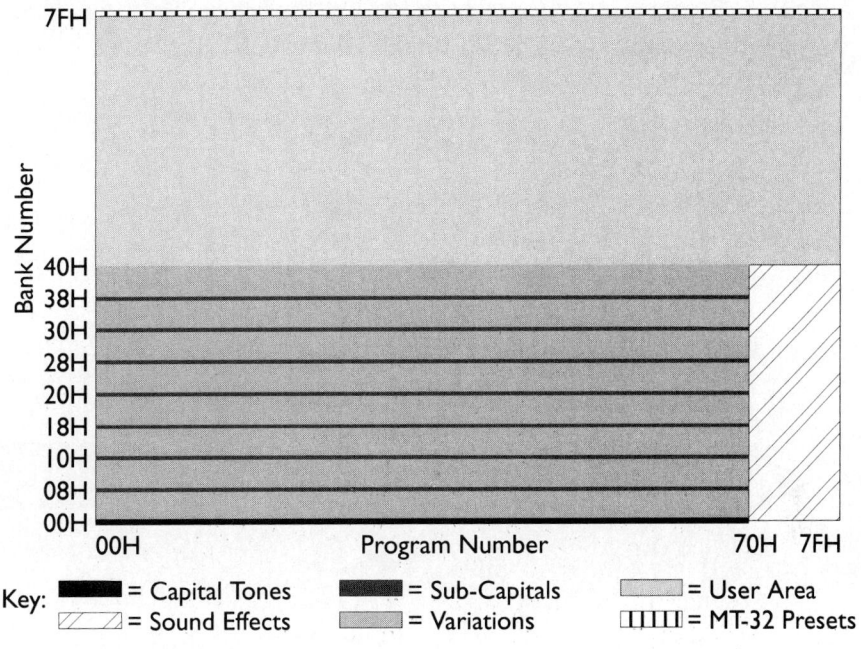

FIGURE 14.1: *Managing the banks in GS format*

It would be a mistake to assume that every instrument that's compatible with the GS standard contains 8,192 sounds. This is why a hierarchical substitution system has been provided—to deal with cases in which a Bank Select message followed by a Program Change message addresses a nonexistent location. When this location corresponds to one of the seven variants of a sub-capital bank, then the same Program Change number is selected within the sub-capital bank. Likewise, when this location corresponds to one of the seven sub-capital banks (i.e., the variants of a capital bank), then the same Program Change number is selected in the capital bank. This system also applied to banks 01H to 07H (with the same Program Change number being selected in bank 00H).

Regardless of the bank they belong to, the sounds that are addressed by Program Change numbers 70H to 7FH are an exception (which simply means that they don't obey the substitution rules described above), because these sounds are reserved for sound effects.

Assigning Drum Sets

A total of 10 drum sets are compatible with the GS format. These sets, which are assigned to MIDI Channel 10, are selected by means of the Program Change messages listed in Table 14.5 below.

TABLE 14.5: *The Ten GS-Compatible Drum Sets*

PROGRAM CHANGE NUMBERS		
DECIMAL	HEX	NAME OF THE SET
1 to 8	(00H to 07H)	The Standard set
9 to 16	(08H to 0FH)	The Room set
17 to 24	(10H to 17H)	The Power set
25 to 32	(18H to 1FH)	The Electronic set
33 to 40	(20H to 27H)	The Jazz set
41 to 48	(28H to 2FH)	The Brush set
49 to 56	(30H to 37H)	The Orchestra set
57 to 64	(38H to 3FH)	The SFX set
65 to 112	(40H to 6FH)	The User set area
113 to 128	(70H to 7FH)	The Optional set area

NOTE: Every sound generator that is compatible with the GS format has at least one standard set that corresponds to Program Change number 00H. The other sets are optional. As you'd expect, the distribution of the drum sets over the keyboard is standardized.

The Implementation Chart

Even though the GS format responds to a certain number of standard System Exclusive (SysEx) messages (as described in the next section), the continuous controllers can have an effect on the sound generator, whether these messages are standardized messages (with an RPN, or Registered Parameter Number) or NRPN messages (that is, messages with a Non Registered Parameter Number).

However, before diving into the implementation of the SysEx messages, it's worth examining in detail a sound-generator implementation chart (as shown in Figure 14.2 below) that's compatible with the GS format. This examination will give you a chance to get acquainted with three of the most recently approved MIDI messages: Legato, All Sounds Off, and RPN Reset. In the descriptions that follow Figure 14.2, the specifications indicated by a set of three dollar signs ($$$) are optional extensions of the GS format.

Model SC-55	MIDI Implementation Chart	Version : 1.00

Function ...		Transmitted	Recognized	Remarks
Basic Channel	Default	X	1 – 16	
	Changed	X	1 – 16 each	Memorized
Mode	Default	X	Mode 3	* 2
	Messages	X	Mode 3, 4 (m = 1)	
	Altered	* * * * * * * * *		
Note Number		X	0 – 127	
	True Voice	* * * * * * * * *	0 – 127	
Velocity	Note ON	X	O	
	Note OFF	X	X	
Aftertouch	Key's	X	* 1	
	Ch's	X	* 1	
Pitch Bender		X	* 1	Resolution: 12 bit
Control Change	0, 32	X	* 3 (MSB only)	Bank Select
	1	X	* 1	Modulation
	5	X	* 3	Portamento time
	6, 38	X	* 3	Data entry
	7	X	* 1	Volume
	10	X	* 1	Panpot
	11	X	* 1	Expression
	64	X	* 1	Hold1
	65	X	* 1	Portamento
	66	X	* 1	Sostenuto
	67	X	* 1	Soft
	91	X	* 3 (Reverb)	Effect1 depth
	93	X	* 3 (Chorus)	Effect3 depth
	98, 99	X	* 1	NRPN LSB, MSB
	100, 101	X	* 1	RPN LSB, MSB
	120	X	O	All sounds off
	121	X	O	Reset all controllers
Prog Change		X	* 1	
	True #	* * * * * * * * *	0 – 127	
System Exclusive		O	O	
System Common	Song Pos	X	X	
	Song Sel	X	X	
	Tune	X	X	
System Real Time	Clock	X	X	
	Commands	X	X	
Aux Messages	Local ON/OFF	X	X	
	All Notes OFF	X	O (123 – 127)	
	Active Sense	O	O	
	Reset	X	X	
Notes		* 1 OX can be selectable.		
		* 2 Recognize as m = 1 even if m ! = 1.		
		* 3 OX can be selectable, only using the receive switch control change (all).		

Mode 1: OMNI ON, POLY	Mode 2: OMNI ON, MONO	O: Yes
Mode 3: OMNI OFF, POLY	Mode 4: OMNI OFF, MONO	X: No

FIGURE 14.2: *A sound-generator implementation chart that's compatible with GS format*

The Data Received

Voice Messages

Note Off

```
8nH kkH vvH
9nH kkH 00H
```

n = the channel number: 0H to FH (that is, 0 to 15)

kkH = the note number: 00H to 7FH (that is, 0 to 127)

vvH = the velocity: 00H to 7FH (that is, 0 to 127)

* Recognized when "Rx.note message = on"

* Recognized, for a drum kit, when "Rx.note off = on" for each instrument

Note On

```
9nH kkH vvH 00H
```

n = the channel number: 0H to FH (that is, 0 to 15)

kkH = the note number: 00H to 7FH (that is, 0 to 127)

vvH = the velocity: 01H to 7FH (that is, 1 to 127)

* Recognized when "Rx.note message = on"

* Recognized, for a drum kit, when "Rx.note on = on" for each instrument

Key-Pressure Aftertouch

```
AnH kkH vvH
```

n = the channel number: 0H to FH (that is, 0 to 15)

kkH = the note number: 00H to 7FH (that is, 0 to 127)

vvH = the velocity: 00H to 7FH (that is, 0 to 127)

* Recognized when "Rx.polyphonic key pressure = on"

Control Change

Bank Select

```
BnH 00H mmH
BnH 20H llH
```

n = the channel number: 0H to FH (that is, 0 to 15)

mmH and llH = the bank number: 00H, 00H to 7FH, 7FH (i.e., from 0000H to 3FFFH, expressed over 14 bits) (that is, 0 to 16,383)

* Only the most significant byte (mmH) is used. The least significant byte is ignored. Thus, only 128 banks are available (1, 128, 256, …, 16,128).

Modulation

```
BnH 01H vvH
```

n = the channel number: 0H to FH (that is, 0 to 15)

vvH = the depth of the modulation: 00H to 7FH (that is, 0 to 127)

* Recognized when "Rx.modulation = on" (the default value), with the modulation action by default having an effect on the pitch)

Portamento Time

```
BnH 05H vvH
```

n = the channel number: 0H to FH (that is, 0 to 15)

vvH = the duration of the portamento: 00H to 7FH (that is, 0 to 127)

Data Entry

```
BnH 06H mmH
BnH 26H llH
```

n = the channel number: 0H to FH (that is, 0 to 15)

mmH and llH = the value of the parameter: 00H, 00H to 7FH, 7FH (that is, 0 to 16,383), as specified by the RPN and/or NRPN messages

Volume

```
BnH 07H vvH
```

n = the channel number: 0H to FH (that is, 0 to 15)

vvH = the volume: 00H to 7FH (that is, 0 to 127)

* The volume can be adjusted for each channel (that is, for each part)

* Recognized when "Rx.volume = on" (the default value)

Panpot

```
BnH 0AH vvH
```

n = the channel number: 0H to FH (that is, 0 to 15)

vvH = the panorama: 00H to 40H to 7FH (that is, left, center, and right)

* Recognized when "Rx.panpot = on" (the default value)

Expression

```
BnH 0BH vvH
```

n = the channel number: 0H to FH (that is, 0 to 15)

vvH = the expression: 00H to 7FH (that is, 0 to 127)

* The expression can be adjusted for each channel (that is, for each part)

* Recognized when "Rx.expression = on" (the default value)

Hold 1

BnH 40H vvH

n = the channel number: 0H to FH (that is, 0 to 15)

vvH = the sustain pedal: 00H to 7FH (with 0 = off)

* Recognized when "Rx.hold1 = on" (the default value)

Portamento

BnH 41H vvH

n = the channel number: 0H to FH (that is, 0 to 15)

vvH = the portamento: 00H to 7FH (with 0 = off)

* Recognized when "Rx.portamento = on" (the default value)

Sostenuto ($$$)

BnH 42H vvH

n = the channel number: 0H to FH (that is, 0 to 15)

vvH = the sostenuto: 00H to 7FH (with 0 = off)

* Recognized when "Rx.sostenuto = on" (the default value)

Soft Pedal

BnH 43H vvH

n = the channel number: 0H to FH (that is, 0 to 15)

vvH = the soft pedal: 00H to 7FH (with 0 = off)

* Recognized when "Rx.soft = on" (the default value)

LGC *(Legato Control)*

```
BnH 54H kkH
```

n = the channel number: 0H to FH (that is, 0 to 15)

kkH = the reference pitch (i.e., the note number): 00H to 7FH
(that is, 0 to 127)

* When a message indicating that a note has been pressed follows
an LGC message, the note in question undergoes a portamento effect. The duration of this effect is equal to the duration specified
by the Portamento Time message. The portamento starts at the
pitch defined by the LGC message and goes on until it reaches
the pitch defined by the Note message. What this means is that
you no longer have to use the Portamento On/Off message for an
individual action.

- Example 1

```
Example 1
90H 3CH 40H      Note On C4
B0H 54H 3CH      LGC (C4)
90H 40H 40H      Note On E4 (portamento from C4 to E4)
80H 3CH 40H      Note Off C4
80H 40H 40H      Note Off E4
```

- Example 2

```
B0H 54H 3CH      LGC (C4)
90H 40H 40H      Note On E4 (portamento from C4 to E4)
80H 40H 40H      Note Off E4
```

Effect 1 Depth *(Reverb Send Depth)*

```
BnH 5BH vvH
```

n = the channel number: 0H to FH (that is, 0 to 15)

vvH = the starting depth of the reverb effect: 00H to 7FH (that
is, 0 to 127)

Effect 3 Depth (Chorus Send Depth)

BnH 5DH vvH

> n = the channel number: 0H to FH (that is, 0 to 15)
>
> vvH = the starting depth of the chorus effect: 00H to 7FH (that is, 0 to 127)

NRPN MSB/LSB ($$$)

BnH 63H mmH
BnH 62H llH

> n = the channel number: 0H to FH (that is, 0 to 15)
>
> mmH = the most significant byte in parameter number NRPN
>
> llH = the least significant byte in parameter number NRPN
>
> * Recognized when "Rx.NRPN = on" (the default value)

After an NRPN parameter has been selected, its value can be modified by means of the Data Entry message. The NRPN messages that are compatible with the GS format are listed in Table 14.6 below (with the least significant byte in the Data Entry message being ignored).

TABLE 14.6: *NRPN Messages That Are Compatible with the GS Format*

MSB AND LSB	DATA-ENTRY MSB	DESCRIPTION
01H 08H	mmH	Vibrato rate (that is, the relative change in the vibrato speed on the specified channel), as indicated by the value of byte mmH: 0EH to 40H to 72H (i.e., −50 to 0 to +50)

TABLE 14.6: *NRPN Messages That Are Compatible with the GS Format (continued)*

MSB AND LSB	DATA-ENTRY MSB	DESCRIPTION
01H 09H	mmH	Vibrato depth (that is, the relative change in the depth of the vibrato on the specified channel), as indicated by the value of byte mmH: 0EH to 40H to 72H (i.e., −50 to 0 to +50)
01H 0AH ($$$)	mmH	Vibrato delay (that is, the relative change in the delay of the vibrato on the specified channel), as indicated by the value of byte mmH: 0EH to 40H to 72H (i.e., −50 to 0 to +50)
01H 20H ($$$)	mmH	TVF cut-off frequency (that is, the relative change in the cut-off frequency of the filter on the specified channel), as indicated by the value of byte mmH: 0EH to 40H to 72H (i.e., −50 to 0 to +50)
01H 21H ($$$)	mmH	TVF resonance (that is, the relative change in the resonance of the filter on the specified channel), as indicated by the value of byte mmH: 0EH to 40H to 72H (i.e., −50 to 0 to +50)

. . . .

TABLE 14.6: *NRPN Messages That Are Compatible with the GS Format (continued)*

MSB AND LSB	DATA-ENTRY MSB	DESCRIPTION
01H 63H	mmH	TVF and TVA envelope attack time (that is, the relative change in the attack time of the filter envelopes and the amplitude on the specified channel), as indicated by the value of byte mmH: 0EH to 40H to 72H (i.e., −50 to 0 to +50)
01H 64H ($$$)	mmH	TVF and TVA envelope decay time (that is, the relative change in the decay time of the filter envelopes and the amplitude on the specified channel), as indicated by the value of byte mmH: 0EH to 40H to 72H (i.e., −50 to 0 to +50)
01H 66H	mmH	TVF and TVA envelope release time (that is, the relative change in the release time of the filter envelopes and the amplitude on the specified channel), as indicated by the value of byte mmH: 0EH to 40H to 72H (i.e., −50 to 0 to +50)
18H rrH ($$$)	mmH	The coarse pitch of a drum instrument (that is, the absolute change in the pitch of the instrument whose note number is equal to rrH), as indicated by the value of byte mmH: 00H to 40H to 7FH (i.e., −64 to 0 to +63 semitones)

TABLE 14.6: *NRPN Messages That Are Compatible with the GS Format (continued)*

MSB AND LSB	DATA-ENTRY MSB	DESCRIPTION
1AH rrH	mmH	The TVA level of a drum instrument (that is, the absolute change in the amplitude of the instrument whose note number is equal to rrH), as indicated by the value of byte mmH: 00H to 7FH (i.e., 0 to 127)
1CH rrH	mmH	The panpot of a drum instrument (that is, the absolute change in the panorama of the instrument whose note number is equal to rrH), as indicated by the value mmH: 00H, 01H to 40H to 7FH (that is, random $$$; left, center, and right)
1DH rrH	mmH	The reverb send depth of a drum instrument (that is, the absolute change in the sending level toward the reverb by the instrument whose note number is equal to rrH), as indicated by the value of byte mmH: 00H to 7FH (i.e., 0 to 127)
1EH rrH ($$$)	mmH	The chorus send depth of a drum instrument (that is, the absolute change in the sending level toward the chorus by the instrument whose note number is equal to rrH), as indicated by the value of byte mmH: 00H to 7FH (i.e., 0 to 127)

RPN MSB/LSB

```
BnH 65H mmH
BnH 64H llH
```

n = the channel number: 0H to FH (that is, 0 to 15)

mmH = the most significant byte in parameter number RPN

llH = the least significant byte in parameter number RPN

* Recognized when "Rx.RPN = on" (the default value)

After an RPN parameter has been selected, its value can be modified by means of the Data Entry message. The RPN messages that are compatible with the GS format are listed in Table 14.7 below.

TABLE 14.7: *RPN Messages That Are Compatible with the GS Format*

MSB AND LSB	DATA-ENTRY MSB AND LSB	DESCRIPTION
00H 00H	mmH —	Pitch Bend sensitivity, with mmH = 00H to 18H (that is, from 0 to 24 semitones). The value of byte llH is ignored, and the default value is two semitones.
00H 01H	mmH llH	Master Fine Tuning, with mmH, llH = 00H, 00H to 40H, 00H to 7FH, and 7FH (that is, from $-8{,}192 \times 100 \ / \ 8{,}192$ to 0 to $+8{,}191 \times 100 \ / \ 8{,}192$ cents).
00H 02H	mmH —	Master Coarse Tuning, with mmH = 28H to 40H to 58H (that is, from -24 to 0 to $+24$ semitones)

TABLE 14.7: *RPN Messages That Are Compatible with the GS Format (continued)*

MSB AND LSB	DATA-ENTRY MSB AND LSB	DESCRIPTION
7FH 7FH	— —	RPN Reset (with the value of the RPN and NRPN parameters being reset). The values of byte mmH and byte llH are ignored.

. . . .

Program Change

CnH ppH

    n = the channel number: 0H to FH (that is, 0 to 15)

    ppH = the program number: 00H to 7FH (that is, 0 to 127)

    * Recognized when "Rx.program change = on" (the default value)

Channel Aftertouch

DnH vvH

    n = the channel number: 0H to FH (that is, 0 to 15)

    vvH = the aftertouch value: 00H to 7FH (that is, 0 to 127)

    * Recognized when "Rx.channel pressure = on"

Pitch Bend Change

EnH llH mmH

    n = the channel number: 0H to FH (that is, 0 to 15)

    mmH, llH = the value: 00H, 00H to 40H, 00H to 7FH, 7FH (that is, −8,192 to 0 to +8,191)

    * Recognized when "Rx.pitch bend = on". The Pitch Bend action is described in the section entitled "Bend controller function" (and by default has an effect on pitch).

Mode Messages

All Sounds Off

```
BnH 78H 00H
```

  n = the channel number: 0H to FH (that is, 0 to 15)

  * The sounds on the specified channel are immediately cut off.

Reset All Controllers

```
BnH 79H 00H
```

  n = the channel number: 0H to FH (that is, 0 to 15)

The controllers are reinitialized to their default values, as listed below:

```
pitch bend              : 64 (center)
polyphonic key pressure : 0 (off)
channel aftertouch      : 0 (off)
modulation              : 0 (off)
expression              : 127 (maximum)
hold 1                  : 0 (off)
portamento              : 0 (off)
sostenuto               : 0 (off)
soft pedal              : 0 (off)
RPN                     : no change
NRPN                    : no change
```

All Notes Off

```
BnH 7BH 00H
```

  n = the channel number: 0H to FH (that is, 0 to 15)

  * The notes on the specified channel are immediately cut off, except if the Hold and/or Sostenuto pedal is being held down.

Omni Off

```
BnH 7CH 00H
```

  n = the channel number: 0H to FH (that is, 0 to 15)

* The Omni Off message is recognized only in the form of an All Notes Off message. The mode is not affected.

Omni On

BnH 7DH 00H

n = the channel number: 0H to FH (that is, 0 to 15)

* The Omni On message is recognized only in the form of an All Notes On message. The mode is not affected.

Mono

BnH 7EH mmH

n = the channel number: 0H to FH (that is, 0 to 15)

* The Mono message is recognized in the form of an All Notes On message. The specified channel changes to Mode 4 (mm = 1), even if mmH has a value other than 1.

Poly

BnH 7FH 00H

n = the channel number: 0H to FH (that is, 0 to 15)

* The Poly message is recognized only in the form of an All Notes On message. The specified channel switches to Mode 3.

Real-Time Messages

Active Sensing

FEH

NOTE: When no MIDI message has been received for a period of 420 milliseconds, and provided that at least one Active Sensing message was received earlier, the instrument performs the following actions before returning to its normal operating mode, without worrying about the time intervals that separate the messages it receives:

```
all sounds off
all notes off
reset all controllers
```

Exclusive Messages

The Exclusive messages that are received are dealt with in the next section.

The Transmitted Data

Active Sensing (Real-Time Messages)

FEH

* Transmitted approximately every 250 milliseconds

Exclusive Messages (Real Time)

The Exclusive messages that are transmitted are dealt with in the next section.

The Syntax of Exclusive Messages

This section discusses the syntax of Exclusive messages.

Implemented Messages

The Exclusive messages that are implemented on every sound generators that is compatible with the GS format are listed below.

One-Way Dump Request (RQ1)

```
F0H (11110000): Exclusive message status byte
41H (01000001): Roland ID
10H:(00010000): unit number (device ID = 17)
```

```
42H (01000010): model or family (model ID = GS format)
11H (00010001): code RQ1 (one-way request)
ddH (0ddddddd): address (start)
eeH (0eeeeeee): address (continuation)
ffH (0fffffff): address (end)
ggH (0ggggggg): size (start)
hhH (0hhhhhhh): size (continuation)
iiH (0iiiiiii): size (end)
ccH (0ccccccc): checksum
F7H (11110111): EOX (end of exclusive)
```

One-Way Dump (DT1)

```
F0H (11110000): Exclusive Message status byte
41H (01000001): Roland ID
10H:(00010000): unit number (device ID = 17)
42H (01000010): model or family ID (model ID = GS format)
12H (00010010): code DT1 (one-way dump)
ddH (0ddddddd): address (start)
eeH (0eeeeeee): address (continuation)
ffH (0fffffff): address (end)
xxH (0xxxxxxx): data
...
ccH (0ccccccc): checksum
F7H (11110111): EOX (end of exclusive)
```

Data Addresses

The memory addresses at which the data resides are indicated in the diagram in Figure 14.3 below. The addresses are expressed in hexadecimal form, distributed over three bytes each consisting of seven bits.

In other words, a capability has been provided that lets you transfer parameters either individually or in the form of a block of data (that is, as a so-called *bulk dump*).

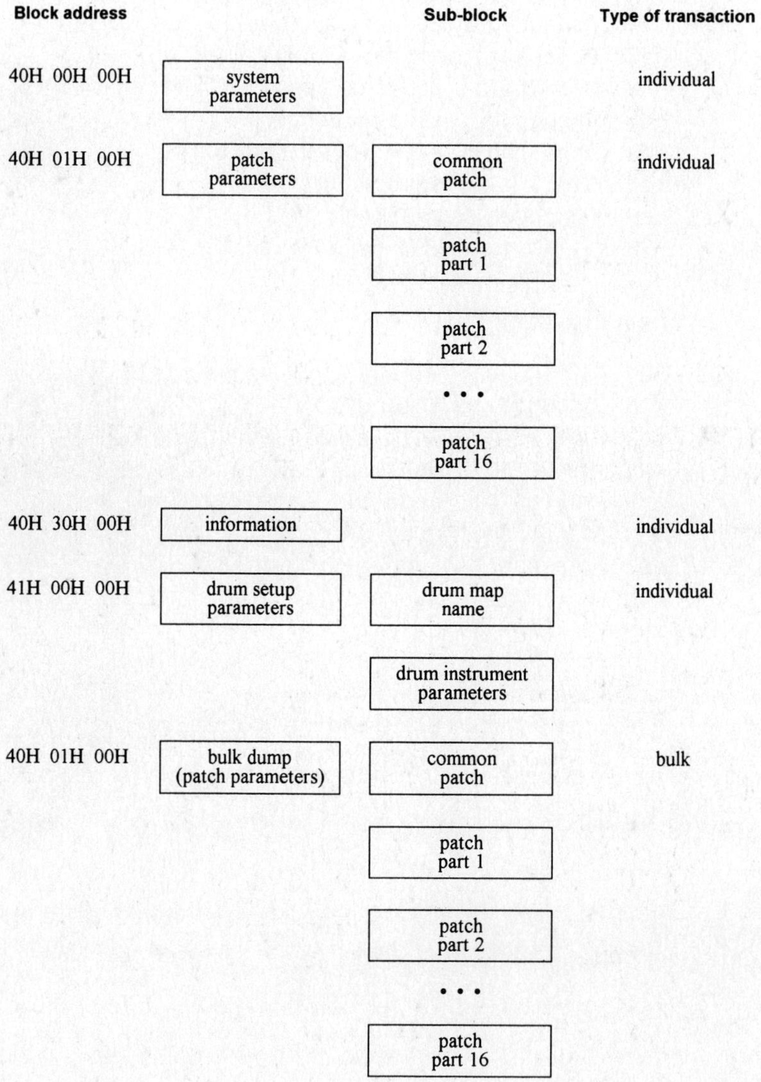

Block address	Sub-block	Type of transaction
40H 00H 00H	system parameters	individual
40H 01H 00H	patch parameters — common patch	individual
	patch part 1	
	patch part 2	
	• • •	
	patch part 16	
40H 30H 00H	information	individual
41H 00H 00H	drum setup parameters — drum map name	individual
	drum instrument parameters	
40H 01H 00H	bulk dump (patch parameters) — common patch	bulk
	patch part 1	
	patch part 2	
	• • •	
	patch part 16	

FIGURE 14.3: *Memory addresses of the data*

Transferring Individual Parameters

Tables 14.8 and 14.9 below shows the details of the individual parameters that can be sent via MIDI. Naturally, each parameter has to be transferred in its entirety. Therefore, when a parameter consists of more than one byte, the addresses indicated by an octothorpe (or pound sign, #) are inaccessible.

System Parameters

TABLE 14.8: *Individual Parameters That Can Be Transferred via MIDI*

ADDRESS	SIZE	RANGE OF VALUES	PARAMETER	DEFAULT VALUE
40H 00H 00H	00H 00H 04H	0018H to 07E8H	Master tune (−100.0 to +100.0)	0400H
40H 00H 01H#			(data expressed in the form of nybbles)	
40H 00H 02H#				
40H 00H 03H#				
40H 00H 04H	00H 00H 01H	00H to 7FH	Master volume (0 to 127)	7FH
40H 00H 05H	00H 00H 01H	28H to 58H	Master key-shift (+/−24)	40H
40H 00H 06H	00H 00H 01H	00H to 7FH	Master pan	40H

TABLE 14.8: *Individual Parameters That Can Be Transferred via MIDI (continued)*

ADDRESS	SIZE	RANGE OF VALUES	PARAMETER	DEFAULT VALUE
40H 00H 7FH	00H 00H 01H	00H	Reset to GSS mode (that is, all of the parameters return to their default values)	

. . . .

Patch Parameters

> * n = the block number (from 0H to FH)
>
> > Part 1 (the default MIDI channel = 1), n = 1H
> >
> > Part 2 (the default MIDI channel = 2), n = 2H
> >
> > Part 3 (the default MIDI channel = 3), n = 3H
> >
> > Part 4 (the default MIDI channel = 4), n = 4H
> >
> > Part 5 (the default MIDI channel = 5), n = 5H
> >
> > Part 6 (the default MIDI channel = 6), n = 6H
> >
> > Part 7 (the default MIDI channel = 7), n = 7H
> >
> > Part 8 (the default MIDI channel = 8), n = 8H
> >
> > Part 9 (the default MIDI channel = 9), n = 9H
> >
> > Part 10 (the default MIDI channel = 10), n = 0H
> >
> > Part 11 (the default MIDI channel = 11), n = AH
> >
> > Part 12 (the default MIDI channel = 12), n = BH

Part 13 (the default MIDI channel = 13), n = CH

Part 14 (the default MIDI channel = 14), n = DH

Part 15 (the default MIDI channel = 15), n = EH

Part 16 (the default MIDI channel = 16), n = FH

X = MIDI channel (0H to FH)

TABLE 14.9: *Addresses of the Patch Parameters*

ADDRESS	SIZE	RANGE OF VALUES	PARAMETER	DEFAULT VALUE
40 01H 10H	00H 00H 10H	00H to 17H	Partial reserve (part 10: drums)	2H
40H 01H 11H#			Part 1	6H
40H 01H 12H#			Part 2	2H
40H 01H 13H#			Part 3	2H
40H 01H 14H#			Part 4	2H
40H 01H 15H#			Part 5	2H
40H 01H 16H#			Part 6	2H
40H 01H 17H#			Part 7	2H
40H 01H 18H#			Part 8	2H
40H 01H 19H#			Part 9	2H
40H 01H 1AH#			Part 11	0H
40H 01H 1BH#			Part 12	0H
40H 01H 1CH#			Part 13	0H
40H 01H 1DH#			Part 14	0H
40H 01H 1EH#			Part 15	0H
40H 01H 1FH#			Part 16	0H

The sum of the partials should never be greater than the number of voices in the sound generator. What this means, for instance, is that if an instrument that has 24 polyphonic voices, the maximum value for the sum of the partials is 17H.

Information (RQ1 Only)

ADDRESS	SIZE	RANGE OF VALUES	PARAMETER
40H 30H 00H	00H 00H 20H	20H to 7FH	system information (ASCII)
… … …#			"GP STANDARD SOUND BOARD VER=1.00"
			47H 50H 20H 53H 54H 41H 4EH 44H 41H 52H 44H 20H 53H
… … …#			4FH 55H 4EH 44H 20H 42H 4FH 41H 52H 44H 20H 56H 45H
40H 30H 1FH#			52H 3DH 31H 2EH 30H 30H
41H m0H 00H	00H 00H 0CH	20H to 7FH	drum map name (ASCII)
… … …#			
… … …#			
41H m0H 0BH#			

ADDRESS	SIZE	RANGE OF VALUES	PARAMETER
41H m1H rrH	00H 00H 01H	00H to 7FH	play key number (coarse pitch) (= BxH 63H 18H 62H rrH 06H vvH)
41H m2H rrH	00H 00H 01H	00H to 7FH	level (TVA level) (= BxH 63H 1AH 62H rrH 06H vvH)
41H m3H rrH	00H 00H 01H	00H to 7FH	assign group number (1 to 127)
41H m4H rrH	00H 00H 01H	00H to 7FH	panpot (random, −63 to +63) (= BxH 63H 1CH 62H rrH 06H vvH)
41H m5H rrH	00H 00H 01H	00H to 7FH	reverb depth (0.0 to 1.0) multiplication coefficient of the reverb depth of the part (= BxH 63H 1DH 62H rrH 06H vvH)
41H m6H rrH	00H 00H 01H	00H to 7FH	chorus depth (0.0 to 1.0) multiplication coefficient of the chorus depth of the part (= BxH 63H 1EH 62H rrH 06H vvH)
41H m7H rrH	00H 00H 01H	00H to 01H	Rx.Note Off (off, on)
41H m8H rrH	00H 00H 01H	00H to 01H	Rx.Note On (off, on)

Drum Setup Parameters

mH = map number (0H = map 1, and 1H = map 2)

rrH = drum part key number (from 00H to 7FH)

Transferring Parameters by Blocks (Bulk Transfers)

Here are the detailed descriptions of the blocks of parameters that can be transferred via MIDI. A bulk dump consists of a packet containing up to 128 bytes.

1) All Patch

Size: $64 + (112 \times 16) = 1,856$

Transmission via nybbles: $1,856 \times 2 = 3,712$ (that is, 1D00H distributed over 2 MIDI data bytes, each of which contains 7 useful bits)

ADDRESS	SIZE	RANGE OF VALUES	PARAMETER
48H 00H 00H	00H 1DH 00H	—	29 packets
… … …#			
… … …#			
48H 1CH 7FH#			

2) Common Patch

Size: 64

Transmission via nybbles: $64 \times 2 = 128$ (that is, 0100H distributed over 2 MIDI data bytes, each of which contains 7 useful bits)

ADDRESS	SIZE	RANGE OF VALUES	PARAMETER
48H 00H 00H	00H 01H 00H	—	1 packet
... ...#			
... ...#			
48H 00H 7FH#			

3) Part Patch

Size: 112

Transmission via nybbles: $112 \times 2 = 224$ (that is, 0160H distributed over 2 MIDI data bytes, each of which contains 7 useful bits)

ADDRESS	SIZE	RANGE OF VALUES	PARAMETER
48H 01H 00H	00H 01H 60H	Part 10	2 packets
... ...#			
... ...#			
48H 02H 5FH#			
48H 02H 60H	00H 01H 60H	Part 1	2 packets
... ...#			
... ...#			
48H 04H 3FH#			

ADDRESS	SIZE	RANGE OF VALUES	PARAMETER
48H 04H 40H	00H 01H 60H	Part 2	2 packets
… … …#			
… … …#			
48H 06H 1FH#			
48H 06H 20H	00H 01H 60H	Part 3	2 packets
… … …#			
… … …#			
48H 07H 7FH#			
48H 08H 00H	00H 01H 60H	Part 4	2 packets
… … …#			
… … …#			
48H 09H 5FH#			
48H 09H 60H	00H 01H 60H	Part 5	2 packets
… … …#			
… … …#			
48H 0AH 3FH#			

ADDRESS	SIZE	RANGE OF VALUES	PARAMETER
48H 0BH 40H	00H 01H 60H	Part 6	2 packets
... ...#			
... ...#			
48H 0DH 1FH#			
48H 0DH 20H	00H 01H 60H	Part 7	2 packets
... ...#			
... ...#			
48H 0EH 7FH#			
48H 0FH 00H	00H 01H 60H	Part 8	2 packets
... ...#			
... ...#			
48H 10H 5FH#			
48H 10H 60H	00H 01H 60H	Part 9	2 packets
... ...#			
... ...#			
48H 12H 3FH#			

ADDRESS	SIZE	RANGE OF VALUES	PARAMETER
48H 12H 40H	00H 01H 60H	Part 11	2 packets
… … …#			
… … …#			
48H 14H 1FH#			
48H 14H 20H	00H 01H 60H	Part 12	2 packets
… … …#			
… … …#			
48H 15H 7FH#			
48H 16H 00H	00H 01H 60H	Part 13	2 packets
… … …#			
… … …#			
48H 17H 5FH#			
48H 17H 60H	00H 01H 60H	Part 14	2 packets
… … …#			
… … …#			
48H 19H 3FH#			

ADDRESS	SIZE	RANGE OF VALUES	PARAMETER
48H 19H 40H	00H 01H 60H	Part 15	2 packets
... ...#			
... ...#			
48H 1BH 1FH#			
48H 1BH 20H	00H 01H 60H	Part 16	2 packets
... ...#			
... ...#			
48H 1CH 7FH#			

MIDI Show Control

The MSC (MIDI Show Control) standard, of which version 1.0 was published on July 25, 1991, lets you control different kinds of devices for stage, multimedia, audiovisual, and other applications. Because MIDI Show Control is of less concern to musicians than it is to stage managers and production personnel, this section will be limited to a brief overview. The entire document, including both the standard itself and its other extensions, is of course available from the IMA.

Message Syntax

The control messages are real-time System Exclusive (SysEx) messages (with sub-ID #1 = 02H), as shown in detail below:

```
F0H          : Exclusive message status byte
7FH          : category = real time
```

```
<device_ID>      : device ID (destination address)
<msc>            : 02H (sub-ID #1)
<command_format>: format of the command
<command>        : command
<data>           : data
F7H              : EOX
```

The maximum size of a message is limited to 128 bytes.

In this version of the standard, communications are unidirectional (that is, from the control unit to the unit that's being controlled). No response is expected or provided for. This way a malfunction in one of the controlled units will not affect any of the other controlled units.

Identifier Syntax

```
<device_ID> = 00H to 6FH: individual
            = 70H to 7EH: group identifiers
            = 7FH        : "all call" identifier
```

Each controlled unit must respond to an "all call" identifier. Each unit has the option of recognizing and accepting one or more individual or group identifiers.

A typical system consists of at least one control unit that is aimed at one or more units that are controlled. There's no reason why any given device can't serve as both a control unit and a controlled unit at the same time—in other words, transmit different commands depending on the commands that it receives.

For informational purposes, a controlled unit can of course transmit to a control unit the names of the commands that it supports. As a result, by polling the set of controlled units, the control unit can also build up and serve as a data base that stores the commands that each device accepts.

The Syntax of Command Formats

```
<command_format>

00H: reserved for future extensions

00H 01H: first extension level
00H 00H 01H: second extension level

01H: lighting (category = general)
02H: moving lighting
03H: color changers
04H: strobes
05H: lasers
06H: chasers

10H: sound (category = general)
11H: music
12H: CD players
13H: EPROM playback
14H: audio tape machines
15H: intercoms
16H: amplifiers
17H: audio effects devices
18H: equalizers

20H: machinery (category = general)
21H: rigging
22H: flys
23H: lifts
24H: turntables
25H: trusses
26H: robots
27H: animation
28H: floats
29H: breakaways
2AH: barges

30H: video (category = general)
31H: video tape machines
```

```
32H: videocassette machines
33H: videodisc players
34H: video switchers
35H: video effects
36H: video character generators
37H: video still stores
38H: video monitors

40H: projection (category = general)
41H: film projectors
42H: slide projectors
43H: video projectors
44H: dissolvers
45H: shutter controls

50H: process control (category = general)
51H: hydraulic oil
52H: H2O (water)
53H: CO2 (carbon dioxide)
54H: compressed air
55H: natural gas
56H: fog
57H: smoke
58H: cracked haze

60H: pyro (pyrotechnics, category = general)
61H: fireworks
62H: explosions
63H: flame
64H: smoke pots

7FH: all types
```

NOTE: MIDI Show Control should never be used as a substitute for the security and safety standards that are currently in effect. The purpose of MIDI Show Control is not to determine whether conditions are satisfactory for sending orders to a controlled unit, but rather to issue an order that will be executed only when optimal precautions have been taken.

Command Syntax

```
<command>

00H           : reserved for future extensions

00H 01H       : first extension level
00H 00H 01H   : second extension level
```

General Commands

Table 14.10 below summarizes the general MIDI Show Control commands.

TABLE 14.10: *General MIDI Show Control Commands*

HEX VALUE	COMMAND	NUMBER OF DATA BYTES
01H	GO	—variable—
02H	STOP	—variable—
03H	RESUME	—variable—
04H	TIMED_GO	—variable—
05H	LOAD	—variable—
06H	SET	4 or 9
07H	FIRE	1
08H	ALL_OFF	0
09H	RESTORE	0
0AH	RESET	0
0BH	GO_OFF	—variable—

Sound Commands

Table 14.11 below summarizes the MIDI Show Control commands that control sounds.

TABLE 14.11: *MIDI Show Control Sound Commands*

HEX VALUE	COMMAND	NUMBER OF DATA BYTES
10H	GO/JAM_CLOCK	—variable—
11H	STANDBY_+	—variable—
12H	STANDBY_–	—variable—
13H	SEQUENCE_+	—variable—
14H	SEQUENCE_–	—variable—
15H	START_CLOCK	—variable—
16H	STOP_CLOCK	—variable—
17H	ZERO_CLOCK	—variable—
18H	SET_CLOCK	—variable—
19H	MTC_CHASE_ON	—variable—
1AH	MTC_CHASE_OFF	—variable—
1BH	OPEN_CUE_LIST	—variable—
1CH	CLOSE_CUE_LIST	—variable—
1DH	OPEN_CUE_PATH	—variable—
1EH	CLOSE_CUE_PATH	—variable—

Data Syntax

`<data>`

When different types of information are specified, the data bytes are separated by a delimitation character, 00H.

Event Numbers

```
<Q_number> 00H <Q_list> 00H <Q_path>
```

The <Q_path> and <Q_list> information is optional. What this means is that you can transmit either:

```
<Q_number> 00H >Q_list>
```

or

```
<Q_number>
```

Expressed in ASCII form, the information uses the digits 0 to 9 (that is, 30H to 39H) as well as the decimal point (2EH). For example, a Q_number, a Q_list, and a Q_path that are equal respectively to 235.6, 36.6, and 59 would be indicated in hex by the following string:

```
32H 33H 35H 2EH 36H 00H 33H 36H 2EH 36H 00H 35H 39H
```

The Time Code

The Time Code is the same one used by the new MIDI Machine Control standard. The format of the Time Code is compatible with the MIDI Time Code.

The Time Code consists of five bytes. The last byte contains either subframes or the provenance of the time code (i.e., the status). The code can be issued either by an SMPTE track or by a sound generator, as the result of a calculation performed on the basis of the tachometry information or from a control track during the fast-forward or high-speed rewinding phase. The Time Code has the following format:

```
hrH mnH scH frH (ffH stH)

hrH = hour, type of code: 0 tt hhhhh
    tt = type
    tt = 00: 24 frames/second
    tt = 01: 25 frames/second
    tt = 10: 30 frames/second (drop-frame)
```

```
   tt = 11: 30 frames/second (non-drop-frame)
   hhhhh = hours: 0 to 23 (00H to 17H)

mnH = minutes: 0 c mmmmmm
   c = bit "color frame"
   c = 0: non-color frame
   c = 1: color frame
   mmmmmm = minutes: 0 to 59 (00H to 3BH)

scH = seconds: 0 k ssssss
   k = reserved: should be equal to zero
   ssssss = seconds: 0 to 59 (00H to 3BH)

frH = frames, fifth-byte identifier, sign: 0 g i fffff
   g = sign bit
   g = 0: positive
   g = 1: negative (when a signed time code is authorized)
   i = identifier of the role of the fifth byte (i.e., the next byte)
   i = 0: subframes
   i = 1: status
   fffff = frames: 0 to 29 (00H to 1DH)

  ffH (i = 1) = subframes: 0 bbbbbbb
   bbbbbbb: 0 to 99 (00H to 63H)

stH (i = 1) = status code: 0 e v d xxxx
   e = type of code
   e = 0: normal time code normal
   e = 1: tachometry or control track
   v = validity (ignore when e = 1)
   v = 0: valid
   v = 1: invalid
   d = video field identifier
   d = 0: no field information in this frame
   d = 1: first frame in a video sequence of four or eight fields
   xxxx = reserved bits:  should be equal to zero
```

The Syntax of MSC Commands and Associated Data

GO (01H)

```
01H        : GO
<Q_number> : optional (required when <Q_list> is transmitted)
00H        : delimiter
<Q_list>   : optional (required when <Q_path> is transmitted)
00H        : delimiter
<Q_path>   : optional
```

This command triggers a transition or a crossfade or lap dissolve toward an event. The transition time is determined by the event with which the controlled unit is involved. When no event number is specified, the event that has the higher or highest number is triggered. When an event number is specified, that event is triggered. If the control unit wants to specify the transition time, it should use the TIMED-GO command.

In a situation in which the controlled units can contain several event lists, if the <Q_number> parameter is not transmitted, then the events whose numbers are greater than the number of the current event that has the same number and that appear on an active list (see the OPEN_CUE_LIST command described below) will "start." If the <Q_number> parameter is transmitted without the <Q_list> parameter, all of the events whose number is equal to the <Q_number> and that belong to an active list will start.

STOP (02H)

```
02H        : STOP
<Q_number> : optional (required when <Q_list> is transmitted)
00H        : delimiter
<Q_list>   : optional (required when <Q_path> is transmitted)
00H        : delimiter
<Q_path>   : optional
```

This command stops any transitions that may be in progress. When no event number is specified, all of the current transitions are stopped. When an event number is specified, only the transition in question is stopped. None of the other transitions is affected.

RESUME (03H)

```
03H          : RESUME
<Q_number> : optional (required when <Q_list> is transmitted)
00H          : delimiter
<Q_list>    : optional (required when <Q_path> is transmitted)
00H          : delimiter
<Q_path>    : optional
```

The stopped transition or transitions resume their operation. When no event number is specified, all of the stopped transitions are resumed. When an event number is specified, only the transition in question resumes its operation. None of the other transitions is affected.

TIMED_GO (04H)

```
04H                   : TIMED_GO
hrH mnH scH frH ffH : time
<Q_number>           : optional (required when <Q_list> is transmitted)
00H                   : delimiter
<Q_list>             : optional (required when <Q_path> is transmitted)
00H                   : delimiter
<Q_path>             : optional
```

This command triggers a transition or a crossfade or lap dissolve toward an event. The transition time is determined by the event with which the controlled unit is involved. When no event number is specified, the event having the next higher number is triggered. When an event number is specified, the related event is triggered.

The time is expressed in standard format (i.e., in terms of the fifth byte, which is type ffH (subframe)). Therefore, it's possible to perform transitions that have a duration of up to 24 hours (and that have a mini-mum duration that can be considered instantaneous). If a controlled unit cannot receive the TIMED_GO command, the unit should interpret the command as a GO command and respond to it without worrying about the time.

In a situation in which the controlled units can contain several event lists, if the <Q_number> parameter is not transmitted, then the events whose numbers are greater than the number of the current event that has the same number and that appear on an active list (see the OPEN_CUE_LIST command described below) will "start." If the <Q_number> parameter is transmitted without the <Q_list> parameter, all of the events whose number is equal to the <Q_number> and that belong to an active list will start.

LOAD (05H)

```
05H         : LOAD
<Q_number> : required
00H         : delimiter
<Q_list>   : optional (required when <Q_path> is transmitted)
00H         : delimiter
<Q_path>   : optional
```

This command places an event in the wait state. It's useful when a certain amount of time is necessary in order to gain access to the event in ques-tion, so that an order that is transmitted later by means of a GO com-mand can be executed instantaneously.

In a situation in which the controlled units can contain several event lists, if the <Q_number> parameter is transmitted without the <Q_list> pa-rameter, all of the events whose number is equal to the <Q_number> and that belong to an active list will be placed in the wait state.

SET (06H)

```
06H                   : SET
ccH ccH               : control number (LSB/MSB)
vvH vvH               : control value (LSB/MSB)
hrH mnH scH frH ffH   : time (optional)
```

Standard control numbers for the lighting category:

```
  0 to 127   : sub-masters
128 to 129   : first-playback masters
130 to 131   : second-playback masters
...
190 to 191   : thirty-second-playback masters
192 to 223   : speed control for the 32 playbacks
224 to 255   : chase-sequence masters
256 to 287   : chase-sequence speed masters
510          : grand master for all of the channels
511          : speed control for all of the crossfades
512 to 1023  : levels of the individual channels
```

This command defines the value of a standard control. The control number and its value are both specified in the form of 14 bits. As an option, the time required by a controller in order to reach its value can be transmitted.

The time is expressed in standard format (i.e., in terms of the fifth byte, which is type ffH (subframe)). Therefore, it's possible to perform transitions that have a duration of up to 24 hours (and that have a minimum duration that can be considered instantaneous). The controlled unit should respond to the SET command even if it cannot receive the time for this command.

FIRE (07H)

```
07H: FIRE
mmH: the macro number
```

This command triggers a pre-programmed macro whose number is specified in terms of seven bits by the mm byte. The macros themselves are programmed directly from the controlled unit, either loaded by means of a MIDI Files dump (i.e., using the MIDI Files file-transfer protocol, which is currently going through the approval process), the ASCII Cue Data format (which is also in the process of being approved), or by any other appropriate means.

ALL_OFF (08H)

```
08H: ALL_OFF
```

This command puts the controlled unit out of service.

RESTORE (09H)

```
09H: RESTORE
```

This command returns the controlled unit to service in a state that is identical to the state the unit was in when it received the ALL_OFF command.

RESET (0AH)

```
0AH: RESET
```

This command reinitializes the controlled unit in a state that is identical to the state the unit was in when it was turned on. It loads the first event on each event list in the appropriate waiting position. The manufacturer of the controlled unit has the option of deciding whether the reinitialization should automatically enable all of the closed event lists (or cue lists) and event path lists (or cue paths).

GO_OFF (0BH)

```
0BH          : GO_OFF
<Q_number> : optional (required when <Q_list> is transmitted)
00H          : delimiter
```

```
<Q_list>     : optional (required when <Q_path> is transmitted)
OOH          : delimiter
<Q_path>     : optional
```

This command triggers a transition or a crossfade or lap dissolve toward the stopped state of an event. The transition time is determined by the event with which the controlled unit is involved. When no event number is specified, the command is applied to the current event. When an event number is specified, the command is applied to the event indicated by the number.

In a situation in which the controlled units can contain several event lists, if the <Q_number> parameter is not transmitted, then all of the current events that appear on an active list (see the OPEN_CUE_LIST command described below) will stop. If the <Q_number> parameter is transmitted without the <Q_list> parameter, all of the events whose number is equal to the <Q_number> and that belong to an active list will stop.

GO/JAM_CLOK (10H)

```
10H          : GO/JAM_CLOK
<Q_number>   : optional (required when <Q_list> is transmitted)
OOH          : delimiter
<Q_list>     : optional (required when <Q_path> is transmitted)
OOH          : delimiter
<Q_path>     : optional
```

This command triggers a transition, such as a crossfade or lap dissolve, toward an event while forcing the time to the starting or go time if the event is an "auto follow" event. The transition time is determined by the event with which the controlled unit is involved. When no event number is specified, the command is applied to the current event. When an event number is specified, the event that has the next higher number is triggered, and the clock for the event list in question "jumps" to the time of the event. If the next event on the list is a manual event (for instance, an event that is not associated with a particular starting time), then the

GO/JAM_CLOK command is ignored. If an event number is specified, then the event indicated by that number will be triggered, and the clock for the event list in question "jumps" to the time of the event—unless the next event on the list is a manual event, in which case no change occurs.

STANDBY_+ (11H)

```
11H: STANDBY_+
<Q_list> : optional
```

This command places the next event (that is, the event whose number is the next higher number after the number of the current event) in the wait state.

If the <Q_list> parameter is not transmitted, then the open list of events containing an event whose number is greater than the number of the current event is used (and the event in question is placed in the wait state). When several event lists each contain an event that is characterized by this same number, then all of these lists are used (and all of the events in question are placed in the wait state). In the opposite case, when the <Q_list> parameter is transmitted, only the event on this list whose number is greater than the number of the current event is placed in the wait state.

STANDBY_— (12H)

```
12H: STANDBY_-
<Q_list> : optional
```

This command places the preceding event (that is, the event whose number is immediately lower than the number of the current event) in the wait state.

If the <Q_list> parameter is not transmitted, then the open list of events containing an event whose number is lower than the number of the current event is used (and the event in question is placed in the wait state). When several event lists each contain an event that is characterized by this same number, then all of these lists are used (and all of the events in question are placed in the wait state). In the opposite case, when the <Q_list> parameter is transmitted, only the event on this list whose number is lower than the number of the current event is placed in the wait state.

SEQUENCE_+ (13H)

```
13H: SEQUENCE_+
<Q_list> : optional
```

This command places the next so-called "parent" event (that is, the event whose number is greater than the number of the current event) in the wait state. The concept of a "parent" event applies to the integer value of the event number—that is, to the part of the number located to the left of the first decimal point. For instance, for a current event whose number is 29.324.98.7 and a list of subsequent events whose numbers are 29.235, 29.4, 29.7, 29.9.876, 36.7, 36.7.832, 36.8, 37, and 37.1, the SEQUENCE_+ command would place the event whose number is 36.7 in the wait state.

If the <Q_list> parameter is not transmitted, then the open list of events containing an event whose number is greater than the number of the current event is used (and the event in question is placed in the wait state). When several event lists each contain an event that is characterized by this same number, then all of these lists are used (and all of the events in question are placed in the wait state). In the opposite case, when the <Q_list> parameter is transmitted, only the event on this list whose number is greater than the number of the current event is placed in the wait state.

SEQUENCE_− (14H)

```
14H: SEQUENCE_−
<Q_list> : optional
```

This command places the preceding so-called "parent" event (that is, the event whose number is greater than the number of the current event) in the wait state. The concept of a "parent" event applies to the integer value of the event number—that is, to the part of the number located to the left of the first decimal point. For instance, for a current event whose number is 37.4.72.18.5 and a list of preceding events whose numbers are 29.325, 29.4, 29.7, 29.9.876, 36.7, 36.7.832, 36.8, 37, and 37.1, the SEQUENCE_– command would place the event whose number is 36.8 in the wait state.

If the <Q_list> parameter is not transmitted, then the open list of events containing an event whose number is lower than the number of the current event is used (and the event in question is placed in the wait state). When several event lists each contain an event that is characterized by this same number, then all of these lists are used (and all of the events in question are placed in the wait state). In the opposite case, when the <Q_list> parameter is transmitted, only the event on this list whose number is lower than the number of the current event is placed in the wait state.

START_CLOCK (15H)

```
15H: START_CLOCK
<Q_list> : optional
```

This command triggers the clock, starting at the time that the clock is currently showing.

When the <Q_list> parameter is not transmitted, the clocks of all of the event lists start. In the opposite case, when the <Q_list> parameter is transmitted, only the clock for the corresponding event list starts.

STOP_CLOCK (16H)

```
16H: STOP_CLOCK
<Q_list> : optional
```

This command stops the clock.

When the <Q_list> parameter is not transmitted, the clocks of all of the event lists stop. In the opposite case, when the <Q_list> parameter is transmitted, only the clock for the corresponding event list stops.

ZERO_CLOCK (17H)

```
17H: ZERO_CLOCK
<Q_list> : optional
```

This command resets the clock to zero (00.00.00.00.00), regardless of whether the clock is stopped or running.

When the <Q_list> parameter is not transmitted, the clocks of all the event lists are reset to zero. In the opposite case, when the <Q_list> parameter is transmitted, only the clock for the corresponding event list is reset to zero.

SET_CLOCK (18H)

```
18H: SET_CLOCK
hrH mnH scH frH ffH: time
<Q_list> : optional
```

This command sets the clock to the specified time, regardless of whether the clock is stopped or running.

When the <Q_list> parameter is not transmitted, the clocks of all of the event lists are set. In the opposite case, when the <Q_list> parameter is transmitted, only the clock for the corresponding event list is set.

MTC_CHASE_ON (19H)

```
19H: MTC_CHASE_ON
<Q_list> : optional
```

This command orders the clock to adjust or synchronize itself with the MIDI Time Code (MTC) messages that it receives. If no MTC message is received, the clock stays in the state it was in (i.e., either stopped or running) when it received this command. The first MTC message updates the clock. If noncontinuous messages are received, the clock displays the last message it received.

When the <Q_list> parameter is not transmitted, the clocks of all of the event lists follow the MIDI Time Code. In the opposite case, when the <Q_list> parameter is transmitted, only the clock for the corresponding event list follows the MIDI Time Code.

MTC_CHASE_OFF (1AH)

```
1AH: MTC_CHASE_OFF
<Q_list> : optional
```

This command orders the clock to ignore the MIDI Time Code (MTC) messages that it receives. After it receives this command, the clock returns to the state it was in (i.e., either stopped or running) when it received the MTC_CHASE_ON command.

When the <Q_list> parameter is not transmitted, the clocks of all the event lists stop following the MIDI Time Code. In the opposite case, when the <Q_list> parameter is transmitted, only the clock for the corresponding event list stops following the MIDI Time Code.

OPEN_CUE_LIST (1BH)

```
1BH: OPEN_CUE_LIST
<Q_list> : required
```

This command activates the event list in question (i.e., so that the MIDI Show Control (MSC) commands have access to the corresponding events).

CLOSE_CUE_LIST (1CH)

```
1CH: CLOSE_CUE_LIST
<Q_list> : required
```

This command deactivates the event list in question (i.e., so that the MIDI Show Control (MSC) commands no longer have access to the corresponding events).

OPEN_CUE_PATH (1DH)

```
1DH: OPEN_CUE_PATH
<Q_list> : required
```

This command activates the event list for the path in question (i.e., so that the MIDI Show Control (MSC) commands have access to the corresponding events).

CLOSE_CUE_PATH (1EH)

```
1EH: CLOSE_CUE_PATH
<Q_list> : required
```

This command deactivates the event list for the path in question (i.e., so that the MIDI Show Control (MSC) commands no longer have access to the corresponding events).

The Bar Marker

This message, transmitted by a sequencer, a drum machine, or any other device, indicates that the next MIDI clock signal (F8H) or the next MTC frame (F1H xxH) marks the start of a new bar. If the receiving unit is stopped, then it can place itself at the corresponding position and immediately display the bar number in question. It is strongly recommended that the bar marker be sent immediately after the last MIDI clock signal or the last MTC frame—that is, so that no delay separates these two messages.

Format: F0H 7FH <device ID> 03H 01H aaH aaH F7H

Type: Universal Real-Time System Exclusive message

```
F0H:           System Exclusive ID
7FH:           category = real time
<device ID>:   device ID number (default = 7FH = all)
<sub-ID#1>:    03H = "notation"-type message
<sub-ID#2>:    01H = bar-marker message
aaH aaH:       bar number, in the form LSB/MSB
               00H 40H =  at the stop
               01H 40H → 00H 00H = countdown
               01H 00H → 7EH 3FH = bar number
               7FH 3FH =  while running, unknown bar number
F7H:           end of exclusive (EOX)
```

The way bar numbers should be interpreted needs some explaining. In the order MSB/LSB, these numbers represent the following values:

```
4000H                     : when stopped
from 40001 to 0000H       : deduction
from 0001H to 3F7EH       : bar number
3F7FH                     : when running, unknown bar number
```

Or, in binary:

```
01000000 00000000                                   : when stopped
from 01000000 00000001 to 00000000 00000000         : deduction
from 00000000 00000001 to 00111111 01111110         : bar number
00111111 01111111                                   : when running,
                                                      unknown bar number
```

Expressed in the form of 14 useful bits (because by definition bit seven in a MIDI byte is zero), these values are indicated in the following way:

```
100000 00000000                                   : when stopped
from 100000 00000001 to 000000 00000000           : deduction
from 000000 00000001 to 011111 11111110           : bar number
011111 11111111                                   : when running,
                                                    unknown bar number
```

Or, in hex:

```
2000H                     : when stopped
from 2001H to 0000H       : deduction
from 0001H to 1FFEH       : bar number
1FFFH                     : when running, unknown bar number
```

The negative data bytes, which are used to make the deduction, are represented in accordance with the so-called "twos complement" method. As you'll recall, this approach consists of starting with the equivalent positive value and inverting all of the bits, then adding 1 to the result. The number of bars deducted is also equal to the number expressed in this way plus 1. In other words, the number of bar 2001H (100000 00000001) corresponds to a deduction of 8,192 bars (−8,191), because after having inverted the bits for the value + 8,191 (1FFFH in hex, or 011111 11111111 in binary) in order to add 1, you get:

```
    100000 00000000  (the bit inversion)
+                 1
    ---------------
  = 100000 00000001
  = 2001H
```

In the same way, bar number 2002H (100000 00000010) corresponds to a deduction of 8,191 bars (−8,190), because after having inverted the bits of the value +8,190 (1FFEH in hex, or 011111 11111110 in binary), in order to add 1, you get:

```
    100000 00000001 (the bit inversion)
+                 1
    ---------------
  = 100000 00000010
  = 2002H
```

And so on, until you get a deduction of two bars, corresponding to bar number 3FFFH (111111 11111111), because after having inverted the bits of the value +1 (0001H in hex, or 000000 00000001 in binary), in order to add 1, you get:

```
    111111 11111110 (the bit inversion)
+                 1
    ---------------
  = 111111 11111111
  = 3FFFH
```

Finally, the value 0000H indicated a deduction of one bar, after which positive values take over in order to count the number of bars in the piece, from 0001H (+1) to 1FFEH (+8,190).

The Time Signature

This message, as transmitted by a sequencer, a drum machine, or any other device, indicates the time signature of a piece (2/4, 4/4, 6/8, 5/4, whatever). The message exists in two forms: one in real time, in which the receiving unit immediately adopts the new time signature, and the other in non-real time. In this form, the receiving unit can display the new time signature right away, but doesn't adopt it until it receives the next Bar Marker message.

Format: F0H 7FH <device ID> 03H 02H lnH nnH ddH ccH bbH [nnH ddH ...] F7H

Type: Universal Real-Time System Exclusive message

```
F0H              : System Exclusive ID
7FH              : category = real time
<device ID>      : ID number of the device (default = 7FH = all)
<sub-ID#1>       : 03H = "notation"-type message
<sub-ID#2>       : 02H = immediate change in the time signature
lnH              : number of bytes to follow
nnH              : numerator of the time signature
ddH              : denominator of the time signature (expressed as a
                   negative power of 2)
ccH              : number of MIDI clock signals per metronome tick
bbH              : number of thirty-second notes per MIDI
                   quarter-note
[nnH ddH ...]    : groups of two additional bytes (numerator
                   and denominator) that define a bar created
                   within a given bar
F7H              : EOX
```

Format: F0H 7FH <device ID> 03H 42H lnH nnH ddH
            ccH bbH [nnH ddH ...] F7H

Type: Universal Real-Time System Exclusive message

```
F0H             : System Exclusive ID
7FH             : category = real time
<device ID>     : ID number of the device (default = 7FH = all)
<sub-ID#1>      : 03H = "notation"-type message
<sub-ID#2>      : 42H = deferred change in the time signature
lnH             : number of bytes to follow
nnH             : numerator of the time signature
ddH             : denominator of the time signature (expressed as
                  a negative power of 2)
ccH             : number of MIDI clock signals per metronome tick
bbH             : number of thirty-second notes per MIDI
                  quarter-note
[nnH ddH ...]   : groups of two additional bytes (numerator
                  and denominator) that define a bar created
                  within a given bar
F7H             : EOX
```

For more information about the nnH, ddH, ccH and bbH bytes, see
Chapter 7.

Master Volume

This message, which is intended primarily for instruments that are compatible with the General MIDI standard, affects not just the volume of
one channel or another (which is the job of Control Change 7), but on
the overall volume of the device as a whole.

Format: F0H 7FH <device ID> 04H 01H vvH vvH F7H

Type: Universal Real-Time System Exclusive message

```
F0H         : System Exclusive ID
7FH         : category = real time
<device ID> : device ID number
```

```
<sub-ID#1>    : 04H = message of the "device control" type
<sub-ID#2>    : 01H = master volume
vvH vvH       : value of the volume over 14 bits (LSB/MSB)
F7H           : EOX
```

Master Balance

This message, which is intended primarily for instruments that are compatible with the General MIDI standard, affects not just the balance of one channel or another (which is the job of Control Change 10), but on the overall balance of the device as a whole.

Format: F0H 7FH <device ID> 04H 02H bbH bbH F7H

Type: Universal Real-Time System Exclusive message

```
F0H           : System Exclusive ID
7FH           : category = real time
<device ID>   : device ID number
<sub-ID#1>    : 04H = message of the "device control" type
<sub-ID#2>    : 02H = master balance
bbH bbH       : value of the balance over 14 bits (LSB/MSB)
F7H           : EOX
```

File Dump

This protocol lets files be exchanged (dumped) between two computers by means of MIDI links—for example, to transfer a piece in MIDI Files format (see Chapter 7) between a hardware sequencer and a computer, or to transfer any file between different kinds of computers. To do this kind of transfer, it's recommended (but not required) that you establish a bi-directional link between the sending unit and the receiving unit by connecting the MIDI Out port of one to the MIDI In port of the other, and vice versa.

Here's the general syntax of the messages:

Format: F0H 7EH <device ID> 07H <sub-ID#2> ssH
... F7H

Type: Universal Non-Real Time System Exclusive message

```
F0H          : System Exclusive ID
7EH          : category = non-real time
<device ID>  : ID number of the unit for which the message is intended
<sub-ID#1>   : 07H = file dump
<sub-ID#2>   : the type of message, i.e.,
             : 01H = dump header
             : 02H = data packet
             : 03H = dump request
ssH          : ID number of the unit sending the message
...
F7H          : EOX
```

The transfer of a file can be triggered either directly by the sending unit or by the receiving unit, which in this case sends a request to the sending unit. This request has the following form:

Dump Request

Format: F0H 7EH ddH 07H 03H ssH <type> <name>
F7H

```
F0H          : System Exclusive ID
7EH          : category = non-real time
<device ID>  : ID number of the unit which is being asked
               to send the dump
<sub-ID#1>   : 07H = file dump
<sub-ID#2>   : 03H = dump request
ssH          : ID number of the unit intended to receive the dump
<type>       : type of file extension (four ASCII bytes,
               over 7 bits)
```

```
<name>      : file name (a variable number of ASCII bytes,
              over 7 bits)
F7H         : EOX
```

Typical recommended file extensions are listed below.

‹TYPE›	RECOMMENDED FILE EXTENSION	MEANING
MIDI	MID	a MIDI file
MIEX	MEX	a MIDIEX file
ESEQ	ESQ	an ESEQ file
TEXT	TXT	a text file (ASCII, 7 bits)
BIN<space>	BIN	a binary file
MAC<space>	MAC	a Macintosh file (with a MacBinary header)

The MacBinary header refers to the file data, accompanied by the information (such as the file type, the program that created the file, etc.) needed by the part of the Macintosh operating system known as the Finder.

Each of the characters in the file name (which can be of any size, with the end delimited by the F7H byte) is represented in ASCII over 7 bits. The name as a whole has to be printable (that is, it has to consist of characters between 20H and 7EH, inclusive). If a file has no name, then the receiving unit will interpret this lack as a request to send the file that's currently residing in memory. This would be the case, for example, with a request addressed directly to a piece of sequencer software on a computer, or even to a hardware sequencer without a disk reader (i.e., a sequencer that is limited to storing data in RAM), which would thereby be asked to send the "current" song.

In response to a Dump Request message, assuming that no file has the name contained in the message, or if there is no name, that no file is present in memory, then the receiving unit has the option of either interrupting the transaction (by sending a Cancel message, as described below), or asking the user to select manually the file to send. In the latter case, a Wait message (described below) is sent to the receiving unit, in order to ask the receiving unit to wait the necessary amount of time.

The transmitted file consists of a so-called "identity card" (i.e., the dump header), followed by a given number of data packets, depending on the length of the file.

The Dump Header

Format: F0H 7EH ddH 07H 01H ssH <type> <length> <name> F7H

```
F0H            : System Exclusive ID
7EH            : category = non-real time
<device ID>    : ID number of the unit receiving the dump
<sub-ID#1>     : 07H = the file dump
<sub-ID#2>     : 01H = the dump header
ssH            : ID number of the unit sending the dump
<type>         : the type of file extension (four
                 ASCII bytes, over 7 bits)
<length>       : the length of the file, expressed over four byte
                 (28 bits), starting with the least significant byte
<name>         : the file name (a variable number of
                 ASCII bytes, over 7 bits)
F7H            : EOX
```

If the length is unknown (i.e., if the file is being converted on the fly), a value of zero should be transmitted.

The Data Packet

Format: F0H 7EH ddH 07H 02H <packet #> <byte count> <data> <checksum> F7H

```
F0H          : System Exclusive ID
7EH          : category = non-real time
<device ID>  : ID number of the device receiving the dump
<sub-ID#1>   : 07H = file dump
<sub-ID#2>   : 02H = data packet
<packet#>    : packet number, expressed as a byte
               (reset to zero every 128 packets)
<byte count> : the size of the packet, reduced by one unit
<data>       : data bytes
<checksum>   : "exclusive OR" (XOR), applied to the bytes from
               7EH inclusive and the end of the data bytes
F7H          : EOX
```

The total size of such a message is a maximum of 137 bytes, with 1 to 128 data bytes (for a <byte count> value between 0 and 127). These bytes are transmitted in so-called "packed" form, with eight MIDI bytes $(8 \times 7 \text{ bits})$ transmitting seven memory bytes $(7 \times 8 \text{ bits})$.

Memory bytes:

```
a7 a6 a5 a4 a3 a2 a1 a0
b7 b6 b5 b4 b3 b2 b1 b0
c7 c6 c5 c4 c3 c2 c1 c0
d7 d6 d5 d4 d3 d2 d1 d0
e7 e6 e5 e4 e3 e2 e1 e0
f7 f6 f5 f4 f3 f2 f1 f0
g7 g6 g5 g4 g3 g2 g1 g0
```

MIDI bytes:

```
0 a7 b7 c7 d7 e7 f7 g7
0 a6 a5 a4 a3 a2 a1 a0
0 b6 b5 b4 b3 b2 b1 b0
0 c6 c5 c4 c3 c2 c1 c0
0 d6 d5 d4 d3 d2 d1 d0
0 e6 e5 e4 e3 e2 e1 e0
0 f6 f5 f4 f3 f2 f1 f0
0 g6 g5 g4 g3 g2 g1 g0
```

If the total number of data bytes to be transmitted isn't a multiple of seven, the last packet will contain fewer than eight bytes. For example:

```
Memory bytes:

a7 a6 a5 a4 a3 a2 a1 a0
b7 b6 b5 b4 b3 b2 b1 b0
c7 c6 c5 c4 c3 c2 c1 c0

MIDI bytes:

0 a7 b7 c7 0  0  0  0
0 a6 a5 a4 a3 a2 a1 a0
0 b6 b5 b4 b3 b2 b1 b0
0 c6 c5 c4 c3 c2 c1 c0
```

The three preceding messages (the Dump Request, the Dump Header, and the Data Packet messages) can be followed by four so-called "hand-shaking" messages (i.e., the Wait, Cancel, Acknowledge, and Non-Acknowledge messages), which are also used by the Sample Dump Standard (see Chapter 10). They can also be followed by a fifth, more recently implemented message, i.e., the End of File message.

ACK (acknowledge)

Format: F0H 7EH <device ID> 7FH ppH F7H

```
F0H         : System Exclusive ID
7EH         : category = non-real time
<device ID> : ID number of the device receiving the dump
<sub-ID#1>  : 7FH = ACK
ppH         : the packet number
F7H         : EOX
```

This message is sent by the receiving unit to let the sending unit know that either a Data Packet message or a File Header message was received correctly, and to invite the sending unit to transmit the next packet. In a sense, this message is a notice of receipt. The contents of the ppH byte usually correspond to the number of the packet that was received—except when a response to a File Header message is involved, in which case the contents of the ppH byte don't really matter.

NAK (non-acknowledge)

Format: F0H 7EH <device ID> 7EH ppH F7H

```
F0H           : System Exclusive ID
7EH           : category = non-real time
<device ID>   : ID number of the device receiving the dump
<sub-ID#1>    : 7EH = NAK
ppH           : the packet number
F7H           : EOX
```

This message is sent by the receiving unit to warn the sending unit that a Data Packet message, whose number is indicated by the ppH byte, was not received correctly (i.e., because the length or checksum was incorrect). The sending unit should then send the same packet again. After three errors in a row, the receiving unit stops sending NAK messages and sends a Cancel message instead.

Cancel

Format: F0H 7EH <device ID> 7DH ppH F7H

```
F0H           : System Exclusive ID
7DH           : category = non-real time
<device ID>   : ID number of the device for which the
                message is intended
<sub-ID#1>    : 7DH = cancel
ppH           : the packet number
F7H           : EOX
```

This message ends the transaction prematurely. It can be sent by the receiving unit to the sending unit, and vice versa, as a result of an erroneous packet number, due to an interruption of the transfer at the user's request, because of an unknown file type, etc.

Wait

Format: F0H 7EH <device ID> 7CH ppH F7H

```
F0H           : System Exclusive ID
7EH           : category = non-real time
<device ID>   : the ID number of the unit for which the
                message is intended
<sub-ID#1>    : 7CH = wait
ppH           : the packet number
F7H           : EOX
```

This message is sent either by the receiving unit, after it receives a File Header message or a Data Packet message, or by the sending unit, after it receives a File Dump Request message. In the first case (i.e., in response to a File Header message), the sending unit should not send anything further until it receives an ACK or Cancel message. In the second case (i.e., in response to a Data Packet message), the sending unit should interrupt the transmission of packets until it receives an ACK, NAK, or Cancel message. In the third and last case (i.e., in response to a File Dump Request message), the receiving unit should wait until it receives a File Header or Cancel message.

End of File

Format: F0H 7EH <device ID> 7BH ppH F7H

```
F0H           : System Exclusive ID
7EH           : category = non-real time
<device ID>   : ID number of the unit sending the dump
<sub-ID#1>    : 7BH = end of file
ppH           : the packet number
F7H           : EOX
```

This message is transmitted by the sending unit after that unit has sent the last packet, in order to inform the receiving unit of the end of the transaction.

It should also be noted that after having sent a Dump Request message, the receiving unit waits to receive a response (either a Dump Header, a Wait message, or a Cancel message) sometime during the next 200 milliseconds. Likewise, after having sent a Dump header, the sending unit waits to receive a response (either an ACK message, a Wait message, or a Cancel message) during the same period of time. If it doesn't get any of these responses, the sending unit treats the link as unidirectional and sends the packets one after another until it reaches the end of the file, without making any attempt to continue the dialogue.

The MIDI Tuning Standard

This extension of the MIDI standard enables the exchange of microtonal scales between different instruments, and also lets the instruments be programmed in real time. Such scales are defined by the fact that each of the 128 MIDI notes they consist of (or, by default, each of the notes that the instrument uses) can be tuned. The frequency of these notes is expressed in the form of three bytes, as indicated below:

```
Oxxxxxxx Oabcdefg Ohijklmn
```

xxxxxxx: the number of the MIDI note between 0 (C-2) and 127 (G8), to which a frequency, expressed in Hz, corresponds (starting with the tempered scale and with reference to A3 at a pitch of 440 Hz).

	the interval between 0 cents, inclusive (0), and 100
abcde-	
fghijklmn:	cents, exclusive (16,383), to be added to the
	preceding frequency. The 100 cents, which as you'll
	recall are equal to one semitone, are divided into
	16,384 intervals of 0.0061035156 cent each (or,
	rounded off, 0.0061 cent each).

As a result, in order to code a given frequency, you start with the MIDI note that has with the closest pitch in Hz (see the table in Chapter 1) and then add the necessary number of cents (that is, from 0 to 16,383 × 0.0061 cent). Here are a few examples:

```
00H 00H 00H =      8.1758 Hz : the pitch of C-2 (tempered scale)
                              (the minimum frequency)
00H 00H 01H =      8.1758 Hz : 8,1758 Hz (C-2) + 0.0061 cent
01H 00H 00H =      8.6620 Hz : the pitch of C#-2 (tempered scale)
0CH 00H 00H =     16.3516 Hz : the pitch of C-1 (tempered scale)
3CH 00H 00H =    261.6256 Hz : the pitch of C3 (tempered scale)
3DH 00H 00H =    277.1826 Hz : the pitch of C#-3 (tempered scale)
44H 7FH 7FH =    439.9984 Hz : 369.994 Hz (F#3) + 16,383 ×
                              0.0061 cent
45H 00H 00H =    440.0000 Hz : the pitch of A3 (tempered scale)
45H 00H 01H =    440.0016 Hz : 440 Hz (A3) + 0.061 cent
78H 00H 00H =  8,372.0181 Hz : the pitch of C8 (tempered scale)
78H 00H 01H =  8,372.0476 Hz : 8,372.0181 Hz (C8) + 0.0061 cent
7FH 00H 00H = 12,543.8540 Hz : the pitch of G8 (tempered scale)
7FH 00H 01H = 12,543.8982 Hz : 12,543.8540 Hz (G8) + 0.0061 cent
7FH 7FH 7EH = 13,289.6567 Hz : 12,543.8540 Hz (G8) + 16,383 × 0.0061 cent
                              (the maximum frequency)
7FH 7FH 7FH = reserved       : no change
```

The value 7FH 7FH 7FH is for the benefit of instruments that use only part of the entire MIDI range from C-2 to G8. When certain tuning messages are transmitted, those instruments can warn the receiving unit about unused notes by associating these three bytes with those notes.

On the functional level, the messages in the MIDI tuning family fall into three categories:

- The transmission of microtonal scales in the form of a dump ((bulk tuning dump request, bulk tuning dump);

- Modification of the pitch of two or more consecutive notes (real time single-note tuning change); and

- Changes in the tuning program and the tuning bank, in the same way as the Program Change and Bank Select messages for sounds.

When one of these three latter types of messages (that is, a real-time single note tuning change, a tuning program change, or a tuning bank change) is received, the instrument should immediately adapt itself to the new pitches, if necessary by making a real-time change in the frequency of the notes that are being played. The instrument has the option of providing a supplementary mode in which that the pitch changes will not affect notes that are being played, but only the notes that are triggered after reception of a real-time single-note tuning-change message, a tuning program message, or a tuning bank message.

Here's the syntax of the various messages:

Bulk Tuning Dump Request

Format: F0H 7EH <device ID> 08H 00H ttH F7H

Type: Universal Non-Real Time System Exclusive message

```
F0H          : System Exclusive ID
7EH          : category = non-real time
<device ID>  : device ID number
08H          : sub-ID#1 = MIDI tuning standard
00H          : sub-ID#2 = bulk dump request
ttH          : number of the tuning program (0 to 127)
F7H          : EOX
```

Bulk Tuning Dump

Format: F0H 7EH <device ID> 08H 01H ttH <tuning name> [xxH yyH zzH] ... <checksum> F7H

```
F0H             : System Exclusive ID
7EH             : category = non-real time
<device ID>     : device ID number
08H             : sub-ID#1 = MIDI tuning standard
01H             : sub-ID#2 = bulk dump reply
ttH             : number of the tuning program
<tuning name>   : name, in the form of 16 characters in ASCII
[xxH yyH zzH]   : frequency of MIDI note 0 (C-2)
[xxH yyH zzH]   : frequency of MIDI note 1 (C#-2)
...
[xxH yyH zzH]   : frequency of MIDI note 127 (G8)
<checksum>      : "exclusive OR" (XOR), applied to the data bytes
F7H             : EOX
```

Real-Time Single-Note Tuning Change

Format: F0H 7FH <device ID> 08H 02H ttH llH [kkH xxH yyH zzH] ... F7H

Type: Universal Real-Time System Exclusive message

```
F0H             : System Exclusive ID
7FH             : category = real time
<device ID>     : device ID number
08H             : sub-ID#1 = MIDI tuning standard
02H             : sub-ID#2 = note change
ttH             : number of the tuning program
llH             : number of notes to be modified (one
                  modification = kkH xxH yyH zzH)
[kkH            : the MIDI note number, and the
xxH yyH zzH]    : frequency of the note as expressed over
                  three bytes (sequence repeated llH times)
F7H             : EOX
```

The Tuning Program and the Tuning Bank

A tuning program or a tuning bank is selected through the transmittal of the registered parameters 00H 03H and 00H 04H, respectively, followed by either a data entry message (indicating the program number or the bank number), or by a data increment message (requesting that the program number or the bank number be incremented), or by a data decrement message (requesting that the program number or the bank number be decremented):

```
BcH (1011cccc) 65H 00H: recorded parameter number (MSB)
BcH (1011cccc) 64H 03H: recorded parameter number (LSB)
BcH (1011cccc) 06H ttH: data entry MSB (program numbers 1 to 128)
```

or

```
BcH (1011cccc) 60H 7FH: data increment
```

or

```
BcH (1011cccc) 61H 7FH: data decrement
```

```
BcH (1011cccc) 65H 00H: recorded parameter number (MSB)
BcH (1011cccc) 64H 04H: recorded parameter number (LSB)
BcH (1011cccc) 06H ttH: data entry MSB (bank numbers 1 to 128)
```

or

```
BcH (1011cccc) 60H 7FH: data increment
```

or

```
BcH (1011cccc) 61H 7FH: data decrement
```

You can get more information about microtonal scales by writing to:

The Just Intonation Network
MIDI Tuning Standard Committee
535 Stevenson Street
San Francisco, CA 94103

I II III IV V VI VII VIII IX X XI XII

CHAPTER 15

MIDI Machine Control:

Data Formats, Messages, and Commands

HILE THE MIDI standard was first designed for musicians to use with electronic musical instruments and the applications derived from them (such as sequencers, score editors, and sound and sample managers), the MIDI Machine Control (MMC) communications protocol is oriented toward recording and production. Largely inspired by the ES-bus standard, it involves essentially devices such as tape recorders, video recorders, Direct to Disk recorders, sequencers, and so on.

The General Syntax of MMC Messages

The MIDI Machine Control protocol, which was first published in January 1992 under the name "MIDI Machine Control 1.0, MIDI 1.0 Recommended Practice RP-013," belongs to the class of real-time System Exclusive messages. It uses two ID numbers (sub-ID#1): one (06H) for commands and the other (07H) for responses. Here's the general syntax of the messages:

Commands

Format: F0H 7FH <device ID> <mcc> <commands...> F7H

Type: universal real time system exclusive

```
F0H: system exclusive identifier
7FH: category = real time
<device ID>: ID number of the "controlled" device (i.e., the device to
which the command is sent)
<mcc>: sub-ID#1 = 06H (where "mcc" stands for "machine control command")
<commands>: one or more commands (up to a maximum of 48 bytes)
F7H: EOX
```

Responses

Format: F0H 7FH <device ID> <mcr> <responses...> F7H

Type: universal real time system exclusive

```
F0H: System Exclusive ID
7FH: category = real time
<device ID>: ID number of the "controlled" device (i.e., the device from
which the response comes)
<mcr>: sub-ID#1 = 07H  (where "mcr" means "machine control response")
<responses>: one or more responses (up to a maximum of 48 bytes)
F7H: EOX
```

The Environment

A typical MIDI Machine Control configuration consists of one or more devices controlled by a single device. Wherever possible, this "controller" device should have as many MIDI In ports as there are devices to be controlled, so that it can receive responses from these devices without having to rely on the use of a Merge box (which is not recommended by the standard, because of the delays it can cause). Another habit that is allowed, but not recommended, is to have two or more controller devices in the same system. The reason it's not recommended (in addition to the fact that each of the controller devices could receive responses that weren't intended for it) is that if you have two or more controller devices, MIDI Machine Control's powerful error-handling procedures won't work. (For more information, see the detailed descriptions of the relevant messages in Chapter 16.)

Transactions

Transactions can be either unidirectional (that is, from the MIDI Out port of the controller device to the MIDI In port of the controlled device) or bidirectional (from the MIDI Out port of the controller device to the MIDI In port of the controlled device and vice-versa). MIDI Machine Control characterizes these links as either "open loop" or "closed loop." When the controller device is turned on, it expects to communicate bidirectionally. If it transmits a command and doesn't get a response within two seconds, it infers that the link is unidirectional. However, there's nothing keeping the controller device from re-checking this condition at regular intervals.

Groups

By definition, a response can only be transmitted to a single controller (specifically, the one that sent the command). However, a command can be addressed to several controlled devices at once. Assume for example that two tape recorders need to be told to stop. In this case the controller would have to send the following messages:

```
F0H 7FH <device ID = tape recorder 1> <mcc> <Stop> F7H
F0H 7FH <device ID = tape recorder 2> <mcc> <Stop> F7H
```

But because MIDI Machine Control lets you define *groups* (defined in detail in Chapter 16)—that is, use a single number to identify several controlled devices—you can replace the two preceding messages with a single message, this way:

```
FOH 7FH <device ID = group 1> <mcc> <Stop> F7H
```

where "group 1" = "tape recorder 1 + tape recorder 2"

You can also send a message to all of the controlled devices in a system simply by assigning the value 7FH ("all call") to the <device ID> byte.

To sum up, then, here are the various roles that the ID number of the controlled device(s) can play in a MIDI Machine Control command:

```
<device ID> = the address of a device (00H to 7EH)
<device ID> = the addresses of a group of devices (00H to 7EH)
<device ID> = the addresses of all of the devices (7FH = "all call")
```

As far as responses go, however, this ID number can represent only one single and unique controlled device, thusly:

```
<device ID> = the address of a device (00H to 7EH)
```

Commands and Responses

Each command is identified by a code from 01H to 77H, followed by one or more data bytes. The value 00H is reserved for future extensions, and the values 78H to 7FH are reserved for handshaking. Here's how the various families of commands are grouped and stored:

COMMAND	MEANING
00H	Reserved for future extensions
01H to 3FH	Commands that don't include any data bytes
40H to 77H	Commands that include a variable number of data bytes, represented in the form <counter> <data bytes>
78H to 7FH	Handshaking (no data bytes)

Each response, which is usually transmitted after a command, is identified by a code from 01H to 77H, followed by a so-called information field, which consists of one or more data bytes The value 00H is reserved for future extensions, and the values 78H to 7FH are reserved for the handshaking procedure. Here's how the various families of responses are grouped and stored:

COMMAND	MEANING
00H	Reserved for future extensions
01H to 1FH	Standard SMPTE timing code (five bytes long)
20H to 3FH	Abbreviated SMPTE timing code (two bytes long)
40H to 77H	Response that includes a variable number of data bytes, represented in the form <counter> <data bytes>
78H to 7FH	Handshaking (no data bytes)

The information fields, which are comparable to internal registers, can be read and also written to. For instance, the Selected Time Code information field contains the current position of a device, expressed in SMPTE form. To determine the value of this time code, the controller device sends a Read command to the controlled device, this way:

```
F0H 7FH <device ID> <mcc> <Read> <counter = 01H> <Selected Time Code> F7H
```

In return the controller device receives the following response:

```
F0H 7FH <device ID> <mcr> <Selected Time Code> <SMPTE code> F7H
```

On the other hand, a Write command, which has the format shown below, doesn't require any response:

```
F0H 7FH <device ID> <mcc> <Write> <counter = O5H> hrH mnH scH frH stH F7H
```

Extensions

With regard to the commands and responses that are reserved for future extensions (that is, the commands and responses identified by the code 00H), two levels have been provided:

```
00H xxH: the first extension level for a command or a response
00H 00H xxH: the second extension level for a command or a response
```

The value xxH (i.e., the code that identifies the command or response), and any accompanying bytes also obey the rules described above. So, for instance, the extended response 00H 27H would be followed by two data bytes.

Comments

1 • In a message of the following type:

```
F0H 7FH <device ID> <mcc or mcr> <counter> <data bytes> F7H
```

the counter indicates the number of data bytes, without including its own length.

2 • The designers of the standard reserved the possibility, for future versions, of redefining some of the variable-length commands or responses by adding bytes to them, provided that the meaning of the original data isn't changed. For example, an message of the following type:

```
F0H 7FH <device ID> <mcc> <counter = 04H> <aaH bbH ccH ddH> F7H
```

could perfectly easily become:

```
F0H 7FH <device ID> <mcc> <counter = 07H> <aaH bbH ccH ddH eeH ffH> F7H
```

However, in such a case the first four bytes (aaH, bbH, ccH, and ddH) have to represent the same information as before, for obvious reasons of compatibility.

3 ▪ Still with regard to variable-length messages, there are three kinds of counters: the ones whose length is predetermined (for example, <counter = 03H>), the ones whose length is only partially defined, because any of the bytes in the information field could give rise to future extensions (for example, <counter = 02H + extension>), and the ones whose length is entirely variable (<counter = variable>).

4 ▪ Because any given number of commands or responses can be sent within a single message, a device has to be able to determine the length of each command or response, regardless of whether it does anything with any particular command or response.

Handshaking

Wait and Resume, which are the only two handshaking messages that are currently defined, are responsible for regulating the exchange of data. They're an exception to the classification scheme that divides messages into commands and responses, since in a sense they belong to both categories. (For more information, see the detailed description of the corresponding messages in Chapter 16.)

To be performed properly, the handshaking operation needs to have a big enough buffer available. Here's what happens: a certain amount of time can elapse between the moment at which, when it reaches the critical threshold, a device sends a Wait command or response and the moment at which no more messages arrive. This means that the following scenario could be played. Device A allows a period of 10 milliseconds for determining that its buffer has exceeded its maximum filling limit (i.e., the limit beyond which the device decides to send a Wait command or response). During this same interval, Device A starts sending a MMC message with the maximum length, i.e., 53 bytes. Therefore, Device A has to wait at least 52×0.32 ms (assuming that the device is making optimal use of the MIDI bandwidth) before being able to send the Wait command or response—a transmission which, under the best of circumstances, will take Device A 6×0.32 ms.

Meanwhile, Device B allows a period of 10 milliseconds for determining that a Wait command or response has arrived. During this same interval, Device B starts sending a MMC message with the maximum length, i.e., 53 bytes. Therefore, Device B has to wait at least 52×0.32 ms (assuming that the device is making optimal use of the MIDI bandwidth) before being able to interrupt any transmission. Furthermore, Device B has to wait for the reception of a Resume command or response before it can go on communicating. In other words, a total of more than 50 ms separates the transmission of the Wait command or response by Device A and the effective acquisition of this message by Device B. During this time, more than 150 bytes have had time to reach Device A. This is the kind of delay that a configuration which consists of several controller and controlled devices, not to mention Merge devices, can aggravate to a significantly annoying degree. It's also why anyone who is developing products that are compatible with MIDI Machine Control should take special care to evaluate the size of the buffer and the location of the buffer's overflow threshold.

Data Formats

Some kinds of data, such as SMPTE code, user bits, running speed, and track status, appear in more than one information field. Here are the formats of the major kinds of data.

SMPTE

The MIDI Machine Control protocol can represent SMPTE time code in two ways: in standard form, which uses five bytes, and in abbreviated form, which uses only two bytes. In standard form, the fifth and last byte represents either the subframes, at a rate of 100 per second, or the status, which combines different pieces of information about the content of the code, including its point of origin (i.e., whether the value is a true SMPTE value, such as one issued through the reading of an audio track, or an update, in particular during fast-forwarding, during which the tape doesn't touch the heads, or from a tachometer, etc.).

```
hrH mnH scH frH (ffH or stH)

hrH = 0tthhhhh
      tt = type of code
           00: 24 frames per second
           01: 25 frames per second
           10: 30 frames per second (drop frame)
           11: 30 frames per second (Nondrop Frame)
      hhhhh = hours (00H to 17H, or 0 to 23 in decimal)

mnH = 0cmmmmmm
      c = color frame indicator
          0 = noncolor frame
          1 = color framed code
      mmmmmm = minutes (00H to 3BH, or 0 to 59 in decimal)

scH = 0ksssssss
      k = blank bit
          0 = normal
          1 = since power-on or the most recent reinitialization
              of the device (via the MMC Reset command); no time
              code has been loaded into this information field
      ssssss = seconds (00H to 3BH, or 0 to 59 in decimal)

frH = 0giffff
      g = sign
```

```
        0 = positive
        1 = negative
    i = fifth-byte ID
        0 = subframes (ffH)
        1 = status (stH)
    fffff = frames (00H to 1DH, or 0 to 29 in decimal)


ffH = 0bbbbbbb
    bbbbbbb = subframes (00H to 63H, or 0 to 99 in decimal)


stH = 0evdnxxx
    e = provenance
        0 = normal time code
        1 = time code updated from a control track (sometimes
            referred to as "CTL"), or on the basis of
            tachometry information
    v = validity (ignored if e = 0)
        0 = the SMPTE value, as validated by the device
        1 = a SMPTE value whose validity hasn't been guaranteed
            by anything
    d = the video field
        0 = this frame is not a "first frame" frame
        1 = the first frame in a sequence of four or eight
            video fields
    n = indicator for the absence of a time code
        0 = a time code has been read
        1 = no time code has been read since power-on or
            since the most recent reinitialization of the device
            (via the MMC Reset command)
    xxx = reserved for future extensions
          (these bits should be equal to zero)
```

The abbreviated form of the time code corresponds to the last two bytes in the standard representation: i.e., frH (ffH or stH). To reduce the density of the messages that are sent, every controlled device that has received the instruction to transmit its SMPTE time to a controller device can use this compressed format—with the provision, of course, that the seconds in the time in question haven't changed since the last transmission.

User Bits

```
u1H u2H u3H u4H u5H u6H u7H u8H u9H

u1H: first binary group (0000aaaa)
u2H: second binary group (0000bbbb)
u3H: third binary group (0000cccc)
u4H: fourth binary group (0000dddd)
u5H: fifth binary group (0000eeee)
u6H: sixth binary group (0000ffff)
u7H: seventh binary group (0000gggg)
u8H: eighth binary group (0000hhhh)
u9H: indicators (00000tji)
```

The nybbles (or half-bytes) from u1H to u8H, and also bits i and j, perform the tasks of encoding binary groups 1 through 8 and bits 27 and 59 of an SMPTE frame (or bits 27 and 43 of a European Broadcasting Union frame), respectively. When bit "t" is set to zero, the eight binary groups represent any kind of information (such as the date of a recording, a tape number, etc.). These groups are then read in the following way:

```
hhhhgggg ffffeeee ddddcccc bbbbaaaa
```

When bit t is set to one, the eight binary groups represent a SMPTE time in DCB format.

Speed

The running speed of a device, which is governed by the Variable Play, Deferred Variable Play, Record Strobe Variable, Search, and Shuttle commands, and also the Velocity Tally information field, are represented in three bytes (shH smH slH), in a whole-number/decimal part format.

```
shH: 0gsssppp
    g = direction
        0 = forward operation
        1 = backward operation
    sss = the number of bits in the whole-number part
```

```
     ppp = most significant bits in the whole-number part
smH: the number of bits to be distributed between the whole-number
     part and the decimal part (Oqqqqqqq)
slH: the decimal part (Orrrrrrr)
```

	BINARY REPRESENTATION		DECIMAL REPRESENTATION	
THE SSS BITS	THE WHOLE- NUMBER PART	THE DECIMAL PART	THE RANGE OF THE WHOLE- NUMBER	THE RESOLUTION OF THE DECIMAL PART
000	ppp .	qqqqqqqrrrrrrr	0 to 7	1/16,384
001	pppq .	qqqqqqrrrrrrr	0 to 15	1/8,192
010	pppqq .	qqqqqrrrrrrr	0 to 31	1/4,096
011	pppqqq .	qqqqrrrrrrr	0 to 63	1/2,048
100	pppqqqq .	qqqrrrrrrr	0 to 127	1/1,024
101	pppqqqqq .	qqrrrrrrr	0 to 255	1/512
110	pppqqqqqq .	qrrrrrrr	0 to 511	1/256
111	pppqqqqqqq .	rrrrrrr	0 to 1023	1/128

For example, a speed of 9.5 centimeters per second would be represented this way:

```
sss = 001 (there are four bits in the whole-number part)
pppq = 1001 (the whole-number part: 9 in decimal)
qqqqqqrrrrrrr = 1000000000000 (the decimal part: 4,096/8,192, or 0.5)
```

That is,

```
Ogsssppp Oqqqqqqq Orrrrrrr = 00001100 01000000 00000000
```

Or even:

```
sss = 111 (there are ten bits in the whole-number part)
pppqqqqqqq = 0000001001 (the whole-number part: 9 in decimal)
rrrrrrr = 1000000 (the decimal part: 64/128, or 0.5)
```

That is:

```
Ogsssppp Oqqqqqqq Orrrrrrr = 00111000 00001001 01000000
```

How Tracks Are Represented

The status of the tracks in a device, which is governed by the Track Record Ready, Track Record Status, Track Sync Monitor, Track Input Monitor, and Track Mute information fields, can be indicated in terms of different numbers of bytes. Each track is coded in the form of a bit, whose values of 0 and 1 correspond respectively to inactive and active status.

```
r0H r1H r2H ...

r0H: Ogfedcba
     a = video
     b = 0 (reserved for future extensions)
     c = track reserved for the time code
     d = auxiliary track A (the control track, or "CTL")
     e = auxiliary track B
     f = track 1 (the left track of a stereo device, or the single track
of a monaural device)
     g = track 2 (the right track of a stereo device)

r1H: Onmlkjih
     h = track 3
     i = track 4
     j = track 5
     k = track 6
     l = track 7
     m = track 8
     n = track 9

r2H: tracks 10 to 16
r3H: tracks 17 to 23
r4H: tracks 24 to 30
r5H: tracks 31 to 37
r6H: tracks 38 to 44
```

```
r7H: tracks 45 to 51
r8H: tracks 52 to 58
r9H: tracks 59 to 65
...
```

In order to keep messages short as possible, MMC doesn't force you to send null bytes (provided, of course, that a null byte isn't followed by any non-null bytes). For example, a 24-track tape recorder on which only the first eight tracks are active would only need two bytes (00000011 01111110) instead of the five bytes (00000011 01111110 00000000 00000000 00000000) that theoretically would be required.

MMC Messages

MIDI Machine Control messages are classified by type, with the meanings listed below:

Comm:	Communications (Wait, Resume, Group)
Ctrl:	Transport (Play, Stop, etc.)
Evnt:	Event
Gen:	Time codes
I/O:	Reading and writing, error handling, etc.
Sync:	Synchronization
Math:	Mathematical operations
MTC:	MIDI Time Code
Proc:	Procedures
Time:	information fields that involve the time code

You'll see the following abbreviations often in the rest of this chapter and in Chapter 16:

ATR:	Audio tape recorder
(ff):	SMPTE code containing a number of subframes
MCP:	Grouped under the heading Motion Control Process (MCS), the Locate and Chase commands, which are mutually exclusive, take priority over the Motion Control State commands.
MCS:	Grouped under the heading Motion Control State (MCS), these twelve commands represent mutually exclusive states. Here's the list: Stop, Pause, Play, Deferred Play, Variable Play, Deferred Variable Play, Fast Forward, Rewind, Search, Shuttle, Step, and Eject
L:	An information field that can only be read
L/R:	An information field that can be read and written to
(st):	SMPTE code containing status byte
VTR:	Video tape recorder. With regard to the MIDI Machine Control protocol, audio devices operate the same way as VTRs, i.e., on the basis of rotating heads

A builder who wants to design a device that's compatible with MIDI Machine Control is under no obligation to implement any particular message(s). However, for the sake of illustration, Table 15.1 and Table 15.2 below specify a so-called "minimum recommended use" for commands and responses, to indicate how each command or response should be implemented in the context of the following four typical applications:

1 • Minimal transport, the absence of a time code, and an open-loop link

2 • Basic transport, the absence of a time code, and the possibility of a closed-loop link

3 • Well-developed transport, the reading of a time code, a closed-loop link, event recognition, and track-by-track recording control

4 • A basic synchronizer and a closed-loop link

TABLE 15.1: *MIDI Machine Control Commands*

CODE	COMMAND	TYPE	NUMBER OF DATA BYTES	MINIMUM RECOMMENDED USE
00H	—reserved for future extensions—			1 2 3 4
01H	Stop (MCS)	Ctrl	—	1 2 3 4
02H	Play (MCS)	Ctrl	—	- 2 3 4
03H	Deferred Play (MCS)	Ctrl	—	1 2 3 4
04H	Fast Forward (MCS)	Ctrl	—	1 2 3 4
05H	Rewind (MCS)	Ctrl	—	1 2 3 4
06H	Record Strobe	Ctrl	—	1 2 3 4
07H	Record Exit	Ctrl	—	1 2 3 4
08H	Record Pause	Ctrl	—	- - - -
09H	Pause (MCS)	Ctrl	—	- - - -
0AH	Eject (MCS)	Ctrl	—	- - - -
0BH	Chase (MCS)	Sync	—	- - - 4
0CH	Command Error Reset	I/O	—	- 2 3 4

TABLE 15.1: *MIDI Machine Control Commands (continued)*

CODE	COMMAND	TYPE	NUMBER OF DATA BYTES	MINIMUM RECOMMENDED USE
0DH	MMC Reset	Ctrl	—	1 2 3 4
40H	Write	I/O	n	1 2 3 4
41H	Masked Write	I/O	n	- - 3 -
42H	Read	I/O	n	- 2 3 4
43H	Update	I/O	n	- 2 3 4
44H	Locate (MCP)	Ctrl	n	1 2 3 4
45H	Variable Play (MCS)	Ctrl	3	- 2 3 4
46H	Search (MCS)	Ctrl	3	- - 3 4
47H	Shuttle (MCS)	Ctrl	3	- - - -
48H	Step (MCS)	Ctrl	1	- - - -
49H	Assign System Master	Sync	1	- - - -
4AH	Generator Command	Gen	1	- - - -
4BH	MIDI Time Code Command	MTC	1	- - - -
4CH	Move	Math	2	1 2 3 4
4DH	Add	Math	3	- 2 3 4
4EH	Subtract	Math	3	- 2 3 4
4FH	Drop Frame Adjust	Math	1	- - 3 4
50H	Procedure	Proc	n	- - 3 4
51H	Event	Evnt	n	- - 3 4
52H	Group	Comm	n	- 2 3 4
53H	Command Segment	Comm	n	- 2 3 4

TABLE 15.1: *MIDI Machine Control Commands (continued)*

CODE	COMMAND	TYPE	NUMBER OF DATA BYTES	MINIMUM RECOMMENDED USE
54H	Deferred Variable Play (MCS)	Ctrl	3	- 2 3 4
55H	Record	Ctrl	3	- - - -
7CH	Wait	Comm	—	- 2 3 4
7FH	Resume	Comm	—	- 2 3 4

TABLE 15.2: *MIDI Machine Control Responses*

CODE	RESPONSE AND INFORMATION ZONE	TYPE	NUMBER OF DATA BYTES	READ/WRITE	MINIMUM RECOMMENDED USE
00H	—reserved for future extensions—				- - - -
01H	Selected Time Code (st)	Time	5	R/W	1 2 3 4
02H	Selected Master Code (st)	Sync	5	R	- - - 4
03H	Requested Offset (ff)	Sync	5	R/W	- - - 4
04H	Actual Offset (ff)	Sync	5	R	- - - 4
05H	Lock Deviation (ff)	Sync	5	R	- - - 4

TABLE 15.2: *MIDI Machine Control Responses (continued)*

CODE	RESPONSE AND INFORMATION ZONE	TYPE	NUMBER OF DATA BYTES	READ/WRITE	MINIMUM RECOMMENDED USE
06H	Generator Time Code (st)	Gen	5	R/W	- - - -
07H	MIDI Time Code Input (st)	MTC	5	R	- - - -
08H	GP0/Locate Point (ff)	Math	5	R/W	1 2 3 4
09H	GP1 (ff)	Math	5	R/W	- 2 3 4
0AH	GP2 (ff)	Math	5	R/W	- 2 3 4
0BH	GP3 (ff)	Math	5	R/W	- 2 3 4
0CH	GP4 (ff)	Math	5	R/W	- - - -
0DH	GP5 (ff)	Math	5	R/W	- - - -
0EH	GP8 (ff)	Math	5	R/W	- - - -
0FH	GP7 (ff)	Math	5	R/W	- - - -
21H	Selected Time Code (st)	Time	2	R/W	1 2 3 4
22H	Selected Master Code (st)	Sync	2	R	- - - 4
23H	Requested Offset (ff)	Sync	2	R/W	- - - 4
24H	Actual Offset (ff)	Sync	2	R	- - - 4
25H	Lock Deviation (ff)	Sync	2	R	- - - 4

TABLE 15.2: *MIDI Machine Control Responses (continued)*

CODE	RESPONSE AND INFORMATION ZONE	TYPE	NUMBER OF DATA BYTES	READ/WRITE	MINIMUM RECOMMENDED USE
26H	Generator Time Code (st)	Gen	2	R/W	- - - -
27H	MIDI Time Code Input (st)	MTC	2	R	- - - -
28H	GP0/Locate Point (ff)	Math	2	R/W	1 2 3 4
29H	GP1 (ff)	Math	2	R/W	- 2 3 4
2AH	GP2 (ff)	Math	2	R/W	- 2 3 4
2BH	GP3 (ff)	Math	2	R/W	- 2 3 4
2CH	GP4 (ff)	Math	2	R/W	- - - -
2DH	GP5 (ff)	Math	2	R/W	- - - -
2EH	GP8 (ff)	Math	2	R/W	- - - -
2FH	GP7 (ff)	Math	2	R/W	- - - -
40H	Signature	I/O	n	R	- 2 3 4
41H	Update Rate	I/O	1	R/W	- 2 3 4
42H	Response Error	I/O	n	—	- 2 3 4
43H	Command Error	I/O	n	R	- 2 3 4
44H	Command Error Level	I/O	1	R/W	- 2 3 4
45H	Time Standard	Time	1	R/W	- 2 3 4
46H	Selected Time Code Source	Time	1	R/W	- - - -

TABLE 15.2: *MIDI Machine Control Responses (continued)*

CODE	RESPONSE AND INFORMATION ZONE	TYPE	NUMBER OF DATA BYTES	READ/WRITE	MINIMUM RECOMMENDED USE
47H	Selected Time Code Userbits	Time	9	R	- - - -
48H	Motion Control Tally	Ctrl	3	R	- 2 3 4
49H	Velocity Tally	Ctrl	3	R	- - - -
4AH	Stop Mode	Ctrl	1	R/W	- - - -
4BH	Fast Mode	Ctrl	1	R/W	- - - -
4CH	Record Mode	Ctrl	1	R/W	- 2 3 4
4DH	Record Status	Ctrl	1	R	- 2 3 4
4EH	Track Record Status	Ctrl	n	R	- - 3 -
4FH	Track Record Ready	Ctrl	n	R/W	- - 3 -
50H	Global Monitor	Ctrl	1	R/W	- - 3 -
51H	Record Monitor	Ctrl	1	R/W	- - - -
52H	Track Sync Monitor	Ctrl	n	R/W	- - - -
53H	Track Input Monitor	Ctrl	n	R/W	- - - -
54H	Step Length	Ctrl	1	R/W	- - - -
55H	Play Speed Reference	Ctrl	1	R/W	- 2 3 -

TABLE 15.2: *MIDI Machine Control Responses (continued)*

CODE	RESPONSE AND INFORMATION ZONE	TYPE	NUMBER OF DATA BYTES	READ/WRITE	MINIMUM RECOMMENDED USE
56H	Fixed Speed	Ctrl	1	R/W	- - - -
57H	Lifter Defeat	Ctrl	1	R/W	- - - -
58H	Control Disable	Ctrl	1	R/W	- - - 4
59H	Resolved Play Mode	Sync	1	R/W	- - - 4
5AH	Chase Mode	Sync	1	R/W	- - - 4
5BH	Generator Command Tally	Gen	2	R	- - - -
5CH	Generator Set Up	Gen	3	R/W	- - - -
5DH	Generator Userbits	Gen	9	R/W	- - - -
5EH	MIDI Time Code Command Tally	MTC	2	R	- - - -
5FH	MIDI Time Code Set Up	MTC	1	R/W	- - - -
60H	Procedure Response	Proc	n	R	- - 3 4
61H	Event Response	Evnt	n	R	- - 3 4
62H	Track Mute	Ctrl	n	R/W	- - 3 -

TABLE 15.2: *MIDI Machine Control Responses (continued)*

CODE	RESPONSE AND INFORMATION ZONE	TYPE	NUMBER OF DATA BYTES	READ/WRITE	MINIMUM RECOMMENDED USE
63H	VITC Insert Enable	Gen	3	R/W	- - - -
64H	Response Segment	Comm	n	—	- 2 3 4
65H	Failure	Ctrl	n	—	- 2 3 4
7CH	Wait	Comm	—		- 2 3 4
7FH	Resume	Comm	—		- 2 3 4

Classification by Type

Table 15.3 below shows the MMC commands and responses arranged in a different way, i.e., by type.

TABLE 15.3: *MMC Commands and Responses, by Type*

CODE	MEANING
READING, WRITING, AND ERROR-HANDING (I/O)	
Commands:	
0CH	Command Error Reset
40H	Write
41H	Masked Write
42H	Read
43H	Update

TABLE 15.3: *MMC Commands and Responses, by Type (continued)*

CODE	MEANING
Information fields:	
40H	Signature
41H	Update Rate
42H	Response Error
43H	Command Error
44H	Command Error Level

TRANSPORT MANAGEMENT	
Commands:	
01H	Stop (MCS)
02H	Play (MCS)
03H	Deferred Play (MCS)
04H	Fast Forward (MCS)
05H	Rewind (MCS)
06H	Record Strobe
07H	Record Exit
08H	Record Pause
09H	Pause (MCS)
0AH	Eject (MCS)
0DH	MMC Reset
44H	Locate (MCP)
45H	Variable Play (MCS)
46H	Search (MCS)
47H	Shuttle (MCS)
48H	Step (MCS)

TABLE 15.3: *MMC Commands and Responses, by Type (continued)*

CODE	MEANING
54H	Deferred Variable Play (MCS)
55H	Record Strobe Variable

Information fields:

48H	Motion Control Tally
49H	Velocity Tally
4AH	Stop Mode
4BH	Fast Mode
4CH	Record Mode
4DH	Record Status
4EH	Track Record Status
4FH	Track Record Ready
50H	Global Monitor
51H	Record Monitor
52H	Track Sync Monitor
53H	Track Input Monitor
54H	Step Length
55H	Play Speed Reference
56H	Fixed Speed
57H	Lifter Defeat
58H	Control Disable
62H	Track Mute
65H	Failure

TABLE 15.3: *MMC Commands and Responses, by Type (continued)*

CODE	MEANING

LOCAL TIME CODE (TIME)

Information fields:

01H	Selected Time Code (st)
21H	Short Selected Time Code (st)
45H	Time Standard
46H	Selected Time Code Source
47H	Selected Time Code Userbits

SYNCHRONIZATION (SYNC)

Commands:

0B	Chase (MCP)
49	Assign System Master

Information fields:

02H	Selected Master Code (st)
03H	Requested Offset (ff)
04H	Actual Offset (ff)
05H	Lock Deviation (ff)
22H	Short Selected Master Code (st)
23H	Short Requested Offset (ff)
24H	Short Actual Offset (ff)
25H	Short Lock Deviation (ff)
59H	Resolved Play Mode
5AH	Chase Mode

TABLE 15.3: *MMC Commands and Responses, by Type (continued)*

CODE	MEANING
TIME-CODE GENERATION	
Command:	
4AH	Generator Command
Information fields:	
06H	Generator Time Code (st)
26H	Short Generator Time Code (st)
5BH	Generator Command Tally
5CH	Generator Set Up
5DH	Generator Userbits
63H	VITC Insert Enable
MIDI TIME CODE	
Command:	
4BH	MIDI Time Code Command
Information fields:	
07H	MIDI Time Code Input (st)
27H	Short MIDI Time Code Input (st)
5EH	MIDI Time Code Command Tally
5FH	MIDI Time Code Set Up

· ·

TABLE 15.3: *MMC Commands and Responses, by Type (continued)*

CODE	MEANING

MATHEMATICAL OPERATIONS THAT AFFECT THE TIME CODE (MATH)

Commands:

4CH	Move
4DH	Add
4EH	Subtract
4FH	Drop Frame Adjust

Information fields:

08H	GP0/Locate Point (ff)
09H	GP1 (ff)
0AH	GP2 (ff)
0BH	GP3 (ff)
0CH	GP4 (ff)
0DH	GP5 (ff)
0EH	GP6 (ff)
0FH	GP7 (ff)
28H	Short GP0/Locate Point (ff)
29H	Short GP1 (ff)
2AH	Short GP2 (ff)
2BH	Short GP3 (ff)
2CH	Short GP4 (ff)
2DH	Short GP5 (ff)
2EH	Short GP6 (ff)
2FH	Short GP7 (ff)

TABLE 15.3: *MMC Commands and Responses, by Type (continued)*

CODE	MEANING
PROCEDURE MANAGEMENT (PROC)	
Command:	
50H	Procedure
Information field:	
60H	Procedure Response
EVENT INITIATION (EVNT)	
Command:	
51H	Event
Information field:	
61H	Event Response
COMMUNICATION	
Commands:	
52H	Group
53H	Command Segment
7CH	Wait
7FH	Resume
Information fields:	
64H	Response Segment
7CH	Wait
7FH	Resume

The Commands

Here's the syntax of each of the commands in the MIDI Machine Control protocol, along with its detailed meaning.

Stop (MCS)

This command orders the device to stop as soon as possible. Any tracks that are being recorded or that are in Rehearsal mode shift out of that mode.

```
01H: Stop
```

Play (MCS)

This command orders the device to shift into Read mode.

```
02H: Play
```

Deferred Play (MCS)

A device that's in the process of executing a Locate command shifts into Read mode only after it has reached the desired point.

```
03H: Deferred Play
```

Fast Forward (MCS)

This command orders the device to shift into Fast Forward mode at top speed. Any tracks that are being recorded or that are in Rehearsal mode shift out of that mode.

```
04H: Fast Forward
```

Rewind (MCS)

This command orders the device to run backward at top speed. Any tracks that are being recorded or that are in Rehearsal mode shift out of that mode.

```
05H: Rewind
```

Record Strobe

When the device is in Read mode, the tracks that are ready to record (that is, the tracks whose bit is set to 1 in the Track Record Ready information field) shift into Record mode or into Rehearsal mode, depending on the value in the Record Mode information field. Otherwise, any tracks that are being recorded or that are in Rehearsal mode shift out of that mode.

When the device is stopped it shifts into Read mode, while the tracks that are ready to record (that is, the tracks whose bit is set to 1 in the Track Record Ready information field) shift into Record mode or into Rehearsal mode, depending on the value in the Record Mode information field.

```
06H: Record Strobe
```

Record Exit

Any tracks that are being recorded or that are in Rehearsal mode shift out of that mode.

```
07H: Record Exit
```

Record Pause

When the device is in Pause mode, it should wait to receive a Record Strobe command or a Record Strobe Variable command and to respond to that command—i.e., by shifting into Record mode as quickly as possible.

With regard to monitoring, the outputs that correspond to the tracks that are ready to record (that is, the tracks whose bit is set to 1 in the Track Record Ready information field) recover the signals that are received at the input.

```
08H: Record Pause
```

Pause (MCS)

This command orders the device to stop as soon as possible. Videotape recorders and other audiovisual devices stop on a frame. In order to minimize wear and tear on the heads, this does not prevent these devices, after a certain amount of time has passed, from allowing the frame image to disappear (that is, to remove the heads from the tape). Reception of a new Pause command has the effect of reactivating the stop frame.

```
09H: Pause
```

Any tracks that are being recorded shift out of Record mode, provided that the device is in the process of recording and can shift into Pause mode. Any tracks that are in Rehearsal mode shift out of that mode.

When such a command is received by a device that isn't equipped with a Pause control, there's nothing keeping the device from executing a simple stop. However, in such a case the Motion Control Tally information field should indicate Pause rather than Stop.

Eject (MCS)

Removable media (such as video cassettes, Digital Audio Tape (DAT), magneto-optical disks, and so on) are ejected. Any tracks that are being recorded or that are in Rehearsal mode shift out of that mode.

Some devices which a priori don't have to worry about executing this command can nevertheless use it for other purposes. This is the case in particular with tape recorders when the tape is taken off one of the reels.

```
OAH: Eject
```

Chase (MCP)

This command orders the device to synchronize itself with a master time code, taking into consideration a possible shift programmed by the user in the Requested Offset information field. This shift represents the difference between the time code of the device (the Selected Time Code) and the master time code (the Selected Master Code):

```
Requested Offset = Selected Time Code – Selected Master Code
```

```
OBH: Chase
```

Command Error Reset

This command reinitializes the indicator for a blocking error in the Command ERror information field. That is, it sets bit "a" to zero, thereby authorizing the device to resume executing the commands that it receives.

```
OCH: Command Error Reset
```

MMC Reset

This command reinitializes the device. Every device that is compatible with MIDI Machine Control should implement this command.

`ODH: MMC Reset`

It does so by:

- Clearing the Update list

- Clearing the procedures

- Clearing the events

- Clearing any group assignments

- Erasing the Command Error information field

- Reinitializing the Command Error Level information field, which takes on the value zero (i.e., ignoring any errors)

- Reinitializing the indicators for the Standard Time Code information fields, which take on their default values

- Reinitializing the mpH byte (i.e., the byte for the last MCP command that was received) for the Motion Control Tally information field, which takes on the value 7FH (i.e., no MCP command is being executed)

- Cancels any de-segmentation or defragmentation that may be in progress

Write

This command writes data in one or more information fields. A given message can contain as many <name of the information field> <corresponding data> pairs as necessary.

```
40H: Write
<counter = variable>: the number of data bytes in the message
<name>: an information field that can be written to
<data>: the data to be written in the information field
<name>: an information field that can be written to
<data>: the data to be written in the information field
<name>: an information field that can be written to
<data>: the data to be written in the information field
...
...
```

Masked Write

This command write certain bits of a byte in an information field that uses the track representation format described earlier in this chapter.

```
41H: Masked Write
<counter = 04H + ext>: the number of data bytes in the message
<name>: an information field that can be read and that uses the track rep-
resentation format
<byte #>: the number of the data byte in which the writing should begin
(starting with zero)
<mask>: the bits that are set to 1 are the ones that should be modified
<data>: the value of the bits to be modified
```

Read

This command reads the contents of one or more information fields.

```
42H: Read
<counter = variable>: the number of data bytes in the message
<name>: an information field that can be written to
<name>: an information field that can be written to
<name>: an information field that can be written to
...
...
```

Update

The first format: Update [Begin]

This command orders the device to transmit immediately the contents of specified information fields (whose names, if they aren't already listed, are added to the Update list), and then to retransmit these contents periodically, provided that the value of the zone has changed since the last retransmission and also provided that a period of time has passed which is equal to or greater than the one specified in the Update Rate information field.

```
43H: Update
<counter = variable>: the number of data bytes in the message
00H: [Begin]
<name>: information field
<name>: information field
<name>: information field
...
...
```

Every information field that has a time code transmits it in standard form (that is, in five bytes) both as the first response to an Update command and also at each retransmission, but only if the value of the seconds byte (scH) has changed since the last response. Otherwise, if the value of the seconds byte *hasn't* changed since the last response, then the time code is retransmitted in abbreviated form (that is, in two bytes).

The second format: Update [End]

This version of the command removes the specified information fields from the Update list. A value of 7FH, appearing instead of a name, interrupts the retransmission of all of the zones on the list.

```
43H: Update
<counter = variable>: the number of data bytes in the message
01H: [End]
```

```
<name>: information field
<name>: information field
<name>: information field
...
...
```

Locate (MCP)

```
The first format: Locate [I/F]
```

This command orders the device whose Selected Time Code information field reflects the value of the timing reference to position itself at a location that corresponds to one of the eight memory areas for the time code (i.e., GP0 through GP7).

```
44H: Locate
<counter = 02H + ext>: the number of data bytes in the message
00H: [I/F]
<name>: 00H = reserved for future extensions
        08H = GP0/Locate Point (the first memory area for the time
        code)
        09H = GP1 (the second memory area for the time code)
        0AH = GP2 (the third memory area for the time code)
        0BH = GP3 (the fourth memory area for the time code)
        0CH = GP4 (the fifth memory area for the time code)
        0DH = GP5 (the sixth memory area for the time code)
        0EH = GP6 (the seventh memory area for the time code)
        0FH = GP7 (the eighth memory area for the time code)
The second format: [Target]
```

This command orders the device whose Selected Time Code information field reflects the value of the timing reference to position itself at a location that corresponds to a SMPTE time.

```
44H: Locate
<counter = 06H>: the number of data bytes in the message
01H: [Target]
hrH mnH scH frH ffH: the SMPTE time
```

Variable Play (MCS)

This command orders the device to shift into Read mode in the specified direction and at the specified speed. If the device in question can't run at that speed, it should still run as close to it as it can.

```
45H: Variable Play
<counter = 03H>: the number of data bytes in the message
shH smH slH: the reading speed
```

Search (MCS)

This command orders the device to move in the specified direction and at the specified speed. If the device in question can't run at that speed, it should still run as close to it as it can.

With regard to monitoring, all that's necessary is for the quality of the signal to make identification possible. If desired, during execution of a Search command an audiovisual device can simply reproduce the (current) frame.

```
46H: Search
<counter = 03H>: the number of data bytes in the message
shH smH slH: the reading speed
```

Shuttle (MCS)

This command orders the device to move in the specified direction and at the specified speed, without necessarily reproducing an image or any sound. If the device in question can't run at that speed, it should still run as close to it as it can.

```
47H: Shuttle
<counter = 03H>: the number of data bytes in the message
shH smH slH: the reading speed
```

Step (MCS)

This command orders the device to move a certain distance in a certain direction. With regard to monitoring, during execution of a Step command an audiovisual device should display an image and hold it once the operation is over, exactly the same way it does in Pause mode. An audiovisual device should produce a sound and, if it can, once the operation is over it should loop a portion located on either side of the point that it reached. Finally, a sequencer should continue with MIDI transmission and, once the operation is over, should take care not to send any messages.

```
48H: Step
<counter = 01H>: the number of data bytes in the message
<steps>: Ogsssssss
        g = direction
        0 = forward operation
        1 = backward operation
        ssssss = the distance to be traveled (expressed
        in terms of a unit specified by the Step Length
        information field, whose default value is a half-frame)
```

Assign System Master

This command activates and selects the master device at the synchronization level, or else deactivates it. Because this command is addressed to all of the devices in a system, the <device ID> number takes on the value 7FH ("all-call").

```
49H: Assign System Master
<counter = 01H>: the number of data bytes in the message
<master device ID>: activation or deactivation of the master device
            00H to 7EH = the ID number for the master device
            7FH = deactivation (so that no device is the
            master device)
```

Generator Command

This command manages the time-code generator.

```
4AH: Generator Command
<counter = 01H>: the number of data bytes in the message
nnH: activity
      00H = stop
      01H = generation of the time code (run)
      02H = copy and/or regeneration of the time code (copy/jam)
```

MIDI Time Code Command

This command manages the production of the time code.

```
4BH: MIDI Time Code Command
<counter = 01H>: the number of data bytes in the message
nnH: activity
      00H = off(no MIDI Time Code)
      01H = the MIDI Time Code is issued from the timing code
      specified by the MIDI Time Code Set Up information field
```

Move

This command reads the time code for an information field, expressed in standard form (that is, in five bytes) with responses from 01H to 1FH), in order to recopy it into another information field that can be written to and that also contains a time code in standard form (that is, with responses from 01H to 1FH, with 02H, 04H, 05H, and 07H being excluded). This command is used particularly to acquire locators on the fly (that is, to recopy information from the Selected Time Code information field into one of the eight memory areas (GP0 to GP7) for the time code).

When the contents of an information field that contains a time code of the "status" (st) type are copied to an information field that contains a time code of the "subframe" (ff) type, bit "i" and the fifth (subframe) byte take on the value zero.

When the contents of an information field that contains a time code of the "subframe" (ff) type are copied to an information field that contains a time code of the "status" (st) type, bits "i" and "n" take on the value 1, while bits "e" and "v" take on the value zero.

```
4CH: Move
<counter = 02H + ext>: the number of data bytes in the message
<destination>: the information field to which the time code is to be
               copied
<source>: the information field from which the time code is to be read
```

Add

This command reads the time codes for two information fields, expressed in standard form (that is, in five bytes) with responses from 01H to 1FH), adds them together, and then recopies the result into another information field that can be written to and that also contains a time code in standard form (that is, with responses from 01H to 1FH, with 02H, 04H, 05H, and 07H being excluded). There's no reason why a <source> information field can't be used as a <destination> information field.

When a <destination> information field contains a time code of the "subframe" (ff) type, bits "c", "k", and "i" in the result take on the value zero.

The number of frames per second, as represented by bits tt, stays the same as in the first source, unless the number is expressed in 30 Drop Frame format. In this case tt = 10 and the value that results from the addition is converted into 30 Nondrop Frame format, with tt = 11. What this amounts to is that the result of an Add command is always expressed without a frame jump.

If the <destination> information field doesn't accept negative results, you have to make the results positive by adding 24 hours.

When a <destination> information field contains a time code of the "status" (st) type, bits "e" and "v" in the result take on the value zero, while bits i and n take on the value 1.

```
4DH: Add
<counter = 03H + ext>: the number of data bytes in the message
<destination>: the information field into which the result
               of the addition is to be copied
<source #1>: the information field from which the first time
             code should be read
<source #2>: the information field from which the second time
             code should be read
```

Subtract

This command reads the time codes for two information fields, expressed in standard form (that is, in five bytes) with responses from 01H to 1FH), subtracts the second value from the first value, and then recopies the result into another information field that can be written to and that also contains a time code in standard form (that is, with responses from 01H to 1FH. Responses 02H, 04H, 05H, and 07H are excluded). The other rules that govern addition apply in the same way to subtraction.

```
4EH: Subtract
<counter = 03H + ext>: the number of data bytes in the message
<destination>: the information field into which the result
               of the subtraction is to be copied
<source #1>: the information field from which the first time
             code should be read
<source #2>: the information field from which the second time
             code should be read
```

Drop Frame Adjust

This command converts the time code for an information field that can
be written to, as expressed in standard form (that is, with responses from
01H to 1FH, with 02H, 04H, 05H, and 07H being excluded), into a 30
Drop Frame time code.

```
4FH: Drop Frame Adjust
<counter = 01H>: the number of data bytes in the message
<name>: the information field in which the time code should
        be converted
```

Procedure

From the point of view of a controlled device, a procedure consists of a
list of commands stored in memory that are executed when the device
receives a Procedure [Execute] command.

```
The first format: [Assemble]
```

This command collects a certain number of commands and stores them
so that they can be executed at a later time.

```
50H: Procedure
<counter = variable>: the number of data bytes in the message
00H: [Assemble]
<procedure>: 00H to 7EH = the ID number of the procedure
                  7FH = reserved for future extensions
<command #1>: any command command other than
        Procedure [Assemble] and Procedure [Execute]
<command #2>: any command command other than
        Procedure [Assemble] and Procedure [Execute]
<command #3>: any command command other than
        Procedure [Assemble] and Procedure [Execute]
...
...
```

The second format: [Delete]

This command removes one or all of the procedures that are stored in memory.

```
50H: Procedure
<counter = 02H>: the number of data bytes in the message
01H: [Delete]
<procedure>: 00H to 7EH = the ID number of the procedure
                to be removed
                    7FH = remove all of the procedures
```

The third format: [Set]

This command determines the procedure that should appear when the Procedure Response information field is read.

```
50H: Procedure
<counter = 02H>: the number of data bytes in the message
02H: [Set]
<procedure>: 00H to 7EH = the ID number of the procedure
                    7FH = all of the procedures
```

The fourth format: [Execute]

This command triggers the execution of a procedure.

```
50H: Procedure
<counter = 02H>: the number of data bytes in the message
03H: [Execute]
<procedure>: 00H to 7EH = the ID number of the procedure to be
            executed
                    7FH = reserved for future extensions
```

Event

From the point of view of a controlled device, an event consists of a command that is stored in memory and programmed for execution at a very specific time (which corresponds to the value stored in one of the eight time-code memory areas).

The first format: [Define]

This command defines an event—that is, the command that it contains—and also the time at which the command should be executed.

```
50H: Event
<counter = variable>: the number of data bytes in the message
00H: [Define]
<event>: 00H to 7EH = the ID number of the event
                7FH = reserved for future extensions
<flags>: 0k0a00dd
        dd = the effect of the direction on the triggering
            00 = the event should be triggered when the device shifts
into forward operation
            01 = the event should be triggered when the device shifts
into backward operation
              10 = the event should be triggered regardless of the
direction
        a = the effect of speed on the triggering
            0 = the event should be triggered when the device reaches
the position that corresponds to the specified time (i.e., the trigger
time) while the device is in Read mode
            1 = the event should be triggered regardless of the operat-
ing speed, after the device has reached or passed the position that
corresponds to the specified time (i.e., the trigger time)
        k = the effect of triggering on the event
            0 = removal of the event after triggering
            1 = retention of the event after triggering
<trigger source>: the information field that specifies the source of the
time code that serves as the triggering reference
                00H = reserved for future extensions
                01H = Selected Time Code
                02H = Selected Master Code
                06H = Generator Time Code
                07H = MIDI Time Code Input
<name>: the name of the information field that specifies the time at
which the event should be initiated (i.e., the trigger time)
        00H = reserved for future extensions
```

```
08H = GP0/Locate Point (the first time-code memory area)
09H = GP1 (the second time-code memory area)
0AH = GP2 (the third time-code memory area)
0BH = GP3 (the fourth time-code memory area)
0CH = GP4 (the fifth time-code memory area)
0DH = GP5 (the sixth time-code memory area)
0EH = GP6 (the seventh time-code memory area)
0FH = GP7 (the eighth time-code memory area)
```

The second format: [Delete]

This command removes one or all of the events that are stored in memory.

```
51H: Event
<counter = 02H>: the number of data bytes in the message
01H: [Delete]
<event>: 00H to 7EH = the ID number of the event to be removed
              7FH = remove all of the events
```

The third format: [Set]

This command determines the event that should appear when the Event Response information field is read.

```
51H: Event
<counter = 02H>: the number of data bytes in the message
02H: [Set]
<event>: 00H to 7EH = the ID number of the event
              7FH = all of the events
```

The fourth format: [Test]

This command causes the immediate execution of the command that contains the event (that is, without waiting for the trigger time), in order to test the execution of the event.

```
51H: Event
<counter = 02H>: the number of data bytes in the message
03H: [Test]
<event>: 00H to 7EH = the ID number of the event to be executed
              7FH = reserved for future extensions
```

Group

This command makes it possible to combine several controlled devices: that is, to assign them a common ID number in addition to their individual ID numbers.

```
The first format: [Assign]
```

This command adds one or more controlled devices to a group. In addition to responding to the commands that are addressed to it individually (that is, the commands whose ID number is the same as the ID number of the device), each device should also respond to the commands that are addressed to the group (that is, the commands whose ID number is the same as the ID number of the group to which the controlled device belongs.

```
52H: Group
<counter = variable>: the number of data bytes in the message
00H: [Assign]
<group>: the group number (00H to 7EH)
<device ID>: the first device to be added to the group
<device ID>: the second device to be added to the group
...
...
```

```
The second format: [Dis-Assign]
```

This command removes one or more of the devices from a group.

```
52H: Group
<counter = variable>: the number of data bytes in the message
01H: [Dis-Assign]
```

```
<group>: the group number
<device ID>: OOH to 7EH =  the first device to be removed from the
            group
                  7FH = remove all of the devices from the group
<device ID>: OOH to 7EH = the second device to be removed from
            the group
...
...
```

Command Segment

When a command or a set of commands exceeds the maximum allowable length of a MIDI Machine Control message (i.e., 48 data bytes, or a total of 53 bytes overall), the command or set of commands can be separated so that the data can be transmitted in the form of two or more segments. Each of these segments should occupy an Exclusive message of its own.

```
53H: Command Segment
<counter = variable>: the number of data bytes in the message
siH: the segment ID (Ofsssssss)
     f = the first segment/the subsequent segments
         1 = the first segment
         0 = the subsequent segments
     ssssss = the segment number (counting backwards to the
              last segment, which is segment zero)
<commands>: the part consisting of the command or the set of commands
```

For instance, a command or a set of commands 100 bytes long would be transmitted this way:

```
FOH 7FH <device ID> <mmc> <Command Segment> <counter = 2EH> 42H <the
first 45 bytes> F7H

FOH 7FH <device ID> <mmc> <Command Segment> <counter = 2EH> 01H <the next
45 bytes> F7H

FOH 7FH <device ID> <mmc> <Command Segment> <counter = OBH> OOH <the last
10 bytes> F7H
```

Deferred Variable Play (MCS)

This command orders the device to shift into Read mode in the specified direction and at the specified speed. If the device in question can't run at that speed, it should still run as close to it as it can. Assuming that the device is in the process of executing a Locate command, it should wait until it reaches the desired point before shifting into Read mode.

```
54H: Deferred Variable Play
<counter = 03H>: the number of data bytes in the message
shH smH slH: the reading speed
```

Record Strobe Variable

When the device is in Read mode, the tracks that are ready to record (that is, the tracks whose bit is set to 1 in the Track Record Ready information field) shift into Record mode or into Rehearsal mode, depending on the value in the Record Mode information field. Otherwise, any tracks that are being recorded or that are in Rehearsal mode shift out of that mode.

When the device is stopped it shifts into Read mode at the speed determined by this command (through bytes shH smH slH), while the tracks that are ready to record (that is, the tracks whose bit is set to 1 in the Track Record Ready information field) shift into Record mode or into Rehearsal mode, depending on the value in the Record Mode information field.

```
55H: Record Strobe Variable
<counter = 03H>: the number of data bytes in the message
shH smH slH: the reading speed
```

Wait

When for any reason (such as a buffer that's full to overflowing) the controller device isn't able to receive any more messages, it sends a Wait command to all of the controlled devices (<device ID> = 7FH: "all-call"). This command asks the controlled devices to interrupt all transmissions within a maximum period of 10 milliseconds and to keep the transmissions in suspense until they're told otherwise.

A controlled device that's in the process of sending a response when it receives a Wait command can continue sending that response, but only until the transmission of the current Exclusive message has been completed.

The Wait command should be the only command in the Exclusive message that carries it.

```
7CH: Wait
```

Resume

When the controller device is again able to receive messages, it sends a Resume command to all of the controlled devices (<device ID> = 7FH: "all-call") to let them know that communications can be picked up again. The Resume command should be the only command in the Exclusive message that carries it.

```
7FH: Resume
```

CHAPTER

16

XIII XIV XV

A
B
C
D
E
F
G
H
I

MIDI Machine Control:

Responses and

Applications

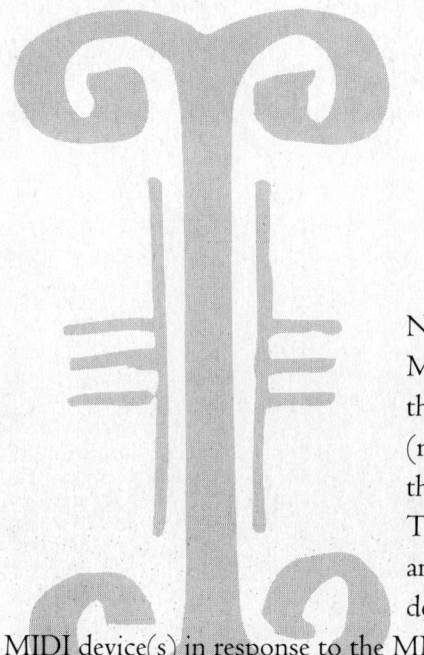

N THE LAST chapter you met the
MIDI Machine Control commands
that are sent from the controlling
(master) MIDI device or devices to
the controlled (slave) MIDI devices.
This chapter introduces the messages
and information that the slave MIDI
devices send back to the master
MIDI device(s) in response to the MMC commands, and also contains
various practical examples of how to implement the MIDI Machine Control protocol. Together, these two chapters provide a comprehensive in-
depth guide to this latest expansion of the MIDI standard.

The MMC Responses

This section describes the syntax of the responses in the MIDI Machine
Control protocol and offers a detailed explanation of the meaning of
each response.

Selected Time Code (read/write)

This time code determines the position of the device in cases in which the position is not derived through the reading of a SMPTE code but instead is the result of a calculation performed on tachymetric information. This field can be written to, so that updates can be performed.

```
01H: Selected Time Code
hrH mnH scH frH stH
```

Table 16.1 below describes in detail the behavior of the time-code status bits in the Selected Time Code field.

TABLE 16.1: *Time-Code Status Bits in the Selected Time Code Information Field*

STATUS BITS	VALUE AFTER THE DEVICE IS TURNED ON, OR AFTER AN MMC RESET COMMAND HAS BEEN RECEIVED	VALUE DURING NORMAL OPERATIONS	INTERPRETATION OF THE BITS IN THE INFORMATION FIELD OF A WRITE COMMAND
tt (time type)	Equal to the value of the corresponding bits in the Time Standard information field, or to a default value stored in the device	If n = 1, either as in the previous column or else as loaded by a Write command or by a "Math" command; if n = 0, as read when the time code is received	Authorized bits tt are written, if bit n of the Write command = 1
c (color frame)	0	If n = 1, c = 0; if n = 0, as read when the time code is received	Bit c is ignored

TABLE 16.1: *Time-Code Status Bits in the Selected Time Code Information Field (continued)*

STATUS BITS	VALUE AFTER THE DEVICE IS TURNED ON, OR AFTER AN MMC RESET COMMAND HAS BEEN RECEIVED	VALUE DURING NORMAL OPERATIONS	INTERPRETATION OF THE BITS IN THE INFORMATION FIELD OF A WRITE COMMAND
k ("blank" bit)	1	k = 0 after the time code has been read from the tape, updated by tachymetric information, or loaded by a Write command or by a "Math" command; otherwise, k = 1	Regardless of its value, bit k is set to zero
g (sign)	0	0	Bit g is ignored
i (the fifth byte)	1	1	Bit i is ignored
e (estimated source)	0	e = 1, only if the most recent change in the value of the time code came either from a control track or from tachymetric information	Regardless of its value, bit e is set to zero

TABLE 16.1: *Time-Code Status Bits in the Selected Time Code Information Field (continued)*

STATUS BITS	VALUE AFTER THE DEVICE IS TURNED ON, OR AFTER AN MMC RESET COMMAND HAS BEEN RECEIVED	VALUE DURING NORMAL OPERATIONS	INTERPRETATION OF THE BITS IN THE INFORMATION FIELD OF A WRITE COMMAND
v (validity)	0	0 or 1, depending on the validity of the code	Regardless of its value, bit v is set to zero
d (video field 1)	0 or 1, depending on whether the first frame in a sequence of four or eight video fields is involved, and provided that this function has been implemented	0 or 1 (as in the previous column)	Bit d is ignored
n (no code)	1	n = 0, only after the time code has been read from tape	Regardless of its value, bit n is set to 1 (indicating that no time code has been read from the tape)

Selected Master Code (read)

The Master Code is the time code with which the devices that have received a Chase command should synchronize themselves.

```
02H: Selected Master Code
hrH mnH scH frH stH
```

The time-code status bits in the Selected Master Code field behave exactly the same way as the time-code status bits in the Selected Time Code field.

Requested Offset (read/write)

This shift represents the difference, as programmed by the user, between the time code of the device (the Selected Time Code) and the master time code (the Selected Master Code):

```
Requested Offset = Selected Time Code – Selected Master Code
```

When it receives a Chase command, a controlled device should synchronize itself with the master time code, in accordance with the shift. This field is expressed in terms of the number of frames, in the form of a Non-drop Frame value.

```
03H: Requested Offset
hrH mnH scH frH ffH
```

Table 16.2 below describes in detail the behavior of the time-code status bits in the Requested Offset field.

TABLE 16.2: *Time-Code Status Bits in the Requested Offset Information Field*

STATUS BITS	VALUE AFTER THE DEVICE IS TURNED ON, OR AFTER AN MMC RESET COMMAND HAS BEEN RECEIVED	VALUE DURING NORMAL OPERATIONS	INTERPRETATION OF THE BITS IN THE INFORMATION FIELD OF A WRITE COMMAND
tt (time type)	— see the next column —	Equal to the value of the corresponding bits in the Selected Time Code information field, except if tt = 10 (Drop Frame), in which case tt = 11 (Nondrop Frame)	Bits tt are ignored
c (color frame)	0	0	Bit c is ignored
k ("blank" bit)	1	k = 1 after a time code has been loaded by a Wait command or by a "Math" command; otherwise, k = 0	Regardless of its value, bit k is set to zero
g (sign)	0	0 or 1, depending on whether the code is positive or negative	Authorized bit g is written

TABLE 16.2: *Time-Code Status Bits in the Requested Offset Information Field (continued)*

STATUS BITS	VALUE AFTER THE DEVICE IS TURNED ON, OR AFTER AN MMC RESET COMMAND HAS BEEN RECEIVED	VALUE DURING NORMAL OPERATIONS	INTERPRETATION OF THE BITS IN THE INFORMATION FIELD OF A WRITE COMMAND
i (the fifth byte)	0	0	If bit i of the Write command = 0, the fifth byte is treated as a set of subframes; if bit i of the Write command = 1, the final data byte is ignored

- -

Actual Offset (read)

This shift represents the difference, as measured at a given time "t", between the time code of the device (the Selected Time Code) and the master time code (the Selected Master Code):

Actual Offset = Selected Time Code – Selected Master Code

This zone is expressed in terms of the number of frames, in the form of a Nondrop Frame value.

```
04H: Actual Offset
hrH mnH scH frH ffH
```

Table 16.3 below describes in detail the behavior of the time-code status bits in the Actual Offset field.

TABLE 16.3: *Time-Code Status Bits in the Actual Offset Information Field*

STATUS BITS	VALUE AFTER THE DEVICE IS TURNED ON, OR AFTER AN MMC RESET COMMAND HAS BEEN RECEIVED	VALUE DURING NORMAL OPERATIONS
tt (time type)	– see the next column –	Equal to the value of the corresponding bits in the Selected Time Code information field, except if tt = 10 (Drop Frame), in which case tt = 11 (Nondrop Frame)
c (color frame)	0	0
k ("blank" bit)	0	0
g (sign)	0	0 or 1, depending on whether the code is positive or negative
i (the fifth byte)	0	0

Lock Deviation (read)

This shift represents the difference, as measured at a given time t, between the time code of the device (the Selected Time Code) and the master time code (the Selected Master Code) to which the shift that was programmed by the user (i.e., the Requested Offset) should be set:

```
Lock Deviation = Actual Offset - Requested Offset
```

This zone is expressed in terms of the number of frames, in the form of a Nondrop Frame value.

```
05H: Lock Deviation
hrH mnH scH frH ffH
```

The time-code status bits in the Lock Deviation field behave exactly the same way as the time-code status bits in the Actual Offset field.

Generator Time Code (read/write)

This message indicates the value of the time code generated by the time-code generator:

```
06H: Generator Time Code
hrH mnH scH frH stH
```

Table 16.4 below describes in detail the behavior of the time-code status bits in the Generator Time Code field.

TABLE 16.4: *Time-Code Status Bits in the Generator Time Code Information Field*

STATUS BITS	VALUE AFTER THE DEVICE IS TURNED ON, OR AFTER AN MMC RESET COMMAND HAS BEEN RECEIVED	VALUE DURING NORMAL OPERATIONS	INTERPRETATION OF THE BITS IN THE INFORMATION FIELD OF A WRITE COMMAND
tt (time type)	Equal to the value of the corresponding bits in the Time Standard information field, or to a default value stored in the device	Either as in the previous column, or as loaded by a "Math" command or by a copy/regeneration operation	Authorized bits tt are written (and determine the time-code counting mode that will be used by the generator)
c (color frame)	0	0	Bit c is ignored
k ("blank" bit)	0	0	Bit k is ignored
g (sign)	0	0	Bit g is ignored
i (the fifth byte)	1	1	Bit i is ignored
e (estimated source)	0	0	Bit e is ignored
v (validity)	0	0	Bit v is ignored

TABLE 16.4: *Time-Code Status Bits in the Generator Time Code Information Field (continued)*

STATUS BITS	VALUE AFTER THE DEVICE IS TURNED ON, OR AFTER AN MMC RESET COMMAND HAS BEEN RECEIVED	VALUE DURING NORMAL OPERATIONS	INTERPRETATION OF THE BITS IN THE INFORMATION FIELD OF A WRITE COMMAND
d (video field 1)	0 or 1, depending on whether the first frame in a sequence of four or eight video fields is involved, and provided that this function has been implemented	0 or 1 (as in the previous column)	Bit d is ignored
n (no code)	0	0	Bit n is ignored

· ·

MIDI Time Code Input (read)

This message indicates the value of the MIDI Time Code:

```
07H: MIDI Time Code Input
hrH mnH scH frH stH
```

Table 16.5 below describes in detail the behavior of the time-code status bits in the MIDI Time Code field.

TABLE 16.5: *Time-Code Status Bits in the MIDI Time Code Information Field*

STATUS BITS	VALUE AFTER THE DEVICE IS TURNED ON, OR AFTER AN MMC RESET COMMAND HAS BEEN RECEIVED	VALUE DURING NORMAL OPERATIONS
tt (time type)	Equal to the value of the corresponding bits in the Time Standard information field, or to a default value stored in the device	If n = 1, as in the previous column; if n = 0, as read when the MIDI Time Code is received
c (color frame)	0	0
k ("blank" bit)	1	After the MIDI Time Code has been received, k = 0; otherwise, k = 1
g (sign)	0	0
i (the fifth byte)	1	1
e (estimated source)	0	0
v (validity)	0	0 or 1, depending on the validity of the code

TABLE 16.5: *Time-Code Status Bits in the MIDI Time Code Information Field (continued)*

STATUS BITS	VALUE AFTER THE DEVICE IS TURNED ON, OR AFTER AN MMC RESET COMMAND HAS BEEN RECEIVED	VALUE DURING NORMAL OPERATIONS
d (video field 1)	0	0
n (no code)	1	After the MIDI Time Code has been received, n = 0; otherwise, n = 1 (i.e., n = k)

GP0/Locate Point (read/write)

This message indicates the value of the first time-code memory area:

```
08H: GP0/Locate Point
hrH mnH scH frH ffH
```

GP1 to GP7 (read/write)

This message indicates the value of the next seven time-code memory areas:

```
09H to 0FH: GP1 to GP7
hrH mnH scH frH ffH
```

Table 16.6 below describes in detail the behavior of the time-code status bits in fields GP0 through GP7.

TABLE 16.6: *Time-Code Status Bits in Information Fields GP0 through GP7*

STATUS BITS	VALUE AFTER THE DEVICE IS TURNED ON, OR AFTER AN MMC RESET COMMAND HAS BEEN RECEIVED	VALUE DURING NORMAL OPERATIONS	INTERPRETATION OF THE BITS IN THE INFORMATION FIELD OF A WRITE COMMAND
tt (time type)	Equal to the value of the corresponding bits in the Time Standard information field, or to a default value stored in the device	As loaded by a Write command or by a "Math" command	Authorized bits tt are written
c (color frame)	0	As loaded by a Write command or by a "Math" command	Authorized bit c is written
k ("blank" bit)	1	k = 1 after a time code has been loaded by a Wait command or by a "Math" command; otherwise, k = 0	Regardless of its value, bit k is set to zero

TABLE 16.6: *Time-Code Status Bits in Information Fields GP0 through GP7 (continued)*

STATUS BITS	VALUE AFTER THE DEVICE IS TURNED ON, OR AFTER AN MMC RESET COMMAND HAS BEEN RECEIVED	VALUE DURING NORMAL OPERATIONS	INTERPRETATION OF THE BITS IN THE INFORMATION FIELD OF A WRITE COMMAND
g (sign)	0	As loaded by a Wait command or by a "Math" command	Authorized bit "i" is written
i (the fifth byte)	0	0	If bit "i" of the Write command = 0, then the fifth byte is treated as a set of subframes; however, if bit "i" of the Write command = 1, then the final data byte is ignored

. . . .

Two-Byte Time Codes

The time codes for the fifteen fields listed below are expressed in abbreviated form, i.e., as two bytes:

```
fr (st/ff)
```

21H Short   Selected Time Code (read)

22H Short   Selected Master Code (read)

23H Short   Requested Offset (read)

24H Short   Actual Offset (read)

25H Short   Lock Deviation (read)

26H Short   Generator Time Code (read)

27H Short   MIDI Time Code Input (read)

28H Short   GP0/Locate Point (read)

29H Short   GP1 (read)

2AH Short   GP2 (read)

2BH Short   GP3 (read)

2CH Short   GP4 (read)

2DH Short   GP5 (read)

2EH Short   GP8 (read)

2FH Short   GP7 (read)

Signature (read)

The information in the Signature message is essentially the MIDI Machine Control equivalent of an implementation chart. Commands and responses are represented by bits, with bits that are set to 1 indicating that the command or response in question is implemented by the device.

```
40H: Signature
<counter = variable>: the number of data bytes in the message
viH: the integer portion of the version number of the MMC protocol
     that is implemented
vfH: the decimal portion of the version number of the MMC protocol
```

```
        that is implemented
vaH: reserved for future extensions (this byte should be set to zero)
vbH: reserved for future extensions (this byte should be set to zero)
<counter 1>: the number of "command" bytes that will follow
c0H: commands 00H to 06H, in the format 0gfedcba
        a = command 00H
        b = command 01H
        c = command 02H
        d = command 03H
        e = command 04H
        f = command 05H
        g = command 06H
c1H: commands 07H to 0DH
c2H: commands 0EH to 14H
c3H: commands 15H to 1BH
c4H: commands 1CH to 1FH, in the format 0000dcba
        a = command 1CH
        b = command 1DH
        c = command 1EH
        d = command 1FH
c5H: commands 20H to 26H
c6H: commands 27H to 2DH
c7H: commands 2EH to 34H
c8H: commands 35H to 3BH
c9H: commands 3CH to 3FH, in the format 0000dcba
        a = command 3CH
        b = command 3DH
        c = command 3EH
        d = command 3FH
c10H: commands 40H to 46H
c11H: commands 47H to 4DH
c12H: commands 4EH to 54H
c13H: commands 55H to 5BH
c14H: commands 5CH to 5FH, in the format 0000dcba
        a = command 5CH
        b = command 5DH
        c = command 5EH
        d = command 5FH
```

```
c15H: commands 60H to 66H
c16H: commands 67H to 6DH
c17H: commands 6EH to 74H
c18H: commands 75H to 7BH
c19H: commands 7CH to 7FH, in the format 0000dcba
       a = command 7CH
       b = command 7DH
       c = command 7EH
       d = command 7FH
c20H to c39H: the first extension level
             (commands 00H 01H to 00H 7FH)
c40H to c09H: the second extension level
             (commands 00H 00H 01H to 00H 00H 7FH)
<counter 2>: the number of "response" bytes that will follow
r0H to r19H: responses 00H to 7FH
r20H to r39H: the first extension level
             (responses 00H 01H to 00H 7FH)
r40H to r59H: the second extension level
             (responses 00H 00H 01H to 00H 00H 7FH)
```

There's no point in transmitting the bytes that represent commands whose code is greater than that of the last command implemented.

In addition to the Signature message, every MMC-compatible device should be able to respond to a MIDI identification-request (Inquiry) message (described in detail in Chapter 4).

A controlled device should understand the 00H (Extension) command, so that it can recognize these messages even if it doesn't implement them. On the other hand, under the current version of MIDI Machine Control (Version 1.0), controlled devices should ignore the 00H response, because no extensions have been defined yet.

The bytes and bits that represent the commands in Version 1.0 of the MIDI Machine Control protocol are listed below, along with their respective hex codes and their English names:

Byte c0H, bit 0 (0000000a)	00H	reserved for future extensions
Byte c0H, bit 1 (000000b0)	01H	Stop (MCS)
Byte c0H, bit 2 (00000c00)	02H	Play (MCS)
Byte c0H, bit 3 (0000d000)	03H	Deferred Play (MCS)
Byte c0H, bit 4 (000e0000)	04H	Fast Forward (MCS)
Byte c0H, bit 5 (00f00000)	05H	Rewind (MCS)
Byte c0H, bit 6 (0g000000)	06H	Record Strobe
Byte c1H, bit 0 (0000000a)	07H	Record Exit
Byte c1H, bit 1 (000000b0)	08H	Record Pause
Byte c1H, bit 2 (00000c00)	09H	Pause (MCS)
Byte c1H, bit 3 (0000d000)	0AH	Eject (MCS)
Byte c1H, bit 4 (000e0000)	0BH	Chase (MCS)

Byte c1H, bit 5 (00f00000)	0CH	Command Error Reset
Byte c1H, bit 6 (0g000000)	0DH	MMC Reset
Byte c10H, bit 0 (0000000a)	40H	Write
Byte c10H, bit 1 (000000b0)	41H	Masked Write
Byte c10H, bit 2 (00000c00)	42H	Read
Byte c10H, bit 3 (0000d000)	43H	Update
Byte c10H, bit 4 (000e0000)	44H	Locate (MCP)
Byte c10H, bit 5 (00f00000)	45H	Variable Play (MCS)
Byte c10H, bit 6 (0g000000)	46H	Search (MCS)
Byte c11H, bit 0 (0000000a)	47H	Shuttle (MCS)
Byte c11H, bit 1 (000000b0)	48H	Step (MCS)
Byte c11H, bit 2 (00000c00)	49H	Assign System Master

Byte c11H, bit 3 (0000d000)	4AH	Generator Command
Byte c11H, bit 4 (000e0000)	4BH	MIDI Time Code Command
Byte c11H, bit 5 (00f00000)	4CH	Move
Byte c11H, bit 6 (0g000000)	4DH	Add
Byte c12H, bit 0 (0000000a)	4EH	Subtract
Byte c12H, bit 1 (000000b0)	4FH	Drop Frame Adjust
Byte c12H, bit 2 (00000c00)	50H	Procedure
Byte c12H, bit 3 (0000d000)	51H	Event
Byte c12H, bit 4 (000e0000)	52H	Group
Byte c12H, bit 5 (00f00000)	53H	Command Segment
Byte c12H, bit 6 (0g000000)	54H	Deferred Variable Play (MCS)
Byte c13H, bit 0 (0000000a)	55H	Record Strobe Variable

| Byte c19H, bit 0 (0000000a) | 7CH | Wait |
| Byte c19H, bit 3 (0000d000) | 7FH | Resume |

Update Rate (read/write)

This message indicates the time interval that separates the sending of the fields whose transmission was requested by the Update command.

```
41H: Update Rate
<counter = 01H>: the number of data byte in the message
<interval>: the time interval, expressed in terms of the
number of frames,
            over 7 bits (with a default value of 01)
```

Response Error (no access)

This message is issued after a Read or Update command has been received, under one of the following three conditions: 1) the field doesn't exist within the controlled device; 2) the field isn't defined by the MMC standard; or 3) the field is defined as being inaccessible.

```
42H: Response Error
<counter = variable>: the number of data byte in the message
<name 1>: the name of the first erroneous field
<name 2>: the name of the second erroneous field
...
...
```

Assume, on the one hand, that a controller device sends a command to a controlled device with the intention of reading three fields, and, on the other hand, that the first two of these zones ("bad1" and "bad2" in the following example) are erroneous. Here's what you'd get as a command:

```
FOH 7FH <device ID> <mcc> <read> <counter = 03H> <bad1> <bad2> <good> F7H
```

And here's what the responses would be:

```
FOH 7FH <device ID> <mcr> <Response Error> <counter = 01H> <bad1> F7H
FOH 7FH <device ID> <mcr> <Response Error> <counter = 01H> <bad2> F7H
FOH 7FH <device ID> <mcr> <good> <data> F7H
```

or possibly:

```
FOH 7FH <device ID> <mcr> <Response Error> <counter = 02H> <bad1> <bad2>
F7H
FOH 7FH <device ID> <mcr> <good> <data> F7H
```

Command Error (read)

```
43H: Command Error
<counter = 04H + ext + counter 1>: the number of data bytes in the
        message
<flags>: 0gfedcba
        a = a so-called "blocking" error (i.e., the Error Halt flag
            is set)
            0 = no interruption (this bit is set to zero when power
                is turned on, or when an MMC Reset or Command Error
                Reset command is received. The commands received by
                the device are executed in the normal way)
            1 = interruption (this bit is set to 1 as soon as an
                "enabled" error (i.e., an error that needs to be
                taken into consideration) occurs. The commands that
                follow the command that caused this error will not be
                executed)
        b = Procedure [Assemble] error
            0 = no error
            1 = error upon verification of a procedure, after
                reception of a Procedure [Assemble] command
        c = Event [Define] error
            0 = no error
            1 = error upon verification of an event, after reception
                of an Event [Define] command
```

```
        d = 0
        e = condition under which a Command Error message is
            transmitted
            0 = in response to a Read command
            1 = automatically, after an "enabled" error has been
                detected
        f = transmission of the last error that was detected
            0 = the Command Error field has not been transmitted
                since the last error occurred (the bit is set to zero
                after an error is detected)
            1 = the Command Error field was transmitted after the
                last error occurred (the bit is set to 1 after this
                message is transmitted)
        g = 0
<level>: the value of the Command Error Level information field
<error>: the error code
            00H = reserved for future extensions
        01H – 7EH = the error code
            7FH: no error has been detected since the device was
                turned on or since an MMC Reset command was
                received
<counter 1>: the number of bytes that will follow
<offset>: the address of the error in the command, starting from zero
          (takes on the value 7FH if the address is unknown or if no
          address can be attributed, as a result of the nature of the
          error itself)
<command string>: the command that was responsible for the error and
                  that is shown in its entirety (except in the case of
                  truncation, or if its length cannot be determined)
```

An error is said to be "enabled" as soon as its code is less than or equal to the value of the Command Error information field. Without executing the command that is responsible for causing the error, the controlled device updates the Command Error information field —that is, it sets the "blocking" error indicator (i.e., the Error Halt flag) to 1—transmits it immediately, and ignores any commands that follow the one that caused the error, until told to do otherwise (that is, until it receives an MMC Reset command or Command Error Reset command).

Errors, which are identified by a code, are divided into three categories—
Major, Immediate Operational, and Implementation—as indicated below:

Major Errors

```
01H = reception buffer overflow
02H = error involving the length of the command
      (e.g., an improperly positioned status byte)
03H = error involving the value of the command counter, which differs
      from the number of bytes in the message
04H = error involving the value of the field counter, which differs
      from the number of bytes in the message in connection with a
      Write command
05H: unauthorized group identification number (7FH)
06H: unauthorized procedure identification number (7FH)
07H: unauthorized event identification number (7FH)
08H: improper extension of a name beyond the second level
      (e.g., 00H 00H 00H instead of 00H 00H <command code>)
09H: segmentation error
```

In the Major category, when a so-called "disabled" error is detected (i.e.,
an error whose code is greater than the value of the Command Error
Level information field), the controlled device does not execute the command that caused the error. Instead, the device updates the Command Error field, but without setting the Error Halt flag. The device ignores any
other commands in an Exclusive message that include the command that
caused the error, and resumes normal operations as soon as possible.

Immediate Operational Errors

```
20H: update list overflow
21H: group buffer overflow
22H: undefined procedure
23H: procedure buffer overflow
24H: undefined event
25H: event buffer overflow
26H: blank time code
```

In the Immediate Operational category, when a so-called "disabled" error is detected (i.e., an error whose code is greater than the value of the Command Error Level information field), the controlled device does not execute the command that caused the error. Instead, the device updates the Command Error field, but without setting the Error Halt flag. The device does execute any other commands in an Exclusive message that include the command the caused the error, and continues with normal operations.

Implementation Errors

```
40H: unimplemented command
41H: a command that includes an unrecognized sub-command
42H: a command that includes unrecognized data
43H: a command that includes an unimplemented field
44H: within a procedure, a Read or Update command that has a field
     with an unimplemented identification number
45H: a non-existent or unimplemented time code serving as the source
     for an event trigger
46H: a nested procedure (i.e., one that includes an [Assemble]
     Procedure command)
47H: a recursive procedure (i.e., one that includes an [Execute]
     Procedure command)
48H: a nested event (i.e., one that includes an Event [Define]
     command)
49H: a Procedure [Assemble] command within an Event [Define] command
60H: an attempt to write to an unimplemented information field
61H: an attempt to write to a "read only" information field
62H: a Write command that contains information fields with
     unrecognized data
63H: a Write command that contains information fields with
     unimplemented names
```

In the Implementation category, when a so-called "disabled" error is detected (i.e., an error whose code is greater than the value of the Command Error Level information field), the controlled device does not execute the command that caused the error. Instead, the device updates the Command Error field, but without setting the Error Halt flag. The device does execute any other commands in an Exclusive message that include the command the caused the error, and continues with normal operations.

When an error is detected during the verification of a procedure or an event, the procedure or the event in question is ignored. Operations resume normally only after an Procedure [Assemble] or Event [Define] command has been received.

Commands that involve first- and second-level extensions also fall under this three-category classification scheme. For instance, commands whose identification numbers are from 00H 20H to 00H 3FH belong to the family of Immediate Operational errors.

Command Error Level (read/write)

This information field lies at the border between "enabled" and "disabled" errors. Errors whose code is greater than the value of the Command Error Level information field are known as "disabled" errors, and must be dealt with, while errors whose code is less than or equal to the value of the Command Error Level information field are known as "enabled" errors, and do not need to be dealt with.

```
44H: Command Error Level
<counter = 01H>: the number of data bytes in the message
vvH: level
        00H = all errors are disabled (the default value)
    00H - 7EH = the errors whose code is less than or equal to this
            value are selectively enabled
        7FH = all errors are enabled
```

Time Standard (read/write)

This information field contains the nominal time code type to be used by the controlled device.

```
45H: Time Standard
<counter = 01H>: the number of data bytes in the message
<type>: 0tt0000
        tt = the number of frames per second
            00 = 24
            01 = 25
            10 = 30 (Drop Frame)
            11 = 30 (Nondrop Frame)
```

Selected Time Code Source (read/write)

This information field indicates the source of the time code that the device will be using.

```
46H: Selected Time Code Source
<counter = 01H>: the number of data bytes in the message
ssH: the source of the time code
     00H = LTC (Longitudinal Time Code)
     01H = VITC (Vertical Interval Time Code)
     02H = updating from a control track ("CTL") or from tachymetric
           data, particularly during fast winding operations
     03H = automatic VITC/LTC
     7FH = as defined by default for the device (i.e., a write-only
           value)
```

Selected Time Code Userbits (read)

This information field contains the value of the user bits as taken from the Selected Time Code information field.

```
47H: Selected Time Code Userbits
<counter = 09H>: the number of data bytes in the message
u1H - u9H: the user bits
```

Motion Control Tally (read)

This information field indicates the activity of the device in terms of transport.

```
48H: Motion Control Tally
<counter = 03H + ext>: the number of data bytes in the message
msH: the last Motion Control State (MCS) command received
     00H = reserved for future extensions
     01H = Stop
     02H = Play
     04H = Fast Forward
     05H = Rewind
     09H = Pause
     0AH = Eject
     45H = Variable Play
     46H = Search
     47H = Shuttle
     48H = Step
mpH: the last Motion Control Process (MCP) command received
     00H = reserved for future extensions
     0BH = Chase
     44H = Locate
     7FH = no MCP command is currently being executed
          ssH: 0bbb0aaa
     aaa = status of the last MCS command received
     bbb = status of the last MCP command received
```

MCS or MCP commands that are responsible for causing an error that belongs to the "Major Error" or "Implementation Error" categories do not need to be mentioned in this information field. (For more details, see the description of the Command Error message given above.) On the other hand, MCS or MCP commands that are responsible for causing an error that belongs to the "Immediate Operational Error" category do need to be mentioned. In such a case, bits aaa or bbb take on the value 010 (i.e., failure).

When the execution of an MCP command is interrupted, either upon reception of an MCS command (except for the Deferred Play and Deferred Variable Play commands, which do not interrupt the positioning), or upon reception of an MMC Rest command, the mpH byte, which indicates the last MCP command that was received, takes on the value 7FH (i.e., indicating that no MCP command is being executed) and bits aaa are set to zero.

Here's a list of the status indicators associated with each MCS command:

```
Stop
000 = stop attempt made
001 = stopped
010 = failure
011 = deduced motion

Fast Forward
000 = attempt to shift into Fast Forward mode
001 = Fast Forward mode achieved
010 = failure
011 = deduced motion

Rewind
000 = attempt to shift into Rewind mode
001 = Rewind mode achieved
010 = failure
011 = deduced motion

Play ("unresolved")
000 = attempt to shift into Read mode
001 = Read mode achieved
010 = failure
011 = deduced motion

Play ("resolved")
000 = in progress
001 = Read mode achieved and resolved (with "servo lock")
010 = failure
101 = Read mode not resolved
```

```
Pause
000 = in progress
001 = paused
010 = failure

Eject
000 = in progress
001 = media ejected or unloaded
010 = failure

Variable Play
000 = in progress
001 = variable-speed Read mode achieved
010 = failure

Search
000 = in progress
001 = Search mode achieved
010 = failure

Shuttle
000 = in progress
001 = Shuttle mode achieved
010 = failure

Step
000 = in progress
001 = shift interval achieved
010 = failure
100 = shift operation not yet completed
```

The four operations (Stop, Fast Forward, Rewind, and Play) which involve deduced motions have the particular feature of not taking place as the result of the reception of a command. Either the device plays the role of a slave and therefore follows the movements of the master device, or else the user manipulates the transport commands for a synchronizer or another interface that is interposed between the master and slave devices, and so on.

Generally speaking, the term "resolve" means that the motor of the device has been locked by means of a servo mechanism. Its play speed should be such that the frames of its timing code (SMPTE, Control Track, etc.) are synchronized with regard to a reference (such as a quartz crystal-based frequency, word sync, a word clock, etc.).

Here's a list of the status indicators associated with each MCP command:

```
Locate
000 = in progress
001 = positioning point reached
010 = failure
100 = in progress, with the Deferred Play command pending
110 = in progress, Deferred Variable Play command pending

Chase
000 = synchronization attempt being made (in Read mode)
001 = synchronization attempt completed (in Read mode)
010 = failure
100 = synchronization attempt being made (in a mode other than Read
      mode, e.g., Fast Forward or Rewind mode)
110 = device stopped, ready to be synchronized (i.e., the device is
      properly positioned)
```

Velocity Tally (read)

This information field indicates the play speed of the device.

```
49H: Velocity Tally
<counter = 03H>: the number of data bytes in the message
shH smH slH: the play speed
```

Stop Mode (read/write)

This information field determines whether the controlled device should go into monitoring mode once it has been stopped as the result of a Stop command.

```
4AH: Stop Mode
<counter = 01H>: the number of data bytes in the message
ccH: monitoring
     00H = no
     01H = yes
     7FH = as defined by default for the device (i.e., a write-only
           value)
```

Fast Mode (read/write)

This information field determines whether the controlled device should go into monitoring mode after it has received a Fast Forward or Rewind command.

```
4BH: Fast Mode
<counter = 01H>: the number of data bytes in the message
ccH: monitoring
     00H = no (forward or backward motion takes place at top speed)
     01H = yes (forward or backward motion takes place at the maximum
           speed that is compatible with proper monitoring)
     7FH = as defined by default for the device (i.e., a write-only
           value)
```

Record Mode (read/write)

This information field determines the behavior of the device after it receives a Record Strobe or Record Strobe Variable command. Tracks that are already being recorded or rehearsed when this information field is changed will not be affected.

```
4CH: Record Mode
<counter = 01H>: the number of data bytes in the message
ddH: the recording mode
     00H = recording has not been activated
     01H = recording (for an audiotape recorder)
         = recording in "insert" mode (for a videotape recorder)
     02H = recording (for an audiotape recorder)
```

```
    = recording in "assemble" mode (for a videotape recorder)
04H = rehearsal
05H = recording (for an audiotape recorder)
    = recording in "crash/full" mode (for a videotape recorder)
7FH = as defined by default for the device (i.e., a write-only
      value)
```

Here's a detailed explanation of these various values:

- Recording (for an audiotape recorder): Recording takes place on the tracks specified by the Track Record Ready information field.

- Rehearse: Recording is simulated, at the monitoring level, but no signals are recorded.

- Recording in "insert" mode (for a videotape recorder): Recording takes place on the tracks specified by the Track Record Ready information field, but the control track ("CTL") is not erased. At the punch-in and punch-out points, the transitions between signals previously recorded on the tape and the new recording take place cleanly, with correct timing.

- Recording in "assemble" mode (for a videotape recorder): Recording takes place on all of the tracks, including the control track. At the punch-in and punch-out points, the transitions between signals previously recorded on the tape and the new recording take place cleanly, with correct timing.

- Recording in "crash/full" mode (for a videotape recorder): Recording takes place on all of the tracks, including the control track. At the punch-in and punch-out points, no attempt is made to cause the transitions between signals previously recorded on the tape and the new recording to take place cleanly or with correct timing.

Record Status (read)

This information field reflects the recording or rehearsal mode of the device.

```
4EH: Track Record Status
<counter = 01H>: the number of data bytes in the message
ssH: 0dcbaaa
    aaaa = Record mode or Rehearsal mode
        0000 = no recording or rehearsal
        0001 = recording (for an audiotape recorder)
               recording in "insert" mode (for a videotape
               recorder)
        0010 = recording in "assemble" mode (for a videotape
               recorder)
        0100 = rehearsal
        0101 = recording in "crash/full" mode (for a videotape
               recorder)
        0110 = record-pause
  b = recording disabled/enabled
    0 = recording enabled at device level
    1 = recording disabled at device level
        (physical protection or write-prevention tabs on the
        media, etc.)
  c = rehearsal disabled/enabled
    0 = rehearsal enabled at device level
    1 = rehearsal disabled at device level
  d = overall track activity indicator
    0 = certain tracks are in Record mode or Rehearsal mode
    1 = no tracks are in Record mode or Rehearsal mode (this
        indicator, which consists of an exclusive OR for the bits
        in the Track Record Status information field, is valid
        only when the value of aaaa is something other than zero)
```

Track Record Status (read)

This information field indicates the tracks that are currently recording or rehearsing.

```
4EH: Track Record Status
<counter = variable>: the number of data bytes in the message
rOH r1H r2H...: the representation of the tracks (see also
                Chapter 15), in the form of a bit map
```

Track Record Ready (read/write)

This information field indicates the tracks that are ready to move into Record mode or Rehearsal mode.

```
4FH: Track Record Ready
<counter = variable>: the number of data bytes in the message
rOH r1H r2H,... : the representation of the tracks (see also
                  Chapter 15), in the form of a bit map
```

Global Monitor (read/write)

This information field selects the device monitoring mode (in Playback or Input mode) for all of the tracks. In Input mode, the outputs pass along the signals that have been recorded on the tape, either by means of the record head (in so-called "synchronous" playback mode), or else by means of the play head (in so-called "repro" playback mode).

```
50H: Global Monitor
<counter = 01>: the number of data bytes in the message
ddH: monitoring mode
     OOH = "synchronous" playback (the default mode)
     01H = input
     02H = "repro" playback
```

With regard to the two playback modes, it's worth noting that apart from professional devices, audiotape recorders generally only have two heads: one for erasing, and the other for reading and recording. For technical reasons, at present it's hard to build heads that perform equally well in reading and recording. This is why professional audiotape recorders often have three heads: one for erasing, one for reading, and one for recording. However, if necessary, the recording head can serve as a play head. This double duty is necessary when you're doing overdubs with a multitrack audiotape recorder, in order to eliminate the delay between the tracks that have already been laid down and the recording that's being made. This mode is often referred to as "synchronous" mode. When you do the mixing, the "real" play head takes over again, for the sake of quality. This mode is often referred to as "repro" or "direct" mode.

Record Monitor (read/write)

This information field selects the conditions under which the outputs pass along the signals that are received at the inputs. These conditions apply only to tracks that are in synchronous playback monitoring mode.

```
51H: Record Monitor
<counter = 01>: the number of data bytes in the message
ddH: track monitoring mode
     00H = only during recording
     01H = during recording or during non-reading
     02H = during recording or in ready-to-record mode
     7FH = as defined by default for the device (i.e., a write-only
           value)
```

Track Sync Monitor (read/write)

In monitoring mode, this information field selects the tracks that will provide synchronous playback. This field takes priority over the Global Monitor information field.

```
53H: Track Input Monitor
<counter = variable>: the number of data bytes in the message
r0H r1H r2H, ...
```

Track Input Monitor (read/write)

This information field selects the tracks whose outputs will pass along the signals that are received at the inputs. This field takes priority over the Global Monitor and Record Monitor information fields.

```
52H: Track Sync Monitor
<counter = variable>: the number of data bytes in the message
r0H r1H r2H, ...
```

Step Length (read/write)

This information field defines the distance unit that will be used by the Step command.

```
54H: Step Length
<counter = 01H>: the number of data bytes in the message
           nnH: the distance unit to be used by the command Step,
           expressed in terms of the number of frames/100 in the
           Step unit (with a default value of 32H, or half a frame)
```

Play Speed Reference (read/write)

This information field is the reference source that determines whether a device should control its speed internally when it is in standard Play mode, or should allow direct play-speed control from an outside source, in Read mode and in the absence of synchronization (i.e., in Chase or Free Resolved Play Mode).

```
55H: Play Speed Reference
<counter = 01H>: the number of data bytes in the message
rrH: reference
     00H = internal
     01H = external
     7FH = as defined by default for the device (i.e., a write-only
           value)
```

Fixed Speed (read/write)

This information field selects a nominal play speed from among the speeds the device offers.

```
56H: Fixed Speed
<counter = 01H>: the number of data bytes in the message
ppH: speed
     ...
     ...
     3FH = the next lower speed below the standard speed
     40H = the medium or "standard" speed
     41H = the next higher speed above the standard speed
     ..
     ..
     7FH = as defined by default for the device (i.e., a write-only
           value)
```

Lifter Defeat (read/write)

This information field defeats the tape lifter mechanism of a controlled reel-to-reel device, thereby allowing the tape to come into contact with the heads, during playing or at any other speed at which the signal needs to be heard.

```
56H: Lifter Defeat
<counter = 01H>: the number of data bytes in the message
ccH: the position of the lifter mechanism
     00H = the lifter mechanism presses the tape against the heads
     01H = the lifter mechanism moves the tape away from the heads
     7FH = as defined by default for the device (i.e., a write-only
           value)
```

Control Disable (read/write)

When the device is no longer controlled, it ignores commands that involve Ctrl-type operations (i.e., handling of transport tasks) and Sync (i.e., synchronization) operations.

```
58H: Control Disable
<counter = 01H>: the number of data bytes in the message
ccH: the device is under control
     00H = yes (the default value)
     01H = no
     7FH = as defined by default for the device (i.e., a write-only
           value)
```

Resolved Play Mode (read/write)

This information field determines the manner in which the device should set its nominal play speed in response to a Play command.

```
59H: Resolved Play Mode
<counter = 01H>: the number of data bytes in the message
ddH: Play mode at nominal speed
     00H = normal
     01H = resolved (Free Resolve Mode)
     7FH = as defined by default for the device (i.e., a write-only
           value)
```

In normal mode, the play speed, regardless of whether it's controlled internally or externally (depending on the value of the Play Speed Reference field), is independent of any reference value. In Free Resolve Mode, the play speed is resolved. In other words, the edges of the frames in the time code of the device (i.e., the Selected Time Code) are synchronized to a reference value (such as a quartz crystal-based frequency, word sync, a word clock, etc.). Videotape recorders and other rotating-head devices, which by definition operate in this manner, don't need to implement this message.

Chase Mode (read/write)

This information field determines how a controlled device synchronizes itself in response to a Chase command.

```
5AH: Chase
<counter = 01H>: the number of data bytes in the message
ddH: the synchronization mode
      00H = absolute (Absolute Standard Mode)
      01H = resolved (Absolute Resolve Mode)
      7FH = as defined by default for the device (i.e., a write-only
            value)
```

In normal mode, the time code of the device (i.e., the Selected Time Code) follows a master reference (i.e., the Selected Master Code), taking into consideration the shift (i.e., the Requested Offset), if one is present. In Resolve mode, the correspondence between the values of these two codes is not significant. The only thing that matters is that the edges of the frames in the time code of the device are synchronized with regard to the edges of the frames in the master reference. This prevents any "slippage" between devices, without requiring the devices to be synchronized with any particular single time reference source.

Generator Command Tally (read)

This information field keeps track of the running state of the time-code generator.

```
5BH: Generator Command Tally
<counter = 02H>: the number of data bytes in the message
ggH: the last command received
      00H = stop
      01H = generation of the time code (run)
      02H = copy/regeneration of the time code (copy/jam)
ssH: 00cb0aaa
      aaa = status
          000 = attempt to execute the command that was received
```

```
        001 = successful execution the command that was received
        010 = failure
  b = the time-code source, for a copy or regeneration
        0 = presence of the time-code source
        1 = loss of the time-code source
  c = external reference, known as "frame sync"
        0 = presence of the external reference
        1 = loss of the external reference
```

Generator Set Up (read/write)

This information field controls the operating modes of the time-code generator.

```
5CH: Generator Set Up
<counter = 03H + ext>: the number of data bytes in the message
<reference>: "frame sync" (0yyy0nnn)
          nnn = the reference, during generation
              000 = internal quartz
              001 = external reference
              010 = internal quartz in "Drop A" mode
              011 = internal quartz in "Drop B" mode
              111 = as defined by default for the device
                    (i.e., a write-only value)
          yyy = the reference, for a copy or regeneration
              000 = edges of the frames of a time code
              001 = external reference
              111 = as defined by default for the device
                    (i.e., a write-only value)
<source>: the time-code source, for a copy or regeneration
        00H = reserved for future extensions
        01H = Selected Time Code (the default value)
        02H = Selected Master Code
        7FH = as defined by default for the device
                (i.e., a write-only value)
<copy/jam>: copy/regeneration mode
```

```
OOH = if the time-code source stops or is lost,
      the copy/regeneration also stops
O1H = if the time-code source stops or is lost,
      the copy/regeneration continues
```

The following chart shows the number of frames per second for the code that's generated, as a function of the type of internal reference:

INTERNAL REFERENCE		TYPE OF CODE		
nnn	24	25	30 Drop Frame	30
000 (normal)	24	25	29.97	30
010 (Drop A)	24	25	29.97	29.97
011 (Drop B)	23.976	24.975	29.97	29.97

Generator Userbits (read/write)

This information field contains the value of the user bits generated by the time code generator.

```
5DH: Generator Userbits
<counter = 09H>: the number of data bytes in the message
u1H through u9H: the user bits
```

MIDI Time Code Command Tally (read/write)

This information field keeps track of the running state of the MIDI Time Code generator.

```
5EH: MIDI Time Code Command Tally
<counter = O2H>: the number of data bytes in the message
mmH: the last command received
     OOH = no MIDI Time Code (off)
```

```
        02H = the MIDI Time Code is issued by the time code specified
                by the MIDI Time Code Set Up information field
ssH: 00000aaa
        aaa = status
            000 = attempt to execute the command that was received
            001 = successful execution the command that was received
            010 = failure
```

MIDI Time Code Set Up (read/write)

This information field controls the operating modes of the MIDI Time Code generator.

```
5EH: MIDI Time Code Command Tally
<counter = 02H + ext>: the number of data bytes in the message
<flags>: 0gfedcba
            a = the "transmit while stopped" flag for the MIDI Time Code
                0 = the transmission of MIDI Time Code messages is
                    suspended as soon as the time-code source which
                    issued the messages has been detected to have
                    stopped
                1 = the transmission of MIDI Time Code messages
                    continues in spite of the stoppage of the time-code
                    source which issued the messages, in a manner
                    determined by bit b
            b = transmission of MIDI Time Code "while stopped"
                (i.e., with bit a = 1)
                0 = Quarter-Frame messages, with no frame incrementing
                1 = Full Messages, sent at regular intervals
            c = high-speed transmission of MIDI Time Code messages
                0 = transmission of MIDI Time Code messages is suspended
                    as soon as the time-code source which issued the
                    messages is detected to be moving at a rate which is
                    more than twice its nominal frame rate
                1 = the transmission of MIDI Time Code messages
                    continues, in spite of the fact that time-code
                    source which issued the messages is detected to be
                    moving at a rate which is more than twice its
                    nominal frame rate, in a manner determined by bit d
```

```
        d = "high-speed" transmission of MIDI Time Code messages
            (i.e., with bit c = 1)
            0 = Quarter-Frame messages
            1 = Full Messages, sent at regular intervals
        e = user bits
            0 = transmission of the user bits is not guaranteed
            1 = transmission of the user bits is guaranteed, as soon
                as their content changes, or at regular intervals
        f = the output port
            0 = the MIDI Time Code messages are physically sent to
                the port which is responsible for transmitting MMC
                responses
            1 = the MIDI Time Code messages are physically sent to a
                port other than the one which is responsible for
                transmitting MMC responses
<source>: the field that specifies the time-code source which issues
                the MIDI Time Code
        00H = reserved for future extensions
        01H = Selected Time Code
        02H = Selected Master Code
        06H = Generator Time Code
        07H = MIDI Time Code Input (in "soft Thru" mode)
        7FH = as defined by default for the device
                (i.e., a write-only value)
```

Procedure Response (read)

This information field enables the controller device to read back any or all of the Procedures.

```
60H: Procedure Response
<counter = variable>: the number of data bytes in the message
<procedure>: 00H to 7EH = the identification number of the procedure
                7FH = invalid identification number

<command #1>
<command #2>
<command #3>
...
...
```

Before this information field is read, the Procedure [Set] command has to program the identification number for the procedure that the controller device wants to read. The procedure in question can be either an individual procedure or all of the procedures that are stored in the memory of the controlled device (as carried by means of as many Procedure Response messages as there are procedures, automatically transmitted one after another). In this latter case, care should be taken to send the value 7FH, rather than a number between 00H and 7EH.

If no procedure stored in the memory of the controlled device corresponds to the identification number for the Procedure [Set] command, or if this command was never sent by the controller device, then before the Procedure Response field is read, the counter and the procedure identification number for this zone will take on the values 00H and 7FH when they are sent, thereby indicating the nullity of the request.

Event Response (read)

This information field allows the controller device to read back any or all of the events.

```
61H: Event Response
<counter = variable>: the number of data bytes in the message
<event>: OOH to 7EH = the identification number of the event
             7FH = invalid identification number
<flags>: OkOaOOdd
        dd = directions
             00 = to be triggered on a shift into forward operation
             01 = to be triggered on a shift into backward operation
             10 = to be triggered regardless of the direction of
                  operation, except for Event [Define] and Procedure
                  [Assemble]
        a = speed
          0 = to be triggered when the corresponding position is
              reached at the specified time (i.e., the trigger
              time), while the device is in play mode
```

```
                1 = to be triggered regardless of the play speed, after
                    the position that corresponds to the specified time
                    (i.e., the trigger time) has been reached or passed
            k = suppression
                0 = the event should be suppressed after triggering
                1 = the event should be preserved after triggering
<trigger source>: the field that specifies the source of the time code
                that serves as a reference for the triggering
                  00H = reserved for future extensions
                  01H = Selected Time Code
                  02H = Selected Master Code
                  06H = Generator Time Code
                  07H = MIDI Time Code Input
hrH mnH scH frH ffH: the time at which the event should be triggered
<command>: the event to be triggered, i.e., any command other than
            Event [Define] and Procedure [Assemble]
```

Before this information field is read, the Event [Set] command has to program the identification number for the event that the controller device wants to read. The event in question can be either an individual event or all of the events that are stored in the memory of the controlled device (as carried by means of as many Event Response messages as there are events, automatically transmitted one after another). In this latter case, care should be taken, via the Event [Set] command, to send the value 7FH, rather than a number between 00H and 7EH.

If no procedure stored in the memory of the controlled device corresponds to the identification number for the Event [Set] command, or if this command was never sent by the controller device, then before the Event Response field is read, the counter and the procedure identification number for this zone will take on the values 00H and 7FH when they are sent, thereby indicating the nullity of the request.

Track Mute (read/write)

This information field indicates the tracks whose output signals will be muted—that is, the tracks that will not pass along any signals. This field takes priority over the Global Monitor, Record Monitor, and Track Sync Monitor information fields.

```
62H: Track Mute
<counter = variable>: the number of data bytes in the message
r0H r1H r2H, ...
```

VITC Insert Enable (read/write)

This information field determines whether a VITC (Vertical Interval Time Code) should be embedded in the video signal that is received by the controlled device. If so, and if that video signal is to be recorded, then the VITC will be recorded along with it.

```
63H: VITC Insert Enable
<counter = 03H>: the number of data bytes in the message
ccH: embedding
      00H = no
      01H = yes
      7FH = as defined by default for the device (i.e., a write-only
            value)
h1H: the number of the first horizontal line for VITC insertion
      0AH to 12H = NTSC
      06H to 14H = PAL
      7FH = as defined by default for the device (i.e., a write-only
            value)
h2H:  the number of the second (non-adjacent) horizontal line for VITC
      insertion (with h2H being greater than h1H)
      0CH to 14H = NTSC
      08H to 16H = PAL
      7FH = as defined by default for the device (i.e., a write-only
            value)
```

Response Segment (not accessible)

When a response or a string of responses exceeds the maximum length for a MIDI Machine Control message (i.e., 48 data bytes, or a total of 53 bytes), the entire response or string of responses can be divided into segments so that the data can be transmitted piece by piece. Each of the segments created in this way should have its own Exclusive message.

```
64H: Response Segment
<counter = variable>: the number of data bytes in the message
siH: identification of the segment (0fsssssss)
     f = the first segment / subsequent segments
         1 = the first segment
         0 = subsequent segments
     ssssss = the number of the segment (counting backward to the
              last one, whose number is equal to zero)
<responses>: part of the response or part of the entire string of
         responses
```

Failure (not accessible)

This information field warns the controller device that a catastrophic problem has just occurred—one that can't be solved without the intervention of the user.

```
65H: Failure
<counter>: the number of data bytes in the message
         (zero, if no data is present)
<data>: an optional ASCII message, intended to be displayed by the
      controller device
```

Wait (not accessible)

When for any reason (such as a buffer overflow, etc.) the controlled device can't receive any more messages, it sends a Wait response to the controller device (<device ID> = 00H to 7EH), to ask the controller device to halt all transmissions for a maximum period of 10 msec, until requested otherwise. A controller device that is in the process of transmitting a command when a Wait response arrives will be permitted to continue that transmission until the end of the current Exclusive message. The Wait response should be the only response carried by the Exclusive message in which it appears.

```
7CH: Wait
```

Resume (not accessible)

When the controlled device is again able to receive messages, it sends a Resume response to the controller device (<device ID> = 00H to 7EH) in order to tell the controller device that communications can be resumed. The Resume response should be the only response carried by the Exclusive message in which it appears.

```
7FH: Resume
```

Typical Applications

To give you a more concrete idea of the capabilities of the MIDI Machine Control protocol, here are a few examples of applications taken from the standard, with comments and annotations.

Looping between Two Points

The purpose of this command is to give the controlled device the order to create a link between Point A and Point B.

```
FOH 7FH <device ID> <mcc> <Write>
<counter = OCH>
<GPO> <point A, expressed in the form of the standard time code>
```

```
<GP1> <point B, expressed in the form of the standard time code>
<Procedure> <counter = 06H>
<[Assemble]> <identification number of the procedure> <Locate>
<counter = 01H>
<GP0> <Deferred Play> <Event>
<counter = 09H>
<[Define]> <identification number of the event>
<Flags = 40H> <Selected Time Code>
<GP1>
<Procedure> <counter = 02H>
<[Execute]> <identification number of the procedure>
<Procedure> <counter = 02H>
<[Execute]> <identification number of the procedure>
F7H
```

A Basic Configuration

The implementation of the controlled device and the sequence of commands shown below are typical of a basic MIDI Machine Control configuration. Communications are unidirectional (i.e., "open loop").

The controlled device implements the following commands: <Stop>, <Deferred Play>, <Fast Forward>, <Rewind>, <Record Strobe>, <Record Exit>, <MMC Reset>, <Write>, <Locate>, and <Move>, as well as the <Selected Time Code> and <GP0/Locate Point> information fields.

The "signature" of the controlled device looks like this:

```
01H 00H 00H 00H
0CH
7BH 41H 00H 00H 00H 00H 00H 00H 00H 00H
11H 20H
02H
02H 02H
```

Now here's a typical command sequence, as transmitted from the controller device to the controlled device, whose identification number (<device ID>), is 01H:

Read:

```
FOH 7FH <device ID> <mcc> <Deferred Play> F7H
```

Stop:

```
FOH 7FH <device ID> <mcc> <Stop> F7H
```

Reinitialization of the counter (the time type is set at 30 frames per second):

```
FOH 7FH <device ID> <mcc> <Write> <counter = 06H> <Selected Time Code>
60H 00H 00H 20H 00H F7H
```

Fast forward:

```
FOH 7FH <device ID> <mcc> <Fast Forward> F7H
```

Stop:

```
FOH 7FH <device ID> <mcc> <Stop> F7H
```

Programming of a locator on the fly:

```
FOH 7FH <device ID> <mcc> <Move>
<counter = 02H>
<GPO/Locate Point> <Selected Time Code>
F7H
```

Play:

```
FOH 7FH <device ID> <mcc> <Deferred Play> F7H
```

Punch-in:

```
FOH 7FH <device ID> <mcc> <Record Strobe> F7H
```

Punch-out:

```
FOH 7FH <device ID> <mcc> <Record Exit> F7H
```

Return to the locator point, followed by a shift into play mode:

```
FOH 7FH <device ID> <mcc> <Locate> <counter = 02H>
<[I/F]> <GPO/Locate Point> <Deferred Play> F7H
```

Return to zero:

```
FOH 7FH <device ID> <mcc> <Locate> <counter = 06H>
<[Target]> 60H OOH OOH OOH OOH F7H
```

MIDI Machine Control and the MIDI Time Code: Example 1

Viewed as the controller device, a sequencer communicates in a unidirectional way (i.e., "open loop") with an audiotape recorder, which is viewed as the controlled device. Even though it doesn't send any responses, the tape recorder does send a SMPTE time code to a unit whose job is to convert that code into a MIDI Time Code and forward it to the sequencer.

The sequencer starts by reinitializing the audiotape recorder, whose identification number (<device ID>), is 01H:

```
FOH 7FH <01H> <mcc> <MMC Reset> F7H
```

By pressing the Play key (assuming that this key also serves to halt Record mode), you give the sequencer the order to shift into play mode:

```
FOH 7FH <01H> <mcc> <Record Exit> <Deferred Play> F7H
```

The audiotape recorder sends the SMPTE signal (30 Nondrop Frame) to the unit whose job is to convert the SMPTE signal into a MIDI Time

Code signal. The sequencer receives the first MTC Quarter Frame messages, from which it reconstructs the value of the time code (01.02.03.04):

```
F1H 04H F1H 20H F1H 23H F1H 30H F1H 42H F1H 50H F1H 61H
F1H 76H F1H 06H ... ...
```

Because the audiotape recorder's Selected Time Code information field isn't updated from the SMPTE signal, but rather on the basis of tachymetric information, there's a possibility that the value in this field may not coincide perfectly with the value of the MIDI Time Code. Furthermore, if the SMPTE code in question was recorded at a speed that was slightly faster or slightly slower than its current playback speed, the shift will be increased proportionally. This is why, in order to minimize this kind of deviation or discrepancy, the sequencer regularly sends the MTC time to the audiotape recorder (in this case, 01.02.03.06), by sending the audiotape recorder the following command:

```
F0H 7FH <01H> <mcc> <Write>
<counter = 06H> <Selected Time Code>
61H 02H 03H 26H 00H F7H
```

By pressing the Record key (thereby causing the sequencer to memorize the current value of the time code, i.e., 01.02.13.20) you instruct the sequencer to shift into Record mode:

```
F0H 7FH <01H> <mcc> <Record Strobe> F7H
```

By pressing the Play key, you instruct the sequencer to exit from Record mode:

```
F0H 7FH <01H> <mcc> <Record Exit> <Deferred Play> F7H
```

By pressing the Stop key, you instruct the sequencer to stop:

```
F0H 7FH <01H> <mcc> <Stop> F7H
```

To hear the result of these operations, you position the sequencer five seconds before the start of the recording. Then, by pressing the Play key, you instruct the sequencer to shift into Play mode:

```
F0H 7FH <01H> <mcc> <Locate>
<counter = 06H> <[Target]>
61H 02H 08H 14H 00H <Deferred Play>
F7H
```

The programming of events, with a view toward achieving fully automatic recording (with the programming of punch-in and punch-out points), as opposed to manual recording, as described here, is completely impossible, thanks to the shift discrepancy mentioned above between the value in the Selected Time Code information field and the value of the MIDI Time Code. This problem can also cause slight errors during positioning.

MIDI Machine Control and the MIDI Time Code: Example 2

While the devices are the same ones discussed above, in this example the audiotape recorder itself handles the conversion of the SMPTE time code into a MIDI Time Code. As a result, the Selected Time Code information field contains a very accurate reflection of the position of the tape.

The sequencer starts by reinitializing the audiotape recorder, whose identification number (<device ID>), is 01H:

```
F0H 7FH <01H> <mcc> <MMC Reset> F7H
```

Then the sequencer inquires about its implementation:

```
F0H 7FH <01H> <mcc> <Read> <counter = 01H> <Signature> F7H
```

In return, the audiotape recorder sends the following response:

```
F0H 7FH <01H> <mcc> <Signature>
<counter = 2EH> 01H 00H 00H 00H
<counter 1 = 14H>
```

```
7FH 61H 00H 00H 00H 00H 00H 00H 00H 00H
7FH 70H 7FH 00H 00H 00H 00H 00H 00H 09H
<counter 2 = 14>
02H 1EH 00H 00H 00H 02H 1EH 00H 00H 00H
3FH 62H 07H 01H 0CH 37H 00H 00H 00H 09H
F7H
```

The sequencer decides to handle errors in the Major and Immediate Operational categories, and then determine the parameters for the time-code generator:

```
F0H 7FH <01H> <mcc> <Write>
<counter = 03H> <Command Error Level>
<counter = 01H> 3FH <Write>
<counter = 04H> <MIDI Time Code Set Up>
<counter = 02H> 00H <Selected Time Code>
F7H
```

By pressing the Play key, you instruct the sequencer to shift into Play mode. The audiotape recorder is then asked to generate the MIDI Time Code:

```
F0H 7FH <01H> <mcc> <Record Exit>
<Deferred Play>
<MIDI Time Code Command>
<counter = 01H> 02H
F7H
```

The sequencer receives the first MTC Quarter Frame (30 Drop Frame) messages, from which it reconstructs the value of the time code (03.02.20.28):

```
F1H 0CH F1H 11H F1H 24H F1H 31H
F1H 42H F1H 50H F1H 63H F1H 74H ... ...
```

The sequencer verifies that the value of the information field Selected Time Code information field is equal to the value of the MIDI Time Code:

```
F0H 7FH <01H> <mcc> <Read>
<counter = 01H> <Selected Time Code>
F7H
```

Right in the middle of MTC frame 03.02.21.00.01, the sequencer responds:

```
F1H 00H F1H 10H F1H 25H F1H 31H F1H 42H ... ...
F0H 7FH <01H> <mcr>
<Selected Time Code> 43H 02H 15H 21H 00H
F7H
... ... F1H 50H F1H 63H F1H 74H ... ...
```

Then, on the fly, you program a punch-in point (03.02.27.08), which the sequencer stores in its memory. Some time later, in the same way you program a punch-out (03.02.41.15), which the sequencer likewise stores in the same way.

You tell the sequencer to position itself a few seconds ahead of the punch-in point, in order to record the first two tracks automatically between the point in question and the punch-out point. During the positioning procedure (whose progress is controlled, because the sequencer tells the audiotape recorder to send it regular updates on the status of the transport), the production of the MIDI Time Code is halted:

```
F0H 7FH <01H> <mcc> <MIDI Time Code Command>
<counter = 01H> 00H <Locate>
<counter = 06H> <[Target]> 43H 02H 16H 08H 00H <Update>
<counter = 02H> <[Begin]> <Motion Control Tally>
F7H
```

The audiotape recorder informs the sequencer about its actions. Then the positioning procedure starts (with a fast rewind operation):

```
F0H 7FH <01H> <mcr> <Motion Control Tally>
<counter = 03H> <Rewind> <Locate> 01H
F7H
```

The positioning process continues. Because it went just a little too far, the audiotape recorder decides to shift into Fast Forward mode:

```
F0H 7FH <01H> <mcr> <Motion Control Tally>
<counter = 03H> <Fast Forward> <Locate> 00H
F7H
```

Then the audiotape recorder actually does shift into Fast Forward mode:

```
F0H 7FH <01H> <mcr> <Motion Control Tally>
<counter = 03H> <Fast Forward> <Locate> 01H
F7H
```

The audiotape recorder then decides to stop:

```
F0H 7FH <01H> <mcr> <Motion Control Tally>
<counter = 03H> <Stop> <Locate> 00H
F7H
```

And then the audiotape recorder actually does stop. The positioning point is reached:

```
F0H 7FH <01H> <mcr> <Motion Control Tally>
<counter = 03H> <Stop> <Locate> 11H
F7H
```

At this point the sequencer instructs the audiotape recorder to stop giving it updates on the status of the transport, and then verifies that the desired position has been reached:

```
F0H 7FH <01H> <mcc> <Update>
<counter = 02H> <[End]> <Read>
<counter = 01H> <Selected Time Code>
F7H
```

In return, the audiotape recorder sends its current position, which is off-set by three frames from the desired position. The sequencer considers this error acceptable:

```
F0H 7FH <01H> <mcc> <Selected Time Code>
43H 02H 16H 25H 00H
F7H
```

The sequencer then sets up the recording parameters (i.e., by putting the first two tracks into Record Ready mode and copying the punch-in and punch-out points into the first two memory areas of the time code), before sending the audiotape recorder the order to send it regular updates on the recording mode:

```
F0H 7FH <device ID> <mcc> <Write>
<counter = 0FH> <Track Record Ready>
<counter = 01H> 60H <GP1> 43H 02H 1BH 08H 00H
<GP2> 43H 02H 29H 0FH 00H <Event>
<counter = 06H> <[Define]> <event = #01>
<flags = 00> <Selected Time Code>
<GP1> <Record Strobe> <Event> <
counter = 06H> <[Define]> <event = #02>
<flags = 00> <Selected Time Code>
<GP2> <Record Exit> <Update>
<counter = 02H> <[Begin]> <Record Status>
F7H
```

The audiotape recorder informs the sequencer about its actions, namely, that at the moment, it isn't recording anything:

```
F0H 7FH <01H> <mcr> <Record Status>
<counter = 01H> 00H
F7H
```

The sequencer shifts into Play mode, and the audiotape recorder is asked to generate the MIDI Time Code:

```
F0H 7FH <01H> <mcc> <Play> <MIDI Time Code Command>
<counter = 01H> 02H
F7H
```

Once the punch-in point (03.02.27.08) has been reached, right in the middle of an MTC frame the audiotape recorder tells the sequencer that it is shifting into Record mode:

```
F1H 08H ... ...
F0H 7FH <01H> <mcr> <Record Status>
<counter = 01H> 01H F7H
F1H 10H F1H 2BH F1H 31H
F1H 42H F1H 50H F1H 63H F1H 74H ... ...
```

Similarly, once the punch-out point (03.02.41.15) is reached, right in the middle of an MTC frame the audiotape recorder tells the sequencer that it is shifting out of Record mode:

```
F1H OEH F1H 1OH F1H 29H F1H 31H
F1H 42H ... ...
FOH 7FH <01H> <mcr> <Record Status>
<counter = 01H> OOH F7H
F1H 50H F1H 63H F1H 74H
```

Once the recording has been completed, the sequencer stops and the audiotape recorder asks it to stop providing information about its recording mode, the production of the MIDI Time Code stops, and the first two tracks exit from Record Ready mode:

```
FOH 7FH <device ID> <mcc> <Stop>
<MIDI Time Code Command>
<counter = 01H> OOH <Update>
<counter = 02H> <[End]> <Write>
<counter = 02H> <Track Record Ready>
<counter = OOH>
F7H
```

Even though the sequencer is responsible for managing the response traffic from the audiotape recorder, in order not to risk delaying the MTC Quarter Frame messages that are being carried physically by the same cable, a sufficiently intelligent controlled device will manage to transmit the responses in question without causing any bottlenecks or traffic jams in the data stream.

Master Devices and Slave Devices

Assume you're working with two controlled devices, such as a videotape recorder and an audiotape recorder. In terms of synchronization, the videotape recorder is designated as the master of the system, and the audiotape recorder is designated as the slave. Both devices communicate in a bidirectional way (i.e., in a closed loop) with a third device, which is the controller.

Each controlled device implements the following commands: <Stop>, <Play>, <Deferred Play>, <Fast Forward>, <Rewind>, <Record Strobe>, <Record Exit>, <Chase>, <Command Error Reset>, <MMC Reset>, <Write>, <Read>, <Update>, <Locate>, <Variable Play>, <Move>, <Add>, <Subtract>, <Drop Frame Adjust>, <Procedure>, <Event>, <Group>, <Command Segment>, <Deferred Variable Play>, <Wait>, and <Resume>.

Each controlled device also implements the following information fields: <Selected Time Code>, <Selected Master Code>, <Requested Offset>, <Actual Offset>, <Lock Deviation>, <GP0/Locate Point>, <GP1>, <GP2>, <GP3>, <Short Selected Time Code>, <Short Selected Master Code>, <Short Requested Offset>, <Short Actual Offset>, <Short Lock Deviation>, <Short GP0/Locate Point>, <Short GP1>, <Short GP2>, <Short GP3>, <Signature>, <Update Rate>, <Response Error>, <Command Error>, <Command Error Level>, <Time Standard>, <Motion Control Tally>, <Record Mode>, <Record Status>, <Control Disable>, <Resolved Play Mode>, <Chase Mode>, <Procedure response>, <Event Response>, <Response Segment>, <Failure>, <Wait>, and <Resume>.

The "signature" of these two controlled devices looks like this:

```
01H 00H 00H 00H
14H
7EH 71H 00H 00H 00H 00H 00H 00H 00H 00H
3DH 60H 7FH 00H 00H 00H 00H 00H 00H 09H
14H
3EH 1EH 00H 00H 00H 3EH 1EH 00H 00H 00H
3FH 62H 00H 38H 00H 33H 00H 00H 00H 09H
```

The controller device starts by reinitializing both of the controlled devices (i.e., the master device and the slave device), whose identification numbers (<device ID>), are 01H and 02H, respectively, before grouping them:

```
FOH 7FH <"all call"> = 7FH> <mcc> <MMC Reset> <Group>
<counter = 04H> <[Assign]>
<Group = 7CH> 01H 02H
F7H
```

The controller device assigns a 30-frame-per-second time code to the two controlled devices and authorizes them to transmit the Command Error information field automatically, regardless of the type of error:

```
FOH 7FH <device group = 7CH> <mcc> <Write>
<counter = 06H> <Time Standard>
<counter = 01H> 03H <Command Error Level>
<counter = 01H> <all = 7FH>
F7H
```

Then, from the controller device, you cause the two controlled devices to shift into Play mode:

```
FOH 7FH <master device = 01H> <mcc> <Play> F7H
```

and

```
FOH 7FH <slave device = 02H> <mcc> <Play> F7H
```

The controller device instructs the two controlled devices to send it regular updates on the value of their time code and also on their transport mode:

```
FOH 7FH <device group = 7CH> <mcc> <Update>
<counter = 03H> <[Begin]> <Selected Time Code>
<Motion Control Tally>
F7H
```

In return, the controlled devices both reply that they are in Play mode: one at position 00.22.05.12 (00H 16H 05H 0CH) and the other at position 10.01.58.28 (0AH 01H 3AH 1CH):

```
FOH 7FH <master device = 01H> <mcr> <Selected Time Code>
60H 16H 05H 2CH 00H <Motion Control Tally>
```

```
<counter = 03H> <Play> 7FH 01H
F7H
```

```
F0H 7FH <slave device = 02H> <mcr> <Selected Time Code>
6AH 01H 3AH 3CH 00H <Motion Control Tally>
<counter = 03H> <Play> 7FH 01H
F7H
```

For the following responses, the controlled devices express the time code in abbreviated form (that is, as two bytes, instead of the five bytes in the standard format), Furthermore, as long as their transport mode stays unchanged, they don't have to give the controller device any information about it:

```
F0H 7FH <master device = 01H> <mcr>
<Short Selected Time Code>
2DH 00H
F7H
```

—which is the same as a SMPTE time of 00.22.05.13.

```
F0H 7FH <slave device = 02H> <mcr> <
Short Selected Time Code> 3DH 00H
F7H
```

—which is the same as a SMPTE time of 10.01.58.29.

The responses continue. Nevertheless, because of a frame change, the slave device has to transmit the time code in standard five-byte format:

```
F0H 7FH <master device = 01H> <mcr>
<Short Selected Time Code> 2EH 00H
F7H
```

—which is the same as a SMPTE time of 00.22.05.14.

```
F0H 7FH <slave device = 02H> <mcr>
<Selected Time Code> 6AH 01H 3BH 20H 00H
F7H
```

—which is the same as a SMPTE time of 10.01.59.00.

Assuming now that the buffer of the controller device has reached its critical filling limit, the Wait command will be sent:

```
F0H 7FH <"all call" = 7FH> <mcc> <Wait> F7H
```

In response, the controlled devices suspend their transmissions, until they receive the Resume command:

```
F0H 7FH <"all call" = 7FH> <mcc> <Resume> F7H
```

Once the Resume command has been received, the responses can continue:

```
F0H 7FH <master device = 01H> <mcr>
<Short Selected Time Code> 30H 00H
F7H
```

—which is the same as a SMPTE time of 00.22.05.16.

```
F0H 7FH <slave device = 02H> <mcr>
<Short Selected Time Code> 22H 00H
F7H
```

—which is the same as a SMPTE time of 10.01.59.02.

From the controller device, you can stop the controlled master device:

```
F0H 7FH <master device = 01H> <mcc> <Stop> F7H
```

This change in the transport mode automatically triggers the transmission of a response by the controlled master device:

```
F0H 7FH <master device = 01H> <mcr> <Motion Control Tally>
<counter = 03H> <Stop> 7FH 01H
F7H
```

Meanwhile, the controlled slave device continues to tell the controller device about its position:

```
F0H 7FH <slave device = 02H> <mcr>
<Short Selected Time Code> 23H 00H
F7H
```

—which is the same as a SMPTE time of 10.01.59.03.

```
F0H 7FH <slave device = 02H> <mcr>
<Short Selected Time Code> 24H 00H
F7H
```

—which is the same as a SMPTE time of 10.01.59.04.

From the controller device, you stop the controlled slave device:

```
F0H 7FH <slave device = 02H> <mcc> <Stop> F7H
```

This change in the transport mode automatically triggers the transmission of a response by the controlled slave device:

```
F0H 7FH <slave device = 02H> <mcr> <Motion Control Tally>
<counter = 03H> <Stop> 7FH 01H
F7H
```

For display purposes, the controller device reads the discrepancy or offset between the time code of the controlled master device and the time code of the controlled slave device:

```
F0H 7FH <slave device = 02H> <mcc> <Read>
<counter = 01H> <Requested Offset>
F7H
```

The controlled slave device provides the response (10.01.59.04 minus 00.22.05.16 = 09.39.53.17, or 09H 27H 35H 11H):

```
F0H 7FH <slave device = 02H> <mcr>
<Requested Offset> 69H 27H 35H 11H 00H
F7H
```

From the controller device, you cause the controlled slave device to shift into Case mode:

```
F0H 7FH <slave device = 02H> <mcc> <Chase> F7H
```

This change in the transport mode automatically triggers the transmission of a response from the controlled slave device:

```
F0H 7FH <slave device = 02H> <mcr> <Motion Control Tally>
<counter = 03H> <Stop> <Chase> 61H
F7H
```

From the controller device, you cause the controlled master device to shift into Play mode:

```
F0H 7FH <master device = 01H> <mcc> <Play> F7H
```

Now the synchronization begins. The controlled master device responds that it is in Play mode, at position 00.22.05.24, while the controlled slave device responds that it is in Chase mode, at position 10.01.59.09:

```
F0H 7FH <master device = 01H> <mcr>
<Short Selected Time Code> 38H 00H <Motion Control Tally>
<counter = 03H> <Play> 7FH 01H
F7H

F0H 7FH <slave device = 02H> <mcr>
<Short Selected Time Code> 29H 00H
<Motion Control Tally>
<counter = 03H> <Play> <Chase> 01H
F7H
```

You decide to observe the deviation between the two devices while they synchronize themselves. To do you, you instruct the controlled slave device to provide regular updated information about the value of the offset or deviation:

```
F0H 7FH <slave device = 02H> <mcc> <Update>
<counter = 02H> <[Begin]> <Lock Deviation>
F7H
```

In reply, the controlled slave device responds:

```
F0H 7FH <slave device = 02H> <mcr> <Lock Deviation>
60H 00H 00H 05H 02H (i.e., a deviation of +5.02 frames)
F7H
```

Meanwhile, the controlled master device continues to keep the controller device informed about its position:

```
F0H 7FH <master device = 01H> <mcr>
<Short Selected Time Code> 39H 00H
```

—which is the same as a SMPTE time of 00.22.05.25.

Once again, the controlled slave device informs the controller device about the offset or deviation that separates it from the controlled master device, and also about its position:

```
FOH 7FH <slave device = 02H> <mcr>
<Short Selected Time Code> 2AH 00H
<Short Lock Deviation> 41H 17H
F7H
```

—which is the same as a SMPTE time of 10.01.59.10 and an offset of −1.17 frames.

Finally, the controlled slave device informs the controller device that the synchronization has been achieved, and also provides an update on its position (in the form of a time code expressed over five bytes, thanks to a frame change):

```
FOH 7FH <slave device = 02H> <mcr>
<Selected Time Code> 6AH 02H 01H 20H 00H F7H
<Short Lock Deviation> 00H 00H <Motion Control Tally>
<counter = 03H> <Play> <Chase> 11H
F7H
```

—which is the same as a SMPTE time of 0.02.01.00 and an offset of zero frames.

Now that the two devices are synchronized, you might want to program an automatic punch-in and punch-out for the controlled slave device. For the sake of clarity, only the Update information fields that are necessary to an understanding of the transactions are mentioned in the following code fragments.

On the fly, you program the punch-in point for each of the two controlled devices, by recopying their current positions into their second time-code memory area (i.e., GP1):

```
FOH 7FH <"all call" = 7FH> <mcc> <Move>
<counter = 02H> <GP1> <Selected Time Code>
F7H
```

Then, shortly after that, you program on the fly the punch-out point for each of the two controlled devices, by recopying their current positions into their third time-code memory area (i.e., GP2):

```
F0H 7FH <"all call" = 7FH> <mcc> <Move>
<counter = 02H> <GP2> <Selected Time Code>
F7H
```

Then you instruct the controller device to perform an automatic punch-in/punch-out. First of all, this operation consists of programming events in the memory of the controlled slave device, so that (only in Play mode and during forward operation) this device will shift into Record mode once it reaches the punch-in point, and then return to Play mode when it reaches the punch-out point. Once these events have been triggered, they will be removed from the memory of the device.

The Record Ready tracks of the controlled slave device are also programmed to shift into Record mode when the device receives a Record Strobe or Record Strobe Variable command. Furthermore, the controller device instructs this controlled slave device to send it regular updates on the status of the recording procedure:

```
F0H 7FH <slave device = 02H> <mcc> <Event>
<counter = 06H> <[define]> <event = #01> <flags = 00H> <Selected Time Code>
<GP1> <Record Strobe> <Event>
<counter = 06H> <[define]> <event = #02> <flags = 00H> <Selected Time Code>
<GP2> <Record Exit> <Write>
<counter = 03H> <Record Mode>
<counter = 01H> 01H <Update>
<counter = 02H> <[Begin]> <Record Status>
F7H
```

In return, the controlled slave device does as it's been told, and transmits the value of the Record Status information field (which in this case indicates that no recording is taking place):

```
F0H 7FH <slave device = 02H> <mcr> <Record Status>
<counter = 01H> 01H F7H
```

After this, the controller device manages the durations of the pre-roll and post-roll periods, which are equal to five and two seconds, respectively. To do so, it tells the controlled master device to position itself five seconds ahead of the punch-in point—that is, the position stored in the second time-code memory area (GP1)—and programs an event whose effect is to trigger the halting of this destination device two seconds after it reaches the punch-out point—that is, the position stored in the third time-code memory area (GP2).

```
FOH 7FH <slave device = 02H> <mcc> <Write>
<counter = 06H> <GPO/Locate Point> 60H 00H 05H 00H <Subtract> <counter
= 03H> <GPO/Locate Point>
<GP1> <GPO/Locate Point> <Locate>
<counter = 02H> <[I/F]> <GPO/Locate Point> <Write>
<counter = 06H> <GP3> 60H 00H 02H 00H 00H <Add>
<counter = 03H> <GP3> <GP3> <GP2> <Event>
<counter = 06H> <[Define]> <event = #01> <flags = 10H> <Selected Time
Code> <GP3> <Stop>
F7H
```

In addition to information about the time codes of the two controlled devices, and also about the deviation between them, the controlled devices also give the controller device information about their transport modes:

```
FOH 7FH <master device = 01H> <mcr> <Motion Control Tally>
<counter = 03H> <Rewind> <Locate> 01H
F7H
```

```
FOH 7FH <slave device = 02H> <mcr> <Motion Control Tally>
<counter = 03H> <Rewind> <Chase> 41H
F7H
```

The controlled master device reaches the pre-roll point before the controlled slave device does:

```
FOH 7FH <master device = 01H> <mcr> <Motion Control Tally>
<counter = 03H> <Stop> <Locate> 11H
F7H
```

```
F0H 7FH <slave device = 02H> <mcr> <Motion Control Tally>
<counter = 03H> <Rewind> <Chase> 41H
F7H
```

In turn, the controlled slave device concludes by reaching the desired position (i.e., the pre-roll point):

```
F0H 7FH <slave device = 02H> <mcr> <Motion Control Tally>
<counter = 03H> <Stop> <Chase> 61H
F7H
```

Once the two devices are properly adjusted, all that's left for the so-called "source" device to do is to instruct the master device to shift into Play mode, so that events can take their course:

```
F0H 7FH <master device = 01H> <mcc> <Play> F7H
```

The controlled master device shifts into Play mode, followed by the controlled slave device, which tries to synchronize itself with it:

```
F0H 7FH <master device = 01H> <mcr> <Motion Control Tally>
<counter = 03H> <Play> 7FH
F7H
```

```
F0H 7FH <slave device = 02H> <mcr> <Motion Control Tally>
<counter = 03H> <Play> <Chase> 01H
F7H
```

A short time later, the controlled slave device informs the controller device that synchronization has been achieved.

```
F0H 7FH <slave device = 02H> <mcr> <Motion Control Tally>
<counter = 03H> <Play> <Chase> 11H
F7H
```

When the device reaches the punch-in point, the first event is triggered. The controlled slave device shifts into Record mode and notifies the controller device accordingly:

```
FOH 7FH <slave device = 02H> <mcr> <Record Status>
<counter = 01H> 01H
F7H
```

Once this command has been executed, the corresponding event is removed from the memory of the device.

When the device reaches the punch-out point, the second event is triggered. The controlled slave device shifts back into Play mode and notifies the controller device accordingly:

```
FOH 7FH <slave device = 02H> <mcr> <Record Status>
<counter = 01H> 00H
F7H
```

Once this command has been executed, the corresponding event is removed from the memory of the device.

Two seconds after it passes the punch-out point, the controlled master device stops. As a result, the controlled slave device also stops:

```
FOH 7FH <master device = 01H> <mcr> <Motion Control Tally>
<counter = 03H> <Stop> 7FH 01H F7H

FOH 7FH <slave device = 02H> <mcr> <Motion Control Tally>
<counter = 03H> <Stop> <Chase> 61H
F7H
```

At the end of the session, the controller device sends the two controlled devices the order to stop giving it regular updates on the value of their time codes, their transport modes, and the value of the offset or deviation that separates them. The controller device also sends the controlled devices a Control Disable command, so that they will ignore the subsequent commands that involve Ctrl-type operations (i.e., transport management maneuvers) and Sync (i.e., synchronization) operations.

```
FOH 7FH <device group = 7CH> <mcc> <Update>
<counter = 02H> <[end]> <all = 7FH> <Write>
```

```
<counter = 03H> <Control Disable>
<counter = 01H> 01H
F7H
```

Finally, you send a command which you assume will read the value of the time-code generator of the controlled master device before starting it up:

```
FOH 7FH <master device = 01H> <mcc> <Read>
<counter = 01H> <Generator Time Code> <Generator Set Up>
<counter = 03H> OOH <Selected Time Code> 01H <Generator
        Command> <counter = 01H> 01H F7H
```

However, on the one hand, this command contains a syntax error (because the Generator Set Up command exists only as a response), and, on the other hand, the controlled master device doesn't have a time-code generator. Therefore, the controlled master device alerts the controller device to the absence of a time-code generator:

```
FOH 7FH <master device = 01H> <mcr> <Response Error>
<counter = 01H> <Generator Time Code>
F7H
```

to indicate that the Generator Set Up command has not been implemented. Because all of the errors have been activated (through the Error Enable command), the controlled master device will not process any further commands until it receives a reinitialization message (in the form of a Command Error Reset message):

```
FOH 7FH <master device = 01H> <mcr> <Command Error>
<counter = OAH> <flags = 11H> <level = 7FH> <error = 40H>
<counter 1 = 06H> <offset = OOH> <Generator Set Up>
<counter = 03> OOH <Selected Time Code> 01H F7H
```

After having acknowledged receipt of the Command Error information field, the controller device transmits a reinitialization message:

```
FOH 7FH <master device = 01H> <mcr> <Command Error Reset> F7H
```

Lastly, a recently developed new protocol may make it easier to transfer musical samples—and to transfer them much more quickly—using the

SCSI ports of musical devices. This data-exchange option is described briefly below.

 MDI

The main purpose of the SMDI (SCSI Musical Data Interchange) protocol is to make it possible to transfer samples between two devices over a SCSI link. The protocol, developed by Peavey Electronics Corp., is intended to provide an alternative to the Sample Dump Standard (SDS), which is fast becoming viewed as an unsuitable way to make this type of transfer, because of the inability of the MIDI flow rate to handle the amounts of data that digital audio requires. However, in terms of syntax, SMDI is modeled to a large extent on SDS.

Although an in-depth examination of SMDI is outside the scope of this book, the protocol is still a subject of immediate interest for MIDI users, because its purpose is to carry MIDI data over SCSI cables. For instance, with SMDI an editing program could send a Note On message to a sampler (so that the edited sound could be heard), or send the sampler the various parameters associated with the samples in the form of SysEx messages (e.g., mapping or envelopes), and so on, without having to use a MIDI link.

Here's the syntax of such a message:

```
53H (01010011): "S" in ASCII (the identifier for an SMDI SCSI message)
4DH (01001101): "M" in ASCII (the identifier for an SMDI SCSI message)
44H (01000100): "D" in ASCII (the identifier for an SMDI SCSI message)
49H (01001001): "I" in ASCII (the identifier for an SMDI SCSI message)
02H (00000010): the identification code for the message (MSB)
00H (00000000): the identification code for the message (LSB)
00H (00000000): the identification subcode for the message (MSB)
00H (00000000): the identification subcode for the message (LSB)
L1H (11111111): the length of the message (MSB)
```

```
L2H (11111111): the length of the message
L2H (11111111): the length of the message (LSB)
<message>      : the MIDI message
```

The length corresponds to the number of MIDI message bytes, which has to be increased by three (i.e., the number of bytes used to indicate this length). Finally, it's worth noting that an SMDI message can only "carry" one MIDI message at a time, and that SMDI messages don't take Running Status into consideration.

I II III IV V VI VII VIII IX X XI XII

A

APPENDIX

XIII XIV XV XVI

C D E F G H I

A Glossary
of MIDIspeak

THIS APPENDIX IS a collection of the most widely used technical terms and other jargon you're likely to encounter in MIDIland. Preference is given to the abbreviated forms of most terms; for instance, if you want to know about beats per minute, look up "B.P.M."

ACIA (Asynchronous Communication Interface Adapter)
A bidirectional interface which ensures that serial digital data is converted into parallel digital data, and vice versa. The microprocessor is connected to the MIDI ports by this type of circuit (see also **UART**).

ACSI (Atari Computer Systems Interface)   An interface, specific to Atari computers, that is dedicated to the connection of peripherals and mass-storage devices. ACSI operates much the same way SCSI (the Small Computer System Interface) does.

Active sensing   An optional MIDI code that lets an instrument detect a connection problem. After it receives a first active sensing code from a transmitting device (i.e., in the form of an FEH status byte), the receiving device waits for up to 300 milliseconds to receive subsequent messages. If it doesn't receive any further messages, the receiving device assumes the connection is defective and reacts appropriately (e.g., a sound generator cuts off all of its voices, and so on).

ADC (Analog to Digital Converter)   A circuit dedicated to converting an analog signal into a digital signal. Used by samplers, Direct to Disk recorders, and other devices. Analog to digital conversion is the process whereby an electrical audio signal is digitized ("sampled").

Additive synthesis   The creation of a timbre by layering or stacking waveforms.

ADSR (attack, decay, sustain, release)   The abbreviation for the four segments that make up the envelope generator(s) or generators of an analog synthesizer and that cause one of the parameters of a sound (primarily its amplitude, but also its timbre, pitch, etc.) to develop over time.

AES (Audio Engineering Society)   The activities of this group, founded in 1948 by a number of representatives of the audio profession, consists of organizing conventions and conferences, publishing a technical journal, distributing pieces of work and documentation, etc.

AES/EBU (Audio Engineering Society/European Broadcasting Union)   This abbreviation refers to a standardized protocol for the exchange of data between tape recorders, samplers, digital audio tape (DAT), Direct to Disk recorders, and other devices.

Aftertouch   The MIDI messages that indicate the amount of pressure applied to the keys on a keyboard after the keys have been pressed down as far as they go. There are two kinds of aftertouch: channel aftertouch (sometimes known as channel pressure) and polyphonic (i.e., note-based) aftertouch.

AI (Advanced Integration)   A synthesis procedure developed by Korg, based on the reading of multiple samples. It's used in the M and T series instruments, including the M1, M1R, M3R, EXM1R, T1, T2, and T3. A more recent version known as AI^2 is used by the 01/W and its derivatives.

AIFF (Audio Interchange File Format)   The format for digital audio files (e.g., samples and Direct to Disk files) that's common to various programs (such as Alchemy and Sound Designer) that run on the Macintosh.

Algorithm   In FM synthesis, the algorithm represents the connection diagram for the carrier operators and modulators.

Aliasing   This type of digital distortion occurs during analog-to-digital conversions. The digitization of a signal whose frequencies are greater than half the sampling frequency (i.e., the Nyquist frequency) causes the appearance of parasitic frequencies that are strictly symmetrical with regard to the sampling frequency (the so-called mirror effect). An anti-aliasing filter located at the input of the sampler, upstream of the converter (such as a low-pass filter with a steep slope, known as an anti-foldback filter) makes it possible to avoid this phenomenon.

Alpha-dial   An endless rotary potentiometer, popularized by Roland synthesizers, used to change the value of a parameter very quickly.

Analog   The representation of a physical phenomenon with the help of a signal whose waveform is equivalent to a continuous variation (i.e., a waveform that consists of an infinite number of values) as opposed to the discontinuous and discrete variations in a digital signal (which consists of a finite number of values). In analog synthesis, the waveform that is created is expressed as an electrical signal whose waveform is equivalent to the continuous variation.

ANSI (American National Standards Institute) The organization which, among others, is responsible for defining certain standards.

ASCII (American Standard Code for Information Interchange) The coding standard for expressing, in the form of a single byte each, the characters and functions (such as line feeds and carriage returns) that appear on an alphanumeric keyboard.

Asynchronous Characteristic of a data-processing link in which each character in the data set is synchronized individually, so that a lack of timing coordination at the transmitting and receiving ends doesn't interfere with the data flow.

AT&T (American Telephone and Telegraph) The type of connectors found on fiber optic cables, particularly in S/PDIF.

ATR Audio tape recorder.

ATRAC (Adaptive TRansform Acoustic Coding) The digital audio data compression algorithm used by the Sony Mini Disc.

Attack The segment of an envelope that expresses the amount of time used by the signal to change from zero amplitude to its maximum amplitude. The **attack rate** is the speed at which a sound reaches its maximum initial volume.

Autolocation The automatic positioning of a recorder (e.g., an audio tape recorder, a video tape recorder, or a sequencer) at a previously stored location.

Automation In audio usage, the automatic recording and reproduction of the changes made by the user in the positions or settings of a group of commands (such as the potentiometers on a mixing console, etc.).

Azimuthing The act of adjusting the heads of a tape recorder.

Backup The procedure for saving and safeguarding a set of data.

899

Bandwidth (Pass band)   The technical characteristic that corresponds to the frequency response of an audio device (for instance, 20 Hz to 20,000 Hz).

Bank   A memory area in which data, particularly voices and Program Change messages, is stored.

Bank Select Message   A special MIDI Control Change message that tells a receiving instrument to change to a different bank.

Bar   A measure of music, or the line that separates one measure from another.

Baud   Unit of measurement indicating the transmission speed of a serial or parallel link in terms of the number of signaling units transmitted per second. A signaling unit can carry any number of bits or fractions of a bit; therefore, there may be little or no correlation between the baud rate and the number of bits transmitted per second. For the sake of safety—and accuracy—"baud" should never be used as a synonym for, or instead of, "bps."

BBS (Bulletin Board System)   A computer system that is located at a remote site and that is accessed by users primarily via modem-based computer communications using telephone lines.

Beam   The ligature or connection line between two musical notes expressed in graphic form.

Beat   A unit of musical time-keeping (see also B.P.M.).

Betacam SP   A type of video tape recorder, created by Sony, which uses $\frac{1}{2}$-inch tape and which has two digital audio tracks.

Betamax   A type of video tape recorder, created by Sony, used by EIAJ-C encoders and decoders (such as the PCM-F1, PCM-701, PCM-601, and PCM-501).

Beta test   An early version of a piece of software, intended to be tested by a given number of users so that corrections and changes can be made before the official release of the product.

Binary   Base 2 numbering system in which the digits (bits) are represented by the values 0 and 1. The raison d'etre of the binary system is directly related to the characteristics of data-processing circuitry, which can't handle more than two states or power levels.

Bit   Short for "binary digit": a number that is either 0 or 1.

BNC (Bayonet Neill Concelman)   A bayonet-type connector that is found on coaxial cables, whether it's a matter of carrying a video signal, a digital audio signal (e.g., SDIF-2, etc.), or a synchronization signal (word clock, word sync, etc.).

Boot   Execution, during power-up of a computer, of a certain number of initialization procedures that reside on a floppy disk or on the computer's hard disk drive.

B.P.M. (Beats Per Minute)   The tempo of a piece of music, expressed in terms of the number of beats per minute (60 BPM, 120 BPM, and so on).

Buffer   A portion of random-access memory (RAM) used for the temporary storage of data for processing purposes.

Bug   A programming error that causes a piece of software to malfunction.

Bulk or Bulk dump   The transfer of the contents of a block of memory between two MIDI devices, such as the transfer of an instrument's internal data to a computer or to a dedicated MIDI data recorder.

Burn-in   SMPTE timing information superimposed on a video frame.

Bus   A parallel link consisting of a set of lines (wires) that connect the various elements of a data-processing system (i.e., the central processing unit, the coprocessor, volatile memory (i.e., RAM), one or more mass-storage devices, etc.). There are three main kinds of buses: data buses, address buses, and command buses.

Byte   A group of eight binary digits (bits). The values of a byte range from 0 to 255 (256 combinations). A kilobyte (K or Kbyte) is equal to 1,024 bytes, a megabyte (MB) is equal to 1,024 Kbytes, and a gigabyte (GB) is equal to 1,024 megabytes.

Carrier   In FM synthesis, the operator whose output, rather than modulating another operator, directly delivers an audio signal in digital form.

CD-A (Compact Disc Audio)   Another name for a CD (compact disc).

CD-G (Compact Disc Graphics)   A conventional compact disc whose R to W "subcodes" contain images.

CD-I (Compact Disc Interactive)   The same size as a standard compact disc (i.e., just under $4^{3}\!/_{4}$ inches), a CD-I disc combines audio data, images, text, etc.

CD-R (Compact Disc Recordable)   A compact disc on which data can be recorded.

CD-ROM (Compact Disc Read-Only Memory)   A specific kind of compact disc, which plays the role of a mass-storage device whose contents can only be read, and which requires a specific reader. CD-ROM discs are used to store large amounts of data (up to 600 megabytes) representing text, images, audio samples, etc.).

CD-ROM XA (Compact Disc Read-Only Memory eXtended Architecture)   An extension of a standard CD-ROM that approaches CD-I, because it allows the mixing (i.e., interlacing) of different types of data (sound, pictures, etc.).

CD-V (Compact Disc Video)   There are three formats. The first (12 cm or 4.75 inches) provides 5 minutes of audio and video plus 15 minutes of audio; the second (20 cm or about 8 inches) offers 40 minutes of audio and video, and the third (30 cm or about 12 inches) gives you 120 minutes of audio and video.

CEDAR (Computer Enhanced Digital Audio Restoration)
A system that makes it possible to restore old recordings (through the elimination of noise, "scratches," etc.).

Cent   A unit of pitch measurement corresponding to one one-hundredth of a semitone.

Channel messages   Messages sent specifically over any one of the 16 discrete MIDI communications channels. These messages include Note On and Note Off, Note Number, Velocity, Program Change, Pitch Bend, Aftertouch, and Controller messages.

Chase-lock   Term used when several recorders are synchronized to a master SMPTE clock by having their running speeds slaved to this reference signal.

Chip   Any integrated circuit (a microprocessor, a memory, etc.).

Click

1 ▪ An audio metronome signal.

2 ▪ Undesirable noise caused by the bad looping of a sample.

Clock   A rhythmic synchronization device that issues logical signals (pulses).

Comma   A pitch interval corresponding to one-ninth of a tone.

Compressor   The amplitude stabilizer for an audio signal.

Continuous controllers   A set of MIDI expression messages (e.g., volume, panorama, modulation, and balance), most of which develop over time in a continuous manner.

Control Change messages   MIDI Channel messages that are used to change a sound while the sound is being played. The 121 MIDI controllers are numbered from 0 to 120. Some (such as linear potentiometers and wheels) are continuous, while others (such as switches) are on-off controllers.

Controller   An interface that converts a musician's physical actions into MIDI codes that can be sent to a sound generator (such as a MIDI keyboard, a MIDI violin, etc.).

CPU (central processing unit)   The part of a computer (usually a single microprocessor chip) that's responsible for managing all of the operational logic and memory organization in the system.

Crossfade looping   A looping technique that consists of taking a portion of the waveform located just ahead of the start of the loop and recopying it and "mixing" it with this loop in a crossfade (in which the end of the portion coincides with the end of the loop). It should be understood that in a crossfade, the volume of the recopied portion gradually decreases (i.e., in a fade-out), while the volume of the loop moves in the opposite direction (i.e., in a fade-in). This way, the transition happens gently.

Crossfading (X-fading)   The crossed attenuation and increase in the amplitudes of both of the overlapping signals, such as between the start and the end of the loop for a sample, between two sound tones that are distributed on a keyboard either horizontally (with the zone being defined by two note numbers), or vertically (with the range of the layer being defined by two velocity values), and so on.

Crosstalk (diaphony)   The interference that occurs when a signal spills over from one track of a tape recorder onto the adjacent track, or from one section of a console onto the neighboring section, etc.

Cue (cue point)   A temporal event referenced by a SMPTE time signal or an MTC clock signal.

Cue list (or cue sheet)   A list of cue points. When a piece of SMPTE or MTC code is being read and the time of an event on the cue list coincides with the time specified in the code, the action that corresponds to the event in question occurs (e.g., the reading of a sample, the transmission of a MIDI message, a punch-in or punch-out, etc.).

Cut-off frequency   The frequency at which a filter stops letting signals pass through it.

CV (Control Voltage)   In analog synthesis, the electrical signal used to indicate the pitch of a sound in the form of a variation in voltage.

DAC (Digital to Analog Converter)   A circuit whose job is to convert digital signals into analog signals. For example, every CD player contains a DAC.

Daisy-chain   The cascade-style connection of several MIDI devices by means of successive MIDI Thru/MIDI In links.

Damper pedal   The sustain pedal.

DAT (Digital Audio Tape)   A digital cassette-based reader and recorder, whose exact terminology is "R-DAT" (Rotary-head Digital Audio Tape), as opposed to "S-DAT" (Stationary-head Digital Audio Tape), which never made it to market.

Data byte   A byte utilized by the MIDI language to indicate the value of an action (i.e., of a status byte), such as the number or

velocity of a note that has been pressed, the position of the Pitch Bend potentiometer, and so on. By definition, the value of bit 7 of a data byte is always equal to zero.

Data compression   A method of storing data, either on disk or in RAM, in compact form.

DASH (Digital Audio Stationary Head)   The digital audio recording format used by various machines with fixed heads (such as those made by Sony, Tascam, and other companies).

dB   The abbreviation of "decibel," which is the unit of measurement for the intensity or strength of a sound.

DCC (Digital Compact Cassette)   A cassette device, developed by Philips, that can read conventional analog cassettes and also read and record specific digital cassettes.

DCO (Digital Controlled Oscillator)   An oscillator utilized by sound generators to deliver a waveform whose pitch is controlled digitally from the keyboard.

DDL (Digital Delay Line)   A digital echo.

Decay   The segment of an envelope that expresses the amount of time used by the signal to change from its maximum amplitude to its sustain phase.

Decimation   When used by certain samplers (particularly to transpose a digital signal downward), this mathematical procedure consists of eliminating a number of samples, X, every Y samples.

Default setting   Sometimes known as the "factory setting," this setting is the value that is set for a parameter when an instrument is initialized.

Delay   An effect that makes it possible to retard a signal within a range that can extend from a few milliseconds to several seconds (i.e., the echo phenomenon).

Detuning   The act of making a slight change in one voice element of a sound relative to another; often used to create a "spread" or "chorus" effect.

Digital   Literally, "using digits." If you're a computer, the digits are zero and 1, which represent the Off and On states. A digital synthesizer produces sounds by arithmetically manipulating a stream of numbers. This stream is then converted into an electrical signal (see **DAC**), and a speaker then converts the electrical signal into an audio signal.

Digital word   A term, analogous to "sample," that's more appropriate in connection with digital recording devices.

DIN (Deutsche Industrie Normen, or German Industrial Standard)   The shorthand term for the standardized set of MIDI connectors, including particularly the five-pin connectors used by MIDI systems.

Direct to Disk   A sampling technique that consists of using a mass storage device (such as a hard disk, an optical disk drive, etc.) instead of volatile memory (i.e., RAM), in order to record and read data in real time, doing it all on a given number of tracks. Although the mass storage device provides a recording capacity that is clearly greater than that of a simple RAM, its access time has to be extremely high. The Direct to Disk recording technique combines the advantages of a multitrack tape recorder and the advantages of a sampler (e.g., unmatched audio quality, the ability to edit recorded data, etc.).

Diskette   A low-capacity magnetic data-storage device (1.44 megabytes for a double-sided, high-density diskette) whose access time is relatively slow.

DOD (Digital Optical Disk) or MOD (Magneto-Optical Disk)   Mass storage device whose removable media look a lot

like compact discs. Technically, DOD, whose access times are currently a lot slower than those of a conventional hard disk (i.e., approximately 50 milliseconds), combines magnetic and optical (i.e., laser-beam) techniques.

Dotted note   A musical note whose nominal time value has been increased by 50 percent, as indicated by the dot. For example, a dotted half-note is equal in length to three quarter-notes; a dotted quarter-note is equal in length to three eighth-notes, and so on.

Download   To receive data from a computer system located elsewhere.

Drive   A disk reader.

Driver   A piece of software that lets a computer send data to, or communicate with, a particular external piece of hardware (such as a printer, disk drive, or sound generator).

Drop-frame (DF)   The term that designates SMPTE code that runs at 29.97 frames per second.

Dropout   Accidental signal loss on a recording medium.

Drum kit   A special kind of synthesizer voice that contains several samples of percussion sounds, with each sound being assigned to a different key on the synthesizer keyboard.

Drum machine   A sound generator that specializes in simulating or reproducing percussive timbres. Almost always associated with a dedicated sequencer.

DSP (Digital Signal Processor)   A special-purpose integrated circuit used in the processing of digital signals, particularly by effects processors, but also by certain types of synthesizers (such as the Kurzweil VAST and others).

Dump   The transfer of data between two MIDI instruments. Used primarily to exchange sounds and samples (see also **Sample Dump Standard**).

Dump request   A request transmitted to a MIDI instrument, asking the instrument to send all or part of the contents of its memory.

Duophonic   Characteristic of an instrument that can generate a maximum of two notes at the same time.

Dynamic allocation   The voice-allocation method used by some MIDI instruments, in which the most recently played notes are given their full shape and value and notes that were played earlier are "robbed" of their characteristics or parameters, as necessary, to support the current notes.

EBU (European Broadcasting Union)   The European SMPTE synchronization rate (i.e., 25 frames per second), which is used by the PAL and SECAM standards.

EDL (Edit Decision List)   Synonym for **cue list**, but used more often in video.

EG (Envelope Generator)   From simple ADSR modules to more complex systems consisting of multiple slopes and plateaus, the purpose of the envelope generator is to cause certain sound parameters to develop over time.

Equalizer   A device whose purpose is to amplify or diminish one or more of the frequency bands in a signal. Equalizers can be graphic, shelving, parametric, or semi-parametric.

EIAJ (Electronics Industries Association of Japan)   The organization which, among other things, is responsible for defining certain standards. (EIAJ-A and EIAJ-C are used by the PCM family of Sony encoders and decoders.)

EPROM   Erasable Programmable ROM; in other words, a read-only memory chip that can be erased and rewritten.

Fade-in   A gradual increase in the amplitude of a signal over time.

Fade-out   A gradual decrease in the amplitude of a signal over time.

Fader (potentiometer)   A linear potentiometer, as opposed to a rotary potentiometer (which is known as a "pot" or "panpot").

Feedback   The effect produced by a signal acting on itself (i.e., a loop). In FM synthesis, an operator that is modulated by its own output.

FFT (Fast Fourier Transform)   This procedure, which is linked to the theorem proposed by the physicist and mathematician Joseph Fourier, makes it possible to use a series of mathematical calculations to break down the harmonic content of a waveform into a series of sinusoidal curves.

FIFO (First In, First Out)   In data processing, a principle in the accumulation or stacking of data characterized by the fact that the first item to be stored will be the first item to be removed from the storage stack (exactly the opposite of what happens with a stack of dinner plates).

Filter   A circuit whose purpose is to attenuate or cut off certain frequencies in a signal.

Floppy   A flexible disk or diskette, as opposed to a hard disk.

FM   Frequency Modulation.

FM synthesis   A principle defined by John Chowning at Stanford University and implemented by Yamaha. FM synthesis is simply an extension of the properties of vibrato. Its major advantage lies in the fact that it can be used to create complex timbres by means of sinusoidal oscillators that modulate one another.

Folder   The storage subdivision in which files are kept in a mass memory device (e.g., a floppy disk or a hard disk).

Formatting   Preparing a magnetic medium (a floppy disk, hard disk, etc.) in such a way that the medium is capable of receiving data.

FPB (Frames Per Beat)   The number of frames per metronome pulse.

FPS (Frames Per Second)   The number of frames per second.

FSK (Frequency-Shift Keying)   A synchronization clock whose frequency is generally too low to be recorded as such on a tape recorder is sometimes represented in the form of an FSK signal that consists of two sufficiently high frequencies that alternate at the rate of the clock in question.

Fundamental   The lowest harmonic of a periodic signal. The frequency of the fundamental determines the overall pitch of the signal.

Gate   An all-or-nothing electrical signal, used particularly by the keyboard of an analog synthesizer to transmit to the sound generator the information relating to the pressing and releasing of keys.

General MIDI   A standard subset of MIDI rules that helps ensure compatibility among different instruments. General MIDI instruments all store sounds in the same memory areas, and always use MIDI Channel 10 for drum parts. They can all play at least 16 sounds at once, and have at least 24-note polyphony.

General MIDI score   A MIDI file that's been optimized for playback by a General MIDI instrument.

Gigabyte (GB)   A unit of memory capacity that corresponds to 1,024 × 1,024 × 1,024 bytes (that is, 1,024 megabytes), or 1,073,741,824 bytes.

GPI (General-Purpose Interface)   An interface dedicated to the remote control of certain functions of video devices from an editing or mixing bench.

Green Book   The document that standardizes the CD-I format.

Handshaking   Procedure, based on a question-and-answer dialog, that lets two data-processing devices communicate with one another.

Hard disk (hard disk drive)   A magnetic substrate that can store an amount of data ranging from 20 megabytes to several hundred megabytes, depending on the manufacturer and model, and whose access times are extremely fast (i.e., several milliseconds).

Harmonic series   A set of frequencies whose values are whole-number multiples of the fundamental frequency.

Header   The information contained in a header, which is a sort of ID card for a file, describes the data that the file contains.

Hertz (Hz)   A unit of frequency that indicates the pitch of a signal, as expressed in terms of the number of periods or cycles per second in the signal.

Hexadecimal   The representation of data in base 16, using the digits 0 through 9 and the letters A through F. This numbering system was designed particularly with a view toward improving the readability of binary data, because two hexadecimal numbers (with 256 values ranging from 00H to FFH) are equivalent to eight binary numbers (with 256 values ranging from 00000000 to 11111111)—that is, to one byte.

Host connection   A connection that lets you link a MIDI instrument directly to a computer, via the computer's serial ports, without needing a separate MIDI interface.

HPF (High-Pass Filter)   A high-pass filter cuts off the harmonics that are located below its cut-off frequency, as a function of its slope, as expressed in terms of decibels per octave.

IEC (International Electronic Commission)   An organization which, among others, is responsible for defining certain standards.

IMA (International MIDI Association)   An international organization which is responsible for distributing to its members all official information relating to the MIDI standard, for overseeing the proper implementation of the information, and so on. The IMA also publishes a monthly bulletin and offers a variety of services.

Implementation   Each builder of MIDI products is required to publish the characteristics of its products in the user manual for each product, in the form of a chart that summarizes the messages that the device sends and receives. This chart is known as the *MIDI implementation chart*.

Initialization   A reset procedure that activates the default values of some or all of the parameters of an instrument or other device.

Interface   The point at which independent systems interact. An interface can exist between two or more machines, or between human beings and one or more machines.

Interpolation   Technique consisting of artificially generating intermediate values (for new samples between the original samples). For example, in order to generate a new sample for each sample, you would calculate the amplitude of the new sample by dividing by two the sum of the amplitude of the two samples on either side of the position to be held by the new sample. Schematically, it involves a kind of smoothing or polishing. The opposite maneuver, involving the removal of samples, is sometimes called *decimation*.

Both of these techniques are used particularly in oversampling, re-sampling, and transposition.

IRT (Institut für Rundfunk Teknik)   The German institute for broadcasting techniques.

ISO (International Standards Organization)   An organization which, among others, is responsible for defining certain standards.

Jam sync   A procedure whose purpose is to replace a defective portion of code with a regenerated portion.

JMSC (Japanese MIDI Standards Committee)   The official organization that includes the majority of the Japanese MIDI instrument builders.

Kilobyte (K or Kbyte)   A unit of memory capacity, equivalent to 1,024 bytes.

LA (Linear Arithmetic)   A digital synthesis procedure developed by Roland and used particularly in that company's D series instrument (the D-50 and D-550, the D-5, D-10, D-110, D-20, and others). The oscillator waveforms are embodied in samples stored in ROM and processed by means of a structure that is functionally similar to that of analog synthesizers.

LAN (Local Area Network)   MediaLink is one example of a LAN applied to MIDI and also to other types of digital information.

Layering   The superimposition of several sounds within the same geographic zone on a keyboard (i.e., within the same tessitura, as delimited by two note numbers). MIDI lets you combine as many as 15 different sounds, including voices from different instruments, to create thick audio textures.

Least Significant Bit (LSB)   Bit 0 in a byte (that is, the bit located the farthest to the right).

Least Significant Byte (LSB) The least significant byte in a group of bytes (that is, the byte located the farthest to the right).

LED (Light Emitting Diode) An electroluminescent diode, used by certain display screens.

LFO (Low Frequency Oscillator) An oscillator whose purpose is to generate low frequencies in order to modulate various parameters of a sound.

LIFO (Last In, First Out) In data processing, a principle in the accumulation or stacking of data characterized by the fact that the last item to be stored will be the first item to be removed from the storage stack (analogous to what happens with a stack of dinner plates).

Local control on/off A function whose purpose is to connect and disconnect the internal link between the keyboard of a MIDI instrument and the instrument's sound generator.

Long word A unit of information consisting of four bytes.

Looping A technique utilized during the processing of a sample. It consists of repeating a certain portion (delimited by the Loop Start and Loop End points) in such a way as to prolong that portion artificially.

LPF (Low-Pass Filter) A low-pass filter cuts off the harmonics that are located beyond its cut-off frequency, as a function of its slope, as expressed in terms of decibels per octave.

LSI (Large Scale Integration) Integrated circuit design and manufacturing procedure that makes it possible to put from 100 to 20,000 transistors on a single chip.

LTC (Longitudinal Time Code) A SMPTE time code physically recorded in audio form on a track on an audio or video tape recorder.

MADI (Multichannel Audio Digital Interface)   A digital interface whose purpose is to carry 56 audio channels, in AES/EBU format, on a single line or wire.

Mapping   The geographical assignment of various timbres to different playing zones on a keyboard, with those zones being delimited by their lower and upper notes (i.e., their tessitura). For example, mapping a drum kit consists of assigning one or more note numbers to each of the different instruments (e.g., the bass drum, the snare drum, etc.). The term also applies to the assignment of notes, programs, and/or channels.

MDR   A MIDI data recorder, i.e., a device that can record and play back MIDI bulk dump data. Many MIDI sequencers and sequencing programs can do this; so can dedicated patch editor/librarian programs and some hardware devices, including the Yamaha SY99 synthesizer.

Megabyte (MB)   A unit of memory capacity that corresponds to $1,024 \times 1,024$ bytes (that is, 1,024 kilobytes), or 1,048,576 bytes.

MEL-2   A digital interface developed by Yamaha.

Merge   A function that ensures the mixing of MIDI data.

MIDI   The Musical Instrument Digital Interface: a standardized digital "language" that lets electronic musical instruments and computers talk to each other and exchange data.

MIDI cable   A special wire that carries MIDI data. The wire has three shielded conductors connected to five-pin DIN plugs at both ends. MIDI cables should usually be no more than 50 yards long.

MIDI channel   Any one of the 16 pathways that the MIDI standard provides for the transmission and reception of data. (The number of the channel over which MIDI data should be transmitted is specified by a number in the MIDI data stream.)

MIDI Clock Signal   A System Real Time message that specifies the tempo of a MIDI sequence. A total of 24 MIDI Clock Signals are issued during each quarter-note.

MIDI connector   A five-pin DIN plug.

MIDI controller   A device that outputs MIDI data. They include instrument controllers (e.g., keyboard, guitar, wind, or drum controllers) or real-time controllers. Real-time controllers are either continuous devices (e.g., wheels, pots, pedals, etc.) or on-off switches. Pitch Bend (usually a wheel or joystick) and After-touch (i.e., channel pressure) are two special kinds of continuous controllers.

MIDI File   The standard format (sometimes referred to as Standard MIDI Files, or SMF) used by computers to encode and store MIDI sequence data. MIDI Files makes it possible to exchange files between different kinds of software (such as sequencers, score editors, etc.).

MIDI interface   A hardware device that lets a computer "speak MIDI" and communicate with MIDI devices such as instruments and synthesizers.

MIDI Manager   An Apple Macintosh system utility that lets you route MIDI signals among various applications.

MIDI port   Any of the physical connections (MIDI In, MIDI Out, and MIDI Thru) through which MIDI data enters or leaves a device.

MIDI software   A computer program that can store, play back, and/or manipulate MIDI data. Typical MIDI software applications include sequencing, notation, and patch editing.

MIDI Time Code (MTC)   A MIDI System Real Time message that assigns a unique address to specified individual moments in time (usually each 120th of a second). MTC is a lot like SMPTE Time Code, except that it's transmitted via MIDI ports and used mainly to synchronize the playback of MIDI files and digital audio, which it does mainly by converting SMPTE data into MIDI messages.

Mixer   A device that blends the audio signals from a variety of sources (instruments, microphones, CD players, etc.). Mixers often contain pots or faders that let you adjust the volume and pan position of each instrument independently.

MMA (MIDI Manufacturers' Association)   The official organization that includes the majority of American MIDI instrument builders.

Modem   A device that converts digital data into an analog signal (and vice versa), in accordance with the MOdulation/DEModulation principle. Modems are used by two correspondents in order to exchange data over telephone lines.

Modulation wheel   The purpose of this continuous MIDI controller, which is generally located near the Pitch Bend wheel, is to modify in real time the various parameters of a sound (e.g., tremolo effects, vibrato effects, etc.).

Modulator   In FM synthesis, the operator whose output will modulate one or more other operators.

Monophonic   Characteristic of an instrument that generates only one note at a time.

Most Significant Bit (LSB)   Bit 7 in a byte (that is, the bit located the farthest to the left).

Most Significant Byte (LSB)   The most significant byte in a group of bytes (that is, the byte located the farthest to the left).

MTC   See **MIDI Time Code.**

MTR   Multitrack Tape Recorder.

Multiplexing   In sampling, this procedure lets a single DAC convert several signals at a time. In reality, because of its inability to handle more than one signal, the DAC proceeds from one signal to another without stopping, alternately converting one portion of one signal and one portion of the other signal during a very short time interval, thereby giving the illusory impression of simultaneous operation.

Multitasking   A data-processing operating system's ability to let several software applications operate simultaneously on a single machine.

Multitimbral (or polytimbral)   The ability of a sound generator to deliver simultaneously several different timbres (i.e., several different sound tones).

MUSICAM (Masking-pattern Universal Sub-band Integrated Coding and Multiplexing)   A digital audio data-compression algorithm (that reaches, just a little, for the acronym).

Muting   The cutting-off of a track on a sequencer, or of a voice on a mixing console. In verb form, you "mute" a track.

NAB (National Association of Broadcasters)   The American association for professional broadcasting personnel.

Noise gate   A device that lets a signal pass only if the signal level exceeds a certain amplitude threshold.

Non-drop frame (NDF)   The term used to designate SMPTE code that runs at 30 frames per second.

NoNoise   A system, developed by Sonic Solutions, that makes it possible to restore old recordings (through the elimination of noise, "scratches," etc.).

Notation software   Any computer program that can display and print MIDI data in the form of standard musical notation. (Some MIDI sequencers have this capability.)

Note Off   The MIDI status of a note that has been released.

Note On   The MIDI status of a note that has been pressed.

NTSC (National Television Standards Committee)   The American video standard, which runs at 30 frames per second in black-and white (non-drop-frame), and at 29.97 frames per second in color (drop-frame). NTSC (sometimes referred to, not entirely facetiously, as "Not The Same Color") is also in effect in Japan, in Canada, and in some other countries.

Nybble   A group of four bits, i.e., a half-byte. Sometimes spelled "nibble."

Nyquist   The frequency that bears the name of this physicist and mathematician is equal to half the sampling frequency, and corresponds to the upper limit of the acceptable pass band when an analog-to-digital conversion takes place. The sampling of a signal that exceeds this limit leads to the occurrence of digital background noise (see **aliasing**).

Offset   The value of a shift. When two tape recorders are synchronized, the offset corresponds to the SMPTE timing difference between the respective codes of the devices.

Operator   In FM synthesis, the operator is an oscillator that can behave either like a carrier or like a modulator, depending on the algorithm that's been selected.

Optocoupler   In the MIDI interface, this circuit converts the information that has been received into light, which is then converted into electricity. By eliminating interference, this optical isolation between the transmitter and the receiver ensures completely reliable communications.

Orange Book   The document that standardizes the format for writable compact discs (either WORM (write once, read many) or WMRA (write many, read always)), with which makers of CD-R discs must comply.

Oscillator   The synthesizer module that is responsible for providing the waveform.

Overflow

1 ▪ Saturation of a buffer.

2 ▪ A function thanks to which the notes that are received by an instrument that has reached the point of polyphonic saturation are retransmitted via the MIDI Out port of the instrument in order to control a second instrument of the same type, set to an identical sound, in order to double the overall level of polyphony.

Oversampling   A technique employed at the input as well as at the output of a digital device (e.g., an ADC or a DAC) in order to improve the quality of the conversions. Without going into gory detail, it can simply be said that the ADC cuts off the signal at a frequency that is X times higher than the frequency at which the ACD stores the data, and that conversely the DAC transmits X times more samples than it reads.

Overtone   A harmonic or partial frequency.

PAL (Phase Alternation Line) The color television standard followed by most European countries, with a few exceptions (such as France and certain Eastern European countries).

PAN (Performing Artists Network) An international BBS that is accessible from about 60 countries. It lets musicians converse through forums and mailboxes, and exchange information such as sounds, samples, sequences, and so on.

Panorama (Pan) The act of positioning sounds between the left and right speakers, to create a stereophonic effect.

Parallel Characteristic of a data link in which the elementary data (i.e., the bits) are transmitted simultaneously over several grouped lines. A parallel 8-bit link makes it possible to send the contents a byte all at once, thereby providing eight times the data density of a serial link.

PASC (Precision Adaptive Sub-band Coding) A data-compression algorithm for digital audio data, similar to MUSICAM, developed by the French CCETT (Common Center for Broadcasting and Telecommunications Research), the German IRT, and Philips, and used by DCC (digital compact cassette) devices.

Patch

1 ▪ One of the many terms used to refer to the memory of a MIDI device (e.g., a sound, a voice, a multitimbral configuration, etc.).

2 ▪ A connection and signal-routing matrix (e.g., an audio patch or a MIDI patch).

Pattern A logical grouping of a certain number of measures or bars in a recording, accomplished with the aid of a sequencer or rhythm box (e.g., an introductory pattern, a couplet, etc.).

PCM (Pulse Code Modulation)   The digitization of an audio signal that has been broken down into samples whose amplitude is measured in order to be coded in binary form.

P.D. (Phase Distortion)   Developed by Casio for the CZ instrument family, the principle of synthesis through phase distortion consists of imposing a change in the phase angle on a co-sinusoidal oscillator so as to obtain complex waveforms.

Performance   A term used by some builders to refer to the set of sounds in a multitimbral configuration.

Peripheral device   In data processing, a device connected to a central processing unit. Screens, hard disks, floppy-disk readers, and printers are all examples of peripheral devices that are linked to computers.

Pitch (frequency)   The relative auditory "highness" or "lowness" of a signal.

Pitch Bend wheel (or Pitch Bender)   A wheel whose purpose is to cause a change, in real time, in the pitch of the notes being played.

Platform   The type of computer with which a MIDI system is working: for instance, a Macintosh platform, an Atari platform, or an IBM platform.

Play list   A synonym for **cue list**.

Polyphony   The number of notes that can be reproduced simultaneously by a sound generator. (The DX7 is polyphonic with 16 voices; the Proteus is polyphonic with 32 voices, etc.)

Polytimbral   A synonym for **multitimbral**. The ability of a sound generator to issue several timbres simultaneously.

Port   A specialized data-processing connector, intended for use in exchanging data between a computer or other device and the

outside world (e.g., the printer port, the modem port, the MIDI port, and so on).

Portamento   An effect that consists of changing from one note to another by gradually sweeping through the range of pitches between these two notes, within a given period of time.

Postproduction   In video, postproduction includes all of the work performed after the raw material is recorded. Audio postproduction (which involves the adjustment and mixing of sounds with the frames) should be distinguished from video postproduction (which involves editing and so on).

Post-roll   The automatic extension of the reading phase for a tape when the tape has reached a predetermined stopping point (such as a punch-out point, a location point, etc.).

PPQN (Pulses Per Quarter-Note)   A synchronization unit, expressed in terms of the number of pulses per quarter-note (for example, 24 PPQN, 48 PPQN, 96 PPQN,etc.).

Pre-roll   A tape recorder that has received an instruction to place itself at a predetermined position on the tape (such as a starting point, a punch-in point, a location point, etc.) will actually position itself a few seconds ahead of that point, depending on the specified pre-roll time. For example, this period makes it possible for two rotating machines to synchronize themselves, for a performer to hear part of the music before starting to make a recording, and so on.

Pro-DAT   Digital Audio Tape that can record a time code which complies with the Pro-R Time standard issued by the IEC.

ProDigi (Professional Digital)   A digital audio recording format used by different fixed-head machines (such as those made by Mitsubishi, Otari, and other companies).

Program Change message   A MIDI channel message that's used to select different voices.

Punch-in   Either programmed or triggered on the fly, this point corresponds to the starting position at which a recorder (i.e., a tape recorder or a sequencer) switches from Read mode to Record mode.

Punch-out   Either programmed or triggered on the fly, this point corresponds to the starting position at which a recorder (i.e., a tape recorder or a sequencer) switches from Record mode to Read mode.

PWM (Pulse Width Modulation)   The modulation of the width of the impulse for a signal that has a square waveform.

Quantization   A way of rounding the value of a piece of digital data to the nearest discrete value, in accordance with a given resolution or interval between the discrete steps, or mapping a continuously variable quantity into a discrete, stepped digital context. Examples include the quantization of MIDI messages in a sequence or the quantization of the samples in a sampled sound, etc. The technique can also be used to correct timing mistakes.

Rack   The standard width of data-processing equipment, musical devices, etc., i.e., 19 inches. Height is measured in terms of the number of unit (1U, 2U, 3U, etc.).

RAM (Random Access Memory)   The type of data storage that allows both reading and writing. It usually contains program information and/or data, but always requires a constant supply of electrical power in order to store data.

Range   A set of frequencies delimited by an upper note and a lower note. Also the customary range of notes or frequencies for a particular instrument or voice.

R-DAT (Rotary-head Digital Audio Tape)   The proper term to use with reference to a DAT device, because these devices use rotating heads.

Real time   Characteristic of a MIDI recording which is accomplished directly, as opposed to a recording which is done in step mode.

Red Book   The document that standardizes the format for compact discs, and with which CD makers must comply.

Release   The segment of an envelope that expresses the amount of time used by the signal to change from its current amplitude to zero amplitude when the note is released.

Remote keyboard   A mute control keyboard whose sole purpose is to transmit MIDI codes. (The keyboard is often provided with a heavy touch and 88 keys.)

Resampling   A simulation procedure based on the resampling calculation of a sample at a sampling frequency that is different from the original frequency. When this new frequency is lower than the original frequency, it makes it possible to save memory but reduces the pass band, whereas in the opposite case (i.e., if the new frequency is higher than the original frequency), the new frequency generally improves the quality of the transposition but takes up more memory space.

Reset   The procedure of re-initializing a data-processing system.

Resolution   The number of finite values utilized to represent a piece of data in digital form (i.e., to quantize the data). Eight-bit resolution involves 256 values; 12-bit resolution involves 4,096 values; 16-bit resolution involves 65,536 values, and so on.

Rest   A silence in a piece of music.

Reverberation (reverb)   The simulation of natural reverberation (i.e., reflection) phenomena, in order to add a sense of spaciousness and ambience to a sound.

ROM (Read-Only Memory)   Memory that can only be read, not written to. It contains unchangeable pre-programmed data relating to a computer's operating system, the factory presets of a synthesizer, and so on, and does not require a constant supply of electricity in order to store data.

RS-232C   An asynchronous EIA (Electronics Industry Association) interface that defines the connection and the electrical standard for serial communication. Its specified maximum data-transmission rate is 20,000 kilobits per second. IBM compatibles use RS232 serial ports.

RS-422   One of the companion interfaces to RS-232C that define balanced and unbalanced high-speed links. RS-422 defines the electrical characteristics for one-megabit-per-second serial communications. Apple Macintosh computers use RS422 serial ports.

Running status   A compression procedure for MIDI data. When the status bytes in a series of successive messages are identical, the status byte is transmitted only once.

Sample   A sound that is sampled, and also each of the digital words that make up the sample (see also **ADC**).

Sample Dump Standard (SDS)   A MIDI protocol that lets samples be transferred.

Sample rate   The sampling rate (or sampling frequency, not to be confused with the frequency of the signal) corresponds to the number of samples taken per second by an analog-to-digital converter. (A compact disk samples at a rate of 44,100 Hz; R-DAT samples at 32,000, 44,100, and 48,000 Hz, and so on.)

Sampler An electronic musical instrument that's based on a sampling technique.

Sampling Measuring a signal electrically at regular intervals, in order to impart to the signal values that can be represented numerically and used directly and immediately by the circuits of a computer.

Sawtooth wave A waveform that consists of the fundamental and all of its harmonics, with the amplitude of each harmonic being inversely proportional to its order or rank (e.g., 1, $\frac{1}{2}$, $\frac{1}{3}$, $\frac{1}{4}$, etc.).

SCMS (Serial Copy Management System) A protection system designed to prevent the making of successive digital copies. Thanks to SCMS, only one first-generation copy of a recording can be made. For example, a DAT cassette that has been recorded digitally from a CD cannot be duplicated digitally on a second DAT cassette.

SCSI (Small Computer System Interface) The high-speed data-transfer protocol dedicated to connecting various peripheral devices and mass storage devices (hard disks, optical disk drives, etc.) to desktop and laptop computers. Apple Macintosh systems have built-in SCSI ports, but IBM PCs and clones can use SCSI too if they add special cards.

SCSI II An improved (i.e., even faster) version of SCSI that is compatible with the earlier version.

S-DAT (Stationary-head Digital Audio Tape) A fixed-head DAT project that was never completed. DCC (digital compact cassette) technology can be considered to be its heir and successor.

SDIF-1 (Sony Digital Interface 1) Derived from SDIF-2, this interface is utilized by the DASH family of tape recorders.

SDIF-2 (Sony Digital Interface 2)   An interface first designed for use with the Sony PCM-1600, PCM-1610, and PCM-1630 instruments (EIAJ-A).

SECAM (Systeme Electronique Couleur Avec Memoire) (electronic color system with memory)   The color television standard used in France, in certain Eastern European countries, and in some African countries, among others.

Serial   Characteristic of a data link in which the various bytes that are carried are broken down, bit to bit, in order to be sent one after another over a single line or wire. MIDI is a serial interface, as are the COM ports (RS-232C) on IBM PCs and the modem and printer ports (RS-422) on Macintoshes.

Serial port   The physical computer connection through which serial data enters and leaves the system.

SFX   Special effects.

Sine wave   A sinusoidal waveform or a smaller periodic sound element, corresponding to a fundamental with no harmonics. According to Fourier's theorem, each complex periodic motion can be broken down into a sum of simple sinusoidal (i.e., harmonic) periodic motions whose frequencies are whole-number multiples of the fundamental.

Slider   A linear potentiometer.

SMPTE (Society of Motion Picture and Television Engineers)
This abbreviation, pronounced "SIMP-tee," refers to a timing synchronization code that assigns a unique address to specified individual moments in time (usually each 120th of a second). SMPTE Time Code consists of hours, minutes, seconds, frames, and subframes. Its major function is to synchronize audio and visual cues with each other.

Soft pedal   The expression pedal stored in the MIDI family of controllers under code 43H (67). This pedal should not be confused with the damper or sustain pedal, which is 40H (64), or with the sostenuto pedal, which is 42H (66).

Song Position Pointer (SPP)   This MIDI System Real Time message describes a particular position within a piece of music, at a resolution of one sixteenth-note. The term also refers to the MIDI counter that counts the number of sixteenth-notes that have passed since the beginning of a piece.

Song Select   A MIDI System Common message that tells a sequencer to select one of the two or more pieces of music stored in its memory.

Sostenuto   The expression pedal stored in the MIDI family of controllers under code 42H (66).

S/PDIF (Sony Philips Digital Interface Format)   A widely utilized public digital audio interface, similar to AES/EBU (the IEC-958-II and EIAJ CP-340 standards).

Spillover   A term that means the same thing as the second definition of **overflow** given above.

Split   The division of a keyboard into several geographic zones that are separated, two by two, by a key number known as the **split point**.

Split point   A separation point that is identified by a note number and that delimits two adjacent geographic zones on a keyboard.

SPP   See **Song Position Pointer**.

Square wave   A waveform that consists of the fundamental and all of its odd-numbered harmonics, with the amplitude of each harmonic being inversely proportional to its order or rank (e.g., 1, $\frac{1}{3}$, $\frac{1}{5}$, $\frac{1}{7}$, etc.).

Stack   See **layering**.

Star network   A star-shaped network of devices within which each MIDI In port of the receiving units is connected to a MIDI Out port that forwards messages from a single transmitting unit (thanks to the addition of a MIDI Thru box, to the multiple outputs of a sequencer, to a master keyboard, to a converter, etc.).

Status byte   The byte that the MIDI language uses to define an action (such as playing a note, pressing the sustain pedal, etc.). By definition, the value of bit 7 of a status byte is {{ALWAYS}} equal to 1.

Step mode   A MIDI recording procedure on a sequencer, thanks to which the information is acquired note by note, by means of a keyboard, a mouse, the pressing of keys on the computer keyboard, or by means of a combination of these various methods.

Streamer   A tape spooler that is dedicated to storing a set of digital data provided by volatile memory (i.e., RAM) or a mass storage device. Also known as a *streaming-tape unit*.

Striping   The recording of a timing code (the "stripe") on the audio track of an audio tape recorder or video tape recorder.

Subtractive synthesis   The creation of a timbre through the filtration of a certain range of frequencies from a waveform (such as a square or sawtooth waveform) that is rich in harmonics.

Sustain

1 ▪ The expression pedal stored in the MIDI family of controllers under code 40H (64).

2 ▪ The segment of an envelope that expresses the stabilization volume of a sound when the sound is held.

Synchronous   Characteristic of a data link in which the timing for sending a block of data (which can contain essentially all of

the characters in the entire message) is coordinated by the transmitter and the receiver at the beginning of the exchange.

Synchronization   The process of having events line up with one another. SMPTE Time Code is often used to make this happen.

Synchronizer   A device whose purpose is to synchronize tape-based devices (e.g., audio and video tape recorders).

Sync-to-tape   A system for the conversion of a clock signal issued by a sequencer in a form that allows the clock signal to be recorded on the audio track of an audio tape recorder or video tape recorder, and vice versa, in order to be able to slave a sequencer to a tape-based device.

Synthesizer   An electronic musical instrument that can produce sounds in the form of audio signals, either by directly manipulating electrical signals (which is what the older, analog synths did), or by using mathematical functions to change a stream of numbers (which is what contemporary digital synths do). Synths also let you change the various parameters (such as pitch, timbre, and amplitude) of a waveform.

SyQuest   A brand of removable hard disks, currently available in 44-, 88-, and 105-megabyte capacities.

SysEx   The abbreviation for "System Exclusive."

System Exclusive   A class of MIDI messages which in particular makes it possible to exchange non-standardized data, because each manufacturer that has an ID number can create this kind of message.

System messages   MIDI data that isn't specific to any single channel. System messages include System Exclusive messages (which involve an instrument's internal data, sometimes called Bulk Dump data), System Real Time messages (sequencer Start, Stop, and Continue commands, and also MIDI Clock Signal and other timing information), and System Common messages (Song Select messages, tuning requests, system resets, etc.).

Threshold   The level at which an event or action is triggered.

Thru box   A box whose job is to duplicate the messages it receives at its MIDI In port and forward them to a given number of MIDI Thru ports, in order to drive several instruments in parallel, reduce the number of delay problems, etc.

Tie   A link or connection.

Timbre   The aural or sonic characteristics that differentiate one sound from other sounds. Sometimes used interchangeably (though not always accurately) with "voice," "patch," or "program."

Time code   A piece of data whose purpose is to express time-related information. Popular examples include SMPTE code and MIDI Time Code.

Time signature   The information that indicates the number of beats in a typical measure in a piece and also what kind of note gets one beat. For instance, in $\frac{2}{4}$ time, there are two beats in each measure and the quarter-note gets one beat. In $\frac{6}{8}$ time there are six beats in each measure and the eighth-note gets one beat. In $\frac{3}{2}$ time there are three beats in each measure and the half-note gets one beat, and so on.

Time stretching and time crunching   Temporal expansion and compression. The purpose of the technique is to extend or shorten the duration of a sample without affecting its pitch—thereby making it possible to transpose the sample upward or downward without affecting its duration.

Timing clock   The MIDI clock pulse (F8H), which is transmitted 24 times per quarter-note for synchronization purposes.

Tone generator   A keyboardless device that outputs audio signal in response to MIDI commands.

TOS links   Connectors that are found in fiber optic cables, particularly in S/PDIF.

Transients   Harmonic components that are responsible for sudden changes in the harmonic spectrum (such as attack transients, damping, etc.).

Tremolo   A cyclic change in amplitude imposed on an audio signal.

Triangle wave   A waveform that consists of the fundamental and a small number of even- and odd-numbered harmonics.

Trigger   A module that is responsible for initiating an action as soon as it detects a given threshold voltage at its input.

True voices   The actual, real tessitura of a sound generator. This range indicates the number of notes of different pitches that can be played.

UART (Universal Asynchronous Receiver/Transmitter)
A bidirectional interface that ensures the conversion of serial data into parallel data, and vice versa. A computer's central processing unit (CPU) is connected to the MIDI ports by means of a circuit of this type (see also **ACIA**).

U-Matic   A type of video tape recorder, created by Sony, that uses $^3/_4$-inch tape and that is used by EIAJ-A encoders and decoders (such as the Sony PCM-1600, PCM-1610, and PCM-1630).

Upload   To send data to a computer system located elsewhere.

Variable Sample Playback   Technique utilized by many samplers to transpose samples. It consists of reading the sample at a sampling frequency that depends on the note that's played on the keyboard. In other words, if a sample were to be transposed one octave upward, it would have to be read twice as fast as before (for example, at 88.2 kHz instead of at 44.1 kHz). In this case the sample would last half as long as it did before.

VCA (Voltage Controlled Amplifier)   A device utilized by analog synthesizers to impose a change in volume on a sound.

VCF (Voltage Controlled Filter)   A device used by analog synthesizers to impose a change in timbre on a sound.

VCO (Voltage Controlled Oscillator)   A device used by analog synthesizers to obtain a waveform whose pitch is controlled by voltage from the keyboard.

VCR   Video cassette recorder.

Velocity   A MIDI message, usually derived from an instrument sensor, indicating the speed at which a note (i.e., a key) has been pressed or released. Velocity messages can alter the volume and/or brightness of a sound.

Vibrato   A cyclic change in pitch imposed on an audio signal.

VITC (Vertical Interval Time Code)   A SMPTE timing code that is recorded jointly with the frame on a video tape recorder, unlike LTC (Longitudinal Time Code), which is recorded on an audio track.

VLSI (Very Large Scale Integration)   Integrated circuit design and manufacturing procedure that makes it possible to put 10,000 to 100,000 transistors on a single chip.

Voice   Any of the sounds that a synthesizer makes. Sometimes used interchangeably (though not always accurately) with "timbre," "patch," or "program."

Volatile   The type of memory whose data is irretrievably lost when the device is turned off. The opposite of *non-volatile*.

Volume   The apparent loudness of a sound.

VTR   Video tape recorder.

Waveform   The shape of a sound wave. Also used with reference to the two- or three-dimensional representation of a sound.

WMRA (Write Many Read Always)   An optical disc that can be written to at will. Magneto-optical discs (MODs) and the Sony Mini Disc are members of the WRMA family.

Word   A piece of data consisting of two bytes.

WORM (Write Once Read Many)   An optical disc that can be written to, once. Current CD-R discs are members of the WRMA family.

Yellow Book   The document that standardizes the format for CD-ROMs.

I II III IV V VI VII VIII IX X XI XII

B

APPENDIX

XIII XIV XV XVI

*U.S., European,
and Japanese
MIDI Manufacturers*

HIS APPENDIX LISTS the current worldwide MIDI manufacturers and their MIDI ID codes, as the codes appear in the instruments made by each company.

MANUFACTURER	MIDI ID CODE
360 Systems	00H 00H 1CH
Ad Lib, Inc.	00H 00H 3FH
ADA Signal Processors	0DH
Adams-Smith	17H
ADB	00H 20H 15H
Akai	47H
AKG Acoustics	0AH
Alesis	00H 00H 0EH
Allen & Heath Brenell	00H 00H 1AH
Allen Organ Co.	00H 00H 35H

MANUFACTURER	MIDI ID CODE
Amek Systems, Ltd.	00H 20H 02H
APHEX	00H 00H 38H
Apple Computer Corp.	11H
ART	1AH
Artisyn	00H 00H 0AH
Audio Architecture	34H
Audio Veritrieb-P. Struven	2CH
Audiomatica	00H 20H 0AH
Avab Electronik Ab	3CH
Axxes	00H 00H 20H
Baldwin	1BH
Blue Sky Logic	00H 00H 2EH
Bontempi/Farfisa	00H 20H 0BH
Breakaway Technologies	00H 00H 25H
Brøderbund Software, Inc.	00H 00H 34H
CAE	00H 00H 26H
Cannon Research Group	00H 00H 2BH
Casio	44H
Clarity	1FH
Clavia Digital Instruments	33H
CTI Audio Inc. (formerly Music Intel. Dev.)	00H 00H 32H
DDA	00H 20H 17H
Digidesign	13H

MANUFACTURER	MIDI ID CODE
Digigram	3DH
Digital Music Corp.	00H 00H 07H
DOD Electronics	00H 00H 10H
Dr.Böhm/Musician International	00H 20H 04H
Dream	00H 20H 00H
Dynacord	30H
E-mu Systems	18H
Elka/General Music	2FH
Encore Electronics	00H 00H 2FH
Ensoniq	0FH
ETA Lighting	00H 00H 3DH
Eventide	1CH
FBT Elettronica	00H 20H 0CH
Fender	08H
Forefront Technology	00H 20H 11H
Fostex	51H
Fujitsu Electronics	4BH
Gallien Krueger	00H 00H 39H
Garfield Electronics	0EH
GeneralMusic Corp.	35H
Grey Matter Response	12H
GT Electronics/Groove Tubes	00H 00H 47H
Gulbransen	09H
Harmony Systems	19H

MANUFACTURER	MIDI ID CODE
Hohner	24H
Hoshino Gakki	4AH
Hotz Instruments Technologies	00H 00H 3CH
IBM Corp.	00H 00H 3AH
IDP	02H
interMIDI, Inc.	00H 00H 4FH
Intone	00H 00H 44H
Inventronics	1DH
IOTA Systems	00H 00H 08H
IVL Technologies	00H 00H 0BH
J.L. Cooper Electronics	15H
Japan Victor	48H
Jeff Tripp/Perfect Fretworks	00H 00H 14H
Jellinghaus MS	27H
JEN	2AH
Jim Marshall Products Limited	00H 20H 16H
Kamiya Studio	46H
KAT	00H 00H 15H
Kawai	40H
Kenton Electronics	00H 20H 13H
KMX 00H	00H 19H
Korg	42H
KTI	00H 00H 24H
Kurzweil	07H

MANUFACTURER	MIDI ID CODE
L.A. Audio (Larking Audio)	00H 20H 0EH
Lake Butler Sound Company	00H 00H 0DH
Lexicon	06H
Lone Wolf	00H 00H 55H
Lowrey	16H
Marquis Music	00H 00H 1EH
Matsushita Communication Industrial	54H
Matsushita Electric	50H
Mesosha	49H
Micon Audio Electronics GmbH	00H 20H 10H
Microsoft	00H 00H 41H
Midori Electronics	53H
Moog	04H
Music Quest	00H 00H 37H
Musonix	00H 00H 64H
New England Digital	00H 00H 09H
Nisshin Onpa	4DH
NSI Corporation	00H 00H 3EH
Oberheim	10H
Opcode	00H 00H 16H
Orban	00H 00H 21H
Palm Tree Instruments	14H
Passac	20H
Passport Designs	05H

MANUFACTURER	MIDI ID CODE
Peavey Electronics	00H 00H 1BH
PianoDisc	00H 00H 2AH
PPG	29H
Quasimidi	3FH
Rane Corp.	00H 00H 17H
Real World Studio	00H 20H 07H
Richmond Sound Design	00H 00H 40H
RJMG/Niche	00H 00H 42H
Rocktron Corp.	00H 00H 29H
Roger Instruments Corp.	00H 00H 2DH
Roland	41H
S&S Research	00H 00H 33H
Sequential Circuits	01H
SIEL	21H
Solton	26H
Sony	4CH
Soundcraft Electronics	39H
Southern Music Systems	00H 00H 0CH
Southworth Music Systems	28H
Spatial Sound/Anadi Inc.	00H 00H 18H
Spectrum Design and Development	00H 00H 1DH
SSL Limited	2BH
Strand Lighting	00H 20H 01H
Studer-Editech	00H 00H 11H

MANUFACTURER	MIDI ID CODE
Suzuki Musical Instrument Mfg.	55H
Synthaxe	22H
t.c. electronics	00H 20H 1FH
TEAC	4EH
The Software Toolwork	00H 00H 42H
Trident Audio	00H 20H 06H
Twister	25H
Uptown	00H 00H 30H
Voce	00H 00H 31H
Voyce Music	0BH
Voyetra/Octave-Plateau	03H
Waldorf Electronics GmbH	3EH
Warner New Media	00H 00H 01H
Waveframe Corp	0CH
Wersi	3BH
Yamaha	43H
Yes Technology	00H 20H 09H
Zero 88 Lighting Limited	00H 20H 0FH
Zeta Systems	00H 00H 1FH
Zoom	52H

I II III IV V VI VII VIII IX X XI XII

C

APPENDIX

A Typical MIDI
Reception Flowchart

THE FLOWCHART shown in Figure C.1 below is taken from the MIDI standard. It shows how a MIDI device receives and stores data, and also introduces certain MIDI programming principles.

The term "FIFO" (First In, First Out) describes one of the two types of stacks that are used in data processing. (A stack is a memory area in which the data to be processed—in this case, MIDI bytes—is stored.) "LIFO" stands for "Last In, First Out." The LIFO stack is like a stack of dinner plates in which the last plate that was placed on the stack is the first one that's taken off the stack, while the FIFO stack is like a stack of glasses in a beverage dispenser, in which the first glass put into position is the first one to be removed. The stack also contains a pointer that indicates the memory address of the height of the stack (i.e., the location of the most recently stored byte).

The MIDI messages that are received at the MIDI In port of the device are read by an endless loop. The first switching operation separates the data bytes from the status bytes by checking bit 7. If bit 7 is set to 1, the byte is a status byte; if bit 7 is set to zero, the byte is a data byte.

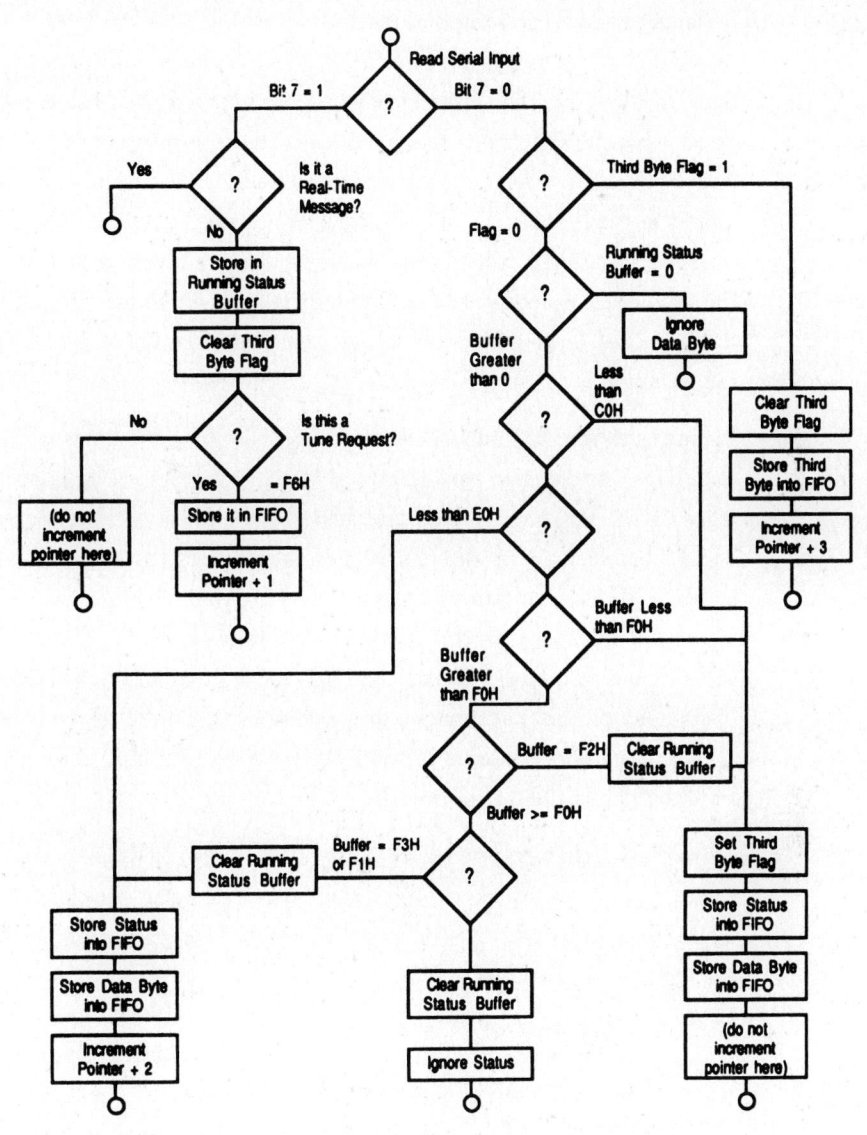

FIGURE C.1: *A typical MIDI reception flowchart*

If the byte is a status byte, the next step is to determine whether the byte belongs to the Real Time family (as it would if bits 3 to 6 were all set to 1). If the byte is a Real Time byte, the message wouldn't contain any data. In that case, the status byte would be ignored (because the flowchart doesn't handle synchronization). But because the program does take Running Status into consideration, every status byte that's received has to be stored in the Running Status Buffer. The exception is the Tuning Request message, which is placed on the stack immediately. This message is the only one (apart from Real Time messages, which are filtered beforehand, and EOX messages, which are handled separately) that doesn't contain data bytes.

A data byte whose so-called *third-byte flag* is set to 1 indicates that a first data byte was received earlier, after a status byte that was something other than a Real Time status byte (because Real Time status bytes can be intercalated between two bytes of any message). When the third-byte flag is set to zero (assuming of course that the byte that's being read is the first byte in the message), and if the Running Status buffer is empty, then the message either includes a data byte that belongs to an Exclusive message (which is ignored, because the program doesn't handle it), or includes an anomaly (such as for instance data received without a preceding status byte), which is likewise ignored.

If the buffer isn't empty, the receiving unit waits for the expected number of data bytes, as indicated by the status byte. A status message lower than C0H (e.g., a Note On, Note Off, Polyphonic Key Pressure, or Control Change message) has two bytes—that is, one byte more than the one that's currently being read. The third-byte flag is then forced to 1, before being stored in the status-byte stack (i.e., held in the buffer, along with the first data byte). At the next reading (in the absence of any anomalies or intercalations of a Real Time status byte), the algorithm switches to the right-hand side of the flowchart to store the second data byte before setting the third-byte flag to zero.

The status messages from C0H (Program Change) to DFH (Channel Pressure) only include one data byte. In these cases, the status message is stored along with the data in progress (i.e., the byte that's currently being read), and the third-byte flag is not set.

Because the E0H to EFH (Pitch Bend) status messages consist of two data bytes, it's logical for these messages to be shifted along the right-hand path.

At this point, the only messages that are left are the status messages from F0H and F7H. (The Real Time messages were filtered earlier, the F6H (Tune Request) message was handled earlier in the left-hand branch, and the F4H and F5H status messages are undefined.) The messages that consist of two data bytes (F1H, which is the MTC Quarter-Frame message, and F3H, which is the Song Select message), along with the messages that contain only one byte (F2H, which is the Song Position Pointer message) are handled in the way described above. However, the Running Status Buffer is cleared, because compression is authorized only for Channel messages (i.e., Voice and Mode messages).

This flowchart filters Exclusive messages. This is why, in the case of an F0H or F7H status message, the Running Status Buffer is cleared and the status message is ignored. The result is that data from F0H to F7H (that is, the contents of the Exclusive message) is not taken into consideration—because the Running Status Buffer is empty.

APPENDIX

D

XIII XIV XV XVI A B

F G H I

MIDI Implementation Charts:

Annotated Examples

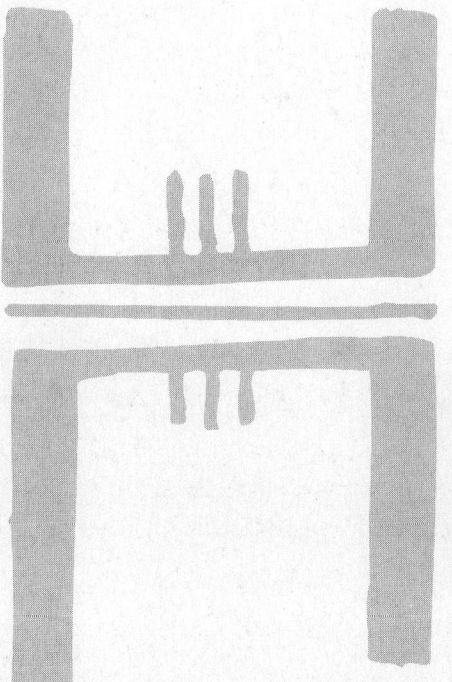

ERE ARE SEVERAL annotated samples of MIDI implementation charts: for the Roland Alpha Juno-1 synthesizer, for the Roland D-550 expander, and for the Ensoniq VFX-SD synthesizer. (If necessary, refer to the general introduction to implementation charts in Chapter 4.)

The Roland Alpha Juno-1 Synthesizer

As shown in Figure D.1 below, the default channels are channels 1 to 16, because their values can be stored in memory.

Even though most monotimbral synthesizers define channels 1 to 16 as the default channels, this chart doesn't indicate that the transmission channel is the same as the reception channel. The Juno-1 only transmits Poly and Omni Off messages; however, it receives all of the Mode messages (Mono, Poly, Omni On, and Omni Off). Nevertheless, because only Mode 1 and Mode 3 are implemented, the Juno-1 is useless as a

Function . . .		Transmitted	Recognized	Remarks
Basic Channel	Default	1 – 16	1 – 16	Memorized
	Changed	1 – 16	1 – 16	
Mode	Default	Mode 3	Mode 1, 3	Memorized
	Messages	POLY, OMNI OFF	MONO, POLY,	
	Altered	* * * * * * * *	OMNI ON/OFF	
			MONO (m ≠ 1) →	
			Mode 1, 3	
Note Number		12 – 108	0 – 127	
	True Voice	* * * * * * * *	12 – 108	
Velocity	Note ON	*	O v = 1 – 127	The velocity value can
	Note OFF	X 9n v = 0	X	be changed by FOOT
				CONTROL volume.
Aftertouch	Key's	X	X	
	Ch's	*	*	
Pitch Bender		*	* 0 – 12 semi	9 bit resolution
Control Change	1	*	*	Modulation
	4	*	*	Foot Control
	5	X	*	Portamento Time
	7	*	*	Volume
	64	*	*	Hold
	65	*	*	Portamento Switch
Prog Change		* 0 – 127	* 0 – 127	
	True #	* * * * * * * *	0 – 127	
System Exclusive		*	*	
System Common	Song Pos	X	X	
	Song Sel	X	X	
	Tune	X	X	
System Real Time	Clock	X	X	
	Commands	X	X	
Aux Messages	Local ON/OFF	X	O	Memorized
	All Notes OFF	O (123)	O (123 – 127)	
	Active Sense	X	O	
	Reset	X	X	
Notes		* Can be set to O or X manually, and memorized.		

Mode 1: OMNI ON, POLY   Mode 2: OMNI ON, MONO   O: Yes
Mode 3: OMNI OFF, POLY   Mode 4: OMNI OFF, MONO   X: No

FIGURE D.1: *The MIDI implementation chart for the Roland Alpha Juno-1 synthesizer* monophonic synthesizer. So, you may ask, why does it receive the Mono message? Good question. Despite the fact that the implementation method masks this function, reception of a BcH 7EH 01H message (Mono Mode with M = 1) activates the chord memory (triggering of 2 to 6 notes through pressure on a single key). This is why the implementation chart indicates that Mode 2 and Mode 4 are interpreted as Mode 1 and Mode 3, except if M = 1. In reality, it would be more accurate to say that Mono mode is not taken into consideration unless M = 1, and then only for an idiosyncratic use that's specific to the Juno-1.

The number of notes transmitted is 96 (MIDI numbers 12 to 108). However, in reality the Juno-1 has a 49-key keyboard that's set by default to transmit notes 48 to 96. The combination of the Octave Transpose and Key Transpose functions lets the tessitura be modified within a range from one octave upward (96 plus 12) to two octaves lower (48 minus 24). The result is that notes 12 to 108 are in fact transmitted. On the other hand, notes 0 to 127 are recognized, with octave folding for notes 12 to 108 (true voice). Note Off messages are transmitted as Note On messages with a Velocity of zero.

The Juno-1 keyboard is not dynamic; therefore, the value of the velocity is constant (i.e., 64, or 40H). However, the velocity can be modified, thanks to the expression pedal (*foot control*). The reception column indicates that the velocity is taken into consideration by the sound-generator section. This means that the Juno-1 can respond to velocity to the extent that the Juno-1 is controlled by a dynamic external keyboard. This is an essential characteristic of a non-dynamic keyboard instrument, which the implementation chart automatically indicates. Fortunately, the Juno-1 correctly interprets a true note-release message (Note Off, 8cH nnH vvH). Even though it accepts Running Status during reception, it uses Running Status during transmission starting only when two consecutive note messages are separated by a sufficiently short period of time.

Furthermore, it's impossible to interrupt from the keyboard a note that's been activated via MIDI, just as it's impossible to interrupt via MIDI a note that's been activated from the keyboard (which is simply an instance of the strict application of the standard). In these examples of the superimposition of a so-called "local" note on a MIDI note, the last velocity received takes precedence over an earlier velocity, regardless of whether the earlier velocity comes from the keyboard or through MIDI.

The transmission of Channel Aftertouch messages relies on the same device used by velocity, because the transmission of aftertouch is activated by an expression pedal. There's only one pedal, and it controls both velocity and aftertouch. In the same way as for velocity, the sound generator of the Juno-1 is sensitive to aftertouch messages received via MIDI.

The Pitch Bend resolution is 9 bits, and therefore is expressed in terms of 512 values (plus or minus 256).

The list of controllers needs no comments, except with regard to the duration of portamento, which is not transmissible.

The Juno-1 has 64 sounds in ROM (preset) and 64 sounds in RAM (internal memory), for a total of 128 Program Change messages. What the chart doesn't show is the option of sending the contents of the editing buffer in the form of System Exclusive (SysEx) messages, by pressing any given program number. (The format of Exclusive data messages is explained in meticulous detail in the user's manual.)

Because the Juno-1 doesn't include a sequencer, there's no need to have any System Common or System Real Time messages.

An All Notes Off message is transmitted each time the last note played on the keyboard is released, even though that note sends its own Note Off message. (This principle is implemented in many Roland devices.) On another level, when the LCD screen of the Juno-1 is set to Local On/Off or Omni On/Off modes, reception of the corresponding messages doesn't automatically update the display, even though the messages

are interpreted correctly. In such a case you first have to select another parameter onscreen, before coming back to find, in a Local or Omni page, the modifications you made via MIDI. This is an example of yet another piece of information that the implementation chart can't provide.

The Roland D-550 Expander

The implementation chart for an expander is characterized by a Transmitted column that's reduced to its most simple expression, because the MIDI Out port of the expander is generally used only to transmit System Exclusive messages.

In the example shown in Figure D.2 below, Mode 4 is implemented. This indicates that controllers with multi-channel transmission, such as MIDI guitars, will derive full benefit from this expander. Reception of Mode 2, which is not recognized, causes the D-550 to switch to Mode 1. You may note in passing the presence of quite a few controllers, including the notorious RPN (Registered Parameter Number).

The implementation chart shown in Figure D.3 below relates exclusively to the so-called "separate" mode of the D-550. In this mode, the four partials of a tone (i.e., the patch) are controlled two by two (the upper tone and the lower tone), over two different MIDI channels. Except for a few details (such as the absence of Mode 1 and of the Balance and Chase controllers, etc.), the information provided in this chart is identical to the information in the preceding one.

Function . . .		Transmitted	Recognized	Remarks
Basic	Default	1 – 16	1 – 16	Memorized
Channel	Changed	1 – 16	1 – 16	
Mode	Default	X	Mode 1, 3, 4	Memorized
	Messages		MONO, POLY,	
	Altered	* * * * * * * * *	OMNI ON/OFF	
			Mode 2 → Mode 1	
Note		X	0 – 127	
Number	True Voice	* * * * * * * * *	12 – 108	
Velocity	Note ON	X	O v = 1 – 127	
	Note OFF	X	X	
Aftertouch	Key's	X	X	
	Ch's	X	*	
Pitch Bender		X	* 0 – 12 semi	9 bit resolution
Control Change	1	X	*	Modulation
	5	X	*	Portamento Time
	7	X	*	Volume
	0, 2 – 4, 8 – 31	X	O	Tone Balance
	6, 38	X	**	Data Entry (MSB, LSB)
	64	X	*	Hold 1
	65	X	*	Portamento SW
	66 – 95	X	O	Chase
	100, 101	X	** (0, 1)	RPC (LSB, MSB)
Prog		X	* 0 – 127	
Change	: True #	* * * * * * * * *	0 – 127	
System Exclusive		*	*	
System Common	: Song Pos	X	X	
	: Song Sel	X	X	
	: Tune	X	X	
System Real Time	: Clock	X	X	
	: Commands	X	X	
Aux Messages	: Local ON/OFF	X	X	
	: All Notes OFF	X	O (123 – 127)	
	: Active Sense	X	O	
	: Reset	X	X	
Notes		* Can be set to O or X manually, and memorized.		
		** RPC = Registered parameter control number.		
		RPC #0: Pitch bend sensitivity		
		RPC #1: Master fine tuning		
		Parameter values are given by Data Entry.		

Mode 1: OMNI ON, POLY	Mode 2: OMNI ON, MONO	O: Yes
Mode 3: OMNI OFF, POLY	Mode 4: OMNI OFF, MONO	X: No

FIGURE D.2: *The MIDI implementation chart for the Roland D-550 expander*

Function . . .		Transmitted	Recognized	Remarks
Basic	Default		1 – 16	Memorized
Channel	Changed		1 – 16	
Mode	Default		Mode 3, 4 (M = 1)	Memorized
	Messages		X	
	Altered	* * * * * * * * *		
Note			0 – 127	
Number	True Voice	* * * * * * * * *	12 – 108	
Velocity	Note ON		O v = 1 – 127	
	Note OFF		X	
Aftertouch	Key's		X	
	Ch's		*	
Pitch Bender			* 0 – 12 semi	9 bit resolution
	1		*	Modulation
	5		*	Portamento Time
	7		X	Volume
	6, 38		**	Data Entry (MSB, LSB)
Control	64		*	Hold 1
Change	65		*	Portamento SW
	100, 101		** (0)	RPC (LSB, MSB)
Prog			X	
Change	: True #	* * * * * * * * *		
System Exclusive			X	
System	: Song Pos		X	
Common	: Song Sel		X	
	: Tune		X	
System	: Clock		X	
Real Time	: Commands		X	
Aux	: Local ON/OFF		X	
Messages	: All Notes OFF		O (123)	
	: Active Sense		O	
	: Reset		X	
Notes		* Can be set to O or X manually, and memorized.		
		** RPC = Registered parameter control number.		
		RPC #0: Pitch bend sensitivity		
		Parameter values are given by Data Entry.		

Mode 1: OMNI ON, POLY   Mode 2: OMNI ON, MONO   O: Yes
Mode 3: OMNI OFF, POLY   Mode 4: OMNI OFF, MONO   X: No

FIGURE D.3: *The MIDI implementation chart for the Roland D-550 expander's "separate" mode*

The Ensoniq VFX-SD Synthesizer

Unlike the procedure used by the Juno-1, the Note On and Note Off
messages (8cH nnH 40H) and, more generally speaking, all of the Channel messages in the VFX-SD are transmitted along with the Running
Status, regardless of the time interval separating them. The remark at the
bottom of the chart in Figure D.4 below indicates that a velocity of 64
(40H) is transmitted for each note that's released.

Some of the available controllers are programmable, while others are governed by the functions for which they were first intended (modulation,
volume, pan, etc.). The Mode row includes the concept of multimode reception (which is not defined by the standard), while Local Mode is
nominally absent. In reality, an equivalent can be obtained through a proprietary procedure in which the VFX-SD manages modes and channels in
its own particular way.

Even though the chart contains enough information to let you estimate
the expressive capabilities of the VFX-SD, you should refer to the operating instructions for further details, particularly with regard to the way
Program Change messages 124 to 127 are used.

. . . .

MODEL: VFX-SD		MIDI Implementation Chart		Version: 1.0
Function . . .		**Transmitted**	**Recognized**	**Remarks**
Basic **Channel**	Default Channel	1 1 – 16	1 1 – 16	
Mode	Default Messages Altered	1 X X	1, 3, 4, Multi X X	Memorized (Global Controllers In MONO Mode)
Note **Number**	True Voice	21 – 108	21 – 108	
Velocity	Note ON Note OFF	O X*	O X	
Aftertouch	Key's Ch's	O O	O O	
Pitch Bender		O	O	

Control
Change
		1 – 95
		1 Mod Wheel
		4 Foot
		7 Volume
		10 Pan
		70 Momentary Patch
		     Select
		71 Timbre Parameter
		72 Release Parameter
		100 Registered Param
		     Select
		101 Registered Param
		     Select
			1 – 95
			1 Mod Wheel
			4 Foot
			7 Volume
			10 Pan
			70 Momentary Patch
			     Select
			71 Timbre Parameter
			72 Release Parameter
			100 Registered Param
			     Select
			101 Registered Param
			     Select
				Programmable

Prog **Change**	: True #	0 – 127	0 – 119, 124 – 127	
System Exclusive		O	O	
System **Common**	: Song Pos : Song Sel : Tune	O O X	O O X	
System **Real Time**	: Clock : Commands	O Clock O Start, Stop, Cont	O Clock O Start, Stop, Cont	
Aux **Messages**	: Local ON/OFF : All Notes OFF : Active Sense : Reset	X X X X	X X X X	
Notes		* A Note Off velocity of 64 is always sent for all keys.		

Mode 1: OMNI ON, POLY	Mode 2: OMNI ON, MONO	O: Yes
Mode 3: OMNI OFF, POLY	Mode 4: OMNI OFF, MONO	X: No

FIGURE D.4: *The MIDI implementation chart for the Ensoniq VFX-SD synthesizer*

I II III IV V VI VII VIII IX X XI XII

£

APPENDIX

XIII   XIV   XV   XVI   A B C D E F G H I

Expressiveness Characteristics

of Typical MIDI Instruments

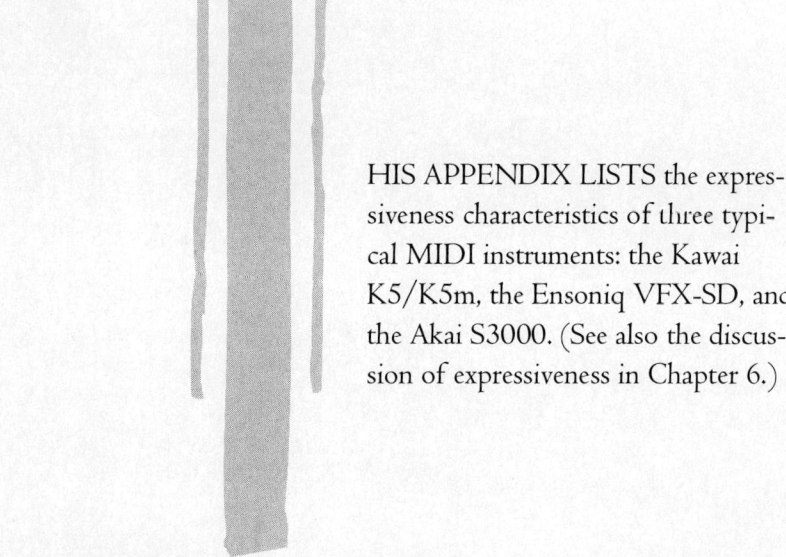

THIS APPENDIX LISTS the expressiveness characteristics of three typical MIDI instruments: the Kawai K5/K5m, the Ensoniq VFX-SD, and the Akai S3000. (See also the discussion of expressiveness in Chapter 6.)

The Kawai K5/K5m

Modulation:

- The filter slope
- The filter cut-off frequency
- The effect of the LFO on pitch
- The effect of the LFO on the amplitude of the selected harmonics

The pressing speed:

- The effect of the envelope on pitch
- The effect of the envelope on amplitude
- The effect of the envelope on the cut-off frequency
- The cut-off frequency
- The filter slope
- The amplitude
- The speed of the selected envelope segments

The release speed:

- The release speed of the envelope segment

Channel Aftertouch:

- Pitch (up to plus or minus two octaves)
- The effect of the LFO on pitch
- The effect of the envelope on amplitude
- The cut-off frequency
- The slope of the filter
- The amplitude

The Ensoniq VFX-SD

In the VFX-SD synthesizer, a modulation source is sent toward any parameter (that is, any destination), whose evolution it controls in accordance with a given ratio (that is, in accordance with a certain depth: for example, plus or minus two semitones for the pitch of an oscillator).

The fifteen modulation sources are grouped as shown in the following list:

Internal modulation sources:

- The LFO
- Envelope 1
- Envelope 2
- The timbre
- The noise generator
- The CV (Control Voltage) pedal
- The mixer (that is, the mixing of two selected sources)

MIDI modulation sources:

- The note number
- An external controller (such as a programmable Control Change message having a value from 01 to 95)
- Aftertouch
- Velocity
- Aftertouch
- Aftertouch plus Velocity
- Modulation
- Modulation plus Aftertouch

These sources are used to modify the following parameters:

- The pitch
- The starting point for the sample (for wave tables)
- The cut-off frequency for the low-pass filter
- The cut-off frequency for the high-pass filter
- The volume

- The panorama
- The LFO (speed and amplitude)

In addition to these programmable modulations, the VFX-SD also implements other controls, as indicated below.

Velocity:

- The starting point for the sample
- The amplitude of the envelope
- The speed of the attack segment
- The response curve for an envelope

Note Number:

- The cut-off frequency
- The amplitude
- The duration of all of the segments of an envelope

The Akai S3000

In the S3000, a modulation source is sent toward any parameter (that is, any destination), whose evolution it controls in accordance with a given ratio (that is, in accordance with a certain depth: for example, plus or minus two semitones for the pitch of an oscillator).

The thirteen modulation sources are grouped as shown in the following list:

Internal modulation sources:

- LFO 1
- LFO 2

- Envelope 1
- Envelope 2

MIDI modulation sources:

- Modulation
- Pitch Bend
- Channel Aftertouch
- Any selected continuous controller (breath, foot, or volume)
- The pressing speed
- The note number
- A fixed value, corresponding to the Pitch Bend value, for which a "snapshot" is taken at the time the note is pressed
- A fixed value, corresponding to the modulation value, for which a "snapshot" is taken at the time the note is pressed
- A fixed value, corresponding to the value of any one of the three selected continuous controllers, for which a "snapshot" is taken at the time the note is pressed

These modulation sources are used to modify the following parameters. Some of these parameters have two or three inputs, which makes them simultaneously accessible to two or three modulation sources—which means that the modulation sources can act in parallel.

Inputs at the Keygroup level:

- The cut-off frequency (times 3)
- The panorama (times 3)
- The pitch (times 2)
- The amplitude (times 2)

Inputs at the Program level:

- The speed of LFO1 (times 1)
- The depth of LFO1 (times 1)
- The delay of LFO1 (times 1)
- The amplitude (times 3)

In addition to these programmable modulations, the S3000 also implements various controls, as indicated below.

Channel Aftertouch:

- Pitch
- The depth of LFO1

Modulation:

- The depth of LFO1

The pressing speed:

- The speed of the attack and release segments of the envelopes
- The depth of LFO1

The release speed:

- The speed of the release segments of the envelopes

The note number:

- The speed of the decay and release segments of the envelopes

APPENDIX

XIII XIV XV XVI A B C D

Test Procedures
and
Hidden Functions

A S NOTED IN Chapter 6, the operating system of most MIDI devices includes hidden functions, such as reinitializations, the display of version numbers, test procedures (including diagnostic aids for use in case of failures), and other functions.

This appendix describes how some of these procedures, which aren't often documented in users' manuals, are launched. In most cases all you have to do is press certain keys (indicated here with square brackets) simultaneously, sometimes while turning on the device. It's worth repeating the warning from Chapter 6: handle these operations with care!

The Boss DR-220

When the device is turned on:

[<] + [>]: reinitialization

The Boss DR-550

When the device is turned on:

[<] + [>]

While the device is on:

[Play]: reinitialization

The Boss DR-550 Mk2

When the device is turned on:

[Tempo] + [>/+1]: the version number

When the device is turned on:

[-1/<] + [>/+1]

While the device is on:

[Start]: reinitialization

The Korg 01/W and 01/WFD

When the device is turned on:

[Reset]: the version number

When the device is turned on:

[Reset] + [Compare] or [3] or [6] or [9]: reinitialization

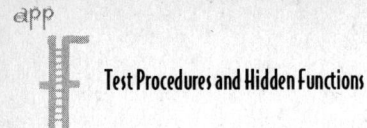

The Korg A1

When the device is turned on:

[Write]: the version number

When the device is turned on:

[-1/v] + [Write]: reinitialization

The Korg A2

Connect the MIDI input to the MIDI output

Insert a RAM card (MCR-03)

When the device is turned on:

[Chain/Effect] + [C]: the test program

[Write]: execution of the current test procedure

[^]: change to the next procedure

[v]: change to the previous procedure

[Bypass]: exit the test program

The Korg A3

Connect the MIDI input to the MIDI output

Insert a RAM card

When the device is turned on:

[Chain/Effect] + [B]: the test program

The Korg A4

When the device is turned on:

[User Preset] + [Write]: the test program

[Write]: execution of the current test procedure

[Mode ^]: change to the next procedure

[Mode v]: change to the previous procedure

The Korg A5

When the device is turned on:

Pedal [Mode] + key [Write]

While the device is on:

Keys [Mode] + [Write] + pedal [SW 1]: reinitialization

When the device is turned on:

[Bypass] + [Mode]: the test program

The Korg DRV2000

[Write] + [Up]: test of the display mechanism

The Korg DSS1

[Data Entry Up] + [Down]: global test

The Korg M1

[Int] + [Card] + [Combi] + [Edit Combi]: reinitialization

The Korg Wavestation and Wavestation A/D

At start-up, as soon as the letters "Korg" appear:

[Cursor v] + [Ten Key 4], then [Init RAM]: reinitialization

The Kurzweil 1000PX

[Program Parameter Up] + [Program Parameter Down]: global test

The Roland A-220

When the device is turned on:

[Utility Memory] + [Output B]: reinitialization

The Roland A-30

When the device is turned on:

[Write]: reinitialization

The Roland A-50 and A-80

While the device is on:

[1] + [2] + [3] + [Channel] (under the menu): the version number

While the device is on:

[1] + [2] + [3] + [Channel] + [v]: reinitialization

The Roland A-880

When the device is turned on:

[Signal] + [Memory]: reinitialization

The Roland AX-1

When the device is turned on:

[Write]: reinitialization

The Roland D-10

When the device is turned on:

[Edit] + [Data Transfer]: the version number

When the device is turned on:

[Tune/Function]: reinitialization

The Roland D-10 and D-20

[Write/Copy] + [Enter]: reinitialization

[Exit] + [Edit]: mode test

List of the Tests:

[Exit] + [Edit]:	RAM + card
[Exit] + [Tune]:	Pitch Bender
[Exit] + [Midi]:	Keyboard
[Exit] + [Write]:	LCD
[Exit] + [Data Transfer]:	LCD
[Exit] + [Enter]:	LED
[Exit] + [Multitimbral]:	Floppy-disk reader
[Exit] + [Compare]:	Converter

The Roland D-110

When the device is turned on:

[Part v] + [Bank v] + [Enter]: the version number

When the device is turned on:

[Write]: reinitialization

[Write/Copy] + [Edit]: reinitialization of RAM, with the factory-installed sounds

The Roland D-20

When the device is turned on:

[Edit] + [Data Transfer]: the version number

When the device is turned on:

[Tune/Function] + [Write]: reinitialization

The Roland D-5

When the device is turned on:

[A/B] + [Bank 8]: the version number

While the device is on:

Shift into ROM Play mode

[Exit] + [Edit] + [Enter], [A/B] + [Bank 7]: reinitialization

The Roland D-50

When the device is turned on:

[0] + [Inc]: the version number

When the device is turned on:

[0] + [Data Transfer]: reinitialization

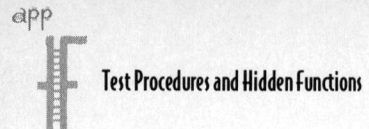

The Roland D-550

When the device is turned on:

[Bank 6] + [Number 6] + [Exit]: the version number

When the device is turned on:

[Bank 2] + [Number 6] + [Enter]: reinitialization

The Roland D-70

When the device is turned on:

[Number 1]: the version number

When the device is turned on:

[Number 8]: reinitialization

The Roland DR-660

When the device is turned on:

[Song] + [7]: the version number

When the device is turned on:

[Reset] + [Rec]

While the device is on:

[Enter]: reinitialization

The Roland DS-70

When the device is turned on:

[^]

While the device is on:

[A], then [C], then [S1]: reinitialization

The Roland E-20, E-30, PRO-E, and RA-50

When the device is turned on:

[Reverb On/Off]: the version number

When the device is turned on:

[Write]: reinitialization

The Roland E-35

When the device is turned on:

[Tone Bank 8]: the version number

When the device is turned on:

[Rec/Punch-In]: reinitialization

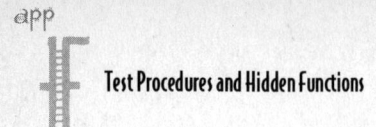

The Roland E-660

When the device is turned on:

[Eq] + [+]: the version number

The Roland E-70

When the device is turned on:

[Enter]: the version number

When the device is turned on:

[Write]: reinitialization

The Roland GP-16

When the device is turned on:

[6] + [7] + [8]: the version number

When the device is turned on:

[6] + [7] + [8]

While the device is on:

[Func], then [Write]: reinitialization

The Roland GR-1

When the device is turned on:

[Value Dec]

While the device is on:

[Enter]: the version number

When the device is turned on:

[Write/Copy]

While the device is on:

[Enter]: reinitialization

The Roland GR-50

When the device is turned on:

[Value v] + [−Page] + [Enter]: the version number

When the device is turned on:

[Value ^] + [Ext] + [Write]: reinitialization

The Roland GS-6

When the device is turned on:

[Noise Suppressor] + [Hum Cancel]: the version number

When the device is turned on:

[Reverb] + [Hum Cancel]: reinitialization

The Roland JD-800

While the device is on:

Shift into Multi mode

[CursorL] + [Cursor R] + [Exit]: the version number

While the device is on:

Shift into Data Transfer mode

[Page ^] × 6, then [Inc/Yes]: reinitialization

The Roland JD-990

When the device is turned on:

[Inc] + [Dec]: the version number

When the device is turned on:

[Inc] + [Dec]

While the device is on:

[F4]: reinitialization

The Roland JV-30

While the device is on:

[Level] + [Pan], [Variation] + [Vibrato], Performance] + [Bank 16]: the version number

While the device is on:

[Chorus] + [Reverb], [Value]: reinitialization

The Roland JV-80

When the device is turned on:

[Number 1]: the version number

When the device is turned on:

[Number 8]

While the device is on:

[Enter]: reinitialization

The Roland JV-880

When the device is turned on:

[Edit] + [Compare]: the version number

When the device is turned on:

[Utility]

While the device is on:

[Data] until Factory Preset, then [Enter]: reinitialization

The Roland JX-1

When the device is turned on:

[Write] + [Flute]: reinitialization

The Roland JW-50

While the device is on:

[Write] + [Song Edit], then [Shift] and [>]: the version number

While the device is on:

[Tune Function] + [F5], then [F4]: reinitialization

The Roland KR-500 and KR-3000

When the device is turned on:

Music Style [A] + [B]: the version number

When the device is turned on:

[From] + [To] + [Write]: reinitialization

The Roland ME-5

When the device is turned on:

[Pedal 1] + [Pedal 2]

While the device is on:

[Write]: reinitialization

The Roland ME-10

When the device is turned on:

[Pedal 1] + [Pedal 2] + [Pedal v] + [Pedal ^]: the version number

When the device is turned on:

[Pedal v]

While the device is on:

[Write]: reinitialization

The Roland MT-32

[Volume] + [3]: global test

The Roland PAD-80

When the device is turned on:

[Up] + [Down]: the version number

When the device is turned on:

[Value <] + [Value >]: reinitialization

The Roland PK-5

When the device is turned on:

[Factory Set]: reinitialization

The Roland PM-16

When the device is turned on:

[Card] + [>] + [Midi]: the version number

When the device is turned on:

[1] + [2]: reinitialization

The Roland R-5

When the device is turned on:

[Condition] + [Exit]: the version number

When the device is turned on:

[Page] + [Select]

While the device is on:

[Enter]: reinitialization

The Roland R-70

When the device is turned on:

[Assign] + [Mixer]: the version number

When the device is turned on:

[MIDI] + [Assign]

While the device is on:

[Yes], then [Yes]: reinitialization

The Roland R-8

When the device is turned on:

[Function] + [Exit]: the version number

When the device is turned on:

[Page] + [Select]

While the device is on:

[Enter]: reinitialization

The Roland R-8 Mk2

[Temp Assgn] + [Exit], then [Enter]: the version number

[Temp Assgn] + [Exit], then [Exit], then [Enter]: reinitialization

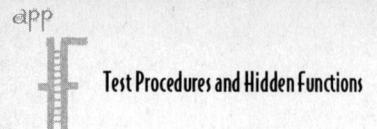

The Roland R-8M

When the device is turned on:

[Cursor <] + [Value v]: the version number

When the device is turned on:

[Cursor >] + [Value ^]: reinitialization

The Roland RA-90

When the device is turned on:

[Sync Start]: the version number

When the device is turned on:

[Write]: reinitialization

The Roland RSP-550

When the device is turned on:

[Program/Page v] + [Value v] + [Param] + [Control]: the version number

When the device is turned on:

[Program/Page v] + [Program/Page ^]

While the device is on:

[Write] x 2: reinitialization

The Roland S-220

[Perform] + [Tune]: converter test

The Roland SC-33

When the device is turned on:

[Low/Sub] + [Utility] + [Number v]: the version number

When the device is turned on:

[Reverb] + [Split]

While the device is on:

[Yes]: reinitialization

The Roland SC-55 and SC-155

When the device is turned on:

[Instrument <] + [Instrument >] + [Midich <] +[Midich >] +: the version number

When the device is turned on:

[Instrument <] + [Instrument >]: reinitialization

The Roland SD-35

[Pause] + [Prog] + [Repeat], then [Stop] + [K-Shift], then [Rec]:
the version number

[Pause] + [Prog] + [Repeat], then [Stop], then [Solo]:
reinitialization

The Roland SE-50

When the device is turned on:

[Number v] + [Value v] + [Utility]: the version number

When the device is turned on:

[Parameter ^] + [Value ^]: reinitialization

The Roland SN-550

When the device is turned on:

[Line Frequency] + [Manual]: the version number

The Roland SPD-11

When the device is turned on:

[Select] + [Edit]: the version number

When the device is turned on:

[v] + [All/Enter]

While the device is on:

[All/Enter]: reinitialization

The Roland SPD-8

When the device is turned on:

[Edit] + [Copy], then [Value v] and [Enter]: reinitialization

The Roland TD-7

When the device is turned on:

[System] + [Edit]: the version number

While the device is on:

[System], then [>] or [<] until INI, then [Enter], then [>] or [<] until HI-HAT, then [Data] until ALL, then [Enter], then [Enter]: reinitialization

The Roland TR-505 and TR-626

When the device is turned on:

[Play] + [A]: reinitialization

The Roland TR-707 and TR-727

When the device is turned on:

[Track] + [A]: reinitialization

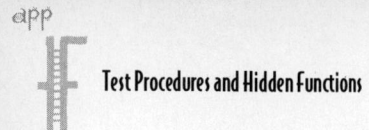

The Roland U-110

When the device is turned on:

[Dec] + [Inc]: the version number

When the device is turned on:

[Part] + [Edit]: reinitialization

The Roland U-20

While the device is on:

Shift into ROM Play mode

[Mark] + [Jump] + [Enter]: the version number

While the device is on:

Shift into ROM Play mode

[Mark] + [Jump] + [Enter], [Mark] + [Jump] + [Number 7], [Enter], [Value ^]: reinitialization

[Part] + [Rhythm]: MODE ROM Play

[Jump] + [Cursor >]: the next test

[Jump] + [Cursor <]: the previous test

[Jump] + [Bank 1-8]: direct selection of the test number

[Jump] + [Number 1-8]: direct selection of the test number

[Jump] + [Exit]: exit test mode

List of the Tests:

1: LCD contrast   (direct access: [Jump] + [Bank 1])

2: LEDs   (direct access: [Jump] + [Bank 2])

3: Internal RAM   (direct access: [Jump] + [Bank 3])

4: The RAM card   (direct access: [Jump] + [Bank 4])

5: The PCM card   (direct access: [Jump] + [Bank 5])

6: The internal PCM   (direct access: [Jump] + [Bank 6])
   ROM

7: The keyboard and   (direct access: [Jump] + [Bank 7])
   switches

8: The converter   (direct access: [Jump] + [Bank 8])

9: The converter   (direct access: [Jump] + [Number 1])

10: MIDI   (direct access: [Jump] + [Number 2])

11: Sound   (direct access: [Jump] + [Number 3])

12: Sound   (direct access: [Jump] + [Number 4])

13: The converter   (direct access: [Jump] + [Number 5])

14: Effects   (direct access: [Jump] + [Number 6])

15: Memory initialization   (direct access: [Jump] + [Number 7])

16: Loading of internal   (direct access: [Jump] + [Number 8])
    sounds

The Roland U-220

While the device is on:

Shift into ROM Play mode

[Jump] + [Value ^], [Mark] + [Jump] + [Enter]: the version number

While the device is on:

Shift into ROM Play mode

[Jump] + [Value ^], [Mark] + [Jump] + [Enter], [Mark] + [Part/Int <], [Enter], [Value v]: reinitialization

[Jump] + [Value ^]: test mode

[Jump] + [Cursor >]: the next test

[Jump] + [Cursor <]: the next test

[Mark] + [Jump] + [Exit]: exit test mode

List of the Tests:

1: LCD + LED	(direct access: [Jump] + [Edit])
2: RAM	(direct access: [Jump] + [Data])
3: The PCM card	(direct access: [Jump] + [Exit])
4: The PCM ROM	(direct access: [Jump] + [Enter])
5: The switches	(direct access: [Jump] + [< Part])
6: MIDI	(direct access: [Jump] + [> Part])
7: The converter	(direct access: [Mark] + [Edit])
8: Sound	(direct access: [Mark] + [Data])

9: Sound   (direct access: [Mark] + [Exit])

10: Effects   (direct access: [Mark] + [Enter])

11: Memory initialization (direct access: [Mark] + [> Part])

12: Loading of internal   (direct access: [Mark] + [< Part])
sounds:

The Roland VP-70

When the device is turned on:

[Play] + [Voice >> MIDI] + [System]: the version number

When the device is turned on:

[Play] + [Voice Exp] + [Voice >> MIDI]: reinitialization

The Yamaha DMP11

[Pre Post] + [Fader flip]: the test program

The Yamaha DX11

[16] + [32] + [Edit], then [Yes]

The Yamaha DX21/27

[Voice 1] + [Voice 2]

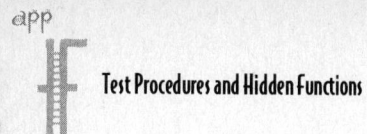

The Yamaha DX7

[16] + [32] + [Function], then [Yes]

The Yamaha DX7II

[16] + [32] + [Edit]

The Yamaha FB01

[System Setup] + [Inst Select] + [Data Entry No.]

The Yamaha PSR400 and PSR500

When the device is turned on:

[Custom Record/End] + [Clear]: reinitialization

When the device is turned on:

Holding down the two rightmost white keys on the keyboard: complete system initialization (wait a few seconds, then turn the instrument off and on again)

The Yamaha PSR5700

When the device is turned on:

[Intro 1] + [Intro 3] + [Demo]: the test program

[Bank 8] + [Number 8]: reinitialization

The Yamaha PSR600

When the device is turned on:

Holding down the two rightmost white keys on the keyboard: complete system initialization (wait a few seconds, then turn the instrument off and on again)

The Yamaha PSR6700

When the device is turned on:

[Panel Registration 8] + [Effect Accomp. 1]: the test program

[Bank 8] + [Number 8]: reinitialization

The Yamaha PSRQ-16

When the device is turned on:

[-] + [+]: reinitialization

When the device is turned on:

Holding down the four rightmost white keys on the keyboard: complete system initialization (wait a few seconds, then turn the instrument off and on again)

The Yamaha QY10

[Menu] + [Enter] + [Oct. Up]: the test program

[Shift], then [Enter]: reinitialization

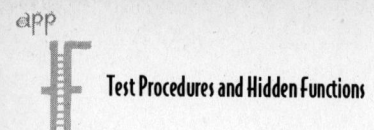

The Yamaha QY20

When the device is turned on:

[-1] + [+1] + [→]: the test program

[F3]: reinitialization

The Yamaha RM50

When the device is turned on:

[Play] + [Macro Play] + [Sound]: the test program

[Sound], then [Yes]: reinitialization

The Yamaha RY10

[Util] + [Memory]: the test program

[+1]: reinitialization

[+1] + [Start/Go]: return to play mode

The Yamaha RY20

[Dec] + [Pattern] + [Perc 2]: the test program

[Stop/Cont]: reinitialization

The Yamaha SY35

When the device is turned on:

[>] + [<] + [Voice]: the test program, with a display of the version number

[Bank Select 4]: reinitialization

[Demo]: return to play mode

The Yamaha SY85

[Shift] + [Store] + [Exit]: the test program

[Menu], then [1]: reinitialization

The Yamaha SY99

[Voice] + [Bank D] + [8]: the test program

[Copy]: reinitialization

The Yamaha TG100

Connect the MIDI input to the MIDI output

Set the Select Host selector to MIDI

When the device is turned on:

[Cursor] + [-/No] + [+/Yes]: the test program

[+/Yes], then [Cursor]: reinitialization

The Yamaha TG500

[Play] + [Utility] + [Exit]: the test program

[Copy] + [Yes]: reinitialization

The Yamaha TX7

[Data Yes] + [Mode]

The Yamaha TX81Z

When the device is turned on:

[Master Volume] + [Cursor]: the test program

Test Procedures in More Detail

In conclusion, here are three examples that show the test procedures in greater detail.

The Yamaha TX802

[8] + [9]: global test

The following information appears:

```
TEST Version Number
Push "Enter"
```

The series consists of 57 tests, which are listed below along with their meanings:

TEST NAME	MEANING OR FUNCTION
TEST-01 RAM	Shifts to TEST-02 if everything happens properly
TEST-02 LCD	All of the segments light up TEST-03 LED: the eight LEDs blink successively and simultaneously

TEST NAME	MEANING OR FUNCTION
TEST-04 to TEST-35	Switch tests. Each of the 32 switches on the front panel switch should be pressed successively and in the order required.
TEST-36 MIDI	Test of the MIDI ports
TEST-37	Test of Type 1 cartridges
TEST-38	Test of Type 2 cartridges
TEST-39	Test of Type 3 cartridges
TEST-40	Cartridge-protection test
TEST-41	Cartridge read/write test
TEST-42 to TEST-55	Test of audio outputs 1 to 8, left and right, headphones, and mixing gates 1 and 2 (through the sending of sinusoidal waveforms)
TEST-56	Total system reinitialization
TEST-57	Loading of factory data

The Roland A-880

You can find the version number for the MIDI A-880 patch by pressing and holding down output buttons No. 1, No. 2, No. 4, and No. 8 while turning on the device. The sum of the values corresponding to the lighted LEDs indicates the version number. For instance,

```
LED number:           1     2     3     4     5     6     7     8
corresponding value: 0.01  0.02  0.04  0.08  0.16  0.32  0.64  1.28
```

For example, when LEDs 1, 3, 6, and 7 are lit, the version number is 1.01, as derived from the following operation:

```
0.01  +  0.04  +  0.32  +  0.64  =  1.01
```

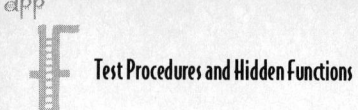
The Casio FZ1

The operating-system test (64K ROM) is run when the instrument is turned on, with a check-sum calculation. The system RAM area is also checked.

The test procedure (i.e., the System Tools option on the main menu) starts if you keep the Display key pressed down while you turn on the instrument.

The Floppy Check sub-menu: the test of the floppy-disk drive is extremely thorough. Among other things, it lets any sector be written to and read, lets the drive heads be aligned, etc., etc.

The LCD Check sub-menu: the display test starts by displaying all of the points on the screen and ends by showing the entire set of displayable characters.

A software option also lets the system run a RAM test (including tests of optional RAM extensions), the switches, the keyboard (for pitch, modulation, aftertouch, etc.), the MIDI ports, the input/output port, and the disk reader.

APPENDIX

G

XIII XIV XV XVI A B C D E F

GenEdit Commands
at a Glance

THE INFORMATION in this appendix is limited to brief comments about data formats and about the sets of instructions that appear in the listings in some of the later chapters in this book. It is by no means an exhaustive description of the GenEdit language, but rather a set of extracts offered for illustrative purposes, so that if you want to work with another language you'll find it easy to convert the various program excerpts that appear in this book.

Variables

. . . .

The 100 general-purpose variables (numbered from V00 through V99) in each segment make it possible to store values. Other variables exist that are dedicated to very specific tasks. All of these latter variables can be read, and some of them can also be written to.

Variables that can be read and written to:

NAME	FUNCTION
PAT	The number of the current patch
CHN	The current MIDI channel
PTR	The current address in the data buffer
NMO	Shifting of the patch name into the data buffer
NML	The number of characters in the patch name
EBL	The number of bytes in the edit buffer

Variables that can be read (but not written to):

NAME	FUNCTION
LPO	The address, in the edit buffer, of the parameter that is being edited

Labels

Labels, which are numbered from L00 through L99 in each segment, are used by the GoTo or GoSub instruction.

Sizes

When it's necessary to specify the size of a value, the following symbols are used:

SYMBOL	MEANING
B	Byte (8 bits)
W	Word (16 bits)

SYMBOL	MEANING
L	Long word (32 bits)

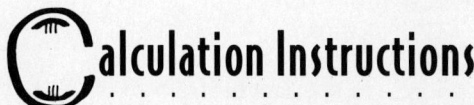alculation Instructions

- **<variable> = <variable operator>**: A calculation is performed on a variable (using one of the operators listed below), and the result is placed in a variable.

OPERATOR	MEANING
Invert	Ones complement
NEG	Negation (twos complement)
NOT	The result is equal to 1 when the value of the variable is equal to 0; otherwise, the result is equal to 0

- **<variable> = <variable variable operator>**
- **<variable> = <constant variable operator>**
- **<variable> = <variable constant operator>**
- **<variable> = <constant constant operator>**

A calculation is performed on constants and variables (using one of the operators listed below), and the result is placed in a variable.

OPERATOR	MEANING
+	Addition
−	Subtraction
*	Multiplication

OPERATOR	MEANING
/	Division
%	Remainder
|	Logical OR
&	Logical AND
^	Logical EXCLUSIVE OR
<<	Left shift in binary (the second parameter, modulo 32, indicates the number of bits by which the shift should be made)
>>	Right shift in binary (the second parameter, modulo 32, indicates the number of bits by which the shift should be made)

- **\<variable\> = \<variable variable operator\>**: Each of the two variables in the operation is evaluated as being either *true* or *false*. A value of zero is treated as false, and every other value is treated as true. The logical operation is then performed (in accordance with one of the three operators listed below), and the result (1 = true and 0 = false) is placed in a variable.

OPERATOR	MEANING
AND	1 if both values are different from 0; otherwise, 0
OR	0 if both values are equal to 0; otherwise, 1
XOR	1 if one of the values is equal to 0 and the other value is equal to 1; otherwise, 0

- **\<variable\> = \<variable variable operator\>**
- **\<variable\> = \<constant variable operator\>**

Both values are considered to be unsigned values. The result is either 0 (false) or 1 (true).

OPERATOR	MEANING
EQ	Equal to
NE	Not equal to
LT	Less than
GT	Greater than
LE	Less than or equal to
GE	Greater than or equal to

Initialization Instructions

- **FormatBank <name of bank> <#patches> <shift>:** This instruction is used by the Initialize segment to format the display of the patch numbers in a bank. The name of the bank is represented by a character string. The <#patches> parameter corresponds to the number of patches per bank, and the <shift> parameter indicates the display offset for the numbers in the bank.

MIDI Byte Transfer Instructions

- **ReceiveData <size> <end byte> <number>:** Reception of a certain number of MIDI bytes (specified by the <size> parameter), which are placed in the data buffer at the address indicated by PTR. The PTR pointer is incremented by one unit each time a piece of data is received. Reception is interrupted prematurely when X end bytes (where the value of X is specified by the <number> parameter) have been received.

- **Receive <byte 1> <byte 2> ... <byte 16>**: Reception of a string of up to 16 bytes (without storing them), whose values are specified in <byte 1> through <byte 16>. If the expected values are not received, an error message is generated.

- **ReceiveAny <number>**: Reception of a certain number of bytes without storing them.

- **TransmitData <size> <end byte> <number>**: Transmission of a certain number of MIDI bytes (specified by the <size> parameter), which are read into the data buffer at the address indicated by PTR. The PTR pointer is incremented by one unit each time a piece of data is transmitted. Transmission is interrupted prematurely when X end bytes (where the value of X is specified by the <number> parameter) have been transmitted.

- **Transmit <byte 1> <byte 2> ... <byte 16>**: Transmission of a string of up to 16 bytes, whose values are specified in <byte 1> through <byte 16>.

- **TransmitVar <variable>**: Transmission of the least significant byte within the <variable> parameter.

Data-Access Instructions

- **<variable> = PeekData <address> <size>**: The value that was read into the data buffer, in accordance with the specified address and size, is placed in <variable>.

- **PokeData <shift> <value> <size>**: A value, whose size is specified, is stored in the data buffer at the specified address.

- **<variable> = PeekEdit <address> <size>**: The value that was read into the edit buffer, in accordance with the specified address and size, is placed in <variable>.

- **PokeEdit <shift> <value> <size>**: A value, whose size is specified, is stored in the edit buffer at the specified address.

- **CopyDtoD <source> <dest> <count> <size>**

- **CopyDtoE <source> <dest> <count> <size>**

- **CopyEtoD <source> <dest> <count> <size>**

- **CopyEtoE <source> <dest> <count> <size>**

Blocks of data are copied between the data buffer and the edit buffer. The letters "D" and "E" indicate the source and the destination, with "D" representing the data buffer and "E" representing the edit buffer; <source> indicate the starting address; <dest> indicates the destination address; and <size> indicates the size of each element.

Instructions Linked to Tables

- **BuildTable <table> <byte 1> <byte 2> … <byte 16>**: The <table> parameter corresponds to a number in the table (from 1 to 16), with each line in the table containing a maximum of 16 bytes.

- **<variable> = PeekTable <table> <shift>**: The value that was read into the table (whose number is specified by the <table> parameter and whose address is specified in the <shift> parameter) is transferred into <variable>.

Display and Acquisition Instructions

- **OpenWindow:** Triggers the opening of a window

- **CloseWindow:** Triggers the closing of a window

A window contains 12 lines, with each line consisting of 38 columns.

- **\<variable\> = InputPatch \<line\> \<col\> \<default\>:** Invites you, the user, to enter a patch number. (GenEdit automatically verifies that the number is located between 1 and 128.)

- **\<variable\> = InputChannel \<line\> \<col\> \<default\>:** Invites you, the user, to enter a channel number. (GenEdit automatically verifies that the number is located between 1 and 16.)

In both of these instructions the \<default\> parameter represents the value that is displayed by default, and the \<line\> and \<col\> parameters specify the position of the value in the window.

Control Instructions

- **Stop:** Ends the execution of the segment

- **Wait \<duration\>:** Causes a pause whose duration is equal to the value of the \<duration\> parameter multiplied by 50 milliseconds (ms)

Control Instructions

```
Loop <repetitions>
    Instruction set
EndLoop
```

The portion of the segment located between the Loop and EndLoop instructions is executed a given number of times (thus forming the loop), with the number of repeated executions being specified by the value of the <repetitions> parameter.

Branching Instructions

- **GoTo <label>:** The segment branches to the instruction located directly after the label.

- **GoSub <label>:** The segment branches to the instruction located directly after the label until it encounters a Return instruction, at which point it returns to the instruction located directly after the GoSub command.

Conditional Branching Instructions

- **If <variable> GoTo <label>:** The segment branches to the instruction located directly after the label, provided that the variable is something other than zero.

- **If <variable> GoSub <label>:** The segment branches to the instruction located directly after the label, provided that the variable is something other than zero, until it encounters a Return instruction, at which point it returns to the instruction located directly after the GoSub command.

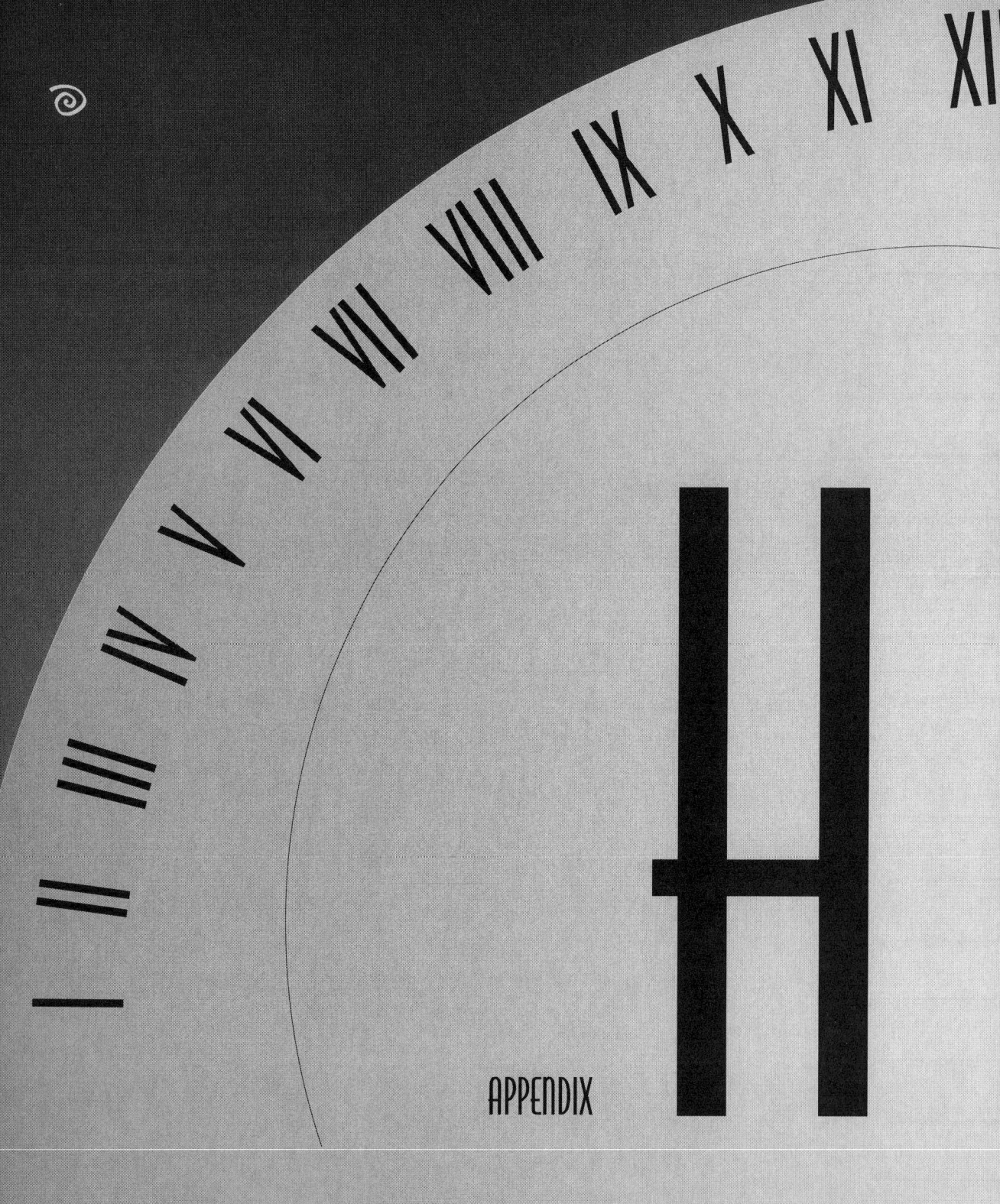

APPENDIX

XIII XIV XV XVI A B C D E F

Edit-Buffer

Parameters

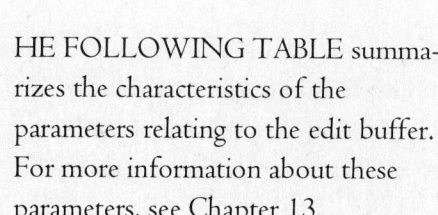

HE FOLLOWING TABLE summarizes the characteristics of the parameters relating to the edit buffer. For more information about these parameters, see Chapter 13.

PARAMETER NAME	NUMBER OF BYTES	ADDRESS IN THE EDIT BUFFER	MINIMUM VALUE	MAXIMUM VALUE
"MULTI VOICE NAME 1"	1	00000	+00020	+00127
"MULTI VOICE NAME 2"	1	00001	+00020	+00127
"MULTI VOICE NAME 3"	1	00002	+00020	+00127
"MULTI VOICE NAME 4"	1	00003	+00020	+00127
"MULTI VOICE NAME 5"	1	00004	+00020	+00127
"MULTI VOICE NAME 6"	1	00005	+00020	+00127
"MULTI VOICE NAME 7"	1	00006	+00020	+00127
"MULTI VOICE NAME 8"	1	00007	+00020	+00127
"MULTI VOICE NAME 9"	1	00008	+00020	+00127

. . . .

PARAMETER NAME	NUMBER OF BYTES	ADDRESS IN THE EDIT BUFFER	MINIMUM VALUE	MAXIMUM VALUE
"MULTI VOICE NAME 10"	1	00009	+00020	+00127
"EFFECT SOURCE SELECT"	1	00010	+00000	+00016
"EFFECT TYPE"	1	00011	+00001	+00034
"OUTPUT LEVEL"	1	00012	+00000	+00100
"PARAMETER 1"	1	00013	+00000	+00100
"PARAMETER 2"	1	00014	+00000	+00100
"PARAMETER 3"	1	00015	+00000	+00100
"VOICE ON/OFF 1"	1	00016	+00000	+00001
"VOICE MEMORY SELECT 1"	1	00017	+00000	+00001
"VOICE NUMBER 1"	1	00018	+00000	+00063
"VOLUME 1"	1	00019	+00000	+00127
"TUNING 1"	1	00020	−00064	+00063
"NOTE SHIFT 1"	1	00021	−00064	+00063
"PAN 1"	1	00022	−00031	+00031
"EFFECT LEVEL 1"	1	00023	+00000	+00100
"RESERVE NOTE 1"	1	00024	+00000	+00016
"VOICE ON/OFF 2"	1	00025	+00000	+00001
"VOICE MEMORY SELECT 2"	1	00026	+00000	+00001
"VOICE NUMBER 2"	1	00027	+00000	+00063
"VOLUME 2"	1	00028	+00000	+00127
"TUNING 2"	1	00029	−00064	+00063

PARAMETER NAME	NUMBER OF BYTES	ADDRESS IN THE EDIT BUFFER	MINIMUM VALUE	MAXIMUM VALUE
"NOTE SHIFT 2"	1	00030	−00064	+00063
"PAN 2"	1	00031	−00031	+00031
"EFFECT LEVEL 2"	1	00032	+00000	+00100
"RESERVE NOTE 2"	1	00033	+00000	+00016
"VOICE ON/OFF 3"	1	00034	+00000	+00001
"VOICE MEMORY SELECT 3"	1	00035	+00000	+00001
"VOICE NUMBER 3"	1	00036	+00000	+00063
"VOLUME 3"	1	00037	+00000	+00127
"TUNING 3"	1	00038	−00064	+00063
"NOTE SHIFT 3"	1	00039	−00064	+00063
"PAN 3"	1	00040	−00031	+00031
"EFFECT LEVEL 3"	1	00041	+00000	+00100
"RESERVE NOTE 3"	1	00042	+00000	+00016
"VOICE ON/OFF 4"	1	00043	+00000	+00001
"VOICE MEMORY SELECT 4"	1	00044	+00000	+00001
"VOICE NUMBER 4"	1	00045	+00000	+00063
"VOLUME 4"	1	00046	+00000	+00127
"TUNING 4"	1	00047	−00064	+00063
"NOTE SHIFT 4"	1	00048	−00064	+00063
"PAN 4"	1	00049	−00031	+00031
"EFFECT LEVEL 4"	1	00050	+00000	+00100

. . . .

PARAMETER NAME	NUMBER OF BYTES	ADDRESS IN THE EDIT BUFFER	MINIMUM VALUE	MAXIMUM VALUE
"RESERVE NOTE 4"	1	00051	+00000	+00016
"VOICE ON/OFF 5"	1	00052	+00000	+00001
"VOICE MEMORY SELECT 5"	1	00053	+00000	+00001
"VOICE NUMBER 5"	1	00054	+00000	+00063
"VOLUME 5"	1	00055	+00000	+00127
"TUNING 5"	1	00056	−00064	+00063
"NOTE SHIFT 5"	1	00057	−00064	+00063
"PAN 5"	1	00058	−00031	+00031
"EFFECT LEVEL 5"	1	00059	+00000	+00100
"RESERVE NOTE 5"	1	00060	+00000	+00016
"VOICE ON/OFF 6"	1	00061	+00000	+00001
"VOICE MEMORY SELECT 6"	1	00062	+00000	+00001
"VOICE NUMBER 6"	1	00063	+00000	+00063
"VOLUME 6"	1	00064	+00000	+00127
"TUNING 6"	1	00065	−00064	+00063
"NOTE SHIFT 6"	1	00066	−00064	+00063
"PAN 6"	1	00067	−00031	+00031
"EFFECT LEVEL 6"	1	00068	+00000	+00100
"RESERVE NOTE 6"	1	00069	+00000	+00016
"VOICE ON/OFF 7"	1	00070	+00000	+00001
"VOICE MEMORY SELECT 7"	1	00071	+00000	+00001

PARAMETER NAME	NUMBER OF BYTES	ADDRESS IN THE EDIT BUFFER	MINIMUM VALUE	MAXIMUM VALUE
"VOICE NUMBER 7"	1	00072	+00000	+00063
"VOLUME 7"	1	00073	+00000	+00127
"TUNING 7"	1	00074	−00064	+00063
"NOTE SHIFT 7"	1	00075	−00064	+00063
"PAN 7"	1	00076	−00031	+00031
"EFFECT LEVEL 7"	1	00077	+00000	+00100
"RESERVE NOTE 7"	1	00078	+00000	+00016
"VOICE ON/OFF 8"	1	00079	+00000	+00001
"VOICE MEMORY SELECT 8"	1	00080	+00000	+00001
"VOICE NUMBER 8"	1	00081	+00000	+00063
"VOLUME 8"	1	00082	+00000	+00127
"TUNING 8"	1	00083	−00064	+00063
"NOTE SHIFT 8"	1	00084	−00064	+00063
"PAN 8"	1	00085	−00031	+00031
"EFFECT LEVEL 8"	1	00086	+00000	+00100
"RESERVE NOTE 8"	1	00087	+00000	+00016
"VOICE ON/OFF 9"	1	00088	+00000	+00001
"VOICE MEMORY SELECT 9"	1	00089	+00000	+00001
"VOICE NUMBER 9"	1	00090	+00000	+00063
"VOLUME 9"	1	00091	+00000	+00127
"TUNING 9"	1	00092	−00064	+00063
"NOTE SHIFT 9"	1	00093	−00064	+00063

. . . .

PARAMETER NAME	NUMBER OF BYTES	ADDRESS IN THE EDIT BUFFER	MINIMUM VALUE	MAXIMUM VALUE
"PAN 9"	1	00094	−00031	+00031
"EFFECT LEVEL 9"	1	00095	+00000	+00100
"RESERVE NOTE 9"	1	00096	+00000	+00016
"VOICE ON/OFF 10"	1	00097	+00000	+00001
"VOICE MEMORY SELECT 10"	1	00098	+00000	+00001
"VOICE NUMBER 10"	1	00099	+00000	+00063
"VOLUME 10"	1	00100	+00000	+00127
"TUNING 10"	1	00101	−00064	+00063
"NOTE SHIFT 10"	1	00102	−00064	+00063
"PAN 10"	1	00103	−00031	+00031
"EFFECT LEVEL 10"	1	00104	+00000	+00100
"RESERVE NOTE 10"	1	00105	+00000	+00016
"VOICE ON/OFF 11"	1	00106	+00000	+00001
"VOICE MEMORY SELECT 11"	1	00107	+00000	+00001
"VOICE NUMBER 11"	1	00108	+00000	+00063
"VOLUME 11"	1	00109	+00000	+00127
"TUNING 11"	1	00110	−00064	+00063
"NOTE SHIFT 11"	1	00111	−00064	+00063
"PAN 11"	1	00112	−00031	+00031
"EFFECT LEVEL 11"	1	00113	+00000	+00100
"RESERVE NOTE 11"	1	00114	+00000	+00016

PARAMETER NAME	NUMBER OF BYTES	ADDRESS IN THE EDIT BUFFER	MINIMUM VALUE	MAXIMUM VALUE
"VOICE ON/OFF 12"	1	00115	+00000	+00001
"VOICE MEMORY SELECT 12"	1	00116	+00000	+00001
"VOICE NUMBER 12"	1	00117	+00000	+00063
"VOLUME 12"	1	00118	+00000	+00127
"TUNING 12"	1	00119	−00064	+00063
"NOTE SHIFT 12"	1	00120	−00064	+00063
"PAN 12"	1	00121	−00031	+00031
"EFFECT LEVEL 12"	1	00122	+00000	+00100
"RESERVE NOTE 12"	1	00123	+00000	+00016
"VOICE ON/OFF 13"	1	00124	+00000	+00001
"VOICE MEMORY SELECT 13"	1	00125	+00000	+00001
"VOICE NUMBER 13"	1	00126	+00000	+00063
"VOLUME 13"	1	00127	+00000	+00127
"TUNING 13"	1	00128	−00064	+00063
"NOTE SHIFT 13"	1	00129	−00064	+00063
"PAN 13"	1	00130	−00031	+00031
"EFFECT LEVEL 13"	1	00131	+00000	+00100
"RESERVE NOTE 13"	1	00132	+00000	+00016
"VOICE ON/OFF 14"	1	00133	+00000	+00001
"VOICE MEMORY SELECT 14"	1	00134	+00000	+00001

· ·

PARAMETER NAME	NUMBER OF BYTES	ADDRESS IN THE EDIT BUFFER	MINIMUM VALUE	MAXIMUM VALUE
"VOICE NUMBER 14"	1	00135	+00000	+00063
"VOLUME 14"	1	00136	+00000	+00127
"TUNING 14"	1	00137	−00064	+00063
"NOTE SHIFT 14"	1	00138	−00064	+00063
"PAN 14"	1	00139	−00031	+00031
"EFFECT LEVEL 14"	1	00140	+00000	+00100
"RESERVE NOTE 14"	1	00141	+00000	+00016
"VOICE ON/OFF 15"	1	00142	+00000	+00001
"VOICE MEMORY SELECT 15"	1	00143	+00000	+00001
"VOICE NUMBER 15"	1	00144	+00000	+00063
"VOLUME 15"	1	00145	+00000	+00127
"TUNING 15"	1	00146	−00064	+00063
"NOTE SHIFT 15"	1	00147	−00064	+00063
"PAN 15"	1	00148	−00031	+00031
"EFFECT LEVEL 15"	1	00149	+00000	+00100
"RESERVE NOTE 15"	1	00150	+00000	+00016
"VOICE ON/OFF 16"	1	00151	+00000	+00001
"VOICE MEMORY SELECT 16"	1	00152	+00000	+00001
"VOICE NUMBER 16"	1	00153	+00000	+00063
"VOLUME 16"	1	00154	+00000	+00127
"TUNING 16"	1	00155	−00064	+00063

PARAMETER NAME	NUMBER OF BYTES	ADDRESS IN THE EDIT BUFFER	MINIMUM VALUE	MAXIMUM VALUE
"NOTE SHIFT 16"	1	00156	−00064	+00063
"PAN 16"	1	00157	−00031	+00031
"EFFECT LEVEL 16"	1	00158	+00000	+00100
"RESERVE NOTE 16"	1	00159	+00000	+00016

APPENDIX

I

XIII XIV XV XVI A B C D E F G

Representative
MIDI
Software Vendors

T

HIS APPENDIX CONTAINS a short sampling of MIDI software manufacturers. Although by no means exhaustive, it includes the major makers of composition and playback programs, and—naturally—sequencer and controller software, editors, and editor/librarians for Atari, Apple (Macintosh), and IBM PC and PC clone computers.

Ars Nova Software
P.O. Box 637
Kirkland, WA 98083
(800) 445-4866
fax (206) 889-0359

Coda Music Technology
6210 Bury Drive
Eden Prairie, MN 55346-1718
(612) 937-9611
(800) 843-2066
fax (612) 937-9760

Digital Music Services
23010 Lake Forest Drive, Suite D-334
Laguna Hills, CA 92653
(714) 951-1159

Dr. T's Music Software
124 Crescent Road
Needham, MA 02194
(617) 455-1454
(800) 989-MIDI
fax (617) 455-1460

Dynaware U.S.A., Inc.
950 Tower Lane, Suite 1150
Foster City, CA 94004
(415) 349-5700
(800) 445-3962
fax (415) 349-5879

Electronic Arts
1450 Fashion Island Blvd.
San Mateo, CA 94404
(415) 571-7171
(800) 245-4525

Great Wave Software
53553 Scotts Valley Drive
Scotts Valley, CA 95066
(408) 438-1990
fax (408) 438-7171

Leigh's Computers
1475 Third Avenue
New York, NY 10028
(212) 879-6257
fax (212) 772-1689

Mark of the Unicorn, Inc.
1280 Massachusetts Ave.
Cambridge, MA 02138
(617) 576-2760
fax (617) 576-3609

Metatec Corp./Nautilus
7001 Discovery Blvd.
Dublin, OH 43017
(614) 776-3165
(800) 637-3472
fax (614) 761-4110

Opcode Systems, Inc.
3950 Fabian Way, Suite 100
Palo Alto, CA 94303
(415) 856-3333
fax (415) 856-3332

Passport Designs, Inc.
100 Stone Pine Road
Half Moon Bay, CA 94019
(415) 726-0280
(800) 443-3210
fax (415) 726-2254

Pyographics
P.O. Box 639
Grapevine, TX 76099
(817) 481-7536
(800) 222-1536
fax (817) 488-9658

Softronics, Inc.
5085 List Drive
Colorado Springs, CO 80919
(719) 593-9540
fax (719) 548-1878

SoundQuest, Inc.
121 West 13th Street, Suite 2
Vancouver, V5Y 1V8 Canada
(604) 874-9499
(800) 667-3998
fax and BBS (604) 874-8971

Soundtrek
3384 Hill Drive
Duluth, GA 30136
(404) 623-0879

Steinberg Jones
17700 Raymer Street, Suite
1001
Northridge, CA 91325
(818) 993-4091
fax (818) 701-7452

Temporal Acuity Products, Inc.
300 120th Ave. N.E., Bldg. 1
Bellevue, WA 98005
(206) 462-1007
(800) 426-2673

Tran Tracks
350 Fifth Ave., Suite 3304
New York, NY 10118
(800) 473-0797 (orders)
(201) 383-6691 (tech support)
fax (201) 383-0797

Twelve-Tone Systems
P.O. Box 760
Watertown, MA 02272
(617) 926-2480
fax (617) 924-6657

INDEX

Note to the Reader:

Boldfaced numbers indicate pages where you will find the principal discussion of a topic or the definition of a term. *Italic* numbers indicate pages where a topic is illustrated in a figure.

E

G

H

A Book Full of Sound and Fury.

500pp. ISBN:1199-8.

The Audible PC is the complete guide to multimedia sound production with Windows. This book is a must for anyone who wants to explore the infinite possibilities of sound.

You'll find product reviews and descriptions, a survey of animation and presentation software, in-depth information on MIDI, sequencers, digital audio, sound cards, and more.

You'll also find a FREE 5¼" disk containing demo versions of two popular PC sound applications—Master Tracks Pro for Windows and Sound Forge.

SYBEX. Help Yourself.

2021 Challenger Drive
Alameda, CA 94501
1-800-227-2346

SYBEX

MAKE A GOOD COMPUTER EVEN BETTER.

COMPUSERVE CIM
MADE SIMPLER.

250pp. ISBN: 1279-X.

POCKET-SIZED PC EXPERTISE.

YES, YOU *CAN* DO WINDOWS.

YOUR GUIDE TO DOS DOMINANCE.

The Musician's Guide to MIDI

GET A FREE CATALOG JUST FOR EXPRESSING YOUR OPINION.

Help us improve our books and get a *FREE* full-color catalog in the bargain. Please complete this form, pull out this page and send it in today. The address is on the reverse side.

Name _____   Company _____

Address _____   City _____ State ____ Zip _____

Phone ( )_____

1. How would you rate the overall quality of this book?

❑ Excellent
❑ Very Good
❑ Good
❑ Fair
❑ Below Average
❑ Poor

2. What were the things you liked most about the book? (Check all that apply)

❑ Pace
❑ Format
❑ Writing Style
❑ Examples
❑ Table of Contents
❑ Index
❑ Price
❑ Illustrations
❑ Type Style
❑ Cover
❑ Depth of Coverage
❑ Fast Track Notes

3. What were the things you liked *least* about the book? (Check all that apply)

❑ Pace
❑ Format
❑ Writing Style
❑ Examples
❑ Table of Contents
❑ Index
❑ Price
❑ Illustrations
❑ Type Style
❑ Cover
❑ Depth of Coverage
❑ Fast Track Notes

4. Where did you buy this book?

❑ Bookstore chain
❑ Small independent bookstore
❑ Computer store
❑ Wholesale club
❑ College bookstore
❑ Technical bookstore
❑ Other _____

5. How did you decide to buy this particular book?

❑ Recommended by friend
❑ Recommended by store personnel
❑ Author's reputation
❑ Sybex's reputation
❑ Read book review in _____
❑ Other _____

6. How did you pay for this book?

❑ Used own funds
❑ Reimbursed by company
❑ Received book as a gift

7. What is your level of experience with the subject covered in this book?

❑ Beginner
❑ Intermediate
❑ Advanced

8. How long have you been using a computer?

years _____
months _____

9. Where do you most often use your computer?

❑ Home
❑ Work

❑ Both
❑ Other _____

10. What kind of computer equipment do you have? (Check all that apply)

❑ PC Compatible Desktop Computer
❑ PC Compatible Laptop Computer
❑ Apple/Mac Computer
❑ Apple/Mac Laptop Computer
❑ CD ROM
❑ Fax Modem
❑ Data Modem
❑ Scanner
❑ Sound Card
❑ Other _____

11. What other kinds of software packages do you ordinarily use?

❑ Accounting
❑ Databases
❑ Networks
❑ Apple/Mac
❑ Desktop Publishing
❑ Spreadsheets
❑ CAD
❑ Games
❑ Word Processing
❑ Communications
❑ Money Management
❑ Other _____

12. What operating systems do you ordinarily use?

❑ DOS
❑ OS/2
❑ Windows
❑ Apple/Mac
❑ Windows NT
❑ Other _____

13. On what computer-related subject(s) would you like to see more books?

_____

_____

_____

_____

14. Do you have any other comments about this book? (Please feel free to use a separate piece of paper if you need more room)

_____

_____

_____

_____

- - - - - - - - - - - - PLEASE FOLD, SEAL, AND MAIL TO SYBEX - - - - - - - - - - - - - -

SYBEX INC.
Department M
2021 Challenger Drive
Alameda, CA
94501